Introduction to Programming with

Visual Basic .NET

Gary J. Bronson
Fairleigh Dickinson University

David Rosenthal
Seton Hall University

Page 490
Splash Screen...

JONES AND BARTLETT PUBLISHERS
Sudbury, Massachusetts
BOSTON   TORONTO   LONDON   SINGAPORE

World Headquarters
Jones and Bartlett Publishers
40 Tall Pine Drive
Sudbury, MA 01776
978-443-5000
info@jbpub.com
www.jbpub.com

Jones and Bartlett Publishers Canada
2406 Nikanna Road
Mississauga, ON L5C 2W6
CANADA

Jones and Bartlett Publishers
International
Barb House, Barb Mews
London W6 7PA
UK

Cover image © Photos.com

Library of Congress Cataloging-in-Publication Data

Bronson, Gary J.
  Introduction to programming using Visual Basic .NET / by Gary Bronson and David Rosenthal.— 1st ed.
    p. cm.
  ISBN 0-7637-2478-5
  1. Microsoft Visual BASIC. 2. BASIC (Computer program language) 3. Microsoft .NET. I. Rosenthal, David A. II. Title.
  QA76.73.B3B7465 2004
  005.13'3—dc22

                                        2004012442

Acquisitions Editor: Stephen Solomon
Production Manager: Amy Rose
Production Assistant: Caroline Senay
Marketing Manager: Matthew Payne
Editorial Assistant: Deborah Arrand
Manufacturing Buyer: Therese Bräuer
Cover Design: Kristin E. Ohlin
Text Design: Anne Spencer
Composition: Northeast Compositors
Technical Artist: George Nichols
Printing and Binding: Malloy, Inc.
Cover Printing: Malloy, Inc.

Printed in the United States of America
08 07 06   10 9 8 7 6 5 4 3 2

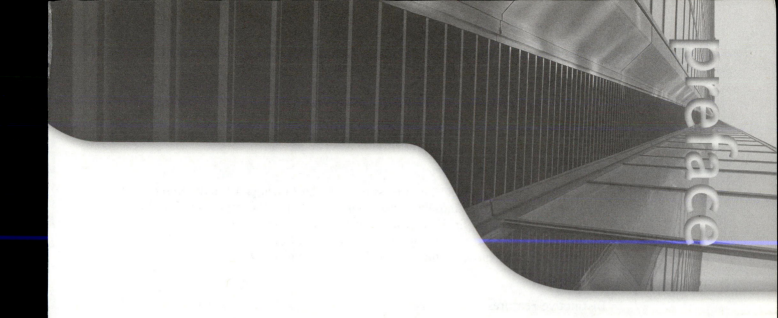

Visual Basic® has emerged as the preeminent programming language for Windows®-based applications. A major reason for this is that Visual Basic® provides a rather complete set of visual objects, such as Buttons, Labels, Text boxes, and List boxes that can easily be assembled into a working graphical user interface (GUI - pronounced goo-eey) and integrated into a Microsoft® Windows® operating system environment. From both a teaching and learning viewpoint, Visual Basic® requires familiarity with three elements, only one of which is common to traditional programming languages such as Basic, Java, and C. These are:

- The new visual objects required in creating a Windows® based graphical user interface;
- The new concept of event-based programming, where the user, rather than the programmer determines the sequence of operations that is to be executed; and
- The traditional concept of procedural program code.

The major objective of this textbook is to introduce each of these elements, within the context of sound programming principles, in a manner that is accessible to the beginning programmer.

Changes from Version 6.0 to Visual Basic .NET

There are new features in Visual Basic® .NET as well as many changes to existing features from Version 6.0. However, since this text is intended for students who are probably not familiar with Visual Basic®, we will not dwell on the differences between Visual Basic® 6.0 and Visual Basic® .NET. Suffice to say that many features and interfaces have changed. It is important to note that Visual Basic® .NET is now a true object-oriented language. In addition there is support of Web programming, which is a key and unique aspect of this new version of Visual Basic®.

Prerequisites

In using this text no prerequisites are assumed. A short Chapter 1 briefly presents computer literacy material for those who need this background. The large numbers of examples and exercises used in the text are drawn from everyday experience and business fields. Thus, an instructor may choose applications and select a topic presentation that matches students' experience for a particular course emphasis.

Distinctive Features

Writing Style We firmly believe that for a textbook to be useful it must provide a clearly defined supporting role to the leading role of the professor. Once the professor sets the stage, however, the textbook must encourage, nurture, and assist the student in acquiring and owning the material presented in class. To do this the text must be written in a manner that makes sense to the student. Thus, first and foremost, we feel that the writing style used to convey the concepts presented is the most important and distinctive aspect of the text.

Flexibility To be an effective teaching resource, a text must provide a flexible tool that each professor can use in a variety of ways, depending on how many programming concepts and programming techniques are to be introduced in a single course, and when they are to be introduced. Accomplished this by partitioning the text into three parts and providing Knowing About sections at the end of most chapters.

Excluding Chapter 1, which presents basic computer literacy material, Part I presents the fundamental visual and procedural elements of Visual Basic® .NET. While presenting this basic material, much of the enrichment material presented in the Knowing About sections can be introduced as desired. For example, the material on Forms Design (Section 3.7) and Programming Costs (Section 6.8) can be introduced almost any time after Chapter 3.

Once Part I is completed, the material in Parts II and III are *interchangeable*. For example, in a more traditional introduction to programming course, Part I would be followed by Chapter 8. However, if a requirement is that the course must emphasize database applications, Part I could just as easily be followed by Chapter 9. In a third instance, if the course is to have a more theoretical slant, Part I can be immediately followed by Chapter 12. In each of these cases, a "pick-and-choose" approach to the Knowing About sections can be applied as these topics are appropriate to the overall course structure and emphasis. Thus, regardless of what the decision is, this book provides a flexible means of customizing a course around the central core topics presented in Part I. This flexibility of topic introduction is illustrated by the following topic dependency chart.

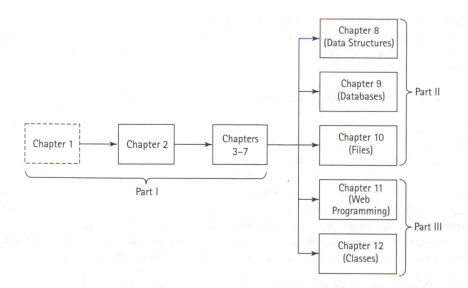

Software Engineering Although this is primarily an introductory Visual Basic® .NET text, as opposed to a CS1 introduction to programming book, the text is meant to familiarize students with the fundamentals of software engineering, from both a procedural and object-oriented viewpoint. This introduction begins in Section 1.2 with the formal introduction of the software development cycle and is a thread that is maintained throughout the text. In some instances this concept material can be skipped. For example, a course could omit Chapter 1 entirely and begin with Chapter 2. Similarly, in a strictly language-oriented course, the introductory section on repetition statements (Section 6.1), which presents the concepts of both pre- and post-test loops, might be omitted. The same is true of the database theory presented in Section 9.1. In most cases, however, the more general programming aspects are interwoven within the text's main language component precisely because the text is meant to both introduce and strengthen the why as well as the *how*.

Program Testing Every single Visual Basic® .NET program in this text has been successfully entered and executed using Microsoft® Visual Basic® .NET. Source code for programs may be accessed at http://computerscience.jbpub.com/bronsonvbnet. This will allow students to both experiment and extend the existing programs and more easily modify them as required by a number of end-of-section exercises.

Pedagogical Features

To facilitate the goal of making Visual Basic .NET accessible as a first level course, the following pedagogical features have been incorporated into the text.

End-of-Section Exercises Almost every section in the book contains numerous and diverse skill builder and programming exercises. Additionally, solutions to selected odd-numbered exercises are provided on the website.

End-of-Chapter Exercises   A set of end-of-chapter programming projects has also been provided. These projects range from the simple to the more complex, and thus provide a spectrum of more challenging assignments than those provided in the end-of-section exercises.

End-of-Chapter Self-Test   Each chapter contains an end-of-chapter self test.

Focus Sections   These sections provide a detailed look at how an actual business system would be developed. The actual practice of applying rapid application development (RAD) techniques to developing the system, from a main menu for a multi-form commercial system to developing real-life operational data entry forms and information forms, such as Splash screens and About dialogs, are presented. Although each section applies specific material developed in the text to the application, the application is meant to illustrate both the need for and application of known techniques. Thus, specific sections can be covered or not, as fits the needs of your class, or the project as a whole can be used as the central element in the course.

Case Studies   A set of case studies that mirror the development of the Focus case is provided. These can be used as semester projects for either individual or group assignment. If assigned as a group project, each member of the group should be responsible for various subsections of the project, with the group as a whole responsible for designing the main menu and interface requirements.

Tips from the Pros   These shaded boxes present useful technical points, programming tips, and programming tricks of a more practical nature that are known and used by professional programmers.

Common Programming Errors and Chapter Review   Each Chapter ends with a section on common programming errors and a review of the main topics covered in the chapter.

Knowing About Sections   Given the many different emphases that can be applied in teaching Visual Basic®, a number of basic and enrichment topics have been included. These sections vary between such basic material as using the Help facility to additional topics, such as defining error types and using the Wizards. The purpose of these sections is to provide flexibility as to the choice of which topics to present and the timing of when to present them.

Programmer Notes   A set of shaded boxes that are primarily meant as a reference for commonly used tasks, such as creating a new project, saving a project, and successfully navigating through the integrated development environment (IDE). They are also used to highlight programming techniques and provide additional concept material.

Appendices

Several appendices are provided that include information on ASCII codes, additional controls, and a glossary of terms.

ACKNOWLEDGMENTS

We would like to express our gratitude to the following individual reviewers:

Melinda C. White	Seminole Community College
Amanda Whaley	Austin Community College
Debra Chapman	University of South Alabama
Kurt Kominek	Northeast State Technical Community College
Chadi Boudiab	Georgia Perimeter College

These reviewers supplied extremely detailed and constructive reviews of several iterations of the text. Their suggestions and comments were very helpful.

Gary Bronson would also like to gratefully acknowledge the encouragement and support of Fairleigh Dickinson University. Specifically, this includes the positive academic climate provided by the university and the direct encouragement and support of the dean, Dr. David Steele and chairperson, Dr. Paul Yoon. Without their support, this text could not have been written.

David Rosenthal would also like to acknowledge the support of Seton Hall University in the development of this book. Without the time and facilities provided, I would have been one of the myriad of would-be authors. Special thanks go to the dean, Dr. Karen Boroff.

Dedicated to our wives Rochelle and Vicki.

contents

4   Controlling Input and Output   197

5   Selection   231

6   Repetition Structures   301

9 Accessing Databases   503

10 Processing Visual Basic Data Files 581

11 Creating Web Applications with Visual Basic .NET 639

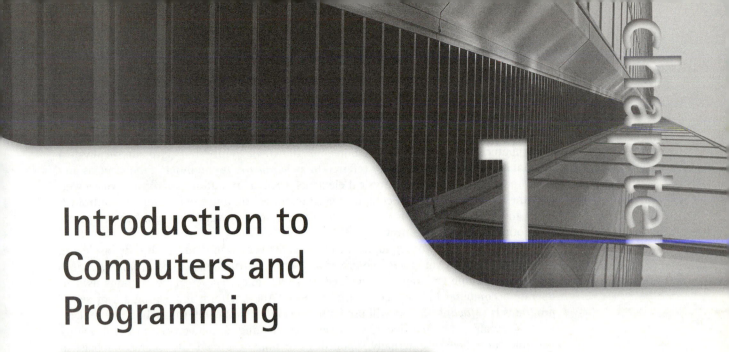

Introduction to Computers and Programming

1.1 Introduction to Programming

A computer, such as the modern notebook shown in Figure 1–1, is made of physical components that are collectively referred to as *hardware*. A computer is the same as any other machine composed of physical elements, such as an automobile or a lawn mower. Like these other machines, a computer must be turned on and then driven, or controlled, to do the task it was meant to do. How this gets done is what distinguishes computers from other types of machinery.

In an automobile, for example, the driver is the person in control who sits inside and directs the car. In a computer, the driver is a set of instructions, called a *program*. More formally, a computer program is defined as a self-contained set of instructions used to operate a computer to produce a specific result. Another term for a program or set of programs is *software*, and we will use both terms interchangeably throughout the text.

Historically, the first recorded attempt at creating a general-purpose calculating machine controlled by externally supplied instructions was made by Charles Babbage in England in 1822. He called it an "analytical engine" (see Figure 1–2). The set of instructions to be put into this machine was developed by Ada Byron, the daughter of the poet Lord Byron. As a result, Ada Byron is considered by some to be the world's first programmer.

Although Babbage's machine was not successfully built in his lifetime, the first practical machine based on his idea was achieved in 1946 with the successful operation of the ENIAC (Electrical Numerical Integrator and Computer) at the University of Pennsylvania. The internal design of ENIAC, which was based on work done by Dr. John V. Atanasoff and Clifford Berry at Iowa State University in 1937, was not a stored-program computer, with the instructions directing its operation stored internally to the machine. Rather, the ENIAC depended on externally connected wires to direct its operation. This

Figure 1–1 *An IBM ThinkPad Notebook Computer*

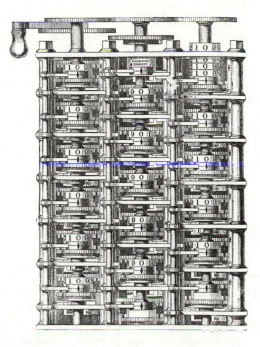

Figure 1-2 *Charles Babbage's Analytical Engine*

meant that reprogramming the ENIAC required changing the external wiring connections to alter the computer's operation.

The final goal of storing both the data to be operated on and the instructions directing these operations within the computer's memory was realized in 1949 at the University of Cambridge. Here the EDSAC (Electronic Delayed Storage Automatic Computer) became the first commercially produced computer to permit instructions stored inside the computer's memory to direct and control the machine's operation. With the successful operation of EDSAC, the theory of a computer program as a stored sequence of instructions, to be executed in order, became a reality that in turn made modern computing possible.

First-Generation and Second-Generation (Low-Level) Languages

Once the goal of a stored program was achieved, the era of programming languages began. The instructions used in EDSAC initiated the *first generation* of such languages, which were also referred to as *machine languages*. These languages consist of a sequence of instructions represented as binary numbers, such as:

```
11000000 00000001 00000010
11110000 00000010 00000011
```

To operate, each new computer type, including modern desktop and notebook computers, requires a machine language program that is compatible with the computer's internal processing hardware. The difference in the processing hardware of early computer types such as IBM, Univac, and Sperry-Rand meant that each of these computer types had its own machine language. This same situation exists today and explains why machine language programs that operate on Intel-based machines, such as IBM Personal Computers (PCs), cannot run on Motorola-based Sun computers or Apple Macintosh computers. As you might expect, it is very tedious and time-consuming to write machine language programs.

One of the first advances in programming was the replacement of machine language binary codes with abbreviated words, such as ADD, SUB, and MUL, to indicate the desired operation, and both decimal numbers and labels to indicate the location of the data. For example, using these words and decimal values, the preceding two machine language instructions might be written as:

```
ADD 1, 2
MUL 2, 3
```

Programming languages that use this type of symbolic notation are referred to as *assembly languages*. Assembly languages formally comprise the *second generation* of computer languages. Since computers can only execute machine language programs, the set of instructions contained within an assembly language program must be translated into a machine language program before it can be executed on a computer (Figure 1–3). Translator programs that translate assembly language programs into machine language programs are known as *assemblers*.

Both first-generation machine languages and second-generation assembly languages are referred to as *low-level languages*. Low-level languages are, by definition, machine-dependent languages, in that programs written in a low-level language can only be run on a particular type of computer. This is because all low-level languages use instructions that are directly tied to specific processing hardware. However, such programs do permit the use of special features of a particular computer and generally execute at the fastest possible levels.

Third-Generation and Fourth-Generation (High-Level) Languages

With the commercial introduction of FORTRAN[1] in 1957, the third generation of languages began. This new generation of computer languages initiated the era of high-level languages. The term *high-level* refers to the fact that the programs written in these languages can be translated to run on a variety of computer types, unlike the low-level lan-

Figure 1–3　*Assembly Programs Must Be Translated*

---

[1]FORTRAN is an acronym for FORmula TRANslation.

guages that are restricted to a particular computer type. If a high-level program is going to be run on an IBM computer, for example, a translator program would produce an IBM machine language program for execution. Similarly, if the program were to be run on another type of computer, a specific translator for that other type of computer would be used. We are still in the era of high-level languages. Figure 1–4 illustrates the relationship and evolution of programming languages. As shown, both third- and fourth-generation languages are considered to be high-level languages. Additionally, as illustrated, third-generation languages include both procedure- and object-oriented languages.

Procedure-Oriented Languages   Third-generation languages grew rapidly to include COBOL, BASIC, Pascal, and C. All of these languages, including FORTRAN, are procedure-oriented languages. The term *procedure-oriented* reflects the fact that the available instructions allow programmers to concentrate on the procedures they are using to solve a problem without regard for the specific hardware that will ultimately run the program. Unlike low-level languages that only permit one mathematical operation per instruction, a single procedural language instruction permits many such operations to be performed. For example, an instruction in a procedure-oriented high-level language to add two numbers and multiply the result by a third number could appear as:

```
answer =  (first + second) * third
```

Typically, a group of such statements are combined together to create a logically consistent set of instructions, called a procedure, which is used to produce one specific result. A complete program can then be composed of multiple procedures that together fulfill the desired programming objective.

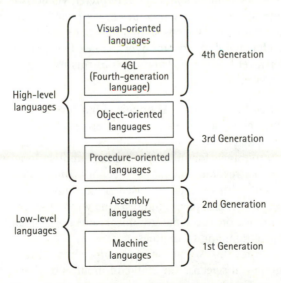

Figure 1–4   *The Evolution of Programming Languages*

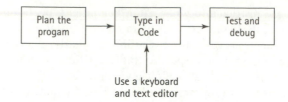

Figure 1–5 *Traditional Procedural Programming Steps to Create a Program*

Until the early 1980s, all new programming languages were predominately high-level procedure-oriented languages. Programs written in these languages typically are produced following the steps shown in Figure 1–5. Here the programmer first plans what the program will do. The required instructions are then entered into the computer using a text-editing program and stored together as a file, which is referred to as the *source program* or *source file*. The source program is then translated into machine language by a translator program and subsequently run on a computer. The final machine language program is referred to as an *executable program*, or as *executable*, for short.

Translation into a machine-language program is accomplished in two ways. When each statement in a high-level language source program is translated individually and executed immediately, the programming language is referred to as an *interpreted language* and the program doing the translation is called an *interpreter*.

When all of the statements in a source program are translated before any one statement is executed, the programming language used is called a *compiled language*. In this case, the program doing the translation is called a *compiler*. Both compiled and interpreted versions of a language can exist, although one typically predominates. Earlier versions of BASIC were interpreted, but VB.NET is complied. Similarly, although C is predominately a compiled language, interpreted versions of C do exist.

Although all high-level source programs must still be translated into machine code to run on a computer, the steps shown in Figure 1–5 that are required to produce a program, have changed dramatically over the last few years with the introduction of a new type of high-level languages. Languages of this new type are referred to as both *object-oriented* and *event-driven*.

Object-Oriented Languages Although high-level languages represented a major advancement over their low-level counterparts, the procedural aspect of high-level languages began to reveal some problems. One of these was the difficulty of reusing procedural programs for new or similar applications without extensive revision, retesting, and revalidation. The second and more fundamental reason for disenchantment with procedural-based programming was the emergence of graphical screens and the subsequent interest in window-based applications. Programming multiple windows on the same graphical screen is virtually impossible using standard procedural programming techniques.

The reason for this is that the major procedural languages were developed before the advent of graphical screens. The standard input and output devices prior to the 1980s all were character-based text, such as that produced by a keyboard and printer, and, as a result, procedural languages were geared to the input, processing, and output of text characters and not to the creation of graphical images such as those shown in Figure 1–6. Clearly, a new way of constructing and then interacting with such images was required.

The solution to producing programs that efficiently manipulate graphical screens and provide reusable windowing code was found in artificial-intelligence-based and simulation programming techniques. The former area, artificial intelligence, contained extensive research on geometrical object specification and recognition. The latter area, simulation, contained considerable background on simulating items as objects with well-defined interactions between them. This object-based paradigm[2] worked well in a graphical windows environment, where each window could be specified as a self-contained object.

An object also is well suited to a programming representation because it can be specified by two basic characteristics: a current *state*, which defines how the object appears at the moment, and a *behavior*, which defines how the object reacts to external inputs. To make this more concrete, consider the screen image reproduced in Figure 1–7.

Figure 1–7 was produced by a very simple Visual Basic Program—one that we will write in the next chapter. As shown, this screen is a graphical user interface (GUI, pronounced "GOO-EE") because it provides a graphical way for the user to interact with the program. An examination of Figure 1–7 reveals that it contains five objects, four of which the user can directly interact with at will. The first object is the window itself, which contains the caption "The Hello Program" and the three buttons at the top of the window. These buttons are the Close button at the upper-left corner of the window and the Maximize and Minimize buttons at the upper-right corner. Within the window illustrated in Figure 1–7 are four basic objects which consist of three buttons and one text box. Each of the buttons has its own caption—Message, Clear, and Exit, respectively. The text box currently contains no text. In object-oriented terms, the three buttons and the

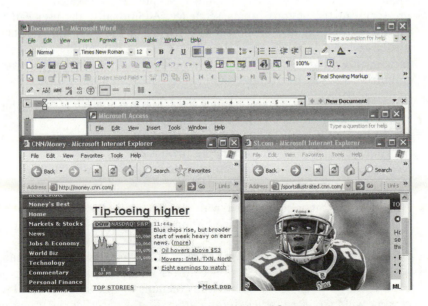

Figure 1–6 *A Multiwindowed Screen*

---

[2]A *paradigm* is a way of thinking about or doing something.

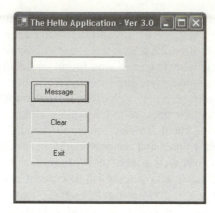

Figure 1–7 *The Screen Image of an Executing Visual Basic Program*

single text box are objects that have been placed on a form when the program was being designed and developed. When the program is run, producing the image shown in Figure 1–7, the form becomes a window. Each object in the window is defined by a set of properties that determine where and how the object appears. The most obvious properties of the buttons are their position on the screen and their captions; each of these properties was set by the programmer.

Events   The most noticeable difference between procedure-based and GUI programs is the manner in which the user interacts with the running program. Take another look at Figure 1–7. Here the user has a number of options from which to choose. The user can press any of the buttons in any sequence. Additionally, the user can push any of the buttons on the top line of the window itself. For the moment, consider only the three buttons labeled <u>M</u>essage, <u>C</u>lear, and E<u>x</u>it. The selection of any one of these buttons will trigger an event, which is a specific procedure that is connected to an object. A user-initiated event can be triggered in one of the following three ways:

- by placing the mouse pointer over a button and clicking the left mouse button (clicking means pushing and releasing the button)
- by simultaneously holding down the Alt key and pressing one of the underlined letters (this is called "activating the hot key")
- by pressing the tab key until the desired button is highlighted with a dotted line and then pressing the Enter key.

(The control that is highlighted with the dotted line is said "to have the focus." As shown in Figure 1–7, the <u>M</u>essage button has the focus, so pressing Enter will activate this control.)

Once a user triggers an event—which in this case is done by simply selecting and activating one of the three button controls in the window—program instructions take over. If the programmer has written instructions for the user-activated event, some processing will take place; otherwise, no processing occurs. For the program shown in Figure 1–7, there are three events for which code was written: If the user activates the

Message button, the message "Hello There World!" is displayed in the text box. Pushing the Clear button results in the text area of the text box being cleared, while pushing the Exit button results in a beep and termination of the program.

Note that the sequence of events—which action is to be taken—is controlled by the user. The user can click any one of the three buttons, in any order, or even run a different Windows program while the Visual Basic program is executing. The user's determination of which event will take place next, as the program is running, is quite a different approach compared to the traditional procedure-based programming paradigm. In a procedure-based program, the decisions about which actions can be taken and in what order are controlled by the programmer when the program is being designed.

Unfortunately, an event-based user graphical interface such as the one illustrated in Figure 1–7 does not eliminate the need for all procedural code. The programmer must still provide the code to appropriately process the events triggered by the user. From a design standpoint, the construction of an object-based program proceeds using the steps shown in Figure 1–8.

The revolutionary aspect of programming languages such as Visual Basic is that they provide a basic set of objects that can be placed on a form while a program is being developed. This is done within an integrated development environment (IDE) that makes creating the graphical interface quite easy. As a result, when using Visual Basic, the programmer does not have to be concerned with writing the code for producing the graphical objects or for recognizing when certain events, such as "mouse was clicked," actually occur. Once the desired objects are selected and placed on the form, Visual Basic takes care of creating the object and recognizing appropriate object events, such as clicking a button. Programming languages that permit the programmer to manipulate graphical objects directly, with the programming language subsequently providing the necessary code to support the selected objects and their interface, are sometimes referred to as visual languages. Visual Basic is an example of a visual language. Using such a language, however, still requires programmer responsibility for:

1. Initially selecting and placing objects on a form when the program is being developed.

2. Writing and including procedural code to correctly process events that can be triggered by a user's interaction with the program's objects when the program is run.

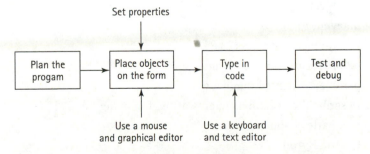

Figure 1–8   *The Steps in Developing an Object-Based Program*

An example of a classic object-oriented language, without the visual programming interface, is C++. The visual language equivalent of C++ is Visual C++.

Finally, sitting between object-oriented languages and visual languages in Figure 1–4 is a group of languages referred to as *4GLs*. These were the initial fourth-generation languages that permitted users to access and format information without the need for writing any procedural code. For example, in a 4GL, both a programmer and user could type the following English-like command to produce a formatted report with the desired information:

```
List the name, starting date, and salary for all employees who
have more than 20 years of service
```

In a 4GL, this request for information causes the program to produce the actual code for satisfying the request without any programmer intervention. Because a similar type of operation occurs in visual languages, where simply placing an object on a form automatically generates the code for each object, visual languages such as Visual Basic are sometimes also classified as 4GLs.

Exercises 1.1

1. Define the following terms:
   a. first-generation language
   b. second-generation language
   c. third-generation language
   d. fourth-generation language
   e. high-level language
   f. low-level language
   g. machine language
   h. assembly language
   i. assembler
   j. interpreter
   k. compiler
   l. object
   m. event
   n. graphical user interface
   o. procedure-oriented language
   p. object-oriented language

2. Describe the accomplishments of the following people:
   a. Charles Babbage
   b. Ada Byron

3. a. Describe the difference between high-level and low-level languages.

b. Describe the difference between procedure-oriented and object-oriented languages.

4. Describe the similarities and differences between procedure-oriented and object-oriented languages.

5. a. To be classified as a fourth generation language (4GL), the language must provide a specific capability. What is this capability?

b. Must a 4GL provide the ability to create event-driven programs?

1.2 Problem Solution and Software Development

Problem solving has become a way of life in modern society because as society has become more complex, so have its problems. Issues such as solid waste disposal, global warming, international finance, pollution, and nuclear proliferation are relatively new, and solutions to these problems now challenge our best technology and human capabilities.

Most solutions to problems require considerable planning and forethought if the solution is to be appropriate and efficient. For example, imagine trying to construct a cellular telephone network or create an inventory management system for a department store by trial and error. Such a solution would be expensive at best, disastrous at worst, and impractical.

Creating a program is no different, because a program is a solution developed to solve a particular problem. As such, creating a program is almost the last step in a process of first determining what the problem is and then what method will be used to solve the problem. Each field of study has its own name for the systematic method used to solve problems by designing suitable solutions. In science and engineering the approach is referred to as the *scientific method*, while in quantitative analysis the approach is referred to as the *systems approach*.

The technique used by professional software developers for understanding the problem that is being solved, and then creating an effective and appropriate software solution, is called the *software development procedure*. This procedure, as illustrated in Figure 1–9, consists of three overlapping phases:

• Design and Development

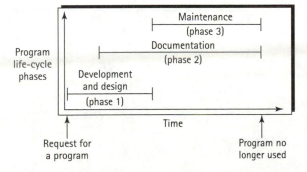

Figure 1–9   *The Three Phases of Program Development*

- Documentation
- Maintenance

As a discipline, *software engineering* is concerned with creating readable, efficient, reliable, and maintainable programs and systems, and uses the software development procedure to achieve this goal.

Phase I. Design and Development

This phase begins with either a statement of a problem or a specific request for a program, which is referred to as a *program requirement*. Once a problem has been stated, or a specific request for a program solution has been made, the design and development phase begins. This phase consists of the four well-defined steps illustrated in Figure 1–10 and summarized below:

1. Analyze the Problem This step is required to ensure that the problem is clearly defined and understood. The determination that the problem is clearly defined can only made when the person doing the analysis understands what output is required and what input will be needed. To accomplish this, the analyst must have an understanding of how the input can be used to produce the desired output. For example, assume that you receive the following assignment:

> *We need a program to provide information about student grades.*
> *—Management*

A simple analysis of this program requirement reveals that it is not a well-defined problem because we do not know exactly what output information is required. As a result, it would be a major mistake to begin writing a program immediately to solve it. To clarify and define the problem statement, your first step should be to contact Management in order to define exactly what information is to be produced (its output) and what data is to be provided (the input). If we are not sure how to obtain the required output from the given input, a more in-depth background analysis may be called for. This typically means obtaining more background information about the problem or application. It also frequently entails doing one or more manual calculations to ensure that we understand the input and how it must be handled to achieve the desired output.

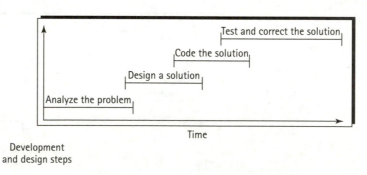

Figure 1–10 *The Development and Design Steps*

2. Develop a Solution   In this step, we identify and select a solution for solving the problem. The solution typically is obtained by a series of refinements, starting with a preliminary solution found in the analysis step, and continuing until an acceptable and complete solution is obtained. This solution must be checked, if it was not checked in the analysis step, to ensure that it correctly produces the desired outputs. The check typically is done by performing one or more manual calculations if they were not already done in the analysis step.

Sometimes the selected solution is quite easy, and sometimes it is quite complex. For example, the solution to determining the dollar value of the change in your pocket or determining the area of a rectangle is quite straightforward and consists of a simple calculation. The construction of an inventory tracking and control system for a department, however, is more complex.

3. Program the Solution   This step, which is also referred to as implementing the solution, consists of translating the solution into a usable application. In Visual Basic, it means constructing a graphical user interface (GUI) and providing the necessary computer instructions which are referred to as *code.*

4. Test and Correct the Application   As its name suggests, this step requires testing the completed application to ensure that it provides a solution to the problem. Any errors that are found during the tests must be corrected.

Listed in Table 1-1 is the relative amount of effort that is typically expended on each of these four development and design steps in large commercial programming projects. As this listing demonstrates, coding is not the major effort in this phase.

Many new programmers have difficulty because they spend the majority of their time writing the program, without spending sufficient time understanding the problem or designing an appropriate solution. In this regard, it is worthwhile to remember the programming proverb, "It is impossible to construct a successful application for a problem that is not fully understood." A somewhat similar and equally valuable proverb, is "The sooner you start programming an application, the longer it usually takes to complete."

Phase II. Documentation

In practice, most programmers forget many of the details of their own programs a few months after they have finished working on them. If they or other programmers must

Table 1-1

Step	Effort
Analyze the Problem	10%
Develop a Solution	20%
Program the Solution	20%
Test the Application	50%

subsequently make modifications to a program, much valuable time can be lost figuring out how the original program works. Good documentation prevents this from occurring.

For every problem solution, there are five document types that should be provided for complete documentation. These include:

1. Initial Application Description
2. Description of Modification and Changes
3. Well-Commented Code Listing
4. Sample Test Runs
5. User's Manual

The documentation phase formally begins in the design phase and continues into the maintenance phase.

Phase III. Maintenance

Maintenance includes the correction of newly found errors and the addition of new features and modifications to existing applications. Figure 1–11 illustrates the relative proportion of time attributable to maintenance compared to development and design.

Using the data provided in Figure 1–11, we see that the maintenance of existing programs currently accounts for approximately 75% of all programming costs. Students generally find this strange because they are accustomed to solving a problem and moving on to a different one. Commercial and scientific fields, however, do not operate this way. In these fields, one application or idea is typically built on a previous one and may require months or even years of work. This is especially true in programming. Once an application is written, which may take weeks or months, maintenance may continue for years as new features are needed. Advances in technology, such as communication, net-

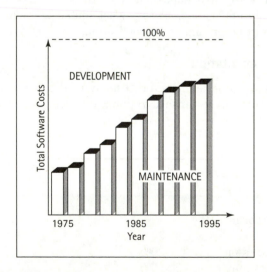

Figure 1–11   *Maintenance is the Predominant Software Cost*

working, fiber optics, new graphical displays, and Web interfaces, constantly demand updated software products.

How easily a program can be maintained (corrected, modified, or enhanced) is related to the ease with which the program can be read and understood, which is directly related to the development and design involved when the program was constructed.

A Closer Look at Phase I

As a result of the fact that the majority of this text is concerned with Phase I of the software development procedure, the four steps required for this phase are described in detail. The use of these steps forms the central focus of our work in creating useful programming solutions.

Step 1: Analyze the Problem   Countless hours have been spent writing computer programs that have never been used or did not produce what the user needed or expected, which can cause considerable animosity between programmer and user. Successful programmers avoid these situations by ensuring that the problem's requirements are understood beforehand. This is the first and most important step in creating an application because this is when the specifications for the final program solution are determined. If the requirements are not fully and completely understood before programming begins, the results are almost always disastrous.

Imagine designing and building a house without fully understanding the architect's specifications. After the house is completed, the architect tells you that a bathroom is required on the first floor, where you have built a wall between the kitchen and the dining room. In addition, that particular wall is one of the main support walls for the house and contains numerous pipes and electrical cables. In this case, adding one bathroom requires a major modification to the basic structure of the house.

Experienced programmers understand the importance of analyzing and understanding a program's requirements before programming the solution, often because they too have constructed programs that later had to be entirely dismantled and redone. The following exercise should give you a sense of this experience.

Figure 1–12 illustrates the outlines of six individual shapes from a classic children's puzzle. Assume that as one or more shapes are given, starting with shapes A and B, an easy-to-describe figure must be constructed.

Typically, shapes A and B are initially arranged to form a square, as illustrated in Figure 1–13. Next, when shape C is considered, it is usually combined with the existing square to form a rectangle, as illustrated in Figure 1–14. Then, when pieces D and E are added, they are usually arranged to form another rectangle, which is placed alongside the existing rectangle to form a square, as shown in Figure 1–15.

Figure 1–12   *Six Individual Shapes*

Figure 1–13 *Typical First Figure*

Figure 1–14 *Typical Second Figure*

Figure 1–15 *Typical Third Figure*

The process of adding new pieces onto the existing structure is identical to constructing a program and then adding to it as each subsequent requirement is understood, rather than completely analyzing the problem before a solution is undertaken. The problem arises when the program is almost finished and a requirement is added that does not fit easily into the established pattern. For example, assume that the last shape (shape F shown in Figure 1–16) is to be added next. This last piece does not fit into the existing pattern that has been constructed. In order to include this piece with the others, the pattern must be completely dismantled and restructured.

Unfortunately, many programmers structure their programs in the same sequential manner used to construct Figure 1–15. Rather than taking the time to understand the complete set of requirements, new programmers frequently start designing a solution based on the understanding of only a small subset of the total requirements. Then, when a subsequent requirement does not fit the existing program structure, the programmer is forced to dismantle and restructure either some parts or all of the application.

Now, let's approach the problem of creating a figure from another view. If we started by arranging the first set of pieces as a parallelogram, all the pieces could be included in the final figure, as illustrated in Figure 1–17.

It is worthwhile to note that the piece that caused us to dismantle the first figure (Figure 1–15) actually sets the pattern for the final figure illustrated in Figure 1–17. This often is the case with programming requirements. The requirement that seems to be the least clear is frequently the one that determines the main interrelationships of the program. It is worthwhile to include and understand all the known requirements before beginning coding. Thus, before any solution is attempted the analysis step must be completed.

The person performing the analysis must initially take a broad perspective, see all of the pieces, and understand the main purpose that the program or system is meant to achieve. The key to success here, which ultimately determines the success of the final

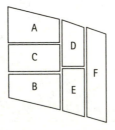

Figure 1–16 *The Last Piece*

Figure 1–17 *Including All the Pieces*

program, is to determine the main purpose of the system from the viewpoint of the person making the request. For large applications, a systems analyst usually conducts the analysis. For smaller applications, the analysis is typically performed directly by the programmer.

Regardless as to how the analysis is done, or by whom, at its conclusion there should be a clear understanding of

- what the system or program must do.
- what reports or outputs must be produced.
- what input is required to create the desired output.

Step 2: Design and Develop a Solution   Once the problem is clearly understood, a solution can be developed. At this point, the programmer is in a similar position to that of an architect who must draw up the plans for a house. The house must conform to certain specifications and meet the needs of its owner, but can be designed and built in many possible ways. This is true for a program as well.

For small applications, the solution may be simple and consist of only one or more calculations that must be performed. More typically, the initial solution must be refined and organized into smaller subsystems, with specifications for how the subsystems will interface with each other. To achieve this goal, the description of the solution starts from the highest level (top-most) requirement and proceeds downward to the parts that must be constructed to achieve this requirement. To make this more meaningful, consider that a computer program is required to track the number of parts in inventory. The required output for this program is a description of all parts carried in inventory and the number of units of each item in stock. The given input includes the initial inventory quantity of each part, the number of items sold, the number of items returned, and the number of items purchased.

For these specifications, a designer could initially organize the requirements for the program into the three sections illustrated in Figure 1–18. This is called a *first-level structure diagram* because it represents the first overall structure of the program selected by the designer.

Once an initial structure is developed, it is refined until the tasks indicated in the boxes are completely defined. For example, both the data entry and report subsections shown in Figure 1–18 would be further refined as follows: the data entry section must

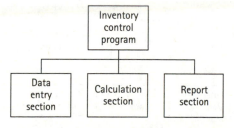

Figure 1–18   *First-Level Structure Diagram*

include provisions for entering the data. Because it is the system designer's responsibility to plan for contingencies and human error, provisions must also be made for changing incorrect data after an entry has been made, and for deleting a previously entered value. Similar subdivisions for the report section can also be made. Figure 1–19 shows a second-level structure diagram for an inventory tracking system that includes these further refinements.

The process of refining a solution continues until the smallest requirement is included within the solution. Note that the design produces a treelike structure where the levels branch out as we move from the top of the structure to the bottom. When the design is complete, each task designated in a box is typically coded with separate sets of instructions that are executed as they are called upon by tasks higher up in the structure.

Step 3: Program the Solution Programming the solution involves translating the chosen design solution into a computer program. In Visual Basic this means creating all of the necessary graphical user interfaces and providing procedural code. If the analysis and solution steps have been performed correctly, this step becomes rather mechanical in nature.

In a well-designed program, the statements making up the procedural code will conform to certain well-defined patterns, or structures, that have been defined in the solution step. These structures consist of the following types:

1. Sequence
2. Selection
3. Iteration
4. Invocation

Sequence defines the order in which instructions within each event procedure are executed by the program. Specifying which instruction comes first, which comes second, and so on, is essential if the procedure is to achieve its purpose.

Selection is the capability to make a choice between different operations, depending on the result of some condition. For example, the value of a number can be checked before a division is performed. If the number is not zero, it can be used as the denomi-

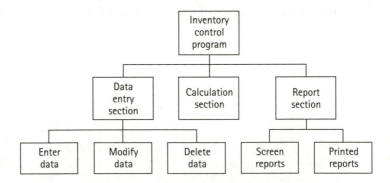

Figure 1–19 *Second-Level Refinement Structure Diagram*

nator of a division operation; otherwise the division will not be performed and the user will receive a warning message.

Repetition (also referred to as looping and iteration) is the same operation being repeated based on the value of a condition. For example, grades might be repeatedly entered and added until a negative grade is entered. In this case, the entry of a negative grade is the condition that signifies the end of the repetitive input and addition of grades. At that point a calculation of an average for all the grades entered could be performed.

Invocation is the summoning into action of a set of procedural code as it is needed. For example, in response to a user-initiated action, such as clicking a button, the event procedure written for this action is called into action or invoked.

Step 4: Test and Correct the Solution   The purpose of testing is to verify that a program works correctly and fulfills its requirements. In theory, testing would reveal all existing program errors (in computer terminology, a program error is called a *bug*[3]). In practice, this would require checking all possible combinations of statement execution. Because of the time and effort required, this is usually an impossible goal, except for extremely simple programs. (Section 5.8 outlines the reasons why this is generally an impossible goal.)

Because exhaustive testing is not feasible for most programs, different philosophies and methods of testing have evolved. At its most basic level, testing requires a conscious effort to ensure that a program works correctly and produces meaningful results. Careful thought must be given to what the test is meant to achieve and the data that will be used in the test. If testing reveals an error (bug), the process of debugging can be initiated, which includes locating and correcting the error, and then verifying the correction. It is important to realize that although testing may reveal an error, it does not necessarily indicate the existence of more errors. Thus, the fact that a test revealed one bug does not indicate that another one is not lurking somewhere else in the program.

Backup   Although not part of the formal design and development process, creating and keeping backup copies of your work at each step in the programming process is critical. This becomes your recovery of last resort should you experience an unforeseen system crash or an unexpected loss of your original work.

Exercises 1.2

1. a. List and describe the four steps required in the design and development stage of an application.

    b. In addition to the development and design stage, what are the other two stages required to produce a program and why are they required?

---

[3]The derivation of this term is rather interesting. When a program stopped running on the MARK I at Harvard University in September 1945, Grace Hopper traced the malfunction to a dead insect in the electrical circuits. She recorded the incident in her logbook at 15:45 hours as "Relay #70.... (moth) in relay. First actual case of bug being found."

2. A note from your department head, Ms. R. Karp says:

   Solve our inventory problems.
                    —R. Karp

   a. What should be your first task?

   b. How would you accomplish this task?

   c. Assuming that everyone cooperates, how long do you think it would take to complete this task?

3. Program development is only one phase in the overall software development procedure. Assuming that documentation and maintenance require 60 percent of the effort in designing a software system, use the table that follows to determine the amount of effort required for initial program coding as a percentage of total software design effort.

Form: Main Menu	Trigger	
Task	Object	Event
Enter Inventory Receipts		
Enter and Process a Mail-in Response		
Enter and Process a Walk-in Request		
Produce Reports		
Exit the System		

4. Many people requesting a program or system for the first time consider coding to be the most important part of program development. They believe that they know what they need and assume that the programmer can begin coding with minimal time spent in analysis. As a programmer, what pitfalls can you envision in working with such people?

5. Many first-time computer users try to contract with programmers for a fixed fee, which means that the total amount to be paid is fixed in advance. What is the advantage to the user in having this arrangement? What is the advantage to the programmer in having this arrangement? What are some disadvantages to both user and programmer in this arrangement?

6. Many programmers prefer to be paid an hourly rate for their work. Why do you think this is so? Under what conditions would it be advantageous for a programmer to give a client a fixed price for the programming effort?

7. Experienced users generally require a clearly written statement of programming work to be done, including a complete description of what the program will do, delivery dates, payment schedules, and testing requirements. What is the advantage to the user in requiring this? What is the advantage to a programmer in working

under this arrangement? What disadvantages does this arrangement have for both user and programmer?

8. Assume that a computer store makes 15 sales per day on average. Assuming that the store is open six days a week and that each sale involves an average of 100 characters, determine the minimum storage that the system must have to keep all sales records for a two-year period.

9. Assume that you are creating a sales recording system for a client. Each sale entered in the system requires that the operator type a description of the item sold, the name and address of the firm buying the item, the value of the item, and a code for the person making the trade. This information consists of a maximum of 300 characters. Estimate the time it would take for an average typist to input 200 sales. (*Hint:* To solve this problem you must make an assumption about the number of words per minute that an average typist can type and the average number of characters per word.)

10. Most commercial printers for personal computers can print at a speed of 165 characters per second. Determine the time it would take to print a complete list of 10,000 records using such a printer, assuming that each record consists of 300 characters.

1.3 Introduction to Modularity

A key feature of a well-designed program is its modular structure. In programming, the term *structure* has two interrelated meanings. The first meaning refers to the program's overall construction which is the topic of this section. The second meaning refers to the form used to carry out individual tasks within a program which is the topic of Chapters 5 and 6. Programs whose structure consists of interrelated screens and tasks, arranged in a logical and easily understandable order to form an integrated and complete unit, are referred to as *modular programs*. As a result of their structure, modular programs are noticeably easier to develop, correct, and modify than programs constructed otherwise. This is because modular programs permit each screen and its associated procedural code to be tested and modified without disturbing other modules and procedural code in the application.

In a modular application, each part of the application is designed and developed to perform a clearly defined and specific function. For example, the first screen presented to a user might include a company logo and a menu consisting of buttons that will activate other screens, as shown in Figure 1-20. Depending on the button clicked by the user, either another screen should appear or some specific task should be accomplished. Each subsequent screen or task should also be designed to produce a clearly understandable and useful result.

The segments used to construct a modular application are referred to as *modules*. In Visual Basic, modules that contain both the visual parts of a program—the screens seen by a user—and the code associated with objects on the screen, are called *form modules*. For each screen in your Visual Basic application you will have one form module. For example, if your program has five screens, it will contain five form modules.

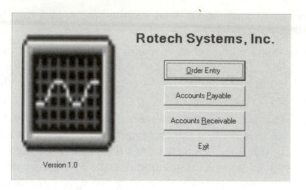

Figure 1–20   *A Sample Opening Screen*

The procedural code that performs actual data processing tasks is most often created in program units called *general procedures*; these are divided into *sub-procedures* and *function procedures*. (We'll refer to function procedures as functions.) Most user-written procedures are stored directly within form modules because they contain the code associated with objects that are on a screen, such as buttons. However, procedural code that will be used by more than one form module must be stored in special code-only modules. Two types of code-only modules exist: *standard* and *class modules*. Figure 1–21 illustrates the interrelationships for an application consisting of two screens and one standard module. As shown, each screen is stored using its own form module which also contains procedures and functions that can only be used by the screen described in the module. Code that is to be shared between the two screens is stored on the standard module. Initially, we will concentrate on single-screen applications that are stored in a single form module.

Procedural Code

Functions and sub-procedures, both of which contain Visual Basic language instructions, are essentially small procedural program units in their own right that must be

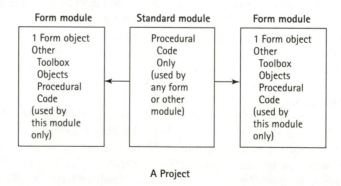

A Project

Figure 1–21   *An Application with Three Modules*

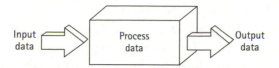

Figure 1–22   *A Procedural Unit Accepts Data, Operates on the Data, and Produces a Result*

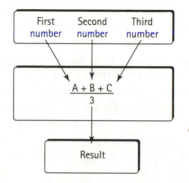

Figure 1–23   *A Procedural Unit that Averages Three Numbers*

capable of receiving data, operating on the data, and producing a result (see Figure 1–22). Typically, a function or sub-procedure performs a single limited task required by the larger application of which it is a part. We will learn about and use both of these unit types, with initial emphasis on procedures.

It is useful to think of both types of program units, functions and sub-procedures, as small machines that transform the data they receive into a finished product. For example, Figure 1–23 illustrates a program unit that accepts three numbers, computes their average, and displays the result.

All procedures have the same structure which is described in detail in Section 2.3.

Aside from functions and sub-procedures which are categories of general procedures, another type of procedure—one that we will be working with extensively—is an *event procedure*. This is a procedure that is called into operation by either a system-initiated or user-initiated event (see Section 1.1) such as clicking the mouse or loading a screen.

Exercises 1.3

1. Describe what information is contained in a form module.

2. Describe the relationship between the information contained in a form module and that contained in a standard module.

3. List two types of programming units that are used to contain procedural code.

4. What is an event procedure?

5. Assuming that btnMessage is the name of a button on a screen, determine what events cause the following procedures to execute:

a. Private Sub btnMessage_Click()

b. Private Sub btnMessage_KeyDown()

Note: Most projects, both programming and nonprogramming, can usually be structured into smaller subtasks or units of activity each of which can be assigned to an individual user screen or window. The development of each screen can often be delegated to a different person so that when all the screens and their associated tasks are finished and integrated, the application is complete. For Exercises 6 through 9, determine a set of screens and tasks that could be used for the application. Be aware that there are many possible solutions for each exercise. The only requirement is that the set of screens and their associated tasks complete the required application. The purpose of these exercises is to have you consider the different ways applications can be structured. Although there is no single correct solution to each problem, there are incorrect solutions and solutions that are better than others. An incorrect solution is one that does not fully solve the problem. One solution is better than another if it more clearly or easily allows a user to operate the application.

6. An inventory application is to be written for entering product data (such as where the product is located in the warehouse and its quantity), for deducting amounts when a product is shipped, and for generating reports (such as quantity on hand and quantity sold for all products).

7. A calculation program is to be written that determines the area of a rectangle.

8. A billing application is to be written that provides the user with three options: one is to enter the items that are to be billed, one is to list all the bills prepared on any given day, and one is to list the twenty most recently billed amounts to any given customer.

9. a. A national medical testing laboratory requires a computer system to prepare its test results daily. Additionally, the laboratory wants the capability to retrieve and output a printed report of all results that meet certain criteria—for example, all results obtained for a particular doctor or all results obtained for hospitals in a particular state. Determine three or four major screens into which this system could be separated.

   b. Suppose someone enters incorrect data for a particular test result and this is discovered after the data has been entered and stored by the system. What additional screens and processing are needed to correct this problem? Discuss why this capability might or might not be required by most applications.

   c. Assume that the capability exists for a user to alter or change data that has been incorrectly entered and stored. Discuss the need for including an audit trail that would allow for a later reconstruction of the changes made, when they were made, and who made them.

1.4 Algorithms

Before the body of any event procedure is written, the programmer must clearly understand what data is to be used, the desired result, and the steps required to produce this result. The procedure (or solution) selected is referred to as an *algorithm*, which is defined as a step-by-step sequence of instructions that must terminate. An algorithm describes how the data is to be processed to produce the desired outputs.

Coding can only begin after we understand the data that we will be using and select an algorithm (the specific steps required to produce the desired result). Writing an event procedure is simply translating a selected algorithm into a language that the computer can use.

To illustrate an algorithm, we will consider a simple problem. Assume that a procedure must calculate the sum of all whole numbers from 1 through 100. Figure 1–24 illustrates three methods we could use to find the required sum. Each method constitutes an algorithm.

Most people who think intuitively would not bother to list the possible alternatives in a detailed step-by-step manner, as we have done here, and then select one of the algorithms to solve the problem. For example, if you had to change a flat tire on your

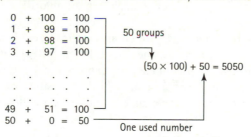

Method 1. Columns: Arrange the numbers from 1 to 100 in a column and add them.

$$
\begin{array}{r}
1 \\
2 \\
3 \\
4 \\
\cdot \\
\cdot \\
\cdot \\
98 \\
99 \\
+100 \\
\hline
5050
\end{array}
$$

Method 2. Groups: Arrange the numbers in convenient groups that sum 100.
Multiply the number of groups by 100 and add in any unused numbers.

$$
\begin{array}{rcrcl}
0 & + & 100 & = & 100 \\
1 & + & 99 & = & 100 \\
2 & + & 98 & = & 100 \\
3 & + & 97 & = & 100 \\
 & & & & \\
\cdot & & \cdot & & \cdot \\
\cdot & & \cdot & & \cdot \\
\cdot & & \cdot & & \cdot \\
49 & + & 51 & = & 100 \\
50 & + & 0 & = & 50
\end{array}
$$

50 groups

$(50 \times 100) + 50 = 5050$

One used number

Method 3. Formula: Use the formula

$$
\text{Sum} = \frac{n(a + b)}{2}
$$

where

n = number of terms to be added
a = first number to be added (1)
b = last number to be added (100)

$$
\text{Sum} = \frac{100(1+100)}{2} = 5050
$$

Figure 1–24   *Summing the Numbers 1 through 100*

car, you would not think of all the steps required—you would simply change the tire or call someone else to do the job. This is an example of intuitive thinking.

However, computers do not respond to intuitive commands. A general statement such as "add the numbers from 1 to 100" means nothing to a computer, because the computer can only respond to algorithmic commands written in an acceptable language such as Visual Basic. To program a computer successfully, you must clearly understand this difference between algorithmic and intuitive commands. You cannot tell a computer to change a tire or to add the numbers from 1 through 100. Instead, you must give the computer a detailed, step-by-step set of instructions that, collectively, forms an algorithm such as the following:

```
Set n equal to 100
Set a = 1
Set b equal to 100
                      n(a + b)
Calculate sum = --------
                         2
Print the sum
```

This set of instructions constitutes a detailed method, or algorithm, for determining the sum of the numbers from 1 through 100. Note that these instructions are not a Visual Basic procedure which must be written in a language to which the computer can respond. This is an algorithm that can be written or described in various ways. When English-like phrases are used to describe the algorithm (the processing steps) as in this example, the description is called *pseudocode*. When mathematical equations are used the description is called a *formula*. When diagrams that employ the symbols shown in Figure 1–25 are used the description is referred to as a *flowchart*. Figure 1–26 illustrates the use of these symbols in depicting an algorithm for determining the average of three numbers.

Because flowcharts are cumbersome to revise and can easily support unstructured programming practices, they have fallen out of favor with professional programmers, while the use of pseudocode to express the logic of algorithms has gained increasing acceptance. In describing an algorithm using pseudocode, short English phrases are used. For example, acceptable pseudocode for describing the steps needed to compute the average of three numbers is:

Input the three numbers into the computer's memory

Calculate the average by adding the numbers and dividing the sum by three

Display the average

An algorithm can only be written using computer-language statements after it has been selected and the programmer understands the steps required. The writing of an algorithm using computer-language statements is called *coding* the algorithm, which is the third step in our program development procedure (see Figure 1–27).

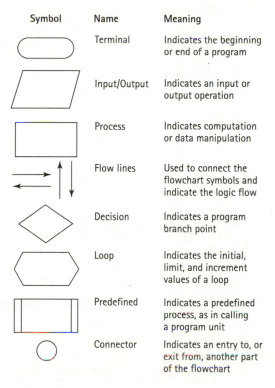

Symbol	Name	Meaning
	Terminal	Indicates the beginning or end of a program
	Input/Output	Indicates an input or output operation
	Process	Indicates computation or data manipulation
	Flow lines	Used to connect the flowchart symbols and indicate the logic flow
	Decision	Indicates a program branch point
	Loop	Indicates the initial, limit, and increment values of a loop
	Predefined	Indicates a predefined process, as in calling a program unit
	Connector	Indicates an entry to, or exit from, another part of the flowchart

Figure 1–25   *Flowchart Symbols*

Exercises 1.4

1. Outline a step-by-step procedure (list the steps) to do these tasks: (**Note:** There is no single correct answer for each of these tasks. The exercise is designed to give you practice in converting intuitive commands into equivalent algorithms, and making the shift between the thought processes involved in the two types of thinking.)

   a. Fix a flat tire.

   b. Make a telephone call.

   c. Go to the store and purchase a loaf of bread.

   d. Roast a turkey.

2. a. Determine the six possible step-by-step procedures (list the steps) to paint the flower shown in Figure 1–28, with the restriction that each color must be completed before a new color can be started. (*Hint:* one of the algorithms is *Use Yellow first, Green second, Black last.*)

   b. Which of the six painting algorithms (series of steps) is best if we are limited to using one paintbrush, and we know that there is no turpentine to clean the brush?

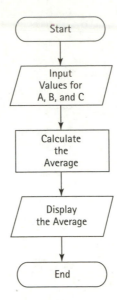

Figure 1–26   *Flowchart for Calculating the Average of Three Numbers*

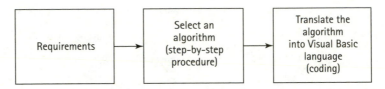

Figure 1–27   *Coding an Algorithm*

3. Determine and write an algorithm (list the steps) to interchange the contents of two cups of liquid. Assume that a third cup is available to hold the contents of either cup temporarily. Each cup should be rinsed before any new liquid is poured into it.

4. Write a detailed set of instructions, using words, to calculate the dollar amount of money in a piggybank that contains *h* half-dollars, *q* quarters, *n* nickels, *d* dimes, and *p* pennies.

5. Write a set of detailed, step-by-step instructions, using words, to find the smallest number in a group of three integers.

6. a. Write a set of detailed, step-by-step instructions, using words, to calculate the change remaining from a dollar after a purchase is made. Assume that the cost of the goods purchased is less than a dollar. The change received should consist of the smallest number of coins possible.

   b. Repeat Exercise 6a, but assume the change is to be given only in pennies.

7. a. Write an algorithm to locate the first occurrence of the name JONES in a list of names arranged in random order.

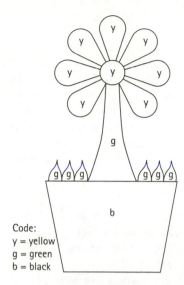

Figure 1–28 *A Simple Paint-by-Number Figure*

b. Discuss how you could improve your algorithm for Exercise 7a if the list of names was arranged in alphabetical order.

8. Write an algorithm to determine the total number of occurrences of the letter *e* in any sentence.

9. Determine and write an algorithm to sort four numbers into ascending order (from lowest to highest).

1.5 Focus on Program Design and Implementation: The Rotech Case and Rapid Application Prototyping

To facilitate the transition from learning Visual Basic fundamentals to producing real-world applications, an actual business application is designed and constructed in this continuing Focus on Program Design and Implementation section. Specifically, we will use rapid application prototyping, a method introduced at the end of this Focus section, to produce a multiscreen business system. To make the design and implementation meaningful, we will concentrate on a specific business application. However, the ideas presented have general applicability to the majority of real-life systems you will encounter as a professional programmer. To reinforce these ideas, a series of business projects is provided, one of which you will design and implement using the techniques presented.

Forms

The vast majority of commercial systems are transaction-oriented, where a *transaction* is defined as a logical unit of work. For example, purchasing an item from a store constitutes a transaction. Adding or delivering a product from inventory is a transaction. Sending an item in the mail is a transaction, and so on. Forms are used to handle transactions that require a user to enter data at the terminal.

A **form** is a computer screen that is the interface for a user to enter data or request information from the system and for displaying screen reports. For example, Figure 1–29 shows a form for user-entered order information.

Once data is entered into a form, an application will perform one or more tasks using the data, such as

- saving the data into a transactions file (for example, storing the data for each sale of merchandise into a file).
- updating another file (for example, deducting a sale from the amount of inventory in an inventory file).
- performing a calculation (for example, computing the total of a bill, including sales tax, for items purchased).
- preparing a report (for example, printing a bill for items purchased or providing a summary list of sales made in each sales region).

Additionally, commercial systems usually perform more than one data entry function. For example, a system might have one form for recording sales, one form for entering returns, one form for maintaining a customer list, one form for maintaining a sales force list, one form for maintaining a list of inventory items, and another form for selecting reports.

A general design approach for a multiform system is to begin the application with a main-menu screen that lists the application's capabilities. This menu screen, a sample of

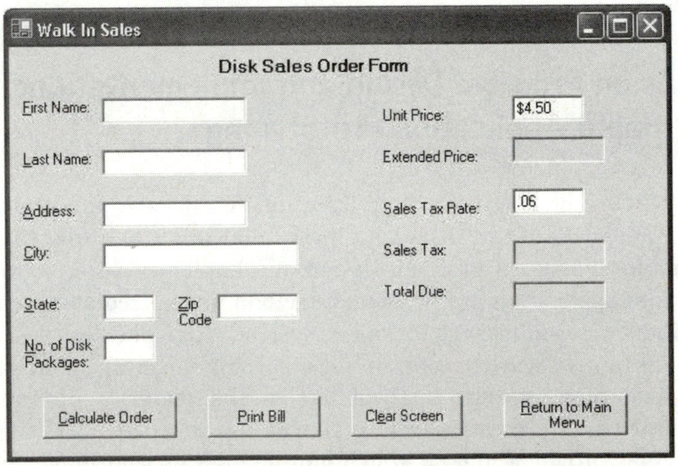

Figure 1–29 *A Sample Order-Entry Form*

Figure 1–30 *A Sample Main Menu Screen*

which is shown in Figure 1–30, then allows the user to select the part of the application with which they wish to work. For example, by selecting the Walk Ins Button shown in Figure 1–30, the user would be presented with the order entry form shown in Figure 1–29.

To understand the forms required for a fully-functioning business system, you need to know the following:

1. The requirements of the system and what the system should accomplish
2. How to design a data entry form (input)
3. How to perform calculations (processing)
4. How to construct reports that are displayed on the screen and reports that produce hard-copy printed documents (output)
5. How to construct a main menu screen and connect it to the other forms in the system
6. How to construct and maintain data files needed by the application

The two most important items in this list are the first and last. Without fully understanding the first item, you cannot build a useful system or use the other items in a positive way. The last item is equally important because the majority of business systems deal with maintaining data stored as data files. These include adding transactions to a transactions file, maintaining a file of inventory items, maintaining a list of customer names and addresses, or maintaining a list of sales representatives. If the correct data is not stored where it is available to the system, the other elements cannot be used to add data to the files, process the data, and create the desired output reports.

The remaining items in the list are really competence elements. They represent the tools that a programmer must have to correctly maintain data files and produce applications that meet the specified requirements. The first eight chapters of this text deal with these competency items which include how to design forms for the input, processing, and output of information. After you also have mastered the material on databases in Chapter 9, you will have the ability to construct a fully functional business system.

Each aspect of Visual Basic is presented in a way that enables you to understand it and make it a part of your programming tool kit. To reinforce how these individual elements are connected in practice, we will also construct a working business application for the following business case.

Rotech Systems, Inc. is a direct-mail firm in the business of warehousing products and distributing them in response to various promotional offers made to the public. For example, direct-mail firms handle the special offers made on cereal boxes requiring you to send in your name and address, a given number of UPC codes, and a shipping and handling fee to receive the offered item. Similarly, computer disk manufacturers frequently offer to send you a free set of disks if you send in the same type of data. These kinds of offers, as well as the ones you see on television for CD and videotape sets, are all handled by direct-mail firms.

Rotech receives the responses by mail, enters the name and address of the person responding, and the type and quantity of each item requested, and prepares a packing slip so that the items can be picked from inventory, packaged, and sent off. It is also Rotech's responsibility to maintain an up-to-date inventory record by keeping track of all product deliveries and disbursements made in response to a specific offer. For now we will consider that the offer is for a package of 10 diskettes. Additionally, the disk manufacturer has asked Rotech to accommodate any walk-in customers. These customers, referred to as walk-in's for short, are people who walk in to Rotech's offices and wish to purchase one or more of the promotional items. Due to good-will considerations, the diskette manufacturer does not want to turn these people away, and has given Rotech permission to sell disk packages to these commercial customers for $4.50 for each package of 10 diskettes. For these sales, a bill that includes a 6% state sales tax must be calculated and printed.

As their in-house programmer, you have been given the task to design and build a program to handle this application.

Tips From the Pros

Developing Commercial Applications

When developing commercial applications, you will mainly be constructing multiform systems that interface with data stored in one or more data files. Most applications, except for very simple calculation programs, deal with extensive amounts of data and must perform many separate business functions. These functions include order entry, invoice preparation, accounts receivable, accounts payable, and maintenance of inventory. In practice, one or more screens are allocated to performing each of these tasks.

The menu system is the easiest part to build and the most user-impressive aspect of this type of application. The menu system tells the user what choices are available and provides a means of navigating between different parts of the system. The most difficult aspects of building a commercial system are constructing the databases and the user-interface that permits storing data into, retrieving data from, and processing the data within the database. Between these two extremes is a range of competency items that includes screen design, performing calculations, correctly formatting output data, and preparing detailed printed reports.

In its most general form, this application contains all of the elements you will encounter in most of your professional programming work. Let's see what these elements are, and how one goes about constructing a working system that correctly, and successfully, handles these elements.

Program Elements

The central feature of most commercial systems is the maintenance of a base of data. The data is stored in a file and is commonly referred to as both a data file and a database. (The term "database" is actually a more encompassing term and is explained in detail in Chapter 9.) Data, either stored in a separate data file or as an integral part of an application, is further subdivided into two types: static and dynamic.

Static data contains data that does not change much from day to day. Although static data must be maintained by additions, deletions, and modifications, few such operations are applied to this type of data on a daily basis. *Dynamic data*, on the other hand, is data that changes frequently, usually on a daily basis.

In our particular application, the product list constitutes the static data. Although there is only one item that we are dealing with, the specifics of the 10-diskette package could change or another item could be added to the offer.

Unlike the product list, the inventory file, which consists of how much of each product is in stock, changes daily. This depends on both receipt of product, which is relatively static, and dispersal of product to the offer's responders. This is a dynamic situation because responses occur on a daily basis. We will also want to keep track of each responder, and for this purpose we will need a transactions data file. This file will consist of the name and address of each responder and the product type and quantity requested. For now, however, do not be concerned with the details of each file. Think instead of the bigger picture, which is that most commercial systems contain two types of data—both static and dynamic—and that much of this data is stored in data files.

Next, every system must generate a series of reports which is the output produced by the system. Reports are categorized as either screen or printed reports. A *screen report* generates its information on a screen, while a *printed report* generates a hard copy on a printer. Typically, a screen report provides a quick response to a single question. For example, in our application such a report might be used to answer the question, "How many packages of diskettes were requested last month from New Jersey?" A printed report for our system includes a packing slip for each request. It also could include a monthly summary of how many diskette packages were distributed in each of the fifty states.

Most systems must also perform some calculations. The calculations can vary from simple addition and subtraction of quantities to and from inventory, to more moderate calculations of invoices for goods sold, or to sophisticated statistical analysis of seasonal fluctuations in product demand. In this category, the Rotech application needs to make relatively minor calculations, adding to and subtracting from the quantity of product held in inventory, as well as calculating invoices for all walk-in sales.[4]

---

[4]In strict business terms, an *invoice* is a direct request for payment while a *bill* is simply a notification statement of money owed for goods or services provided.

Finally, the last item that each system must provide is a series of forms that are used by the operator for entering all requests and producing all reports. This is the system's visual interface. Access to these forms will be provided by a menu system, which gives the operator a visual means of selecting a desired form and moving between forms. Figure 1–31 illustrates how these system elements are related within a typical commercial system and how an application's interface elements and code are linked to accomplish specific tasks.

In this text we will present each menu choice as a button, as shown in Figure 1–30. (An alternate method, using a menu bar, is presented in Section 11.4). When a user selects a menu item by clicking the desired button, another form appears. On this next form, which can be one of many, the user may then enter additional data and/or request that a certain task be completed.

Systems Analysis and Design

The traditional method of designing an application, that existed prior to the introduction of visual languages such as Visual Basic, was to always start with a detailed systems analysis. This detailed analysis, which is also required with Visual Basic (but later in the development cycle), defines exactly what the system must accomplish:

- What reports or outputs the system must produce
- What inputs are required to produce the desired output
- The number of users the system has to accommodate
- The average number of transactions that must be processed in a given time period, usually per hour or per day
- The maximum number of transactions that must be processed in a given time period, usually per hour or per day
- The type of data that has to be stored by the system

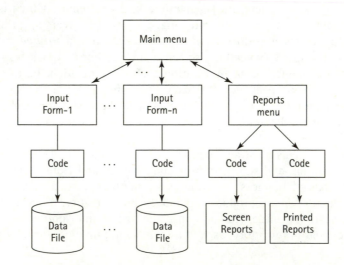

Figure 1–31 *Components of a Typical Business System*

- The maximum amount of data the system is required to store
- Backup procedures in case the system crashes (fails)
- Security procedures for gaining access to the system
- Interface requirements with other systems

The first questions that need to be asked when doing an analysis should always involve determining the motivation of the person making the request and his or her expectations for the program. For example, questions such as, "What is the main problem you are having with your present system?" and, "What are the main tasks that the new system must fulfill?" are ways of eliciting useful and necessary information from the requester. Additional questions include, "If you could make a wish list of everything you want from the system, what would it be?" Later you can rank the wish list by those items that are essential, those that are very useful but not essential, and those that would be nice to have but could be omitted if necessary due to cost, equipment, or time constraints.

These questions are always asked so that the analyst can see the request from the requester's perspective. Frequently, a simple initial request for a program conceals many expectations that are not initially verbalized. It is the job of the analyst to uncover these expectations before the system is assembled. The analysis is complete when the objectives of the system or program have been understood and all of the algorithms for completing each task are fully known.

Rapid Application Prototyping

As a result of the ease with which visual interfaces can be constructed and modified, a more recent approach to designing an application is to start implementing a system before the systems analysis has been completed. This newer approach is referred to as *rapid application prototyping*, and is the development approach we will use in this text for our Rotech System project. It consists of the following procedure:

1. Gain a cursory understanding of the data used and the reports required by the system.
2. Construct a menu system that can be tested by the user—initially, selecting a menu item will only bring up a blank form that performs no processing.
3. Complete each form, which includes any input, processing, output, or calling of additional forms, and modify the menu system as you gain a complete understanding of the data, input, reporting requirements, and processing tasks.

In this rapid prototyping procedure, the user becomes an integral part of the development process. As you show the user the menu system, she or he can tell you if you have correctly captured all of the required tasks. As you fully understand the data and reporting requirements, you add functionality to the menu and each form, so that a selection ultimately leads to completing a desired task rather than bringing up a blank form. In this manner, you get valuable user feedback on the menu's completeness and the ease of using each form, allowing you to modify elements of the application based on this feedback.

The advantage of rapid prototyping is that you get both user buy-in and ownership, in addition to getting early warning of anything the user doesn't like about the system or of elements of the system that are not operating as they should. Users that are actively involved in the design of the system—how it looks, how it works, and how it evolves—tend to take real ownership of the system, have a vested interest in seeing that the system succeeds, to alert you to potential pitfalls early in the development cycle. Because *the success of a system is directly related to a user's perceived ease of use of both menus and data-entry forms*, and also to a user's perception that the system is accomplishing what she or he expects it to accomplish, it is in your interest as an applications programmer to get the user involved early. Make special note of the word *perceived* here. Even if your system is operationally correct and really can accomplish what it is supposed to accomplish, if the user does not perceive it to be easy to use and functionally successful, your system will be judged unsuccessful. This may seem unfair, but it is how business systems are judged.

To begin a rapid prototype development, you initially present the user with the first menu screen that she or he will see when the application is run. This menu is easily created using the techniques presented in Chapter 2 where one is constructed for the Rotech application in the Project Planning and Implementation Focus section.

Task Trigger List (TTL) Tables

One of the first elements used in developing an application and constructing a main menu is a table that lists the tasks required by the system and the events that will "trigger" (that is, activate) each task. This table, referred to as a Task Trigger List (TTL) table, initially contains only the major tasks that your system must accomplish. As your understanding of the system develops, additional tasks are added to the list. When you have completed the system's design, the TTL table will contain all of the tasks performed by the system and the events by which each task is executed. Table 1–2 contains an initial TTL table for our Rotech Systems application.

Note that Table 1–2 essentially lists items that would be included in a first-level structure diagram, but both the objects and events used to trigger each task and the form to which each task will be attached have been omitted. Clicking a button contained on the main menu screen will trigger each task in this initial TTL table. Thus, the *objects* used to activate the tasks in the initial TTL list will be a set of buttons, and the specific *event* that triggers execution of a task will be the clicking of an appropriate but-

Table 1–2   Initial Rotech Systems TTL Table

Form: Main Menu	Trigger	
Task	Object	Event
Enter Inventory Receipts		
Enter and Process a Mail-in Response		
Enter and Process a Walk-in Request		
Produce Reports		
Exit the System		

ton. In the next Focus section, you will have the necessary information for completing Table 1–2 using the correct form, object, and event names. The completed initial table is then used to construct a working main menu.

Programming Projects

Note: For each selected project, do the following:

- Define what constitutes the static and dynamic data.
- List the data that you think should be stored in its own data file.
- List the information that should be included with each transaction.
- Construct an initial TTL table (list only the tasks, not the form, objects, or events).

Also note that your instructor may assign one of these projects as a semester project. In this case, you will be required to construct a suitable application following the development procedure presented for the Rotech Systems case in subsequent Focus sections.

Case Study 1   You have been asked to construct a billing system for a local lawyer. The billing system is meant to produce an invoice for the number of hours that the lawyer has worked for the client. The lawyer does not have many clients and is content to enter the name, address, and past due amount for each client. Currently, the lawyer charges $100 for each hour of time spent with a client.

Case Study 2   You have been asked by a local oil company to construct a notification system for its customers. The system is meant to produce an invoice that notifies a customer that a delivery of oil was made, the amount of oil that was delivered, and the total bill for the delivery. The company currently has 500 customers that it supplies with home heating oil, and the current retail price of the heating oil is $1.25 per gallon.

Case Study 3   You have been asked to construct a point-of-sale system for a local bookstore. The store currently has an inventory of 400 books identified by an ISBN number, author, title, quantity in stock, and quantity on order. Your system must calculate a bill, including sales tax, when books are purchased, and deduct the number of books purchased in each sale from inventory. Additionally, the system must add to inventory when a shipment of books comes in or an item is returned.

Case Study 4   You have been asked to design a billing system for a local newspaper delivery service. The service delivers the local morning newspaper and has three rates: $2.50 per week for weekday delivery, $1.50 for Sunday delivery, and $3.50 for customers that get both weekday and Sunday delivery. Currently, the news delivery service has 200 customers.

Case Study 5   You have been asked to construct a system for a local dry-cleaning company that currently serves about 600 active customers. The company provides dry cleaning of pants, shirts, blouses, dresses, suits, and outerwear at prices of $3.00, $1.50, $2.50, $4.00, $5.00, and $10.00, respectively.

Case Study 6 You have been asked to construct a billing system for a local psychologist whose practice consists of seeing patients either individually or in groups. The psychologist charges $100 a session for individual therapy and $35 a session for group therapy. Currently the psychologist has an active patient list of 25 patients.

Case Study 7 A small municipal bond trading firm maintains a list of approximately 100 municipal bonds that it owns as part of its bond inventory. A bond is identified by a 10-digit CUSIP number, an issuer's name, a maturity date, a coupon rate, and a price. The firm deals with approximately 100 other bond firms. Your system must record each bond purchase and sale. The firm has 30 transactions a day on average. Each transaction must record the sales person, the firm bought from or sold to, the amount of bonds in the transaction, the type of transaction (purchase or sale), the price of the bond, the quantity of bonds transacted, and the CUSIP number of the bond. Currently the firm has five sales people.

1.6 Knowing About: Computer Hardware

All computers, from large supercomputers costing millions of dollars to smaller desktop personal computers, must perform a minimum set of functions and provide the capability to:

1. Accept input.
2. Display output.
3. Store information in a logically consistent format (traditionally binary).
4. Perform arithmetic and logic operations on either the input or stored data.
5. Monitor, control, and direct the overall operation and sequencing of the system.

Figure 1–32 illustrates the computer hardware components that support these capabilities. These physical components are collectively referred to as *hardware*.

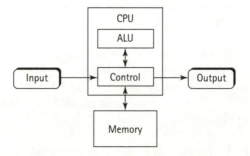

Figure 1–32 *Basic Hardware Units of a Computer*

Memory Unit   This unit stores information in a logically consistent format. Typically, both instructions and data are stored in memory, usually in separate and distinct areas.

Each computer contains memory of two fundamental types: RAM and ROM. *RAM,* which is an acronym for *Random Access Memory*, is usually volatile, which means that whatever is stored there is lost when the computer's power is turned off. Your programs and data are stored in RAM while you are using the computer. The size of a computer's RAM memory is usually specified in terms of how many bytes of RAM are available to the user. Personal Computer (PC) memories currently consist of 64 million to 1 trillion bytes. A million bytes is denoted as a megabyte, or MB for short, and a trillion bytes is denoted as a gigabyte, or GB for short.

ROM, which is an acronym for *Read Only Memory*, contains fundamental instructions that cannot be lost or changed by the casual computer user. ROM contains instructions necessary for loading anything else into the machine when it is first turned on and any other instructions the manufacturer requires to be permanently accessible when the computer is turned on. ROM is *nonvolatile*; its contents are not lost when the power is turned off.

Control Unit   The control unit directs and monitors the overall operation of the computer. It keeps track of where in memory the next instruction resides, issues the signals needed to both read data from and write data to other units in the system, and executes all instructions.

Arithmetic and Logic Unit (ALU)   The ALU performs all the arithmetic and logic functions, such as addition, subtraction, comparison, and so on, provided by the system.

Input/Output (I/O) Unit   This unit provides access to and from the computer. It is the interface to which peripheral devices such as keyboards, cathode ray screens, and printers are attached.

Secondary Storage   Because RAM memory in large quantities is still relatively expensive and volatile, it is not practical as a permanent storage area for programs and data. Secondary or auxiliary storage devices are used for this purpose. Although data has been stored on punched cards, paper tape, and other media in the past, virtually all secondary storage is now done on magnetic tape, magnetic disks, and optical storage media.

The surfaces of magnetic tapes and disks are coated with a material that can be magnetized by a write head, and the stored magnetic field can be detected by a read head. Current tapes are capable of storing thousands of characters per inch of tape, and a single tape may store up to hundreds of megabytes. Tapes, by nature, are sequential storage media, allowing data to be written or read in one sequential stream from beginning to end. Should you desire access to a block of data in the middle of the tape, you must scan all preceding data on the tape to find the block you want. Because of this, tapes are primarily used for mass backup of the data stored on large-capacity disk drives.

A more convenient method of rapidly accessing stored data is provided by a *direct access storage device (DASD)*, where any one file or program can be written or read independent of its position on the storage medium. The most popular DASD in recent years has been the magnetic disk. A *magnetic hard disk* consists of either a single rigid platter or several platters that spin together on a common spindle. A movable access arm positions the read/write heads over, but not quite touching, the recordable surfaces.

In optical media, data is stored by using laser light to change the reflective surface properties of a single removable disk identical to an audio compact disk. The disk is called a *CD-ROM* and is capable of storing several thousand megabytes.[5] Although most CD-ROMs are currently read-only devices, erasable technology is now widely available that permits the user to record, erase, and reuse data on optical media. In addition, technology now exists to read data stored in DVD format. DVDs allow for approximately 10 times the capacity of CD-ROMs.

Hardware Evolution

In the first commercially available computers of the 1950s, all hardware units were built using relays and vacuum tubes. The resulting computers were extremely large pieces of equipment, capable of making thousands of calculations per second and costing millions of dollars. With the introduction of transistors in the 1960s, both the size and cost of computer hardware were reduced. The transistor was approximately one-twentieth the size of its vacuum tube counterpart. The transistor's small size allowed manufacturers to combine the arithmetic and logic unit with the control unit into a single new unit. This combined unit is called the *central processing unit (CPU)*. The combination of the ALU and control units into one CPU made sense because a majority of control signals generated by a program are directed to the ALU in response to arithmetic and logic instructions within the program. Combining the ALU with the control unit simplified the interface between these two units and provided improved processing speed.

The mid-1960s saw the introduction of integrated circuits (ICs), resulting in still another significant reduction in the space required to produce a CPU. Initially, integrated circuits were manufactured with up to 100 transistors on a single 1 cm^2 chip of silicon. Such devices are referred to as small-scale integrated (SSI) circuits. Current versions of these chips contain from hundreds of thousands to over a million transistors and are referred to as very large-scale integrated (VLSI) chips. VLSI chip technology has provided the means of transforming the giant computers of the 1950s into today's desktop personal computers. The individual units required to form a computer (CPU, memory, and I/O) are now all manufactured on individual VLSI chips. The single-chip CPU is referred to as a *microprocessor*. Figure 1–33 illustrates how these chips are connected internally within current personal computers.

Concurrent with the remarkable reduction in computer hardware size, there has been an equally dramatic decrease in cost and increase in processing speeds. Equivalent computer hardware that cost over a million dollars in 1950 can now be purchased for less than five hundred dollars. If the same reductions occurred in the automobile industry, for example, a Rolls-Royce car could now be purchased for ten dollars! The processing speeds of current computers have also increased by a factor of a thousand over their

---

[5]A thousand megabytes is referred to as a gigabit.

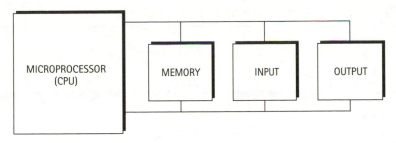

Figure 1–33   *VLSI Chip Connections for a Desktop Computer*

1950s predecessors, with the computational speeds of current machines being measured in both millions of instructions per second (MIPS) and billions of instructions per second (BIPS).

Bits and Bytes

It would be very convenient if a computer stored numbers and letters inside its memory and arithmetic and logic units the way that people do. The number 126, for example, would then be stored as 126, and the letter A stored as the letter A. Unfortunately, due to the physical components used in building a computer, this is not the case.

The smallest and most basic data item in a computer is called a *bit*. Physically, a bit is really a switch that can either be open or closed. By convention, the open and closed positions of each switch are represented by 0 and 1, respectively.

A single bit that represents the values 0 and 1, by itself, has limited usefulness. All computers, therefore, group a set number of bits together, both for storage and transmission. The grouping of eight bits to form a larger unit is a universal computer standard referred to as *byte*. A single byte consisting of eight bits, where each bit is either a 0 or 1, can represent any one of 256 distinct patterns. These consist of the pattern 00000000 (all eight switches open) to the pattern 11111111 (all eight switches closed), and all possible combinations of 0s and 1s in between. Each of these patterns can be used to represent either a letter of the alphabet, other single characters such as a dollar sign or a comma, a single digit, or numbers containing more than one digit. The patterns of 0s and 1s used to represent letters, single digits, and other single characters are called *character codes*. (One such code, called the ANSI code, is presented in Section 3.1.) The patterns used to store numbers are called *number codes*.

Words

One or more bytes may themselves be grouped into larger units, called *words*, facilitating faster and more extensive data access. For example, retrieving a word consisting of four bytes from a computer's memory results in more information than that obtained from retrieving a word consisting of a single byte. Such retrieval is also considerably faster than four individual byte retrievals. This increase in speed and capacity, however, is achieved by an increase in the computer's cost and complexity.

Table 1–3   Integer Values and Word Size

Word Size	Maximum Integer Value	Minimum Integer Value
1 Byte	127	−128
2 Bytes	32,767	−32,768
4 Bytes	2,147,483,647	−2,147,483,648

Early personal computers, such as the Apple IIe and Commodore, internally stored and transmitted words consisting of single bytes. The AT&T 6300 and IBM-PC/XT use word sizes consisting of two bytes, while Digital Equipment, Data General, and Prime minicomputers store and process words consisting of four bytes each. Supercomputers, such as the CRAY-1 and Control Data 7000, have six-byte and eight-byte words, respectively.

The number of bytes in a word determines the maximum and minimum values that can be represented by the word. Table 1–3 lists these values for 1-byte, 2-byte, and 4-byte words. (Each of the values listed can be derived using 8-bit, 16-bit, and 32-bit value boxes, respectively.)

In addition to representing integer values, computers must also store and transmit numbers containing decimal points, mathematically referred to as real numbers. The codes used for real numbers are more complex than those used for integers but still depend on a two's complement type of representation.

1.7 Common Programming Errors and Problems

The most common errors associated with the material presented in this chapter are as follows:

1. A major programming error made by most beginning programmers is the rush to create and run an application before fully understanding what is required, including the algorithms that will be used to produce the desired result. This results in a lack of documentation or even a program outline. Simply checking the selected algorithm written in pseudocode can catch many problems.

2. A second major error is not backing up a program. Many new programmers make this mistake until they lose a program that has taken considerable time to code.

3. The third error made by many new programmers is the failure to understand that computers respond only to explicitly-defined algorithms. Telling a computer to add

a group of numbers is quite different than telling a friend to add the numbers. The computer must be given the precise instructions in a programming language.

1.8 Chapter Review

Key Terms

algorithm
analysis
assembler
assembly language
coding
compiler
design and development
documentation
function
hardware
high-level language
low-level language
machine language
object-oriented
procedure-oriented

programming
programming language
pseudocode
refinement
repetition
secondary storage
selection
sequence
software
software development procedure
software engineering
software maintenance
sub procedure
testing

Summary

1. The first recorded attempt at creating a self-operating computational machine was by Charles Babbage in 1822.

2. The ENIAC (Electrical Numerical Integrator and Computer) was the first operational digital computer. It became operational in 1946 and depended on externally connected wires to direct its operation. The internal design of ENIAC was based on work done previously by Dr. John V. Atanasoff and Clifford Berry at Iowa State University in 1937.

3. The EDSAC (Electronic Delayed Storage Automatic Computer) became the first commercially produced computer to permit instructions stored inside the computer's memory to direct and control the machine's operation. Prior to this, computers used external wiring to direct their operation.

4. Programming languages come in a variety of forms and types. Machine-language programs contain the binary codes that can be executed by a computer. Assembly languages permit the use of symbolic names for mathematical operations and memory addresses. Machine and assembly languages are referred to as *low-level languages*.

5. *High-level languages* are programming languages that are written using instructions that resemble a written language, such as English, and can be run on a variety of computer types. Compiler languages require a compiler to translate the

program into machine code, while interpreter languages require an interpreter to do the translation.

6. *Procedure-oriented* languages consist of a series of procedures that direct the operation of a computer.

7. *Object-oriented* languages permit the use of objects within a program. Each object is defined by its properties, such as its size and color.

8. Event-based programs execute program code depending on what events occur, which in turn depends on what the user does.

9. GUIs are graphical user interfaces that provide the user with objects that recognize events, such as clicking a mouse.

10. An *algorithm* is a step-by-step sequence of instructions that describes how a computation is to be performed.

Test Yourself—Short Answer

1. A set of instructions to tell the computer what to do is called a _____ .

2. An example of a *high-level* language is _____ .

3. All high-level languages must be translated into _____ before they can be executed on the computer.

4. A programming language that is translated into executable code, line by line, as it is executed is called an _____ language.

5. A programming language that translates all of the code into executable statements before any execution takes place is called a _____ language.

6. The editor that is used in creating a graphical interface is a _____ editor.

7. The phase of software development that accounts for more than 75% of overall system cost for the majority of systems is _____ of the system.

8. The four steps required in the development and design phase of a program are _____ , _____ , _____ , and _____ .

9. Of the four steps required in the development and design phase of a program, the step that requires the most effort in large commercial systems is _____ .

10. The visual parts of a Visual Basic program are stored in _____ modules.

Introduction to Visual Basic .NET

In this chapter we begin learning about the fundamentals of programming and Visual Basic .NET. First we examine the two elements that are required by every practical Visual Basic program: the screens and instructions seen by the user, and the "behind the scenes" processing that is done by the program. We then present the basic design windows that you must be familiar with to produce such programs. Finally, we show you how to use these design windows to create the visual user interface, or GUI, and then add processing instructions.

2.1   Elements of a Visual Basic Application

Visual Basic was initially introduced in 1991 as the first programming language that directly supported programmable graphical user interfaces using language-supplied objects. From that time until 2002, there were five other versions released, each version having features that increased the power of the language. In 2001, Microsoft released the .NET (pronounced "dot net") platform. Visual Basic .NET, or VB.NET, is an upgrade to the last version of VB (version 6.0) that conforms to the .NET platform. As you will see in subsequent chapters, the changes in VB.NET allow programmers to write Web or desk-top applications within the same language. In addition, VB.NET is fully object-oriented as opposed to prior versions that had many, but not all, of the elements of an object-oriented language. This book is based on VB.NET. In the balance of the book we will sometimes refer to Visual Basic as VB, omitting .NET.

From a programming viewpoint, Visual Basic is an object-oriented language that consists of two fundamental parts: a visual part and a language part. The visual part of the language consists of a set of objects, while the language part consists of a high-level procedural programming language. These two elements of the language are used together to create applications. An *application* is simply a Visual Basic program that can be run under the Windows operating system. The term *application* is preferred to the term *program* for two reasons: one, it is the term selected by Microsoft to designate any program that can be run under its Windows Operating System (all versions) and two, it is used to avoid confusion with older procedural programs that consisted entirely of only a language element. Thus, for our purposes we can express the elements of a Visual Basic application as:

```
Visual Basic Application = Object-Based Visual Part +
Procedural-Based Language Part
```

Thus, learning to create Visual Basic applications requires being very familiar with both elements, visual and language.

The Visual Element

From a user's standpoint, the visual part of an application is provided within a window. This is the graphical interface that allows the user to see the input and output provided by the application. This user interface is referred to as the *graphical user interface* (GUI). From a programmer's perspective the GUI is constructed by placing a set of visual objects on a blank window, or form, when the program is being developed. For example, consider Figure 2-1, which shows how a particular application would look to the user. From a programmer's viewpoint, the application shown in Figure 2-1 is based on the design form shown in Figure 2-2. The points displayed on the form are a design grid used to arrange objects on the form and are only displayed during design time.

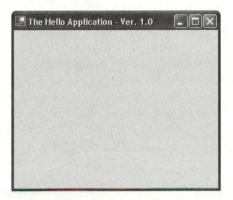

Figure 2-1   *A User's View of an Application*

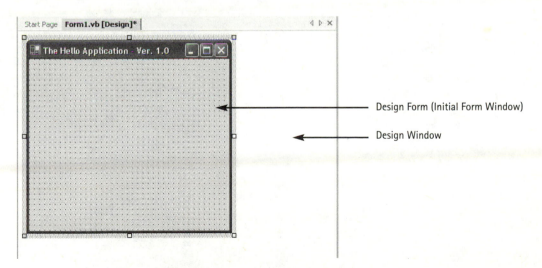

Figure 2-2   *The Design Form on which Figure 2-1 is Based*

The programmer can place various objects on this form, which is itself a Visual Basic object. When an application is run, the form becomes a window that provides the background for the various objects placed on the form by the programmer. The objects on the window become the controls used to direct program events. Let's take a moment to look at the objects provided in the Visual Basic Toolbox. The standard object Toolbox, which is illustrated in Figure 2–3, contains the objects we will use in constructing each graphical user interface.

Figure 2–3 *The Standard Visual Basic Toolbox*

Programmer Notes

Forms and Controls

When an application is being designed, a *form* is a container upon which controls are placed. When an application is executed, the form becomes either a window or a dialog box. Forms can be of two types: SDI or MDI. The acronym SDI stands for Single Document Interface, which means that only one window at a time can be displayed by an application. SDI applications can have multiple windows, but a user can only view one window at a time. The acronym MDI refers to Multiple Document Interface, which means the application consists of a single "parent" or main window that can contain multiple "child" or internal windows. For example, the Notepad application supplied with the Windows operating system is an SDI application, while Excel and Access are both MDI applications.

A control is an object that can be placed on a form, and has its own set of recognized properties, methods, and events. Controls are used to receive user input, display output, and trigger event procedures.

A majority of applications can be constructed using a minimal set of objects provided by the standard object Toolbox. This minimal set consists of the Label, TextBox, and Button objects. The next set of objects that are more frequently found in applications include the CheckBox, RadioButton, ListBox, and ComboBox. Finally, the Timer and PictureBox can be used for constructing interesting moving images across the window. Table 2–1 lists these object types and describes what each object is used for. The remaining sections of the text will describe the use of objects in the toolbox, with special emphasis on the four objects (Label, TextBox, Button, and ListBox) that you will use in almost every application that you develop.

In addition to the basic set of controls provided in VB, a great number of objects can be purchased either for special purpose applications or to enhance standard applications.

Table 2–1   Fundamental Object Types and Their Uses

Object Type	Use
Label	Create text that a user cannot directly change.
TextBox	Enter or display data.
Button	Initiate an action, such as a display or calculation.
CheckBox	Select one option from two mutually exclusive options.
RadioButton	Select one option from a group of mutually exclusive options.
ListBox	Display a list of items from which one can be selected.
ComboBox	Display a list of items from which one can be selected, as well as permit users to type the value of the desired item.
Timer	Create a timer to automatically initiate program actions.
PictureBox	Display text or graphics.

Don't be overwhelmed by all of the available controls. At a minimum, you will always have the objects provided by the standard Toolbox available to you, and these are the ones we will be working with. Once you learn how to place the basic control objects on a form, you will also understand how to place the additional objects, because every object used in a Visual Basic application, whether it is selected from a standard or purchased control, is placed on a form in the same simple manner. Similarly, each and every object contains two basic characteristics: properties and methods.

An object's *properties* define particular characteristics of the object. For example, the properties of a text box include the location of the text box on the form, the color of the box (the background color), the color of text that will be displayed in the box (the foreground color), and whether it is read-only or can also be written to by the user.

Methods are predefined procedures that are supplied with the object for performing specific tasks. For example, you can use a method to move an object to a different location or change its size.

Additionally, each object from the Toolbox recognizes certain actions. For example, a button recognizes when the mouse pointer is pointing to it and the left mouse button is clicked. These types of actions are referred to as *events*. In our example, we would say that the button recognizes the mouse-click event. However, once an event is activated, we must write our own procedures to do something in response to the event. This is where the language element of Visual Basic comes into play.

The Language Element

Before the advent of GUIs, computer programs consisted entirely of a sequence of instructions. Programming was the process of writing these instructions in a language to which the computer could respond. The set of instructions and rules that could be used to construct a program were called a programming language. Frequently, the word *code* was used to designate the instructions contained within a program. With the advent of graphical user interfaces the need for code (program instructions) has not gone away—rather, it forms the basis for responding to the events taking place on the GUI. Figure 2–4 illustrates the interaction between an event and a program code.

As illustrated in Figure 2–4, an event, such as clicking the mouse on a button, sets in motion a sequence of actions. If code has been written for the event, the code is exe-

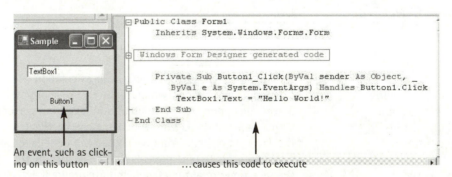

Figure 2–4 *An Event "Triggers" the Initiation of a Procedure*

cuted; otherwise the event is ignored. This is the essence of GUIs and event-driven applications—the selection of executed code depends on what events occur, which ultimately depends on what the user does. The programmer must still write the code that performs the desired action.

Visual Basic is a high-level programming language that supports all of the procedural programming features found in other modern languages. These include statements to perform calculations, permit repetitive instruction execution, and allow selection between two or more alternatives.

With these basics in mind, it is now time to create our first Visual Basic application. In the next section, we introduce the Visual Basic programming environment and create an application that uses only a single object: the form itself. We will then add additional objects and code to create a more complete Visual Basic application.

Exercises 2.1

1. List the two elements of a Visual Basic Application.

2. What is the purpose of a GUI and what elements does a user see in a GUI?

3. What does a Visual Basic toolbox provide?

4. Name and describe the four most commonly used Toolbox objects.

5. When an application is run, what does a design form become?

6. What is executed when an event occurs?

2.2   Getting Started in Visual Basic

It's now time to begin designing and developing Visual Basic programs. To do this, you will have to bring up the opening Visual Basic screen and understand the basic elements of the Visual Basic development environment. Visual Studio is the integrated development environment (IDE, pronounced as both I-D-E, and IDEE) used to create, test, and debug projects. Developers can also use Visual Studio to create applications using languages other than Visual Basic, such as C# and Visual C++. To bring up the opening Visual Basic screen, either click the Microsoft Visual Studio .NET icon (see Figure 2–5), which is located within the Microsoft Visual Studio .NET Group, or, if you have a shortcut to Visual Basic .NET on the desktop, double-click this icon.

When you first launch Visual Basic .NET, the Start Page similar to the one shown in Figure 2–6 will appear. While this page provides links to Web pages to help developers find useful information, we will be concerned only with the following three areas: the central rectangle displaying recent programs, the Open Project button, and the New Project button. Clicking on any of the recent programs causes VB.NET to retrieve the program and load it into the IDE. Clicking the Open Project button opens a standard Windows file dialog box permitting you to retrieve a previously saved Visual Basic program and load it into the IDE. Clicking the New Project button opens the dialog box shown in Figure 2–7. This dialog box provides a choice of eleven project types, shown

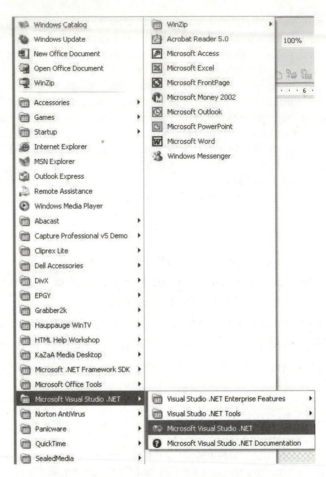

Figure 2–5 *The Microsoft Visual Studio .NET Icon within the Visual Studio .NET Group*

in Table 2–2. In this text, we will be concerned with Windows Applications and ASP.NET Web Applications.

Click the New project button to open the New Project Dialog box displayed in Figure 2–7. Click the OK button to create a new project. Don't be concerned with the Name and Location, as the goal here is to display the IDE screen as shown in Figure 2–8

The four windows shown in Figure 2–8 are, as marked, the Toolbox window, the Initial Form window, the Solution window, and the Properties window. Additionally, directly under the Title bar at the top of the screen sits a Menu bar and a Toolbar, which should not be confused with the Toolbox window. Table 2–3 lists a description of each of these components. Before examining each of these components in depth, it will be useful to consider the IDE as a whole and how it uses standard Windows keyboard and mouse techniques.

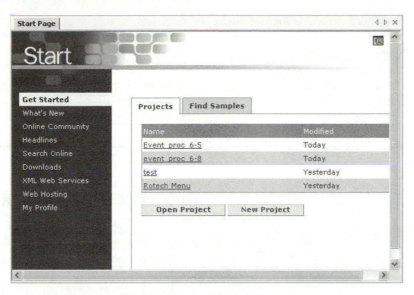

Figure 2-6 *The Visual Basic .NET Start Page*

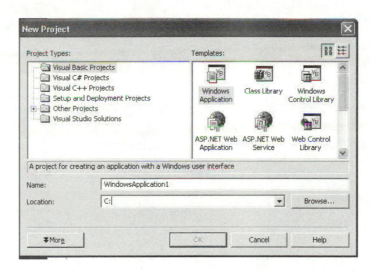

Figure 2-7 *New Project Dialog*

The IDE as a Windows Workspace

The IDE consists of three main components: a GUI designer, a code editor, and a debugger. In the normal course of developing a Visual Basic program, you will use each of these components. Initially, we will work with GUI designer, which is the screen shown in Figure 2-8. The screen is actually composed of a main "parent" window containing multiple "child" windows.

Table 2–2   Eleven Project Types

Windows Application	Class Library
Windows Control Library	ASP .NET Web Application
ASP.NET Web Service	Web Control Library
Console Application	Windows Service
Empty Project	Empty Web Project
New Project in Existing Folder	

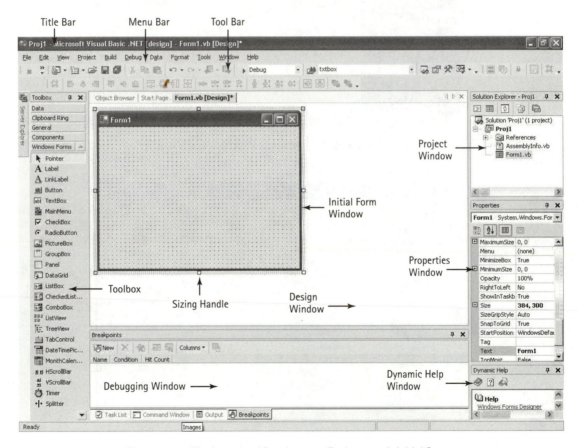

Figure 2–8   *The Integrated Development Environment's Initial Screen*

As a Windows-based application, each child window within the overall parent window, as well as the parent window itself, can be resized and closed in the same manner as all windows. To close a window you can double-click the X in the upper right-hand corner of each window. Windows can be resized by first moving the mouse pointer to a window's border. Then, when the pointer changes to a double-headed arrow, click and drag the border in the desired direction. You can move each window by clicking the mouse within the window's Title bar, and then dragging the window to the desired position on the screen.

Table 2-3   Initial Development Screen Components

Component	Description
Title Bar	The colored bar at the top edge of a window that contains the window name.
Menu Bar	Contains the names of the menus that can be used with the currently active window. The menu bar can be modified, but cannot be deleted from the screen.
Toolbar	Contains icons that provide quick access to commonly used Menu Bar commands. Clicking an icon, which is referred to as a button, carries out the designated action represented by that button.
Layout Toolbar	Contains buttons that enable you to format the layout of controls on a form. These buttons enable you to control aligning, sizing, spacing, centering, and ordering controls.
Toolbox	Contains a set of controls that can be placed on a Form window to produce a graphical user interface (GUI).
Initial Form Window	The form upon which controls are placed to produce a graphical user interface (GUI). By default, this form becomes the first window that is displayed when a program is executed.
Properties Window	Lists the property settings for the selected Form or control and permits changes to each setting to be made. Properties such as size, name, and color, which are characteristics of an object, can be viewed and altered either from an alphabetical or category listing.
Solution Window	Displays a hierarchical list of projects and all of the items contained in a project. Also referred to as both the Solution Resource Window and the Solution Explorer.
Form Layout Window	Provides a visual means of setting the Initial Form window's position on the screen when a program is executed.

As with any other Windows application, Visual Basic makes use of a menu bar to provide an interface to the programmer. For example, if you wish to save a program you have been working on and start a new one, you would choose the File item from the menu bar, which will bring up the File submenu shown in Figure 2-9. From this menu you can save the current project by using the Save All option, then click the New option and click Project (Figure 2-10). The New Project dialog box appears. To access an existing program, you can also use the menu bar File item, except you would then click Open and click Project to reopen a previously saved program. Similarly, these two options can also be activated by clicking the appropriate icons on the Toolbar located immediately under the Menu bar.

Once a program has been opened, you can always use the View item on the menu bar to display any windows that you need. For example, if either the Properties or Toolbox windows are not visible on the development screen, select the View item from the

Figure 2–9   *The File SubMenu*

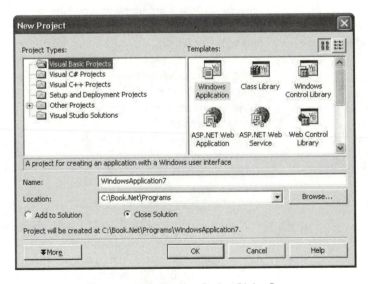

Figure 2–10   *The New Project Dialog Box*

menu bar. This will open the View submenu illustrated in Figure 2–11. From this submenu, click the Properties Window or click Toolbox and then click a Toolbox item to open the desired window. Note in Figure 2–11 that all Visual Basic's windows are listed in the View submenu.

Having examined the Menu bar and how it is used to configure the development screen, make sure that you go back to the initial development screen shown in Figure 2–8. If any additional windows appear on the screen, close them by clicking each win-

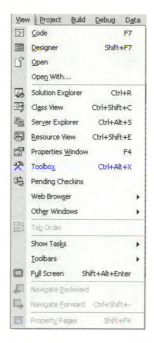

Figure 2–11   *The View SubMenu*

dow's close button (the box with the X in the upper right corner). The window does not have to be active to do this.

Note that the caption within the top title bar of the screen shown in Figure 2–8 contains the words *Microsoft Visual Basic* [design]. The word [design] in the top Title bar caption is important because it indicates that we are in the design phase of a Visual Basic program. At any point within our development, we can run the program and see how it will look to the user.

Once the design windows are visible, creating a Visual Basic application requires the following three steps:

1. Create the graphical user interface (GUI).

2. Set the properties of each object on the interface.

3. Write the code.

The foundation for creating the GUI (Step 1) is the Initial Form window. It is on this design form that we place various objects to produce the interface we want users to see when the program is executed. When the program is run, the design form becomes a window and the objects that we place on the design form become visual controls that are used to input data, display output, and activate events. The objects that we can place on the design form are contained within the Toolbox. The Toolbox drop-down list is shown in Figure 2–12. The visual controls we will be using are under the Windows Forms drop-down list.

Figure 2–12   *The Standard Object Toolbox*

Programmer Notes

Opening the Basic Design Windows

To create a Visual Basic program, you will need the following three windows: the Toolbox window for selecting objects, a Form window for placing objects, and a Properties window for altering an object's properties. Additionally, the Solution Explorer window should be visible when you begin. If any of these windows are in the background, clicking on them will activate them and bring them to the foreground, or you may use the following procedures:

For a Form window:

For a new project, first click File from the menu bar, click New from the submenu, and click Project (or use the hot key sequence Alt+F, then N, then P). This will open a new Form window.

For an existing project, click File from the menu bar, click Open from the submenu, and then click Project (or use the hot key sequence Alt+ F, then O, then P). This will open a project window. Then select the project file.

For a Toolbox window:

To either activate an existing Toolbox window or open one if it is not on the screen, do either of the following:

- Click View and then click Toolbox.
- Use the hot key sequence Alt+V and then press the X key (Alt+V / X).

For a Properties window:

To activate an existing Properties window or open one if it is not on the screen, do one of the following:

- Click View and then click Properties Window.
- Use the hot key sequence Alt+V, and then press the W key (Alt+V / W).
- Press the F4 function key.

For a Solution Explorer window:

To activate an existing Solutions window or open one if it is not on the screen, do one of the following:

- Click View and then click Solution Explorer.
- Use the hot key sequence Alt+V and then press the P key (Alt+V / P).

Don't be confused by all of the available objects. Simply realize that Visual Basic provides a basic set of object types that can be selected to produce a graphical user interface. The balance of this book explains what some of the more important objects represent and how to design a Visual Basic application using them. To give you an idea of how simple it is to design such an interface, move the mouse pointer to the Button object in the Toolbox and double-click the Button icon. Note that a Button object appears in the form. Placing any object from the Toolbox onto the form is this simple. Now click the newly created button within the form and press the Delete key to remove it.

Setting an Object's Properties

As previously stated, all objects on a form have properties, which define where on the form the object will appear (the object's vertical and horizontal position relative to the left-hand corner of the form), the color of the object, its size, and various other attributes. To understand these properties, we will now examine the most basic object in Visual Basic: the form. Like any other object, the Form object has properties that define how it will appear as a screen when the program is run. As an introduction to the ease with which properties are set, we will first explore the Form object's properties. To do this, you need to have a basic design screen open (see Figure 2–8).

First, click the Properties window to activate it. The Properties window, which should appear as shown in Figure 2–13, is used for setting and viewing an object's properties.

The Properties window allows properties to be listed in alphabetic order, by property name, or by property category. By default, the properties are sorted by category. To change to property categories, click the first button on the Properties window toolbar. To switch back to alphabetic sort, click the second button on the Properties window toolbar. When viewed by category, individual properties are grouped according to appearance, font, position, behavior, and so on.

No matter the order of properties selected, the first box within a Properties window is the *ObjectIdentification box*, located immediately under the window's Title bar. This box lists the name of the object and its object type. In Figure 2–13 the name of the object is Form1 and its type is Form.

The two columns within the Properties window are where individual object properties are identified. The column on the left is the properties list, which provides the names of all the properties of the object named in the object box. The column to the right is the settings list, which provides the current value assigned to the property on the left. The currently selected property is the one that is highlighted. For example, the

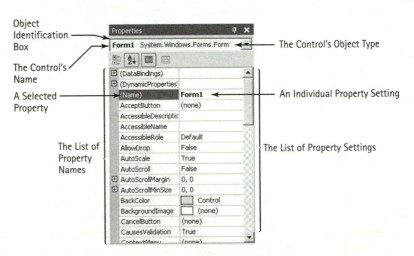

Figure 2–13 *The Properties Window*

Name property is highlighted in Figure 2–13. The value assigned to a highlighted property can be changed directly in the property settings list.

Take a moment now and, using the keyboard arrows, move down through the Properties window. Observe that each property is highlighted as it is selected, and that the description of the highlighted property is displayed in the description box at the bottom of the window.[1] Now move back up until the **Name** property at the top of the alphabetical list is highlighted. The name Form1 shown in the figure is the default name that Visual Basic gives to the first Form object provided for a new program. If a second form were used, it would be given the default name Form2, the third form would be named Form3, and so on.

The Name Property   There is nothing inherently wrong with keeping the default name that Visual Basic provides for each Form object that you use. However, good programming practice requires that all Form and other object names be more descriptive and convey some idea about what the object is used for. The names that are allowed for all objects, of which a Form is one, are also used to name other elements in the Visual Basic programming language and are collectively referred to as *identifiers*. Identifiers can be made up of any combination of letters, digits, or underscores (_) selected according to the following rules:

1. The first character of an identifier must be a letter.
2. Only letters, digits, or underscores may follow the initial letter. Blank spaces, special characters, and punctuation marks are not allowed. Use the underscore or capital letters to separate words in an identifier consisting of multiple words.
3. An identifier can be no longer than 1016 characters.
4. An identifier cannot be a keyword. (A *keyword* is a word that is set aside by the language for a special purpose.)[2]

Using these rules, development teams may then use whatever naming conventions they choose. In this book, form names begin with `frm` and our first form will always be given the name `frmMain`. To assign this name to our current form, do the following: if the name property is not already highlighted, click the name property and change the name to `frmMain` by directly typing in the settings list to the right of the **Name** property. The name change takes effect when you either press the Enter key, move to another property, or activate another object.

---

[1]The description box can be toggled on or off by clicking the right mouse button from within the Properties window.

[2]More specifically, an identifier cannot be a restricted keyword. A restricted keyword is a word that is set aside by the language for a specific purpose and can only be used in a specified manner. Examples of such words are If, Else, and Loop. Other languages refer to such words as reserved words. Use the Help Facility and search for "Word Choice" to find a table of keywords.

Programmer Notes

The Properties Window

The Properties window is where you set an object's initial properties. These are the properties that the object will exhibit when the application is first run. These properties can be altered later, using procedural code.

To Activate the Properties Window:

To activate a particular object's Properties window, first click the object to select it and then press the F4 function key. You can also click View and then click Properties Window (or use the hot-key sequence Alt+V, then W). This will activate the Properties window for the currently active object. Once the Properties window is active, clicking the down-facing arrowhead to the right of the object identification box will activate a drop-down list that can be used to select any object on the form, including the form itself.

To Move to a Specific Property:

First, make sure that the Properties window is active. You can then cursor up or down through the properties by using the up and down arrow keys or by simply clicking the desired property with the mouse.

The Text Property   A form's name property is important to the programmer when developing an application. However, it is the form's **Text** property that is important to the user when a program is run, because it is the **Text** property that the user sees within the window's Title bar when an application is executing.

To change the **Text** property, select it from the Properties window. To do this, make sure the Properties window is selected and use the arrow keys to position the cursor on the **Text** property. Now change the caption to read:

```
The Hello Application - Version 1 (pgm2-1).
```

If the caption is larger than the space shown in the settings box, as is shown in Figure 2–14, the text will scroll as you type it in. When you have changed the text, the design screen should appear as shown in Figure 2–14.

Before leaving the Properties window to run our application, let's take a moment to see how properties that have restricted values can also be changed.

We changed both the **Name** and **Text** properties by simply typing new values. Certain properties have a fixed set of available values. For example, the **Cursor** property, which determines the type of cursor that will appear when the program runs, can be selected from a list of defined cursors. Similarly, the **Font** property, which determines the type of font used for an object's displayed text can only be selected from a list of available fonts. Likewise, the **BackColor** and **ForeColor** properties, which determine the background color and the color of text displayed in the foreground, can only be selected

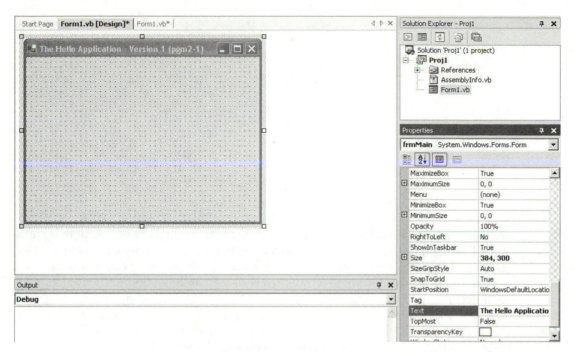

Figure 2–14   *The Design Screen after the Text Property Change*

from a predefined palette of colors. When one of these properties is selected, either a down-facing arrowhead property button (▼) or an ellipses (...) property button will appear to the right of the selected setting. Clicking this button will show you the available settings. You can then make a selection by clicking the desired value. In the case of colors, a palette of available colors is displayed, and clicking on a color sets the numerical code for the chosen color as the property's value.

The Solution Explorer Window   Although Visual Basic was initially designed as a tool to build smaller desktop applications, it has expanded in scope to allow for the construction of enterprise-wide systems. To support this capability, Visual Basic .NET has adopted a more complex, but logical, way to associate different elements of an application. At the top level is a *solution* file. A solution consists of a set of projects. Only in cases of a complex application will there be more than one project. For all examples and assignments in this book, there will be only one project. A project consists of all the programming components we write. We have just seen one of these components: a form. There are many others that we can use to build an application. All of these components are associated together under the project.

The Solution Explorer window displays a hierarchical list of projects and components contained in a project, as shown in Figure 2–15. As files are added or removed from a project, Visual Basic reflects all of your changes within the displayed hierarchical tree.

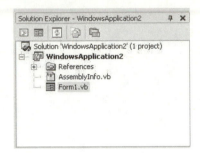

Figure 2–15 *Solution Explorer Window*

The hierarchical tree uses the same folder tree structure found in Windows, which means that you can expand and contract tree sections by clicking on the plus (+) and minus (−) symbols, respectively. As always, sections of the tree that are hidden from view due to the size of the window can be displayed using the attached scroll bars.

The Solution Explorer window is extremely useful in providing a visual picture of the project files and in providing a rapid means of accessing, copying, and deleting files associated with a project. For example, if a Form object is not displayed on the design screen, you can make it visible by double-clicking the desired Form object from within the hierarchical tree. In a similar manner, you can expand a folder or bring up both code and visible objects by clicking one of the five icons shown in Figure 2–15. Two further items relating to the Solution Explorer window are worth noting. First, Visual Basic assigns default names to solutions (Solution1), projects (Project1), and forms (Form1). These names can be changed by selecting the solution, project, or form with the Solution Explorer and right-clicking to open a menu. Select the Rename menu option and enter the new name.

Second, it is worth noting that the first two items in the View submenu, Code and Object, have icons identical to those displayed in the Solution Explorer window shown in Figure 2–15. Thus, both code and objects can be displayed by using either the View submenu or the Solution Explorer window.

Running an Application

At any time during program development, you can run your program using one of the following three methods:

1. Select the Debug Menu and click Start.
2. Press the F5 function key.
3. Use the hot key sequence Alt+D, then press the S key.

If you do this now for Program 2–1, the program will appear as shown in Figure 2–16. **Before doing so, change the Name property of the Form back to Form1. (You had changed it to frmMain.) We will explain later why this is necessary.**

Notice that when the program is run, the form becomes a standard window. Thus, even though we have not placed any objects on our form or added any code to our pro-

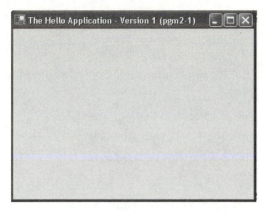

Figure 2–16   *The Form as a Window When the Application is Run*

gram, we can manipulate the window using standard window techniques. For example, you can click the Maximize or Minimize buttons, move or resize the window, and close the application by double-clicking the Close (X) button.

A useful feature of Visual Basic is that you can run your program at any point within its development process. This permits you to check both the look of the graphical user interface and the operation of any code that you write while the program is being developed, rather than at the end of the design process. As you write more involved programs, it is a good idea to get into the habit of checking program features as they are added by running the program.

To clearly distinguish between when a program is being developed and when it is being executed, Visual Basic uses the terms *design time* and *run time*. *Design time* is defined as the time when a Visual Basic application is being developed. During design time, objects are placed on a form, their initial properties are set, and program code is written. *Run time* is defined as the time a program is running. During run time, each form becomes a window, and the windows and controls respond to events, such as a mouse-click, by invoking the appropriate procedural code. Run time can be initiated directly from design time by pressing the F5 function key (or any of the other methods listed in the accompanying Programmer Notes on Running an Application). Although in this section we have changed object properties in design time, we will see in Section 2.4 that an object's properties can also be changed at run time.

Saving and Recalling a Project

In the next section, we will add three Button objects and one Text box to our form. Then, in Section 2.4, we will complete our application by adding program code. Before doing so, let's make sure that you can save and then retrieve the work we have completed so far.

Programmer Notes

Running an Application

While creating a Visual Basic application, you can run the application at any time using one of the following procedures:

1. Select the Debug Menu and select Start.
2. Use the hot key sequence Alt+D, then press the S key (Alt+D / S).
3. Press the F5 function key.

Unlike our current program which consists of a single form, a program can consist of many forms, additional code modules containing program code, and third-party supplied objects. A *form* contains the data for a single Form object, information for each object placed on the form (in this case there are none), all event code related to these objects, and any general code related to the form as a whole. A *code module* contains procedural code (no objects) that will be shared between two or more forms. It is for this reason that a separate project file, with its own name, is used. The project file keeps track of all forms, and any additional code and object modules.

To save an application, first click the File menu and then click Save All. At this point all the forms, code modules and ancillary files will be saved in a folder. The name of the folder will be the project name. You can also click the SaveAll icon in the Standard Toolbar (see Figure 2–17). It is recommended that you save your solution often to prevent accidental loss of work.

To retrieve a project, select Open Solution from the File menu, at which point an Open Solution dialog box similar to the one shown in Figure 2–17 is displayed. Select the folder with the correct solution name. A second file dialog box will appear. Within

Figure 2–17 *The Open Solution Dialog Box*

Figure 2–18 *Visual Basic's Standard Toolbar*

this dialog box a file with the project name and a file type of Visual Studio Solution will appear. After this file is selected, the forms that comprise your project will reappear.

Using the Toolbar

Once you have become comfortable with the menu bar items and see how they operate and interconnect, you should take a closer look at the Standard Toolbar. For the most commonly used features of Visual Basic, such as opening a solution file, saving a solution, and running or stopping an application, click on the appropriate toolbar icon to perform the desired operation. Figure 2–18 illustrates the Standard Toolbar and identifies the icons that you will use as you progress in designing Visual Basic applications. To make sure the Standard Toolbar is visible, select the Toolbar item from the View menu. When this item is selected, a menu listing the available toolbars is displayed. Make sure that a check mark (v) appears to the left of the Standard item. The most useful Standard Toolbar buttons are represented by the Save All, Start, and Stop Debugging icons.

Exercises 2.2

1. Describe the difference between design time and run time.

2. a. Name the three windows that should be visible during an application's design.

   b. What are the steps for opening each of the windows listed in your answer to Exercise 2a?

   c. In addition to the three basic design windows, what two additional windows may also be visible on the design screen?

3. What two **Form** properties should be changed for every application?

4. What does a form become during run time?

5. List the steps for creating a Visual Basic application.

6. Determine the number of properties that a Form object has. (*Hint:* Activate a form's property window and count the properties.)

7. a. Design a Visual Basic application that consists of a single form with the heading `Test Form`. The form should not have a minimize button nor a maximize button, but should contain a close control button. (*Hint:* Locate these properties in the Properties window and change their values from **True** to **False**.)

   b. Run the application you designed in Exercise 7a.

8. By looking at the screen, how can you tell the difference between design time and run time?

2.3 Adding an Event Procedure

In the previous section, we completed the first two steps required in constructing a Visual Basic application:

1. Create the GUI.
2. Set initial object properties.

Now we will finish the application by completing the third step:

3. Adding procedural code.

At this point our simple application, pgm2-1, produces a blank window when it is executed. If you then click anywhere on the window, nothing happens. This is because no event procedures have been included for the form. We will complete the application by providing a mouse click event procedure that displays a message whenever the application is running and the mouse is clicked anywhere on the application's window.

In a well-designed program, each procedure will consist of a set of instructions necessary to complete a well-defined task. Although a procedure can be initiated in a variety of ways, a procedure that is executed (called into action, or *invoked*) when an event occurs is referred to as an *event procedure* or *event handler*. The general structure of an event procedure is illustrated in Figure 2–19.

The first line of a procedure is always a header line. A *header line* begins with the optional keyword **Private**[3] and must contain the keyword **Sub** (which derives from the word Subprogram), the name of the procedure, and a set of parentheses. For event procedures, the name consists of an object identification, an optional underscore character (_), a valid event for the object, the parameters in parentheses, the keyword **Handles** followed by the object identification, an underscore character, and a valid event. If the object is the form itself, the object name Form is used. For example, the header line

```
Private Sub Form1_Click(ByVal sender As Object, ByVal e As _
    System.EventArgs) Handles MyBase.Click
```

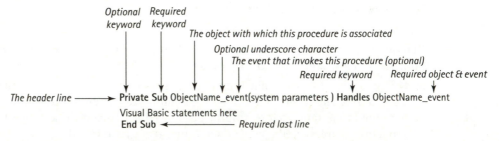

Figure 2–19   *The Structure of an Event Procedure*

---

[3]The significance of the keyword Private is explained in Chapter 7.

denotes an event procedure that will be activated when the mouse is clicked on the form. The values between the parentheses are used for transmitting data to and from the procedure when it is invoked. Data transmitted in this fashion are referred to as *arguments* of the procedure. Note that for forms, the object identification after the **Handles** keyword is `MyBase`, while for controls on the form the object identification is the name of the control (e.g., txtBox1). The last line of each procedure consists of the keywords **End Sub**. Finally, all statements from the header line up to and including the terminating **End Sub** statement are collectively referred to as the procedure's *body*.

For a form's mouse click event, the required procedure's structure is:

```
Private Sub Form1_Click(ByVal sender As Object, ByVal e As _
    System.EventArgs) Handles MyBase.Click
        ' Visual Basic statements in here
End Sub
```

The first and last lines of a procedure, consisting of the header line and terminating body line **End Sub**, are referred to as the procedure's *template*. Note that if the form is named `frmMain`, the procedure is named `frmMain_Click`. As shown in Figure 2-20, event procedure templates need not be manually typed because they are automatically provided in Visual Basic's Code window.

Before activating the Code window, we need to decide what Visual Basic statements will be included in the body of our event procedure. In this section, we present an easy way for displaying an output message—the MessageBox.Show method.

The MessageBox.Show Method[4]

Visual Basic provides a number of built-in methods in addition to methods for constructing event procedures. The **MessageBox.Show** method is used to display a box with a user-supplied message inside. The message box also contains a title and an icon. For example, the boxes illustrated in the next several figures all were created using the

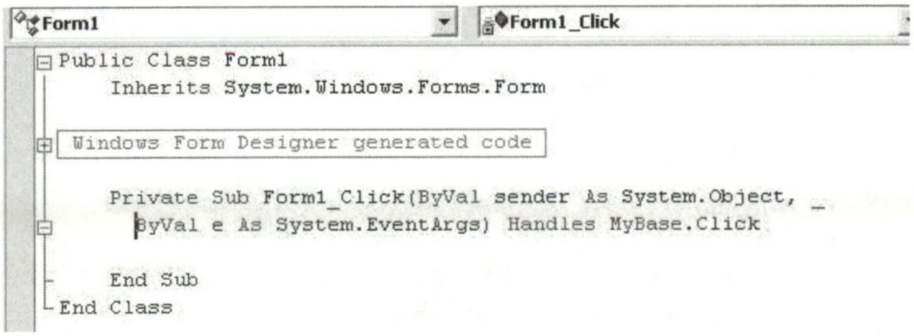

Figure 2–20 *The Code Window, Showing a Click Event Procedure Template*

---

[4]In previous versions of Visual Basic, the MsgBox function was used to display a message box. Although this function may still be used, the MessageBox class replaces this function with MessageBox.Show as the method used to display a message box.

MessageBox.Show method. The MessageBox.Show method has the following general formats:

```
MessageBox.Show(text)
MessageBox.Show(text, caption)
MessageBox.Show(text, caption, buttons)
MessageBox.Show(text, caption, buttons, icon)
MessageBox.Show(text, caption, buttons, icon, defaultbutton)
```

Messages, such as those displayed in message boxes, are called *strings* in Visual Basic. A *string* consists of a group of characters made up of letters, numbers, and special characters, such as the exclamation point. The beginning and end of a string of characters are marked by double quotes ("string in here").[5] The argument *text* appears in the message box window and it may be a literal string enclosed in quotes or a string variable. The string *caption* is displayed in the message box's title bar. If *caption* is not specified, as in the preceding form, the title bar is empty. Figure 2–21 shows the message box displayed as a result of the following statement:

```
MessageBox.Show("This is the text")
```

This is the simplest form of the message box. Figure 2–22 displays a message from the following statement, which includes a title (caption):

```
MessageBox.Show("This is the text", "This is the caption")
```

The word *buttons* specifies the types of buttons that are displayed. The value for *buttons* can be one of the following:

```
MessageBoxButtons.AbortRetryIgnore
MessageBoxButtons.OK
MessageBoxButtons.OKCancel
MessageBoxButtons.RetryCancel
MessageBoxButtons.YesNo
MessageBoxButtons.YesNoCancel
```

If the value is MessageBoxButtons.AbortRetryIgnore, then the Abort, Retry, and Ignore buttons are all displayed in the message box. The string following the period indicates which buttons are displayed (e.g., Yes and No for YesNo). If this argument is not specified, the OK button is displayed as shown in the previous two figures. The following statement displays a message box with two buttons, as shown in Figure 2–23.

```
MessageBox.Show("Are you sure you want to delete the record?", _
   "Customer Records", MessageBoxButtons.YesNo)
```

---

[5]Strings are discussed in detail in Chapter 3.

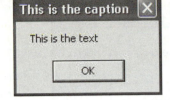

Figure 2-21   *A Simple Message Box*   Figure 2-22   *A Message Box with Title*   Figure 2-23   *A Message Box with Title and Yes/No Buttons*

Table 2-4   MessageBox.Show Icons

Values for Icon	Icon
MessageBoxIcon.Asterisk	The Letter i
MessageBoxIcon.Information	The Letter i
MessageBoxIcon.Error	The Letter X
MessageBoxIcon.Hand	The Letter X
MessageBoxIcon.Stop	The Letter X
MessageBoxIcon.Exclamation	Exclamation Point
MessageBoxIcon.Warning	Exclamation Point
MessageBoxIcon.Question	Question Mark

Table 2-4 lists the values for the *icon* argument and shows what the icons look like. Note that some values display the same icon as other values. An icon is displayed to the left of the message.

For example, the statements:

```
MessageBox.Show("Record has been deleted.", "Customer Records", _
    MessageBoxButtons.OK, MessageBoxIcon.Information)

MessageBox.Show("Data entered is invalid. Try Again", "Invalid Data", _
    MessageBoxButtons.OK, MessageBoxIcon.Warning)
```

produced the message boxes shown in Figures 2-24 and 2-25. These message boxes include an information icon.

The information icons (Asterisk and Information) should be used when you are displaying an information message box with only an OK button. The stop icons (Error, Hand, and Stop) should be used when the message displayed is indicating a serious

Figures 2–24 and 2–25 *Message Boxes with Title, OK Button, and Information Icon*

problem that needs to be corrected before the program can continue. The exclamation icons (Exclamation and Warning) should be used when the user must make a decision before the program can continue; this would not be used with only an OK button. The question icon can be used when a question needs to be answered.

The last optional argument to the MessageBox.Show method, as shown in the fifth format above, is the *defaultbutton*. This argument specifies which button to select as the default button, as there may be three buttons displayed in the message box (e.g., Yes, No, Cancel). The default button is the button that has focus when the message box is displayed, and is the button that is clicked when the user presses the Enter key. If this argument is not specified, the default is that the leftmost button is the default. The values for this argument are:

```
MessageBoxDefaultButton.Button1
MessageBoxDefaultButton.Button2
MessageBoxDefaultButton.Button3
```

where `MessageBoxDefaultButton.Button1` specifies the leftmost button (and is the default), `MessageBoxDefaultButton.Button2` specifies the second button from the left, and `MessageBoxDefaultButton.Button3` specifies the third button from the left.

After the user clicks on a button in the message box, the message box is closed. The return value of the call to the MessageBox.Show method indicates which button the user clicked. This is useful in code to determine what action to take. The return values may be one of the following:

```
DialogResult.Abort
DialogResult.Cancel
DialogResult.Ignore
DialogResult.No
DialogResult.OK
DialogResult.Retry
DialogResult.Yes
```

The following code gives an example of how the return value may be used:

```
Dim msgresult as Integer

msgresult = MessageBox.Show("Press OK to Delete", "Confirm Delete", _
    MessageBoxButtons.OKCancel, MessageBoxIcon.Stop, _
    MessageBoxDefaultButton.Button2)

If msgresult = DialogResult.OK Then
    . . .
```

Figure 2–26 shows the message box that is displayed by this call to **MessageBox.Show**. It is important to note that, in this example, the second button, Cancel, is the default button. The user has to move focus to the OK button to confirm the deletion. If the OK button is clicked, the return value is `DialogResult.OK`.

The message boxes shown are all special cases of a more general type of box referred to as a dialog box. A *dialog box* is any box that appears which requires the user to supply additional information to complete a task. In the case of the message boxes illustrated in this section, the required additional information is simply that the user must either click the OK box or press the Enter key to permit the application to continue.

Now let's include a **MessageBox.Show** method on our form so that the statement will be executed when the mouse is clicked. The required procedure is:

```
Private Sub Form1_Click(ByVal sender As Object, ByVal e As _
    System.EventArgs) Handles MyBase.Click
  MessageBox.Show("Hello World!", "Sample")
End Sub
```

To enter this code, first make sure that you are in design mode and have a form named Form1 showing on the screen, as illustrated in Figure 2–27.

To open the Code window, do any one of the following:

- If the Code window is visible, click on it.

Figure 2–26   *A Message Box with Default Button Argument Changed*

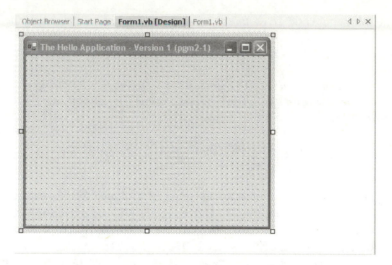

Figure 2–27   *The Form1 Form in Design Time*

- Double-click anywhere on the Form window.
- Select the Code option from the View menu.
- Press the F7 method key anywhere on the design form.
- Select the View Code icon from the Project Window.

Any of these actions will open the Code window shown in Figure 2–28.

The class drop-down should display Form1 and the method drop-down should display Form1_Load. This indicates that the current class is Form1 and the method is Load, which in this case is an event. Note that a code stub (template) for the Form1_Load procedure is auto-

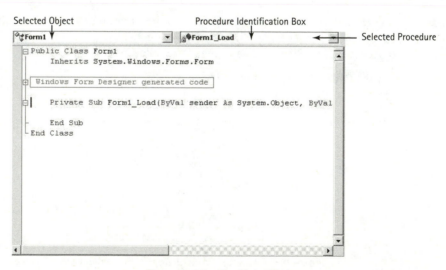

Figure 2–28   *The Code Window*

matically supplied within the Code window. Note, too, that the Code window displays all procedures and declarations that have been written, with each procedure separated by a line. When the Code window is not large enough to display either all procedures or even all of a single procedure, the scroll bars can be used to bring sections of code within the visible window area.

When you have the Code window shown in Figure 2–28 visible, click the down arrowhead (▼) to the right of the selected class box. Then select (*Base Class Events*). Click the down-facing arrowhead in the method box. This produces the window shown in Figure 2–29. Here the drop-down list can be scrolled to provide all of the events associated with the selected object.

To select the **Click** procedure, do either of the following:

- Using the list's scroll bar, locate the word **Click**, and then click on this keyword.
- Using the up-arrow cursor key, highlight the word **Click**, and press Enter.

Either of these actions will add the following lines to the Code window:

```
Private Sub Form1_Click(ByVal sender As Object, ByVal e As _
    System.EventArgs) Handles MyBase.Click


End Sub
```

In your code window, the first statement beginning with `Private` fits on one line. However, this line will not fit on a page of this book. To continue a Visual Basic statement on the next line, type a space followed by the underscore symbol (" _").

You are now ready to add code to the Form1 Click event. Type the line,

```
MessageBox.Show("Hello World!", "Sample")
```

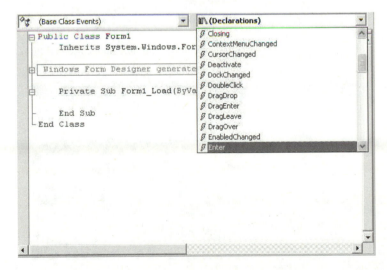

Figure 2–29   *The List of Events Associated With a Form*

between the header line `Private Sub Form1_Click` (*parameters*) and the terminating line `End Sub`. When this task is completed, the procedure should appear as shown below:

```
Private Sub Form1_Click(ByVal sender As Object, ByVal e As _
     System.EventArgs) Handles MyBase.Click
  MessageBox.Show("Hello World!", "Sample")
End Sub
```

Note that we have indented the single Visual Basic statement using three spaces. Although this is not required, indentation is a sign of good programming practice. Here it permits the statements within the procedure to be easily identified.

Our event procedure is now complete and you can close the Code window. When you run the program, the application should appear as shown in Figure 2–30. Clicking anywhere on the window will create the window shown in Figure 2–31. To remove the

Figure 2–30   *The Initial Run Time Application Window*

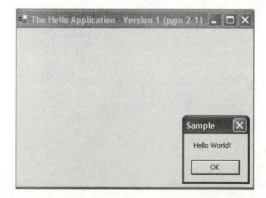

Figure 2–31   *The Effect of the Mouse Click Event*

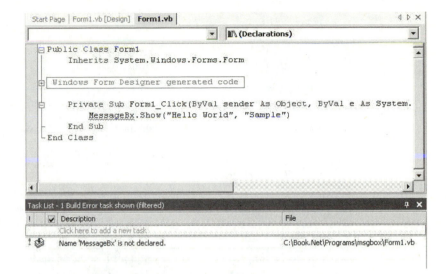

Figure 2-32a   *Notification of an Error*

Figure 2-32b   *Identification of the Invalid Statement and its Procedure*

message box, press either the escape (Esc) or Enter key, or click the OK Button. After performing this test, save the application using the Save All option from the File menu.

Correcting Errors

If you incorrectly typed the message box statement in your procedure, when the program is run the code box containing this procedure would automatically be displayed with the highlight placed on the incorrect statement. For example, if you inadvertently spelled **MessageBox** as MessageBx, the window shown in Figure 2-32a would appear. If you then clicked No in the message box, Figure 2-32b would appear. Below the Code window, a new window would appear listing all the errors detected. In this case only one error was found: Visual Basic could not interpret MessageBx. If you double-clicked MessageBx in the Task List window, Visual Basic would position the cursor in the Code window beside the statement in question. Note that even before you tried running the program, Visual Basic would underline, with a blue saw-toothed line, parts of statements that it could not interpret. Once you corrected the error, you could re-run the program.

Programmer Notes

Code Editor Options

The Visual Basic Editor provides a number of options that are useful when you are entering code into the Code window. These include the following:

Color Coded Instructions

The Visual Basic Editor displays procedural code in a variety of user-selected colors. By default, the following color selections are used:

Keywords—Blue

Comments—Green

Errors—Blue, saw-toothed underline

Other Text—Black

Completing a Word

Once you have entered enough characters for Visual Basic to identify a work, you can have the Editor complete the word.

Quick Syntax Information:

If you are trying to complete a statement, such as a MessageBox.Show statement, and forget the required syntax, you can ask the editor to provide it. You activate this option by placing the insertion cursor (the vertical insert line) over the piece of code in question.

Exercises 2.3

1. Define the following terms:
   a. event-procedure
   b. dialog box
   c. method
   d. header line
   e. argument
   f. template

2. a. What window do you use to enter the code for an event procedure?

   b. List two ways of activating the window you listed as the answer for Exercise 2a.

3. Using the Code window, determine how many event procedures are associated with a form.

4. Design and run the application presented in this section using the MessageBox.Show method in the form's click event procedure.

2.4 Adding Controls

Although the application presented in the previous section is useful in introducing us to the basic design-time windows needed for developing Visual Basic applications, it is not a very useful application in itself. To make it useful, we will have to add additional

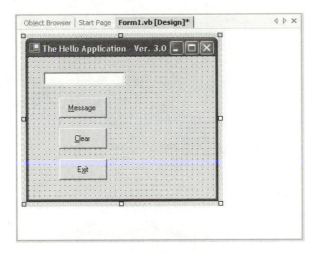

Figure 2-33 *Program 2-3's Interface*

objects and event procedures to the form. Adding objects to the form creates the final graphical interface that the user will see and interact with when the program is run. Adding event procedures to the objects then brings them "to life," so that when they are selected something actually happens. In this section, we present the basic method for placing objects on a form, and in the next section we will attach specific event procedures to these objects.

Objects selected from the Toolbox and placed on a form are referred to as *controls*. Placing objects on a Form is quite simple, and the same method is used for all objects.

The simplest procedure is to double-click the desired Toolbox object. This causes an object of the selected type to be automatically placed on the Form. Once this is done you can change its size or position, and set any additional properties such as its name, text, or color. These latter properties are modified from within the Properties window or in the Design window, and determine how the object appears when it is first displayed during run time.

By far the most commonly used Toolbox objects are the Button, TextBox, and Label. For our second application, we will use the first two of these object types—the Button and TextBox—to create the design-time interface shown in Figure 2-33.

Adding a Button

To place a button on the form, double-click the Button icon. Double-clicking this icon causes a button with eight small squares, referred to as *sizing handles*, to be placed on the form, as shown in Figure 2-34. The fact that the sizing handles are visible indicates that the object is *active*, which means that it can be moved, resized, and have its other

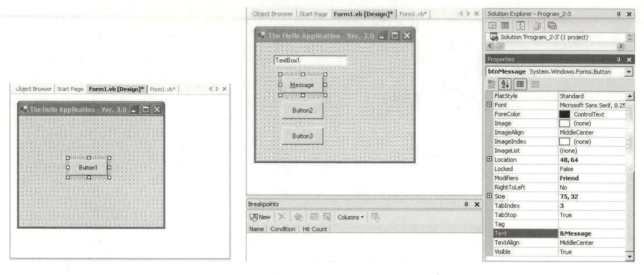

Figure 2–34   *The First Button Placed on the Form*

properties changed. To deactivate the currently active object, use the mouse to click any-where outside of it. Clicking on another object will activate the other object, while click-ing on an area of the form where no object is located activates the Form object itself.

The active object, which should now be the button just placed on the form, can be moved by placing the mouse pointer anywhere inside the object (but not on the sizing handles), holding down the mouse's left button, and dragging the object to its desired new position. Do this now and place this first button in the position of the Message button shown in Figure 2–33. Your form should now look like the one shown in Fig-ure 2–35.

Once you have successfully placed the first button on the form, either use the same procedure to place two more buttons in the positions shown in Figure 2–36, or use the alternative procedure given in the Programmer Notes box on page 82. Included in this box are additional procedures for resizing, moving, and deleting an object. Controls do not have to line up perfectly, but should be placed neatly on the form.

Adding a TextBox Control

Text boxes can be used for both entering data and displaying results. In our current application, we will use a text box for output by displaying a message when one of the form's buttons is clicked.

To place a TextBox object on a form, double-click the TextBox icon, as we did when we placed the three-button object. If you happen to double-click the wrong icon, simply activate it and press the Delete key to remove it. Once you have placed a text box on the form, move and resize it so that it appears as shown in Figure 2–37.

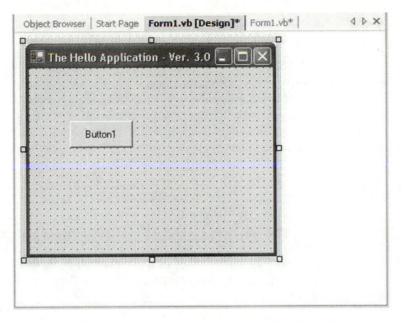

Figure 2–35   *The Final Placement of the First Button*

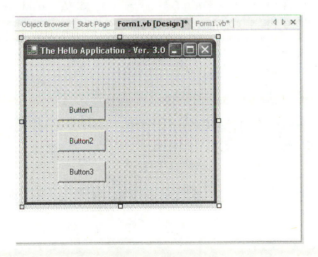

Figure 2–36   *Placement of Three Buttons on the Form*

Programmer Notes

Creating and Deleting Objects

To Add an Object:

Either:

Double-click the desired object in the toolbox. Doing this places a presized object on the form.

Or:

Click the desired object in the Toolbox and then move the mouse pointer onto the form. When the mouse pointer moves onto the form, it will change to a crosshair cursor. Hold the left mouse button down when the crosshairs are correctly positioned for any corner of the object and drag the mouse diagonally away from this corner, in any direction, to generate the opposite corner. When the object is the desired size, release the left mouse button.

To Resize an Object:

Activate the object by clicking inside it. Place the mouse pointer on one of the sizing handles, which will cause the mouse pointer to change to a double-sided arrow, <=>. Hold down the left mouse button and move the mouse in the direction of either arrowhead. Release the mouse button when the desired size is reached. You can also hold down the Shift key while pressing any of the four arrow keys to resize the object. Pressing the up and down arrow keys will decrease and increase the height; pressing the right and left arrow keys will increase and decrease the width.

To Move an Object:

Whether the object is active or not, place the mouse pointer inside the object and hold down the left mouse button. Drag the object to the desired position and then release the mouse button. You can also press one of the four arrow keys to move the object in the direction of the arrow. Holding down the Control key while pressing an arrow key will move the object in smaller increments.

To Delete an Object:

Activate the object by clicking inside it, and then press the Delete key.

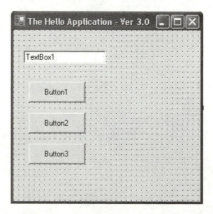

Figure 2–37 *Placement of the TextBox*

Table 2–5   Program 2–3's Initial Properties Table

Object	Property	Setting
Form	Name	frmMain[6]
	Text	The Hello Application—Ver. 3.0
Button	Name	btnMessage
	Text	&Message
Button	Name	btnClear
	Text	&Clear
Button	Name	btnExit
	Text	E&xit
TextBox	Name	txtDisplay
	Text	(blank)

Setting the Initial Object Properties

At this point we have assembled all of the Form controls that are required for our application. We still need to change the default names of these objects and set the Text properties of the buttons to those previously shown in Figure 2–33. After that, we can add the code so that each button performs its designated task when it is clicked. Let's now change the initial properties of our four objects to make them appear as shown in Figure 2–33. Table 2–5 lists the desired property settings for each object, including the Form object.

Programmer Notes

Changing the Name of a Form

When executing an application, Visual Basic needs to know the name of the form with which to start the application. So far we have only created small programs with one form. In subsequent chapters we will build applications with multiple forms.

By default, Visual Basic assumes that the name of the first form of the application is Form1. If we change the name of the form in the Property Window, even in a one-form application, Visual Basic will generate the following error message when we try to run the program:

'Sub Main' was not found in 'Project_1.Form1'.

To fix this error, there are two options.

1. Double-click the above error. This will cause the dialog box shown in Figure 2–38 to appear, prompting us to confirm that frmMain is the first form to be executed. Double

---

[6]Be sure to read the Programmer Notes on changing Form names. If the actions in the Note are not taken, the program may never run.

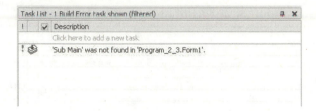

Figure 2–38 *Error Dialog Caused by New Form Name*

click Project_1.frmMain and then click OK. This will only have to be done once because the specification that frmMain is the initial form will be saved with other project information.

2. In the Solution Explorer, highlight Project 1, right-click it, and then choose Properties. The form shown in Figure 2–39 will appear. From the Startup Object, select the new form name, in this case frmMain.

Before we set the properties listed in Table 2–5, two comments are in order. The first concerns the ampersand (&) symbol that is included in the Text property of all of the buttons. This symbol should be typed exactly as shown. Its visual effect is to cause the character immediately following it to be underlined. Its operational effect is to create an accelerator key. An *accelerator key*, which is also referred to as a hot key sequence (or hot key, for short), is simply a keyboard shortcut for a user to make a selection. When used with a button it permits the user to activate the button by simultaneously pressing the Alt key and the underlined letter key, rather than either clicking with the mouse or activating the button by first selecting it and then pressing the Enter key.

The second comment concerns the Text property for a text box, shown in the last line in Table 2–5. For a text box, the Text setting determines what text will be displayed in the text box. As shown in Figure 2–37, the initial data shown in the text box is

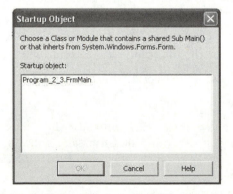

Figure 2–39 *Dialog Box to Change the Startup Form Name*

TextBox1, which is the default value for this property. The term (blank) means that we will set this value to a blank.

Also note that, although we are setting the initial properties for all of the objects at the same time, this is not necessary. We are doing so here to show the various setting methods in one place. In practice, we could just as easily have set each object's properties immediately after it was placed on the form.

Recall from the Programmer Notes box on page 59 that a Properties window can be activated in a variety of ways: by pressing the F4 function key or by selecting Properties from the Window menu (which can also be obtained by the hot key sequence ALT+V, followed by S). Now, however, we have five objects on the design screen: the form, three buttons, and a text box. To select the properties for a particular object, you can use any of the options listed in the Programmer Notes box on page 59.

The simplest method is to first activate the desired object by clicking it, then press the F4 function key, and then scroll to the desired property. Because an object is automatically activated just after it is placed on a form, this method is particularly useful for immediately changing the object's properties. This sequence of adding an object and immediately changing its properties is the preferred sequence for many programmers.

An alternative method is to open the Properties window for the currently active object, no matter what it is, and then click on the downward-facing arrowhead key (▼) to the right of the object's name (see Figure 2–40). The pull-down list that appears contains the names of all objects associated with the form. Clicking the desired object name

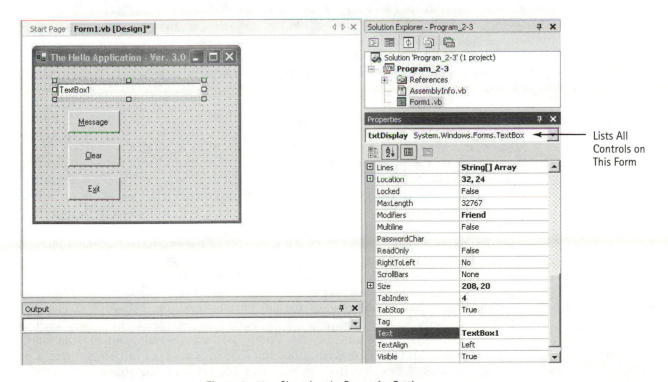

Figure 2–40 *Changing the Properties Settings*

in the list both activates the desired object and opens its Properties window. This method is particularly useful when changing the properties of a group of objects by sequencing through them after all objects have been placed on the form. Using either of these methods, alter the initial properties to those listed in Table 2–5.

At this stage, you should see the design screen shown in Figure 2–40. Within the context of developing a complete program, we have achieved the first two steps in our three-step process. They are:

1. Create the GUI.
2. Set the properties of each object on the interface.

We will complete the third and final step of writing the code in the next section. However, before doing so, run the application by pressing the F5 function key. Despite the fact that clicking on any of the buttons produces no effect (because we have not yet attached any code to these buttons), we can use the application to introduce two important concepts connected with any form: focus and tab sequence.

Programmer Notes

Activating the Properties Window for a Specific Object

1. Activate the object by clicking it, and then press the F4 function key.
2. Activate the Properties window for the currently selected object or form, whatever it may be, by either pressing the F4 key or selecting the Properties option from the Windows menu (Alt+V / S). Then change to the desired object from within the Properties window by clicking the underlined down arrow to the right of the object's name and then selecting the desired object from the pull-down list.

Looking at the Focus and Tab Sequence

When an application is run and a user is looking at the form, only one of the form's controls will have *input focus*, or focus, for short. The control with focus is the object that will be affected by pressing a key or clicking the mouse. For example, when a button has the focus, its caption will be surrounded by a dotted rectangle, as shown in Figure 2–41. Similarly, when a text box has the focus, a solid cursor appears, indicating that the user can type in data.

An object can only receive focus if it is capable of responding to user input through either the keyboard or mouse. As a result, controls such as labels can never receive the focus. In order to receive the focus a control must have its **Enabled, Visible,** and **TabStop** properties set to **True.** As the default settings for all three properties are **True,** they do not usually have to be checked for normal tab operation. By setting a control's Enabled property to **True,** you permit it to respond to user-generated events, such as pressing a key or clicking a mouse. The **Visible** property determines whether an object will actually be visible on the form during run time (it is always available for view during design time). A **True TabStop** setting forces a tab stop for the object, while a **False**

Figure 2–41 *A Button With and Without Focus*

value causes the object to be skipped over in the tab stop sequence. A control capable of receiving focus, such as a button, can receive the focus in one of three ways:

1. A user clicks the object.
2. A user presses the tab key until the object receives the focus.
3. The code activates the focus.

To see how the first method operates, press the F5 function key to execute the Hello Application (Program 2-3). Once the program is executing, click on any of the form objects. As you do, notice how the focus shifts. Now, press the tab key a few times and see how the focus shifts from control to control. The sequence in which the focus shifts from control to control as the tab key is pressed is called the *tab sequence*. This sequence is initially determined by the order in which controls are placed on the form. For example, assume you first created buttons named btnCom1, btnCom2, and btnCom3, respectively, and then created a text box named txtText1. When the application is run, the btnCom1 button will have the focus. As you press the tab key, focus will shift to the btnCom2 button, then to the btnCom3 button, and finally to the text box. Thus, the tab sequence is btnCom1 to btnCom2 to btnCom3 to txtText1. (This assumes that each control has its **Enabled**, **Visible**, and **TabStop** properties all set to True.)

You can alter the default tab order obtained as a result of placing controls on the form by modifying an object's **TabIndex** value. Initially, the first control placed on a form is assigned a **TabIndex** value of 0, the second object is assigned a **TabIndex** value of 1, and so on. To change the tab order, you have to change an object's **TabIndex** value and Visual Basic will renumber the remaining objects in a logical order. For example, if you have six objects on the form with **TabIndex** values from 0 to 5, and you change the object with value 3 to a value of 0, the objects with initial values of 0, 1, and 2 will have their values automatically changed to 1, 2, and 3, respectively. Similarly, if you change the object with a **TabIndex** value of 2 to 5, the objects with initial values of 3, 4, and 5 will have their values automatically reduced by one. Thus, the sequence from one object to another remains the same for all objects, except for the insertion or deletion of the altered object. However, if you become confused, simply reset the complete sequence in the desired order by manually starting with a **TabIndex** value of 0 and then assigning values in the desired order. A control whose **TabStop** property has been set to

False maintains its **TabIndex** value, but is simply skipped over for the next object in the tab sequence. Be sure to check all the **TabIndex** values after any changes to the form have been made. In Chapter 3, we will describe another way to set the **TabIndex** values.

The Format Menu Option[7]

The Format menu option provides the ability to align and move selected controls as a unit, as well as lock controls and make selected controls the same size. This is a great help in constructing a consistent look on a form that contains numerous controls. In this section, we will see how this menu option is used.

As a specific example using the Format menu, consider Figure 2–42, showing two buttons on a design form. To align both controls and make them the same size, first you must select the desired controls. This can be done by clicking the form and dragging the resulting dotted line to enclose all of the controls that you wish to format, as illustrated in Figure 2–42, or by holding the Shift key down and clicking the desired controls.

Once you have selected the desired controls for formatting, the last selected object will appear with solid grab handles. For example, in Figure 2–43 it is Button2. The solid grab handles designate the control that is the *defining control*, setting the pattern for both sizing and aligning the other selected controls. If this control is not the defining control that you want, select another by clicking it.

Having selected the desired defining control, click on the Format menu bar and then select the desired Format option. For example, Figure 2–44 illustrates the selection for making all controls within the dotted lines the same size. Within this submenu, you have the further choice of making either the width, height, or both dimensions of all controls equal to the defining control's respective dimensions. The choice shown in this figure would make all selected controls equal in both width and height to the defining control. You can also use the Layout Toolbar, as shown in Figure 2–8, instead of using the Align submenu.

You can also change the size of a control by selecting the control in design mode and using the Shift and arrow keys. In addition to sizing controls, you may also want to

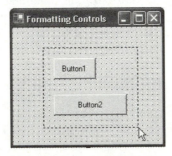

Figure 2–42   *Preparing Two Controls for Formatting*

---

[7]This topic may be omitted on first reading with no loss of subject continuity.

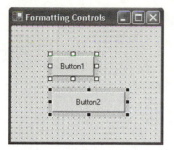

Figure 2-43 *Locating the Defining Control*

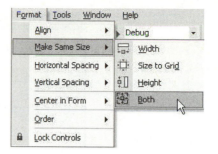

Figure 2-44 *Making Controls the Same Size*

align a group of controls within a form. Figure 2–45 illustrates the options that are provided for the <u>A</u>lign submenu. As shown, controls may be aligned in seven different ways, the first six of which are aligned relative to the position of the defining control. Choosing any one of these first six options will move all other formatted controls in relation to the defining control. The position of the defining control *is not* altered.

An additional and very useful feature of the Format selection process is that all selected controls can be moved as a unit. To do this, click within one of the selected controls and drag the control. As the control is dragged, all other selected controls will move as a group while maintaining their relative positions to each other.

Finally, as shown in Figures 2–44 and 2–45, the <u>F</u>ormat submenu provides a number of other Format choices, the effects of which are obvious, except perhaps for the <u>L</u>ock control. This control locks all controls on the form in their current positions and prevents you from inadvertently moving them once you have placed them. Because this control works on a form-by-form basis, only controls on the currently active form are locked, and controls on other forms are unaffected.

The Label Control

When you create a GUI application, you need to make clear what the purpose of a form is and what sort of data should be entered into a text box. The Label control is used to provide the user with information. As such, labels appear as headings within a form or next to a control to let the user know the control's purpose. For example, in Figure

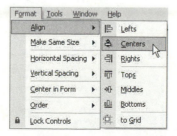

Figure 2-45 *Aligning Controls to the Defining Control*

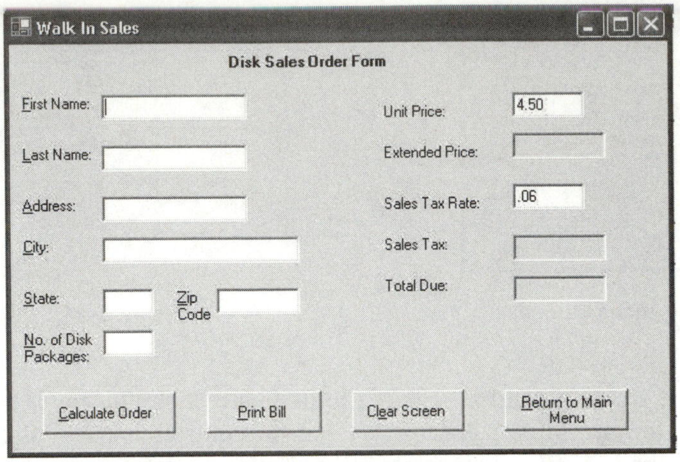

Figure 2–46 *A Form with Labels*

2-46, the heading *Disk Order Sales Form* is a label. Additionally, the text located to the left of each text box is also a label. As the text within a button is provided by the button's Text property, buttons rarely have labels associated with them.

Creating a label is very simple; all that is required is selecting the Label icon from the Toolbox and setting both its **Text** and **Font** properties. By definition, a label is a read-only control that cannot be changed by a user directly. The text displayed by a label is determined by its **Text** property, which can be set at design time or at run time under program control. The **Text** property's value is displayed in a style using the information provided by the **Font** property. For example, Figure 2–47 shows the Font property's setting box as it appears when the Font property was selected for the heading used in Figure 2–46. In particular, notice that the highlighted **Font** property has an ellipsis box (the box with the three dots) to the right of the MS Sans Serif setting. The

Figure 2–47 *Selecting the Font Property*

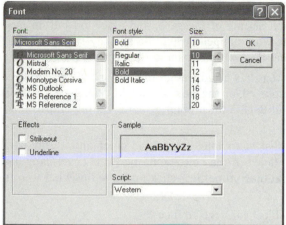

Figure 2–48a *The Font Dialog Box*   **Figure 2–48b** *The Font Properties Expanded*

ellipsis box appears when the **Font** property is selected, and clicking this box causes the **Font** dialog box shown in Figure 2–48a to appear.

In the **Font** dialog box, you set the label's font type, style, and size. The size is specified in points, and there are 72 points to an inch. Note that the label used as a heading in Figure 2–46 uses a Microsoft Sans Serif font type and is displayed in bold with a point size of 10. The type size used for all of the other labels is 8.25 points, the default. To make the form easily readable, you should try to avoid using a point size smaller than 8 points on any form. Figure 2–48b shows what is displayed in the properties window if you click on the + to the left of the **Font** property.

Although it is the label's **Text** property that is displayed on an application's interface, an additional useful property is the **AutoSize**. If the **AutoSize** property is set to False, you must manually adjust the physical size of the label at design time, using the sizing handles to fit the text. It is generally easier to set the **AutoSize** property to True. Then, as you type in the text, the label will automatically expand its width to the right to fit the text. However, you should take care that the size of the control is not too large and does not impact the other controls.

Exercises 2.4

1. Determine how many event procedures are available for a Button control. (*Hint:* Activate the Code window for a form that has a Button control and count the available procedures.)

2. Determine how many properties can be set for a text box control.

3. Determine if a label has a **TabStop** property.

4. What is the difference between the **Name** and **Text** properties?

5. How is a hot (accelerator) key created for a button?

6. Create a button named btnInput having a **Text** setting of <u>V</u>alues.

7. Create a button named btnDisplay having a Text setting of Display.

8. Assume that one button has a Text setting of Mess_age, and a second button has a Text setting of Displ_ay. Determine what happens when the hot key sequence Alt+A is pressed twice. Do this by creating the two buttons and running the program.

9. Create a text box named txtOne that has a red foreground color and a blue background color. The initial text displayed in the box should be Welcome to Visual Basic. (*Hint:* Use the **ForeColor** and **BackColor** properties—click on the ellipsis (...) to bring up the available colors.)

10. Create a text box named txtTwo that has a blue foreground color and a gray background color. The initial text displayed in the box should be High-Level Language. (*Hint:* Use the **ForeColor** and **BackColor** properties—click on the ellipsis (...) to bring up the available colors.)

11. What are the three ways that an object can receive focus?

12. To receive focus in the tab sequence, what three properties must be set to True?

13. a. Create a graphical user interface that contains two buttons and two text boxes. The names of these controls should be btnOne, btnTwo, txtFirst, and txtSecond. Set the tab sequence so that tab control goes from txtFirst to txtSecond to btnOne to btnTwo.

    b. For the tab sequence established in Exercise 13a, set the TabStop property of btnOne to False and determine how the tab sequence is affected. What was the effect on the objects' TabIndex values?

    c. For the tab sequence established in Exercise 13a, set the TabStop property of btnOne to True and its Visible property to False. What is the run time tab sequence now? Did these changes affect any object's TabIndex Values?

    d. For the tab sequence established in Exercise 13a, set the TabStop property of btnOne to True, its Visible property to **True**, and its **Enabled** property to **False**. What is the run time tab sequence now? Did these changes affect any object's **TabIndex** values?

    e. Change the tab sequence so that focus starts on txtFirst, and then goes to btnOne, txtSecond, and finally btnTwo. For this sequence, what are the values of each object's **TabIndex** property?

2.5   Adding Additional Event Procedures

Now that we have added four objects to Program 2-3 (The Hello Application, Version 3.0, shown in Figure 2–40), we will need to supply these objects with event code. Although each object can have many events associated with it, one of the most commonly used events is the clicking of a button. For our Hello Application, we will initially create three mouse click event procedures, each of which will be activated by clicking one of the three buttons. Two of these event procedures will be used to change the text displayed in the text box, and the last will be used to exit the program.

To change an object's property value while a program is running, a statement is used that has the syntax:

```
Object.Property = value
```

The term to the left of the equals sign identifies the desired object and property. For example, btnMessage.Name refers to the **Name** property of the control named btnMessage, and txtDisplay.Text refers to the **Text** property of the control named txtDisplay. The period between the object's name and its property is required. The value to the right of the equal sign provides the new setting for the designated property. The equal sign is used as an assignment operator where the value on the right is 'assigned' to the object on the left.

For our program, we want to display the text `Hello World!` when the button named btnMessage is clicked. This requires that the statement

```
txtDisplay.Text = "Hello World!"
```

be executed for the click event of the btnMessage control. Notice that this statement will change a property of one object, the TextBox object, using an event procedure associated with another object, a Button object. Now let's attach this code to the btnMessage button so that it is activated when this control is clicked. The required event procedure code is:

```
Private Sub btnMessage_Click(ByVal sender As System.Object, ByVal e As _
    System.EventArgs) Handles btnMessage.Click

   txtDisplay.Text = "Hello World!"
End Sub
```

To enter this code, double-click the btnMessage control. (Make sure you have the design form shown in Figure 2–33 on the screen). This will open the Code window shown in Figure 2–49. As always, the stub for the desired event is automatically supplied for you, requiring you to complete the procedure's body with your own code. You might also notice that the keywords `Private`, `Sub`, `ByVal`, `As`, and `End` are displayed in a different color than the procedure's name.[8]

Also, note that the first statement above beginning with `Private` is too long to fit on one line in this book. To continue a Visual Basic statement on the next line, type a space followed by the underscore symbol (" _") and indent the continued statement.

The object identification box should display btnMessage and the procedure identification box should display Click. This indicates that the current object is the btnMessage control and that the procedure we are working on is for the **Click** event. If either of

---

[8]Typically, the color for keywords is blue and is automatically supplied when a keyword is typed.

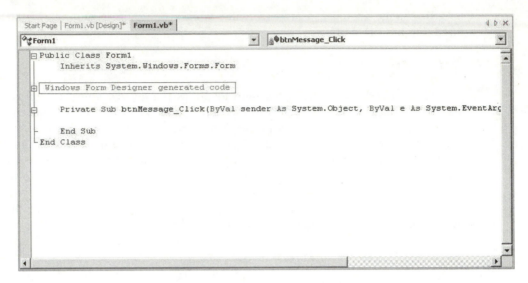

Figure 2–49 *The Code Window*

these boxes does not contain the correct data, click the underlined arrow to the right of the box and then select the desired class and method. Note that when you click on the arrow to the right of the class name box, a drop-down list appears which lists all of the form's objects, including the form itself.

When the Code window looks like the one shown in Figure 2–49, type in the line

```
txtDisplay.Text = "Hello World!"
```

between the header line, Private Sub btnMessage_Click(), and terminating End Sub line, so that the complete procedure appears as

```
Private Sub btnMessage_Click(ByVal sender As System.Object, ByVal e As _
    System.EventArgs) Handles btnMessage.Click
  txtDisplay.Text = "Hello World!"
End Sub
```

After your procedure is completed, press the F5 function key to run the program. When the program is running, activate the btnMessage control by either clicking it, tabbing to it and pressing the Enter key, or using the hot key combination Alt+M. When any one of these actions is performed, your screen should appear as shown in Figure 2–50.

One of the useful features of Visual Basic is the ability to run and test an event procedure immediately after you have written it, rather than having to check each feature after the whole application is completed. You should get into the habit of doing this as you develop your own programs.

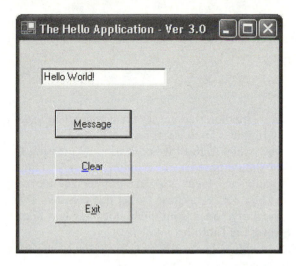

Figure 2–50   *The Interface Produced by Clicking the Message Button*

Now let's finish our second application by attaching event code to the click events of the remaining two buttons, and then fixing a minor problem with the TextBox control.

Bring up the Code window for the btnClear button by double-clicking this control after you have terminated program execution and are back in the design mode. When the Code window appears, add the single line

```
txtDisplay.Text = ""
```

between the procedures header (Private Sub) and terminating line (End Sub).

When this is completed, the procedure should appear as follows:

```
Private Sub btnClear_Click(ByVal sender As System.Object, ByVal e As _
    System.EventArgs) Handles btnClear.Click
  txtDisplay.Text = ""
End Sub
```

The string "", with no spaces, is called the *empty string.* This string consists of no characters. Setting the Text property of the text box to this string value will have the effect of clearing the text box of all text. Note that a value such as "   ", which consists of one or more blank spaces, will also clear the text box. However, a string with one or more blank spaces is not an empty string, which is defined as a string having *no* characters.

When this procedure is completed, use the arrow to the right of the class name box in the Code window to switch to the btnExit control. (You can also double-click the btnExit control to open the Code window.) The event procedure for this event should be:

```
Private Sub btnExit_Click(ByVal sender As System.Object, ByVal e As _
    System.EventArgs) Handles btnExit.Click
  Beep()
  End
End Sub
```

Beep is an instruction that causes the computer to make a short beeping sound. The keyword End terminates an application.

You are now ready to run the application by pressing the F5 function key. Running the application should produce the window shown in Figure 2–51. Note that when the program is initially run, focus is on the btnMessage button and the text box is empty. The empty text box occurs because we set this control's **Text** property to a blank during design time. Similarly, focus is on the btnMessage box because this was the first control added to the Form (its **TabIndex** value is 0).

Now click the M̲essage control to activate the btnMessage_Click() procedure and display the message shown in Figure 2–52.

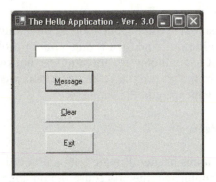

Figure 2–51   *The Initial Run Time Window*

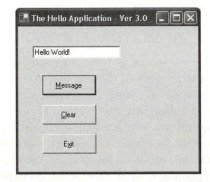

Figure 2–52   *The Run Time Window after the Message Button is Clicked*

Clicking the <u>C</u>lear button invokes the `btnClear_Click()` procedure, which clears the text box, whereas clicking the E<u>x</u>it button invokes the `btnExit_Click()` procedure. This procedure causes a short beep and terminates program execution.

Comments

Comments are explanatory remarks made within a program. When used carefully, comments can be helpful in clarifying what the complete program is about, what a specific group of statements is meant to accomplish, or what one line is intended to do.

Comments are indicated by using an apostrophe or the keyword **Rem,** which is short for Remark. Using an apostrophe is the preferred method and it will be used in this book. For example, the following are comment lines:

```
' this is a comment
' this program calculates a square root
```

With one exception, comments can be placed anywhere within a program and have no effect on program execution. Visual Basic ignores all comments—they are there strictly for the convenience of anyone reading the program. The one exception is that comments cannot be included at the end of a statement that is continued on the next line.

A comment can always be written either on a line by itself or on the same line as a program statement that is not continued on the next line. When written on a line by itself, either an apostrophe or the keyword **Rem** may be used. When a comment is written on the same line as a program statement, the comment must begin with an apostrophe. In all cases, a comment only extends to the end of the line it is written on. For example, the following event procedure illustrates the use of comments.

```
' This is the click event procedure associated with the Exit
Private Sub btnExit_Click(ByVal sender As System.Object, ByVal e As _
    System.EventArgs) Handles btnExit.Click
  Beep() 'This causes a short beep
  End   ' This ends the application
End Sub
```

If you need to create multiline comments, each line must begin with an apostrophe. Typically, many comments are required when using unstructured programming languages. These comments are necessary to clarify the purpose of either the program itself or individual sections and lines of code within the program. In Visual Basic, the program's inherent modular structure is intended to make the program readable, making the use of extensive comments unnecessary. However, if the purpose of a procedure or any of its statements is still not clear from its structure, name, or context, include comments where clarification is needed.

Statement Categories

You will have many statements at your disposal while constructing your Visual Basic event procedures. All statements belong to one of two broad categories: executable statements and nonexecutable statements. An *executable statement* causes some specific action to be performed by the compiler or interpreter. For example, a MessageBox.Show statement or a statement that tells the computer to add or subtract a number is an executable statement. A nonexecutable statement is a statement that describes some feature of either the program or its data but does not cause the computer to perform any action. An example of a nonexecutable statement is a comment statement. As the various Visual Basic statements are introduced in the upcoming sections, we will point out which ones are executable and which are nonexecutable.

A Closer Look at the TextBox Control

Text boxes form a major part of most Visual Basic programs, because they can be used for both input and output purposes. For example, run the Program 2-3 (see Figure 2–51) again, but this time click on the text box. Note that a cursor appears in the text box. At this point, you can type in any text that you choose. The text that you enter will stay in the text box until you click on one of the buttons, either changing the text to Hello World!, clearing the Text box of all text, or terminating the program.

Because we have constructed the program to use the text box for output display purposes only, we would like to alter the operation of the text box so that a user cannot enter data into it. To do this, we set the text box's Enter event to immediately put focus on one of the buttons. The following procedure accomplishes this:

```
Private Sub txtDisplay_Enter(ByVal sender As Object, ByVal e As _
    System.EventArgs) Handles txtDisplay.Enter

  btnMessage.Focus()
End Sub
```

Enter this procedure now in the text box's Code window. When you first open the Code window for the TextBox object (by either pressing the Shift+F4 keys or using the View menu), the Code window may appear as shown in Figure 2–53. If this happens, click the underlined arrow to the right of the class name box and select the txtDisplay object. Then click the Method Name underlined arrow and choose the Enter event.

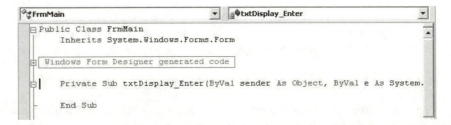

Figure 2–53   *The Code Window*

Focus is a method in which the Button object sets the focus on its object.[9] Thus, when a user clicks on the text box, it will trigger the txtDisplay_Enter() procedure, which in turn will call the **Focus** method of the btnMessage button. This method will set the focus on the <u>M</u>essage Button.

Note that when you initially entered characters in the text box, before we deactivated it for input, the entered characters were actually accepted as a string of text. This is always true of a text box—all data entered or displayed is considered a string. As we will see in the next chapter, when we want to use a text box to input a number, such as 12356, we will have to carefully check that a string representing an invalid number, such as 123a56, is not inadvertently entered. This type of validation is necessary because the text box does not filter out unwanted characters from an input or displayed string.

Exercises 2.5

1. a. Determine the events that can be associated with a button. (*Hint:* Create a button and use the Code window to view its various events.)

   b. List the event names for each event that can be associated with a button.

2. Repeat Exercise 1a for a Text box.

3. Repeat Exercise 1a for a Label.

4. List the objects and the events that the following procedures refer to:

   a. `Private Sub btnDisplay_Click(ByVal sender As Object, ByVal e As _`
      `System.EventArgs) Handles btnDisplay.Click`

   b. `Private Sub btnBold_Leave(ByVal sender As Object, ByVal e As _`
      `System.EventArgs) Handles btnBold.Leave`

   c. `Private Sub txtInput_Enter(ByVal sender As Object, ByVal e As _`
      `System.EventArgs) Handles txtInput.Leave`

   d. `Private Sub txtOutput_Leave(ByVal sender As Object, ByVal e As _`
      `System.EventArgs) Handles txtOutput.Leave`

5. Using the correspondence shown here, follow the instructions below:

Event Name	Event
Click	Click
DblClick	Double click
Enter	Enter
Leave	Leave

   a. Write the header line for the double-click event associated with a Label control named lblFirstName.

   b. Write the header line for the lost focus event of a text box named txtLastName.

   c. Write the header line for the got focus event of a text box named txtAddress.

---

[9]An alternative solution is to set the Locked property of the text box to True. With this property set to True, the text box is locked from receiving any input and effectively becomes a read-only box. However, it still can be clicked on and receive focus.

6. Write instructions that will display the following message in a text box named txtTest:

   a. Welcome to Visual Basic

   b. Now is the time

   c. 12345

   d. 4 * 5 is 20

   e. Vacation is near

7. For each of the following procedures, determine the event associated with the button btnDisplay and what is displayed in the text box named txtOut:

   a.
```
Private Sub btnDisplay_Click(ByVal sender As Object, ByVal e As _
    System.EventArgs) Handles btnDisplay.Click

  txtOut.Text = "As time goes by"

End Sub
```

   b.
```
Private Sub btnDisplay_Enter(ByVal sender As Object, ByVal e As _
    System.EventArgs) Handles btnDisplay.Enter

  txtOut.Text = "456"

End Sub
```

   c.
```
Private Sub btnDisplay_Leave(ByVal sender As Object, ByVal e As _
    System.EventArgs) Handles btnDisplay.Leave

  txtOut.Text = "Play it again Sam"

End Sub
```

   d.
```
Private Sub btnDisplay_Enter(ByVal sender As Object, ByVal e As _
    System.EventArgs) Handles btnDisplay.Enter

  txtOut.Text = "          "

End Sub
```

8. a. **TextAlign** is the name of a property that can be set for a text box. What do you think this property controls?

   b. What display do you think the following procedure produces when the button btnOne is clicked?

```
Private Sub btnOne_Click(ByVal sender As System.Object, _

  ByVal e As System.EventArgs) Handles BtnOne.Click


  txtBox1.TextAlign = HorizontalAlignment.Center

  txtBox1.Text = "Computers"

End Sub
```

For Exercises 9 and 10, create the given interface and initial properties. Then complete the application by writing code to perform the stated task.

9.

Object	Property	Setting
Form	Name	frmMain
	Text	Messages
Button	Name	btnGood
	Text	&Good
Button	Name	btnBad
	Text	&Bad
Text box	Name	txtMessage
	Text	(blank)

When a user clicks the btnGood button, the message *Today is a good day!* should appear in the text box, and when the btnBad button is clicked, the message *I'm having a bad day today!* should be displayed.

10. Write a Visual Basic application having three buttons and one text box that is initially blank. Clicking the first button should produce the message *See no evil.* Clicking the second button should produce the message *Hear no evil*, and clicking the third button should produce the message *Speak no evil* in the text box.

2.6 Focus on Program Design and Implementation: Creating a Main Menu

Most commercial applications perform multiple tasks, with each task typically assigned its own form. For example, one form might be used for entering an order, a second form for entering the receipt of merchandise into inventory, and a third form used to specify information needed to create a report.

Although each additional form can easily be added to an existing project using the techniques presented later in this section, there is the added requirement for activating each form in a controlled and user-friendly manner. This activation can be accomplished using an initial main menu form that is displayed as the application's opening window. This menu of choices provides the user with a summary of what the application can do, and is created as either a set of buttons or as a menu bar. Here, we show how to rapidly prototype a main menu consisting of buttons, using the Rotech Systems case (see Section 1.5) as an example. The procedure for constructing a menu bar is presented in Section 1.5.

Button Main Menus

The underlying principle involved in creating a main menu screen is that a user can easily shift from one form to a second form by pressing a button. How this works for two screens is illustrated in Figure 2–54. Here, pressing the button shown on the Main Menu form causes the second form to be displayed. Similarly, pressing the second form's button redisplays the Main Menu form.

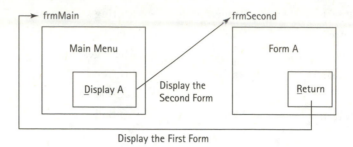

Figure 2–54   *Switching Between Two Screens*

Figure 2–55   *A Sample Main Menu Screen*

The switching between screens that is provided by the scheme shown in Figure 2–54 can easily be extended to produce a main menu screen, a sample of which is shown in Figure 2–55. For this screen there would be four additional screens, with each screen displayed by clicking one of the buttons on the main menu. In a completed application, each additional screen is different, but each screen would have a Return button to display the main menu screen again.

The menu options shown in this figure would be provided as the first operational form presented to the user. The term *operational form* means that the form is used to interact directly with the operational part of the system to perform a task, unlike an information form. *Information forms* are purely passive forms that provide information about the application, and which, if omitted from the system, would not stop the system from performing its intended functions. Examples of information forms are an opening splash screen containing general advertising information that is displayed for a few seconds before the first operational form is presented, an About Box providing information about the application (such as author, copyright holder, and version number), and Help forms providing assistance on how to use various application features. An application's initial main menu screen is constructed from the information contained in the system's

Table 2–6   The Initial Rotech Systems TTL Table

Form: Task	Trigger Object	Event
Enter Inventory Receipts Enter & Process a Mail-in Response Enter & Process a Walk-in Request Produce Reports Exit the System		

initial TTL table. We will construct the Rotech Systems main menu to provide access to the tasks listed in the TTL table developed in Section 1.5, and reproduced here for convenience as Table 2-6.

Because each menu option in our main menu is to be activated by the clicking of a button, we can now easily complete Table 2-6. The form that we will use to activate these tasks is a Main Menu form. Each object used to trigger the listed task will be a button, and each event trigger will be a button's Click event. After names have been assigned arbitrarily to each button, the completed initial TTL table is listed as Table 2–7.

Tips From The Pros

Creating a Main Menu

The development of a menu system is quite easy, provides one of the most visually impressive functioning parts of a system, and actually demands the least in terms of programming competency. To develop a menu, follow these steps:

1. Make the opening application's form a Main Menu form, which is a form that contains buttons used to display other forms.

2. Initially, add a single new form to the project, which ultimately will be replaced by an operational form. (Later on, additional new forms will be added, one for each operational form required by the project.)

3. Provide the new form with a button having a caption such as Return to Main Menu form. This button is referred to as the Return button.

4. Attach three lines of code to the new form's Return button's Click event.

These three lines of code appear as:

```
Dim frmMainRef As New frmMain()

Me.Hide                ' this is a valid statement

frmMainRef.Show        ' replace frmMain with any valid form name
```

The first code line creates a reference to the form frmMain. It is needed in order to refer to existing forms. (The New keyword is explained more fully in Chapter 12.) The second code line is an instruction to hide the current form from view, while the third line displays the frmMain form. As a result, if the Main Menu form is named frmMain, the statement frmMainRef.Show displays the Main Menu form when the Return button is pressed. In general, each new form will have more than one button. However, one button should always return the user directly to the Main Menu.

5. Attach three similar lines of code to each Main Menu button used to display a new form. These lines of code take the form:

```
Dim frmDesiredRef As New frmDesired()
Me.Hide                ' this is a valid statement
frmDesired.Show        ' replace frmDesired with any valid form name
```

Initially, all Main Menu buttons will be used to display the same form added in Step 2. The reason for using the Hide method rather than the Close method is based on the assumption that we will be returning to each form many times, so we try to keep each form in memory to minimize loading times.

The information in Table 2–7 tells us that, operationally, our main menu will consist of five buttons, with each button's Click event used to display another form. Specifically, clicking on the btnInvRec button will activate an operational form for entering inventory receipts. Clicking the btnMailin button will activate an operational form for entering an order for the promotional 10-diskette pack. Clicking the btnWalkin button will activate an operational form for entering a walk-in order. Clicking the btnReport button will activate an operational form for producing reports, and clicking the btnExit button will terminate program execution. By using this information, and adding an information label to the Main Menu form, we construct Table 2–8 displaying the initial Main Menu properties table.

Table 2–7   The Completed Initial Rotech Systems TTL Table

Form: Main Menu Task	Trigger Object	Event
Enter Inventory Receipts	btnInvRec	Click
Enter & Process a Mail-in Response	btnMailins	Click
Enter & Process a Walk-in Request	btnWalkins	Click
Produce Reports	btnReport	Click
Exit the System	btnExit	Click

Table 2–8   The Rotech Systems Main Menu Properties Table

Object	Property	Setting
Form	Name	frmMain
	Text	Main Menu
Button	Name	btnMailins
	Text	&Mail Ins
	TabIndex	0
Button	Name	btnWalkins
	Text	&Walk Ins
	TabIndex	1
Button	Name	btnInvRec
	Text	&Inventory Receipts
	TabIndex	2
Button	Name	btnReports
	Text	&Reports
	TabIndex	3
Button	Name	btnExit
	Text	E&xit
	TabIndex	4
Label	Name	lblHeader
	Text	Rotech Systems Disk Promotion Program
	Font	MS Sans Serif, Bold, Size = 10

Figure 2–56 illustrates a form having the properties described by Table 2–8. Specifically, we have chosen to group the two buttons associated with order entry (Mail Ins and Walk Ins) in one column, align the two remaining buttons in a second column, and center the Exit button below and between the two columns. If there were an even number of buttons, we could have aligned them vertically into two columns, including the Exit button as the last button in the second column, and made all the buttons the same size. Figures 2–57 and 2–58 show two alternatives to Figure 2–56. In each case, the size and placement of each button is determined by the programmer, with the only overriding design consideration at this point being that the size of each button within a grouping should be the same and that the buttons should align in a visually pleasing manner. Although we will give a number of form design guidelines in Section 3.6, the basic rule is to produce a functionally useful form that is dignified and not ornate. The design and colors of your form should always be appropriate to the business whose application you are producing.

We have given the *Mail Ins* button the initial input focus because of the majority of times a user will be interacting with it and the fact that it deals with the system's most dynamic data.. Thus, by simply pressing the Enter key, a user will activate the most commonly used button in the menu. The tab sequence then ensures a smooth transition that moves the focus from the *Mail Ins* button down the first column to

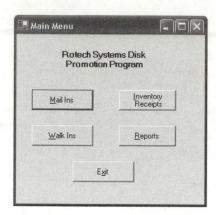

Figure 2–56 *Rotech's Initial Main Menu Form*

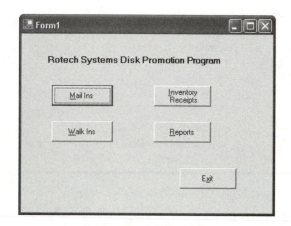

Figure 2–57 *A Possible Main Menu Layout*

Figure 2–58 *Another Main Menu Layout*

the top of the second column of buttons, where the *Inventory Receipts* button is located, and then down this column, over to the *Exit* button, and back to the top of the first column.

In reviewing Figure 2–56, note that the window furnishes information about the application and provides a current list of available choices shown as a sequence of buttons. We now need to add additional forms and provide code so that pressing any of the buttons, except the *Exit* button, hides the current Main Menu form and displays the new form appropriate to the selected menu choice. Pressing the *Exit* button performs the normal operation of ending program execution.

Adding a Second Form

At this stage in our application's development we have neither sufficient understanding of the system's requirements nor sufficient knowledge of Visual Basic to construct a

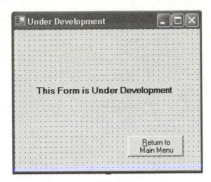

Figure 2-59   *The Project's "Under Development" Form*

meaningful form to carry out the tasks indicated by the Main Menu. We can, however, easily add a second form, shown in Figure 2-59, to indicate that the form is under development. Note that this second form contains a Label object and a Button object, the same types of objects included in our Main Menu form. The properties for this second form are listed in Table 2-9. Because this form performs the single task of returning to the Main Menu form, a TTL table listing this single task is not created.

To add this second form to our project, select the Add Windows Form item from the Project menu, as shown in Figure 2-60. This will open the Add New Item dialog box shown in Figure 2-61, from which you should select the Windows Form icon under the Templates category. This will add the second form to the Project Explorer Window, as shown in Figure 2-62. Once you have generated this new form, configure it with the objects and properties listed in Table 2-9.

The form you have just created is an example of a stub form. The functional use of a stub form is simply to see that an event is correctly activated. In our particular case, it will be used to test the operation of the Main Menu to ensure that it correctly displays a second form and provides a return back to the Main Menu from the newly developed

Table 2-9   The "Under Development" Form's Properties Table

Object	Property	Setting
Form	Name	frmStub
	Text	Under Development
Button	Name	btnReturn
	Text	&Return to Main Menu
Label	Name	lblReturn
	Text	This Form is Under Development
	Font	MS Sans Serif, Bold

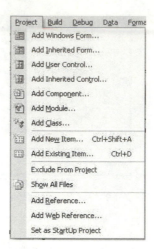

Figure 2-60 *Adding a Second Form Using the Project Menu*

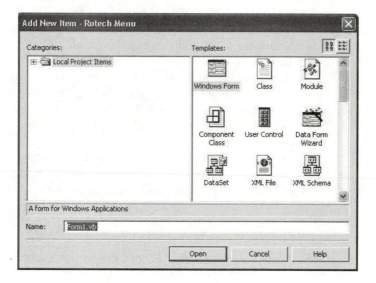

Figure 2-61 *The Add New Item Dialog Box*

form. To do this, we now have to add the code that correctly shows and hides forms from the user's view.

Displaying and Hiding Forms

The Visual Basic methods provided for displaying and hiding forms from a user's view are listed in Table 2-10. When a project is first executed, the default is to automatically load and display the project's opening form. Other forms must then be loaded into

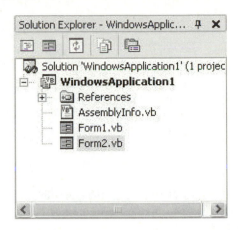

Figure 2–62 *The Solution Explorer Window Showing Two Forms*

Table 2–10   Form Display Statements and Methods

Instruction	Type	Syntax	Example	Description
Show	Method	Form-nameRef.Show()	frmStubRef.Show()	Displays a form. If the variables for the form are not already loaded into memory, they will be before the form is displayed.
Hide	Method	Me.Hide()	Me.Hide()	Hides a Form object, but does not unload its variables from memory.
Close	Method	Me.Close()	Me.Close()	Hides a Form object and unloads its variables from memory.

memory before they can be displayed, and forms that are no longer needed should be unloaded to conserve memory space. Note that in order to use the Show method, we need to create a reference to the forms that are being manipulated. In Table 2–10, we use Form-nameRef and frmStubRef to designate this reference. To hide or close a form, use Me to refer to the form that should be hidden.

Using the methods listed in Table 2–10, we easily can write event procedures to hide the Main Menu form and load and display the Under Development stub form when any Main Menu button, except the Exit button, is pressed. The required event procedure codes are:

Main Menu Event Procedures

```
Private Sub btnMailins_Click(ByVal sender As Object, ByVal e As _
    System.EventArgs) Handles btnMailins.Click
  Dim frmStubRef As New frmStub()
```

```
   Me.Hide()
   frmStubRef.Show()
End Sub

Private Sub btnWalkins_Click(ByVal sender As Object, ByVal e As _
    System.EventArgs) Handles btnWalkins.Click
   Dim frmStubRef As New frmStub()
   Me.Hide()
   frmStubRef.Show()
End Sub

Private Sub btnInvrec_Click(ByVal sender As Object, ByVal e As _
    System.EventArgs) Handles btnInvrec.Click
   Dim frmStubRef As New frmStub()
   Me.Hide()
   frmStubRef.Show()
End Sub

Private Sub btnReports_Click( ByVal sender As Object, ByVal e As _
    System.EventArgs) Handles btnReports.Click
   Dim frmStubRef As New frmStub()
   Me.Hide()
   frmStubRef.Show()
End Sub

Private Sub btnExit_Click(ByVal sender As Object, ByVal e As _
    System.EventArgs) Handles btnExit.Click
   Beep()
   End
End Sub
```

Each of these **Click** event procedures causes the frmMain form to be hidden and the frmStub form to be displayed whenever any Main Menu button is pressed, except for the Exit button. The code for the stub form's return button's **Click** event is:

```
Private Sub btnReturn_Click( ByVal sender As Object, ByVal e As _
    System.EventArgs) Handles btnReturn.Click
   Dim frmMainRef As New frmMain()
   Me.Hide()
   frmMainRef.Show()
End Sub
```

The Return button simply hides the current stub form and displays the initial frm-Main window. The advantage of using a stub form is that it permits us to run a complete application that does not yet meet all of its final requirements. As each successive form is developed, the display of the stub form can be replaced with a display of the desired form. This incremental, or stepwise, refinement of the program is an extremely powerful development technique used by professional programmers. Another advantage to this rapid application prototyping technique is that, as new features are required, additional buttons can easily be added to the Main Menu form.

One modification that can be made to our Main Menu form is to have each button call a single, centrally placed, general-purpose procedure that would then make the choice of which form to hide and display based on the button pressed. We consider this approach in Chapter 7 after both selection statements and general-purpose procedures are presented. You will encounter both the current technique and the general-purpose procedure technique in practice, and which one you adopt for your programs is more a matter of style than substance.

Note: The Rotech Systems project, as it exists at the end of this section, can be found on the website http://computerscience.jbpub.com/bronsonvbnet in the ROTECH2 *folder as project* rotech2. *Note that rotech2 and all subsequent projects are also folders.*

Exercises 2.6

1. Implement the two screens and the relationship between the two forms previously shown in Figure 2–54. When a user presses the single button on the form with the label Main Menu, the screen labeled Form A should appear. When the Return button on Form A is pressed, the form labeled Main Menu should appear.

2. a. Implement the three screens and the relationship shown in the accompanying figure. The Main Menu form should have a single button that displays Form A. Form A should have two buttons: one to return to the Main Menu and one to display Form B. Form B should also have two buttons: one to return control to Form A and one to return control directly to the Main Menu.

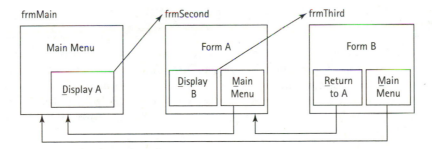

   b. Add a fourth form with the label Form C to the project created for Exercise 2a. This form is to be displayed using a button on Form B. In this case, how many buttons should Form B contain for controlling the display of forms? Note that when forms are chained together in the manner shown, there are at most three buttons: one button to "back up" one level and return to the immediately preceding screen, one button to return directly to the Main Menu, and a third button to call the next form in the chain. For multilevel forms, it is also convenient to provide a "hot key" (such as the F10 function key that can be used on all forms) to return directly to the Main Menu form. A second "hot key" (such as the F9 function key) always redisplays the preceding form. (How to create this type of "hot key" is presented in Section 6.7.)

3. Either create the menu system developed in this section or locate and load the project from the *http://computerscience.jbpub.com/bronsonvbnet* website (project rotech2 in the rotech2 folder).

4. a. Add a new form, with the following properties, to the Rotech project:

Object	Property	Setting
Form	Name	frmWalkIn
	Text	Walk In Processing Form
Button	Name	btnReturn
	Text	&Return to Main Menu
Label	Name	lblReturn
	Text	This Form is Under Development
	Font	MS Sans Serif, Bold, Size = 10

This new form's button should return control to the Main Menu form when the button is clicked.

b. Modify the Main Menu Walk In button's **Click** event so that it displays the form you created in Exercise 4a, rather than displaying the frmStub form.

5. (Case study)

For your selected case project (see project specifications at the end of Section 1.5), complete the project's initial TTL table and then create a working Main Menu that corresponds to the data in the completed table. Additionally, add an Under Development stub form to the project and verify that a user can successfully cycle between forms.

2.7 Knowing About: The Help Facility

No matter how experienced you become at using Visual Basic, there will be times when you'll need some help in either performing a particular task, looking up the exact syntax of a statement, or finding the parameters required by a built-in function. For these tasks you can use Visual Basic's Help Facility. Help includes the entire reference manual, programming examples, and the complete Microsoft Development Network (MSDN) Library.

To access the Help Facility, select either the Contents, Search, or Index options from the Help menu, as shown in Figure 2-63. When any of these options is selected, the screen shown in Figure 2-58 will be displayed.

Note that this main help window is divided into two panes. The left pane, which is referred to as the Navigation pane, contains the three tabs labeled Contents, Index, and Search. Each of these tabs provides a different way of accessing information from the help facility, as summarized in Table 2-11. The right section, which is the Documentation pane, displays all information retrieved from the Library. Note on the left side the words `Filtered by`. This should typically be set to `Visual Basic and Related` when you're developing a Visual Basic project.

As shown in Figure 2-64, the Contents tab, because it is on top of the other tabs, is the currently active tab. This happened because the Contents option was selected from

Figure 2–63   *The Help Menu Options*

Table 2–11   The Help Tabs

Tab	Description
Contents	Displays a Table of Contents for the documentation. This table can be expanded to display individual topic titles; double-clicking a title displays the associated documentation in the Documentation pane.
Index	Provides both a general index of topics and a text box for user entry of a specific topic. Entering a topic causes focus to shift to the closest matching topic within the general index. Double-clicking an index topic displays the associated documentation in the Documentation pane.
Search	Provides a means of entering a search word or phrase. All topics matching the entered word(s) are displayed in a List box. Clicking on a topic displays the corresponding documentation in the Documentation pane.

the Help menu (see Figure 2–64). If either the Index or Search options had been selected, the same main help window would appear, except that the respective Index or Search tab would be active. However, no matter which tab is currently active you can switch from one tab to another by clicking on the desired tab.

The Contents Tab

The Contents tab provides a means of browsing through all of the available reference material and technical articles contained within Visual Studio .NET, and specifically within Visual Basic .NET. This tab provides a table of contents of all of the material and displays the topics using the standard Windows tree view. For example, if you expand the topic Visual Studio .NET shown in Figure 2–64 by clicking on the plus sign box [+], and then expand the Introducing Visual Studio .NET topic, you will see the tree shown in Figure 2–65. The information provided in the documentation pane was displayed by

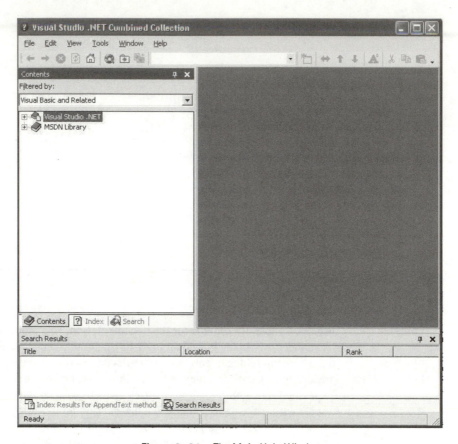

Figure 2–64   *The Main Help Window*

double-clicking on the page highlighted in the Navigation pane. A hard copy of the displayed page is obtained by either selecting the Print option from the File menu or right-clicking in the Documentation pane and selecting the Print option.

A very useful feature of the documentation is the hyperlink embedded within the displayed documentation text. By positioning the mouse on underlined text and clicking, the referenced text will be displayed. This permits you to rapidly jump from topic to topic, all while staying within the Documentation pane.

The Index Tab

As shown in Figure 2–66, the Index tab is on top of the other tabs, which makes it the active tab. This tab operates much like an index in a book, with one major improvement: In a book, after looking up the desired topic, you must manually turn to the refer-

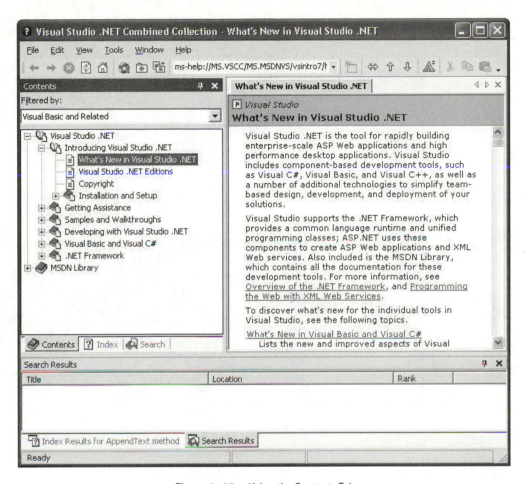

Figure 2–65   *Using the Contents Tab*

enced page or pages. In the help facility, this "look up and display" is automatic once you indicate the desired topic. Selection of the topic is accomplished by double-clicking on an item within the list of topics contained in the list box (this is the box located at the bottom of the tab). To locate a topic, you can either type the topic's name within the tab's Keyword text box, which causes the item to be highlighted in the ListBox, or use the scroll bar at the right of the list box to manually move to the desired item.

For example, in Figure 2–67, the topic AppendText Method has been typed in the Look For: text box, and the list box entry for this topic has been selected. As each letter is typed in the text box, the selected entry in the list box changes to match the input letters as closely as possible. In this case, because there are multiple library entries for the highlighted topic, if you double-click the highlighted topic, the Multiple Topics dialog box shown in Figure 2–68 appears. By double-clicking the desired item directly in

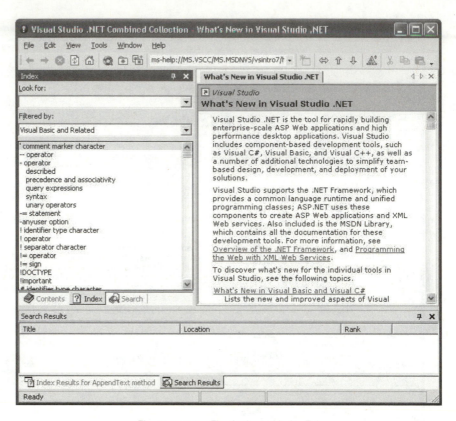

Figure 2–66   *The Activated Index Tab*

the list box, the documentation for the selected topic is displayed in the Documentation area. Figure 2–69 illustrates the documentation for the item highlighted in Figure 2–68.

A useful feature of the help facility is that once you have selected and displayed the desired topic, you can easily generate a hard copy of the information. This is accomplished by either selecting the Print item from the File menu button at the top of the MSDN Library window, or by using the context menu provided by clicking the right mouse button from within the displayed information.

The Search Tab

The Search tab, shown as the active tab in Figure 2–70, permits you to search for the words entered in the tab's text box in either the complete MSDN Library or sections of it. When creating a search phrase, you should enclose a phrase within double quotes

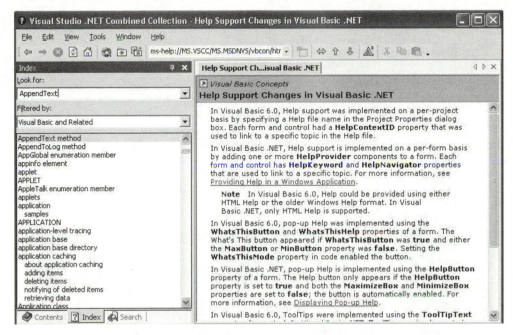

Figure 2–67   *The Index Tab with a Typed Entry*

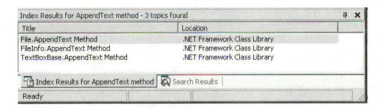

Figure 2–68   *The Multiple Topics Dialog Box*

and make use of Boolean operators to limit the search. For example, using the filter "Visual Basic and Related," a list of two topics was generated for the phrase "sqrt method" when the List Topics button shown in Figure 2–70 was pressed. The double quotes direct the search to look for the words "sqrt method" together. If the double quotes are omitted, the search finds all occurrences of either the word "sqrt" or the word

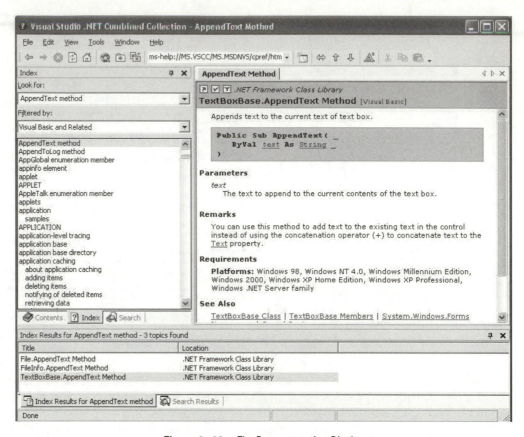

Figure 2–69 *The Documentation Display*

"method," and returns ten matches. The documentation shown in Figure 2–70 was displayed by clicking the second topic listed in the list box. As an aid to reading the help text, it is sometimes useful to have the search words highlighted in the help text. This can be accomplished by checking the box "Highlight search hits (in topics)" located below the search button.

Dynamic Help

Dynamic Help is an excellent way to get information about the IDE and its features. The Dynamic Help window displays a list of help topics that changes as you perform operations. This window occupies the same location as the Properties window. If the Dynamic Help window is not open, click Help on the menu bar and then click Dynamic Help. When you click a word or component such as a form or control, links to relevant articles appear in the Dynamic Help window. This window also has a toolbar that provides access to the **Contents, Index,** and **Search** Help features. Figure 2–71 shows a Dynamic Help window.

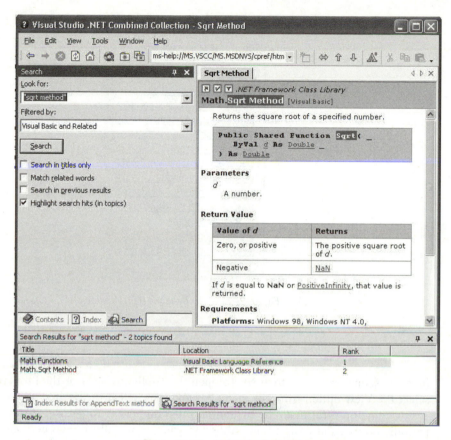

Figure 2–70   *Using the Search Tab*

Context-Sensitive Help

A quick way to view Help on any topic is to use context-sensitive Help. This is similar to dynamic help, except that it immediately displays a relevant article rather than presenting a list of articles. To use this facility, select an object such as a form or control and press F1. You can also highlight a word in a line of code and press F1 to get information on that topic.

2.8   Common Programming Errors and Problems

One of the most frustrating problems when learning Visual Basic is not being able to locate all of the elements needed to create an application. For example, you may not have the Form object, Toolbox, nor Properties window on the design screen. To bring up the form, either retrieve an existing project or select New Project from the File menu

Figure 2–71 *The Dynamic Help Window*

(hot key sequence Alt+F, then N). To open the Toolbox object or the Properties window, select the <u>V</u>iew option from the menu bar and then select the desired window.

A common error made by beginning programmers is forgetting to save a project at periodic intervals at design time. Although you can usually forego periodic saves, every experienced programmer knows the agony of losing work as a result of a variety of mistakes or an unexpected power outage. To avoid this, you should develop the habit of periodically saving your work.

2.9 Chapter Review

Key Terms

accelerator key	dialog box
code module	empty string
Code window	event
button	executable statement
comment	focus
controls	form
design screen	Form module
design time	graphical user interface

hot key

identifier

label

menu bar

methods

MessageBox.Show

nonexecutable statement

properties

run time

sizing handles

string

text box

toolbar

Toolbox

Summary

1. An object-oriented language permits the use and creation of new object types.
2. Visual Basic .NET is a true object-oriented language.
3. Event-based programs execute program code depending on what events occur, which depends on what the user does.
4. GUIs are graphical user interfaces that provide the user with objects that recognize events such as clicking a mouse.
5. An *application* is any program that can be run under a Windows Operating System.
6. The term *design time* refers to the period of time during which a Visual Basic application is being developed under control of Visual Basic.
7. The term *run time* refers to the period of time when an application is executing.
8. A Visual Basic program consists of a visual part and a language part. The visual part is provided by the objects used in the design of the graphical user interface, whereas the language part consists of procedural code.
9. The basic steps in developing a visual basic program are:
   a. Creating the GUI.
   b. Setting the properties of each object on the interface.
   c. Writing procedural code.
10. A form is used during design time to create a graphical user interface for a Visual Basic application. At run time the form becomes a window.
11. The most commonly placed objects on a form are buttons, labels, and text boxes.
12. Each object placed on a form has a name property. Development teams may choose guidelines for naming objects but in this book, form names begin with the prefix frm, text boxes begin with txt, and buttons begin with btn. Names must be chosen according to the following rules:
    a. The first character of the name must be a letter.
    b. Only letters, digits, or underscores may follow the initial letter. Blank spaces, special characters, and punctuation marks are not allowed; use the underscore or capital letters to separate words in an identifier consisting of multiple words.
    c. A name can be no longer than 1016 characters.
    d. A name should not be a keyword.

Test Yourself–Short Answer

1. A Visual Basic programmer works with the application in two modes: run time and _____.

2. The letters GUI are an acronym for _____ .

3. There are two basic parts to a Visual Basic application; they are: _____ and _____ .

4. At run time, a form becomes a _____ .

5. Using the right-click mouse button will produce a _____ .

6. List the three design steps required in creating a Visual Basic application.

7. What is the difference between the **Name** property and the **Text** property?

8. Write a Visual Basic statement to clear the contents of a text box named txtText1.

9. Write a Visual Basic statement to clear a form.

10. Write a Visual Basic statement to place the words "**Welcome to Visual Basic**" in a text box named txtWelcome.

Programming Projects

Note: On all programming projects that you submit, include your name (or an identification code, if you have been assigned one), and the project number in the lower left-hand corner of the form.

1. a. Create the run time interface shown in Figure 2–72. The application should display the message "My first Visual Basic Program" in a text box when the first button is clicked, and the message "Isn't this neat?!?" when the second button is clicked. Both messages should be in MS Sans Serif, 18 point, bold font.

Figure 2–72

b. (Extra Challenge) Make the label appear randomly on the form by using the intrinsic function RND, the form's Width and Height properties, and the label's Left property.

2. Create the form shown in Figure 2–73 that displays a label with the caption text `Hello World`. The form should have four buttons. One button should have the caption <u>I</u>nvisible, and when this button is pressed the `Hello World` caption should become invisible, but should have no effect on any other label. A second button, with the caption <u>N</u>ew Message, should make the `Hello World` caption invisible and display the text `This is a New Message`. Both messages should be in MS Sans Serif, 14 point, bold font. The third button, with the caption

Reset, should make the Hello World caption reappear. Finally, an Exit button should terminate the program.

Figure 2–73

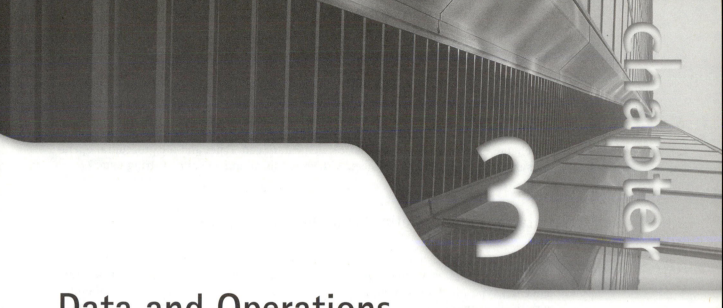

Data and Operations

Visual Basic programs process different types of data in different ways. For example, calculating a company's income tax requires mathematical operations on numerical data, whereas sorting a list of names requires comparison operations using alphabetic data. In this chapter, we introduce Visual Basic's elementary data types and the procedural operations that can be performed on them, with emphasis on numerical and string data.

3.1 Data Types, Arithmetic Operations, and Strings

Visual Basic distinguishes between a number of fundamental types of data, such as integers, real numbers, character strings, Boolean, and so on. Table 3–1 lists all of the fundamental types, including their storage size and range of values. (If you are unfamiliar with the concept of a byte, review Section 1.6.) In this section, we introduce the numerical, string, and Boolean types. The remaining types are introduced in later sections.

Integers

An integer in Visual Basic is any positive or negative number without a decimal point or fractional part. Examples of valid integer values are:

$$6 \quad -12 \quad +35 \quad 1000 \quad 186 \quad -25821 \quad +42$$

Table 3–1 Fundamental Visual Basic Data Types

Type	Bytes of Storage	Range of Values
Byte	1	0 to 255
Integer	4	−2,147,483,648 to 2,147,483,647
Long	8	−9,223,372,036,854,775,808 to 9,223,372,036,854,775,807
Short	2	−32,768 to 32,767
Single	4	−3.402823E38 to +3.402823E38
Double	8	−1.79769313486231E308 to +1.79769313486231E308
Char	2	Any Unicode character
String	2 per char	0 to approximately 2 billion Unicode characters
Boolean	1	True or False
Decimal	16	−79,228,162,514,264,337,593,543,950,335 to 79,228,162,514,264,337,593,543,950,335 with 29 Significant digits
Date	8	00:00:00 on January 1, 0001 to 11:59:59 on December 31, 9999
Object	4	(Reference to an object)

As these examples illustrate, integers may either be signed (have a leading + or − sign) or unsigned (no leading + or − sign). No commas, decimal points, or special symbols, such as the dollar sign, are allowed. Examples of invalid integers are:

$187.62   3,532   4.   8,634,941   2,371.98   +7.0

An integer can be any value between −2,147,483,648, which is the smallest (most negative) value, to +2,147,483,647, which is the largest (most positive) value. These values are defined by the 4-byte storage size required for all integers.[1] If the program requires values outside of the integer range, a long integer can be used. This long integer, referred to as a Long, can store values in the range from approximately −9.2E18 to 9.2E18.

Floating Point Values

A floating point value, which is also called a real number, is any signed or unsigned number having a decimal point. Examples of floating point values are:

+10.625   5.   −6.2   3251.92   0.0   0.33   −6.67   +2.

Note that the numbers 5., 0.0, and +2. are classified as floating point numbers, while the same numbers written without a decimal point (5, 0, +2) would be integer values. As with integer values, special symbols, such as the dollar sign and the comma, are not permitted in real numbers. Examples of invalid real numbers are:

5,326.25   24   123   6,459 $10.29

Visual Basic supports two different categories of floating point numbers: single and double. The name *single* is derived from the term *single precision number*, and double is derived from the term *double precision number*. The difference between these two types of numbers is the amount of storage allocated for each type. Visual Basic requires a double precision number to use twice the amount of storage as that of a single precision number. In practice, this means that a single precision constant in Visual Basic retains six decimal digits to the right of the decimal point and double precision constants retain fourteen digits.

Exponential Notation

Floating point numbers can be written in exponential notation, similar to scientific notation and commonly used to express both very large and very small numbers in a compact form. The following examples illustrate how numbers with decimals can be expressed in exponential and scientific notation.

---

[1]It is interesting to note that in all cases, the magnitude of the most negative number allowed is always one more than the magnitude of the most positive integer. This is due to the method most commonly used to represent integers, called the two's complement representation.

Decimal Notation	Exponential Notation	Scientific Notation
1625.	1.625E3	1.625×10^3
63421.	6.3421E4	6.3421×10^4
.00731	7.31E-3	7.31×10^{-3}
.000625	6.25E-4	6.25×10^{-4}

In exponential notation, the letter E stands for exponent. The number following the E represents a power of 10 and indicates the number of places the decimal point should be moved to obtain the standard decimal value. The decimal point is moved to the right if the number after the E is positive, or moved to the left if the number after the E is negative. For example, the E3 in the number 1.625E3 indicates that the decimal place should be moved three places to the right, so that the number becomes 1625. The E-3 in the number 7.31E-3 indicates that the decimal point should be moved three places to the left, so that 7.31E-3 becomes .00731.

Booleans

There are only two Boolean data values in Visual Basic. These values are the constants

    True   False

The words **True** and **False** are restricted keywords in Visual Basic.

Boolean data is useful in programming because all programming languages have the ability to select a course of action based on the state of a programmer-specified condition. Any condition has one of two possible outcomes—either the condition is satisfied or it is not. In computer terms, a condition that is satisfied is considered **True**, and a condition that is not satisfied is considered **False**. The two Boolean constants in Visual Basic correspond to these outcomes and are used extensively in programs that incorporate decision-making statements.

Numeric Operations

Integers and real numbers may be added, subtracted, multiplied, divided, and raised to a power. The symbols for performing these and other numeric operations in Visual Basic are listed in Table 3–2.

Each of these numeric operators is referred to as a *binary operator* because it requires two operands. A *simple numeric expression* consists of a numeric operator connecting two arithmetic operands and has the syntax:

    operand *operator* operand

Examples of simple numeric expressions are:

6 + 2

17 − 5

$$12.75 + 9.3$$

$$0.06 * 14.8$$

$$26.7 / 3.03.1416 \char`\^ 2$$

The spaces around the arithmetic operators in these examples are inserted strictly for clarity and may be omitted without affecting the value of the expression.

Other types of operators, known as relational operators and logical operators, are described in Section 5.2.

Expression Types A numeric expression containing only integers is called an *integer expression.* The result of an integer expression can be either an integer or a floating point value. For example, 8 / 4 is the integer 2, while 15 / 2 is the floating point value 7.5. Similarly, an expression containing only floating point operands (single and double precision) is called a *floating point expression.* The result of such an expression can also be either an integer or a floating point value. An expression containing both integer and floating point operands is called a *mixed-mode expression.*

Integer Division Operator A special numeric operation supplied in Visual Basic is integer division, designated by the slash operator, (\). This operator divides two numbers and provides the result as an integer. When the result of the division is not an integer, the result is truncated (that is, the fractional part is dropped). Thus, 15 \ 2 is 7. This is calculated by first performing the normal division, 15 / 2 = 7.5, and then truncating the result to 7.

When an operand used in integer division is a floating point number, the floating point number is automatically rounded to the nearest integer before the division is performed. Thus,

14.6 \ 2 is calculated as 15 / 2 = 7.5, which is then truncated to 7

14 \ 2.8 is calculated as 14 / 3 = 4.667, which is then truncated to 4

14.6 \ 2.8 is calculated as 15 / 3 = 5, which is left as the integer 5

Table 3–2   Visual Basic's Numeric Operators

Operator	Operation
+	Addition
−	Subtraction
*	Multiplication
/	Division
\	Integer Division
^	Exponentiation (raising to a power)
Mod	Return a remainder

The Mod Operator   There are times when we would like to retain the remainder of an integer division. To do this, Visual Basic provides an arithmetic operator that captures the remainder when two integers are divided. This operator, called the modulus operator, uses the symbol Mod. For example,

```
9 Mod 4 is 1
17 Mod 3 is 2
14 Mod 2 is 0
```

Note that in each case the result of the numeric expression is the remainder produced by the division of the second integer into the first. If any of the numbers used in the expression is a floating point number, the division is carried out and the floating-point remainder is returned.

```
19 Mod 6.7 is 5.6
10.6 Mod 4.2 is 2.2
```

A Unary Operator (Negation)   Besides the binary operators for addition, subtraction, multiplication, and division, Visual Basic also provides a few unary operators. One of these unary operators uses the same symbol that is used for binary subtraction ($-$). The minus sign used in front of a single numerical operand negates (reverses the sign of) the number. This operator can be used with all numeric types except the Byte type, because bytes can only be positive values.

Strings

The third basic data type recognized by Visual Basic is a string. Strings were introduced in the previous chapter. To review, a string value consists of one or more characters that are enclosed within double quotes. Examples of valid character constants are:

```
"A"
"**&!#!!"
"$3,256.22"
"25.68"
"VELOCITY"
"HELLO THERE WORLD!"
```

The number of characters within a string determines the length of the string. For example, the length of the string value "$3,256.22" is nine and the length of the string constant "A" is one. Should it be required to include a double quote within a string constant, two double quotes are used. For example, in the string "They said ""Hello"" to me" the length of the string is 23 characters.

```
They(space)said(space)"Hello"(space)to(space)me
```

Table 3–3 The ANSI Uppercase Letter Codes

Letter	ANSI Code	Letter	ANSI Code
A	01000001	N	01001110
B	01000010	O	01001111
C	01000011	P	01010000
D	01000100	Q	01010001
E	01000101	R	01010010
F	01000110	S	01010011
G	01000111	T	01010100
H	01001000	U	01010101
I	01001001	V	01010110
J	01001010	W	01010111
K	01001011	X	01011000
L	01001100	Y	01011001
M	01001101	Z	01011010

String constants typically are represented in a computer using the ANSI codes. ANSI, pronounced "AN-see," is an acronym for American National Standards Institute. This code assigns individual characters to specific bit patterns. Table 3–3 lists the correspondence between bit patterns and the uppercase letters of the alphabet used by the ANSI code. Note that Visual Basic now stores string characters in Unicode, a coding system that uses 2 bytes to store each character. With this system, all characters and symbols in foreign languages can be represented. When foreign symbols are not being used, only the first byte of each character is used and this byte is the same as the ANSI codes below. Thus for English characters, the second byte is not used.

Using Table 3–3, we can determine how the string constant "SMITH," for example, is stored inside the computer. Using the Unicode system and the ANSI code, this sequence of characters requires ten bytes of storage (two bytes for each letter, where only the first letter is used) and would be stored as illustrated in Figure 3–1.

String Concatenation   String concatenation means the joining of two or more strings into a single string. Although string concatenation is not an arithmetic operation, it is the only operation that directly manipulates string data. Visual Basic provides two symbols, the ampersand (&) and the plus sign (+), for performing string concatenation. Both symbols produce the same effect when applied to string data. However, it is recommended that you use the ampersand so the use of the plus sign is not confused with the addition operator. For example, the expression

```
"Hot" & " " & "Dog"
```

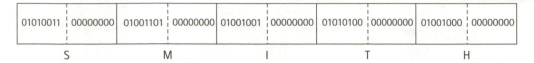

Figure 3-1 *The Letters SMITH Stored Inside a Computer*

concatenates the three individual strings, "Hot", " ", and "Dog" into the single string "Hot Dog".

Displaying Numeric Expressions and Strings   The value of any numeric expression can be displayed using a call to the `MessageBox.Show` method. For example, the value of the expression 0.06 * 14.8 can be displayed using the following statement:

```
MessageBox.Show (0.06 * 14.8)
```

Here, the expression, with no surrounding double quotes, is included directly in the `MessageBox.Show` statement. When this statement is executed, the indicated multiplication is performed and the output 0.888 is displayed in the message box. If quotes had been used, the string "0.06 * 14.8" would be displayed instead of having the numbers multiplied.

Another way to display a value and/or string is to use a text box. By default, the Text property of a text box is a single line, but this can be changed to Multiline if necessary by changing the **Multiline** property to True. For example, after a text box named txtDisplay has been created on a form, the statement

```
txtDisplay.Text = "The value of the expression 0.06 * 14.8 is " & 0.06 * 14.8
```

contains two items that will be printed within a text box on the form. The first item is a message, which is enclosed in double quotes, and the second item is an arithmetic expression. When an arithmetic expression is used, the numerical result of the expression is displayed. Event Procedure 3-1 illustrates this statement within the context of a complete `frmMain_Click` event procedure.

Note the continuation character used for lines that are too long. To continue a Visual Basic statement on the next line, type a space followed by the underscore symbol (" _").

Event Procedure 3-1

```
Private Sub frmMain_Click(ByVal sender As Object, ByVal e As _
    System.EventArgs) Handles MyBase.Click
```

```
txtDisplay.Text = "The value of the expression 0.06 * 14.8 is _
   " & 0.06 * 14.8
End Sub
```

When this event procedure is executed, the display produced on the screen is:

The value of the expression 0.06 * 14.8 is 0.888

See if you can determine the output that is produced by the Event Procedure 3–2. Note that in order to get strings to be displayed on a new line in a multiline text box, you need to concatenate a new line character at the end of the string. The newline character is stored in the constant ControlChars.NewLine. The control character CrLf could also be used in this procedure instead of NewLine. CrLf stands for Carriage-return Line-feed and is equivalent to the NewLine character. Both of these control characters force the subsequent text to be placed on a new line.

Event Procedure 3–2

```
Private Sub frmMain_Click(ByVal sender As Object, ByVal e As _
   System.EventArgs) Handles MyBase.Click
  txtDisplay.Text = "0.06 * 14.8" & ControlChars.NewLine
  txtDisplay.Text = txtDisplay.Text & (0.06 * 14.8) & ControlChars.NewLine
  txtDisplay.Text = txtDisplay.Text & "0.06 * 14.8 is " & (0.06 * 14.8)
End Sub
```

Because the txtDisplay text box has its **Multiline** property set to True, Event Procedure 3–2 causes three lines of output to be displayed in the text box. In the first statement, the characters 0.06 * 14.8 are enclosed in double quotes, causing these characters to be displayed exactly as typed. In the second statement, the 0.06 * 14.8 are not in double quotes, causing the calculation to be performed and 0.888 to be displayed. Finally, the last statement has 0.06 * 14.8 both in quotes and not in quotes, causing the following to be displayed:

0.06 * 14.8 is 0.888

Program 3–1 illustrates using a multiline text box to display the results of simple arithmetic expressions within the context of a complete program. The interface for this project is shown in Figure 3–2. As illustrated, the form contains a button and a text box. The objects and properties for Program 3–1 are shown in Table 3–4.

For this application, the only procedure will be for the button's click event. The required code is listed in Program 3–1's Event Code.

Program 3–1's Event Code

```
Private Sub btnOps_Click(ByVal sender As Object, ByVal e As _
   System.EventArgs) Handles btnOps.Click
```

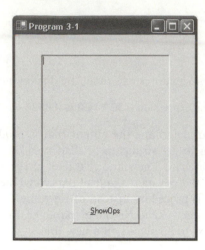

Figure 3–2 *Program 3–1's Interface*

Table 3–4   The Properties Table for Program 3–1

Object	Property	Setting
Form	Name	frmMain
	Text	Program 3–1
Text Box	Name	txtDisplay
	TabStop	False
	Multiline	True
	Text	(blank)
Button	Name	btnOps
	Text	&ShowOps

```
    txtDisplay.Clear()
    txtDisplay.Text = "OPERATION" & ControlChars.CrLf
    txtDisplay.Text = txtDisplay.Text & "15.2 + 2 = " & 15.2 + 2 & _
       ControlChars.CrLf
    txtDisplay.Text = txtDisplay.Text & "15.2 - 2 = " & 15.2 - 2 & _
       ControlChars.CrLf
    txtDisplay.Text = txtDisplay.Text & "15.2 * 2 = " & 15.2 * 2 & _
       ControlChars.CrLf
    txtDisplay.Text = txtDisplay.Text & "15.2 / 2 = " & 15.2 / 2 & _
       ControlChars.CrLf
    txtDisplay.Text = txtDisplay.Text & "15.2 ^ 2 = " & 15.2 ^ 2 & _
       ControlChars.CrLf
End Sub
```

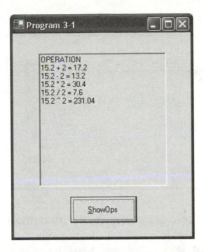

Figure 3–3   *The Output Displayed by Program 3–1*

Note that the first line of the procedure uses the text box's `Clear` method. This method is used to clear a text box. Using the `Clear` method is an alternative to setting the Text property to the null string, as was done earlier, using

```
txtDisplay.Text = ""
```

The output displayed in the text box by Program 3-1's event procedure when the button is clicked is shown in Figure 3-3.

Operator Precedence and Associativity

In addition to simple numeric expressions such as 5 + 12 and .08 * 26.2, we frequently need to create more complex expressions. Visual Basic requires that certain rules be followed when writing expressions containing more than one operator. These rules are as follows:

1. Two binary operators must never be placed adjacent to one another. For example, 12 / Mod 6 is invalid because the two binary operators / and Mod are placed next to each other. However, the expression 12 / −6 is valid and does not violate this rule because the "−" here is recognized as a unary operator that simply makes the +6 a −6. Thus, the result of this expression is −2.

2. Parentheses may be used to form groupings, and all expressions enclosed within parentheses are evaluated first. For example, in the expression (6 + 4) / (2 + 3), the 6 + 4 and 2 + 3 groupings are evaluated first to yield 10 / 5. The 10 / 5 is then evaluated to yield 2. Sets of parentheses may also be enclosed by other parentheses. For example, the expression (2 * (3 + 7)) / 5 is valid. When parentheses are used within

Table 3–5 Arithmetic Operator Precedence and Associativity

Operation	Operator	Associativity
Exponentiation	^	left to right
Negation (unary)	-	left to right
Multiplication and division	* /	left to right
Integer division	\	left to right
Modulo arithmetic	Mod	left to right
Addition and subtraction	+ -	left to right

parentheses, the expressions in the innermost parentheses are always evaluated first. The evaluation continues from innermost to outermost parentheses until the expressions of all parentheses have been evaluated. The number of right-facing parentheses, "(," must always equal the number of left-facing parentheses, ")," so that there are no unpaired sets.

3. Parentheses cannot be used to indicate multiplication; the multiplication operator must be used. For example, the expression (3 + 4) (5 + 1) is invalid. The correct expression is (3 + 4) * (5 + 1).

As a general rule, parentheses should be used to specify logical groupings of operands and to indicate clearly the intended order of arithmetic operations to both the computer and any programmer reading the expression. In the absence of parentheses, expressions containing multiple operators are evaluated by the priority, or precedence, of each operator. Table 3–5 lists both the precedence and associativity of the operators considered in this section.

The precedence of an operator establishes its priority relative to all other operators. Operators at the top of Table 3–5 have higher priority than operators at the bottom of the table. In expressions with multiple operators, the operator with the higher precedence is used before an operator with a lower precedence. For example, in the expression 6 + 4 / 2 + 3 the division is done before the addition, yielding an intermediate result of 6 + 2 + 3. The additions are then performed to yield a final result of 11.

When the minus sign precedes an operand, as in the expression −A ^ B, the minus sign negates (reverses the sign of) the number with a higher priority level than all other operators except exponentiation. For example, the expression −6 ^ 2 is calculated as −(6^2), which equals −36.

Expressions containing operators with the same precedence are evaluated according to their associativity. This means that evaluation for addition and subtraction, as well as multiplication and division, is from left to right and successive exponents are evaluated from right to left as each operator is encountered. For example, in the expression 8 + 40 / 8 * 2 + 4, the multiplication and division operators are of higher precedence than the addition operator and are evaluated first. However, both the multiplication and division operators are of equal priority. Therefore, these operators are evaluated according to their left-to-right associativity, yielding the following:

$$8 + 40 / 8 * 2 + 4 =$$
$$8 + \quad 5 * 2 + 4 =$$
$$8 + \quad\quad 10 + 4$$

The addition operations are now performed, again from left to right, yielding the following:

$$18 + 4 = 22$$

When two exponentiation operations occur sequentially, the resulting expression is evaluated from left to right. Thus, the expression 2^2^4 is evaluated as 4^4, which equals 256.

Exercises 3.1

1. Determine data types appropriate for the following data:
   a. the average of four speeds
   b. the number of transistors in a circuit
   c. the length of the Golden Gate Bridge
   d. the part numbers in a machine
   e. the distance from Brooklyn, NY to Newark, NJ
   f. the names of circuit components

2. Convert the following numbers into standard decimal form:

   6.34E5   1.95162E2   8.395E1   2.95E–3   4.623E–4

3. Write the following decimal numbers using exponential notation:

   126.656.23   3426.95   4893.2   .321   .0123   .006789

4. Show how the name KINGSLEY would be stored inside a computer that uses the ANSI code. That is, draw a figure similar to Figure 3–1 for the letters KINGSLEY.

5. Repeat Exercise 4 using the letters of your last name.

6. Listed below are correct algebraic expressions and the incorrect Visual Basic expressions corresponding to them. Find the errors and write corrected Visual Basic expressions.

Algebra Expression	Visual Basic
a. (2)(3) + (4)(5)	(2)(3) + (4)(5)
b. $\dfrac{6 + 18}{2}$	6 + 18 / 2
c. $\dfrac{4.5}{12.2 - 3.1}$	4.5 / 12.2 − 3.1
d. 4.6(3.0 + 14.9)	4.6(3.0 + 14.9)

    e. (12.1 + 18.9)(15.3 − 3.8)   (12.1 + 18.9)(15.3 − 3.8)

7. Determine the value of the following expressions:

    a. 3 + 4 * 6

    b. 3 * 4 / 6 + 6

    c. 2.0 * 3 / 12 * 8 / 4

    d. 10 * (1 + 7.3 * 3)

    e. 20 − 2 / 6 + 3

    f. 20 − 2 / (6 + 3)

    g. (20 − 2) / 6 + 3

    h. (20 − 2) / (6 + 3)

8. Assuming that DISTANCE has an integer value of 1, V has the integer value 50, N has the integer value 10, and T has the integer value 5, evaluate the following expressions:

    a. N / T + 3

    b. V / T + N − 10 * DISTANCE

    c. V − 3 * N + 4 * DISTANCE

    d. DISTANCE / 5

    e. 18 / T

    f. −T * N

    g. −V / 20

    h. (V + N) / (T + DISTANCE)

    i. V + N / T + DISTANCE

9. Enter and run Program 3–1 on your computer system.

10. Because Visual Basic uses different representations for storing integer, real, and string values, discuss how a program might alert Visual Basic to the data types of the various values it will be using.

3.2   Variables and Declaration Statements

All data used in an application is stored and retrieved from the computer's memory unit. Conceptually, individual memory locations in the memory unit are arranged like the rooms in a large hotel. Like hotel rooms, each memory location has a unique address ("room number"). Before high-level languages such as Visual Basic existed, memory locations were referenced by their addresses. For example, storing the integer values 45 and 12 in memory locations 1652 and 2548 (see Figure 3–4), respectively, required instructions equivalent to:

put a 45 in location 1652

put a 12 in location 2548

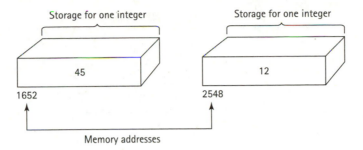

Figure 3–4 *Enough Storage for Two Integers*

Adding the two numbers just stored and saving the result in another memory location, such as location 3000, required a statement comparable to the following:

add the contents of location 1652

to the contents of location 2548

and store the result in location 3000

Clearly this method of storage and retrieval is a cumbersome process. In high-level languages like Visual Basic, symbolic names are used in place of actual memory addresses. Symbolic names used in this manner are called variables. A *variable* is simply a name given by the programmer to a memory storage location. The term variable is used because the value stored in the variable can change. For each name that the programmer uses, the computer keeps track of the corresponding actual memory address. In our hotel room analogy, this is equivalent to putting a name on the door of a room and referring to the room by this name, such as the BLUE room, rather than using the actual room number.

In Visual Basic the selection of variable names is left to the programmer, as long as the following rules are observed:

1. The name must begin with a letter or an underscore.
2. The name can only consist of letters, numeric digits, or underscores.
3. The name cannot exceed 16,383 characters.
4. The name cannot be a Visual Basic keyword, such as **Integer**.

A variable name should also be a mnemonic. A *mnemonic* (pronounced ni-MONic) is a memory aid that should convey information about what the name represents. For example, a mnemonic name for a variable used to store a total value would be sum or total. Similarly, the variable name width is a good choice if the value stored in the variable represents a width. Variable names that give no indication of the value stored, such as r2d2, linda, bill, and dude, should not be selected.

Now, assume the first memory location illustrated in Figure 3–4, assigned address 1652, is given the name num1. Also assume that memory location 2548 is given the

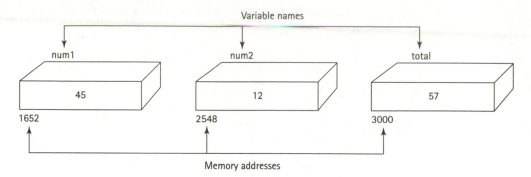

Figure 3–5 *Naming Storage Locations*

variable name num2, and memory location 3000 is given the variable name total, as illustrated in Figure 3–5.

Using these variable names, Visual Basic statements enable you to store 45 in location 1652, 12 in location 2548, and add the contents of these two locations, as shown below:

```
num1 = 45
num2 = 12
total = num1 + num2
```

These statements are called *assignment statements* because they tell the computer to assign (store) a value into a variable. Assignment statements always have an equal (=) sign and one variable name immediately to the left of the equal sign. The value on the right of the equal sign is determined first and this value is assigned to the variable on the left of the equal sign. The blank spaces in the assignment statements are inserted for readability. We will have more to say about assignment statements in the next section, but for now we can use them to store values in variables.

A variable name is useful because it frees the programmer from concern over where data is physically stored inside the computer. We simply use the variable name and let the computer worry about where in memory the data is actually stored. Before storing a value into a variable, however, we must clearly define the type of data that is to be stored in it. This requires telling the computer, in advance, the names of the variables that will be used for integers, the names that will be used for real numbers, and the names that will be used to store the other Visual Basic data types.

Declaration Statements

Naming a variable and specifying the data type that can be stored in it are accomplished using *declaration statements*. Declaration statements placed within a procedure are nonexecutable statements that have the general syntax

```
Dim variable-name As data-type
```

where *data-type* designates any of the Visual Basic data types listed in Table 3–1, such as `Integer`, `Boolean`, and `String`. *Variable-name* is a user-selected variable name. For example, the declaration statement

```
Dim total As Integer
```

declares total as the name of a variable capable of storing an integer value. Variables used to hold single-precision values are declared using the keyword `Single`; variables that are used to hold double-precision values are declared using the keyword `Double`; variables that are used to hold Boolean values are declared using the keyword `Boolean`, and variables used to hold strings are declared using the keyword `String`. For example, the statement

```
Dim firstnum As Single
```

declares `firstnum` as a variable that can be used to store a single precision value (a number with a decimal point). Similarly, the statement

```
Dim secnum As Double
```

declares `secnum` as a variable that can be used to store a double precision value, and the declaration statements

```
Dim logical As Boolean
Dim message As String
```

declare `logical` as a Boolean variable and `message` as a string variable.

Although declaration statements may be placed anywhere within a procedure, most declarations are typically grouped together and placed immediately after the procedure's header line, known as the procedure declaration. In all cases, however, a variable must be declared before it can be used.[2]

Program 3–2 illustrates using declaration statements within the context of a complete application. Except for the Form and Button text properties, the application interface, shown in Figure 3–6, is essentially the same as used in Program 3–1. As illustrated, the form contains a button and a multiline text box. The objects and properties for Program 3–2 are shown in Table 3–6.

For this application, the only procedure is for the button's click event. The required code is listed in Program 3–2's Event Code. Note that we introduce the **AppendText** method for the TextBox control. This method appends the text in the parameter to whatever exists in the text box at the time. More precisely, it is appending the text to the Text property of the text box.

---

[2]In Visual Basic, the Option Explicit option is turned on by default, meaning that all variables must be declared before being used. It is highly recommended that this option remain on, but it can be turned off.

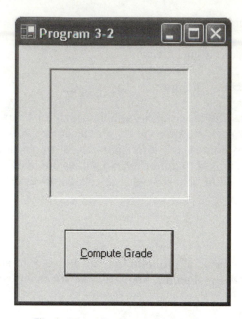

Figure 3-6 *Program 3-2's Interface*

Table 3-6 **The Properties Table for Program 3-2**

Object	Property	Setting
Form	Name	frmMain
	Text	Program 3-2
Text Box	Name	txtDisplay
	TabStop	False
	Multiline	True
	Text	(blank)
Button	Name	btnOps
	Text	&Compute Grade

Program 3-2's Event Code

```
Private Sub btnOps_Click(ByVal sender As Object, _
    ByVal e As System.EventArgs) Handles btnOps.Click
  Dim grade1 As Single 'declare grade1 as a Single
  Dim grade2 As Single 'declare grade2 as a Single
  Dim total As Single 'declare total as a Single
  Dim average As Single 'declare average as a Single

  grade1 = 85.5
```

```
    grade2 = 97
    total = grade1 + grade2
    average = total / 2
    txtDisplay.AppendText("grade1 is " & grade1 & ControlChars.NewLine)
    txtDisplay.AppendText("grade2 is " & grade2 & ControlChars.NewLine)
    txtDisplay.AppendText("The average grade is " & average)
End Sub
```

Although the placement of the declaration statements in the event procedure is straightforward, note the blank line after these statements. Placing a blank line after variable declarations is a common programming practice that improves both a procedure's appearance and readability. We will adopt this practice for all of our procedures. The output displayed by Program 3-2's event procedure when the button is clicked is shown in Figure 3-7.

Single-line Declarations

Visual Basic permits combining multiple declarations into one statement, using the syntax:

```
Dim var-1 As data-type, var-2 As data-type,...,var-n As data-type
```

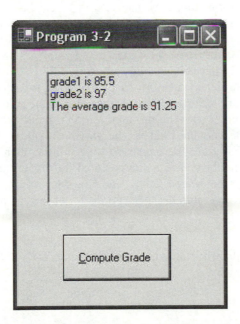

Figure 3-7 *The Output Displayed by Program 3-2*

Using this syntax, the four individual declaration statements used in Program 3-2 can be combined into the single declaration statement:

```
Dim grade1 As Single, grade2 As Single, total As _
    Single, average As Single
```

When all variables are the same type, as in this example, this declaration can be further simplified to the following single-line declaration

```
Dim grade1, grade2, total, average As Single
```

Initialization

The first time a value is stored in a variable, the variable is said to be *initialized*. In Visual Basic, all numeric variables are initialized, by default, to zero. Thus, if you print the value of a declared numeric variable before you explicitly assign it a value, the displayed value will be 0. Similarly, all strings are initialized to zero-length strings containing no characters at all.

Specifying Storage Allocation Declaration statements perform both a software and a hardware function. From a software perspective, declaration statements provide a convenient, up-front list of all variables and their data types. In addition to this software role, declaration statements also serve a distinct hardware task: Each data type has its own storage requirements (see Table 3-1), and Visual Basic can only allocate sufficient storage for a variable after it knows the variable's data type. Because variable declarations provide this information, they also inform Visual Basic of the physical memory storage that must be reserved for each variable. (In the hotel analogy introduced at the beginning of this section, this is equivalent to connecting adjoining rooms to form larger suites.)

Figure 3-8 illustrates the series of operations set in motion by declaration statements in performing their memory allocation function. As illustrated, declaration statements cause sufficient memory to be allocated for each data type and also "tag" the reserved memory locations with a name. This name is, of course, the variable's name.

A programmer uses the declared variable name within a program to reference the contents of the variable (that is, the variable's value). Where in memory this value is stored is generally of little concern to the programmer. However, Visual Basic must be concerned with where each value is stored. In this task, Visual Basic uses the variable's name to locate the desired value. Knowing the variable's data type allows Visual Basic to access the correct number of locations for each type of data.

Exercises 3.2

1. State whether the following variable names are valid or not. If they are invalid, state the reason why.

```
prod_a      c1234       abcd        -c3         12345
newbal      Print       $total      new bal     a1b2c3d4
9ab6        sum.of      average     grade1      fin_grade
```

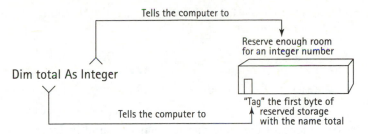

Figure 3–8a *Defining the Integer Variable Named total*

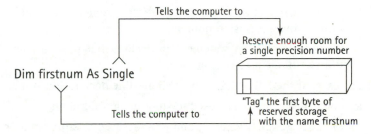

Figure 3–8b *Defining the Single Variable Named firstnum*

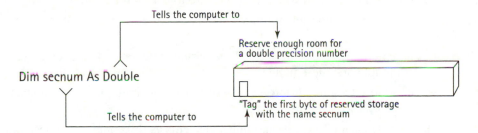

Figure 3–8c *Defining the Double Variable Named secnum*

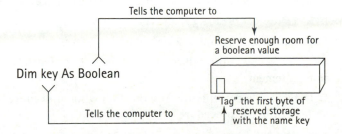

Figure 3–8d *Defining the Logical Variable Named key*

2. a. State whether the following variable names are valid or not. If they are invalid, state the reason why.

salestax	a243	r2d2	first_num	cc_a1
harry	sue	c3p0	average	sum
maximum	okay	a	awesome	goforit
3sum	for	tot.a1	c$five	newpay

   b. List which of the valid variable names found in Exercise 2a should not be used because they clearly are not mnemonics.

3. a. Write a declaration statement to declare that the variable count will be used to store an integer.

   b. Write a declaration statement to declare that the variable grade will be used to store a single precision number.

   c. Write a declaration statement to declare that the variable yield will be used to store a double precision number.

4. For each of the following, write a single-line declaration statement:

   a. num1, num2, and num3 used to store integer numbers

   b. grade1, grade2, grade3, and grade4 used to store single precision numbers

   c. tempa, tempb, and tempc used to store double precision numbers

   d. message1 and message2 used to store strings

5. For each of the following, write a single-line declaration statement:

   a. firstnum used to store an integer and secnum used to store a single precision number

   b. speed used to store a single precision number and distance used to store a double precision number

   c. years to store an integer, yield to store a single precision number, and maturity used to store a string

6. Rewrite each of these declaration statements as three individual declarations.

   a. Dim month As Integer, day As Integer, year As Integer

   b. Dim hours As Single, rate As Single

   c. Dim price As Double, amount As Double, taxes As Double

   d. Dim inkey As String, choice As String

7. a. Enter and run Program 3–2 on your computer.

   b. Rewrite the event procedure in Program 3–2 so that it uses a single-line declaration statement.

8. a. Determine what event invokes the following procedure and the effect of each statement in the procedure.

   ```
   Private Sub btnButton1_Click(ByVal sender As Object, _
   ```

```
      ByVal e As System.EventArgs) Handles btnButton1.Click
    Dim num1 As Integer, num2 As Integer, total As Integer
    num1 = 25
    num2 = 30
    total = num1 + num2
    txtDisplay.Text = num1 & " + " & num2 & " = " & total
  End Sub
```

    b. What is the output that will be printed when the event procedure listed in Exercise 8a is run?

9. Write a Visual Basic program that stores the sum of the integer numbers 12 and 33 in a variable named sum. Have your program display the value stored in sum, along with an appropriate message telling the user what is being displayed. The display should appear in a text box when a button is clicked. There should also be a button to clear the text box display.

10. Write a Visual Basic program that stores the value 16 in the integer variable named length and the value 18 in the integer variable named width. Have your program calculate the value assigned to the variable perimeter, using the assignment statement

```
perimeter = 2 * (length + width)
```

and display the value stored in the variable perimeter. The display should appear in a text box when a button is clicked. There should also be a second button to clear the text box display. Be sure to declare all the variables as integers at the beginning of the event procedure.

11. Write a Visual Basic program that stores the integer value 16 in the variable num1 and the integer value 18 in the variable num2. Have your program calculate the total of these numbers and their average. The total should be stored in an integer variable named total and the average in an integer variable named average. (Use the statement average = total/2, to calculate the average.) The display of the total and average should appear in a text box when a button is clicked There should also be a second button to clear the text box display. Be sure to declare all the variables as integers at the beginning of the event procedure.

12. Repeat Exercise 11, but store the number 15 in num1 instead of 16. Using a pencil, write down the average of num1 and num2. What do you think your program will store in the integer variable that you used for the average of these two numbers? What change must you make in the event procedure to ensure that the correct answer will be printed for the average?

13. Write a Visual Basic program that stores the number 105.62 in the variable firstnum, 89.352 in the variable secnum, and 98.67 in the variable thirdnum. Have your program calculate the total of the three numbers and their average. The total should be stored in the variable total and the average in the variable average. (Use the

statement *average = total /3* to calculate the average.) The display of the total and average should appear in a text box when a button is clicked. There should also be a second button to clear the text box display. Be sure to declare all the variables as either Single or Double at the beginning of the event procedure.

14. Every variable has at least two items associated with it. What are these two items?

For Exercises 15 through 17, use the storage allocations given in Table 3–1 and assume that variables are assigned storage in the order they are declared.

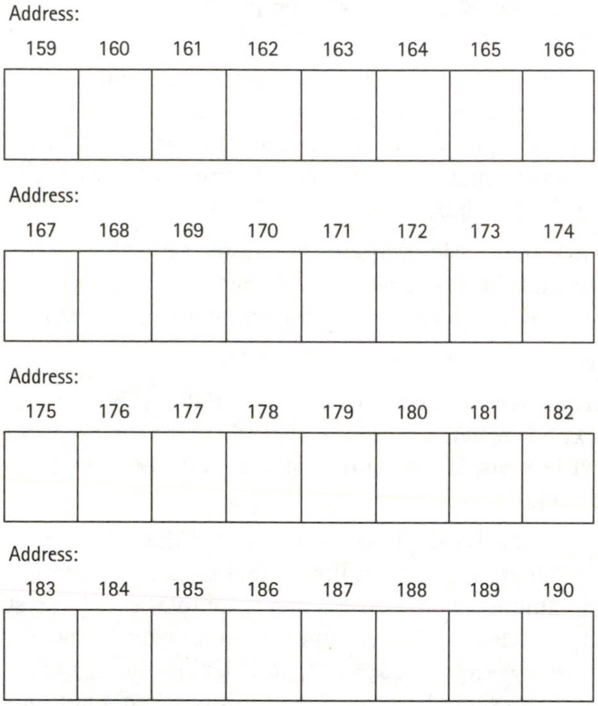

Address:

159	160	161	162	163	164	165	166

Address:

167	168	169	170	171	172	173	174

Address:

175	176	177	178	179	180	181	182

Address:

183	184	185	186	187	188	189	190

Figure 3–9 *Memory Bytes for Exercises 15, 16, and 17*

15. Using Figure 3-9, and assuming that the variable name `miles` is assigned to the byte at memory address 159, determine the addresses corresponding to each variable declared in the following statements:

```
Dim miles As Single
Dim count As Integer, num As Integer
Dim distance As Double, temp As Double
```

16. a. Using Figure 3-9, and assuming that the variable name `rate` is assigned to the byte having memory address 159, determine the addresses corresponding to each variable declared in the following statements. Also, fill in the appropriate bytes

with the data stored in each string variable (use letters for the characters, not the computer codes that would actually be stored).

```
Dim rate As Single
Dim message As String
Dim taxes As Double
Dim num As Integer, count As Integer


message = "OKAY"
```

b. Repeat Exercise 16a, but substitute the actual byte patterns that a computer using the ANSI code would use to store the characters in the message variable. (*Hint:* Use Table 3–2.)

17. a. Using Figure 3–9, and assuming that the variable named `message` is assigned to the byte at memory address 159, determine the addresses corresponding to each variable declared in the following statements. Also, fill in the appropriate bytes with the data stored in the variables (use letters for the characters and not the computer codes that would actually be stored).

```
Dim message As String


message = "HAVE A WONDERFUL DAY"
```

b. Repeat Exercise 17a, but substitute the actual byte patterns that a computer using the ANSI code would use to store the characters in each of the declared variables. (*Hint:* Use Table 3–2.)

3.3 Named Constants

Literal data is any data within a procedure that explicitly identifies itself. For example, the constants 2 and 3.1416 in the assignment statement

```
circumference = 2 * 3.1416 * radius
```

are also called literals because they are literally included directly in the statement. Additional examples of literals are contained in the following Visual Basic assignment statements. See if you can identify them.

```
perimeter = 2 * length * width
y = (5 * p) / 7.2
salestax = 0.05 * purchase
```

The literals are the numbers 2, 5, and 7.2, and 0.05 in the first, second, and third statements, respectively.

Frequently, literal data used within a procedure have a more general meaning that is recognized outside the context of the procedure. Examples of these types of constants include the number 3.1416, which is the value of π accurate to four decimal places, 32.2 ft/sec^2, which is the gravitational constant, and the number 2.71828, which is Euler's number accurate to five decimal places.

Certain other constants appearing in a procedure are defined strictly within the context of the application being programmed. For example, in a procedure to determine bank interest charges, the value of the interest rate takes on a special meaning. Similarly, in determining the weight of various sized objects, the density of the material being used takes on a special significance. Constants such as these are sometimes referred to as both *manifest constants* and *magic numbers*. By themselves, the constants are quite ordinary, but in the context of a particular application they have a special ("manifest" or "magical") meaning. Frequently, the same manifest constant appears repeatedly within the same procedure. This recurrence of the same constant throughout a procedure is a potential source of error, should the constant have to be changed. For example, if either the interest rate changes or a new material is employed with a different density, the programmer has the cumbersome task of changing the value of the magic number everywhere it appears in the procedure. However, multiple changes are subject to error. If just one value is overlooked and not changed, or if the same value used in different contexts is changed when only one of the values should have been changed, the result obtained when the procedure is run will be incorrect.

To avoid the problems of having such constants spread throughout a procedure, and to clearly permit identification of more universal constants, such as π, Visual Basic allows the programmer to give these constants their own symbolic names. As a result, instead of using the constant value throughout the procedure, the symbolic name is used instead. If the number ever has to be changed, the change need only be made once, at the point where the symbolic name is equated to the actual constant value. Equating numbers to symbolic names is accomplished using the **Const** statement. The syntax for this statement within a form's procedure is:

```
Const name As data-type = expression
```

For example, the number 3.1416 can be equated to the symbolic name PI using the Const statement

```
Const PI As Single = 3.1416
```

Constants used in this fashion are called *named constants*. The constant's name must be selected using the same rules as those for choosing a variable's name.

Once a constant has been named, the name can be used in any Visual Basic statement in place of the number itself. For example, the assignment statement

```
circumference = 2 * PI * radius
```

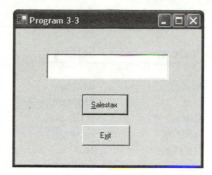

Figure 3–10 *Program 3-3's Interface*

uses the named constant PI. This statement must appear after the declaration of the named constant is made. Within a Form module, all Const statements must be placed in one of the following locations:

- in the Declarations section of the form; or
- anywhere within a procedure, though for clarity they are usually placed immediately after the procedure's declaration.

In the first case, the constant can be used by all procedures connected to the form and its objects. In the second case, the constant can only be used within the procedure from its point of declaration to the end of the procedure. In this case, the constant is said to be local to the procedure declaring it.

Although we have typed the named constant PI in uppercase letters, lowercase letters could have been used. In Visual Basic it is common to use uppercase letters for named constants, at least for the initial letter of the name. In this way, whenever a programmer sees an initial uppercase letter in a procedure, he or she will know the name is a named constant defined in a **Const** statement, not a variable name declared in a declaration statement.

Program 3–3 illustrates the use of the **Const** statement declared within an event procedure. The interface for this project is shown in Figure 3-10. As illustrated, the GUI consists of two buttons and a multiline text box. The objects and properties for Program 3-3 are shown in Table 3-7.

For this application the only procedures will be for the button **Click** events. The required procedures are listed in Program 3-3's Event Code.

Program 3–3's Event Code

```
Private Sub btnTax_Click(ByVal sender As Object, ByVal e As _
    System.EventArgs) Handles btnTax.Click
    Const TAXRATE As Single = 0.05
    Dim amount, taxes, total As Single
```

Table 3–7   The Properties Table for Program 3–3

Object	Property	Setting
Form	Name	frmMain
	Text	Program 3–3
Text Box	Name	txtDisplay
	TabStop	False
	Multiline	True
Button	Name	btnTax
	Text	&Salestax
Button	Name	btnExit
	Text	E&xit

```
txtDisplay.Clear()
amount = Val(InputBox("Enter the amount purchased", "Input Box", "0"))
taxes = TAXRATE * amount
total = amount + taxes
txtDisplay.Text = "The sales tax is " & Format(taxes, "Currency") & _
    ControlChars.NewLine & "The total bill is " & FormatCurrency(total)

End Sub

Private Sub btnExit_Click(ByVal sender As Object, ByVal e As _
    System.EventArgs) Handles btnExit.Click
  Beep()
  End
End Sub
```

The output displayed in the multiline text box, when the button is clicked and an input value of 1.81 is entered in the InputBox dialog, is shown in Figure 3–11.

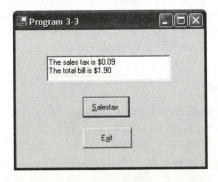

Figure 3–11   *A Sample Output Displayed by Program 3–3*

The advantage of using a named constant such as PI is that it clearly identifies the value 3.1416 in terms recognizable to most people. The advantage of using the named constant TAXRATE in Program 3–3 is that it permits a programmer to change the value of the sales tax, when required, without having to search through the procedure to see where it is used. However, a natural question arises as to the actual difference between named constants and variables.

The value of a variable can be altered anywhere within a program. By its nature, a named constant is a constant value that must not be altered after it is defined. Naming a constant, rather than assigning its value to a variable, ensures that the value in the constant cannot be subsequently altered. Whenever a named constant appears in an instruction, it has the same effect as the constant it represents. Thus, TAXRATE in Program 3–3 is simply another way of representing the number 0.05. Since TAXRATE and the number 0.05 are equivalent, the value of TAXRATE may not be subsequently changed within the program. Once TAXRATE has been defined as a constant, an assignment statement such as

```
TAXRATE = 0.06
```

is meaningless and will result in an error message, because TAXRATE is not a variable. Because TAXRATE is only a substitute for the value 0.05, this last statement is equivalent to writing the invalid statement 0.05 = 0.06.

In addition to using the **Const** statement to name constants, as in Program 3–3, this statement can also be used to equate the value of a constant expression to a symbolic name. A constant expression is an expression consisting of operators and constants only (no variables or intrinsic functions are allowed). For example, the statement:

```
Const CONVERT As Single = 3.1416/180
```

equates the value of the constant expression 3.1416/180 to the symbolic name CONVERT. The symbolic name, as usual, can be used in any statement following its definition. For example, because the expression 3.1416/180 is required for converting degrees to radians, the symbolic name selected for this conversion factor can be conveniently used whenever such a conversion is required.

As previously defined, a named constant can also be used in a subsequent Const statement. For example, the following sequence of statements is valid:

```
Const PI As Single = 3.1416
Const CONVERT As Single = PI/180
```

Because the constant 3.1416 has been equated to the symbolic name PI, it can be used legitimately in any subsequent definition, even within another Const statement.

An interesting modification to the `Const` statement is that the *As data-type* clause may be omitted. When the data type is not explicitly declared, Visual Basic will select the data type that is most appropriate for the value. For example, if you use the statement

```
Const PI = 3.14159265358979
```

which has 14 digits of precision after the decimal point, Visual Basic will automatically make this a Double value.

Finally, you can place more than one constant declaration on a line, as long as a comma separates each constant assignment. For example, the following Const statement is valid:

```
Const PI = 3.1415, CONVERT = 360/PI
```

Exercises 3.3

1. Rewrite the following event procedure using a Const statement for the constant 3.1416.

```
Private Sub frmMain_Click(ByVal sender As Object, _
    ByVal e As System.EventArgs) Handles MyBase.Click
  Dim radius, area, circumference As Single
  radius = Val( InputBox("Enter a radius:", "Input Dialog", "0"))
  circumference = 2 * 3.1416 * radius
  area = 3.1416 * radius ^ 2
  txtShow.Text = "The area of the circle is " & area
End Sub
```

2. Rewrite the following procedure so that the variable prime is changed to a named constant.

```
Private Sub frmMain_Click(ByVal sender As Object, _
    ByVal e As System.EventArgs) Handles MyBase.Click
  Dim prime, amount, interest As Single
  prime = 0.08     ' prime interest rate
  amount = Val(InputBox("Enter the amount", "Input Dialog", "0"))
  interest = prime * amount
  txtDisplay.Text = "The interest earned is" & interest & " _
    dollars"
End Sub
```

3. Rewrite the following procedure to use the named constant FACTOR in place of the expression (5/9) used in the procedure.

```
Private Sub frmMain_Click(ByVal sender As Object, _
    ByVal e As System.EventArgs) Handles MyBase.Click
  Dim fahren, celsius As Single
```

```
fahren = Val(InputBox("Enter a temperature in degrees _
    Fahrenheit",,"0"))
celsius = (5/9) * (fahren - 32)
txtDisplay.Text = "The equivalent Celsius temperature is " & _
    celsius
End Sub
```

3.4 Assignment Statements

We have already used simple assignment statements in the previous section. An assignment statement provides the most basic way to both assign a value to a variable and to perform calculations. This statement has the following syntax:

variable = *expression*

The simplest expression in Visual Basic is a single constant, and in each of the following assignment statements, the expression to the right of the equal sign is a constant:

```
length = 25
width = 17.5
```

In each of these assignment statements, the value of the constant to the right of the equal sign is assigned to the variable on the left side of the equal sign. It is extremely important to note that the equal sign in Visual Basic does not have the same meaning as an equal sign in algebra. The equal sign in an assignment statement tells the computer to first determine the value of the expression to the right of the equal sign and then to store (or assign) that value in the variable to the left of the equal sign. In this regard, the Visual Basic statement `length = 25` is read as "length is assigned the value 25." The blank spaces in the assignment statement are inserted for readability only.

Recall from the previous section that when a value is assigned to a variable for the first time, the variable is said to be *initialized*. Although Visual Basic automatically initializes all explicitly declared variables to zero, the term *initialization* is frequently used to refer to the first time a user places a value into a variable. For example, assume the following statements are executed one after another:

```
temperature = 68.2
temperature = 70.6
```

The first assignment statement assigns the value of 68.2 to the variable named `temperature`. If this is the first time a user-assigned value is stored in the variable, it is also acceptable to say that "temperature is initialized to 68.2." The next assignment statement causes the computer to assign a value of 70.6 to `temperature`. The value 68.2 that was in `temperature` is overwritten with the new value of 70.6, because a variable can only store one value at a time. In this regard, it is sometimes useful to think of the variable to the left of the equal sign as a temporary parking spot in a huge parking lot. Just as an individual parking spot can only be used by one car at a time, each variable can only store one value at a time. The "parking" of a new value in a variable automatically causes the computer to remove any value previously parked there.

In its most common form, a Visual Basic expression is any combination of constants, variables, and operators that can be evaluated to yield a value.[3] Thus, the expression in an assignment statement can be used to perform calculations using the arithmetic operators introduced in Section 3.1 (see Table 3–3). Examples of assignment statements using expressions containing these operators are:

```
sum = 3 + 7
difference = 15 - 6
taxes = 0.05 * 14.6
tally = count + 1
newtotal = 18.3 + total
price = 6.58 * quantity
totalweight = weight * factor
average = sum / items
newval = number ^ power
```

In an assignment statement, the equal sign always directs the computer to first calculate the value of the expression to the right of the equal sign and then store this value in the variable to the left of the equal sign. For example, in the assignment statement `totalweight = weight * factor`, the expression `weight * factor` is first evaluated to yield a value. This value, which is a number, is then stored in the variable `totalweight`.

When writing assignment statements, you must be aware of two important considerations: Because the expression to the right of the equal sign is evaluated first, all variables used in the expression must be assigned values if the result is to make sense. For example, the assignment statement `totalweight = weight * factor` will only cause a valid number to be stored in `totalweight` if the programmer first takes care to put valid numbers in `weight` and `factor`. Thus, the sequence of statements:

```
weight = 155.0
factor = 1.06
totalweight = weight * factor
```

---

[3]Expressions can also include functions, which are presented in the next section.

weight	factor	totalweight
155	1.06	164.30

Figure 3-12 *Values Stored in the Variables*

ensures that we know the values being used to obtain the result that will be stored in the variable to the left of the equal sign. Figure 3-12 illustrates the values stored in the variables `weight`, `factor`, and `totalweight`.

The second consideration to keep in mind is that, because the value of an expression is stored in the variable to the left of the equal sign, there must be only one variable listed in this position. For example, the following assignment statement is invalid:

```
amount + extra = 1462 + 10 - 24
```

The right-side expression evaluates to the integer 1448, which can only be stored in a variable. Because amount + extra is not the valid name of a memory location (it is not a valid variable name), Visual Basic does not know where to store the value 1448.

Program 3-4 illustrates the use of assignment statements to calculate the volume of a cylinder. As illustrated in Figure 3-13, the volume of a cylinder is determined by the formula, Volume = $\pi\ r^2 h$, where r is the radius of the cylinder, h is its height, and π is the constant 3.1416 (accurate to four decimal places).

The interface for Program 3-4 is shown in Figure 3-14. For this application, the only procedure is for the button's **Click** event. The required code is listed in Program 3-4's Event Code. Note that because only one line of output is produced, the Multiline property of the text box is kept at False, the default value. The objects and properties for Program 3-4 are shown in Table 3-8.

Program 3-4's Event Code

```
Private Sub btnVol_Click(ByVal sender As Object, _
    ByVal e As System.EventArgs) Handles btnVol.Click
  Dim radius, height, volume As Single
```

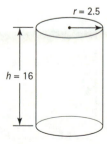

Figure 3-13 *Determining the Volume of a Cylinder*

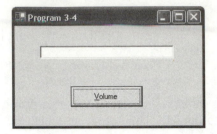

Figure 3–14 *Program 3–4's Interface*

Table 3–8 The Properties Table for Program 3–4

Object	Property	Setting
Form	Name	frmMain
	Text	Program 3–4
Text Box	Name	txtDisplay
	TabStop	False
	Text	(blank)
Button	Name	btnVol
	Text	&Volume

```
  txtDisplay.Text = ""
  radius = 2.5
  height = 16.0
  volume = 3.1416 * radius ^ 2 * height
  txtDisplay.Text = "The volume of the cylinder is " & volume
End Sub
```

The output displayed in the text box by this event code, when the button is clicked, is shown Figure 3–15.

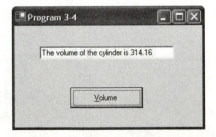

Figure 3–15 *The Output Displayed by Program 3–4*

Note the order in which statements are executed in the event procedure. The procedure begins with the header line and continues sequentially, statement by statement, until the End Sub statement is encountered. All procedures execute in this manner. The computer works on one statement at a time, executing that statement with no knowledge of what the next statement will be. This explains why all variables used in an expression must have values assigned to them before the expression is evaluated.

When the computer executes the statement volume = 3.1416 * radius ^ 2 * height, it uses whatever value is stored in the variables radius and height at the time the assignment statement is executed. If no values have been specifically assigned to these variables before they are used in the assignment statement, the procedure uses whatever values happen to occupy these variables when they are referenced (in Visual Basic all numeric variables are automatically initialized to zero). The procedure does not look ahead to see that you might assign values to these variables later in the program.

Assignment Variations

Although only one variable is allowed immediately to the left of the equal sign in an assignment expression, the variable on the left of the equal sign can also be used on the right of the equal sign. For example, the assignment statement total = total + 20 is valid. Clearly, in an algebraic equation total could never be equal to itself plus 20. But in Visual Basic, the statement total = total + 20 is not an equation; it is a statement that is evaluated in two distinct steps. The first step is to calculate the value of total + 20. The second step is to store the computed value in total. See if you can determine the output of Event Procedure 3–3, when the form Click event is triggered:

Event Procedure 3–3

```
Private Sub frmMain_Click(ByVal sender As Object, ByVal e As _
    System.EventArgs) Handles MyBase.Click
  Dim total As Integer

  total = 15
  txtDisplay.AppendText("The number stored in total is " & total & _
    ControlChars.NewLine)
  total = total + 25
  txtDisplay.AppendText("The number now stored in total is " & total)
End Sub
```

The assignment statement total = 15 assigns the value in total to the number 15, as shown in Figure 3–16.

The first AppendText method statement causes both a message and the value stored in total to be displayed on the form. The output produced by this statement for the form Click event is:

```
The number stored in total is 15
```

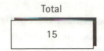

Figure 3–16 *The Integer 15 Is Stored in total*

The second assignment statement in the procedure, `total = total + 25` causes the computer to retrieve the 15 stored in `total` and add 25 to this number, yielding the number 40. The number 40 is then stored in the variable on the left side of the equal sign, which is the variable `total`. The 15 that was in `total` is simply erased and replaced; it is overwritten with the new value of 40, as shown in Figure 3–17. The second line of output is

```
The number now stored in total is 40
```

Accumulating

Assignment expressions such as `total = total + 25` are very common in programming and are required in accumulating subtotals when data is entered one number at a time. For example, if we want to add the numbers 96, 70, 85, and 60 in calculator fashion, the following statements could be used:

Statement	Value in total
`total = 0`	0
`total = total + 96`	96
`total = total + 70`	166
`total = total + 85`	251
`total = total + 60`	311

The first statement initializes the total to 0. This removes any number ("garbage" value) stored in the memory locations corresponding to total and ensures that we start with 0. (This is equivalent to clearing a calculator before doing any computations.) As each number is added, the value stored in total is increased accordingly. After completion of the last statement, total contains the total of all the added numbers.

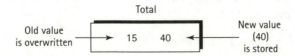

Figure 3–17 `total = total + 25` *Causes a New Value to be Stored in total*

The form's Click procedure listed in Event Procedure 3–4 illustrates the effect of these statements by displaying total's contents after each addition is made.

Event Procedure 3–4

```
Private Sub frmMain_Click(ByVal sender As Object, ByVal e As _
    System.EventArgs) Handles MyBase.Click
  Dim total As Integer

  total = 0
  txtDisplay.AppendText("The value of total is initially set to " & total _
    & ControlChars.NewLine)
  total = total + 96
  txtDisplay.AppendText("  total is now " & total & ControlChars.NewLine)
  total = total + 70
  txtDisplay.AppendText("  total is now " & total & ControlChars.NewLine)
  total = total + 85
  txtDisplay.AppendText("  total is now " & total & ControlChars.NewLine)
  total = total + 60
  txtDisplay.AppendText("  The final value in total is " & total)
End Sub
```

The output produced by the form's Click event in Event Procedure 3–4 is:

```
The value of total is initially set to 0
  total is now 96
  total is now 166
  total is now 251
  The final value in total is 311
```

Although it is easier to add the numbers by hand than to use the sequence of assignment statements listed, these statements do illustrate the subtotaling effect of repeated assignment statements having the form:

```
variable = variable + new value
```

We will find many important uses for this type of statement when we become more familiar with the various loops introduced in Chapter 6.

Counting

A variation of the accumulating assignment statement is the counting statement. Counting statements have the form:

```
variable = variable + fixed number
```

Examples of counting statements are:

```
sum = sum + 1
totalStudents = totalStudents + 1
count = count + 1
m = m + 2
number = number + 3
```

In each of these examples, the same variable is used on both sides of the equal sign. After the statement is executed, the value of the respective variable is increased by a fixed amount. In the first three examples, the variables `sum`, `totalStudents`, and `count` have all been increased by one. In the next example, `count` has been increased by two and in the final example, the variable number has been increased by three. Typically, integer variables with very simple names such as `i`, `j`, `k`, `1`, `m`, and `n`,[4] or more mnemonic names, such as `count`, are used for counter variables. The following sequence of statements illustrates the use of a counter.

Statement	Value in COUNT
count = 0	0
count = count + 1	1
count = count + 1	2
count = count + 1	3
count = count + 1	4

The form's **Click** event listed in Event Procedure 3–5 illustrates the effect of these statements within the context of a complete procedure.

Event Procedure 3–5

```
Private Sub frmMain_Click(ByVal sender As Object, ByVal e As _
    System.EventArgs) Handles MyBase.Click
  Dim count As Integer

  count = 0
  txtDisplay.AppendText("The initial value of count is " & count & _
    ControlChars.NewLine)
  count = count + 1
  txtDisplay.AppendText("  count is now " & count & ControlChars.NewLine)
  count = count + 1
```

---

[4]This is a carryover from the original version of the first high-level language, FORTRAN, in which any variable beginning in these letters was created as an integer variable.

```
  txtDisplay.AppendText("  count is now " & count & ControlChars.NewLine)
  count = count + 1
  txtDisplay.AppendText("  count is now " & count & ControlChars.NewLine)
  count = count + 1
  txtDisplay.AppendText("  count is now " & count & ControlChars.NewLine)
End Sub
```

The output produced by the form's **Click** event in Event Procedure 3–5 is:

```
The initial value of count is 0
  count is now 1
  count is now 2
  count is now 3
  count is now 4
```

Visual Basic also supports combined operators. For example,

```
count = count + 1
```

can also be written as

```
count += 1
```

Although combined operators are available for many operations, the most commonly used ones are for addition (+=) and subtraction (-=).

Type Conversions

It is important to understand that data type conversions take place across the assignment statement. As a result, the expression on the right side of the assignment operator is converted to the data type of the variable to the left of the assignment operator. For example, consider the evaluation of the expression

```
average = total / 2
```

where `total` is an integer variable having a stored value of 15 and `average` also is an integer variable. The result of the expression `total / 2` will be 7.5. However, because the left side of the assignment operator is an integer variable, the value of the expression `total / 2` is rounded to an integer value and stored in the variable `average`. At the completion of this assignment statement, the value stored in `average` is 8.

Automatic type conversions due to assignment take place whenever possible. For example, consider the following section of code:

```
Dim s As String, number As Integer

s = "55"
number = s
```

Here, the value 55 is stored in `number`. However, if the string "AB" is stored in s, the error

```
Cast from string "AB" to type 'Integer' is not valid.
```

will be displayed when the assignment statement number = s is executed.

To avoid unintentional conversions and type mismatch errors, the general rule is always to use the same types of variables on each side of the equal sign; that is, the integer types (byte, integer, and long) should be used with integer types, floating point types (single and double) with floating point types, strings with strings, and so on.

In addition to data type conversions that are made automatically across an equal sign, Visual Basic also provides for explicit user-specified type conversions. These conversion functions are presented in the next section.

Exercises 3.4

1. Write an assignment statement to calculate the circumference of a circle having a radius of 3.3 inches. The equation for determining the circumference (c) of a circle is $c = 2 \pi r$, where r is the radius and π equals 3.1416.

2. Write an assignment statement to calculate the area of a circle. The equation for determining the area (a) of a circle is $a = \pi r2$, where r is the radius and $\pi = 3.1416$.

3. Write an assignment statement to convert temperature in degrees Fahrenheit to degrees Celsius. The equation for this conversion is *Celsius = 5/9 (Fahrenheit − 32)*.

4. Write an assignment statement to calculate the round trip distance (d) in feet for a trip that is *s* miles long, one way.

5. Write an assignment statement to calculate in inches the length of a line that is measured in centimeters. Use the fact that there are 2.54 centimeters in one inch.

6. Write an assignment statement to calculate the value, in dollars, of an amount of money in francs. Assume that five francs are worth one dollar.

7. Determine the output of the following procedure:

```
Private Sub frmMain_Click(ByVal sender As Object, ByVal e As _
    System.EventArgs) Handles MyBase.Click
    ' a procedure illustrating integer truncation
   Dim num1 As Integer, num2 As Integer
   txtDisplay.Clear()
   num1 = 9/2
   num2 = 17/4
   txtDisplay.AppendText("The first integer displayed is " & _
     num1 & ControlChars.NewLine)
   txtDisplay.AppendText("The second integer displayed is " & _
     num2)
End Sub
```

8. Determine the output produced by the following procedure:

```
    Private Sub frmMain_Click(ByVal sender As Object, ByVal e As _
        System.EventArgs) Handles MyBase.Click
      Dim average As Single
      txtDisplay.Clear()
      average = 26.27
      txtDisplay.AppendText("The average is " & average & _
        ControlChars.NewLine)
      average = 682.3
      txtDisplay.AppendText("The average is " & average & _
        ControlChars.NewLine)
      average = 1.968
      txtDisplay.AppendText("The average is " & average & _
        ControlChars.NewLine)
    End Sub
```

9. Determine the output produced by the following procedure:

```
    Private Sub frmMain_Click(ByVal sender As Object, ByVal e As_
        System.EventArgs) Handles MyBase.Click
      Dim sum As Single
      txtDisplay.Clear()
      sum = 0.0
      txtDisplay.AppendText("The sum is " & sum & _
        ControlChars.NewLine)
      sum = sum + 26.27
      txtDisplay.AppendText("The sum is " & sum & _
        ControlChars.NewLine)
      sum = sum + 1.968
      txtDisplay.AppendText("The final sum is " & sum & _
        ControlChars.NewLine)
    End Sub
```

10. a. Determine what each statement causes to happen in the following procedure.

```
      Private Sub frmMain_Click(ByVal sender As Object, ByVal e As _
          System.EventArgs) Handles MyBase.Click
        Dim num1 As Integer, num2 As Integer
        Dim num3 As Integer, total As Integer
        txtDisplay.Clear()
        num1 = 25
        num2 = 30
```

```
            total = num1 + num2
            txtDisplay.AppendText(num1 & " + " & num2 & " = " &
                total & ControlChars.NewLine)
        End Sub
```

b. What output will be produced when the event procedure listed in Exercise 10a is triggered by clicking the screen?

11. Determine and correct the errors in the following procedures.

a.

```
        Private Sub frmMain_Click(ByVal sender As Object, ByVal e As _
            System.EventArgs) Handles MyBase.Click
            width = 15
            area = length * width
            txtDisplay.Text = "The area is " & area
        End Sub
```

b.

```
        Private Sub frmMain_Click(ByVal sender As Object, ByVal e As _
            System.EventArgs) Handles MyBase.Click
            Dim length As Integer, width As Integer, area As Integer
            area = length * width
            length = 20
            width = 15
            txtDisplay.Text = "The area is " & area
        End Sub
```

c.

```
        Private Sub frmMain_Click(ByVal sender As Object, ByVal e As _
            System.EventArgs) Handles MyBase.Click
            Dim length As Integer, width As Integer, area As Integer
            length = 20
            width = 15
            length * width = area
            txtDisplay.Text = "The area is & area
        End Sub
```

12. Determine the output produced by the following event procedure.

```
        Private Sub frmMain_Click(ByVal sender As Object, ByVal e As _
            System.EventArgs) Handles MyBase.Click
```

```
Dim sum As Integer
sum = 0
sum = sum + 96
sum = sum + 70
sum = sum + 85
sum = sum + 60
txtDisplay.AppendText("The value of sum is initially set to " & sum)
txtDisplay.AppendText("  sum is now " & sum & ControlChars.NewLine)
txtDisplay.AppendText("  sum is now " & sum & ControlChars.NewLine)
txtDisplay.AppendText("  sum is now " & sum & ControlChars.NewLine)
txtDisplay.AppendText("  The final sum is " & sum)
End Sub
```

13. Using Program 3–3, determine the volume of cylinders having the following radii and heights.

Radius (in.)	Height (in.)
1.62	6.23
2.86	7.52
4.26	8.95
8.52	10.86
12.29	15.35

3.5 Using Intrinsic Functions

As we have seen, assignment statements can be used to perform numeric computations. For example, the assignment statement

```
tax = rate * income
```

multiplies the value in `rate` with the value in `income` and then assigns the resulting value to `tax`. Although the common numeric operations, such as addition, subtraction, and so on, are easily accomplished using Visual Basic's numeric operators, no such operators exist for finding the square root of a number, the absolute value of a number, and other useful mathematical values. To facilitate the calculation of such quantities as well as the conversion between data types, and other useful operations, Visual Basic .NET provides a set of preprogrammed routines, referred to as *intrinsic functions*, that can be included in a procedure. A number of mathematical functions[5] are found in the System.Math class of Visual Basic .NET.

Before using one of Visual Basic's intrinsic functions, you must know the following:

- The name of the desired intrinsic function
- The name of the library or class in which the function exists
- What the intrinsic function does
- The type of data required by the intrinsic function
- The data type of the result returned by the intrinsic function

In practice, all functions operate in a manner similar to sub procedures, with one major difference: *A function always directly returns a single value.* This is an extremely important difference because it allows functions to be included within expressions.

To illustrate the use of a Visual Basic intrinsic function, consider the function named Sqrt, which calculates the square root of a number. Because this is in the Math class, Math. must precede Sqrt. The square root of a number is computed using the expression

```
Math.Sqrt(number)
```

where the function's name—in this case Math.Sqrt—is followed by parentheses containing the number for which the square root is desired. The parentheses following the function name effectively provide a "funnel" through which data can be passed to the function (see Figure 3–18). The items that are passed to the function through the parentheses are called *arguments* of the function and constitute its input data. For example, the following expressions are used to compute the square root of the arguments 4, 17, 25, 1043.29, and 6.4516:

```
Math.Sqrt(4)

Math.Sqrt(17)

Math.Sqrt(25)

Math.Sqrt(1043.29)

Math.Sqrt(6.4516)
```

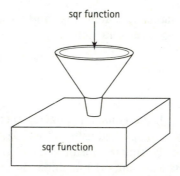

Figure 3–18   *Passing Data to the Sqrt Function*

---

[5]The mathematical functions are actually methods in Visual Basic .NET. However, for simplicity, we will refer to them as functions.

The argument to the `Sqrt` function can be any numeric expression that results in a positive value.[6] The `Sqrt` function computes the square root of its argument and returns the result. The values returned by `Sqrt` function for the previous expressions are:

Expression	Value Returned
`Math.Sqrt(4)`	2
`Math.Sqrt(17)`	4.12310562561766
`Math.Sqrt(25)`	5
`Math.Sqrt(1043.29)`	32.3
`Math.Sqrt(6.4516)`	2.54

Although we have used the square root function to illustrate how intrinsic functions are used, the most useful functions for commercial purposes are those that deal with formatting numbers, converting between data types, and operating on string data. Other functions in the Math Library include `Round(x)`, which rounds a Double value x to the nearest integer value, `Floor(x)` which rounds a value down to the smallest Integer less than or equal to x, and `Abs(x)` which returns the absolute value of a number. Table 3–9 lists commonly used conversion functions. For those functions below that return a numeric value (e.g., `Cint`), if the expression converts to a value that is outside the range for that type, an error during execution is generated. When these functions are used in a program, they do not need to be preceded by any library name (e.g., they do not need `Math.`). The formatting functions and string manipulation functions are presented in Sections 4.2 and 7.3, respectively.

Exercises 3.5

1. List the four items that you must know before using a Visual Basic intrinsic function.

2. How many values does a call to a single Visual Basic function return?

3. Write function calls to determine:

   a. The square root of 6.37.

   b. The square root of $x - y$.

   c. The square root of $a^2 - b^2$.

4. For $a = 10.6$, $b = 13.9$, $c = -3.42$, determine the value of:

   a. `CInt(a)`

   b. `CInt(b)`

   c. `CInt(c)`

   d. `CInt(a) + b`

   e. `CType(a, Integer) + b + c`

   f. `CType(a+b, Integer)`

   g. `CInt(a + b + c)`

---

[6]A negative argument value results in the error message "Invalid procedure call" when the function is used.

Table 3–9   Visual Basic's Conversion Functions

Function Name and Argument(s)	Description and Returned Value
Asc(string)	Converts the first character in the string to an Integer representing the ANSI code for that character.
Chr(val)	Returns the string consisting of the character with ANSI value val.
CBool(expression)	Converts an expression to a Boolean value. If an expression is zero, False is returned; otherwise, True is returned.
CByte(expression)	Converts an expression to a Byte which can hold the values 0 through 255. The expression is rounded if it is a fractional number.
CChar(expression)	Converts a string expression to a Char. If the string contains more than one character, only the first character is returned.
CDate(expression)	Converts an expression to a Date.
CDbl(expression)	Converts a numeric or string expression to a Double.
CDec(expression)	Converts a numeric or string expression to a Decimal.
CInt(expression)	Converts a numeric or string expression to an Integer.
CLng(expression)	Converts a numeric or string expression to a Long.
CObj(expression)	Converts an expression to an object.
CShort(expression)	Converts a numeric or string expression to a Short.
CSng(expression)	Converts a numeric or string expression to a Single.
CStr(expression)	Converts a numeric, Boolean, Date, or string expression to a String.
CType (expression, type)	Converts an expression to the type specified by the second argument. For example, CType(exp, Integer) is equivalent to CInt(exp).
Val(string)	Returns the first number in the string. (The function stops reading the string at the first nonnumeric character, except for a period, which is recognized as a decimal point.)

5. Determine the returned value for the following function calls:

   a. Val("")

   b. Val("abc")

   c. Val("123abc")

   d. Val(123.4abc")

   e. Val(123.5.6abc")

   f. Val(123abc.456"}

6. Write one Visual Basic Program that displays the value of each of the function calls listed in Exercise 5.

3.6 Focus on Program Design and Implementation: Creating an Operational Form[7]

Currently, the Rotech Systems application consists of a main menu and stub form, with sufficient event code to permit a user to cycle between forms. In this Focus section, we make the main menu's <u>W</u>alk In button operational, so that it calls a new form that calculates and prints out invoices for walk-in customers. This is done using the following three steps:

Step 1: Add a new Walk In stub form to the project.
   a. Provide the Walk In stub form with a single button that returns control to the Main Menu.
   b. Save the new form.
Step 2: Link the new stub form to the main menu.
   a. Modify the main menu <u>W</u>alk In button to display the new Walk In stub form rather than the Under Development stub form.
   b. Verify that a user can correctly cycle between the main menu and the new stub form.
Step 3: Modify the Walk In stub form.
   a. Change the stub form to a fully functional operational form that performs its intended operational task.
   b. Verify that the new form performs correctly.

The first two steps are "cookbook" items because the same procedure is used whenever we modify an application to have the main menu call a new stub form rather than the generic Under Development stub form. Here is the procedure for performing these two steps, as they apply to our new Walk In form:

Step 1: Add a new stub form to the project

Add a new form by either following the procedure used in the previous Focus section for the Under Development stub form or the summary procedure listed in this section's Programmer Notes box. Provide this new form with the following properties and make the form look like the form shown in Figure 3–19.

Object	Property	Setting
Form	Name	frmWalkIn
	Text	Walk In Sales
Button	Name	btnReturn
	Text	&Return to Main Menu
Label	Name	lblHeader
	Text	Disk Sales Order Form
	Font	MS Sans Serif, Bold

[7]Unless subsequent Focus sections are to be covered, the material in this section may be omitted with no loss of subject continuity.

This new form's button should return control to the main menu form when the button is clicked. This is done using the following event code:

```
Private Sub btnReturn_Click(ByVal sender As Object, ByVal e As _
    System.EventArgs) Handles btnReturn.Click
  Dim frmMainRef As New frmMain()

  Me.Close()
  frmMainRef.Show()
End Sub
```

We have chosen to close the form rather than merely hide it, because the form will not be used extensively. When the form is not in use, we might as well close it altogether instead of keeping it in memory. Note that the statement Me.Close() can be replaced by the statement frmWalkIn.Close(). Once this is done, save the new form in the file named frmWalkin using the Save As option from the File menu.

Programmer Notes

Adding a New Form:

To add a new form to an existing project:

1. Select the Add Windows Form item from the Project menu.
2. Select the Windows Form icon.
3. Enter a name for the form.
4. Click Open to add the new form to the project.

This procedure displays a new form and adds this new form to the Project Explorer Window. To switch between forms, simply click on the desired form in the Project Explorer Window.

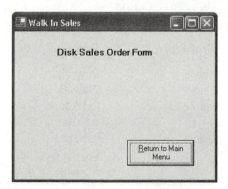

Figure 3–19 *The New Stub Walk In Form*

Step 2: Link the new stub form to the Main Menu

Link the new stub form to the main menu by modifying one line in the main menu Walk In button's Click event code. Specifically, change the second line within the button's existing Click event procedure from frmStubRef.Show to frmWalkRef.Show. The completed event procedure should now be:

```
Private Sub btnWalkins_Click(ByVal sender As Object, ByVal e As _
    System.EventArgs) Handles btnWalkins.Click
  Dim frmWalkRef As New frmWalkIn()

  Me.Hide()
  frmWalkRef.Show()     'this is the changed line
End Sub
```

Once this change is made, verify that the new Walk In form is displayed when the main menu Walk In button is clicked, and that the new form's Return button successfully redisplays the Main Menu form.

  (Note: At this stage, the project consists of three forms: a Main Menu form, an Under Development stub Form, and a stub WalkIn Form. The project, as it currently exists, can be found as the rotech3a project in the ROTECH3a folder at http://computerscience.jbpub. com/bronsonvbnet.)

  The remaining task is to modify the stub WalkIn form illustrated in Figure 3–19 to that shown in Figure 3–20. As seen in Figure 3–20, the form has an input section for entering a customer's name, address, and the number of diskette boxes purchased. Also

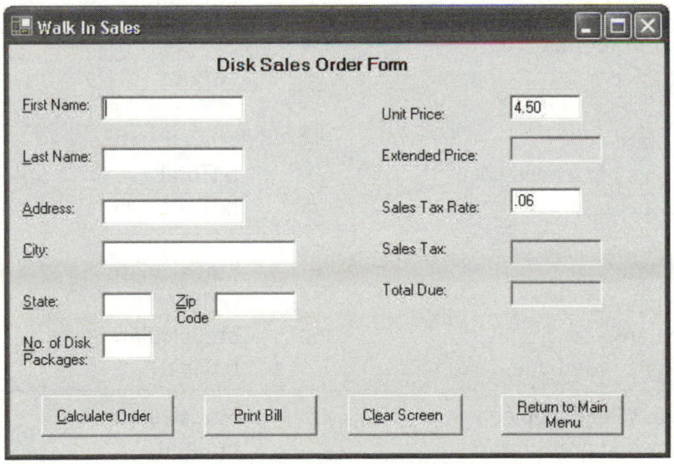

Figure 3–20   *The Completed WalkIn Form*

included on the form are four buttons, whose function is indicated by their captions, and an output section for listing the total amount of the purchase. Recall from the original project specification given in Section 1.5 that the price of a box of diskettes is $4.50 and the sales tax rate is currently 6%.

The WalkIn form's required tasks are listed in the TTL Table 3–10. Note that the tasks have been organized by function—that is, input, output, and processing. The input tasks are all performed using text boxes, as is the output. In some cases, such as when calculating and displaying the extended price, two objects are required. In this case, a **Click** event is used to perform the calculation and force the display, while the output text box requires no event because it is a passive recipient of the calculated data.

The properties provided to the objects listed in the TTL table are listed in Table 3–11, used to produce the form previously shown in Figure 3–20.

Table 3–10 The WalkIn Form's TTL Table

Form: WalkIn (Order Entry)		Trigger
Task	Object	Event
Obtain customer data		
First name	txtFname	user entry
Last name	txtLname	user entry
Address	txtAddr	user entry
City	txtCity	user entry
State	txtState	user entry
Zip code	txtZip	user entry
Disk packs ordered	txtQuantity	user entry
Display output data		
Unit price	txtPrice	initial text with user over-write
Calculate and	btnCalculate	Click
display extended price	txtTotal	none
Sales tax rate	txtTrate	initial text with user over-write
Calculate and	btnCalculate	Click
display tax due	txtTax	none
Calculate and	btnCalculate	Click
display total due	txtFinal	none
Compute screen invoice	btnCalculate	Click
Compute and print Invoice	btnPrint	Click
Clear all screen inputs	btnClear	Click
Return to Main Menu	btnReturn	Click

Table 3–11   The WalkIn Form's Properties Table

Object	Property	Setting
Form	Name	frmWalkIn
	Text	Walk In Sales
Label	Name	lblHeader
	Text	Disk Sales Order Form
	Font	MS Sans Serif, Bold, Size = 10
Label	Name	lblFname
	Text	&First Name:
	TabIndex	0
TextBox	Name	txtFname
	Text	(blank)
	TabIndex	1
Label	Name	lblLname
	Text	&Last Name:
	TabIndex	2
TextBox	Name	txtFname
	Text	(blank)
	TabIndex	3
Label	Name	lblAddr
	Text	&Address:
	TabIndex	4
TextBox	Name	txtAddr
	Text	(blank)
	TabIndex	5
Label	Name	lblCity
	Text	&City:
	TabIndex	6
TextBox	Name	txtCity
	Text	(blank)
	TabIndex	7
Label	Name	lblState
	Text	&State:
	TabIndex	8
TextBox	Name	txtState
	Text	(blank)
	TabIndex	9
Label	Name	lblZip
	Text	&Zip:
	TabIndex	10

(continued)

Table 3–11 (continued)

Object	Property	Setting
TextBox	Name	txtZip
	Text	(blank)
	TabIndex	11
Label	Name	lblQuantity
	Text	&No. of Disk Packages:
	TabIndex	12
TextBox	Name	txtQuantity
	Text	(blank)
	TabIndex	13
Label	Name	lblPrice
	Text	Unit Price:
	TabIndex	14
TextBox	Name	txtPrice
	Text	4.50
	TabIndex	15
Label	Name	lblTrate
	Text	Sales Tax Rate:
	TabIndex	16
TextBox	Name	txtTrate
	Text	.06
	TabIndex	17
Button	Name	btnCalculate
	Text	&Calculate Order
	TabIndex	18
Button	Name	btnPrint
	Text	&Print Bill
	TabIndex	19
Button	Name	btnClear
	Text	Cl&ear Screen
	TabIndex	20
Button	Name	btnReturn
	Text	&Return to Main Menu
	TabIndex	21
Label	Name	lblExt
	Text	Extended Price:
TextBox	Name	txtTotal
	TabStop	False
	ReadOnly	True
	Text	(blank)

(continued)

Table 3–11 (continued)

Object	Property	Setting
Label	Name	lblTax
	Text	Sales Tax:
TextBox	Name	txtTax
	TabStop	False
	ReadOnly	True
	Text	(blank)
Label	Name	lblFinal
	Text	Total Due:
TextBox	Name	TxtFinal
	TabStop	False
	ReadOnly	True
	Text	(blank)

Except for the quantity of objects placed on the WalkIn form, there is nothing significantly different here from the forms you have been using throughout the text. However, it is worth reviewing the **TabIndex** numbers in the Properties table and the reason for their assignment. Note that in each case a text box's corresponding label is given a **TabIndex** number that is one less than the number assigned to the text box. Also note the labels corresponding to text boxes that will be used for input have been assigned an access key. Activating a label's access key will cause the program to attempt to move focus to the label, but labels cannot receive focus, so the focus automatically shifts to the object having the next highest **TabIndex** value. As a result of giving the associated text box the next **TabIndex** value in sequence, we have provided a means for users to tab into a text box using an access key.

Tips From The Pros

Providing Text Boxes with Access Keys:

We cannot directly provide a text box with an access key that will move focus to it. A useful and common work-around is to provide an access key within a Label control associated with the text box. This can always be done, because most input text boxes require an associated label. And if a label is not actually required, we provide one anyway.

The next step is to manipulate the label's access key to move the focus to the text box. This is accomplished by providing the text box with a **TabIndex** value that is one higher than its associated label. Because a label cannot receive focus, when the user activates the label's access key focus will automatically shift to the object having the next highest **TabIndex** value. In this case, it is the text box. From a user's viewpoint, it makes sense that the access key contained within the label forces the focus into the text box, because it is the text box, and not the label, that the user interacts with. Thus, the operation of the label's access key will appear natural and correct to a user.

The **TabIndex** value of each control can be set by typing the value in each control's property window. However, a simpler way is to use the **Tab Order** feature. To set the tab order on the controls, display the form design and do the following:

1. On the **View** menu, choose **Tab Order**. This activates the tab order selection mode on the form. The **TabIndex** property appears in the upper left corner of each control.

2. Click the controls sequentially to establish the tab order desired. You can click on a control multiple times to reach the desired value of **TabIndex**.

3. After this has been completed, choose **Tab Order** from the View menu again to deactivate tab order mode.

Adding the Event Code

All that remains to complete our sales order form is to provide Click events so that each button performs the task assigned to it in the TTL table. Except for the Printing task, which is developed in the next Focus section, the required event code is rather simple and is listed as Rotech Event Code–Version 1.

Rotech Event Code–Version 1

```
Private Sub btnCalculate_Click(ByVal sender As System.Object, _
    ByVal e As System.EventArgs) Handles btnCalculate.Click
  Dim sTotal, sTaxes, sFinal As Single

  txtTotal.Clear()
  txtTax.Clear()
  txtFinal.Clear()

  'Calculate and display new values
  sTotal = Val(txtQuantity.Text) * Val(txtPrice.Text)
  sTaxes = Val(txtTrate.Text) * sTotal
  sFinal = sTotal + sTaxes
  txtTotal.Text = sTotal
  txtTax.Text = sTaxes
  txtFinal.Text = sFinal
End Sub

Private Sub btnClear_Click(ByVal sender As Object, ByVal e As _
    System.EventArgs) Handles btnClear.Click
```

```
   txtTotal.Clear()
   txtTax.Clear()
   txtFinal.Clear()
   txtLname.Clear()
   txtFname.Clear()
   txtAddr.Clear()
   txtCity.Clear()
   txtState.Clear()
   txtZip.Clear()
   txtQuantity.Clear()
End Sub

Private Sub btnReturn_Click(ByVal sender As Object, ByVal e As _
   System.EventArgs) Handles btnReturn.Click
   Dim frmMainRef As New frmMain()
   Me.Hide()
   frmMainRef.Show()
End Sub
```

Each of these **Click** event codes should look familiar to you. Working from the bottom up, the Return button's code closes the current form and shows the Main Menu form. The Clear button clears out the text boxes by calling the Clear method for each text box. Finally, the Calculate button's Click event declares three single precision variables and uses these variables to store, and then display, the calculated values of price, sales tax, and total amount due for the order.

Areas of Programmer Concern

The form that has been developed in this section contains a number of areas that would be of concern to a professional programmer. As these concerns are neither immediately apparent nor restricted to our order entry form, but represent more general problems encountered in all commercial applications, we will take a moment to consider them.

The first and most noticeable concern when the form is activated is that displayed dollar values are not output in conventional currency format with a leading dollar sign and two digits following the decimal point. We address and rectify this problem in the next Focus section, after the material on output formatting is presented.

The second problem with the form is that pressing the Enter key does not shift the focus from the current text box to the next one. Users expect this type of operation— when they press the Enter key it signifies the end of the current input, at which point the focus should automatically shift to another object. Providing this feature requires correctly determining when the Enter key is pressed, and then taking action. Detecting when a particular key is pressed is presented in Chapter 5, and in that chapter's Focus section we show how to use this detection to shift the input focus.

A third concern is that the form provides no user-input validation, which is a very serious flaw in the application. For example, if a user inadvertently enters the letters "abc" into the txtQuantity box, the application will crash. At some point in every system's lifetime, incorrect types of data are entered. Therefore the application must provide some type of input validation to prevent a user from crashing the system simply by entering the wrong data type. This concern is addressed in the Focus section in Chapter 6, after Visual Basic's looping facilities are presented.

Our fourth item of concern is that we have not provided the WalkIn form's <u>P</u>rint button with any event code. As a result, if a user clicks this button, nothing will happen. The obvious and correct solution to this problem is to have the button display a stub form. Because we will provide the code for this button's **Click** event as the next item in our application's development (in the next Focus section), we can temporarily leave this button as is.

A more subtle problem with our sales order form is that the product is hard-coded into the form. Thus, if an additional product is added to the promotion, the form itself must be modified, requiring action by a programmer. For many systems that are only used for the duration of a single promotion, such as the Rotech application, this is not a problem. However, many systems need to provide a choice among many items, any of which can be purchased and any of which can change. For these situations, asking the client to call you each time an addition or modification needs to be made will only cause frustration for both of you. A better approach is to provide the application with a list of products, and give the user the means to add items to the list, delete items from the list, and modify existing products already in the list. The means of doing this is presented in the Focus section in Chapter 8.

In practice, a programmer handles each of these concerns as a normal course of constructing a commercial application, using standard techniques known to all professional programmers. By the time you finish this course, you too should have a good understanding of how to address these concerns and how to correctly incorporate their use within your VB applications. However, don't be discouraged about how much is still to be done. If you have completed the Rotech project to this point, you have built a solid foundation for your own programming work.

(Note: The Rotech Systems project, at the stage of development begun in this section, can be found at http://computerscience.jbpub.com/bronsonvbnet in the ROTECH2 *folder as project* rotech2. *The project, as it exists at the end of this section, can be found in the* ROTECH3 *folder as project* rotech3. *If you are developing the system yourself, following the procedures given in this section, we suggest that you first copy all of the files in the* ROTECH2 *folder onto your system, and then work out of this latter folder. When you have finished your changes, you can compare your results to the files in the ROTECH3 folder.)*

Exercises 3.6

1. Either construct the Rotech system as it has been developed in this section or locate and load the project from http://computerscience.jbpub.com/bronsonvbnet.

2. Modify the Rotech project so that pressing the <u>P</u>rint Bill button displays a new form. This new form should have two buttons: one that returns control to the WalkIn form and one that returns control directly to the Main Menu form.

Figure 3–21   *The Mail In Order Form*

3. Add a new form to the Rotech application to handle the Mail In orders. This form should look like Figure 3–21.

   (*Hint:* Either start from scratch by adding a new form, setting the form's Name property to frmMailIn, and adding the required controls, or make a copy of the existing Walk In form using the method described in the Programmer Notes box that follows, and then modify the copied form. Additionally, the project with a copied MailIn form that must now be modified can be found in the ROTECH3b folder, as project rotech3b, at http://computerscience.jbpub.com/bronsonvbnet.)

4. (Case study) For your selected project (see project specifications at the end of Section 1.5), design an appropriate order entry form. To do this you can either make a preliminary pencil sketch or start designing it directly on a new form within Visual Basic's IDE. Be sure to construct a TTL table for the new form and save this table as part of your project's documentation.

3.7   Knowing About: The Basics of Form Design[8]

The purpose of a form is to permit the user to interact with the application in a convenient way. In this section we present basic guidelines for using controls to create easy to use, attractive forms.

In designing a form it is useful to always remember that the form's main purpose is to control the flow of information to and from a user. It is also useful to understand that when a user views a screen, the user's eye will be attracted to a graphic first and then to text. When a user views text, a user will automatically start at the left top corner of the screen and move across and down the screen. Finally, users will judge an application

---

[8]The material in this section may be omitted with no loss of subject continuity.

based on how your screens look and how easy it is to use these screens and complete the tasks that the application is meant to accomplish. With this in mind, the following guidelines should always be observed, unless a special situation demands otherwise.

1. General Design Considerations

- Place frequently read information toward the top left or top center of a screen. Because this is where a user's eye normally focuses, it decreases eye movement and increases the screen's usability.
- Margins should be consistent around the screen, and should consist of a minimum of two dots from the screen's edge.
- Keep at least 40% of a screen's overall area blank.
- Make sure that all controls are surrounded by blank spaces.
- Buttons within a column or row should be the same size. They can all be touching or separated from each other by one or two pixels. The most commonly used button should be placed either at the top of the left-most column of buttons or at the left side of a row of buttons.
- When placing Label or TextBox controls in a line across the screen, make sure that the line is filled no more than 75% with controls.
- Don't make a form larger than the screen's physical size. Although users can use scroll bars to access these areas, they are not used to doing so.
- Create additional forms as needed with buttons that allow the user to switch between forms.
- Design inconspicuous forms. Each form should be useful yet unobtrusive. In this way, users should remember and refer to each operational form by its function, such as the WalkIn form, and not by its color or graphic.

2. Label and Text Considerations

- Use labels to describe the purpose of a form and what information is being asked for or displayed.
- Provide every text box with a label. If the text box is used for input, provide the label with an access key and give it a TabIndex number that is one less than its associated text box. This permits the user to force the focus onto the text box by activating the label's access key.
- All labels should be positioned either above or to the left of their respective text boxes. When placed above a text box, the label should align with the box's left side. When placed to the left of a text box, all labels in a column should be left-aligned.
- Use only one or two fonts that are easy to read, and use them for all text on the form. Generally, avoid script fonts (fonts that resemble handwriting) because they are harder to read than nonscript fonts.
- Use a point size of 8 or more; smaller point sizes are difficult to read. To distinguish important data or make titles clearly identifiable, use larger point sizes.
- For multiword labels, adopt a consistent style of either capitalizing all words that should be capitalized in the label or only capitalizing the first word.

- Do not use exotic fonts that may not be available on a user's computer.
- Do not use underlining or italics, as they both make text hard to read.

3. Color Considerations

- Use colors to create a soothing effect, rather than a dazzling, frenetic effect. Users quickly tire and become irritated when required to view a "glittering" or glaring form over an extended period of time. Blue colors tend to be soothing while "hot" colors, such as vivid pink or violet, tend to be distracting.
- Use only two or, at most three, complimentary colors within a single form, in addition to white, gray, or black. Numerous colors tend to distract users.
- Use a darker color to emphasize headings or titles.
- Use different color combinations among multiple forms to create a coding scheme for your application. For example, a blue and white color scheme might be used for a mail-in order entry form and a red and gray scheme for a walk in order entry form. These color schemes can be used on more than one form.
- Be cautious of using certain colors together as individuals may have trouble distinguishing between them. For example, color-deficient or color-blind users may not be able to tell the difference between red and green or red and blue patterns.

3.8   Common Programming Errors and Problems

Part of learning any procedural programming language is making the elementary mistakes commonly encountered as you begin to use the language. These mistakes vary with each programming language and tend to be frustrating. The more common errors made when initially programming procedural code in Visual Basic are as follows:

1. Misspelling the name of a method—for example, typing `ApendText` instead of `AppendText`. A simple way to detect this is to type all entries in the Code Window in lower case. Keywords will then be automatically capitalized correctly and displayed in blue (or any other color selected under the Tools Options). Any misspelled word will not be converted, making it easier to detect.

2. Forgetting to close string messages to be displayed by the `MessageBox.Show` method within double quote symbols.

3. Incorrectly typing the letter O for the number zero (0), and vice versa.

4. Incorrectly typing the letter l, for the number 1, and vice versa.

5. Forgetting to declare all the variables used in a program. This error is detected by Visual Basic, and an error message is generated for all undeclared variables.[9]

6. Storing an inappropriate data type value in a declared variable. This results in the assigned value being converted to the data type of the declared variable.

---

[9]An error is not generated if the user has turned off Option Explicit.

7. Using a variable in an expression before an explicit value has been assigned to the variable. Whatever value happens to be in the variable will be used when the expression is evaluated, and the result is usually incorrect.

8. Using an intrinsic function without providing the correct number of arguments of the proper data type.

9. Being unwilling to test an event procedure in depth. After all, you wrote the procedure and so assume it is correct, or you would have changed it before it was run. It can be very difficult to completely test your own software. As a programmer, you must constantly remind yourself that thinking your program is correct does not make it so. Finding errors in your own program is a sobering experience, but one that will help you become a master programmer.

One of the more fundamental errors mentioned in Chapter 1 is presented again here. A major programming error that almost all beginning programmers make is the rush to code and run a program before fully understanding what is required by each procedure. A symptom of this haste to get a program entered into the computer is the lack of either an outline of each proposed procedure or a written procedure itself. You can catch many problems by visually checking each procedure, either handwritten or listed from the computer, before it is ever run, and then testing it for a variety of inputs that a user might enter.

3.9 Chapter Review

Key Terms

accumulating	integer number
ANSI	intrinsic function
assignment	long
associativity	mixed-mode
counting	mnemonic
declaration	named constant
double	precedence
double precision number	single
expression	string
floating point number	type conversions
integer	variable

Summary

1. Four types of data were introduced in this chapter: integer, floating point, Boolean, and string. Each of these types of data is typically stored in a computer using different amounts of memory.

2. Every variable in a Visual Basic program should be declared to confirm the type of value it can store. Declarations within a function or sub procedure may be placed anywhere after the function or procedure declaration, but are usually placed together at the top of a procedure. Single variable declarations use the syntax

    Dim *var-1* As *data-type*

An example of using this syntax is

```
Dim quantity as Double
```

Multiple variable declarations may also be made on the same line using the syntax

```
Dim var-1 As data-type, var-2 As data-type,..., var-n As data-type
```

An example using this syntax is

```
Dim amount As Single, price as Double, count As Integer
```

3. Declaration statements always play a software role of defining a list of a procedure's valid variable names. They also play a hardware role, because they cause memory storage locations to be set aside for each declared variable.

4. An *expression* is any combination of constants, variables, operators, and functions that can be evaluated to yield a value.

5. Expressions are evaluated according to the precedence and associativity of the operators used in the expression.

6. Assignment statements are used to store values in variables. The general syntax for an assignment statement is

```
variable = expression
```

7. Visual Basic provides intrinsic functions for calculating mathematical and string computations.

8. Data passed to a function are called *arguments* of the function. Arguments are passed to an intrinsic function by including each argument, separated by commas, within the parentheses following the function's name. Each function has its own requirements for the number and data types of the arguments that must be provided.

9. Every intrinsic function operates on its arguments to calculate a single value. To effectively use an intrinsic function, you must know what the function does, the name of the function, the library in which the function exists, the number and data types of the arguments expected by the function, and the data type of the returned value.

10. A Const statement is used to equate a constant to a symbolic name. The syntax of this statement is

```
Const name As data-type = constant expression
```

where a constant expression can only include constants and operators (no variables or intrinsic functions). For example, the number 3.1416 can be equated to the symbolic name PI using the Const statement

```
Const PI As Single = 3.1416
```

Once a symbolic name has been equated to a value, another value may not be assigned to the symbolic name.

Test Yourself–Short Answer

1. Give an example of an **expression**.
2. Give an example of an **assignment**.
3. Name three Visual Basic **keywords**.

4. Define variable.
5. List the rules for naming a variable.
6. Declare a variable called PayAmt. It should be able to hold a decimal value.
7. Declare a variable called DeptName. It should hold alphabetic characters.
8. Create code that will force you to declare all of your variables.
9. Create code that will declare a variable to hold the count of students riding a bus. Use the data type best suited to the number anticipated.
10. Create code that will store the sum of the numbers 78 and 2. The variable **sum** has been declared as an integer.

Programming Projects

1. Construct a program that uses integer and string variables and the operations that can be performed on them. Follow the instructions below.
   a. Integers
      i. Open a new project and change the form's Text to "VB.NET Data Types".
      ii. On your form, create an Exit button named btnExit that can be used to end the program.
      iii. On your form, create a text box and button control named txtDisplay1 and btnDisplay1, respectively. Set the text of the Button control to "Display results".
      iv. Add the following commands to the Button control's Click event procedure, and run your program.

```
txtDisplay.AppendText(1 & ControlChars.NewLine)

txtDisplay.AppendText(3 + 4 & ControlChars.NewLine)

txtDisplay.AppendText(3 + 4 - 5 & ControlChars.NewLine)

txtDisplay.AppendText(3 + 4 * 5 - 10 / 2 & ControlChars.NewLine)

txtDisplay.AppendText(3 / 4 & 6 / 4 & 8 / 4 & ControlChars.NewLine)

txtDisplay.AppendText(6 ^ 2 & 3 ^ 2 ^ 2 & ControlChars.NewLine)

txtDisplay.AppendText(3 & 4 & 5 & 7-1 & ControlChars.NewLine)
```

      v. Now, add a button that causes the following code to be executed:

```
Dim a, b, c As Integer

a = 5

b = 2

txtDisplay.AppendText(a + b & a - b & ControlChars.NewLine)

txtDisplay.AppendText(a * b & a / b & ControlChars.NewLine)

txtDisplay.AppendText(a ^ b & b ^ a & ControlChars.NewLine)

txtDisplay.AppendText((a + b) / b * a - 13 & ControlChars.NewLine)

txtDisplay.AppendText(((a - 3) * b) - 13 * 2 & ControlChars.NewLine)
```

      vi. Now add a button to calculate and display the following:
         ? a * b where a = 10 and b = 7

? the average speed of a plane that traveled 600 miles in 2.5 hours

? the square root of 15

  b. Strings

  i. Create a new text box named txtDisplay2 and a button that activates the
  following code when it is clicked:

```
Dim today As String   ' string variables
Dim fday As String
Dim tdate as String   ' today's date, as a string
txtDisplay2.AppendText("Hello" & ControlChars.NewLine)
txtDisplay2.AppendText("There!"  & ControlChars.NewLine)
today = "01/24/04"
txtDisplay2.AppendText(today & ControlChars.NewLine)
fday = "Friday"
txtDisplay2.AppendText("Today is " & ControlChars.NewLine)
txtDisplay2.AppendText(fday & " - " & today & ControlChars.NewLine)
tdate = fday + " - " + today
txtDisplay2.AppendText(tdate & ControlChars.NewLine)
txtDisplay2.AppendText("400 + 125 = " & 400 + 125)
```

Adding two strings is called concatenation. The strings are simply
"strung" together. Adding two integers adds up the numbers.

  ii. Add a new button that executes the following code:

```
Dim irate, net, principal As Single
Dim phrase As String
irate = 0.065
principal = 1000
phrase = "The balance after a year is "
net = (1 + irate) * principal
txtDisplay2.AppendText("Using an interest rate of " &
    ControlChars.NewLine)
txtDisplay2.AppendText(irate * 100 & "%" & ControlChars.NewLine)
txtDisplay2.AppendText(phrase & net & ControlChars.NewLine)
```

  iii. Create one last text box named txtDisplay3, and a button to activate the
  following code:

```
Dim n1, n2, n3 As Integer
Dim f1, f2, f3 As Single
Dim s1, s2, s3 As String
n1 = 3
n2 = 4
```

```
n3 = 5
f1 = 3
f2 = 4
f3 = 5
s1 = "3"
s2 = "4"
s3 = "5"
txtDisplay3.AppendText(n1 * n2 * n3 & n1 * Val(s2) * n3 & _
    ControlChars.NewLine)
n2 = n3 / n1
f2 = f3 / f1
txtDisplay3.AppendText(n2 & f2 & ControlChars.NewLine)
txtDisplay3.AppendText(n1+n2+n3 & s1+s2+s3 & ControlChars.NewLine)
txtDisplay3.AppendText(s1 & n2 & f2 & ControlChars.NewLine)
txtDisplay3.AppendText(ControlChars.NewLine)
txtDisplay3.AppendText(Val(s1) + n2 + f2 & Val(s1)+ n2+ Int(f2) & _
    ControlChars.NewLine)
```

2. **Extra Challenge:**
   a. Use the Help Facility to obtain information on the string functions Left, Right, Mid, and InStr.[10]

      Based on this documentation determine:
      i. What does the Left function do?
      ii. What does the Right function do?
      iii. What does the Mid function do?
      iv. What is the exact value of the expression Str(3.1415)?
      v. What does the InStr function return?
   b. Create a text box and a button to activate the following code:

```
Dim s1 As String
Dim f1 As Single
s1 = "Hello There, World!"
txtDisplay4.AppendText(Microsoft.VisualBasic.Left(s1, 5) & _
    ControlChars.NewLine)
txtDisplay4.AppendText(Mid(s1,7,5) & ControlChars.NewLine)
txtDisplay4.AppendText(Microsoft.VisualBasic.Right(s1,6) & _
    ControlChars.NewLine)
```

---

[10]The namespace qualifier Microsoft.VisualBasic must be added in front of the Left and Right function names so that the correct string functions are used.

```
txtDisplay4.AppendText(Instr(s1,"W") & ControlChars.NewLine)
f1 = 3.1415927
txtDisplay4.AppendText("/" & Str(f1) & "/" & Mid(Str(f1),4,4) _
    & ControlChars.NewLine)
txtDisplay4.AppendText((s1) + Str(f1))
```

   c. Answer the following questions. (*Hint:* Use the results of Exercise 1.)

      i. What happens when you divide two integers together and store the result in an integer variable?

      ii. What happens when you divide two integers together and store the result in a single precision variable?

      iii. Is $3 \char94 2 \char94 2$ equal to 81?

      iv. What is the value of the expression 3 + 4 * 5?

      v. What is the value of the expression (3 + 4) * 5?

      vi. What is the value of the expression "3 + 4 * 5"?

      vii. What is the value of the expression "(3 + 4) * 5"?

      viii. What happens when two strings are added together?

      ix. What does an apostrophe do in Visual Basic?

      x. What does a colon do in Visual Basic?

      xi. True or False: An assignment statement takes the right hand side of an equation and assigns it to the left hand side.

      xii. Is the statement a + b = c + 5 a valid Visual Basic statement? Why or why not?

      xiii. What type of data does the `Val` function expect to operate on and what data type does it return?

3. Create a project that can be used by a business person on their laptop computer to determine exchange rates for China, Japan, England, and France. A form for this project is shown in Figure 3–22. For this project, assume that there are 8.3 yuan per dollar, 120 yen per dollar, 0.6 pounds per dollar, and 5 francs per dollar.

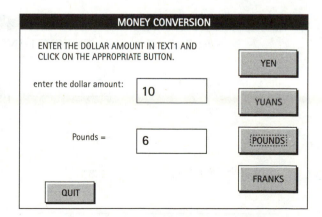

Figure 3–22 *Form for Project 3*

4. You're the owner of a clothing store. Business has been slow and you have too much of last season's merchandise, so you decide to have a sale. Everything in the store will be 45% off. Write a program that will allow the clerk to enter the original price, then press a button and view the discounted price, with the 6% sales tax added. A suggested form for this project is shown in Figure 3–23.

   a. The following formulas are needed for the CALCULATE button.
      DISCOUNTED PRICE = .55 * ORIGINAL PRICE
      TAX = .06 * DISCOUNTED PRICE
      FINAL PRICE = DISCOUNTED PRICE + TAX

   b. The CLEAR button clears the values in the text box and the three labels used for the discounted price, tax, and final price.

5. You believe that in ten years you will need money to start a new business. At present you have about $10,000, which you can invest in a savings account or CD. Create a Visual Basic Project that will allow you to experiment with different interest rates to see how much money you will have in this savings account or CD in ten years. The formula needed for this *future value* program is: *future value = present value * (1 + interest rate) ^ years*

   where the present value = $10,000, the interest rate is variable, and the years = 10. (This problem assumes that interest is compounded annually.)

   You may prefer to use the FV (future value) function built in to Visual Basic rather than the above formula. Information on this function can be obtained using the Help facility. In calculating the future value, construct a form similar to that shown in Figure 3–24.

6. Create an application that permits a user to compare the cost of ordering equipment via mail order or buying the equipment locally. It is assumed that the local delivery entails no delivery charge, but a sales tax of 6% is charged, whereas the mail order has no sales tax, but requires a $100 shipping and handling charge. Using your application, fill out the following table:

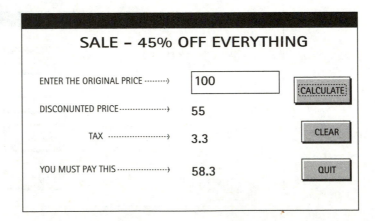

Figure 3–23   *Suggested Form for Project 4*

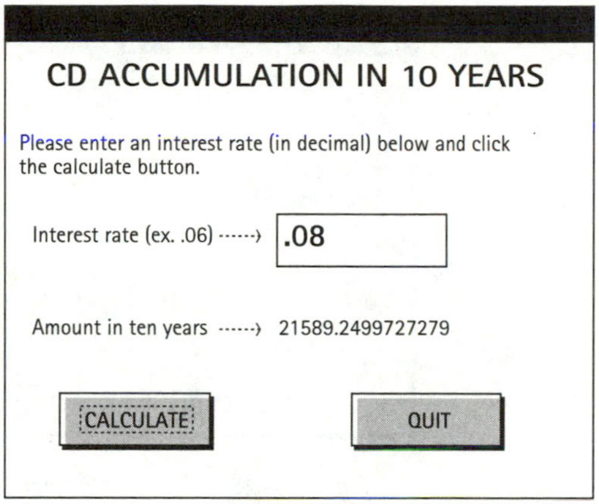

CD ACCUMULATION IN 10 YEARS

Please enter an interest rate (in decimal) below and click the calculate button.

Interest rate (ex. .06) ·······⟶   .08

Amount in ten years ·······⟶   21589.2499727279

| CALCULATE | | QUIT |

Figure 3–24   *Form for Project 5*

Base Item Cost	Total Mail Order Cost	Total Local Order Cost
$ 500		
$1000		
$1500		
$2000		
$2500		
$3000		
$3500		
$4000		
$4500		
$5000		

Note: The following Motel 8 project is used in subsequent End-of-Chapter Programming Projects. You will be required to modify and enhance your solution to this project as new Visual Basic capabilities are introduced in subsequent chapters.

7. **The Motel 8 Project:** A night's stay at Motel 8 costs $30 per adult and $10 per child. There is no discount for a multiple night stay. Additionally, there is a 5% state and local tax that is computed on the sum of the nightly charges. Figure 3–25 shows the form to be used for Project 7.

   Requirements: When the user clicks the Calc button, your program should calculate and display the total charge. Clicking the New button should blank all

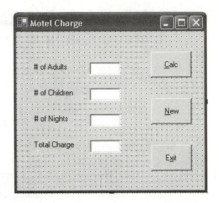

Figure 3–25   *Form for Project 7*

text boxes and give the focus to the # of adults text box. The Exit button should end the program. Additionally:

Ensure that the tab sequence is txtAdults, txtChildren, txtNights, btnCalc, btnNew, and btnExit.

Use the VAL function to convert input in text boxes to numeric values.

In the Declaration section of your program, declare variables to hold values of # of adults, # of children, # of nights (all Integer variables), and total charge (a Currency variable).

Object	Property	Setting
Form	Name	frmMotelCharge
	Text	Room Charge
Label	Name	lblAdults
	Text	# of Adults
TextBox	Name	txtAdults
	Text	(blank)
Label	Name	lblChildren
	Text	# of Children
TextBox	Name	txtChildren
	Text	(blank)
Label	Name	lblNights
	Text	# of Nights
TextBox	Name	txtNights
	Text	(blank)
Label	Name	lblTotCharge
	Text	Total Charge
TextBox	Name	txtTotCharge
	Text	(blank)
	TabStop	False

Object	Property	Setting
Button	Name	btnCalc
	Text	&Calc
Button	Name	btnNew
	Text	&New
Button	Name	btnExit
	Text	E&xit

Note: The following Local Car Rental Company project is used in subsequent end-of-chapter Programming Projects. You will be required to modify and enhance your solution to this project as new Visual Basic capabilities are introduced in subsequent chapters.

8. The Local Car Rental Company rents cars for $29.95 per day with unlimited mileage. There is a refueling fee of $12.95, regardless of what the level of fuel is when the car is returned. Write a program that will permit the user to input the customer's first and last names and the number of days that the car was rented. The program should compute the total charge for the car rental. Figure 3–26 shows the form to be used for Project 8.

Requirements: When the user clicks the Calc button, your program should calculate and display the total charge. Clicking the New button should blank all text boxes and give the focus to the first name text box. The Exit button should end the program. Additionally:

Ensure that the tab sequence is txtFirstName, txtLastName, txtDays, btnCalc, btnNew, and btnExit.

Use the Val function to convert input in the # of Days text box to an integer numerical value.

Declare variables to hold values of # of days and total charge in the Declaration section of the program.

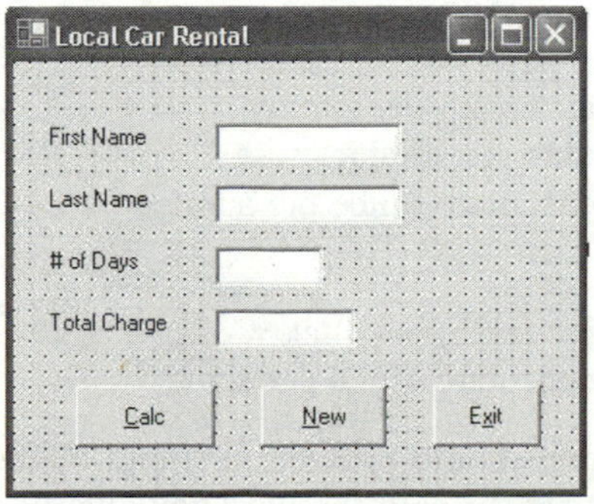

Figure 3–26 *Form for Project 8*

Object	Property	Setting
Form	Name	frmCarRental
	Text	Local Car Rental Company
Label	Name	lblFirstName
	Text	First Name
TextBox	Name	txtFirstName
	Text	(blank)
Label	Name	lblLastName
	Text	Last Name
TextBox	Name	txtLastName
	Text	(blank)
Label	Name	lblDays
	Text	# of Days
TextBox	Name	txtDays
	Text	(blank)
Label	Name	lblTotCharge
	Text	Total Charge
TextBox	Name	txtTotCharge
	Text	(blank)
	TabStop	False
Button	Name	btnCalc
	Text	&Calc
Button	Name	btnNew
	Text	&New
Button	Name	btnExit
	Text	E&xit

9. The LoCal Ice Cream Shoppe has asked you to write a program that will calculate the quantities of ice cream, nuts, and chocolate sauce they will probably need on the next day based on an estimate of the next day's sales. The following is a list of the quantities used in their sundaes and shakes (their only products).

Sundaes:
Ounces of ice cream per sundae   7
Ounces of nuts per sundae   1
Ounces of chocolate sauce per sundae   2

Shakes:
Ounces of ice cream per shake   12
Ounces of chocolate sauce per shake   1

Your program should provide for input of the estimated amount of sundaes and shakes that will be sold the next day and display the quantities needed. The out-

Figure 3–27   *Form for Project 9*

put list should display the amount of ice cream in gallons, nuts in pounds, and sauce in quarts. Figure 3–27 shows the form to be used for Project 9.

Object	Property	Setting
Form	Name	frmIceCream
	Text	LoCal Ice Cream Shoppe
Label	Name	lblSundaes
	Text	Sundae Estimate
TextBox	Name	txtSundaes
	Text	(blank)
Label	Name	lblShakes
	Text	Shake Estimate
TextBox	Name	txtShakes
	Text	(blank)
Label	Name	lblGalIcecream
	Text	Gallons of Ice Cream
TextBox	Name	txtGalIceCream
	Text	(blank)
Label	Name	lblNuts
	Text	Pounds of Nuts
TextBox	Name	txtLbsNuts
	Text	(blank)
Label	Name	lblChocolate
	Text	Quarts of Chocolate Sauce
TextBox	Name	txtQtsChocolate
	Text	(blank)

Button	Name	btnCalc
	Text	&Calc
Button	Name	btnNew
	Text	&New
Button	Name	btnQuit
	Text	&Quit

10. Create an application that permits a user to determine how much an item depreciates over a five-year time span using a straight-line, declining balance, and sum of the years' digits depreciation methods. The application should allow the user to:

a. Input the item's original cost and its salvage value at the end of 5 years.

b. Enter the depreciation year of interest, which should be an integer from 1 to 5.

c. Exit the program.

The required formulas are as follows:

Yearly straight line depreciation = (cost − salvage value)/5

Double declining depreciation = .4 * (cost − previous years depreciation)

Sum of the years digits depreciation = (6 − year)/15 * cost

Use a form of your own choosing for this application.

Controlling Input and Output

Goals

In previous chapters we explored how data is stored and processed using variables and assignment statements. In this chapter, we complete this exploration by presenting additional input, output, and processing capabilities. On the input side, we show how both the InputBox function and TextBox control can be used to obtain data from a user while an application is executing. On the output side, we show how numerical data can be displayed in a text box and formatted using the various Format functions.

4.1 Interactive User Input

Data for applications that are going to be executed only once may be included directly in the appropriate procedure. For example, if we want to multiply the numbers 30.5 and 0.06, we could use the Event Procedure 4–1.

Event Procedure 4–1

```
Private Sub frmMain_Click(ByVal sender As Object, _
    ByVal e As System.EventArgs) Handles MyBase.Click
  Dim num1, num2, product As Single
  num1 = 30.5
  num2 = 0.06
  product = num1 * num2
  txtDisplay.Text = num1 & " times " & num2 & " is " & product
End Sub
```

The output displayed by Event Procedure 4–1 is

```
30.5 times 0.06 is 1.83
```

Event Procedure 4–1 can be shortened to the simpler Event Procedure 4–2. However, both procedures suffer from the same basic problem: they must be rewritten in order to multiply other numbers. Neither procedure allows the user to substitute different values in the multiplication operation.

Event Procedure 4–2

```
Private Sub frmMain_Click(ByVal sender As Object, _
    ByVal e As System.EventArgs) Handles MyBase.Click
  txtDisplay.Text = "30.5 times 0.06 is " & 30.5 * 0.06
End Sub
```

Except for the programming practice they provide, event procedures that perform a single, simple calculation are clearly not very useful. After all, it is simpler to use a calculator to multiply two numbers than to enter and run either Event Procedure 4–1 or 4–2.

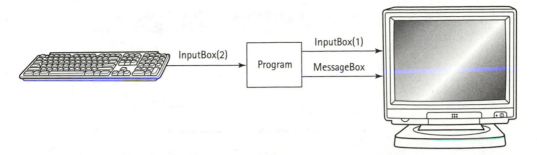

Figure 4–1   *An InputBox Dialog and a MessageBox.Show Dialog*

This section outlines two commonly used techniques for permitting a user to enter data into an executing Visual Basic application by using the InputBox intrinsic function and the TextBox control.

The InputBox Intrinsic Function

The `InputBox` intrinsic function provides a simple means for a user to enter a single input into a procedure while it is executing. A call to this function creates a dialog box that permits a user to enter a string. The entered string, which frequently is converted to either an integer or a floating-point number, is then stored directly in a variable. Figure 4–1 shows the relationship between an InputBox function used for entering string data, and a `MessageBox.Show` statement used for displaying string data. (Recall from Section 2.3 that a dialog is any box requiring the user to supply additional information to complete a task.)

The most commonly used syntax for calling the `InputBox` function is

```
InputBox(prompt, title, default)
```

where *prompt* is a required string and both *title* and *default*, which are also strings, are optional. If a title string is used, it is displayed in the title bar of the dialog box; otherwise, the name of the project is placed in the title bar. If a default string is provided, it is placed within the input area of the dialog box. A *prompt* is a message telling a user that input is required. The prompt, which is always required, is displayed as a string within the input dialog box. For example, the second statement of

```
Dim stringinput As String
stringinput = InputBox("Enter a value", "Input Dialog")
```

calls the `InputBox` function with the arguments "`Enter a value`", which is the prompt, "`Input Dialog`", which is the title, and no default argument. When this statement is executed, the input dialog box shown in Figure 4–2 is displayed.

Figure 4–2 *A Sample InputBox Dialog*

Further examples of the `InputBox` function are:

```
stringinput = InputBox("Enter a Value")
stringinput = InputBox("Enter a Value", "Sample", "5")
stringinput = InputBox("Enter a Value",, "10")
number = Val(InputBox("Enter a number between 1 and 10"))
```

In the first three examples, the prompt "Enter a Value" is displayed. In both the first and third examples, the title bar is used to display the application's name, while in the second example, the title bar displays "Sample". The second and third examples provide default string values of 5 and 10 in the text input area. Note that in the third example, where a default value is provided with no explicit title, the title argument is left blank but is separated from both the prompt and the default value by a comma. The last example uses the `Val` function to convert the string result to a numeric variable.

Once an input dialog box is displayed, the keyboard is continuously scanned for data. As keys are pressed, the `InputBox` function displays the data within the input area of the dialog. When either the Enter key is pressed or one of the two buttons in the box is clicked, input stops and the entered text is stored in the variable on the left side of the assignment statement. The procedure then continues execution with the next statement after the call to InputBox.

Program 4–1 illustrates using an `InputBox` function within the context of a complete application. The interface for this project is shown in Figure 4–3. As illustrated, the GUI consists of two buttons and a text box. Table 4–1 shows the objects and properties for Program 4–1.

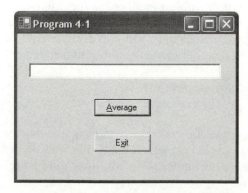

Figure 4–3 *Program 4–1's Interface*

Table 4–1   The Properties Table for Program 4–1

Object	Property	Setting
Form	Name	frmMain
	Text	Program 4–1
TextBox	Name	txtDisplay
	Text	(blank)
	TabStop	False
Button	Name	btnInput
	Text	&Average
Button	Name	btnExit
	Text	E&xit

For this application, the only procedure is the button Click event, which is listed in Program 4–1's Event Code. Note the use of the `Val` function to convert the string returned from InputBox to a numeric value.

Program 4–1's Event Code

```
Private Sub btnInput_Click(ByVal sender As System.Object, _
    ByVal e As System.EventArgs) Handles btnInput.Click
  Dim num1, num2, average As Single

  num1 = Val(InputBox("Enter a number", "Input Dialog", "0"))
  num2 = Val(InputBox("Great! Now enter another number", _
    "Input Dialog", "0"))
  average = (num1 + num2) / 2
  txtDisplay.Text = "The average of " & num1 & " and " & num2 & " is " & _
    average
End Sub
```

The first input dialog box displayed by Program 4–1's event procedure is shown in Figure 4–4. The number 15 displayed in the input area of the dialog box is the value that was entered from the keyboard. Before this value is entered, the dialog displays a 0, which is the default provided in the InputBox function call.

Note that the dialog box prompt tells the user to enter a number. After this dialog box is displayed, the `InputBox` function puts the application into a temporary paused state for as long as it takes the user to type in a value. The user signals to the `InputBox` function that the data entry is finished by clicking one of the buttons. If the user clicks the OK button (or presses the Enter key when this button is in focus), the entered value is stored in the variable on the left side of the assignment statement, in this case `num1`, and the application is taken out of its pause. Program execution then proceeds with the next statement, which in Program 4–1's event procedure is another call to an `InputBox` function. The second `InputBox` dialog and the data entered in response to it are shown in Figure 4–5.

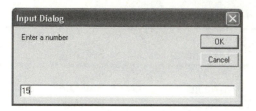

Figure 4–4 *The First Dialog after Data is Entered*

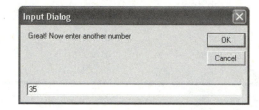

Figure 4–5 *The Second InputBox Dialog after Data is Entered*

While the second dialog is displayed, the application is again put into a temporary waiting state while the user types a second value. This second number is stored in the variable num2. Based on these input values, the output produced by Program 4-1 is shown in Figure 4-6.

We now explain why a default value of 0 was used for each InputBox dialog. The reason touches on a much broader issue of constant concern to all good programmers.

A default value will handle the case where a user presses the OK button accidentally before any value is entered. Remember that the InputBox function actually accepts and returns a string, which allows a user to type in any text. Using a string as input provides a safety precaution because the programmer has no control over what a user might happen to enter. Accepting the input as a string ensures that whatever is typed will be accepted initially. After the data is entered, however, the programmer should

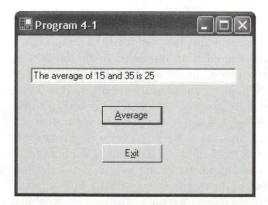

Figure 4–6 *A Sample Output Produced by Program 4-1*

validate the entered data. For example, if a number is required, the procedure should check that only digits, and possibly one decimal point, have been entered. Whenever invalid data is detected, an error message should be displayed and the user should be given an opportunity to reenter valid data. Validating user input requires the selection statements presented in Chapter 5, so for now we can provide only minimal protection against invalid data entry. This is the reason for the default value.

If no default is provided and a user accidentally clicks the OK button before any data is entered, the string returned from the dialog will contain no characters at all. Now note that in Program 4–1's event procedure, the first assignment statement stores the entered and returned value in the variable num1, which is declared as a Single. In executing this assignment, if the Val function were not used, Visual Basic would automatically convert the returned string, if possible, into a single precision number before storing it in num1. (If this is unfamiliar to you, refer to the type Conversions presented in Section 3.3). Thus, if the user enters only digits and possibly a single decimal point into the input dialog, the conversion can be made. If an entered string cannot be converted, the error message *Type mismatch* is displayed. Because an empty string has no valid numerical value, clicking the OK button when no default or value has been entered would also cause a *Type mismatch* error. Providing a zero default prevents this error from occurring. However, it is strongly recommended that the Val function be used to convert the result to a number because it is being assigned to a numeric variable. Note also that if the user clicks the Cancel or Close button, the InputBox function returns an empty string.

Before leaving Program 4–1's event procedure, note the parentheses in the following statement:

```
average = (num1 + num2) / 2
```

The parentheses here are required to produce a correct calculation. Without these parentheses, the only number that would be divided by two is the value in num2 (because division has a higher precedence than addition). Refer back to Chapter 3 for a discussion on operator precedence.

The TextBox Control Reconsidered

The most versatile and commonly used object for interactive input is the TextBox control. This control permits the user to enter a string, which is then stored as the value for the text box's Text property. A TextBox control for input is almost always used in conjunction with a Label control, where the label acts as a prompt and the text box provides the actual means for the user to input data. For example, consider the interface shown in Figure 4–7. Here the label is Enter a Fahrenheit Temperature: and the text box provides an input area.

Creating a label is simple; you select the Label control from the toolbox and set its Text property. By definition, a Label control is a read-only control—the user cannot alter it while the programming is executing.

The text box provides the actual means for a user to enter data while a program is executing. All data entered in the text box is assumed by Visual Basic to be string data. This means that if numbers are to be input, the entered string must be converted to

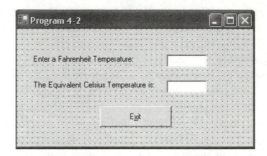

Figure 4–7   *Program 4–2's User Interface*

numerical data either explicitly or implicitly. It also means that some data validation is typically required to ensure that a user does not enter data that will cause the application to crash.

For example, consider the interface for Program 4–2 that is shown in Figure 4–7, where the user is prompted to enter a temperature in degrees Fahrenheit.

Once a user enters a Fahrenheit temperature, the program will compute the corresponding temperature in degrees Celsius and display the calculated value in the output text box. The properties for Program 4–2 are listed in Table 4–2.

Table 4–2   Program 4–2's Property Table

Object	Property	Setting
Form	Name	frmMain
	Text	Program 4–2
Label	Name	lblFahr
	Text	Enter a Fahrenheit Temperature:
	AutoSize	True
TextBox	Name	txtFahr
	Text	(blank)
Label	Name	lblCelsius
	Text	The Equivalent Celsius Temperature is:
	AutoSize	True
TextBox	Name	txtCelsius
	Text	(blank)
Button	Name	btnExit
	Text	E&xit

Now consider Program 4–2's event code, paying particular attention to the text box Enter and Leave functions, because these are two of the three events primarily used in processing text box data:

Program 4–2's Event Code

```
Private Sub txtFahr_Enter(ByVal sender As Object, ByVal e As _
    System.EventArgs) Handles txtFahr.Enter
  txtCelsius.Text = ""
End Sub

Private Sub txtFahr_Leave(ByVal sender As Object, ByVal e As _
    System.EventArgs) Handles txtFahr.Leave
  Dim celsius As Single

  celsius = 5 / 9 * (Val(txtFahr.Text) - 32)
  txtCelsius.Text = celsius
End Sub

Private Sub btnExit_Click(ByVal sender As System.Object, ByVal e As _
    System.EventArgs) Handles btnExit.Click
  Beep()
  End
End Sub
```

The **Enter** event is triggered when an object receives focus and is used to perform any pre-processing associated with a user control. In Program 4–2, we use the text box's **Enter** event to clear the output text box of any data prior to allowing a user to enter a new Fahrenheit temperature. This is done to ensure that a previously calculated Celsius temperature does not appear while the user is typing in new data.

The actual calculation and display of a Celsius temperature is performed by the text box's **Leave** event. This event is triggered when the text box loses focus, which occurs when the user signals completion of data entry either by pressing the TAB key or clicking on another control. The actual computation in the **Leave** event consists of the single calculation celsius = (5 / 9) * (Val(txtFahr.Text) - 32), which converts a Fahrenheit temperature to its Celsius equivalent. Figure 4–8 illustrates a completed run using Program 4–2. Note that the focus in this figure is on the E<u>x</u>it button.

Before leaving Program 4–2, take a closer look at the assignment statement used to calculate a Celsius value and notice the term Val(txtFahr.Text). The term txtFahr.Text accesses the data value entered in the text box and stored in its Text property, which is a string value. Using this string as an argument to the Val function explicitly converts the string into a numerical value. Specifically, the Val function

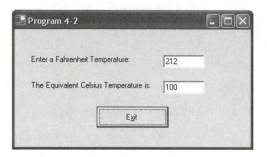

Figure 4–8 *A Sample Run Using Program 4–2*

converts string data into numerical data for as many characters in the string as can be recognized as a number (see Table 3–9). Although the `Val` function will recognize a period as a decimal point, it stops the conversion at the first character that it cannot recognize as part of a number. For example, if the user enters the data 212abc, the `Val` function returns the number 212. The function also returns a numerical value of zero if the string does not begin with either a digit or a decimal point.

The purpose of using the `Val` function is that it prevents the program from crashing if the user types in a nonnumeric input, such as the characters abc. For example, without the `Val` function the assignment statement would appear as:

```
celsius = (5 / 9) * (txtFahr.Text - 32)
```

This statement operates correctly when a user enters any string that can be considered to be a number, such as 212, because the string is automatically converted to a numeric value within the expression (`txtFahr.Text - 32`). However, if a user inadvertently types in a string such as 212a, the program stops and produces the message "`Cast from string '212a' to type 'Double' is not valid`," because the entered string cannot be converted into a numerical value. Using the `Val` function ensures that this error will not occur, because the string is always converted to a numerical value prior to being processed as part of the calculation.

A First Look at User–Input Validation

Validating user input and ensuring that a program does not crash as a result of unexpected input are best practices that ensure a well-constructed program. Programs that respond effectively to unexpected user input are referred to as "bullet-proof" programs, and one of your jobs as a programmer is to produce this type of program.

Program 4–2 touches on the topic of validating user input by employing one of the more commonly used techniques associated with text box input. This is to explicitly convert string data to numerical data, using the `Val` function when a numerical value is expected. The conversion is done in the **Leave** event code, immediately after the user has finished using the text box. Clearly, this is an ideal place to verify and validate data. This is one of the primary uses of the **Leave** event—to verify and validate data, before any computation is made. Visual Basic also provides the events **Validating** and **Validated**. These could be used instead of **Enter** and **Leave** but will not be discussed.

Another important type of validation occurs directly as the user is entering data. Typically, this type of validation is made using the **KeyPress** and **KeyDown** events. Each of these events returns the key just pressed and permits action to be taken before the key's value is accepted into the input string. The **KeyDown** event occurs before the **KeyPress** event, and the **KeyUp** event occurs when the user releases the key. The difference between these events is the amount of information returned. The **KeyPress** event receives only the ANSI value of a character key as an argument, while the **KeyDown** event can detect and process the function, cursor, and shift keys in addition to the printable character keys. However, this type of validation is based on selecting desired characters and rejecting others from the entered string. The methods for performing such selections are described in the next chapter.

Exercises 4.1

1. Write assignment statements that store the returned value from an input box dialog in a variable named test for the following input dialog specifications. Because the InputBox function returns a string, use a conversion function (such as Val), where necessary:

   a. `prompt = Enter a grade`
      `title = Input dialog`
      `default = 0`

   b. `prompt = Enter a temperature`
      `title = Data Analysis`
      `default = 98.6`

   c. `prompt = Enter an interest rate`
      `title = Yield Analysis`
      `default = 0`

   d. `prompt = Enter a name`
      `the title should be the application's name`
      `no default value`

   e. `prompt = Enter a price`
      `the title should be the application's name`
      `default = 12.50`

2. Determine what value is placed in the variable num1 in Program 4.1's event procedure if the Cancel button on the input dialog box is clicked.

3. a. By hand, write a Visual Basic event procedure named btnTax_Click that can be used to display the following prompt in an input dialog box:

   `Enter the amount of the bill:`

After accepting a value for the amount of the bill, your procedure should calculate the sales tax, assuming a tax rate of 6 percent. The display of the sales tax as a dollar amount should appear in a text box named txtDisplay when a button is clicked. A second button should be provided to terminate the application.

b. Include the event procedure written for Exercise 3b in a working program. For testing purposes, verify your program using an initial amount of $36.00. After manually checking that the result produced by your program is correct, use your program to complete the following table:

Amount (dollars)	Sales Tax (dollars)
36.00	
40.00	
52.60	
87.95	
125.00	
182.93	

4. a. Write a Visual Basic program that can be used to convert Celsius temperatures to their equivalent Fahrenheit values. Use a label to display the following prompt:

`Enter the temperature in degrees Celsius:`

After accepting a value entered from the keyboard into a text box, the program should convert the entered temperature to degrees Fahrenheit, using the equation *Fahrenheit = (9.0 / 5.0) * Celsius + 32.0*. The program should then display the temperature in degrees Fahrenheit, in a clearly labeled text box named txtDisplay. A button should be provided to terminate the application.

b. Verify your program by first calculating the Fahrenheit equivalent of the following test data by hand, and then using your program to see if it produces the correct results.

`Test data set 1: 0 degrees Celsius.`

`Test data set 2: 50 degrees Celsius`

`Test data set 3: 100 degrees Celsius`

When you are sure your procedure is working correctly, use it to complete the following table:

Celsius	Fahrenheit
45	
50	
55	
60	
65	
70	

5. Write and execute a Visual Basic program that displays the following prompts, using two Label controls:

```
Enter the length of the office:

Enter the width of the office:
```

Have your program accept the user input in two text boxes. When a button is clicked, your program should calculate the area of the office and display the area in a text box. This display should be cleared whenever the input text boxes receive the focus. A second button should be provided to terminate the application. Verify your procedure using the following test data:

```
Test data set 1: length = 12.5, width = 10

Test data set 2: length = 12.4, width = 0

Test data set 3: length = 0, width = 10
```

6. a. Write and execute a Visual Basic program that displays the following prompts and uses two text boxes to receive the input data.

```
Enter the miles driven:

Enter the gallons of gas used:
```

The program should calculate and display the miles per gallon in a text box when a button is clicked. Use the equation *miles per gallon = miles / gallons used*. The display should be cleared whenever one of the text boxes gets the focus. A second button should be provided to terminate the application. Verify your procedure using the following test data:

```
Test data set 1: Miles = 276, Gas = 10 gallons.

Test data set 2: Miles = 200, Gas = 15.5 gallons.
```

b. When you have completed your verification, use your procedure to complete the following table:

Miles Driven	Gallons Used	MPG
250	16.00	
275	18.00	
312	19.54	
296	17.39	

c. For the procedure written for Exercise 6a, determine how many verification runs are required to ensure that the procedure is working correctly. Give a reason supporting your answer.

7. Write a Visual Basic Program that displays the following prompts:

```
Enter the length of the swimming pool:

Enter the width of the swimming pool:

Enter the average depth of the swimming pool:
```

Have your program accept the user input in three text boxes. When a button is clicked, your program should calculate the volume of the swimming pool and display the volume in a text box. This display should be cleared whenever the input text box receives focus. Provide a second button to terminate the application. When calculating the volume, use the equation

volume = length * width * average depth

8. a. Write and execute a Visual Basic program that provides three text boxes for the input of three user input numbers. There should be a single label prompt that tells the user to enter three numbers in the boxes. When the user clicks a button, the program should calculate the average of the numbers and then display the average in a clearly labeled text box. The displayed value should be cleared whenever one of the text boxes receives focus. Provide a second button to terminate the application. Verify your procedure using the following test data:

   Test data set 1: 100, 100, 100

   Test data set 2: 100, 50, 0

   b. When you have completed your verification, use your program to complete the following table:

Numbers	Average
92, 98, 79, 85	
86, 84, 75, 86	
63, 85, 74, 82	

9. Program 4–1 prompts the user to input two numbers, where the first value entered is stored in `num1` and the second value is stored in `num2`. Using this procedure as a starting point, rewrite the procedure so that it swaps the values stored in the two variables.

10. Write a Visual Basic program that prompts the user to type in an integer number. Have your procedure accept the number as an integer and immediately display the integer. Run your procedure three times. The first time you run the procedure, enter a valid integer number; the second time, enter a floating point number; and the third time, enter the string "`Help`". Using the output display, see what numbers your procedure actually accepted from the data you entered.

11. Repeat Exercise 10, but have your procedure declare the variable used to store the number as a single precision floating point variable. Run the procedure three times. The first time, enter an integer; the second time, enter a decimal number with less than fourteen decimal places; the third time, enter a number having more than fourteen decimal places; and the fourth time, enter the string "`Oops`". Using the output display, keep track of what number your procedure actually accepted from the data you typed in. What happened, if anything, and why?

12. a. Why most successful applications procedures contain extensive data input validity checks? (*Hint:* Review Exercises 10 and 11.)

    b. What do you think is the difference between a data type check and a data reasonableness check?

c. Assume that a procedure asks the user to enter the speed and acceleration of a car. What are some checks that could be made on the data entered?

4.2 Formatted Output

Although it is essential that an application display correct results, it is also important that it present these results attractively. Most applications are judged on their ease of data entry and the style and presentation of their output. For example, displaying a monetary result as 1.897256 is not in keeping with accepted report conventions. The display should be either $1.90 or $1.89, depending on whether rounding or truncation is used.

Formatting Functions

Visual Basic provides several intrinsic functions that perform formatting. These functions all return a string. Note that you can change the default format for all these functions by changing your computer's regional settings. Table 4–3 lists the format functions and includes a description of each.

Formatting Currency The `FormatCurrency` function returns a string of characters formatted as dollars and cents with a dollar sign, commas, and two digits to the right of the decimal point.

This function takes a number of optional arguments. The general form of the function call is:

```
FormatCurrency (Numerical Expression [, NumberofDecimalPositions
[,Include Leading Digit,
[, UseParensForNegative
[,GroupingForDigits]]]])
```

Table 4–3 Format Functions

Name	Description
FormatCurrency	Returns an expression formatted as a currency value using a currency symbol such as dollars and cents.
FormatNumber	Returns an expression formatted as a number including commas and a decimal point.
FormatPercent	Returns an expression formatted as a percentage with a trailing percent character.
FormatDateTime	Returns an expression formatted as a date or time or both.

The only required argument is the number you want to format, which is the first argument. It may also be useful to use the second argument, which specifies the number of Decimal Positions desired. For more information on the other arguments, see Visual Basic's Help.

The following are examples of calls to `FormatCurrency` and the return value of each.

```
FormatCurrency (1234.89)        $1,234.89
FormatCurrency (1234.89,2)      $1,234.89
FormatCurrency (1234.89,0)      $1,235
FormatCurrency (1234.896,2)     $1,234.90
```

Formatting Numbers   The `FormatNumber` function is similar to the `FormatCurrency` function. By default, it returns a string containing a number formatted to two decimal places with commas included. The general form of the function call is:

```
FormatNumber (Numerical Expression [, NumberofDecimalPositions
[,Include Leading Digit,
[, UseParensForNegative
[,GroupingForDigits]]]])
```

The following are examples of calls to `FormatNumber` and the return value of each.

```
FormatNumber (1234.89)          1,234.89
FormatNumber (1234.89,2)        1,234.89
FormatNumber (1234.89,0)        1,235
FormatNumber (1234.896,2)       1,234.90
FormatNumber (1234.89653,3)     1,234.897
```

Formatting Numbers as Percents   The `FormatPercent` function returns a string containing a number formatted as a percent. The function multiplies the argument by 100, adds a percent sign, and rounds it to two decimal places. The general form of the function call is:

```
FormatPercent (Numerical Expression [, NumberofDecimalPositions
[,Include Leading Digit,
[, UseParensForNegative
[,GroupingForDigits]]]])
```

The following are examples of calls to `FormatPercent` and the return value of each.

```
FormatPercent(.58)          58.00%
FormatPercent(.58, 1)       58.0%
FormatPercent(.5868)        58.68%
FormatPercent(.58687)       58.69%
FormatPercent(.58687,0)     59%
```

Table 4-4   Values of the *NamedFormat* argument

Value	Description
DateFormat.GeneralDate	If the first argument contains a date, it formats it as a ShortDate. If there is a time part, it formats it the same way as a LongTime. If the *NamedFormat* argument is omitted, DateFormat.GeneralDate is the default. An example is "2/7/2004 8:25:14 AM".
DateFormat.LongDate	Formats a date in long format, which contains the day of the week, month, day, and year. The time is not reported. An example is "Friday, February 07, 2004".
DateFormat.ShortDate	Formats a date in short format, which contains the month, day and year. An example is "2/7/2004".
DateFormat.LongTime	Formats a time in long format, which contains the hour, minutes, seconds, and an AM/PM indicator. The date is not reported. An example is "8:25:14 AM".
DateFormat.ShortTime	Formats a time in short format, which contains two digits for the hours and two digits for the minutes. The time is given in 24 hour format and the date is not reported. An example is "13:35".

Formatting Dates and Times   The FormatDateTime function takes a Date data type as an argument and formats it as a date and/or time. The values returned depend on the regional settings on your computer. The formats below are based on U.S. settings. The general form of the function call is:

```
FormatDateTime (Expression[, NamedFormat])
```

The values of the *NamedFormat* argument are shown in Table 4-4.

Exercises 4.2

1. Determine and write out the display produced by the following statements:

```
FormatNumber (5,2)
FormatNumber (5)
FormatNumber (56829,1)
FormatNumber (5.26)
FormatNumber (5.267,2)
FormatNumber (53.264,0)
```

2. Write out the display produced by the following statements:

```
FormatPercent (126.27,0)
FormatPercent (.825)
FormatPercent (1.756,1)
```

3. Write out the display produced by the following statements:

```
FormatCurrency (26.27, 0)
FormatCurrency (682.3)
FormatCurrency (1.968, 2)
FormatCurrency (26.27 + 682.3 + 1.968)
```

4.3 Printer Output[1]

Visual Basic provides a powerful mechanism for generating printed output. Unfortunately the power comes at the expense of additional complexity. What follows are the steps needed to generate printed output. In order not to get bogged down, we will forgo a detailed explanation of every step of this process. The text and examples will provide you with sufficient understanding to generate output for the assignments in the remainder of the book.

Microsoft Windows provides a set of interfaces, known as the Graphical Device Interface (GDI), that displays information on screens and printers. GDI+ is the latest version of these interfaces that allows application programmers to display information on a screen or printer without having to be concerned about the details of a particular display device. The programming interfaces that follow are for printing, such as DrawString, are part of the System.Drawing namespace of GDI+.

In order to generate printed output, Visual Basic requires that we add a **PrintDocument** control to a project. This control is located at the bottom of the list of controls as shown in Figure 4–9. When you drag this control onto the form (or double-click using the left mouse button) does not remain on the form (Figure 4–10). Instead, it is placed in an area below the form called the component tray. This area is provided for controls, like PrintDocument, that are not displayed during the execution of the program.

The next step is to activate printing using a button that will generate output. The code to cause the printing is

```
PrintDocument1.Print()
```

where PrintDocument1 is the Printer control and Print is a method to activate printing.

The final step is to add code that will actually have the details of what we wish to print out. This code will be associated with a PrintDocument event. Therefore we will

---

[1]Sections 4.3 and 4.4 deal with printing in Visual Basic; because this is a complex topic, the instructor may choose to delay this topic until a later time.

Figure 4–9   *PrintDocument Control*

return to the design view and double-click the PrintDocument control in the component tray. This will bring us to the PrintPage event code section. The statement that prints text is as follows:

```
e.Graphics.DrawString("Hello World", fntArial, Brushes.Black, x, y)
```

Let's break down this statement. The `e.Graphic.DrawString` is one method used to perform printing.[2] It needs the following five parameters:

1. the text to print out. (In this case, the text is "Hello World".)

2. a font. (We need to create a variable, fntArial, which will hold the specifications of the font.)

3. a color in which to print. (For now we will always use `Brushes.Black`. To print in a different color, simply change Black to another color that is supported.)

---

[2]*e* is a parameter in an event procedure declaration that may contain values passed by the object that triggered the event. The use of the *e* parameter is different for different events.

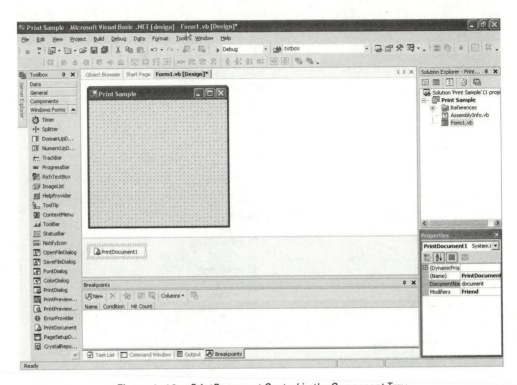

Figure 4–10 *PrintDocument Control in the Component Tray*

4. an *x* or horizontal coordinate on the page to indicate where to start printing. (We will use a variable, *x*, to indicate this.)

5. a *y* or vertical coordinate on the page to to indicate where to start printing. (We will use a variable, *y*, to indicate this.)

The last step is to create and initialize the three variables fntArial, *x*, and *y*. We will look at each one individually.

To create the fntArial variable, use the following statement:

```
Dim fntArial As New Font("Arial", 10)
```

This statement creates an instance of a Font object and initializes it to an Arial 10-point font. Instead of Arial, we could have substituted any supported font and set the point size to any supported value.

The creation of the *x* and *y* variables is accomplished by means of the following three statements:

```
Dim x, y As Single

x = e.MarginBounds.Left
y = e.MarginBounds.Top
```

The statements `e.MarginBounds.Left` and `e.MarginBounds.Top` are the coordinates of the top left of the page. In every program that we print, we will initialize x and y to these coordinates.

Putting these statements all together, we get the following:

```
Dim fntArial As New Font("Arial", 10)
Dim x, y As Single

x = e.MarginBounds.Left
y = e.MarginBounds.Top

e.Graphics.DrawString("Hello World", fntArial, Brushes.Black, x, y)
```

To print additional lines, continue to use the e.Graphics.DrawString method for each line that will be printed. Unfortunately the y, or vertical, coordinate needs to be adjusted for each subsequent print. Specifically, the coordinate has to be adjusted by the height of a character of the selected font. The height of character printed can be retrieved using the GetHeight property of the font. So after each line is printed (using `e.Graphics.DrawString`), the following line must follow:

```
y = y + font.GetHeight
```

4.4 Focus on Program Design and Implementation: Formatting and Printer Output

Using this chapter's information on formatting and printer output, we can address two problems associated with the WalkIn form developed in the previous Focus section.[3] Figure 4–11 illustrates a sample completed order entry form for which the <u>C</u>alculate Order button was pressed. As shown, the calculated dollar amounts are not formatted in conventional currency notation. Also, at this stage in its development, the form's <u>P</u>rint button has no associated code. Both of these problems are corrected in this Focus section. It is also necessary to add a PrintDocument control to the WalkIn form. Note again that this control is only visible during design-time.

You can modify the text boxes' displayed dollar values by using the FormatCurrency function when displaying the values in the variables sTotal, sTaxes, and sFinal and assigning them to the Text property of the various output text boxes. Making these replacements in the <u>C</u>alculate Order button's **Click** event procedure and using the Val

---

[3]The Rotech application, as it exists at the start of this Focus section, can be found as the rotech3 project in the ROTECH3 folder on the http://computerscience.jbpub.com/bronsonvbnet website.

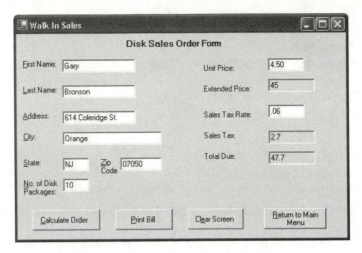

Figure 4–11   *A Filled-in WalkIn Order Form*

and CDec conversion functions to convert all text box data into numerical values, provides the following event code:

```
Private Sub btnCalculate_Click(ByVal sender As System.Object, ByVal e As _
    System.EventArgs) Handles btnCalculate.Click
  Dim sTotal, sTaxes, sFinal As Single

  txtTotal.Clear()
  txtTax.Clear()
  txtFinal.Clear()

  'Calculate and display new values
  sTotal = Val(txtQuantity.Text) * Cdec(txtPrice.Text)
  sTaxes = Val(txtTrate.Text) * sTotal
  sFinal = sTotal + sTaxes
  txtTotal.Text = FormatCurrency(sTotal)
  txtTax.Text = FormatCurrency(sTaxes)
  txtFinal.Text = FormatCurrency(sFinal)
End Sub
```

Figure 4–12 illustrates a sample output produced using this modified **Click** event code. As shown, each calculated amount is now formatted in conventional currency notation. Note that we also have modified the displayed unit price to show a dollar sign. Because a text box displays string data, all that was required for this was to set the Text property to the string $4.50 at design time. However, when this is done, the conversion of this string into an equivalent numerical value cannot be accomplished using the Val function. The reason for this is that the Val function stops reading a string at the first

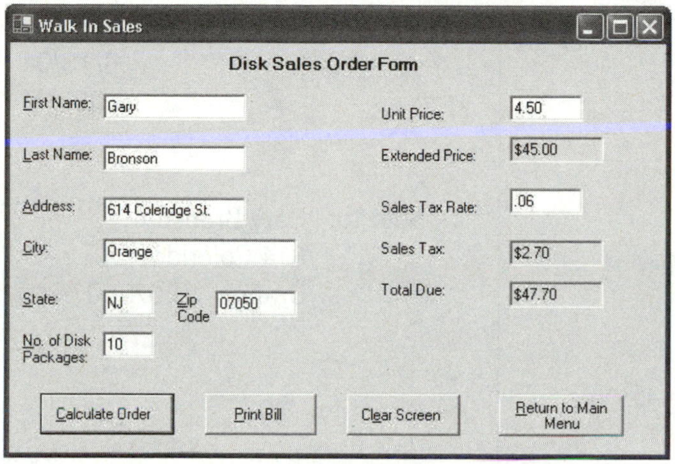

Figure 4–12 *Formatting the Calculated Dollar Amounts*

nonnumerical character, including both dollar signs and commas. Thus, the value of the expression Val ($4.50) is 0, not 4.50.

All that remains now is to add code to the Print button's **Click** event, so that a bill is printed when this button is pressed. In practice, the bill is printed either on a preprinted form or a blank piece of paper. The entire bill, including Rotech's name and address, is printed under control of the Print button's **Click** event. To illustrate the main points required for this event code, we will produce a simpler bill, a sample of which is shown in Figure 4–13.

As a practical matter, the Print button should also calculate the bill, because users would quickly tire of pressing the Calculate Order button before pressing the Print button each time something on the form changes.[4] Anticipating this, we will make the system easier to use by duplicating the Calculate Order button's calculate and display code and including it within the Print button's **Click** event code. If a customer only wants to know the final price, the user can press the Calculate Order button. However, to produce a bill, the Print button must be pressed. (It will not matter whether the Calculate Order button was or was not pressed first.) The required event code for the Print button is:

```
Private Sub btnPrint_Click(ByVal sender As System.Object, _
    ByVal e As System.EventArgs) Handles btnPrint.Click
  Dim sTotal, sTaxes, sFinal As Single

  txtTotal.Clear()
```

---

[4]Or, more likely, they would just press the Print button anyway, get a blank printed bill and complain that the system did not correctly compute the bill. At this point, after explaining the proper operation of the system, you would be asked to make the correction so that the Calculate button need not be pressed first. These are the types of situations that you should anticipate before the user brings them to your attention.

```
                                           6/15/04
                                           9:39 AM



                    Sold to:  Gary Bronson
                              614 Coleridge St.
                              Orange, NJ 07050



                    Quantity:  10
                    Unit Price:      $4.50
                    Total:           $45.00
                    Sales tax:       $2.70
                    Amount Due:      $47.50
```

Figure 4–13 *A Sample Printed Bill*

```
    txtTax.Clear()
    txtFinal.Clear()

    'Calculate and display new values
    sTotal = Val(txtQuantity.Text) * Cdec(txtPrice.Text)
    sTaxes = Val(txtTrate.Text) * sTotal
    sFinal = sTotal + sTaxes
    txtTotal.Text = FormatCurrency(sTotal)
    txtTax.Text = FormatCurrency(sTaxes)
    txtFinal.Text = FormatCurrency(sFinal)

    'Invoke Printing
    PrintDocument1.Print()
End Sub

Private Sub PrintDocument1_PrintPage(ByVal sender As System.Object, _
    ByVal e As System.Drawing.Printing.PrintPageEventArgs) _
    Handles PrintDocument1.PrintPage
```

```
Dim font As New Font("Courier New", 12)
Dim x, y As Single

x = e.MarginBounds.Left
y = e.MarginBounds.Top

e.Graphics.DrawString("", font, Brushes.Black, x, y)
y = y + font.GetHeight
e.Graphics.DrawString("", font, Brushes.Black, x, y)
y = y + font.GetHeight

e.Graphics.DrawString(Space(20) + FormatDateTime(Now, _
   DateFormat.ShortDate), font, Brushes.Black, x, y)
y = y + font.GetHeight
e.Graphics.DrawString(Space(20) + FormatDateTime(Now, _
   DateFormat.LongTime), font, Brushes.Black, x, y)
y = y + font.GetHeight

e.Graphics.DrawString("", font, Brushes.Black, x, y)
y = y + font.GetHeight
e.Graphics.DrawString("", font, Brushes.Black, x, y)
y = y + font.GetHeight

e.Graphics.DrawString("Sold to: " & txtFname.Text + _
   " " & txtLname.Text, font, Brushes.Black, x, y)
y = y + font.GetHeight
e.Graphics.DrawString(Space(9) & txtAddr.Text, font, _
   Brushes.Black, x, y)
y = y + font.GetHeight
e.Graphics.DrawString(Space(9) & txtCity.Text & " " _
   & txtState.Text & " " & txtZip.Text, font, Brushes.Black, x, y)
y = y + font.GetHeight

e.Graphics.DrawString("", font, Brushes.Black, x, y)
y = y + font.GetHeight
e.Graphics.DrawString("", font, Brushes.Black, x, y)
y = y + font.GetHeight
```

```
e.Graphics.DrawString("Quantity:" & Space(1) & txtQuantity.Text, _
   font, Brushes.Black, x, y)
y = y + font.GetHeight
e.Graphics.DrawString("Unit Price:" & Space(2) &
   FormatCurrency(txtPrice.Text), font, Brushes.Black, x, y)
y = y + font.GetHeight
e.Graphics.DrawString("Total:" & Space(6) & txtTotal.Text, _
   font, Brushes.Black, x, y)
y = y + font.GetHeight
e.Graphics.DrawString("Sales tax:" & Space(3) & txtTax.Text, _
   font, Brushes.Black, x, y)
y = y + font.GetHeight
e.Graphics.DrawString("Amount Due:" & Space(1) & txtFinal.Text, _
   font, Brushes.Black, x, y)
End Sub
```

In reviewing this event code, pay particular attention to the lines of code where the date and time are printed (because almost all printed forms require this type of information) and how spacing within a line is controlled by the Space function. In practice, each of these items would be determined by your particular application, but the syntax required to set each item is always the same as that shown here. Also note that when the PrintPage routine exits, it forces a page to eject from the printer.

Exercises 4.4

(Note: The Rotech Systems project, at the stage of development begun in this section, can be found at http://computerscience.jbpub.com/bronsonvbnet in the ROTECH3a folder as project rotech3a. If you are developing the system yourself by following the procedures given in this section, we suggest that you first copy all of the files in the ROTECH3a folder onto your system and then work out of this latter folder. When you have finished your changes, you can compare your results to the files in the ROTECH4 folder.)

1. Either construct the Rotech system as it has been developed in this section or locate and load the project at http://computerscience.jbpub.com/bronsonvbnet.

2. Modify the Rotech project so that pressing the Print Packing Slip button on the MailIn form causes the printer to print a packing slip. (*Note:* The MailIn form is contained within the current Rotech application stored at http://computerscience.jbpub.com/bronsonvbnet as project rotech4 within the rotech4 folder.)

3. Using the Help facilities' Index tab, obtain information on the CDec conversion function used within both Click event procedures presented in this section.

4. Using the Help facilities' search tab, enter the string "Formatting Numbers, Dates, and Times" (do not include the double quotes) and search for any information on these topics.

5. (Case study) For your selected project (see project specifications at the end of Section 1.5) complete the order entry form you developed in the previous chapter. Your order entry form should now be able to calculate the total amount due on the entered order and print a bill for the order.

4.5 Common Programming Errors and Problems

The common programming errors and problems associated with the material presented in this chapter are:

1. Calling the **InputBox** function without assigning its return value to a variable. The **InputBox** function is useless without assigning its return value.

2. Forgetting to use the **Val** function when the value of the **InputBox** function is assigned to a numeric variable.

3. Forgetting to clear the Text property of a TextBox control that will be used for input purposes, unless an initial value is to be inserted in the text box.

4. Mixing up the argument order in the various formatting functions.

4.6 Chapter Review

Key Terms

FormatCurrency function	InputBox
FormatDateTime function	Label
FormatNumber function	MessageBox.Show
FormatPercent function	PrintDocument Control

Summary

1. The InputBox function permits a user to enter a single value into an executing procedure. A commonly used syntax for calling this function is

```
InputBox(prompt, title, default)
```

where *prompt* is a required string and both *title* and *default*, which are also strings, are optional. If a title string is used, it is displayed in the title bar of the dialog box; otherwise, the application's project name is placed in the title bar. If a default string is provided, it is placed within the input area of the dialog box. A *prompt* is a message telling a user that input is required. The prompt, which is always required, is displayed as a string within the input dialog box. For example, the statement

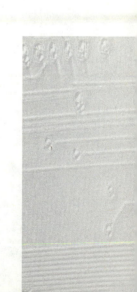

```
stringinput = InputBox("Enter a value", "Input Dialog", "0")
```

calls the **InputBox** function with the arguments " Enter a value ", which is the prompt; "Input Dialog", which is the title; and a default string value of 0. Here the returned value is assigned to the variable stringinput.

2. Text boxes are the most commonly used method of providing interactive user input. The data entered into a text box becomes the value of the text box's Text property, and is always stored as a string. In addition to being set at run time by the user, the Text property can also be set at design time and at run time under program control. The Text property value is accessed using the standard object dot notation, in which the property name is separated from the object name using a dot. For example, the identifier txtInput.Text refers to the Text property of a text box named txtInput.

3. A Label control is commonly used as a prompt for a text box.

Test Yourself—Short Answer

1. What value will result when the following is executed?

```
Val(2345)
Val(218 Main Street)
Val(0)
Val(R456)
```

2. Write code using the various Format functions that will obtain the following results from the given number:

Number	Result
22345	$22,345.00
5.26	5.2600
.7685	77%

3. What is the difference between **KeyPress** and **KeyDown**?

4. A form has two text boxes, txtNum1 and txtNum2. How would you blank out txtNum2 whenever the user leaves the txtNum1 field?

5. When asking a user to enter a number in a text box called txtNum, describe why

```
Dim x as Integer
x = Val(txtNum.Text)
```

is better than

```
Dim x as Integer
x = txtNum.Text
```

6. Write the code that will generate the following output on the printer using any font you like:

```
Hello World
Goodbye World
```

7. You are writing a program that needs to convert kilos to pounds. What line of code would you include in your program to help perform conversions?

8. Write a statement that will prompt the user, in a dialog box, for a random number. If the user presses enter in response to the prompt, the statement should return 85.

9. There is a built-in function named Now that returns the current date and time. Write the code that would display just the current date in a text box named txtTime.

Programming Projects

1. a. Implement a simple calculator like the one shown in Figure 4–14. An executable example of the calculator can be found at http://computerscience. jbpub.com/bronsonvbnet as simpcalc.exe. Your calculator should have the following features:

   i. The buttons perform the indicated operation on the two text fields and display the answer in the text box to the right of the Answer Label.

   ii. When the calculator starts up, the first text box field, to the right of the Label Num 1, has the focus.

   iii. The tab key switches between the two text box fields.

   iv. The Clear button clears the text boxes and the answer, and sets the focus to the first text box.

   v. The End button ends the program.

   Hints:

   - Create a form having the following controls: 3 TextBox controls, 3 Label controls, and 6 Button controls.
   - Set the properties for all of the controls. Start with each control's name!
   - Deactivate the **TabStop** property for all but the two text boxes, and set the **TabIndex** property of the text boxes to 1 and 2, respectively.
   - Write the code for each button's Click event procedure. The Clear button should call the **Focus** method for the first text box.

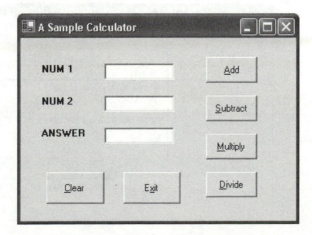

Figure 4–14 *Form for Project 1*

b. Extra challenges:
   i. Add a Square Root button that calculates the square root of the answer.
   ii. Add a Negate button that negates (changes the sign of) the answer.

2. Create a project that will compare the income (after one year) from a tax-exempt municipal bond to a taxable bond with similar risk. It is assumed that the municipal bond has a 5% interest rate and that $1000 will be invested in either type of bond. This project should allow users to enter their income tax rate and the interest available on the taxable bond.

   The formula for calculating the income from the *taxable bond* is as follows:

   Income = (1000 * Bond interest rate) * (1 − Tax rate)

   The tax exempt bond will earn $50 (1000 * .05). This amount is entered in a Label. A possible form for this project is shown in Figure 4–15.

3. Create an application that permits a user to determine how much an item depreciates over a five-year time span. Use straight line, declining balance, and sum of the years digits depreciation methods. The application should allow the user to:
   a. Input the item's original cost and salvage value at the end of 5 years.
   b. Enter the depreciation year of interest, which should be an integer from 1 to 5.
   c. Exit the program.

   The required formulas are as follows:
   Yearly straight line depreciation = (cost − salvage value)/5
   Double declining depreciation = .4 * (cost − previous years depreciation)
   Sum of the years digits depreciation = (6 − year)/15 * cost

   Use the form shown in Figure 4–16.

4. a. Create a project that will permit users to determine the value of their current portfolio of stocks. A suggested form is shown in Figure 4–17. The requirements for this project are:

TAX FREE MUNIES VS. TAXABLE BONDS

DETERMINING WHETHER TAX EXEMPT MUNICIPAL BONDS ARE
A BETER INVESTMENT THAN SIMILAR RISK TAXABLE BONDS.

MUNIES	TAXABLE BONDS
Annual interest income from $1000 of tax exempt municipal bonds at 5% interest is	ENTER INTEREST RATE (IN DECIMAL) [ ] ENTER TAX RATE (IN DECIMAL) [ ]
50 dollars	[CALCULATE] [QUIT] AFTER TAX INTEREST INCOME FROM TAXABLE BOND IS dollars

Figure 4–15   *Form for Project 2*

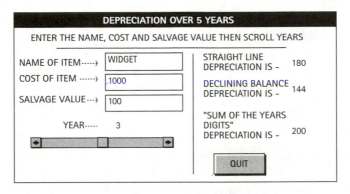

Figure 4–16 *Form for Project 3*

PORTFOLIO EVALUATION					
STOCK NAME	no. shares	purchase price	amt. invested	current price	INCREASE OR DECREASE
BORLAND	200	20	4000	18	–400
IBM	500	90	45000	100	5000
NOVELL	300	18	5400	20	600
TOTALS			54400		5200

UPDATE   QUIT   CURRENT PORTFOLIO VALUE – 59600

Figure 4–17 *Form for Exercise 4*

    i. The stock names (Borland, IBM, Novell), the number of shares, and their purchase price are all entered at design time.

    ii. The amount invested is calculated when the form is loaded.

    iii. The current prices are entered with an InputBox when the UPDATE button is clicked.

    iv. After the current prices are entered, the increase or decrease totals and current portfolio value are calculated.

b. The user knows that he or she will need to provide the purchase date on each stock for the IRS. This date has to be reported on schedule D (capital gains). Change this form so that, if the stock name is clicked, a message box appears reporting the purchase date for that stock. Similar click procedures should be written for the other stock name labels.

5. **a.** Develop an application that will calculate the Economic Order Quantity (EOQ). EOQ is the most cost effective order quantity when dealing with production inventories and materials orders. A suggested form is shown in Figure 4–18. It uses the annual demand, holding cost, and ordering cost to determine this quantity. The equation for the EOQ is:

$$EOQ = \sqrt{2\ (\text{Annual demand})\ (\text{Ordering cost})\ /\ \text{Holding cost}}$$

  i. The user should enter the three quantities (Annual demand, Ordering cost, and Holding cost) using text boxes.
  ii. The EOQ should appear on the form in a Label.
  iii. An Exit button should be included.

b. (Extra challenge) Add an <u>A</u>bout button that displays the About box shown in Figure 4–19. *Hint:* An About box is simply another form that must be dis-

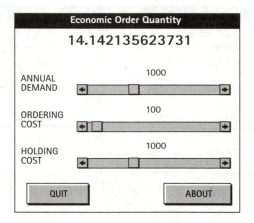

Figure 4–18   *Form for Project 5a*

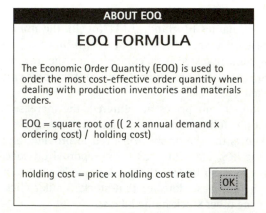

Figure 4–19   *Form for Project 5b*

played and hidden in the same manner as all other forms. You can create the form by adding controls to a new form or you can change the default controls within the About Box provided when you select this form from the Add Form dialog box (see Figure 3–26). Additionally, an About Box is further described in Section 8.6, when one is added to the Rotech project.

6. This assignment is a modification to the Motel 8 project (Section 3.9, Programming Projects, Project 8).

   a. Use constants (in your Declaration section) to assign values for Cost per Adult (Integer value 30), Cost per Child (Integer value 10), and State-Local Tax (Currency value 0.05). Additionally, use a Currency format to display the total charges.

   b. Add named constants to your project to hold values for the Daily Charge (Currency value 29.95) and Refueling Fee (Currency value 12.95).

7. You have been asked to write a program that will help new employees at the local Burger House return the correct change. The point of sale terminal displays the amount of change to be returned to the customer but does not tell the employee how to choose the coins. Your program will be used to train new employees to make change in the most efficient manner.

Program Requirements:

Your program will permit an integer value to be entered and will compute and display the number of quarters, dimes, nickels, and pennies for the value entered. Output is computed, beginning with quarters and ending with pennies. For example, for change of 68 cents, your program should display 2 quarters, 1 dime, 1 nickel, and 3 pennies. All program variables should be declared as integers. *Hint:* Use integer division and integer remainder operators (\ and Mod) in your calculations. Create a form like the one shown in Figure 4–20.

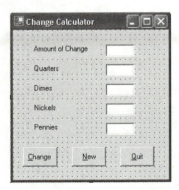

Figure 4–20   *Form for Project 7*

Selection

Goals

A decision requires making a choice between two or more alternatives. Given the dual nature of Visual Basic, decisions can be implemented by both graphical and procedural means.

The graphical features consist of Toolbox control objects specifically designed to provide a selection of input choices. These controls are listed in Table 5–1. The first three—the CheckBox, ListBox, and RadioButton controls—are presented in Section 5.1. Additional controls are described in Appendix B.

On the procedural side, selection statements are used to make decisions on what action or computation should be performed based upon either an expression or property value. Examples of such basic decisions include setting a type as bold only if a check box has been selected, performing division only if the divisor is not zero, printing different messages depending upon the value of a grade received, and so on. In this way, selection statements determine the flow of control of procedural code execution based on tested conditions being True or False.

The term flow of control refers to the order in which a program's procedural code statements are executed. Unless directed otherwise, the normal flow of control for procedural statements within an event procedure is sequential. This means that once the procedure is invoked, the statements within that procedure are executed in sequence, one after the other.

Selection statements, presented in this chapter starting with Section 5.2, permit this sequential flow of control to be altered in precisely defined ways. Specifically, selection statements determine the procedural code to be executed next, based on a comparison operation. Repetition statements, which are used to repeat a set of procedural code, can also alter a procedure's flow of control. They are presented in Chapter 6.

5.1 Selection Controls

Except for the ComboBox control, which is a combination of a ListBox control and a TextBox control, all of the controls listed in Table 5–1 limit the user to selecting from a

Table 5–1 Selection Controls

Control	Use
CheckBox	A Yes/No toggle selection.
RadioButton	Select only one option from a group.
ListBox	Select one or more options from a predefined list.
ComboBox	Select from a predefined list or type in a selection.
Horizontal and Vertical Scroll Bar	Select a number from a sequential range of numbers.

predefined set of choices. However, both the ComboBox and the TextBox controls are less restrictive. What this means in practice is that the procedural code used to decide what was entered in either a text box or combo box is generally more complex than that needed for the other controls listed in Table 5–1. We will see an example of this in Section 5–3, where the input from a text box is processed to ensure that a user types in a legitimate value. The advantage of the controls listed in Table 5–1 (with the exception of the ComboBox control), is that they force a user to choose between programmer-defined choices. In this section, we present the CheckBox and RadioButton input controls.

The CheckBox Control

The CheckBox control provides a user with a simple Yes-or-No, or alternatively On-or-Off, option. For example, in the interface shown in Figure 5–1 there are two check boxes. The properties table for this interface is listed in Table 5–2.

As illustrated on Figure 5–1, both check boxes are unchecked. These settings are initially set at design time using the check box's **Checked** property and can be altered by the user at run time by either clicking the box, pressing the space key when the box has focus, or using the hot key sequence defined for the box.

Each check box in an application is independent of any other check box. This means that the choice made in one box has no effect on, nor depends on, the choice made in another check box. As such, check boxes are useful for providing a set of one or more options that can be in effect at the same time. For example, in the interface shown in Figure 5–1, the check box options consist of a set of two check boxes that permit independent selection of how the text is to be displayed. Selecting or deselecting Bold has no effect on the choice for Italic or nonItalic.

Because of their On/Off nature, check boxes are also known as toggle selections, where a user can effectively toggle or switch back and forth between a check mark and no check mark. If no check mark appears in a box, clicking on it changes its **Checked** property to True and causes a check to appear; otherwise, if the box has a check, clicking on it changes the **Checked** property to False and causes the check to be erased.

Figure 5–1   *An Interface with Two Check Boxes*

Table 5–2   The Properties Table for Figure 5–1

Object	Property	Setting
Form	Name	frmMain
	Text	Program 5–1
Label	Name	lblDisplay
	Text	The font will change here
CheckBox 1	Name	chkItalic
	Text	&Italic
	Checked	False
	Checkstate	Unchecked
CheckBox 2	Name	chkBold
	Text	&Bold
	Checked	False
	Checkstate	Unchecked
Button	Name	btnExit
	Text	E&xit

Program 5–1's Event Code

```
Private Sub chkItalic_CheckedChanged(ByVal sender As Object, ByVal e As _
    System.EventArgs) Handles chkItalic.CheckedChanged
  lblDisplay.Font = New Font(lblDisplay.Font.Name, lblDisplay.Font.Size, _
    lblDisplay.Font.Style Xor FontStyle.Italic)
End Sub

Private Sub chkBold_CheckedChanged(ByVal sender As Object, ByVal e As _
    System.EventArgs) Handles chkBold.CheckedChanged
  lblDisplay.Font = New Font(lblDisplay.Font.Name, lblDisplay.Font.Size, _
    lblDisplay.Font.Style Xor FontStyle.Bold)
End Sub

Private Sub btnExit_Click(ByVal sender As Object, ByVal e As _
    System.EventArgs) Handles btnExit.Click
  Beep()
  End
End Sub
```

Although a check box allows a user to easily make a selection, the programmer must still provide the code for appropriate action when the selection is made. In Program 5–1's event code, the **CheckedChanged** events for both the Bold and Italic check boxes are used to change the font of the displayed text, **lblDisplay.Font**. To enable the font to be changed, the programmer must set the Font property to a **Font** object. The **Font** object is an advanced topic touched upon briefly in the Printer Output section of Chapter 4. For the purpose of this book, no further explanation is needed.

The RadioButton Control

The RadioButton control provides a user with a set of one or more choices, only one of which can be selected. Radio buttons always operate as a group, where selecting one radio button immediately deselects and clears all the other buttons in the group. Thus, the choices in a radio button group are mutually exclusive. Radio buttons operate in the same manner as the channel selector buttons provided on radios, where selecting one channel automatically deselects all other channels.

As an example using radio buttons, consider a form that requires information on the marital status of an employee. As the employee can be either Single, Married, Divorced, or Widowed (see Figure 5–2), selection of one category automatically means the other categories are not selected. This type of choice is ideal for a radio button group, as shown in Figure 5–2, where the group consists of four individual radio buttons.

Each radio button placed on a form is automatically part of the same group. To create separate groups of radio buttons, place the radio buttons in a GroupBox or Panel. The GroupBox and Panel controls are known as container controls because these are designed to hold or 'contain' other controls. All radio buttons placed directly on a form constitute a single group. To create separate groups within either a GroupBox or Panel requires drawing these controls on the form *before* placing a radio button within them. Placing a radio button outside of a GroupBox or Panel and then dragging it into the control, or drawing a GroupBox or Panel around existing radio buttons, will not produce the same result. In either of these cases, the radio buttons will still be part of their original group location.

Figure 5–2   *A Radio Button Group*

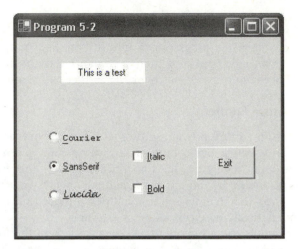

Figure 5–3 *An Interface with a Radio Button Group*

For example, in the interface shown in Figure 5–3 we have added a radio button group to the interface previously used in Program 5–1. This radio button group consists of three individual radio buttons with the captions **Courier**, SansSerif, and *Lucida*, respectively. We will use these buttons to select the style of print that is displayed in the label box. Because these styles are mutually exclusive in that only one style can be displayed at a time, the choice of radio buttons for this selection is appropriate. The properties table for this interface is listed in Table 5–3.

Note in the Properties Table 5–3 that only one of the radio button **Checked** properties has been set to **True**. Setting the second radio button **Checked** value to **True** automatically sets the remaining radio button's **Checked** property to **False**. The event code for these radio buttons follows. The remaining event code for Program 5–2 is the same as listed for Program 5–1.

Program 5–2's RadioButton Event Code

```
Private Sub radCourier_Click(ByVal sender As Object, ByVal e As _
    System.EventArgs) Handles radCourier.Click
  lblDisplay.Font = New Font("Courier New", lblDisplay.Font.Size)
End Sub

Private Sub radSansSerif_Click(ByVal sender As Object, ByVal e As _
    System.EventArgs) Handles radSansSerif.Click
  lblDisplay.Font = New Font("Microsoft Sans Serif", lblDisplay.Font.Size)
End Sub

Private Sub radLucida_Click(ByVal sender As Object, ByVal e As _
    System.EventArgs) Handles radLucida.Click
```

Table 5-3 Program 5-2's Property Table

Object	Property	Setting
Form	Name	frmMain
	Text	Program 5-2
Label	Name	lblDisplay
	Text	This is a test
	Font.Name	Microsoft Sans Serif
CheckBox 1	Name	chkItalic
	Text	&Italic
	Checked	False
CheckBox 2	Name	chkBold
	Text	&Bold
	Checked	False
RadioButton 1	Name	radCourier
	Text	&Courier
	Font.Name	Courier New
	Checked	False
RadioButton 2	Name	radSansSerif
	Text	&SansSerif
	Font.Name	Microsoft Sans Serif
	Checked	True
RadioButton 3	Name	radLucida
	Text	&Lucida
	Font.Name	Lucida Handwriting
	Checked	False
Button	Name	btnExit
	Text	E&xit

```
    lblDisplay.Font = New Font("Lucida Handwriting", lblDisplay.Font.Size)
End Sub
```

Note that the event code for a radio button group does not require any selection statements. This is because only one radio button can be in effect at a time. Thus, the Click event for each button can unilaterally change the text box's **Font** property.

When Program 5-2 is executed, and before any check box or radio button is checked, the typeface of the text in the label is determined by the label box **Font.Name** property values set at design time (see Table 5-3). For these values, the text "This is a test" would appear as shown in Figure 5-3.

The user can now change the font of the text illustrated in Figure 5-3 by using the check boxes and radio buttons. A radio button is selected at run time in one of three ways:

- Click the desired button.
- Tab to the radio button group and use the arrow keys.
- Use the access (hot) keys.

For example, if the user checks the Bold and Italic check boxes and the Courier radio button, the text will appear as shown in Figure 5–4. If the user unchecks the Italic check box, checks the Bold check box, and selects the Lucida radio button, the text will appear as shown in Figure 5–5.

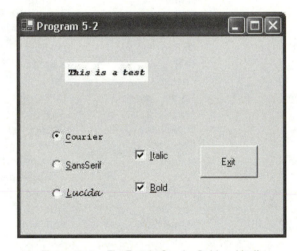

Figure 5–4   *The Text in Courier Bold and Italic*

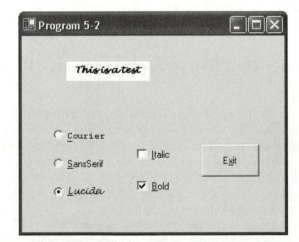

Figure 5–5   *The Text in Lucida Bold*

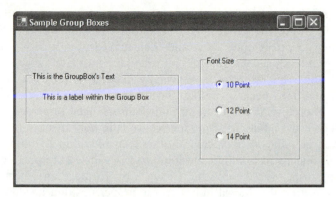

Figure 5–6 *The GroupBox*

The GroupBox Control

Group boxes, two of which are shown in Figure 5–6, are extremely useful for providing clearly defined visual areas and for grouping controls together. This is especially important when you need to have two or more groups of radio buttons on the same form. Because all radio buttons placed directly on a form, no matter where they are placed, constitute a single group of buttons, the only way to create additional groupings is to use either a GroupBox control or Panel control. All radio buttons placed within either of these two controls constitute a separate grouping of buttons. The main difference between these two controls is that a GroupBox can display a caption (text) and does not include scrollbars, whereas Panels do not include a caption, but can include scrollbars.

A GroupBox is placed on a form in the same manner as all other Toolbox controls—either by clicking the control, or clicking and dragging the control to the desired location. As with all controls, the GroupBox control can be resized using its resizing handles.

Besides setting the group box's size and position, the only other values that should be explicitly set at design time are its Text property (caption) and the Text's font properties.

A group box, which can be used to group a set of other controls, such as radio buttons, is referred to as a *container control*. The primary container control is a form, because all other controls are contained within it.

The relationship between a container control and all its internal controls is referred to as a *parent and child relationship*. In this relationship, the position of all child controls is relative to the upper Left and Top of its parent control. This means that if the parent control is moved, all of its internal child controls move with it as a group and retain their relative positions within the parent control. Additionally, a child control cannot be moved outside of the parent.

When using a group box to group a set of controls, such as radio buttons or check boxes, *you must always draw the group box first, and then place the controls within the group box.*[1] Doing this produces two important effects: First, it ensures that all of the controls within the Group box will automatically move when the Group box itself is relocated (controls drawn first and then moved onto a Group box will not move with the Group box); second, it forces all internal controls to be grouped together as an individual unit. This last effect is especially important when you need a separate grouping of radio buttons because, unlike Check boxes, only one radio button can be active in a group. Therefore, if two or more radio buttons need to be active at the same time, you must construct additional container controls to hold them.

Additionally, when placing another control within a Group box, double clicking the desired object's icon within the toolbox *will not* work; doing so only places the object on the Form, over the existing Group box. To place an object within the Group box, click and drag the desired object to the proper position inside the Group box and then release the mouse button.

The ListBox Control

The ListBox control is extremely useful for presenting a small list of items. The list of items can be used for selection by the user or just as output. A list box appears as a rectangle that displays rows of text. If the number of rows is too large to fit within the rectangle, Visual Basic automatically provides a vertical scroll bar on the right side of the list box. A list box is shown in Figure 5–7.

Each line of output in a list box is referred to as an **Item**. The set of Items can be specified at design time by changing the Items property. In addition, the set of Items can be changed at run time with procedural code. To add to the Items list at run time, the

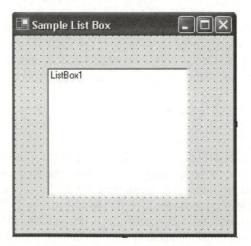

Figure 5–7   *ListBox control*

---

[1]If you have existing controls that need to be grouped together, select all of the controls and then cut and paste them into an existing GroupBox or Panel control.

`Items.Add` method is used. Unlike the text box method `AppendText`, when `Items.Add` is invoked, the text is displayed on the next line; you do not have to explicitly add a NewLine control character. This is because the TextBox control has a single property (Text) for storing and displaying information. Even when a text box has multiple lines, all these lines are actually associated with the single Text property. However, the List-Box control can reference multiple text values.

Figure 5–8 displays a form that has a list box, which we will use to demonstrate how to add and clear text. Table 5–4 is the Property Table for this form.

To add text to the list box at design time, select the Items property and click the ellipsis. This will bring up a dialog box that will allow the entry of text. Figure 5–9 shows this filled in with one line: `First line from design time`. After entering the

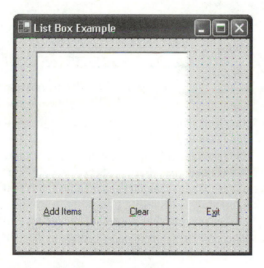

Figure 5–8 *List Box User Interface*

Table 5–4   Property Table for List Box Example

Object	Property	Setting
Form	Name	frmMain
	Text	List Box Example
ListBox	Name	lstTest
Button	Name	btnAdd
	Text	&Add
Button	Name	btnClear
	Text	&Clear
Button	Name	btnExit
	Text	E&xit

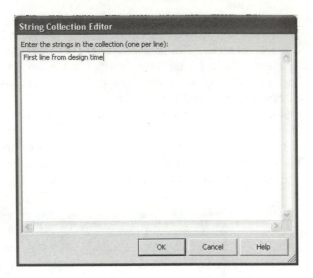

Figure 5–9 *List Box Item's Property*

desired text, click OK. The list box in the design screen will now display what was entered in the previous dialog box.

To show how text can be added to the list box at run time, see the code in Event Procedure `ListBox.Add`. All that is needed to add items is a call to the `Items.Add` method. Successive calls to this method will add the text to a new line in the list box. While this example only adds string constants to the list box, variables can also be displayed. Simply enter the variable instead of the string constant between the parentheses. Figure 5–10 shows what the program will display after the btnAdd button is clicked.

Figure 5–10 *Sample Run of List Box program*

Event Procedure ListBox Add

```
Private Sub btnAdd_Click(ByVal sender As System.Object, ByVal e As _
    System.EventArgs) Handles btnList.Click
  lstTest.Items.Add("Second Line at run-time")
  lstTest.Items.Add("End of adding")
End Sub
```

Another method that is commonly used is Items.Clear, which removes all items from the list box. The Event code below demonstrates how it is invoked. After you click the btnClear button, the list box lstTest will be blank.

Event Procedure ListBox Clear

```
Private Sub btnClear_Click(ByVal sender As System.Object, ByVal e As _
    System.EventArgs) Handles btnList.Click
  lstTest.Items.Clear()
End Sub
```

The ListBox control is a very complex control with many more useful features. For more information on this control, refer to Appendix B.

Exercises 5.1

1. Determine whether the following choices should be presented on a GUI using either check boxes or radio buttons:

   a. The choice of air conditioning or no air conditioning on a new automobile order form.

   b. The choice of automatic or manual transmission on a new automobile order form.

   c. The choice of AM/FM, AM/FM Tape, or AM/FM CD radio on a new automobile order form.

   d. The choice of a tape backup system or no tape backup system on a new computer order form.

   e. The choice of a 14-, 15-, or 17-inch color monitor on a new computer order form.

   f. The choice of a CD-ROM drive or not on a new computer order form.

   g. The choice of a 4-, 6-, or 8-speed CD-ROM drive on a new computer order form.

   h. The choice of a 100, 120, or 200 MHZ Pentium processor on a new computer order form.

2. Enter and run Program 5–1 on your computer.

3. a. Modify Program 5–1 so that the choices presented by the check boxes are replaced by buttons. (*Hint:* Each check box can be replaced by two buttons.)

   b. Based on your experience with Exercise 3a, determine what type of input choice is best presented using a check box rather than buttons.

4. a. Modify Program 5–1 so that the choices presented by the check boxes are replaced by radio buttons.

   b. Based on your experience with Exercise 4a, determine what type of input choice is best presented using a check box rather than a radio button.

5. Enter and run Program 5–2 on your computer.

5.2 Relational Expressions

Besides providing computational capabilities (addition, subtraction, multiplication, division, and so on), all programming languages provide procedural operations for comparing quantities. Because many decision-making situations can be reduced to the level of choosing between two quantities, this comparison capability can be very useful.

The expressions used to compare quantities are called relational expressions. A *simple relational expression* consists of a relational operator that compares two operands, as shown in Figure 5–11.

Although each operand in a relational expression can be any valid Visual Basic expression, the relational operators must be one of those listed in Table 5–5. These relational operators can be used with all Visual Basics data types, but must be typed exactly as given in Table 5–5. For example, the following examples are all valid:

```
age > 40        length <= 50       temp > 98.6
3 < 4           flag = done        id_num = 682
day <> 5        2.0 > 3.3          hours > 40
```

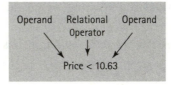

Figure 5–11 *Structure of a Simple Relational Expression*

Table 5–5 Relational Operators

Operator	Meaning	Example
<	Less than	age < 30
>	Greater than	height > 6.2
<=	Less than or equal to	taxable <= 20000
>=	Greater than or equal to	temp >= 98.6
=	Equal to	grade = 100
<>	Not equal to	number <> 250

whereas the following are invalid:

```
length =< 50    ' operator out of order
2.0 >> 3.3      ' invalid operator
```

Relational expressions are sometimes called conditions, and we will use both terms to refer to these expressions. Like all Visual Basic expressions, relational expressions are evaluated to yield a result. For relational expressions this result is one of the Boolean values: **True** or **False**. For example, the expression 3 < 4 is always **True**, and the expression 2 > 3 is always **False**. Thus, the event code

```
Private Sub Form_Click(ByVal sender As System.Object, ByVal e As _
    System.EventArgs) Handles Form.Click
  txtDisplay1.Text = "The value of 3 < 4 is " & (3 < 4)
  txtDisplay2.Text = "The value of 2 > 3 is " & (2 > 3)
End Sub
```

can be used to display the value of the expressions 3 < 4 and 2 > 3, respectively, and produce the display:

```
The value of 3 < 4 is True
The value of 2 > 3 is False
```

The value of a relational expression such as hours > 40 depends on the value stored in the variable hours. In Visual Basic, a condition such as this is typically used as part of a selection statement. In these statements, which are presented in the next section, the selection of the statement to be executed next is based on the value of the condition (**True** or **False**).

In addition to numerical operands, character data can also be compared using relational operators. For example, in the ANSI code, the letter "A" is stored using a code having a lower numerical value than the letter "B", the code for a "B" is lower in value than the code for a "C", and so on. For character sets coded in this manner, the following conditions are evaluated as listed below.

Expression	Value
'A' > 'C'	False
'D' <= 'Z'	True
'E' = 'F'	False
'G' >= 'M'	False
'B' <> 'C'	True

Comparing letters is essential in alphabetizing names or using characters to select a particular option.

Finally, two string expressions can be compared using relational operators. Each character in a string is stored in binary using the ANSI code. In this code, a blank precedes (is less than) all letters and numbers; the letters of the alphabet are stored in order from A to Z; and the digits are stored in order from 0 to 9. It is important to note that in ANSI the digits come before, or are less than, the letters.

When two strings are compared, their individual characters are compared one character pair at a time (both first characters, then both second characters, and so on). If no differences are found, the strings are equal; if a difference is found, the string with the first lower character is considered the smaller string. If all characters are the same, but the end of the first string is reached before the end of the second string, the first string is considered less than the second string. Thus,

"JONES" is less than "SMITH" because the first 'J' in JONES is less than the first 'S' in SMITH.

"Hello" is less than "hello" because the first 'H' in Hello is less than the first 'h' in hello.

"Hello" is less than "Hello " because the second string is longer.

"Hello" is greater than "Good Bye" because the first 'H' in Hello is greater than the first 'G' in Good Bye.

"Behop" is greater than "Beehive" because the third character, the 'h', in Behop is greater than the third character, 'e', in Beehive.

"123" is greater than "1227" because the third character, '3', in 123 is greater than the third character, '2', in 1227.

"123" is less than "1237" because the first three characters are the same, but the first string is shorter.

Note that it is very important that the items being compared are the same type of data, that is, that numerical values are compared to numerical values and strings are compared to strings. If you try to compare two different types of data, you will get a run-time error.

Logical Operators

In addition to using simple relational expressions as conditions, more complex conditions can be created using the logical operators And, Or, Xor, and Not.

When the And operator is used with two simple expressions, the condition is true only if both individual expressions are true by themselves. Thus, the compound condition

```
(age > 40) And (term < 10)
```

is **True** only if age is greater than 40 **and** term is less than 10.

The logical Or operator is also applied between two expressions. When using the Or operator, the condition is satisfied if either one or both of the two expressions is **True**. Thus, the compound condition

```
(age > 40) Or (term < 10)
```

will be **True** if either `age` is greater than `40`, `term` is less than `10`, **or** both conditions are **True**. The `Xor`, or exclusive Or operator, is similar to the Or operator but not used as often. It operates on two expressions but evaluates to **True** only when one of the two expressions is **True**. If both expressions are **True** or both are **False**, the overall expression is **False**.

For the declarations

```
Dim i, j As Integer
Dim a, b As Single
Dim complete As Boolean
```

the following represent valid conditions:

```
a > b
(i = j) Or (a < b) Or complete
(a/b > 5) And (i <= 20)
```

Before these conditions can be evaluated, the values of `a`, `b`, `i`, `j`, and `complete` must be known. Assuming

```
a = 12.0
b = 2:0
i = 15
j = 30
complete = False
```

the previous expressions yield the following results:

Expression	Value
`a > b`	`True`
`(i = j) Or (a < b) Or complete`	`False`
`(a/b > 5) And (i <= 20)`	`True`
`(i <= j) Xor (b < a)`	`False`

The `Not` operator is used to change an expression to its opposite state; that is, if the expression is **True**, then the `Not` expression is **False**. Similarly, if an expression is False, then the `Not` expression is **True**. For example, assuming the number `26` is stored in the variable `age`, the expression `age > 40` is **False** and the expression `Not(age > 40)` is **True**. Because the `Not` operator is used with only one expression, it is a unary operator.

Relational and logical operators have a hierarchy of execution similar to the arithmetic operators. Table 5–6 lists the precedence of these operators in relation to the other operators we have used. Because relational operators have a higher precedence than logical operators, the parentheses in an expression such as

```
(age > 40) And (term < 10)
```

Table 5-6   Precedence of Operators

Operation	Operator	Associativity
Exponentiation	^	left to right
Negation	-	left to right
Multiplication and Division	* /	left to right
Integer Division	\	left to right
Modulo arithmetic	Mod	left to right
Addition and Subtraction	+ -	left to right
String Concatenation	&	left to right
Equality	=	left to right
Inequality	<>	left to right
Less than	<	left to right
Greater than	>	left to right
Less than or equal to	<=	left to right
Greater than or equal to	>=	left to right
Not	Not	left to right
And	And	left to right
Or	Or	left to right
Xor	Xor	left to right

are not strictly needed. The evaluation of this expression is identical to the evaluation of the expression:

```
age > 40 And term < 10
```

The following example illustrates the use of an operator's precedence and associativity to evaluate relational expressions, assuming the following declarations and assignments:

```
Dim i, j, k As Integer
Dim x As Single
Dim key As String
i = 5
j = 7
k = 12
x = 22.5
key = "m"
```

Expression	Equivalent Expression	Value
i + 2 = k - 1	(i + 2) = (k - 1)	False
3 * i - j < 22	(3 * i) - j < 22	True
i + 2 * j > k	(i + (2 * j)) > k	True
k + 3 >= -j + 3 * i	(k + 3) <= ((-j) + (3*i))	False
"a" <> "b"	"a" <> "b"	True
key > 'p'	key > "p"	True
25 >= x + 10.2	25 >= (x + 10.2)	False

As with arithmetic expressions, parentheses can be used both to alter the assigned operator priority and to improve the readability of relational and logical expressions. Because expressions within parentheses are evaluated first, the following complex condition is evaluated as:

```
(6 * 3 = 36 / 2) Or (13 < 3 * 3 + 4) And Not (6 - 2 < 5) =
      (18 = 18) Or  (13 < 9 + 4)    And Not (4 < 5) =
        (True) Or  (13 < 13)     And Not (True) =
        (True) Or      (False)   And (False) =
        (True) Or (False) =
                  True
```

A Numerical Accuracy Problem

A problem that can occur with Visual Basic's relational expressions is a subtle numerical accuracy problem relating to floating point and double precision numbers. As a result of the way computers store these numbers, tests for equality of floating point and double precision values and variables using the relational operator, =, should be avoided.

Many decimal numbers, such as 0.1, for example, cannot be represented exactly in binary using a finite number of bits. Thus, testing for exact equality for such numbers can fail. When equality of noninteger values is desired, it is better to require that the absolute value of the difference between operands be less than some extremely small value. Thus, for noninteger numerical operands, the general expression

```
operand_1 = operand_2
```

should be replaced by the condition

```
Math.Abs(operand_1 - operand_2) < 0.000001
```

where the value 0.000001 can be altered to any other acceptably small value. If the difference between the two operands is less than 0.000001 (or any other user-selected amount), the two operands are considered essentially equal. Because the Absolute Value function is part of the Math Class, you must use `Math.Abs` to access the function.

For example, if *x* and *y* are single precision variables, a condition such as

```
x/y = 0.35
```

should be programmed as

```
Math.Abs(x/y - 0.35) < 0.000001
```

This latter comparison ensures that slight inaccuracies in representing noninteger numbers in binary do not affect evaluation of the tested condition. Because all computers have an exact binary representation of zero, comparisons for exact equality to zero don't encounter this numerical accuracy problem.

Exercises 5.2

1. Determine whether the value of each of the following expressions is **True** or **False**. Assume $a = 5$, $b = 2$, $c = 4$, $d = 6$, and $e = 3$.

   a. `a > b`

   b. `a <> b`

   c. `d Mod b = c Mod b`

   d. `a * c <> d * b`

   e. `d * b = c * e`

   f. `Not (a = b)`

   g. `Not (a < b)`

2. Write relational expressions to express the following conditions (use variable names of your own choosing) (see Exercise 5.1):

   a. A person's age is equal to 30.

   b. A person's temperature is greater than 98.6.

   c. A person's height is less than 6 feet.

   d. The current month is 12 (December).

   e. The letter input is m.

   f. A person's age is equal to 30 and the person is taller than 6 feet.

   g. The current day is the 15th day of the 1st month.

   h. A person is older than 50 or has been employed at the company for at least 5 years.

   i. A person's identification number is less than 500 and the person is older than 55.

   j. A length is greater than 2 feet and less than 3 feet.

3. Determine the value of the following expressions, assuming $a = 5$, $b = 2$, $c = 4$, and $d = 5$.

   a. `a = 5`

b. b * d = c * c

c. d Mod b * c > 5 Or c Mod b * d < 7

4. Using parentheses, rewrite the following expressions to correctly indicate their order of evaluation. Then evaluate each expression, assuming all variables are integers and that $a = 5$, $b = 2$, and $c = 4$.

a. a / b <> c And c / b <> a

b. a / b <> c Or c / b <> a

c. b Mod c = 1 And ab Mod c = 1

d. b Mod c = 1 Or a Mod c = 1

5. Write a Visual Basic program to determine the value of the condition (2 > 1) >= (2 < 1). What does your result tell you about how Visual Basic orders a **True** value relative to a **False** value?

5.3 The If–Then–Else Structure

The **If–Then–Else** structure directs a procedure to perform a series of one or more instructions based on the result of a comparison. For example, the state of New Jersey has a two-level state income tax structure. If a person's taxable income is less than $20,000, the applicable state tax rate is 2%. For incomes exceeding $20,000, a different rate is applied. The **If–Then–Else** structure can be used in this situation to determine the actual tax, based on whether the taxable income is less than or equal to $20,000. The general syntax of an **If–Then–Else** structure is:

```
If (condition) Then
  statement(s)
Else
  statement(s)
End If
```

This structure consists of three separate Visual Basic parts, each of which must reside on a line by itself: an **If** statement having the form If `condition` Then, an Else statement consisting of the keyword `Else`, and an `End If` statement consisting of the keywords `End` and `If`.

The condition in the `If` statement is evaluated first. If the condition is **True**, the first set of statements is executed. If the condition is **False**, the statements after the keyword **Else** are executed. Thus, one of the two sets of statements is always executed depending on the value of the condition. The flowchart for the **If–Then–Else** structure is shown in Figure 5–12.

As a specific example of an **If–Then–Else** statement, we will construct a Visual Basic application for determining New Jersey income taxes. As previously described,

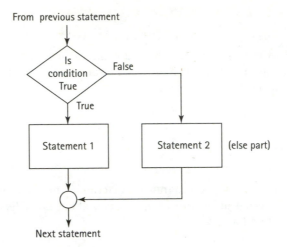

From previous statement

Figure 5–12 *The If-Then-Else Flowchart*

these taxes are assessed at 2% of taxable income for incomes less than or equal to $20,000. For taxable incomes greater than $20,000, state taxes are 2.5% of the income that exceeds $20,000 plus a fixed amount of $400. The expression to be tested is whether taxable income is less than or equal to $20,000. An appropriate **If-Then-Else** statement for this situation is:

```
If taxable <= 20000.00 Then
   taxes = 0.02 * taxable
Else
   taxes = 0.025 * (taxable - 20000.00) + 400.00
End If
```

Recall that the relational operator <= represents the relation less than or equal to. If the value of `taxable` is less than or equal to `20000.00`, the condition is **True** and the statement `taxes = 0.02 * taxable` is executed. If the condition is **False**, the `Else` part of the statement is executed. Note that although there is only one statement to execute under both conditions, you may have multiple statements. Program 5–3 illustrates the use of this statement within the context of a complete application. The interface for this program is shown in Figure 5–13.

The properties table for Program 5–3 is given in Table 5–7. Note that the **TabStop** property for the Taxes Text box has been set to **False**. Thus, the user can only tab between the Income text box, the Calculate button, and the E**x**it button. Now look at Program 5–3's event code. Note that the Text box's **Enter** event is used to clear the text boxes. This ensures that whenever a user moves into the Income text box to enter an income value, both text boxes will be cleared. Doing this prevents the situation of a previously calculated tax amount being visible for a newly entered income level before the

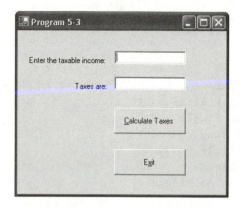

Figure 5–13   *The Interface for Program 5–3*

Table 5–7   Program 5–3's Property Table

Object	Property	Setting
Form	Name	frmMain
	Text	Program 5-3
Label	Name	lblIncome
	Text	Enter the taxable income:
TextBox	Name	txtIncome
	TabStop	True
	Text	(blank)
Label	Name	lblTaxes
	Text	Taxes are:
TextBox	Name	txtTaxes
	TabStop	False
	Text	(blank)
Button	Name	btnCalculate
	Text	&Calculate Taxes
Button	Name	btnExit
	Text	E&xit

user moves off the text box. The actual calculation and display of the taxes due on the entered amount uses an **If-Then-Else** statement within the btnCalculate_Click event.

Program 5–3's Event Code

```
Private Sub txtIncome_Enter(ByVal sender As Object, ByVal e As _
    System.EventArgs) Handles txtIncome.Enter
```

```
      txtTaxes.Text = ""
      txtIncome.Text = ""
  End Sub

  Private Sub btnCalculate_Click(ByVal sender As Object, ByVal e As _
      System.EventArgs) Handles btnCalculate.Click
    Const HIGHRATE As Single = 0.025
    Const LOWRATE As Single = 0.02
    Const FIXED As Single = 400.0
    Const CUTOFF As Single = 20000.0
    Dim taxable, taxes As Single

    taxable = Val(txtIncome.Text)
    If taxable <= CUTOFF Then
      taxes = LOWRATE * taxable
    Else
      taxes = HIGHRATE * (taxable - CUTOFF) + FIXED
    End If

    txtTaxes.Text = FormatCurrency(taxes)
  End Sub

  Private Sub btnExit_Click(ByVal sender As Object, ByVal e As _
      System.EventArgs) Handles btnExit.Click
    Beep()
    End
  End Sub
```

Figures 5–14 and 5–15 illustrate the interface for two different values of taxable income. Observe that the taxable income shown in Figure 5–14 was less than $20,000, and the tax is correctly calculated as 2% of the number entered. In Figure 5–15, the tax-

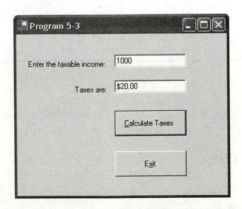

Figure 5–14　*Entering a Taxable Income Less Than $20,000*

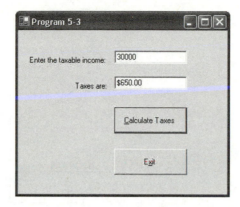

Figure 5–15   *Entering a Taxable Income Greater Than $20,000*

able income is more than $20,000, and the `Else` part of the **If-Then-Else** statement was used to yield a correct tax computation of:

```
0.025 * ($30,000 - $20,000) + $400 = $650
```

One-Way Selection and the Single-line If-Then Statement

As we have seen, the **If-Then-Else** structure that we have been using consists of three separate Visual Basic parts: an **If-Then** part, an `Else` part, and an `End If` part. Any number of valid Visual Basic statements can be included with the `If` and `Else` parts of the structure. However, as a multiline statement, it must always be used with an `End If` statement. Use of the `Else` statement is optional. When the `Else` statement is not used, the `If` statement takes the shortened and frequently useful form:

```
If condition Then
 statement(s)
End If
```

The statement or statements following the `If` condition are only executed if the condition is true. Figure 5–16 illustrates the flowchart for this combination of statements. This modified form of the `If` statement is called a *one-way If structure*. Program 5–4 uses this statement to selectively display a message in a text box for cars that have been driven more than 3,000 miles. The program's interface is shown in Figure 5–17 and its Properties table is listed in Table 5–8.

If only one statement is to be executed if the condition is true and there is no `Else` statement, you may use a single-line **If-Then** statement without the `End If` as follows:

```
If condition Then statement
```

Note that this must all be typed in one line as in the following example:

```
If taxable <= CUTOFF Then taxes = LOWRATE * taxable
```

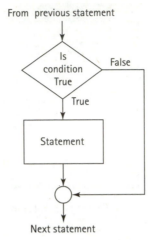

From previous statement

Figure 5–16   *Flowchart for One-Way If Structure*

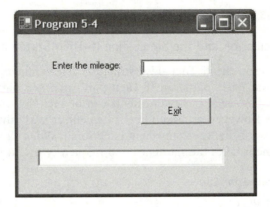

Figure 5–17   *Program 5–4's Interface*

Programmer Notes

What is a Flag?

In current programming usage, the term **flag** refers to an item, such as a variable or argument, that sets a condition usually considered to be active or inactive. Flags are typically used in selecting actions based on the following pseudocode:

If the flag is set
  do the statements here
Else

Table 5–8   The Properties Table for Program 5–4

Object	Property	Setting
Form	Name	frmMain
	Text	Program 5–4
Label	Name	lblMiles
	Text	Enter the mileage:
TextBox	Name	txtMiles
	Text	(blank)
TextBox	Name	txtError
	TabStop	False
	Text	(blank)
Button	Name	btnExit
	Text	E&xit

> *do the statements here*
> *End If*
>
> where the flag being set means that the flag has a value that is **True**. Similarly, selection can also be based on the fact that the flag is not set, which corresponds to a **False** condition.
>
> Although the exact origin of this term in programming is not known, it probably comes from the use of real flags to signal a condition, such as the Stop, Go, Caution, and Winner flags commonly used at car races.

Note in the event code for Program 5–4 that the text box **Enter** event is used to clear the text boxes of any text. The actual calculation is contained in the text box **Leave** event, which uses a one-way If statement to check the value in the text box and display the message This car is over the mileage limit only if mileage is greater than LIMIT.

Program 5–4's Event Code

```
Private Sub txtMiles_Enter(ByVal sender As Object, ByVal e As _
    System.EventArgs) Handles txtMiles.Enter
  txtError.Text = ""
  txtMiles.Text = ""
End Sub

Private Sub txtMiles_Leave(ByVal sender As Object, ByVal e As _
    System.EventArgs) Handles txtMiles.Leave
```

```
    Const LIMIT As Single = 3000.0
    Dim mileage As Single

    mileage = Val(txtMiles.Text)
    If mileage > LIMIT Then
      Beep()
      txtError.Text = "This car is over the mileage limit"
    End If
End Sub

Private Sub btnExit_Click(ByVal sender As Object, ByVal e As _
    System.EventArgs) Handles btnExit.Click
  Beep()
  End
End Sub
```

Figure 5–18 illustrates the case where the input data causes the statements within the **If** to be executed. In Figure 5–19 the input data is below the LIMIT so that the message is not printed.

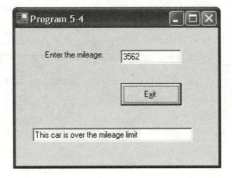

Figure 5–18   *Entering Mileage Greater than the Limit*

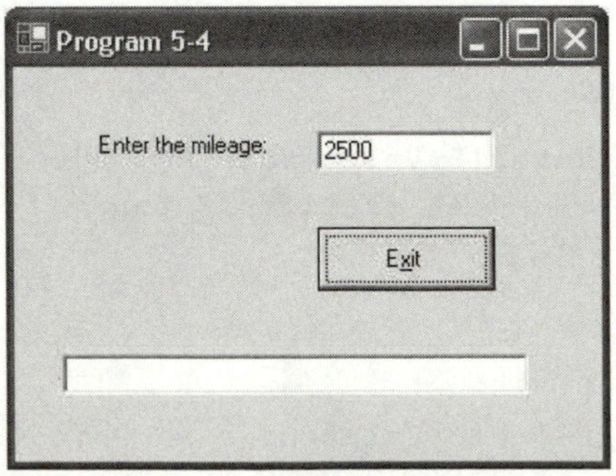

Figure 5–19   *Entering Mileage Below the Limit*

Nested If Statements

As noted above, an **If-Then-Else** statement can contain simple compound statements and any valid VB.NET statements can be used, including another **If-Then-Else** statement. Thus, one or more **If-Then-Else** statements can be included within either part of an **If-Then-Else** statement. For example, substituting the one-way `If` statement

```
If hours > 6 Then
  txtDisplay.Text = "snap"
End If
```

for *statement1* in the following

```
If hours < 9 Then
  statement1
Else
  txtDisplay.Text = "pop"
End If
```

results in the nested **If** statement

```
If hours < 9 Then
  If hours > 6 Then
    txtDisplay.Text = "snap"
  Endif
Else
  txtDisplay.Text = "pop"
Endif
```

The process of nesting `If` statements can be extended indefinitely, so the `txtDisplay.Text = "snap"` statement could itself be replaced by either a complete **If-Then-Else** statement or another one-way `If` statement.

Input Data Validation

`If` statements can be used to select appropriate processing paths as in Programs 5–3 and 5–4. These statements can also validate input data and prevent undesirable data from being processed at all. For example, a date such as 5/33/98 contains an obviously invalid day. Similarly, division of any number by zero within a program, such as 14/0, should not be allowed. Both of these examples illustrate the need for a technique referred to as *defensive programming*, in which code is used to check for improper input data before attempting to process it further. The defensive programming technique of checking user input data for erroneous or unreasonable data is called *input data validation*. We now have the tools to supply input data validation to Program 5–3.

Clearly, Program 5–3 expects that the user will enter a number and not a text string into the text box. To ensure that only numerical data is entered, we can validate each typed character and reject any keystrokes that do not result in one of the characters

0–9. This can be done using the text box's **KeyPress** event. This event enables us to examine and respond to the keystrokes made by a user. It should be noted that, in general, the e parameter may contain values passed by the object that caused the event to occur. The type of event procedure being called determines the uses of this parameter. In the KeyPress event procedure, the e parameter is useful. The declaration for this event, created by Visual Basic, is

```
Private Sub text-box-name_KeyPress(ByVal sender As Object, ByVal e As _
    System.Windows.Forms.KeyPressEventArgs) Handles text-box-name.KeyPress
```

where the argument **e.KeyChar**[2] provides the ANSI value as a string of the key that was pressed. (Appendix A lists the ANSI values for each character.) Note that non-ANSI keys such as the arrow keys, Ctrl, and Shift keys will not cause this event. Using a one-way **If** statement, this value can be compared to the ANSI values of the characters 0–9 using the following code:

```
If Asc(e.KeyChar) < Asc("0") Or Asc(e.KeyChar) > Asc("9") Then
  e.Handled = True
  Beep()
End If
```

The **Asc** function in this code takes the string value in e.KeyChar and returns the ANSI value as an integer. For example, the value returned by Asc("0") is 48 and the value returned by Asc("9") is 57. Thus, the If statement checks whether the ANSI value of the typed character is outside the range 48 to 57, and is thus invalid. If the key is outside of this range, the computer will beep. When e.Handled is set to **True**, the system will not process this event and the character that was typed does not get displayed in the text box. This effectively intercepts each key and replaces any nonnumeric key with no key. In this manner, each keystroke is checked as the user enters data. The complete event code that can be used for this input validation is listed below:

```
Private Sub txtIncome_KeyPress(ByVal sender As System.Object, _
    ByVal e As System.Windows.Forms.KeyPressEventArgs) Handles _
    txtIncome.KeyPress

  If Asc(e.KeyChar) < Asc("0") Or Asc(e.KeyChar) > Asc("9") Then
    e.Handled = True
    Beep()
  End If
End Sub
```

Before leaving this key-checking procedure, there is one additional verification we can make. Most users expect that pressing the **Enter** key will terminate data input. Of

---

[2]e is a parameter in an event procedure declaration that may contain values passed by the object that triggered the event. The use of the e parameter is different for different events.

course, this is not the case for text boxes, where the user must either press the Tab key, click on another object, or use hot keys to move off the box. However, we can check the value of the key just pressed to determine if it was the **Enter** key. Because the ANSI value of the **Enter** key is 13, this check takes the form:

```
Const ENTER = Chr(13)      ' the ANSI value of the Enter key
If e.KeyChar = ENTER Then
  btnExit.Focus()
End If
```

The Chr function returns the string consisting of the character with ANSI value of the argument. In this example, 13 is the ANSI value of the Enter key. This code simply checks whether the key just pressed is the **Enter** key. If it is, the focus is set to the **btnExit** object using the **Focus** method. Including this code with the prior check for a digit key results in the following event procedure:

```
Private Sub txtIncome_KeyPress(ByVal sender As System.Object, _
    ByVal e As System.Windows.Forms.KeyPressEventArgs) Handles
txtIncome.KeyPress
  Const ENTER = Chr(13) ' the ANSI value of the Enter key

  If e.KeyChar = ENTER Then
    btnExit.Focus()
  Else
    If Asc(e.KeyChar) < Asc("0") Or Asc(e.KeyChar) > Asc("9") Then
      e.Handled = True
      Beep()
    End If
  End If
End Sub
```

Note in the code above that we can use an If statement within another If statement. There are no restrictions on the statements we can use for either the statements after the If or the Else. However, for each If statement there must be a matching End If statement.

Programmer Notes

Validating Input Using the KeyPress Event

KeyPress event procedures are often used to validate user input for TextBox controls. When a text box has focus and the user presses a key, the character typed is automatically appended to the text box's Text property if there is no **KeyPress** Event procedure. If there is a procedure, however, the following occurs:

1. The ANSI value of the typed key is stored in the **KeyChar** property of the object reference parameter `e`.

   This value may then be accessed using `e.KeyChar`.

2. Visual Basic starts executing the **KeyPress** event procedure.

3. The event procedure code written by the user would normally examine the value of e.KeyChar and set e.Handled to True if the character is not valid. When this occurs, the character does not get appended to the text box's **Text** property. When the value of the **Handled** property is False (which is the default), the character is appended to the text box's **Text** property and displayed.

Exercises 5.3

1. Write appropriate **If–Then–Else** statements for each of the following conditions:

   a. If `angle` is equal to 90 degrees, print the message `The angle is a right angle`; else print the message `The angle is not a right angle`.

   b. If the temperature is above 100 degrees, display the message `above the boiling point of water`; else display the message `below the boiling point of water`.

   c. If the number is positive, add the number to `possum`; else add the number to `negsum`.

   d. If the slope is less than 0.5, set the variable `flag` to zero; else set `flag` to one.

   e. If the difference between `num1` and `num2` is less than 0.001, set the variable `approx` to zero; else calculate `approx` as the quantity `(num1 - num2) / 2.0`.

   f. If the difference between `temp1` and `temp2` exceeds 2.3 degrees, calculate error as `(temp1 - temp2) * factor`.

   g. If `x` is greater than `y` and `z` is less than 20, read in a value for `p`.

   h. If `distance` is greater than 20 and less than 35, read in a value for `time`.

2. Write **If–Then–Else** statements corresponding to the conditions illustrated by each of the following flow charts.

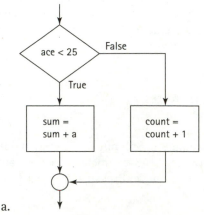

a.

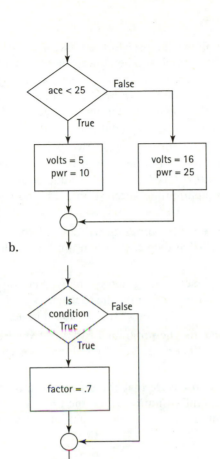

b.

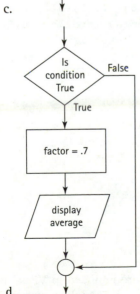

c.

d.

3. Write a Visual Basic program that allows the user to input two numbers. If the first number entered is greater than the second number, the program should print the message The first number is greater in a text box named txtDisplay; otherwise it should print the message The first number is smaller. Test your program by entering the numbers 5 and 8 and then using the numbers 11 and 2. What do you think your program will display if the two numbers entered are equal? Test this case.

4. a. If money is left in a particular bank for more than two years, the interest rate given by the bank is 5.5 percent, otherwise the interest rate is 3 percent. Write a Visual Basic program that uses a text box to accept the number of years into the variable nyrs and display the appropriate interest rate in another text box, depending on the input value.

   b. How many runs should you make for the program written in Exercise 4a to verify that it is operating correctly? What data should you input in each of the program runs?

5. a. In a pass/fail course, a student passes if the grade is greater than or equal to 70 and fails if the grade is lower. Write a program that accepts a grade and prints the message A passing grade or A failing grade, as appropriate.

   b. How many runs should you make for the program written in Exercise 5a to verify that it is operating correctly? What data should you input in each of the program runs?

6. A student wrote the following code to ensure that the input into a text box was a number and to set the focus on the btnExit button when the Enter key was pressed. When testing the code, the student noticed that the focus did not shift when the Enter key was pressed. Determine the error.

```
Private Sub txtMiles_KeyPress(ByVal sender As Object, ByVal e As _
    System.Windows.Forms.KeyPressEventArgs) Handles txtMiles.KeyPress
  Const ENTER = Chr(13) ' the ANSI value of the Enter key

  If Asc(e.KeyChar) < Asc("0") Or Asc(e.KeyChar) > Asc("9") Then
    e.Handled = True
    Beep()
  Else
    If e.KeyChar = ENTER Then
      btnExit.Focus()
    End If
  End If
End Sub
```

5.4 The If–Then–ElseIf Structure

A modification to the **If-Then-Else** selection structure provided in Visual Basic uses an ElseIf part. When an **ElseIf** is included within an **If-Then-Else** statement, the complete syntax is:

```
If condition-1 Then
     statement(s)
ElseIf condition-2 Then
     statement(s)
ElseIf condition-3 Then
     statement(s)
ElseIf condition-4 Then
          :
Else
     statement(s)
End If
```

Each condition is evaluated in the order it appears in this structure. For the first condition that is **True**, the corresponding statements between it and the next immediately following `ElseIf` or `Else` statement are executed; control is then transferred to the statement following the final `End If` statement. Thus, if condition-1 is True, only the first set of statements between condition-1 and conditon-2 is executed; otherwise, condition 2 is tested. If condition 2 is then true, only the second set of statements is executed; otherwise, condition 3 is tested. This process continues until a condition is satisfied or the `End If` statement is reached. The final `Else` statement, which is optional, is only executed if none of the previous conditions is satisfied. This serves as a default or "catch-all" case that is frequently useful for detecting an error condition. Although only three `ElseIf` parts are illustrated, any number of `ElseIf` parts may be used in the structure, which must be terminated with an `End If` statement.

As a specific example, consider the following **If-Else-ElseIf** statement:

```
If Marcode = "M" Then
  txtDisplay.Text = "Individual is married."
ElseIf Marcode = "S" Then
  txtDisplay.Text = "Individual is single."
ElseIf Marcode = "D" Then
  txtDisplay.Text = "Individual is divorced."
ElseIf Marcode = "W" Then
  txtDisplay.Text = "Individual is widowed."
Else
  txtDisplay.Text = "An invalid code was entered."
End If
```

Execution through this `If` statement begins with the testing of the expression `Marcode` = "M". If the value in `Marcode` is an `M`, the message Individual is married is displayed, no further expressions in the structure are evaluated, and execution resumes with the next statement immediately following the `End If` statement. If the value in `Marcode` is not an `M`, the expression `Marcode` = "S" is tested, and so on, until a **True** condition is found. If none of the conditions in the chain is **True**, the message "An invalid code was entered" is displayed. In all cases, execution resumes with whatever statement immediately follows the End If statement. Program 5–5 uses this **If-Then-Else** statement within a complete program. The interface and properties for Program 5–5 are illustrated in Figure 5–20 and Table 5–9, respectively. It is also important to note that in this example, the value of Marcode must be an upper case letter; lower case letters are not accepted.

Since the message in the text box depends on the text box input, we will use our standard procedure of clearing the text box when the text box gets the focus, and calculate the message to be displayed, based on the text box's data when the text box loses the focus. This is accomplished by the text box **Enter** and **Leave** event code. Within the

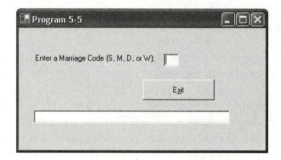

Figure 5–20   *Program 5–5's Interface*

Table 5–9   Program 5–5's Property Table

Object	Property	Setting
Form	Name	frmMain
	Text	Program 5–5
Label	Name	lblMcode
	Text	Enter a Marriage Code (S, M, D, or W):
TextBox	Name	txtMcode
	Text	(blank)
TextBox	Name	txtDisplay
	TabStop	False
	Text	(blank)
Button	Name	btnExit
	Text	E&xit

Leave event code, the message that is displayed in the second text box depends on the user input value for `Marcode`.

Program 5-5's Event Code

```
Private Sub txtMcode_Enter(ByVal sender As Object, _
    ByVal e As System.EventArgs) Handles txtMcode.Enter
  txtDisplay.Text = ""
End Sub

Private Sub txtMcode_Leave(ByVal sender As Object, _
    ByVal e As System.EventArgs) Handles txtMcode.Leave
  Dim Marcode As String

  Marcode = txtMcode.Text
  If Marcode = "M" Then
    txtDisplay.Text = "Individual is married."
  ElseIf Marcode = "S" Then
    txtDisplay.Text = "Individual is single."
  ElseIf Marcode = "D" Then
    txtDisplay.Text = "Individual is divorced."
  ElseIf Marcode = "W" Then
    txtDisplay.Text = "Individual is widowed."
  Else
    txtDisplay.Text = "An invalid code was entered."
  End If
End Sub

Private Sub txtMcode_KeyPress(ByVal sender As Object, ByVal e As _
    System.Windows.Forms.KeyPressEventArgs) Handles txtMcode.KeyPress
  Const ENTER = Chr(13) ' the ANSI value of the Enter key

  If e.KeyChar = ENTER Then
    btnExit.Focus()
  End If
End Sub

Private Sub btnExit_Click(ByVal sender As System.Object, ByVal e As _
    System.EventArgs) Handles btnExit.Click
  Beep()
  End
End Sub
```

As a final example illustrating the **If-Else** chain, we calculate the monthly income of a computer salesperson using the following commission schedule:

Monthly Sales	Income
greater than or equal to $50,000	$375 plus 16 percent of sales
less than $50,000 but greater than or equal to $40,000	$350 plus 14 percent of sales
less than $40,000 but greater than or equal to $30,000	$325 plus 12 percent of sales
less than $30,000 but greater than or equal to $20,000	$300 plus 9 percent of sales
less than $20,000 but greater than or equal to $10,000	$250 plus 5 percent of sales
less than $10,000	$200 plus 3 percent of sales

The following **If-Then-Else** chain can be used to determine the correct monthly income, where the variable MonthlySales is used to store the salesperson's current monthly sales:

```
If MonthlySales >= 50000.00 Then
   income = 375.00 + 0.16 * MonthlySales
ElseIf MonthlySales >= 40000.00 Then
   income = 350.00 + 0.14 * MonthlySales
ElseIf MonthlySales >= 30000.00 Then
   income = 325.00 + 0.12 * MonthlySales
ElseIf MonthlySales >= 20000.00 Then
   income = 300.00 + 0.09 * MonthlySales
ElseIf MonthlySales >= 10000.00 Then
   income = 250.00 + 0.05 * MonthlySales
Else
   income = 200.000 + 0.03 * MonthlySales
End If
```

Note that this example makes use of the fact that the chain is stopped once a **True** condition is found. This is accomplished by checking for the highest monthly sales first. If the salespersons monthly sales are less than $50,000, the **If-Then-ElseIf** chain continues checking for the next highest sales amount, until the correct category is obtained.

Program 5–6 uses this **If-Then-ElseIf** chain to calculate and display the income corresponding to the value of monthly sales input in the text box by the user. The interface and properties for Program 5–6 are illustrated in Figure 5–21 and Table 5–10, respectively.

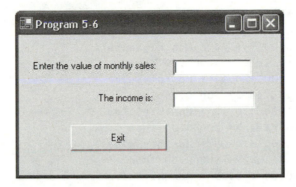

Figure 5–21   *Program 5–6's Interface*

Table 5–10   Program 5–6's Property Table

Object	Property	Setting
Form	Name	frmMain
	Text	Program 5–6
Label	Name	lblSales
	Text	Enter the value of monthly sales:
Label	Name	lblIncome
	Text	The income is:
TextBox	Name	txtSales
	Text	(blank)
TextBox	Name	txtIncome
	TabStop	False
Button	Name	btnExit
	Text	E&xit

Program 5–6's Event Code

```
Private Sub txtSales_Enter(ByVal sender As Object, _
    ByVal e As System.EventArgs) Handles txtSales.Enter
  txtIncome.Text = ""
  txtSales.Text = ""
End Sub

Private Sub txtSales_Leave(ByVal sender As Object, _
    ByVal e As System.EventArgs) Handles txtSales.Leave
  Dim MonthlySales, income As Single
```

```
MonthlySales = Val(txtSales.Text)
If MonthlySales >= 50000.00 Then
   income = 375.00 + 0.16 * MonthlySales
ElseIf MonthlySales >= 40000.00 Then
   income = 350.00 + 0.14 * MonthlySales
ElseIf MonthlySales >= 30000.00 Then
   income = 325.00 + 0.12 * MonthlySales
ElseIf MonthlySales >= 20000.00 Then
   income = 300.00 + 0.09 * MonthlySales
ElseIf MonthlySales >= 10000.00 Then
   income = 250.00 + 0.05 * MonthlySales
Else
 income = 200.00 + 0.03 * MonthlySales
End If


txtIncome.Text = FormatCurrency(income)
End Sub

Private Sub txtSales_KeyPress(ByVal sender As Object, ByVal e As _
   System.Windows.Forms.KeyPressEventArgs) Handles txtSales.KeyPress
Const ENTER = Chr(13) ' the ANSI value of the Enter key
Const DECPOINT = Chr(46) ' the ANSI value of the decimal point

If e.KeyChar = ENTER Then
   btnExit.Focus()
ElseIf (Asc(e.KeyChar) < Asc("0") Or Asc(e.KeyChar) > Asc("9")) And _
      e.KeyChar <> DECPOINT Then
   e.Handled = True
   Beep()
End If
End Sub

Private Sub btnExit_Click(ByVal sender As Object, _
   ByVal e As System.EventArgs) Handles btnExit.Click
Beep()
End
End Sub
```

The selection code contained within the **Leave** event is simply the **If-Then-Else** statement previously presented. However, a new feature of the event code is contained within the **KeyPress** event procedure. Note that we have included the ANSI code for the decimal point and have included the decimal point as one of the valid keys that may be

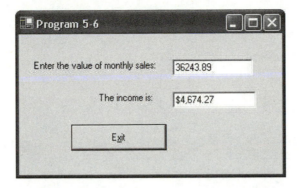

Figure 5–22 *A Sample Run Using Program 5–6*

pressed by a user when entering a number. Figure 5–22 illustrates a sample run using Program 5–6.

Exercises 5.4

1. Modify Program 5–5 to accept both lowercase and uppercase letters as marriage codes. For example, if a user enters either an m or an M, the program should display the message `Individual is married`.

2. Write If statements corresponding to the conditions illustrated in each of the following flowcharts.

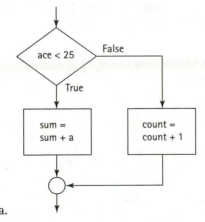

a.

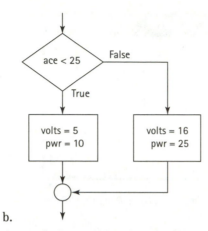

b.

3. An angle is considered acute if it is less than 90 degrees, obtuse if it is greater than 90 degrees, and a right angle if it is equal to 90 degrees. Using this information, write a Visual Basic program that accepts an angle, in degrees, and displays the type of angle corresponding to the degrees entered.

4. The grade level of undergraduate college students is typically determined according to the following schedule:

Number of Credits Completed	Grade Level
Less than 32	Freshman
32 to 63	Sophomore
64 to 95	Junior
96 or more	Senior

Using this information, write a Visual Basic program that accepts the number of credits a student has completed, determines the student's grade level, and displays the grade level.

5. A student's letter grade is calculated according to the following schedule:

Numerical Grade	Letter Grade
Greater than or equal to 90	A
Less than 90 but greater than or equal to 80	B
Less than 80 but greater than or equal to 70	C
Less than 70 but greater than or equal to 60	D
Less than 60	F

Using this information, write a Visual Basic program that accepts a student's numerical grade, converts the numerical grade to an equivalent letter grade, and displays the letter grade.

6. The interest rate used on funds deposited in a bank is determined by the amount of time the money is left on deposit. For a particular bank, the following schedule is used:

Time on Deposit	Interest Rate
Greater than or equal to 5 years	7.5 percent
Less than 5 years but greater than or equal to 4 years	7.0 percent
Less than 4 years but greater than or equal to 3 years	6.5 percent
Less than 3 years but greater than or equal to 2 years	5.5 percent
Less than 2 years but greater than or equal to 1 year	4.65 percent
Less than 1 year	3.58 percent

Using this information, write a Visual Basic program that accepts the time that funds are left on deposit and displays the interest rate corresponding to the time entered.

7. Using the commission schedule from Program 5-6, a student coded the text box's **Leave** event procedure as follows:

```
Private Sub txtSales_Leave(ByVal sender As Object, _
    ByVal e As System.EventArgs) Handles txtSales.Leave
  Dim MonthlySales, income As Single

  MonthlySales = Val(txtSales.Text)
  If MonthlySales >= 50000.00 Then
    income = 375.00 +.16 * MonthlySales
  End If
  If MonthlySales >= 40000.00 & MonthlySales < 50000.00 Then
    income = 350.00 +.14 * MonthlySales
  End If
  If MonthlySales >= 30000.00 & MonthlySales < 40000.00 Then
    income = 325.00 +.12 * MonthlySales
  End If
  If MonthlySales >= 20000.00 & MonthlySales < 30000.00 Then
    income = 300.00 +.09 * MonthlySales
  End If
  If MonthlySales >= 10000.00 & MonthlySales < 20000.00 Then
    income = 250.00 +.05 * MonthlySales
  End If
  If MonthlySales < 10000.00 Then
    income = 200.00 +.03 * MonthlySales
  End If

  txtIncome.Text = FormatCurrency(income)
End Sub
```

a. Will this code produce the same output as Program 5–6?

b. Which program is better and why?

8. a. Will the following event code produce the same result as that used in Program 5–6?

```
Private Sub txtSales_Leave(ByVal sender As Object, _
    ByVal e As System.EventArgs) Handles txtSales.Leave
  Dim MonthlySales, income As Single

  MonthlySales = Val(txtSales.Text)
  If MonthlySales < 10000.00
      income = 200.00 +.03 * MonthlySales
  ElseIf MonthlySales >= 10000.00 Then
      income = 250.00 +.05 * MonthlySales
  ElseIf MonthlySales >= 20000.00 Then
      income = 300.00 +.09 * MonthlySales
  ElseIf MonthlySales >= 30000.00 Then
      income = 325.00 +.12 * MonthlySales
  ElseIf MonthlySales >= 40000.00 Then
      income = 350.00 +.14 * MonthlySales
  ElseIf MonthlySales >= 50000.00 Then
      income = 375.00 +.16 * MonthlySales
  End If
  txtIncome.Text = FormatCurrency(income)
End Sub
```

b. What does the event procedure do?

c. For what values of monthly sales does this procedure calculate the correct income?

9. a. Write a Visual Basic program that accepts two real numbers from a user, using individual text boxes, and a select code, using a radio box group. If the entered select code is 1, have the program add the two previously entered numbers and display the result; if the select code is 2, the second number should be subtracted from the first number; if the select code is 3, the numbers should be multiplied; and if the select code is 3, the first number should be divided by the second number.

b. Determine what the program written in Exercise 9a does when the entered numbers are 3 and 0, and the select code is 3.

c. Modify the program written in Exercise 9a so that division by 0 is not allowed and so that an appropriate message is displayed when such a division is attempted.

10. a. Write a program that displays the following two labels:

Enter a month (use a 1 for Jan, etc.):

Enter a day of the month:

Have your program accept a user input number in a Text box and store the number in a variable named month, in response to the first label prompt. Similarly, have it accept and store a number entered in a second text box in the variable named day in response to the second label prompt. If the month entered is not between one and twelve inclusive, print a message informing the user that an invalid month has been entered. If the day entered is not between one and thirty-one, print a message informing the user that an invalid day has been entered.

b. What will your program do if the user types a number with a decimal point for the month? How can you ensure that your If statements check for an integer number?

c. In a non-leap year, February has 28 days, the months January, March, May, July, August, October, and December have 31 days, and all other months have 30 days. Using this information, modify the program written in Exercise 10a to display a message when an invalid day is entered for a user-entered month. For this program, ignore leap years.

11. All years that are evenly divisible by 400 or are evenly divisible by four and not evenly divisible by 100, are leap years. For example, because 1600 is evenly divisible by 400, the year 1600 was a leap year. Similarly, since 1988 is evenly divisible by four, but not by 100, the year 1988 was also a leap year. Using this information, write a Visual Basic program that accepts the year as a user input, determines if the year is a leap year, and displays an appropriate message that tells the user if the entered year is or is not a leap year.

12. Based on an automobile's model year and weight, the state of New Jersey determines the weight class and registration fee using the following schedule:

Model Year	Weight	Registration class	Fee
1970 or earlier	less than 2,700 lbs	1	$16.50
	2,700 to 3,800 lbs	2	25.50
	more than 3,800 lbs	3	46.50
1971 to 1979	less than 2,700 lbs	4	27.00
	2,700 to 3,800 lbs	5	30.50
	more than 3,800 lbs	6	52.50
1980 or later	less than 3,500 lbs	7	19.50
	3,500 or more lbs	8	52.50

Using this information, write a Visual Basic program that accepts the year and weight of an automobile and determines and displays the weight class and registration fee for the car.

5.5   The Select Case Structure

An alternative to the **If-Then-ElseIf** structure presented in the previous section is the **Select-Case** structure. The syntax of the **Select-Case** construct is:

```
Select Case expression
  Case value_1
     statement(s)
  Case value_2
     statement(s)
        :
  Case value_n
     statement(s)
  Case Else
     statement(s)
End Select   ' End of Select Structure
```

The Select Case structure uses three Visual Basic statements, a single Select Case statement, one or more Case statements, and a required End Select statement. Let us see how these statements are used. The Select Case statement, which has the general form:

```
Select Case expression
```

identifies the start of the Select Case construct. The expression in this statement is evaluated and the result of the expression is compared to various alternative values contained within each Case statement.

Internal to the Select Case construct, the Case statement, which has the general syntax

```
Case list of values
```

is used to identify individual values that are compared to the value of the Select Case expression. The expression's value is compared to each of these Case values, in the order that these values are listed, until a match is found. Execution then begins with the statement immediately following the matching Case and ends when either the next Case or End Select statement is encountered. The Select Case structure is then exited and program execution continues with the statement following the End Select statement, which formally ends the Select Case construct. Thus the value of the expression determines where in the Case construct execution actually begins, as illustrated in Figure 5–23.

Any number of Case labels may be contained within a Select Case structure, in any order; the only requirement is that the values in each Case statement must be of the same type as the expression in the Select Case statement. However, if the value of the expression does not match any of the case values, no statement within the Case construct is executed unless a Case Else statement is encountered. The Case Else statement is optional and produces the same effect as the last Else in an If-ElseIf structure. If the value of the Select Case expression does not match any of the Case values, and the Case Else statement is present, execution begins with the statement following the word Else.

Once an entry point has been located by the Select Case structure, all further case evaluations are ignored and execution continues until either a Case or End Select statement is encountered.

When writing a Select Case structure, you can use multiple case values to refer to the same set of statements; the Case Else is optional. For example, consider the following:

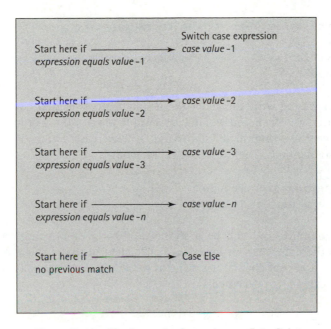

Figure 5–23 *The Expression Determines an Entry Point*

```
Select Case number
  Case 1
    MessageBox.Show("Have a Good Morning")
  Case 2
    MessageBox.Show("Have a Happy Day")
  Case 3, 4, 5
    MessageBox.Show("Have a Nice Evening")
End Select
```

If the value stored in the variable number is 1, the message Have a Good Morning is displayed. Similarly, if the value of the variable number is 2, the second message is displayed. Finally, if the value of number is 3 or 4 or 5, the last message is displayed. Because the statement to be executed for these last three cases is the same, the cases for these values can be consecutively grouped as shown in the example. Also, because there is no Case Else, no message is printed if the value of number is not one of the listed case values. Although it is good programming practice to list case values in increasing order, the Select Case statement does not require this. A Select Case statement may have any number of case values, in any order; only the values being tested for need to be listed.

A Select Case structure can also be used to test the value of a string expression. For example, assuming that letter is a string variable, the following Select Case statement is valid:

```
Select Case letter
  Case "a", "e", "i", "o", "u", "A", "E", "I", "O", "U"
```

```
      txtDisplay.Text = "The character is a vowel"
   Case Else
      txtDisplay.Text = "The character is not a vowel"
End Select
```

Another way to write the above set of statements is to first convert the letter to a lower-case letter, and then you would only need to specify the five lowercase vowels. One way to convert a string to all uppercase or lowercase letters is to use the `ToUpper` or `ToLower` methods. The form of these methods is:

stringexpression.ToUpper
stringexpression.ToLower

stringexpression can be a string expression or a string variable and the method returns the uppercase (or lowercase) equivalent of that string expression. A call to these methods does not change the value of the original string. For example, after the following statements are executed,

```
strngvar = "This is a STRING"
upperstrngvar = strngvar.ToUpper
```

the variable `upperstrngvar` is set to "THIS IS A STRING".
    Using the `ToLower` method, the above code would be rewritten as:

```
Select Case letter.ToLower
   Case "a", "e", "i", "o", "u"
      txtDisplay.Text = "The character is a vowel"
   Case Else
      txtDisplay.Text = "The character is not a vowel"
End Select
```

Exercises 5.5

1. Rewrite the following `If-Else` chain using a `Select Case` statement:

```
If let_grad = "A"
  lstDisplay.Items.Add("The numerical grade is between 90 and 100")
ElseIf let_grad = "B"
  lstDisplay.Items.Add("The numerical grade is between 80 and 89.9")
ElseIf let_grad = "C"
  lstDisplay.Items.Add("The numerical grade is between 70 and 79.9")
ElseIf let_grad = "D"
  lstDisplay.Items.Add("How are you going to explain this one?")
Else
```

```
lstDisplay.Items.Add("Of course I had nothing to do with my grade.")
lstDisplay.Items.Add("It must have been the professor's fault.")
End If
```

2. Rewrite the following `If-Else` chain using a `Select Case` statement:

```
If res_typ = 1
  a = b + c
ElseIf res_typ = 2
  a = b * c
ElseIf res_typ = 3
    a = b / c
ElseIf res_typ = 4
  a = 4
ElseIf res_typ = 5
  a = c/b
ElseIf res_typ = 6
  a = b + c/d
End If
```

3. Each disk drive in a shipment of these devices is stamped with a code from 1 through 4, indicating the following drive manufacturers:

Code	Disk Drive Manufacturer
1	3M Corporation
2	Maxell Corporation
3	Sony Corporation
4	Verbatim Corporation

Write a Visual Basic program that accepts the code number as an input, and based on the value entered, displays the correct disk drive manufacturer.

5.6   Focus on Program Design and Implementation: Controlling Focus and On–the–Fly Data Validation[3]

Figure 5–24 illustrates the Rotech project's current Walk In order-entry form. With the information provided in this chapter, we can now provide this form with two additional features required of all commercial applications: focus control features that automatically move the focus to the next input control when the Enter key is pressed and input

---

[3]The Rotech project, as it should exist at the start of this section (which includes all of the capabilities built into it through the end of Section 4.4) can be found at http://computerscience.jbpub.com/bronsonvbnet in the ROTECH4 folder as project rotech4.

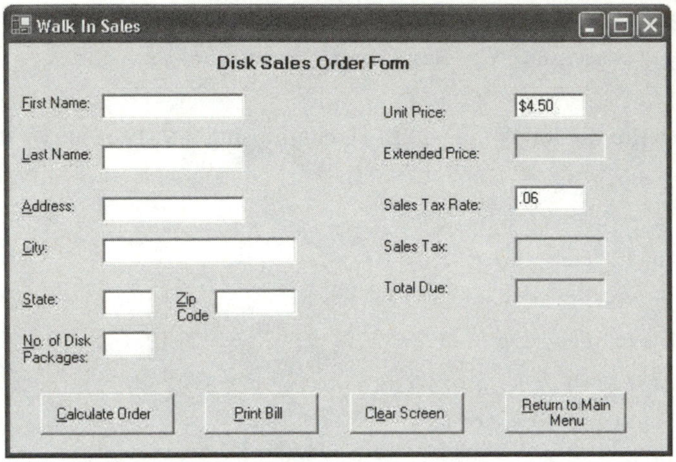

Figure 5–24   *The Current Walk In Order Entry Form*

data validation, so that a user cannot enter data that will cause the program to crash. We start by providing the focus control feature.

Focus Control

The **TabIndex** property controls how focus shifts when a user presses either the Tab key or the Shift-Tab keys together. Pressing the tab key moves the focus to the control with the next highest **TabIndex** value, while the Shift-Tab keys move the focus in the opposite direction. In addition to this operation, users expect that when they press the Enter key, input to the current control will stop and focus will shift to the next input control. Unfortunately, this operation is not built into Visual Basic. To force this type of focus shift, we can use each control's **KeyPress** event to detect when the Enter key has been pressed, and then use the **Leave** method to explicitly shift the focus to another control when the detection is made. Event Procedure 5–1 illustrates the code that can be used for the First Name text box shown in Figure 5–24 (named txtFname) to shift focus to the Last Name text box (named txtLname) when the Enter key is pressed. If this code is unfamiliar to you, review Section 5.3's Input Data Validation section, where the code is described in detail.

Event Procedure 5–1

```
Private Sub txtFname_KeyPress(ByVal sender As Object, _
    ByVal e As System.Windows.Forms.KeyPressEventArgs) Handles _
    txtFname.KeyPress
  Const ENTER = Chr(13) ' the ANSI value of the Enter key

  If  e.KeyChar = ENTER Then
    txtLname.Focus()
  End If
End Sub
```

One drawback to Event Procedure 5-1's code is that the name of the control to which the focus is shifted must be included with the Focus method. That is, there is no Visual Basic statement that uses the TabIndex values to focus on the next TabIndex value. Event Procedures 5-2 illustrate the complete set of procedures, including Event Procedure 5-1 that can be used to control the shifting of focus by using the Enter button for Rotech's WalkJn order entry form.

Event Procedures 5-2

```
Private Sub txtFname_KeyPress(ByVal sender As Object, _
    ByVal e As System.Windows.Forms.KeyPressEventArgs) Handles _
    txtFname.KeyPress
  Const ENTER = Chr(13) ' the ANSI value of the Enter key

  If e.KeyChar = ENTER Then
    txtLname.Focus()
  End If
End Sub

Private Sub txtLname_KeyPress(ByVal sender As Object, _
    ByVal e As System.Windows.Forms.KeyPressEventArgs) Handles _
    txtLname.KeyPress
  Const ENTER = Chr(13) ' the ANSI value of the Enter key

  If e.KeyChar = ENTER Then
    txtAddr.Focus()
  End If
End Sub

Private Sub txtAddr_KeyPress(ByVal sender As Object, _
    ByVal e As System.Windows.Forms.KeyPressEventArgs) Handles _
    txtAddr.KeyPress
  Const ENTER = Chr(13) ' the ANSI value of the Enter key

  If e.KeyChar = ENTER Then
    txtCity.Focus()
  End If
End Sub

Private Sub txtCity_KeyPress(ByVal sender As Object, _
    ByVal e As System.Windows.Forms.KeyPressEventArgs) Handles _
    txtCity.KeyPress
  Const ENTER = Chr(13) ' the ANSI value of the Enter key

  If e.KeyChar = ENTER Then
    txtState.Focus()
```

```
      End If
End Sub


Private Sub txtState_KeyPress(ByVal sender As Object, _
    ByVal e As System.Windows.Forms.KeyPressEventArgs) Handles _
    txtState.KeyPress
  Const ENTER = Chr(13) ' the ANSI value of the Enter key

  If e.KeyChar = ENTER Then
    txtZip.Focus()
  End If
End Sub


Private Sub txtZip_KeyPress(ByVal sender As Object, _
    ByVal e As System.Windows.Forms.KeyPressEventArgs) Handles _
    txtZip.KeyPress
  Const ENTER = Chr(13) ' the ANSI value of the Enter key

  If e.KeyChar = ENTER Then
    txtQuantity.Focus()
  End If
End Sub


Private Sub txtQuantity_KeyPress(ByVal sender As Object, _
    ByVal e As System.Windows.Forms.KeyPressEventArgs) Handles _
    txtQuantity.KeyPress
  Const ENTER = Chr(13) ' the ANSI value of the Enter key

  If e.KeyChar = ENTER Then
    btnCalculate.Focus()
  End If
End Sub
```

In reviewing the procedures contained within Event Procedures 5–2, note that all procedures are essentially copies of Event Procedure 5–1, with the only difference being the object named for the Focus method. Thus, once you have coded one of these procedures, you can use standard copy-and-paste techniques to include the code within each subsequent event procedure, and then change the object named to receive focus.

Also, note that the last event procedure listed shifts the focus to the Calculate button rather than to the Print button. Although most of the time a user will want to print a bill from the order entry form, shifting focus to the Calculate button prevents a user from inadvertently printing a bill by unintentionally pressing the Enter key one too many times. Pressing the Enter key while the focus is on the Calculate button will simply fill in the order form with the calculated data, and still force the user to make a conscious choice of either tabbing over to the <u>P</u>rint button or using this button's access key when a bill is needed.

On-the-Fly Input Data Validation

The user input to the Walk In form that can easily cause the system to crash is the quantity of disks ordered. If the data entered is not numeric or cannot be converted to numeric data, the system will crash when it uses this quantity to calculate a total amount. The surest way to guarantee correct data is to verify each keystroke made by the user as data is being entered. This type of input data validation—where each keystroke is checked immediately after being pressed—is referred to as on-the-fly validation. For our particular case, the entered data must be an integer, which means each key pressed should be either the Enter key or correspond to a digit between 0 and 9. This type of validation was presented in Section 5.3, and the relevant code is repeated below for convenience:

```
If Asc(e.KeyChar) < Asc("0") Or Asc(e.KeyChar) > Asc("9") Then
   e.Handled = True
   Beep()
End If
```

This code can easily be incorporated into the existing **If** statement within the txtQuantity text box **KeyPress** event code listed in Event Procedure 5–2. Doing so provides the code listed in Event Procedure 5–3. Note that in this code we have also added a Message box to inform the user that an incorrect character was entered. However, the code does not check that the number is reasonable.

Event Procedure 5–3

```
Private Sub txtQuantity_KeyPress(ByVal sender As Object, _
   ByVal e As System.Windows.Forms.KeyPressEventArgs) Handles
   txtQuantity.KeyPress
  Const ENTER = Chr(13) ' the ANSI value of the Enter key

  If e.KeyChar = ENTER Then
    btnCalculate.Focus()
  ElseIf  Asc(e.KeyChar) < Asc("0") Or  Asc(e.KeyChar) > Asc("9") Then
    e.Handled = True
    Beep()
    MessageBox.Show("You can only enter a number here.", _
        "Data Entry Error", MessageBoxButtons.OK, MessageBoxIcon.Error)
  End If
End Sub
```

Exercises 5.6

(Note: The Rotech Systems project, at the stage of development begun in this section, can be found at http://computerscience.jbpub.com/bronsonvbnet in the ROTECH4 folder as project rotech4. The project, as it exists at the end of this section, can be found in the ROTECH5 folder as project rotech5. If you are developing the system yourself, following the procedures given in this section, we suggest that you first copy all of the files in the ROTECH4 folder onto your system, and then work out of this latter folder. When you have finished your changes, you can compare your results to the files in the ROTECH5 folder.)

1. a. Either add the data validation and Enter key focus shifting code described in this section to the Rotech system or locate and load the project from http://computerscience.jbpub.com/bronsonvbnet.

   b. Test that the Enter key correctly shifts control focus as expected, and that the data validation procedure works correctly when a quantity is entered in the Walk In Order Entry Form.

2. Add the same type of focus shifting and input data validation to Rotech system's Mail In form as was made to the Walk In form.

3. Using the Help facility's Index tab, obtain information on the **Focus** method used within all of the **Click** event procedures presented in this section.

4. a. Modify the Walk In form's <u>P</u>rint button's event code to provide the following two features:

      i. If both the first and last name text boxes are blank, the name printed on the bill and displayed in the txtFname Text box should be "Cash".

      ii. If no quantity is entered in the quantity text box, a message box should be displayed indicating that a bill will not be printed unless an amount is entered.

   b. Would you classify the data validation code written for Exercise 4a as on-the-fly validation? Why or why not?

5. (Case study) For your selected project (see project specifications at the end of Section 1.5), complete the order entry form you developed in Chapter 4 by adding appropriate input data validation and Enter key-activated focus shifting.

5.7 Knowing About: Errors, Testing, and Debugging

The ideal in programming is to efficiently produce readable, error-free programs that work correctly and can be modified or changed with a minimum of testing required for reverification. In this regard, it is useful to know the different types of errors that can occur, when they are detected, and how to correct them.

Design-time and Run-time Errors

A program error can be detected at various times:

1. During design time

2. During run time

3. After the program has been executed and the output is being examined

4. Never

Errors detected by the compiler are formally referred to as *design-time* errors, and errors that occur while the program is being run are formally referred to as *run-time* errors.

Methods are available for detecting errors both before and after a program has been executed. The method for detecting errors after a program has been executed is called *program verification and testing.* The method for detecting errors before a program is run is called *desk checking* because the programmer sits at a desk or table and checks the program, by hand, for syntax and logic errors.

Syntax and Logic Errors

There are two primary types of errors, referred to as syntax and logic errors. A *syntax* error is an error in the structure or spelling of a statement. For example, the statements

```
If a < b
  MessageBox.Show("There are four syntax errors here)
  MsgBox.Show(" can you find tem")
End
```

contain four syntax errors. These errors are:

1. The keyword `Then` is missing in the first line.

2. A closing double quote is missing in line two.

3. The keyword `MessageBox.Show` is misspelled in line three.

4. The `End` keyword in line four should be `End If`.

All of these errors will be detected by Visual Basic when the program is translated for execution. This is true of all syntax errors, because they violate the basic rules of the language.[4] In some cases the error message is clear and the error is obvious; in other cases it takes a little detective work to understand the error message. Note that the misspelling of the word them in the third line is not a syntax error. Although this spelling error will result in an undesirable output line being displayed, it is not a violation of Visual Basic's syntactical rules. It is simply a typographical error, commonly referred to as a "typo."

Logic errors result directly from some flaw in the program's logic. These errors, which are never caught during translation, may be detected either by desk-checking, by program testing, by accident when a user obtains an obviously erroneous output, while

---

[4]However, they may not all be detected at the same time. Frequently, one syntax error masks another error, and the second error is only detected after the first error is corrected.

the program is executing, or never. If the error is detected while the program is executing, a run-time error occurs that results in an error message being generated and/or abnormal and premature program termination.

Because logic errors may not be detected during translation, they are always more difficult to detect than syntax errors. If not detected by desk checking, a logic error most often will reveal itself in one of three ways:

1. **No output**

   This is caused either by an omission of an output statement or by a sequence of statements that inadvertently bypasses an output statement.

2. **Unappealing or misaligned output**

   This is caused by an error in an output statement.

3. **Incorrect numerical result**

   This is caused either by incorrect values assigned to the variables used in an expression, the use of an incorrect arithmetic expression, an omission of a statement, a round-off error, or the use of an improper sequence of statements.

Sometimes faulty or incomplete program logic will cause a run-time error. Examples of this type of logic error are attempts to divide by zero or to take the square root of a negative number.

Testing and Debugging

In theory, a comprehensive set of test runs would reveal all possible program errors and ensure that a program will work correctly for any and all combinations of input and computed data. In practice, this requires checking all possible combinations of event activation and statement execution. Due to the time and effort required, this is an impossible goal, except for extremely simple programs. Let us examine why this is so. Consider the following event code that is activated on a button **Click** event:

```
Private Sub btnTest_Click (ByVal sender As System.Object, _
    ByVal e As System.EventArgs) Handles btnText.Click
  Dim num As Integer

  num = Val(txtDisplay.text)
  If num = 5 Then
    MessageBox.Show("Bingo!")
  Else
    MessageBox.Show("Bongo!")
  End If
End Sub
```

This event code has two paths that can be traversed when the event code is activated. The first path, which is executed when the input number is 5, consists of the statement:

```
MessageBox.Show("Bingo!")
```

The second path, which is executed whenever any number except 5 is input, consists of the statement:

```
MessageBox.Show("Bongo!")
```

To test each possible path through this event code requires two activations of the **Click** event, with a judicious selection of test input data to ensure that both paths of the **If** statement are exercised. The addition of one more **If-Else** statement in the program increases the number of possible execution paths by a factor of two and requires four (2^2) runs of the program for complete testing. Similarly, two additional **If-Else** statements increase the number of paths by a factor of four and require eight (2^3) runs for complete testing, and three additional **If-Else** statements would produce a program that required sixteen (2^4) test runs.

Now consider a modestly sized application consisting of only ten event procedures, with each procedure containing five **If-Else** statements. Assuming the procedures are always activated in the same sequence, there are 32 possible paths through each module (2 raised to the fifth power) and more than 1,000,000,000,000,000 (2 raised to the fiftieth power) possible paths through the complete application (all modules executed in sequence). The time needed to create individual test data to exercise each path and the actual computer run time required to check each path make the complete testing of such a program impossible.

The inability to fully test all combinations of statement execution sequences has led to the claim that there is no error-free program. It has also led to the realization that any testing should be well thought out to maximize the possibility of locating errors. At a minimum, test data should include appropriate values for input values, illegal input values that the program should reject, and limiting values that are checked by selection statements within the program.

Another important realization is that, although a single test can reveal the presence of an error, it cannot guarantee the absence of one. The fact that one error is revealed by a particular verification run does not indicate that another error is not lurking somewhere else in the program. Also, the fact that one test revealed no errors does not indicate that there are no errors.

Although there are no hard and fast rules for isolating the cause of an error, some useful techniques can be applied. The first of these is preventive. Many errors are introduced by the programmer in the rush to code and run a program before fully understanding what is required and how the result is to be achieved. A symptom of this haste to get a program entered into the computer is the lack of an outline of the proposed program (pseudocode or flowcharts) or a hand-written program. Many errors can be eliminated simply by desk-checking a copy of each procedure before it is ever entered or translated.

A second useful technique is to mimic the computer and execute each statement, by hand, as the computer would. This means writing down each variable as it is encountered in the program and listing the value that should be stored in the variable, as each input and assignment statement is encountered. Doing this also sharpens your programming skills, because it requires that you fully understand what each statement in your program causes to happen. Such a check is called *program tracing*.

A third debugging technique is to use one or more diagnostic `MessageBox.Show` statements to display the values of selected variables. In this same manner, another use of `MessageBox.Show` statements in debugging is to immediately display the values of all input data. This technique is referred to as *echo printing* and is useful in establishing that the computer is correctly receiving and interpreting the input data.

The fourth and most powerful debugging technique is to use the debugger that comes with Visual Basic. The debugger is discussed in Chapter 7.

Finally, no discussion of program verification is complete without mentioning the primary ingredient needed for successful isolation and correction of errors: the attitude and spirit you bring to the task. Because you wrote the program, your natural assumption is that it is correct, or you would have changed it before it was executed. It is extremely difficult to back away and honestly test and find errors in your own software. As a programmer, you must constantly remind yourself that just because you *think* your program is correct does not make it so. Finding errors in your own programs is a sobering experience, but one that will help you become a better programmer. It can also be exciting and fun, if approached as a detection problem with you as the detective.

5.8 Common Programming Errors and Problems

The common programming errors related to Visual Basic's selection statements include the following:

1. Omitting the keyword **Then** from an **If** and **Else** statement
2. Writing the keyword **ElseIf** as the two words **Else** and **If**
3. Trying to use a logical operator without a relational expression or logical variable immediately following it. For example, the expression

   ```
   age >= 35 And < 40
   ```

   is invalid. The expression

   ```
   age >= 35 And age < 40
   ```

   using the **And** operator to connect the two relational expressions is valid.
4. This error presents a typical debugging problem. Here an **If** statement appears to select an incorrect choice and the programmer mistakenly concentrates on the tested condition as the source of the problem. For example, assume that the following **If-Else** statement is part of your program:

   ```
   If key = "F" Then
     temp = (5.0 / 9.0) * (temp  - 32.0)
     txtDisplay.Text = "Conversion to Celsius completed"
   Else
     temp = (9.0 / 5.0) * temp + 32.0
     txtDisplay.Text = "Conversion to Fahrenheit completed"
   End If
   ```

This statement will always display "Conversion to Celsius completed" when the variable key contains an F. Therefore, if this message is displayed when you believe the variable key does not contain an F, investigation of the key's value is called for. As a general rule, whenever a selection statement does not act as you think it should, be sure to test your assumptions about the values assigned to the tested variables by displaying these values. If an unanticipated value is displayed, you have at least isolated the source of the problem to the variables themselves, rather than the structure of the **If-Then** statement. From there you will have to determine where and how the incorrect value was obtained.

5.9 Chapter Review

Key Terms

CheckBox control	logical operators
condition	nested **If**
flag	one-way selection
GroupBox control	RadioButton control
If-Then-Else structure	**Select Case** structure
input data validation	simple relational expression
ListBox control	

Summary

1. Relational expressions, which are also called *simple conditions*, are used to compare operands. The value of a relational expression is either **True** or **False**. Relational expressions are created using the following relational operators:

Relational Operator	Meaning	Example
<	Less than	`age < 30`
>	Greater than	`height >6.2`
<=	Less than or equal to	`taxable <= 20000`
>=	Greater than or equal to	`temp >= 98.6`
=	Equal to	`grade = 100`
<>	*Not equal to*	`number <> 250`

2. More complex conditions can be constructed from relational expressions using Visual Basic's **And, Or,** and **Not** logical operators.

3. An **If** statement is used to select one or more statements for execution based on the value of a condition. The single-line **If** statement has the form:

> If *condition* **Then** *statement*

and is used without an **End If** statement. Additionally, one **Else** statement and any number of ElseIf statements may be used with an **If** statement to provide multiple selection criteria; this must be followed by an **End If** statement. The common selection structures that can be created using an **If** statement include the following forms:

a. Form 1: Simple If:

> If *condition* **Then**
>   *statement(s)*
> **End If**

Here, the statements between the **If** and **End If** statements are only executed if the condition being tested is true. The **If** and **End If** statements must be written on separate lines.

b. Form 2: Simple If Else:

> If *condition* **Then**
>   *statement(s)*
> **Else**
>   *statement(s)*
> **End If**

This is a two-way selection structure. Here the **Else** statement is used with the **If** to select between two alternative sets of statements based on the value of a condition. If the condition is **True**, the first set of statements is executed; otherwise, the set of statements following the keyword **Else** is executed. The **If**, **Else** and **End If** statements must be written on separate lines.

c. Form 3: Simple If-ElseIf-Else:

> If *condition-1* **Then**
>   *statement(s)*
> ElseIf *condition-2* **Then**
>   *statement(s)*
> **Else**
>   *statement(s)*
> **End If**

This is a three-way selection structure. Once a condition is satisfied, only the statements between that condition and the next **ElseIf** or **Else** are executed, and no further conditions are tested. The **Else** statement is optional, and the statements corresponding to the **Else** statement are only executed if neither condition-1 nor condition-2 is **True**. The **If**, **ElseIf**, **Else**, and **End If** statements must be written on separate lines.

d. Form 4: Multiple **Else-Ifs:**

If *condition-1* **Then**
  statement(s)
ElseIf *condition-2* **Then**
  statement(s)

    .
    .
    .

ElseIf *condition-n* **Then**
  statement(s)
Else
  statement(s)
End If

This is a multiway selection structure. Once a condition is satisfied, only the statements between that condition and the next **ElseIf** or **Else** are executed, and no further conditions are tested. The **Else** statement is optional, and the statements corresponding to the **Else** statement are only executed if none of the conditions tested are **True**. The **If**, **Else**, and **End If** statements must be written on individual lines.

Test Yourself–Short Answer

1. The `Select Case` statement always ends with the statement _____.
2. If you click a grayed Check box, what will happen?
3. If your form has a single group of 5 check boxes and a single group of 5 radio buttons, how many of the check boxes can be true at the same time? _____ How many of the radio buttons can be true at the same time? _____
4. Write a `Select Case` statement that will check the value of a variable myNum and process as follows:

myNum Value	Required Processing
1 or 7 or 15	Add 100 to myNum
2 or 9 or 21	Add 150 to myNum
3 or 6 or 13	Add 200 to myNum
none of the above	print "Can't find it"

Programming Projects

1. Implement a calculator similar to the one pictured in Figure 5-25. Although you are free to design your calculator interface and functionality however you like, the button operation must be consistent with a typical calculator.

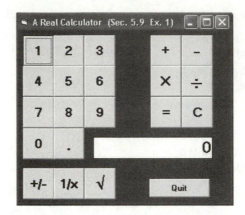

Figure 5–25 *Form for Project 1*

Requirements:
   i. There can only be one number display (like a calculator).
   ii. Your calculator must have support for: addition, subtraction, multiplication, and division.
   iii. Your calculator needs to have (at least) the following features:
   • A square root function
   • An additive inverse function (+/– key to negate the display)
   • A multiplicative inverse function (1/x to get the reciprocal of the display)
   • A clear key.
   iv. The Divide button needs to check for divide by zero using an **If-Then** statement.

Although you can start with the simple calculator completed for Programming Project 1 in the previous chapter, significant redesign will need to be done.

2. Create the interface shown in Figure 5-26. Using the interface to select a desired display, you should be able to update the text in the text box by clicking the update button. Also, make sure that each group of radio and check boxes is enclosed within their own Group box.

To do this Project:
   i. Create the interface (the form and its controls).
   ii. Add Visual Basic to the "Update" button's **Click** event procedure. This code will consist of a series of **If-Then** type statements to set the properties of the Text box.
   iii. Be sure to put the Group box on the interface first, and then place the desired set of radio boxes or check boxes within the Group box.

3. Change the RETIREMENT PARTY Form created in Program 1 from Chapter 2 by increasing the size of the form to accommodate the following additions:

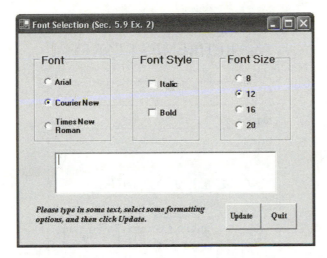

Figure 5–26 *Form for Project 2*

i. A line at the bottom of the invitation area named linBase. This line will be used to determine the area to be printed.

ii. Two check boxes that will be used to select bold and italic fonts for the invitations title.

iii. Three radio buttons in a Group box that will be used to color the invitation title.

Your Form should look like that shown in Figure 5–27.

4. Create a program that will calculate the cost of the purchase of donuts. Below is a list of the types of donuts offered and their price at Dopey's Donut Shop. Dopey needs a program that will calculate the cost of a donut purchase (price per donut × quantity of that donut) with the tax added (6 percent sales tax).

Donut Type	Cost
Chocolate frost cake	50
Cherry vanilla cake	60
Plain glazed yeast	40
German chocolate cake	55
Plain cake	35

A suggested form for this programming project is shown in Figure 5–28.

5. Create a project that calculates the user's actual tax rate by including social security and Medicare contributions in the tax rate. The user is asked to indicate his or her tax rate (choices are presented in radio buttons and a Group box), enter his or her monthly income, enter the amount of this monthly income devoted to social security, and and enter the amount devoted to Medicare. The user then clicks on a calculate button which uses the following formulas:

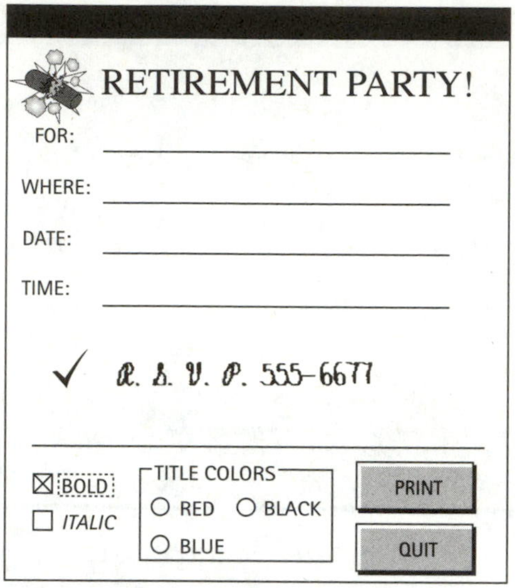

Figure 5–27 *Form for Project 3*

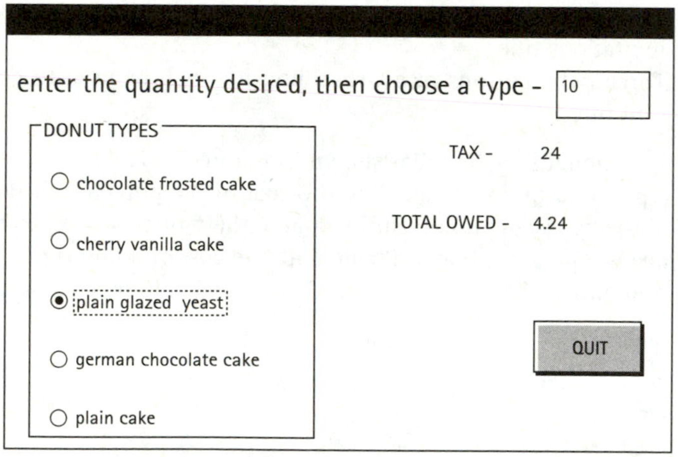

Figure 5–28 *Suggested Form for Project 4*

*Percent used for SS = $ amount to SS/ monthly income * 100*
*Percent used for medicare = $ amount to medicare/ monthly income * 100*

The radio button choice can be saved in an invisible label and then used as follows.

Users actual tax rate = percent used for SS
                    + percent used for medicare
                    *+ income tax rate (saved in label) * 100*

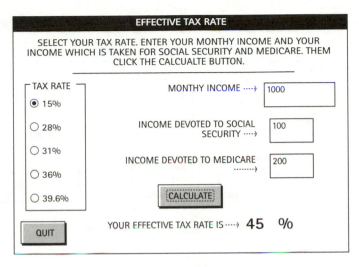

Figure 5–29 *Suggested Form for Project 5*

(*Note:* A person's tax rate is actually slightly lower than the 15 percent to 39.6 percent used for exemptions.)

A suggested form for this project is shown as Figure 5–29.

6. Develop a program for Rambling Wreck Auto Rentals to determine the daily rental rate on its vehicles. The daily rate is calculated as follows:

    i. Base rate for sedans is $30(convertible) and $25(hardtop); for minivans it is $32; and for trucks it is $35.

    ii. All convertibles are sedans.

    iii. If the vehicle is large, the day rate increases by 10%.

    iv. After the above has been calculated, if the vehicle is rented on the weekend, the day rate is cut by 50%.

    v. If the renter requires insurance, $5 is added to the day rate.

    vi. The day rate is calculated in a calculate button and displayed in currency format.

A suggested form for this project is shown in Figure 5–30.

7. This assignment is a modification to the Motel 8 Project (Section 3.9, Exercise 8).

Additional Program Requirements: Motel 8 requires at least one adult registered in each room. Therefore, if the number of adults text box is left empty, display a message box indicating the need for at least one adult in the room. Use the vbCritical type and reposition the focus to the number of adults text box. (*Hint:* Take a look at both the **Leave** and **Enter** event procedures.)

Additionally, the entry in the number of nights text box should be a positive value (Integer). If the value in the number of nights text box is not a positive value, display a message box indicating the need for a positive value for number of nights. Use the vbCritical type and reposition the focus to the number of nights text box.

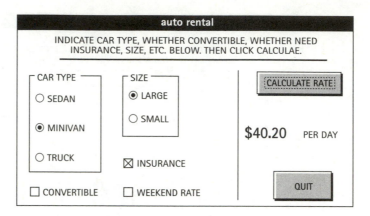

Figure 5–30 *Form for Project 6*

The customer will be given a 15% discount (before state and local taxes are computed) when the number of nights is greater than four. Use a constant to represent the discount value.

8. This assignment is a modification to Local Car Rental Company Project (Section 3.9, Exercise 9).

Additional Program Requirements: For all miles in excess of 200 per day, there is a $0.10 per mile charge, which means that the first 200 miles per day are free. Use constants to represent the number of miles per day (200) over which mileage will be charged and the per mile charge (0.10).

There is no refueling fee charge if the car is returned with a full tank; otherwise, the customer is charged the $12.95 refueling fee regardless of the amount of fuel in the tank (not full). Use a check box (chkTankFull) to indicate that the car was returned with a full tank.

All input fields (txtFirstName, txtLastName, txtDays) must contain text. Use a message box to alert the user of any empty text box and reset the focus to the appropriate empty field. A suggested form is shown in Figure 5–31.

9. **The State Utilities Commission Project**

Note: The following State Utilities project is used in subsequent End-of-Chapter Programming Projects. You will be required to modify and enhance your solution to this project as new Visual Basic capabilities are introduced in subsequent chapters.

The commission has ruled that the company you work for, Municipal Power and Light, overcharged customers for two months during the previous year. To compensate the customer, the commission has ordered the company to decrease each customer's bill next month by 12%.

The state levies a 3.5% utility tax and the city levies a 1.5% utility tax, both of which must be applied to the customer's bill before it is discounted. (The state

Figure 5–31 *Form for Project 8*

and city want their taxes on the full, undiscounted amount, and the 12% discount does not apply to the utility taxes.) Municipal Power and Light charges are as follows:

kWh Used	Cost Scale
less than 1000	$0.052 per kWh used
at least 1000 but less than 1300	$0.052 per kWh for first 1000 kWh used
	$0.041 per kWh for kWh used over 1000
at least 1300 but less than 2000	$0.052 per kWh for first 1000 kWh used
	$0.041 per kWh for next 300 kWh used
	$0.035 per kWh for kWh used over 1300
at least 2000	$0.052 per kWh for first 1000 kWh used
	$0.041 per kWh for next 300 kWh used
	$0.035 per kWh for next 700 kWh used
	$0.03 per kWh for kWh used over 2000

Input for your program should include the customer name and number of kWhs used during the current month. Output should include:

    base, undiscounted, untaxed bill amount
    discount amount
    state utility tax amount
    city utility tax amount
    total amount due

Remember that the state and city taxes are computed on the first amount in the above list. Your solution should use a form like that shown in Figure 5–32.

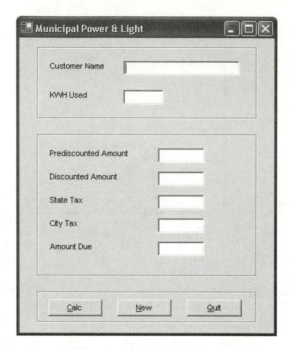

Figure 5–32 *Form for Project 9*

Object	Property	Setting
Form	Name	frmPowerBill
	Text	Municipal Power & Light
GroupBox	Name	grpInput
Label	Name	lblCustomer
	Text	Customer Name
TextBox	Name	txtCustomer
	Text	(blank)
Label	Name	lblkWhUsed
	Text	kWh Used
TextBox	Name	txtKWHUsed
	Text	(blank)
GroupBox	Name	grpOutput
Label	Name	lblPreDiscountAmt
	Text	Prediscounted Amount
TextBox	Name	txtPreAmt
	Text	(blank)
Label	Name	lblDiscountAmt
	Text	Discounted Amount

TextBox	Name	txtDiscountAmt
	Text	(blank)
Label	Name	lblStateTax
	Text	State Tax
TextBox	Name	txtStateTax
	Text	(blank)
Label	Name	lblCityTax
	Text	City Tax
TextBox	Name	txtCityTax
	Text	(blank)
Label	Name	lblAmtDue
	Text	Amount Due
TextBox	Name	txtAmtDue
	Text	(blank)
GroupBox	Name	grpCommands
Button	Name	btnCalc
	Text	&Calc
Button	Name	btnNew
	Text	&New
Button	Name	btnQuit
	Text	&Quit

Repetition Structures

Goals

The applications examined so far have illustrated the programming concepts involved in input, output, assignment, and selection capabilities. By this time you should have gained enough experience to be comfortable with these concepts and the mechanics of implementing them using Visual Basic. However, many problems require a repetition capability, in which the same calculation or sequence of instructions is repeated, over and over, using different sets of data. Examples of such repetition include continual checking of user data entries until an acceptable entry, such as a valid password, is made; counting and accumulating running totals; and recurring acceptance of input data and recalculation of output values that only stop upon entry of a designated value.

This chapter explores the different methods that programmers use to construct repeating sections of code and how they can be implemented in Visual Basic. A repeated procedural section of code is commonly called a loop, because after the last statement in the code is executed, the program branches, or loops back to the first statement and starts another repetition. Each repetition is also referred to as an iteration or pass through the loop.

6.1 Introduction

The real power of most computer programs resides in their ability to repeat the same calculation or sequence of instructions many times over, each time using different data, without the necessity of rerunning the program for each new set of data values. This ability is realized through repetitive sections of code. Such repetitive sections are written only once, but include a means of defining how many times the code should be executed.

Constructing repetitive sections of code requires four elements:

1. A *repetition statement* that both defines the boundaries containing the repeating section of code and controls whether the code will be executed or not. There are three different forms of Visual Basic repetition structures: **Do While** structures, **For** structures, and **Do/Loop Until** structures.

2. A *condition* that needs to be evaluated. Valid conditions are identical to those used in selection statements. If the condition is **True**, the code is executed; if it is **False**, the code is not executed.

3. A *statement* that initially *sets the condition*. This statement must always be placed before the condition is first evaluated, to ensure correct loop execution the first time.

4. A *statement* within the repeating section of code that *allows the condition to become False*. This is necessary to ensure that, at some point, the repetitions stop.

Pretest and Posttest Loops

The condition being tested can be evaluated either at the beginning or the end of the repeating section of code. Figure 6–1 illustrates the case where the test occurs at the beginning of the loop. This type of loop is referred to as a *pretest loop*, because the condition is tested before any statements within the loop are executed. If the condition is

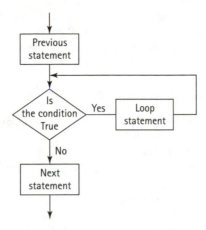

Figure 6–1   *A Pretest Loop*

True, the executable statements within the loop are executed. If the initial value of the condition is **False,** the executable statements within the loop are never executed, and control transfers to the first statement after the loop. To avoid infinite repetitions, the condition must be updated within the loop. Pretest loops are also referred to as *entrance-controlled loops.* Both the Do While and For loop structures are examples of such loops.

A loop that evaluates a condition at the end of the repeating section of code, as illustrated in Figure 6–2, is referred to as a *posttest* or *exit-controlled loop.* Such loops always execute the loop statements at least once before the condition is tested. Because

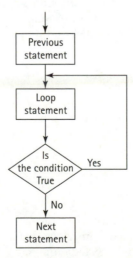

Figure 6–2   *A Posttest Loop*

the executable statements within the loop are continually executed until the condition becomes **False,** there must always be a statement within the loop that updates the condition and permits it to become **False.** The **Do /Loop Until** construct is an example of a posttest loop.

Fixed Count Versus Variable Condition Loops

In addition to where the condition is tested (pretest or posttest), repeating sections of code are also classified as to the type of condition being tested. In a *fixed-count loop,* the condition is used to keep track of how many repetitions have occurred. For example, we might want to produce a very simple fixed design such as:

```
* * * * * * * * * * * * * * * * * * * * * * * *
* * * * * * * * * * * * * * * * * * * * * * * *
* * * * * * * * * * * * * * * * * * * * * * * *
* * * * * * * * * * * * * * * * * * * * * * * *
```

In each of these cases, a fixed number of calculations is performed or a fixed number of lines is printed, at which point the repeating section of code is exited. All of Visual Basics repetition statements can be used to produce fixed-count loops.

In many situations, the exact number of repetitions is not known in advance or the items are too numerous to count beforehand. For example, if we are working with a large amount of market research data, we might not want to take the time to count the number of actual data items that must be entered and so we would use a variable-condition loop. In a *variable-condition loop,* the tested condition does not depend on a count being achieved, but rather on a variable that can change interactively with each pass through the loop. When a specified value is encountered, regardless of how many iterations have occurred, repetitions stop. All of Visual Basic's repetition statements can be used to create variable-condition loops. In this chapter we will encounter examples of both fixed-count and variable-condition loops.

6.2 Do While Loops

In Visual Basic, a `Do While` loop is constructed using the following syntax:

```
Do While expression
    statement(s)
Loop
```

The expression contained after the keywords `Do While` is the condition tested to determine if the statements provided before the `Loop` statement are executed. The expression is evaluated in exactly the same manner as that contained in an If-Else statement—the difference is in how the expression is used. As we have seen, when the expression is **True** in an **If-Else** statement, the statement or statements following the expression are executed once. In a `Do While` loop, the statement or statements following the expression are executed repeatedly as long as the expression remains **True**. Considering the expression and the statements following it, the process used by the computer in evaluating a `Do While` loop is:

1. Test the expression.

2. If the expression is **True**:

    a. Execute all statements following the expression up to the `Loop` statement.

    b. Go back to step 1.

    Else

    Exit the `Do While` statement and execute the next executable statement following the `Loop` statement.

Note that step 2b forces program control to be transferred back to step 1. This transfer of control back to the start of a `Do While` statement, in order to reevaluate the expression, is what forms the loop. The `Do While` statement literally loops back on itself to recheck the expression until it becomes **False**. This means that somewhere in the loop, it must be possible to alter the value of the tested expression so that the loop ultimately terminates its execution.

This looping process produced by a `Do While` statement is illustrated in Figure 6-3. A diamond shape is used to show the two entry and two exit points required in the decision part of the `Do While` statement.

To make this process more understandable, consider the code segment below. Recall that the statement `lstDisplay.Items.Add(count)` will display each value of count into a List Box.

```
Do While count <= 10
  lstDisplay.Items.Add(count)
Loop
```

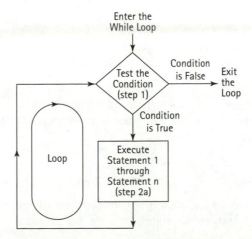

Figure 6–3   *Anatomy of a Do While Loop*

Although this loop structure is valid, the alert reader will realize that we have created a situation in which the `lstDisplay` statement either is called forever (or until we stop the program) or it is not called at all. Let us examine why this happens.

If `count` has a value less than or equal to 10 when the expression is first evaluated, the `lstDisplay` statement is executed. When the `Loop` statement is encountered, the structure automatically loops back on itself and retests the expression. Because we have not changed the value stored in `count`, the expression is still true and the `lstDisplay` statement is again executed. This process continues forever, or until the program containing this statement is prematurely stopped by the user. However, if count starts with a value greater than 10, the expression is false to begin with and the `lstDisplay` statement is never executed.

How do we set an initial value in `count` to control what the `Do While` statement does the first time the expression is evaluated? The answer is to assign values to each variable in the tested expression before the `Do While` statement is encountered. For example, the following sequence of instructions is valid:

```
Dim count As Integer
count = 1
Do While count <= 10
  lstDisplay.Items.Add(count)
Loop
```

Using this sequence of instructions, we ensure that `count` starts with a value of 1. We could assign any value to `count` in the assignment statement—the important thing is to assign a value. In practice, the assigned value depends upon the application.

We must still change the value of `count` so that we can finally exit the `Do While` loop. This requires an expression such as `count = count + 1` to increment the value of `count` each time the `Do While` statement is executed. All that we have to do is add a statement within the `Loop` structure that modifies count's value so that the loop ultimately terminates. For example, consider the following expanded loop:

```
count = 1    ' initialize count
Do While count <= 10
  lstDisplay.Items.Add(count)
  count = count +  1  ' increment count
Loop
```

Note that the `Do While` structure begins with the keywords `Do While` and ends with the keyword `Loop`. For this particular loop, we have included two statements within the `Loop` structure:

```
lstDisplay.Items.Add(count)
count = count +  1  ' increment count
```

Now we need to analyze the complete section of code to understand how it operates. The first assignment statement sets `count` equal to 1. The `Do While` structure is then entered and the expression is evaluated for the first time. Because the value of count is less than or equal to 10, the expression is **True** and the two statements internal to the **Loop** structure are executed. The first statement within the loop is a lstDisplay statement that displays the value of count. The next statement adds 1 to the value currently stored in count, making this value equal to 2. The Do While statement now loops back to retest the expression. Since count is still less than or equal to 10, the loop statements are executed once again. This process continues until the value of count reaches 11. Event Procedure 6–1 illustrates these statements within the context of a complete **Button1_Click** event procedure:

Event Procedure 6–1

```
Private Sub frmMain_Click(ByVal sender As Object, _
    ByVal e As System.EventArgs) Handles MyBase.Click
  Dim count As Integer

  count = 1   ' initialize count
  Do While count <= 10
    lstDisplay.Items.Add(count)
    count = count + 1  ' increment count
  Loop
End Sub
```

The output that will appear on the screen in the List Box when Event Procedure 6–1 is activated is:

```
1
2
3
4
5
6
7
8
9
10
```

There is nothing special about the name count used in Event Procedure 6–1. Any valid integer variable could have been used.

Note that if a text box had been used instead of a list box, the lstDisplay.Items.Add(count) statement would be replaced with txtDisplay.AppendText(' ' & count) and the output would be:

```
1 2 3 4 5 6 7 8 9 10
```

Before we consider other examples of the Do While statement, two comments concerning Event Procedure 6–1 are in order. First, the statement count + 1 can be replaced with any statement that increases the value of count. A statement such as count = count + 2, for example, would cause every second integer to be displayed. Second, it is the programmer's responsibility to ensure that count is changed in a way that ultimately leads to a normal exit from the Do While statement. For example, if we replace the expression count + 1 with the expression count - 1, the value of count will never exceed 10 and an infinite loop will be created. An *infinite loop* is a loop that never ends. With the above example, the computer continues to display numbers, until you realize that the program is not working as you expected.

Now that you have some familiarity with the Do While structure, see if you can read and determine the output of Event Procedure 6–2.

Event Procedure 6–2

```
Private Sub frmMain_Click(ByVal sender As Object, ByVal e As _
    System.EventArgs) Handles MyBase.Click
  Dim I As Integer

  I = 10    ' initialize I
  Do While I >= 1
    lstDisplay.Items.Add(I)
    I = I - 1        ' subtract 1 from I
  Loop
End Sub
```

The assignment statement in Event Procedure 6–2 initially sets the integer variable I to 10. The Do While statement then checks to see if the value of I is greater than or equal to 1. While the expression is **True**, the value of I is displayed by the lstDisplay statement and the value of I is decremented by 1. When I finally reaches zero, the expression is **False** and the program exits the Do While statement. Thus, the following display is obtained when Event Procedure 6–2 is activated:

```
10
9
8
7
6
5
4
3
2
1
```

To illustrate the power of the Do While loop, consider the task of printing a table of numbers from 1 to 10 with their squares and cubes. This can be done with a simple Do While statement, as illustrated by Event Procedure 6–3.

Event Procedure 6–3

```
Private Sub frmMain_Click(ByVal sender As Object, _
    ByVal e As System.EventArgs) Handles MyBase.Click
  Dim num As Integer

  num = 1
  lstDisplay.Items.Clear()  ' clear the List box
  lstDisplay.Items.Add("NUMBER SQUARE CUBE")
  Do While num < 11
    lstDisplay.Items.Add("        " & num & "                " & (num ^ 2) _
      & "          " & (num ^ 3))
    num = num + 1
  Loop
End Sub
```

When Event Code 6–3 is activated, the following display is produced in the List box:

NUMBER	SQUARE	CUBE
1	1	1
2	4	8
3	9	27
4	16	64
5	25	125
6	36	216
7	49	343
8	64	512
9	81	729
10	100	1000

Note that the expression used in Event Procedure 6–3 is num < 11. For the integer variable num, this expression is exactly equivalent to the expression num <= 10. The choice of which to use is entirely up to you.

If we want to use Event Procedure 6–3 to produce a table of 1,000 numbers, all that needs to be done is to change the expression in the Do While statement from num < 11 to num < 1001. Changing the 11 to 1001 produces a table of 1,000 lines—not bad for a simple five-line Do While structure.

All the program examples illustrating the Do While statement are examples of fixed-count loops because the tested condition is a counter that checks for a fixed number of repetitions. A variation on the fixed-count loop can be made, where the counter is not incremented by one each time through the loop, but by some other value. For example, consider the task of producing a Celsius to Fahrenheit temperature conversion table. Assume that Fahrenheit temperatures corresponding to Celsius temperatures ranging from 5 to 50 degrees are to be displayed in increments of five degrees. The desired display can be obtained with the following series of statements:

```
celsius = 5        ' starting Celsius value
Do While celsius <= 50
  fahren =  9.0/5.0  * celsius + 32.0
  lstDisplay.Items.Add(celsius & " " & fahren)
  celsius = celsius + 5
Loop
```

As before, the Do While loop consists of everything from the words Do While through the Loop statement. Prior to entering the Do While loop, we have made sure to assign a value to the counter being evaluated and there is a statement to alter the value of celsius within the loop (in increments of 5), to ensure an exit from the Do While loop. Event Procedure 6–4 illustrates the use of this code within the context of a complete Form_Click event.

Event Procedure 6–4

```
' A procedure to convert Celsius to Fahrenheit

Private Sub frmMain_Click(ByVal sender As Object, _
    ByVal e As System.EventArgs) Handles MyBase.Click
  Const MAX_CELSIUS As Integer = 50
  Const START_VAL As Integer = 5
  Const STEP_SIZE As Integer = 5

  Dim celsius As Integer
  Dim fahren As Single

  lstDisplay.Items.Clear()
  lstDisplay.Items.Add("Degrees" & "      Degrees")
  lstDisplay.Items.Add("Celsius" & "      Fahrenheit")

  celsius = START_VAL
  Do While celsius <= MAX_CELSIUS
    fahren = (9.0 / 5.0) * celsius + 32.0
    lstDisplay.Items.Add("    " & celsius & "               " & fahren)
    celsius = celsius + STEP_SIZE
  Loop

End Sub
```

After this code is activated, the list box will display:

```
Degrees    Degrees
Celsius    Fahrenheit
  5          41
 10          50
 15          59
 20          68
 25          77
 30          86
 35          95
 40         104
 45         113
 50         122
```

Exercises 6.2

1. Rewrite Event Procedure 6–1 to print the numbers 2 to 10 in increments of two. The list box in your program should display the following:

   2

   4

   6

   8

   10

2. Rewrite Event Procedure 6–4 to produce a table that starts at a Celsius value of -10 and ends with a Celsius value of 60, in increments of ten degrees.

3. a. Using the following code, determine the total number of items displayed. Also determine the first and last numbers printed.

   ```
   Dim num As Integer
   Num = 0
   Do While Num <= 20
       Num = Num + 1
       lstDisplay.Items.Add(Num)
    Loop
   ```

   b. Enter and run the code from Exercise 3a as a Button_Click event procedure to verify your answers to the exercise.

   c. How would the output be affected if the two statements within the compound statement were reversed; i.e., if the lstDisplay statement were made before the n = n + 1 statement?

4. Write a Visual Basic program that converts gallons to liters. The program should display gallons from 10 to 20 in one-gallon increments and the corresponding liter equivalents. Use the relationship of 3.785 liters to a gallon.

5. Write a Visual Basic program to produce the following display within a multiline text box.

```
0
 1
  2
   3
    4
     5
      6
       7
        8
         9
```

6. Write a Visual Basic program to produce the following displays within a list box.

```
a. ****       b.     ****
     ****            ****
     ****            ****
     ****            ****
```

7. Write a Visual Basic program that converts feet to meters. The program should display feet from 3 to 30 in three-foot increments and the corresponding meter equivalents. Use the relationship of 3.28 feet to a meter.

8. A machine purchased for $28,000 is depreciated at a rate of $4,000 a year for seven years. Write and run a Visual Basic program that computes and displays in a suitably sized list box a depreciation table for seven years. The table should have the following form:

Year	Depreciation	End-of-year value	Accumulated depreciation
1	4000	24000	4000
2	4000	20000	8000
3	4000	16000	12000
4	4000	12000	16000
5	4000	8000	20000
6	4000	4000	24000
7	4000	0	28000

9. An automobile travels at an average speed of 55 miles per hour for four hours. Write a Visual Basic program that displays in a list box the distance driven, in miles, that the car has traveled after 0.5, 1.0, 1.5 hours, and so on. until the end of the trip.

10. An approximate conversion formula for converting temperatures from Fahrenheit to Celsius is:

Celsius = (Fahrenheit − 30) / 2

a. Using this formula, and starting with a Fahrenheit temperature of zero degrees, write a Visual Basic program that determines when the approximate equivalent Celsius temperature differs from the exact equivalent value by more than four degrees. (*Hint:* Use a `Do While` loop that terminates when the difference between approximate and exact Celsius equivalents exceeds four degrees.)

b. Using the approximate Celsius conversion formula given in Exercise 10a, write a Visual Basic program that produces a table of Fahrenheit temperatures, exact Celsius equivalent temperatures, approximate Celsius equivalent temperatures, and the difference between the exact and approximate equivalent Celsius values. The table should begin at zero degrees Fahrenheit, use two-degree Fahrenheit increments, and terminate when the difference between exact and approximate values differs by more than four degrees. Use a list box to display these values.

6.3   Interactive Do While Loops

Combining interactive data entry with the repetition capabilities of the `Do While` loop produces very adaptable and powerful programs. To understand the concept involved, consider Program 6-1, where a `Do While` statement is used to accept and then display four user-entered numbers, one at a time. Although it uses a very simple idea, the program highlights the flow of control concepts needed to produce more useful programs. Figure 6-4 shows the interface for Program 6-1.

For this application the only procedure code is the **Click** event, which is listed in Program 6-1's event code.

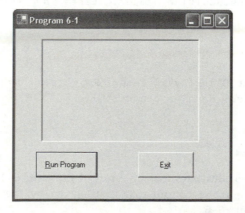

Figure 6-4   *Program 6-1's Interface*

Table 6–1   The Properties Table for Program 6–1

Object	Property	Setting
Form	Name	frmMain
	Text	Program 6–1
ListBox	Name	lstDisplay
Button	Name	btnRun
	Text	&Run Program
Button	Name	btnExit
	Text	E&xit

Program 6–1's Event Code

```
Private Sub btnRun_Click(ByVal sender As Object, _
    ByVal e As System.EventArgs) _Handles btnRun.Click
  Const MAXNUMS As Integer = 4
  Dim count As Integer
  Dim num As Single

  lstDisplay.Items.Clear()
  lstDisplay.Items.Add("This Program will ask you to enter " & MAXNUMS _
    & " numbers")

  count = 1
  Do While count <= MAXNUMS
    num = Val(InputBox("Enter a number", "Input Dialog", 0))
    lstDisplay.Items.Add("The number entered is " & num)
    count = count + 1
  Loop
End Sub

Private Sub btnExit_Click(ByVal sender As Object, ByVal e As _
    System.EventArgs) Handles btnExit.Click
  Beep()
  End
End Sub
```

Figure 6–5 illustrates a sample run of Program 6–1 after four numbers have been input. The InputBox control that is displayed by the program for the data entry is shown in Figure 6–6.

Let us review the program to clearly understand how the output illustrated in Figure 6–5 was produced. The first message displayed is caused by execution of the first

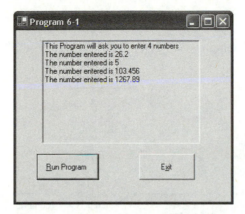

Figure 6–5   *A Sample Run of Program 6–1*

Figure 6–6   *The InputBox Displayed by Program 6–1*

lstDisplay statement. This statement is outside and before the Do While loop, so it is executed once before any statement within the loop.

Once the Do While loop is entered, the statements within the loop are executed while the test condition is **True**. The first time through the loop, the following statement is executed:

```
num = Val(InputBox("Enter a number", "Input Dialog", "0"))
```

The call to the InputBox function displays the InputBox shown in Figure 6–6, which forces the computer to wait for a number to be entered at the keyboard. Once a number is typed and the Enter key is pressed, the **lstDisplay** statement within the loop displays on a new line the number that was entered. The variable count is then incremented by one. This process continues until four passes through the loop have been made and the value of count is 5. Each pass causes the InputBox to be displayed with the message The number entered is. Figure 6–7 illustrates this flow of control.

Program 6–1 can be modified to use the entered data rather than simply displaying it. For example, let us add the numbers entered and display the total. To do this we must be very careful about how we add the numbers, because the same variable, num, is used

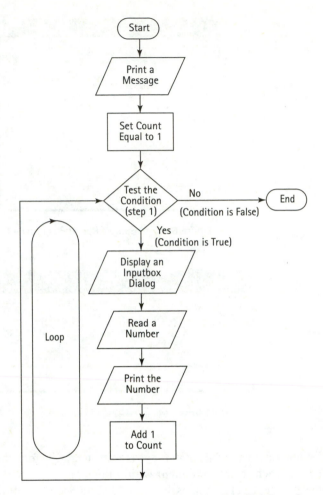

Figure 6–7 *Flow of Control Diagram for the btnRun Click Event Procedure*

for each number entered. As a result, the entry of a new number in Program 6–1 automatically causes the previous number stored in num to be lost. Thus, each number entered must be added to the total before another number is entered. The required sequence is:

```
Enter a number
Add the number to the total
```

How do we add a single number to a total? A statement such as total = total + num is the solution. This is the accumulating statement introduced in Section 3.3. After each number is entered, the accumulating statement adds the number to the total, as

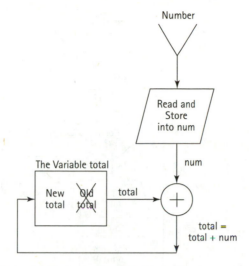

Figure 6-8   *Accepting and Adding a Number to a Total*

illustrated in Figure 6-8. The complete flow of control required for adding the numbers is illustrated in Figure 6-9.

Observe that in Figure 6-9 we have made a provision for initially setting the total to zero before the Do While loop is entered. If we cleared the total inside the Do While loop, it would be set to zero each time the loop was executed and any value previously stored would be erased. As indicated in the flow diagram shown in Figure 6-9, the statement total = total + num is placed immediately after the call to the **InputBox** function. Putting the accumulating statement at this point in the program ensures that the entered number is immediately added to the total.

Program 6-2 incorporates the necessary modifications to Program 6-1 to total the numbers entered. The significant difference between Program 6-1 and Program 6-2 is the Run Program button event code. The event code for Program 6-2 is shown below.

Program 6-2's Event Code

```
Private Sub btnRun_Click(ByVal sender As Object, _
    ByVal e As System.EventArgs) Handles btnRun.Click
  Const MAXNUMS As Integer = 4
  Dim count As Integer
  Dim num, total As Single

  lstDisplay.Items.Clear()
  lstDisplay.Items.Add("This Program will ask you to enter " & MAXNUMS & _
      " numbers")
  count = 1
  Do While count <= MAXNUMS
    num = Val(InputBox("Enter a number", "Input Dialog", 0))
```

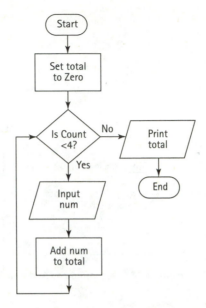

Figure 6–9 *Accumulation Flow of Control*

```
    total = total + num
    lstDisplay.Items.Add("The number entered is " & num)
    lstDisplay.Items.Add("The total is now " & total)
    count = count + 1
  Loop
  lstDisplay.Items.Add("The final total is " & total)

End Sub
```

Let us review this event code. The variable `total` was created to store the total of the numbers entered. Prior to entering the `Do While` statement, the value of `total` is set to zero. This ensures that any previous value present in the storage locations assigned to the variable `total` is erased. Within the `Do While` loop, the statement `total = total + num` is used to add the value of the entered number into `total`. As each value is entered, it is added into the existing `total` to create a new `total`. Thus, `total` becomes a running subtotal of all the values entered. Only when all numbers are entered does `total` contain the final sum of all the numbers. After the `Do While` loop is finished, the last `lstDisplay` statement displays the final sum.

Using the same data we entered in the sample run for Program 6–1, the sample run of Program 6–2 produces the total shown in Figure 6–10.

Having used an accumulating assignment statement to add the numbers entered, we can now go further and calculate the average of the numbers. However, first we have to determine whether we calculate the average within the `Do While` loop or outside of it.

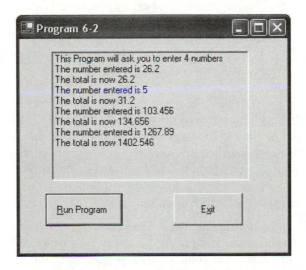

Figure 6–10   *A Sample Run of Program 6–2*

In the case at hand, calculating an average requires that both a final sum and the number of items in that sum be available. The average is then computed by dividing the final sum by the number of items. We must now answer the questions "At what point in the program is the correct sum available, and at what point is the number of items available?" In reviewing Program 6–2's event code, we see that the correct sum needed for calculating the average is available after the Do While loop is finished. In fact, the whole purpose of the Do While loop is to ensure that the numbers are entered and added correctly to produce a correct sum. With this as background, see if you can read and understand the event code used in Program 6–3.

Program 6–3's Event Code

```
Private Sub btnRun_Click(ByVal sender As Object, _
  ByVal e As System.EventArgs) Handles btnRun.Click
Const MAXNUMS As Integer = 4
Dim count As Integer
Dim num, total, average As Single

lstDisplay.Items.Clear()
lstDisplay.Items.Add("This Program will ask you to enter " & MAXNUMS & _
    " numbers")
count = 1
Do While count <= MAXNUMS
  num = Val(InputBox("Enter a number", "Input Dialog", 0))
  total = total + num
  lstDisplay.Items.Add("The number entered is " & num)
  count = count + 1
```

```
Loop
Average = total/MAXNUMS
lstDisplay.Items.Add("The average of these numbers is " & average)
End Sub
```

Program 6-3 is almost identical to Program 6-2, except for the calculation of the average. We have also removed the constant display of the total within and after the Do While loop. The loop in Program 6-3 is used to enter and add four numbers. Immediately after the loop is exited, the average is computed and displayed.

A sample run of Program 6-3 is illustrated in Figure 6-11.

The Do Until Loop Structure

In a Do While Loop structure, the statements within the loop are executed as long as the condition is **True**. A variation of the Do While loop is the Do Until loop which executes the statements within the loop as long as the condition is **False**. The syntax of a Do Until loop is:

```
Do Until condition
    statement(s)
Loop
```

The Do Until loop, like its Do While counterpart, is an entrance-controlled loop. Unlike the Do While loop, which executes until the condition becomes **False**, a Do Until loop executes until the condition becomes **True**. If the condition tested in a Do Until loop is **True** to begin with, the statements within the loop will not execute at all. Do Until loops are not used extensively for two reasons. First, most practical programming problems require performing a repetitive set of tasks while a condition is **True**. Second, if an entrance-controlled loop is required until a condition becomes **True**, it can always be

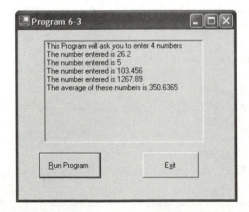

Figure 6-11 *A Sample Run of Program 6-3*

restated as a loop that needs to be executed while the same condition remains **False**, using the following syntax:

```
Do While Not condition
   statement(s)
Loop
```

Sentinels

All of the loops we have created thus far have been examples of fixed-count loops, where a counter controls the number of loop iterations. By means of a `Do While` statement, variable-condition loops may also be constructed. For example, when entering grades we may not want to count the number of grades that will be entered, preferring to enter the grades one after another and, when finished, typing in a special data value to signal the end of data input.

In computer programming, data values used to signal either the start or end of a data series are called *sentinels*. The sentinel values selected must not conflict with legitimate data values. For example, if we were constructing a program to process a student's grades, assuming that no extra credit is given that could produce a grade higher than 100, we could use any grade higher than 100 as a sentinel value. Program 6–4 illustrates this concept. In Program 6–4's event procedure, the grades are serially requested and accepted until a number larger than 100 is entered. Entry of a number higher than 100 alerts the program to exit the `Do While` loop and display the sum of the numbers entered. Figure 6–12 shows the interface for Program 6–4.

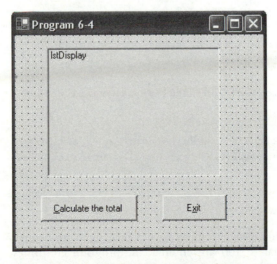

Figure 6–12   *Program 6–4's Interface*

Table 6-2   The Properties Table for Program 6-4

Object	Property	Setting
Form	Name	frmMain
	Text	Program 6-4
ListBox	Name	lstDisplay
	TabStop	False
Button	Name	btnRun
	Text	&Calculate the total
Button	Name	btnExit
	Text	E&xit

Program 6-4's Event Code

```
Private Sub btnRun_Click(ByVal sender As Object, _
    ByVal e As System.EventArgs) Handles btnRun.Click
  Const HIGHGRADE As Integer = 100
  Dim grade, total As Single

  grade = 0
  total = 0
  lstDisplay.Items.Clear()
  lstDisplay.Items.Add("To stop entering grades, type in")
  lstDisplay.Items.Add("any number greater than 100.")

  Do While grade <= HIGHGRADE
    grade = Val(InputBox("Enter a grade", "Input Dialog", "0"))
    lstDisplay.Items.Add("The grade just entered is " & grade)
    total = total + grade
  Loop
  lstDisplay.Items.Add("The total of the valid grades is " & total - grade)
End Sub

Private Sub btnExit_Click(ByVal sender As Object, _
    ByVal e As System.EventArgs) Handles btnExit.Click
  Beep()
  End
End Sub
```

A sample run using Program 6-4 is illustrated in Figure 6-13. As long as grades less than or equal to 100 are entered, the program continues to request and accept additional data. For example, when a number less than or equal to 100 is entered, the pro-

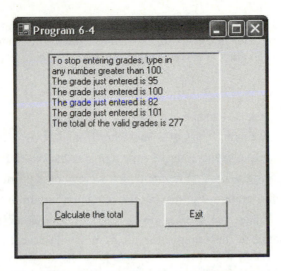

To stop entering grades, type in
any number greater than 100.
The grade just entered is 95
The grade just entered is 100
The grade just entered is 82
The grade just entered is 101
The total of the valid grades is 277

Figure 6–13 *A Sample Run Using Program 6–4*

gram adds this number to the total. When a number greater than 100 is entered, the program exits the loop and displays the sum of the grades.

Note that the event procedure used in Program 6–4 differs from previous examples in that termination of the loop is controlled by an externally supplied value rather than a fixed count condition. The loop in Program 6–4 will continue indefinitely until the sentinel value is encountered.

Breaking Out of a Loop

It is sometimes necessary to prematurely break out of a loop when an unusual error condition is detected. The Exit Do statement allows you to do this. For example, execution of the following Do While loop is immediately terminated if a number greater than 76 is entered.

```
count = 1
Do While count <= 10
  num = Val(InputBox("Enter a number", "Input Dialog", "0"))
  If num > 76 Then
    lstDisplay.Items.Add("You lose!")
    Exit Do       ' break out of the loop
  End If
  lstDisplay.Items.Add("Keep on trucking!")
  count = count + 1
Loop
' break jumps to here
```

The Exit Do statement violates pure structured programming principles because it provides a second, nonstandard exit from a loop. This statement should be used with extreme caution since it makes debugging more difficult.

Exercises 6.3

1. Write a Do While loop to achieve the following:

   a. Display the multiples of 3 backward from 33 to 3, inclusive.

   b. Display the capital letters of the alphabet backward from Z to A.

2. Rewrite Program 6–2 to compute the average of eight numbers.

3. Rewrite Program 6–2 to display the following prompt in an InputBox:

   `Please type the total number of data values to be averaged`

   In response to this prompt, the program should accept a user-entered number from the InputBox and then use this number to control the number of times the **Do While** loop is executed. Thus, if the user enters 5 in the InputBox, the program should request the input of five numbers, and display the total after five numbers have been entered.

4. a. Write a Visual Basic program to convert Celsius degrees to Fahrenheit. The program should request the starting Celsius value, the number of conversions to be made, and the increment between Celsius values. The display should have appropriate headings and list the Celsius value and the corresponding Fahrenheit value. Use the relationship: Fahrenheit = 9.0 / 5.0 * Celsius + 32.0.

   b. Run the program written in Exercise 4a on a computer. Verify that your program starts at the correct Celsius value and contains the exact number of conversions specified in your input data.

5. a. Modify the program written in Exercise 4b, to request the starting Celsius value, the ending Celsius value, and the increment. Instead of the condition checking for a fixed count, the condition will check for the ending Celsius value.

   b. Run the program written in Exercise 5a on a computer. Verify that your output starts and ends at the correct values.

6. Rewrite Program 6–3 to compute the average of ten numbers.

7. Rewrite Program 6–3 to display the following prompt in an InputBox:

   `Please type the total number of data values to be averaged`

   In response to this prompt, the program should accept a user-entered number from the InputBox and then use this number to control the number of times the **Do While** loop is executed. Thus, if the user enters 6, the program should request the input of six numbers and display the average of the next six numbers entered.

8. By mistake, a programmer put the statement average = total / count within the Do While loop immediately after the statement total = total + num in Program 6–3. Thus, the Do While loop becomes:

   `count = 1`

```
total = 0
Do While count <= MAXNUMS
   num = Val(InputBox("Enter a number", "Input Dialog", "0"))
   total = total + num
   lstDisplay.Items.Add("The number just entered is " & num)
   average = total / count
   count = count + 1
Loop
lstDisplay.Items.Add("The average of these numbers is " & average)
```

Will the program yield the correct result with this Do While loop?

From a programming perspective, which Do While loop is better and why?

9. a. The following data was collected on a recent automobile trip.

	Mileage	Gallons
Start of trip:	22495	Full tank
	22841	12.2
	23185	11.3
	23400	10.5
	23772	11.0
	24055	12.2
	24434	14.7
	24804	14.3
	25276	15.2

Write a Visual Basic program that accepts a mileage and gallons value and calculates the miles-per-gallon (mpg) achieved for that segment of the trip. The miles-per-gallon is obtained as the difference in mileage between fill-ups divided by the number of gallons of gasoline used.

b. Modify the program written for Exercise 9a to additionally compute and display the cumulative mpg achieved after each fill-up. The cumulative mpg is calculated as the difference between the mileage at each fill-up and the mileage at the start of the trip, divided by the sum of the gallons used to that point in the trip.

10. a. A bookstore summarizes its monthly transactions by keeping the following information for each book in stock:

   International Standard Book Number (ISBN)

   Inventory balance at the beginning of the month

   Number of copies received during the month

   Number of copies sold during the month

   Write a Visual Basic program that accepts this data for each book, and then displays the ISBN and an updated book inventory balance using the relationship:

New balance = Inventory balance at the beginning of the month

+ Number of copies received during the month

− Number of copies sold during the month

Your program should use a `Do While` loop with a fixed count condition, so that information on only three books is requested.

b. Run the program written in Exercise 10a on a computer. Review the display produced by your program and verify that the output produced is correct.

11. Modify the program you wrote for Exercise 10a to keep requesting and displaying results until a sentinel identification value of 999 is entered. Run the program on a computer.

6.4 For/Next Loops

As we have seen, the condition used to control a `Do While` loop can be used either to test the value of a counter or to test for a sentinel value. Loops controlled by a counter are referred to as *fixed-count* loops, because the loop is executed a fixed number of times. The creation of fixed-count loops always requires initializing, testing, and modifying the counter variable. The general form we have used for these steps has been:

```
Initialize counter
Do While counter <= final value
        statement(s)
        counter = counter + increment
Loop
```

The need to initialize, test, and alter a counter to create a fixed-count loop is so common that Visual Basic provides a special structure, called the `For/Next` loop, that groups all of these operations together on a single line. The general form of a `For/Next` loop is:

```
For variable = start To end Step increment
    statement(s)
Next variable
```

Although the `For/Next` loop looks a little complicated, it is really quite simple if we consider each of its parts separately. A `For/Next` loop begins with a `For` statement. This statement, beginning with the keyword `For`, provides four items that control the loop: a variable name, a starting value for the variable, an ending value, and an increment value. Except for the increment, each of these items must be present in a `For` statement, including the equal sign and the keyword `To`, used to separate the starting and ending values. If an increment is included, the keyword **Step** must also be used to separate the increment value from the ending value.

The variable name can be any valid Visual Basic name and is referred to as the *loop counter* (typically the counter is chosen as an integer variable); *start* is the starting (initializing) value assigned to the counter; *end* is the maximum or minimum value the counter can have and determines when the loop is finished; and *increment* is the value that is added to or subtracted from the counter each time the loop is executed. If the increment is omitted, it is assumed to be 1. Examples of valid For statements are as follows:

```
For count = 1 To 7 Step 1
For I = 5 To 15 Step 2
For kk = 1 To 20
```

In the first For statement, the counter variable is named count, the initial value assigned to count is 1, the loop will be terminated when the value in count exceeds 7, and the increment value is 1. In the next For statement, the counter variable is named I, the initial value of I is 5, the loop will be terminated when the value in I exceeds 15, and the increment is 2. In the last For statement, the counter variable is named kk, the initial value of kk is 1, the loop will be terminated when the value of kk exceeds 20, and a default value of 1 is used for the increment.

For each For statement there must be a matching Next statement. The Next statement both defines where the loop ends and is used to increment the counter variable by the increment amount defined in the For statement. If no increment has been explicitly listed in the For statement, the counter is incremented by one.

The Next statement formally marks the end of the loop and causes the counter to be incremented. It then causes a transfer back to the beginning of the loop. When the loop is completed, program execution continues with the first statement after the Next statement.

Consider the loop contained within Event Procedure 6–5 as a specific example of a For/Next loop.

Event Procedure 6–5

```
Private Sub frmMain_Click(ByVal sender As Object, _
    ByVal e As System.EventArgs) Handles MyBase.Click
  Dim count As Integer

  lstDisplay.Items.Clear()
  lstDisplay.Items.Add("NUMBER    SQUARE")

  For count = 1 To 5
    lstDisplay.Items.Add("        " & count & "            " & count*count)
  Next count

End Sub
```

When Event Procedure 6–5 is executed, the following display is produced in the List box lstDisplay:

```
NUMBER    SQUARE
  1         1
  2         4
  3         9
  4         16
  5         25
```

The first line displayed by the program is produced by the lstDisplay statement placed before the For statement. The statements within the For/Next loop produce the remaining output. This loop begins with the For statement and ends with the Next statement.

The initial value assigned to the counter variable count is 1. Because the value in count does not exceed the final value of 5, the statements in the loop, including the Next statement, are executed. The execution of the lstDisplay.Items.Add statement within the loop produces the following display:

```
1          1
```

The Next statement is then encountered, incrementing the value in count to 2, and control is transferred back to the For statement. The For statement then tests whether count is greater than 5 and repeats the loop, producing the following display:

```
2          4
```

This process continues until the value in count exceeds the final value of 5, producing the complete output of numbers and squares displayed above. For comparison purposes, a Do While loop equivalent to the For/Next loop is contained in Event Procedure 6–5:

```
count = 1
Do While count <= 5
  lstDisplay.Items.Add("      " & count & "          " & count*count)
  count = count + 1
Loop
```

As seen in this example, the difference between the For/Next and Do While loops is the placement of the initialization, condition test, and incrementing items. The grouping together of these items in a For statement is very convenient when fixed-count loops must be constructed. See if you can determine the output produced by Event Procedure 6–6.

Event Procedure 6–6

```
Private Sub frmMain_Click(ByVal sender As Object, _
    ByVal e As System.EventArgs) Handles MyBase.Click
  Dim count As Integer
```

```
   For count = 12 To 20 Step 2
      lstDisplay.Items.Add(count)
   Next count
End Sub
```

The loop starts with count initialized to 12, stops when count exceeds 20, and increments count in steps of 2. The actual statements executed include all statements following the **For** statement, up to and including the **Next** statement. The output produced by Event Procedure 6–6 is:

```
12
14
16
18
20
```

For/Next Loop Rules

Now that we have seen a few simple examples of For/Next loop structures, it is useful to summarize the rules that all For/Next loops must adhere to:

1. The first statement in a For/Next loop must be a For statement and the last statement in a For/Next loop must be a Next statement.
2. The For/Next loop counter variable may be either a real or integer variable.
3. The initial, final, and increment values may all be replaced by variables or expressions, as long as each variable has a value previously assigned to it and the expressions can be evaluated to yield a number. For example, the For statement:

   ```
   For count = begin To begin + 10 Step Augment
   ```

   is valid and can be used as long as values have been assigned to the variables begin and augment before this For statement is encountered in a program.
4. The initial, final, and increment values may be positive or negative, but the loop will not be executed if any one of the following is true:
a. The initial value is greater than the final value and the increment is positive.
b. The initial value is less than the final value and the increment is negative.
5. An infinite loop is created if the increment is zero.
6. An Exit For statement may be embedded within a For/Next loop to cause a transfer out of the loop.

Once a For/Next loop is correctly structured, it is executed as follows:[1]

---

[1]The number of times that a For/Next loop is executed is determined by the expression:
```
INT((final value - initial value + increment)/increment)
```

Step 1. The initial value is assigned to the counter variable.

Step 2. The value in the counter is compared to the final value.

For positive increments, if the value is less than or equal to the final value, then:

All loop statements are executed; and

The counter is incremented and step 2 is repeated.

For negative increments if the value is greater than or equal to the final value, then:

All loop statements are executed.

The counter is decremented and step 2 is repeated,

Else

The loop is terminated.

It is extremely important to realize that no statement within the loop should ever alter the value in the counter because the Next statement increments or decrements the loop counter automatically. The value in the counter may itself be displayed, as in Event Procedures 6–5 and 6–6, or used in an expression to calculate some other variable. However, it must never be used on the left-hand side of an assignment statement or altered within the loop. Also note that when a For/Next loop is completed, the counter contains the last value that exceeds the final tested value.

Figure 6–14 illustrates the internal workings of the For/Next loop for positive increments. To avoid the necessity of always illustrating these steps, a simplified flowchart symbol has been created. Using the following flowchart symbol to represent a For/Next statement

complete For/Next loops alternatively can be illustrated as shown on Figure 6–15.

To understand the enormous power of For/Next loops, consider the task of printing a table of numbers from 1 to 10, including their squares and cubes, using a For/Next statement. Such a table was previously produced using a Do While loop in Event Procedure 6–3. You may wish to review Event Procedure 6–3 and compare it to Event Procedure 6–7 to get a further sense of the equivalence between For/Next and Do While loops. Both Event Procedures 6–3 and 6–7 produced the same output.

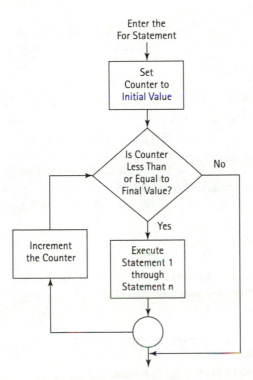

Figure 6-14 *For/Next Loop Flowchart for Positive Increments*

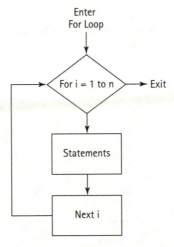

Figure 6-15 *Simplified For/Next Loop Flowchart*

Programmer Notes

Which Loop Should You Use?

Beginning programmers frequently ask which loop structure they should use—a **For** or **Do While** loop?

In Visual Basic, the answer is relatively straightforward, because the **For** statement can be used only to construct fixed-count loops. Although both **For** and **Do While** loops in Visual Basic create pretest loops, generally you should use a **For/Next** loop when constructing fixed-count loops and **Do While** loops when constructing variable-condition loops.

Event Procedure 6–7

```
Private Sub frmMain_Click(ByVal sender As Object, _
    ByVal e As System.EventArgs) Handles MyBase.Click
  Dim num As Integer

  lstDisplay.Items.Add("NUMBER SQUARE CUBE")
  For num = 1 To 10
    lstDisplay.Items.Add("      " & num & "           " & num ^ 2 & "          " _
       & num ^ 3)
  Next num
End Sub
```

When Event Code 6–6 is activated, the following display is produced in the list box lstDisplay:

NUMBER	SQUARE	CUBE
1	1	1
2	4	8
3	9	27
4	16	64
5	25	125
6	36	216
7	49	343
8	64	512
9	81	729
10	100	1000

Simply changing the number 10 in the For/Next statement of Program 6–11 to 1000 creates a loop that is executed 1,000 times and produces a table of numbers from 1 to

1000. As with the `Do While` loop, this small change produces an immense increase in the processing and output provided by the program.

Exercises 6.4

Note: in all the problems listed below, output should be displayed in a ListBox control.

1. Write individual **For** statements for the following cases:

   a. Use a counter named I that has an initial value of 1, a final value of 20, and an increment of 1.

   b. Use a counter named `count` that has an initial value of 1, a final value of 20, and an increment of 2.

   c. Use a counter named J that has an initial value of 1, a final value of 100, and an increment of 5.

   d. Use a counter named `count` that has an initial value of 20, a final value of 1, and an increment of -1.

   e. Use a counter named `count` that has an initial value of 20, a final value of 1, and an increment of -2.

   f. Use a counter named `count` that has an initial value of 1.0, a final value of 16.2, and an increment of 0.2.

   g. Use a counter named `xcnt` that has an initial value of 20.0, a final value of 10.0, and an increment of -0.5.

2. Determine the number of times that each **For/Next** loop is executed for the statements written for Exercise 1.

3. Determine the value in `total` after each of the following loops is executed.

   a.
   ```
   total = 0
   For I = 1 To 10
      total = total + I
   Next I
   ```

   b.
   ```
   total = 1
   For count = 1 To 10
      total = total * 2
   Next count
   ```

   c.
   ```
   total = 0
   For I = 10 To 15
      total = total + I
   Next I
   ```

   d.
   ```
   total = 50
   For I = 1 To 10
      total = total - I
   Next I
   ```

e. ```
total = 1
For icnt = 1 To 8
  total = total * icnt
Next icnt
```

f. ```
total = 1.0
For J = 1 To 5
  total = total / 2.0
Next J
```

4. Determine the errors in the following **For/Next** statements:

a. `For I = 1,10`

b. `For count 5,10`

c. `For JJ = 1 To 10 Increment 2`

d. `For kk = 1, 10, -1`

e. `For kk = -1, -20`

5. Determine the output of the following **For** loop:

```
Dim I As Integer
For I = 20 To 0 Step -4
  lstDisplay.Items.Add(I)
Next I
```

6. Modify Event Procedure 6–7 to produce a table of the numbers 0 through 20 in increments of 2, with their squares and cubes.

7. Modify Event Procedure 6–7 to produce a table of numbers from 10 to 1, instead of 1 to 10 as it currently does.

8. Write a Visual Basic program that uses a `For/Next` loop to accumulate the sum 1 + 2 + 3 + ... + N, where N is a user-entered integer number. Then evaluate the expression $N*(N + 1)/2$ to verify that this expression yields the same result as the loop.

9. a. An old Arabian legend has it that a fabulously wealthy but unthinking king agreed to give a beggar one cent and double the amount for 64 days. Using this information, write, run, and test a Visual Basic program that displays how much the king must pay the beggar on each day. The output of your program should appear as follows:

```
Day          Amount Owed
 1               0.01
 2               0.02
 3               0.04
 .                .
 .                .
 .                .
64                .
```

b. Modify the program you wrote for Exercise 9a to determine on which day the king will have paid a total of one million dollars to the beggar.

10. Write and run a program that calculates and displays the amount of money available in a bank account that initially has $1,000 deposited in it and earns 8% interest a year. Your program should display the amount available at the end of each year for a period of ten years. Use the relationship that the money available at the end of each year equals the amount of money in the account at the start of the year plus 0.08 times the amount available at the start of the year.

11. A machine purchased for $28,000 is depreciated at a rate of $4000 a year for seven years. Write and run a Visual Basic program that uses a For/Next loop to compute and display a seven-year depreciation table. The table should have the form:

```
Depreciation Schedule
                          End-of-year        Accumulated
Year     Depreciation        value          depreciation
----     ------------     -----------        ------------
 1           4000            24000               4000
 2           4000            20000               8000
 3           4000            16000              12000
 4           4000            12000              16000
 5           4000             8000              20000
 6           4000             4000              24000
 7           4000                0              28000
```

12. A well-regarded manufacturer of widgets has been losing 4% of its sales each year. The annual profit for the firm is 10% of sales. This year, the firm has had $10 million in sales and a profit of $1 million. Determine the expected sales and profit for the next 10 years. Your program should complete and produce a display as follows:

```
Sales and Profit Projection
Year            Expected sales          Projected profit
----            --------------          ----------------
 1               $10000000                $1000000
 2               $ 9600000                $ 960000
 3                   .                        .
 .                   .                        .
 .                   .                        .
 .                   .                        .
10                   .                        .
----------------------------------------------------------
Totals:      $      .                 $     .
```

13. According to legend, the island of Manhattan was purchased from its Native American population in 1626 for $24. Assuming that this money was invested in a Dutch bank paying 5 percent simple interest per year, construct a table showing how much money the Indians would have at the end of each twenty year period, starting in 1626 and ending in 2006.

6.5 Nested Loops

There are many situations in which it is very convenient to have a loop contained within another loop. Such loops are called *nested loops*. A simple example of a nested loop is:

```
For I = 1 To 4     '<-- Start of Outer Loop
  lstDisplay.Items.Add("I is now " & I)
  For J = 1 To 3  '<-- Start of Inner Loop
    lstDisplay.Items.Add("  J = " & J)
  Next J          '<-- End of Inner Loop
Next I            '<-- End of Outer Loop
```

The first loop, controlled by the value of I, is called the *outer loop*. The second loop, controlled by the value of J, is called the *inner loop*. Note that all statements in the inner loop are contained within the boundaries of the outer loop, and that we have used a different variable to control each loop. For each single trip through the outer loop, the inner loop runs through its entire sequence. Thus, each time the I counter increases by one, the inner For/Next loop executes completely. This situation is illustrated in Figure 6–16.

To understand the concept involved, consider Program 6–5, which uses a nested For/Next loop. Figure 6–17 shows the interface for Program 6–5.

For this application, the procedure code for the Button **Click** events is listed in Program 6–5's event code.

Program 6–5's Event Code

```
Private Sub btnRun_Click(ByVal sender As Object, _
    ByVal e As System.EventArgs) Handles btnRun.Click
  Dim I, J As Integer

  lstDisplay.Items.Clear()
  For I = 1 To 4     '<-- Start of Outer Loop
    lstDisplay.Items.Add("I is now " & I)
    For J = 1 To 3 '<-- Start of Inner Loop
      lstDisplay.Items.Add("  J = " & J)
    Next J          '<-- End of Inner Loop
  Next I            '<-- End of Outer Loop

  End Sub

  Private Sub btnExit_Click(ByVal sender As Object, _
    ByVal e As System.EventArgs) Handles btnExit.Click
  Beep()
  End
End Sub
```

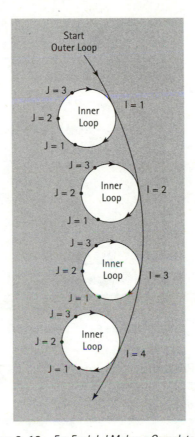

Figure 6–16   *For Each I, J Makes a Complete Loop*

Figure 6–18 illustrates the display produced when Program 6–5 is executed.

When you are creating nested loops using any of Visual Basic's loop structures (and the various structures can be nested within one another), the only requirements that must be adhered to are the following:

1. An inner loop must be fully contained within an outer loop.
2. The inner loop and outer loop control variables cannot be the same.
3. An outer loop control variable must not be altered within an inner loop.

Let us use a nested loop to compute the average grade for each student in a class of 10 students. Each student has taken four exams during the course of the semester. The final grade for each student is calculated as the average of the four examination grades. The pseudocode for this example is:

```
Do 10 times
  Set student total to zero
  Do 4 times
    Read in a grade
    Add the grade to the student total
```

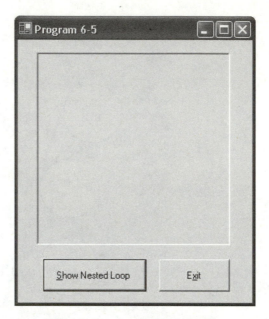

Figure 6–17 *Program 6-5's Interface*

Table 6–3   The Properties Table for Program 6–5

Object	Property	Setting
Form	Name	frmMain
	Text	Program 6–5
ListBox	Name	lstDisplay
Button	Name	btnRun
	Text	&Show Nested Loop
Button	Name	btnExit
	Text	E&xit

```
   End inner Do
Calculate student's average grade
Print student's average grade
End outer Do
```

As described in the pseudocode, an outer loop consisting of 10 passes will be used to calculate the average for each student. The inner loop will consist of four passes, with one examination grade entered in each inner loop pass. As each grade is entered, it is added to the total for the student, and at the end of the loop, the average is calculated

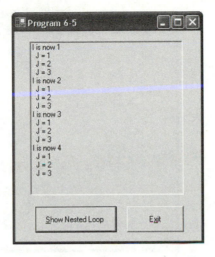

Figure 6-18 *The Display Produced by Program 6-5*

and displayed. Program 6-6 uses a nested loop to make the required calculations. Figure 6-19 shows the interface for Program 6-6.

For this application, the procedure code for the Button Click event is listed in Program 6-6's event code.

Program 6-6's Event Code

```
Private Sub btnRun_Click(ByVal sender As Object, _
    ByVal e As System.EventArgs) Handles btnRun.Click
  Const MAXSTUDENTS As Integer = 10
  Const NUMGRADES As Integer = 4
  Dim i, j As Integer
  Dim grade, total, average As Single

  ' This is the start of the outer loop
  For i = 1 To MAXSTUDENTS
    total = 0
    ' This is the start of the inner loop
    For j = 1 To NUMGRADES
      grade = Val(InputBox("Enter an exam grade for this student", _
          "Input Dialog", "0"))
      total = total + grade
    Next j   ' End of inner loop
    average = total / NUMGRADES
    lstDisplay.Items.Add("The average for student " & i & " is " & _
                        average)
  Next i 'End of outer loop
End Sub
```

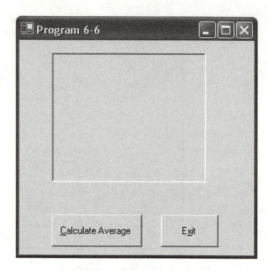

Figure 6–19   *Program 6–6's Interface*

Table 6–4   The Properties Table for Program 6–6

Object	Property	Setting
Form	Name	frmMain
	Text	Program 6–6
ListBox	Name	lstDisplay
Button	Name	btnRun
	Text	&Calculate Average
Button	Name	btnExit
	Text	E&xit

```
Private Sub btnExit_Click(ByVal sender As Object, ByVal e As _
    System.EventArgs) Handles btnExit.Click
  Beep()
  End
End Sub
```

In reviewing Program 6–6, pay particular attention to the initialization of `total` within the outer loop before the inner loop is entered; `total` is initialized 10 times, once for each student. Also note that the average is calculated and displayed immediately after the inner loop is finished. Because the statements that compute and print the average are also contained within the outer loop, 10 averages are calculated and displayed. The entry and addition of each grade within the inner loop uses summation techniques we have seen before that should now be familiar to you.

It may be useful to provide a way out of this program to avoid having to enter four grades for 10 students. With the code above, clicking the `Cancel` button in the `InputBox` dialog box just enters a 0 for that particular grade and continues. However, to have the `Cancel` terminate the program, the code must examine the return value of `InputBox`. When the user clicks on Cancel, the return value for InputBox is set to the null string "". An If statement can check for this value and if it is equal to the null string, then you want to exit from the For loop. However, just doing that only exits from the inner For loop. To completely exit from the program, you need to put another check in the outer For loop with a second Exit For. It is also important to note that the conversion of the return value to an integer using the Val function needs to be done after the return value is checked for equality with the null string. So a string variable `returnval` has been added to the program. The following code provides a way to terminate Program 6–6:

```
Private Sub cmdRun_Click(ByVal sender As Object, _
    ByVal e As System.EventArgs) Handles cmdRun.Click
  Const MAXSTUDENTS As Integer = 10
  Const NUMGRADES As Integer = 4

  Dim i, j As Integer
  Dim grade, total, average As Single
  Dim returnval As String

  ' This is the start of the outer loop
  For i = 1 To MAXSTUDENTS
    total = 0
    ' This is the start of the inner loop
    For j = 1 To NUMGRADES
      returnval = InputBox("Enter an exam grade for this student", _
          "Input Dialog", "0")
      If returnval = "" Then 'InputBox canceled
        Exit For  ' exit inner loop
      End If
      grade = Val(returnval)
      total = total + grade
    Next j   ' End of inner loop
    If returnval = "" Then
      Exit For  ' exit outer loop
```

```
        End If
    average = total / NUMGRADES
    lstDisplay.Items.Add("The average for student " & i & " is " & _
                        average)
  Next i    ' End of outer loop
End Sub
```

Exercises 6.5

Note: in all the problems listed below, output should be displayed in a ListBox control.

1. Four experiments are performed, with each experiment consisting of six test results. The results for each experiment follow. Write a program using a nested loop to compute and display the average of the test results for each experiment.

1st experiment results:	23.2	31.5	16.9	27.5	25.4	28.6
2nd experiment results:	34.8	45.2	27.9	36.8	33.4	39.4
3rd experiment results:	19.4	16.8	10.2	20.8	18.9	13.4
4th experiment results:	36.9	39.5	49.2	45.1	42.7	50.6

2. Modify the program written for Exercise 1 so that the user enters the number of test results for each experiment. Write your program so that a different number of test results can be entered for each experiment.

3. a. A bowling team consists of five players. Each player bowls three games. Write a Visual Basic program that uses a nested loop to enter each player's individual scores and then computes and displays the average score for each bowler. Assume that each bowler has the following scores:

1st bowler:	286	252	265
2nd bowler:	212	186	215
3rd bowler:	252	232	216
4th bowler:	192	201	235
5th bowler:	186	236	272

   b. Modify the program written for Exercise 3a to calculate and display the average team score. (*Hint:* Use a second variable to store the total of all the players' scores.)

4. Rewrite the program written for Exercise 3a to eliminate the inner loop. To do this, you will have to input three scores for each bowler rather than one at a time.

5. Write a program that calculates and displays values for Y when:

   $Y = X * Z/(X - Z)$

   Your program should calculate Y for values of X ranging between 1 and 5, and values of Z ranging between 2 and 10. X should control the outer loop and be incremented in steps of one, and Z should be incremented in steps of two. Your program should also display the message Value Undefined when the X and Z values are equal.

6. Write a program that calculates and displays the yearly amount available if $1,000 is invested in a bank account for 10 years. Your program should display the amounts available for interest rates from 6% to 12% inclusively, in 1% increments. Use a nested loop, with the outer loop controlling the interest rate and the inner loop controlling the years. Use the relationship that the money available at the end of each year equals the amount of money in the account at the start of the year, plus the interest rate times the amount available at the start of the year.

7. In the Duchy of Penchuck, the fundamental unit of currency is the Penchuck Dollar (PD). Income tax deductions are based on Salary in units of 10,000 PD and on the number of dependents the employee has. The formula, designed to favor low-income families, is:

Deduction PD = Dependents * 500 + 0.05 * (50,000 − Salary)

Beyond 5 dependents and beyond 50,000 PD, the Deduction does not change. There is no tax—hence no deduction—on incomes of less than 10,000 PD. Based on this information, create a table of Penchuck income tax deductions, with Dependents 0 to 5 as the column headings and salary 10000, 20000, 30000, 40000, and 50000 as the rows.

6.6   Exit-Controlled Loops

The `Do While` and `For/Next` loops are both entrance-controlled loops, meaning that they evaluate a condition at the start of the loop. A consequence of testing a condition at the top of the loop is that the statements within the loop may not be executed at all.

There are cases, however, where we always require a loop to execute at least once. For such cases, Visual Basic provides two exit-controlled loops, the `Do/Loop Until` and `Do/Loop While` structures. Each of these loop structures tests a condition at the bottom of a loop, ensureing that the statements within the loop are executed at least one time.

The Do/Loop Until Structure

The syntax for the most commonly used exit-controlled loop is:

```
Do
    statement(s)
Loop Until condition
```

The important concept to note in the `Do/Loop Until` structure is that all statements within the loop are executed at least once before the condition is tested, and the loop is repeated until the condition becomes **True** (in other words, the loop executes while the condition is **False**). A flowchart illustrating the operation of the `Do/Loop Until` loop is shown in Figure 6–20.

As illustrated in Figure 6–20, all statements within the `Do/Loop Until` loop are executed once before the condition is evaluated. Then, if the condition is **False**, the statements within the loop are executed again. This process continues until the condition becomes **True**.

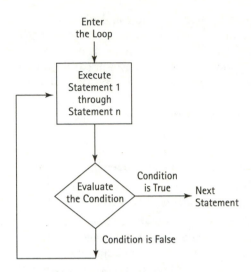

Figure 6-20 *The Do/Loop Until Loop's Flowchart*

As an example of a **Do/Loop Until** structure, consider the following loop:

```
i = 0
Do
   lstDisplay.Items.Add(i)
   i = i + 5
Loop Until i > 20
```

The output produced in the list box lstDisplay by this code is:

```
0
5
10
15
20
```

The important point to note here is that the condition is tested after the statements within the loop structure have been executed, rather than before. This ensures that the loop statements are always executed at least once. Also note that exit-controlled loops require you to correctly initialize all variables used in the tested expression before the loop is entered, in a manner similar to that used in entrance-controlled loops. Similarly, within the loop itself, these same variables must be altered to ensure that the loop eventually terminates.

The Do/Loop While Structure

In a `Do/Loop Until` structure, the statements within the loop are executed as long as the condition is **False**. A variation of the `Do/Loop Until` structure is the `Do/Loop While` structure, which executes the statements within the loop as long as the condition is **True**. The syntax of a `Do/Loop While` loop is:

```
Do
  statement(s)
Loop While condition
```

The `Do/Loop While` structure, like its `Do/Loop Until` counterpart, is an exit-controlled loop. Unlike the `Do/Loop Until` loop, which executes until the condition becomes **True**, a `Do/Loop While` structure executes until the condition becomes **False**. If the condition tested in a `Do/Loop While` loop is **False** to begin with, the statements within the loop will execute only once.

Validity Checks

Exit-controlled loops are particularly useful for filtering user-entered input and validating that the correct type of data has been entered. For example, assume that a program is being written to provide the square root of any number input by the user. For this application, we want to ensure that a valid number has been entered. Any invalid data, such as a negative number or nonnumeric input, should be rejected and a new request for input should be made until the user actually enters a valid number. Program 6–7 illustrates how this request can be accomplished easily using a `Do/Loop Until` structure. Figure 6–21 shows the interface for Program 6–7.

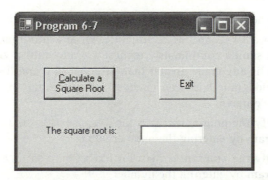

Figure 6–21   *Program 6–7's Interface*

Program 6–7's Event Code

```
Private Sub btnRun_Click(ByVal sender As Object, _
    ByVal e As System.EventArgs) Handles btnRun.Click
  Dim num As String

  Do
    txtSquare.Clear()
    num = InputBox("Enter a number", "Input Request", "0")
    If IsNumeric(num) And Val(num) >= 0 Then
      txtSquare.Text = Math.Sqrt(num)
    Else
      MessageBox.Show("Invalid data was entered", "Error Message", _
          MessageBoxButtons.OK, MessageBoxIcon.Error)
    End If
  Loop Until IsNumeric(num) And Val(num) >= 0
End Sub

Private Sub btnExit_Click(ByVal sender As Object, _
    ByVal e As System.EventArgs) Handles btnExit.Click
  Beep()
  End
End Sub
```

Note that in the run button **Click** code, a request for a number is repeated until a valid number is entered. This code is constructed so that a user cannot "crash" the program by entering either a nonnumeric string or a negative number. This type of user input validation is essential for programs that are to be used extensively by many people, and is a mark of a professionally written program.

Although this example is showing the validity check on exit in a **Do/Loop Until** structure, a validity check could also be done on entrance in a **Do/While** structure.

Exercises 6.6

Note: in all the problems listed below, output should be displayed in a ListBox control.

1. a. Using a `Do/Loop Until` structure, write a program to accept a grade. The program should continuously request a grade until a valid grade is entered. A valid grade is any grade greater than or equal to 0 and less than or equal to 101. After a valid grade has been entered, your program should display the value of the grade entered.

   b. Modify the program written for Exercise 1a so that it allows the user to exit the program by entering the number 999.

   c. Modify the program written for Exercise 1b so that it allows the user to exit the program by entering the number 999.

   d. Modify the program written for Exercise 1c so that it automatically terminates after five invalid grades are entered.

2. a. Modify the program written for Exercise 1a as follows: If the grade is less than 0 or greater than 100, your program should print an appropriate message informing the user that an invalid grade has been entered; otherwise, the grade should be added to a total. When a grade of 999 is entered, the program should exit the repetition loop and compute and display the average of the valid grades entered.

    b. Run the program written in Exercise 2a on a computer and verify the program using appropriate test data.

3. a. Write a program to reverse the digits of a positive integer number. For example, if the number 8735 is entered the number displayed should be 5378. *Hint:* Use an exit-controlled loop, and continuously strip off and display the units digit of the number. If the variable num initially contains the number entered, the units digit is obtained as num Mod 10. After a units digit is displayed, dividing the number by 10 sets up the number for the next iteration. Thus, 8735 Mod 10 is 5 and 8735 / 10 is 873. The loop should repeat as long as the remaining number is not zero.

    b. Run the program written in Exercise 3a on a computer and verify the program using appropriate test data.

4. a. The outstanding balance on Rhona Karp's car loan is $8,000. Each month, Rhona is required to make a payment of $300, which includes both interest and principal repayment of the car loan. The monthly interest is calculated as 0.10/12 of the outstanding balance of the loan. After the interest is deducted, the remaining part of the payment is used to pay off the loan. Using this information, write a Visual Basic program that produces a table indicating the beginning monthly balance, the interest payment, the principal payment, and the remaining loan balance after each payment is made. Your output should resemble and complete the entries in the following table until the outstanding loan balance is zero.

Beginning Balance	Interest Payment	Principal Payment	Ending Loan Balance
---------	--------	---------	----------
8000.00	66.67	233.33	7766.67
7766.67	64.73	235.28	7531.39
75531.39	.	.	.
.	.	.	.
.	.	.	.
.	.	.	0.00

    b. Modify the program written in Exercise 4a so that the total of the interest and principal paid is displayed at the end of the table produced by your program.

5. Write, run, and test a Visual Basic program that prompts the user for the amount of a loan, the annual percentage rate, and the number of years of the loan, using InputBox functions that display the following prompts:

    What is the amount of the loan?
    What is the annual percentage rate?
    How many years will you take to pay back the loan?

From the input data, produce a loan amortization table similar to the one shown below:

Amount	Annual % Interest	Years	Monthly Payment
1500	14	1	134.68

Payment Number	Interest Paid	Principal Paid	Cumulative Interest	Total Paid to Date	New Balance Due
1	17.50	117.18	17.50	134.68	1382.82
2	16.13	118.55	33.63	269.36	1264.27
3	14.75	119.93	48.38	404.04	1144.34
4	13.35	121.33	61.73	538.72	1023.01
5	11.94	122.75	73.67	673.40	900.27
6	10.50	124.18	84.17	808.08	776.09
7	9.05	125.63	93.23	942.76	650.46
8	7.59	127.09	100.81	1077.45	523.37
9	6.11	128.57	106.92	1212.13	394.79
10	4.61	130.07	111.53	1346.81	264.72
11	3.09	131.59	114.61	1481.49	133.13
12	1.55	133.13	116.17	1616.17	0

In constructing the loop necessary to produce the body of the table, the following initializations must be made:

```
New balance due = Original loan amount
Cumulative interest = 0.0
Paid to date = 0.0
Payment number = 0
Monthly Interest Rate = Annual Percentage Rate / 1200
```

$$\text{Monthly Payment} = \frac{(\text{Loan Amount}) * (\text{Monthly Interest Rate})}{1 - (1 + \text{Monthly Interest Rate})^{-(\text{Number of Months})}}$$

Within the loop, the following calculations and accumulations should be used:

Payment number   = Payment number + 1

Interest paid   = New balance due * Monthly interest rate

Principal paid   = Monthly payment - Interest paid

Cumulative interest = Cumulative interest + Interest paid

Paid to date   = Paid to date + Monthly payment

New balance due   = New balance due - Principal paid

6. Modify the program written for Exercise 5, to prevent the user from entering an illegal value for the interest rate. That is, write a loop that asks the user repeatedly for the annual interest rate, until a value between 1.0 and 25.0 is entered.

6.7 Focus on Program Design and Implementation:[2] After-the-Fact Data Validation and Creating Keyboard Shortcuts[3]

In the last Focus Section, keystroke input validation was applied to the Rotech Walk In order entry forms quantity text box. This type of validation consists of checking each entered character and only permitting selected keys to be entered as valid input data. In addition to this keystroke-by-keystroke data validation, overall validation of a completed input entry is also used to ensure that: (1) a required field has not been skipped over; and (2) that data contained within a field is reasonable. This second type of data validation is referred to as after-the-fact validation.

As a practical example of this type of data validation, consider Rotech's Mail In form, a copy of which is shown in Figure 6–22.

In an extreme situation, a user could enter no data at all into any of the input text boxes shown in Figure 6–22 and still attempt to print out a packing slip. Even using keystroke validation for the quantity text box won't help, because a user can simply skip this box without entering any quantity into it. After-the-fact validation can be used to correct this type of situation. Specifically, for the Mail In form, we will apply after-the-fact validation to ensure the following requirements are met:

Figure 6–22 *The Rotech Mail In Form*

---

[2]This section can be omitted with no loss of subject continuity, unless the Rotech project is being followed.

[3]The Rotech project, as it should exist at the start of this section (which includes all of the capabilities built into it through the end of Section 5.6) can be found at http://computerscience.jbpub.com/bronsonvbnet in the ROTECH5 folder as project rotech5.

A packing slip will not be prepared if any name or address fields are empty or if there is not a positive number in the quantity text box. We will also assume that each customer is limited to a maximum of 5 free disk packages, so the quantity cannot exceed this value.

In addition, we will add after-the-fact data validation to ensure that the Walk In form adheres to the following requirements:

A bill will be printed only if the quantity field contains a positive number. Because the customer is purchasing disk packs, there will be no limit check on the maximum number that can be entered for this quantity. Additionally, if both the first and last name fields have been left blank, the bill will be made out to Cash.[4]

There are two predominant techniques for informing a user that a particular data entry item has either been filled in incorrectly or is missing completely. In the first method, each individual field is examined and a message displayed, one at a time, for each incorrectly completed item. For more than two fields, this method tends to annoy users and should be avoided. For example, assume that you inform the user that the Address item has not been filled in. Then, after the user corrects this field, you provide another message that the City item is missing. After this item is entered, another message appears indicating that the State has not been entered. From a user's standpoint, this is extremely annoying. A much better scheme is to provide a single message that gives a complete list of all missing items.

Figure 6–23 shows how such a message would look, assuming that all of the Mail In form's name and address fields were left empty when the P̲rint Packing S̲lip button was pressed. Note that the message box lists all of the missing address items. The quantity input, which is not part of the address data, will be given its own set of error messages. Figures 6–24 and 6–25 show the two possible error messages that a user could receive for this input. Thus, a user will receive at most two separate error messages (one for the address data and one for the quantity input), which is within most user's tolerance zone. Clearly, these error messages can and will recur if the user does not correct the problem. However, this recurrence will not be blamed on the system, but rather on the user's inattention to detail.

Figure 6–23 *A Sample Address Information Error Message*

---

[4]This is a common custom in business. For customers who do not wish to give their names or addresses, the transaction is simply posted as a cash transaction.

Figure 6–24   *The Error Message for a Missing Quantity*

Figure 6–25   *The Error Message for Too Large a Quantity*

Event Procedure 6–8 illustrates the code used in the Rotech application to validate the Mail In form's input before a packing slip is printed. The first item to note is that, from a user's viewpoint, the procedure is meant to print a packing slip. However, from a programming viewpoint, the majority of the procedure is concerned with validating data. This is true for most real-world code; the code itself should validate all data and ensure that any data required for processing cannot inadvertently cause the system to crash or produce inappropriate results. For example, it is the program's responsibility not to print a packing slip with a blank address or an unreasonable quantity of product. All the validation in the world cannot stop a user from entering a misspelled name or a nonexistent address, but that is an error that cannot be fixed by the application. Note that the control character CrLf is used in this procedure. This stands for Carriage-return Linefeed and is equivalent to the NewLine character.

Event Procedure 6–8

```
Private Sub btnPrint_Click(ByVal sender As Object, _
    ByVal e As System.EventArgs) Handles btnPrint.Click
  Dim strErrorPrompt, strErrorMsg, strErrorMin, strErrorMax As String
  Dim strListEmptyBoxes As String  ' the list of empty Text boxes

  Const MAXALLOWED As Integer = 5

  'Set the standard strings that will be printed
  strErrorPrompt = "Data Entry Error"
  strErrorMsg = "The following data needs to be entered: " & _
      ControlChars.CrLf
```

```
        strListEmptyBoxes = ""
        strErrorMin ="You must enter the No. of disk packages ordered."
        strErrorMax = "The quantity ordered cannot exceed " & Str(MAXALLOWED)

        'Locate all empty name and address text boxes
        If txtFname.Text.Length = 0 Then
          strListEmptyBoxes = strListEmptyBoxes & "First Name " & ControlChars.CrLf
        End If
        If txtLname.Text.Length = 0 Then
          strListEmptyBoxes = strListEmptyBoxes & "Last Name " & ControlChars.CrLf
        End If
        If txtAddr.Text.Length = 0 Then
          strListEmptyBoxes = strListEmptyBoxes & "Address " & ControlChars.CrLf
        End If
        If txtCity.Text.Length = 0 Then
          strListEmptyBoxes = strListEmptyBoxes & "City " & ControlChars.CrLf
        End If
        If txtState.Text.Length = 0 Then
          strListEmptyBoxes = strListEmptyBoxes & "State " & ControlChars.CrLf
        End If
        If txtZip.Text.Length = 0 Then
          strListEmptyBoxes = strListEmptyBoxes & "Zip Code "
        End If


        ' Inform the user of all empty text boxes
        If strListEmptyBoxes.Length > 0 Then
          MessageBox.Show(strErrorMsg & strListEmptyBoxes, strErrorPrompt, _
              MessageBoxButtons.OK, MessageBoxIcon.Error)

        ElseIf Val(txtQuantity.Text) < 1 Then
          MessageBox.Show(strErrorMin, strErrorPrompt, MessageBoxButtons.OK, _
              MessageBoxIcon.Error)
        ElseIf Val(txtQuantity.Text) > MAXALLOWED Then
          MessageBox.Show(strErrorMax, strErrorPrompt, MessageBoxButtons.OK, _
              MessageBoxIcon.Error)

        Else ' Print the packing slip
          PrintDocument1.Print()
        End If
    End Sub

    Private Sub PrintDocument1_PrintPage(ByVal sender As System.Object, _
        ByVal e As System.Drawing.Printing.PrintPageEventArgs) _
        Handles PrintDocument1.PrintPage
      Dim font As New Font("Courier New", 12)
```

```
Dim x, y As Single

x = e.MarginBounds.Left
y = e.MarginBounds.Top

e.Graphics.DrawString("", font, Brushes.Black, x, y)
y = y + font.GetHeight
e.Graphics.DrawString("", font, Brushes.Black, x, y)
y = y + font.GetHeight

e.Graphics.DrawString(Space(20) + FormatDateTime(Now, _
    DateFormat.GeneralDate), font, Brushes.Black, x, y)
y = y + font.GetHeight

e.Graphics.DrawString("", font, Brushes.Black, x, y)
y = y + font.GetHeight
e.Graphics.DrawString("", font, Brushes.Black, x, y)
y = y + font.GetHeight

e.Graphics.DrawString(Space(5) & "To: " & txtFname.Text + _
    " " & txtLname.Text, font, Brushes.Black, x, y)
y = y + font.GetHeight
e.Graphics.DrawString(Space(9) & txtAddr.Text, font, _
    Brushes.Black, x, y)
y = y + font.GetHeight
e.Graphics.DrawString(Space(9) & txtCity.Text & " " _
    & txtState.Text & " " & txtZip.Text, font, Brushes.Black, x, y)
y = y + font.GetHeight

e.Graphics.DrawString("", font, Brushes.Black, x, y)
y = y + font.GetHeight
e.Graphics.DrawString("", font, Brushes.Black, x, y)
y = y + font.GetHeight

e.Graphics.DrawString("Quantity:" & Space(1) & txtQuantity.Text, _
    font, Brushes.Black, x, y)
End Sub
```

Now look at the first section of code printed in black in Event Procedure 6–8. Note that the maximum allowable disk order quantity and all of the standard messages used as prompts in Figures 6–23 through 6–25 have been assigned at the top of this section, near the beginning of the procedure. The advantage of this is that if any change must be made to any of these values, the value can be easily located and modified.

Now note that the name and address validation code at the end of this first black section consists of a series of six individual If statements. Within each statement an individual text box string is checked using the Length method. The *Length method* returns a string's length, consisting of the total number of characters in the string. A length of zero means that the string has no characters, indicating that no data has been entered for it. For each text box that has no data, the name of the equivalent data field and a carriage return-line feed combination are appended to the string variable named `strListEmptyBoxes`. Thus, after the last If statement is executed, this string variable will contain a list of all empty name and address items.

Tips from the Pros

Checking for Completed Inputs

The method used in Event Procedure 6–8 individually tests and identifies each text box that contains an empty string. When this individual identification is not necessary, a much quicker validation can be obtained by multiplying the length of all the input strings together. Then, if one or more of the strings is empty, the result of the computation will be zero.

As a specific example, assume that you need to check that three text boxes, named `txtPrice`, `txtQuantity`, and `txtDescription`, have all been filled in. The following code does this:

```
If (txtPrice.Text.Length * txtQuantity.Text.Length * _
    txtDescription.Text.Length) = 0 Then
  MessageBox.Show("One or more of the fields has not been filled in!")
Endif
```

Note that this code does not identify which, or how many, of the input items are blank. However, if one or more of the items is blank, at least one of the operands in the multiplication will be zero, and the result of the computation is zero. Note that this is the only way a zero will result, because if all of the inputs are filled in the result of the multiplication will be a positive number. Thus, a zero result ensures that at least one of the inputs has not been filled in.

This programming trick is very prevalent in real-world applications, and you are certain to see many applications of it in your programming work.

Finally, look at the second section of code printed in black, containing the validation code for the quantity of disk packages ordered. Here there are two possibilities—either the quantity has been left blank or the number of ordered packages exceeds the value in the MAXALLOWED named constant. (We don't have to check for either a negative or fractional value being entered, because the key stroke validation will prevent a minus sign or period from being entered.) The two `ElseIf` statements within this second black region check for each of these conditions.

The Walk In form's after-the-fact validation is listed as Event Procedure 6–9. As most of the code listed in this procedure was previously described in Section 4.4, we will only comment on the code specifically added for data validation. The first black section provides the prompts that we will use for an error Message box, which is the same as that previously illustrated in Figure 6–24 for the Mail In form. The second black section contains two individual If statements. The first If statement checks that both a first name and last name have been entered; if not, the string Cash is substituted for the first name. (See this section's Tips From the Pros box in this section for an alternative way of making this check.) The second If statement validates the number of disks ordered is greater than zero.

Event Procedure 6–9

```
Private Sub btnPrint_Click(ByVal sender As Object, _
    ByVal e As System.EventArgs) Handles btnPrint.Click
  Dim stotal, staxes, sfinal As Single
  Dim strErrorPrompt As String
  Dim strErrorMin As String

  'Set the standard strings that will be printed
  strErrorPrompt = "Data Entry Error"
  strErrorMin = "You must enter the No. of disk packages ordered."

  'Clear out the text boxes
  txtTotal.Clear()
  txtTax.Clear()
  txtFinal.Clear()

  'Calculate and display new values
  sTotal = Val(txtQuantity.Text) * CDec(txtPrice.Text)
  sTaxes = Val(txtTrate.Text) * sTotal
  sFinal = sTotal + sTaxes
  txtTotal.Text = FormatCurrency(sTotal)
  txtTax.Text = FormatCurrency(sTaxes)
  txtFinal.Text = FormatCurrency(sFinal)

  ' Validate the Name and Quantity
  If txtFname.Text.Length = 0 AND txtLname.Text.Length = 0 Then
    txtFname.Text = "Cash"
  End If
  If Val(txtQuantity.Text) < 1 Then
    MessageBox.Show(strErrorMin, strErrorPrompt, MessageBoxButtons.OK, _
        MessageBoxIcon.Error)
  Else ' Print a Bill
    PrintDocument1.Print()
  End If
End Sub

Private Sub PrintDocument1_PrintPage(ByVal sender As System.Object, _
    ByVal e As System.Drawing.Printing.PrintPageEventArgs) _
    Handles PrintDocument1.PrintPage
```

```
Dim font As New Font("Courier New", 12)
Dim x, y As Single

x = e.MarginBounds.Left
y = e.MarginBounds.Top

e.Graphics.DrawString("", font, Brushes.Black, x, y)
y = y + font.GetHeight
e.Graphics.DrawString("", font, Brushes.Black, x, y)
y = y + font.GetHeight

e.Graphics.DrawString(Space(20) + FormatDateTime(Now, _
    DateFormat.ShortDate), font, Brushes.Black, x, y)
y = y + font.GetHeight
e.Graphics.DrawString(Space(20) + FormatDateTime(Now, _
    DateFormat.LongTime), font, Brushes.Black, x, y)
y = y + font.GetHeight

e.Graphics.DrawString("", font, Brushes.Black, x, y)
y = y + font.GetHeight
e.Graphics.DrawString("", font, Brushes.Black, x, y)
y = y + font.GetHeight

e.Graphics.DrawString("Sold to: " & txtFname.Text + _
    " " & txtLname.Text, font, Brushes.Black, x, y)
y = y + font.GetHeight
e.Graphics.DrawString(Space(9) & txtAddr.Text, font, _
    Brushes.Black, x, y)
y = y + font.GetHeight
e.Graphics.DrawString(Space(9) & txtCity.Text & " " _
    & txtState.Text & " " & txtZip.Text, font, Brushes.Black, x, y)
y = y + font.GetHeight

e.Graphics.DrawString("", font, Brushes.Black, x, y)
y = y + font.GetHeight
e.Graphics.DrawString("", font, Brushes.Black, x, y)
y = y + font.GetHeight

e.Graphics.DrawString("Quantity:" & Space(1) & txtQuantity.Text, _
    font, Brushes.Black, x, y)
y = y + font.GetHeight
e.Graphics.DrawString("Unit Price:" & Space(2) & _
    FormatCurrency(txtPrice.Text), font, Brushes.Black, x, y)
y = y + font.GetHeight
```

```
e.Graphics.DrawString("Total:" & Space(6) & txtTotal.Text, _
    font, Brushes.Black, x, y)
y = y + font.GetHeight
e.Graphics.DrawString("Sales tax:" & Space(3) & txtTax.Text, _
    font, Brushes.Black, x, y)
y = y + font.GetHeight
e.Graphics.DrawString("Amount Due:" & Space(1) & txtFinal.Text, _
    font, Brushes.Black, x, y)
End Sub
```

Using Function Keys as Keyboard Shortcuts

Many applications reserve the Function keys (F1, F2, and so on) for use as keyboard shortcuts. A keyboard shortcut is a single key, or combination of keys, that performs a distinct task no matter when or where it is pressed in the application.

For example, a common practice is to allocate the F1 key as the keyboard shortcut for calling up a Help screen, so that whenever this key is pressed a Help screen appears. Another use is to allocate a function key as a "Return to Main Menu" keyboard shortcut. Using the designated key (no matter where it is pressed in an application) guarantees hiding/unloading of the currently displayed form and display of the Main Menu form. For applications with long chains of forms, where one form is used to call another, a specific function key can also be used as a "Return to Main Menu" keyboard shortcut. By pressing the designated key, the user recalls the previous form. This permits a user to back up as many forms as necessary, even to the point of recalling the first screen displayed by the application.

The first requirement for capturing a pressed function key, independent of which specific control has the focus when the key is pressed, is to set a form's **KeyPreview** property to **True**. Doing this ensures that no matter which control has focus, the keyboard events **KeyDown**, **KeyUp**, and **KeyPress** will be invoked as Form events before they are invoked for any control placed on a form. Because the form keyboard events supercede all other control keyboard events, the desired function key is detected as a `Form` event first and is recognized as such no matter where on the form or within a control that the key is pressed.

As a specific example, assume that we want to make the F11 key a "Return to Main Menu" keyboard shortcut. The following event code does this:

```
Private Sub Form1_KeyDown(ByVal sender As Object, _
    ByVal e As System.Windows.Forms.KeyEventArgs) Handles MyBase.KeyDown
  If e.KeyCode = System.Windows.Forms.Keys.F11 Then  ' check for F11 key
    Dim frmMainRef as New frmMain()
    e.Handled = True
    Me.Hide()
    frmMainRef.Show()
  End If
End Sub
```

In this event code, we check for the constant `System.Windows.Forms.Keys.F11`, which is the named constant for the **KeyCode** returned by the F11 key. When the F11 function key is pressed, the If statement first sets e.Handled to **True** to ensure that the key is not passed on to the specific control currently having the focus. Then the current Form is hidden, and the frmMain form is displayed. Assuming this is the name of the Main Menu form, the user now sees this form displayed.

All that remains is to explicitly set each form's **KeyPreview** property to **True**, which is necessary to ensure that the **Form-level Keyboard event** is triggered. This is easily done within the code that displays each form for which we want the function keys to be active at the form level. For example, the following event code, which is used to display the Walk In form from Rotech's Main Menu screen, illustrates how this form's **Key-Preview** property is set before the form is displayed.

```
Private Sub btnWalkins_Click(ByVal sender As System.Object, _
    ByVal e As System.EventArgs) Handles btnWalkins.Click
  Dim frmWalkRef as New frmWalkIn()

  frmWalkRef.KeyPreview() = True
  Me.Hide
  frmWalkRef.Show()
End Sub
```

Although the example presented here applies to the F11 key, it is easily extended to any key for which you know the **KeyCode**. Exercise 4 in the exercise set for Section 6.7 shows how to obtain these codes using the Help facility.

Finally, as a technical note, a **KeyCode** is recognized within all keyboard event procedures, while the **e.Keychar** codes used in last chapter's Focus section are only recognized within **KeyPress** events.

Exercises 6.7

(Note: The Rotech Systems project, at the stage of development begun in this section, can be found at http://computerscience.jbpub.com/bronsonvbnet in the ROTECH5 folder as project rotech5. The project, as it exists at the end of this section, can be found in the ROTECH6 folder as project rotech6. If you are developing the system yourself, following the procedures given in this section, we suggest that you first copy all of the files in the ROTECH5 folder onto your system, and then work out of this latter folder. When you have finished your changes you can compare your results to the files in the ROTECH6 folder.)

1. a. Either add the data validation code described in this section to Rotech Mail In and Walk In forms or locate and load the project at the JBWEB website.

   b. Test that the data validation procedures work correctly for each form.

2. a. Make the F11 function key a keyboard shortcut for both the Mail In and Walk In forms, as described in this section.

   b. Test the keyboard shortcut created in Exercise 2a to ensure that it works correctly for both the Mail In and Walk In forms.

3. Using the Help facilities' Index tab, obtain information on the **KeyPreview** method used to create the keyboard shortcut described in this section.

4. Using the Help facility, obtain information on the **KeyCode** constant names and values used for all of the function keys. *Hint:* Enter the words `Keycode Constants` in the Index tabs text box.

5. The key stroke validation used for the quantity text box in both the Mail In and Walk In forms is a bit too restrictive because it does not permit entry of the backspace key to delete an entered digit (a user can still use the arrow keys and the delete key to edit the text box's data). Using the fact that the named constant for the backspace key is `vbKeyBack`, which you can verify by completing Exercise 4, modify the keystroke validation for the txtQuantity text box to permit entry of the backspace key.

6. Event Procedure 6–8 uses the following series of six individual `If` statements to check each name and address text box:

```
If txtFname.Text.Length = 0 Then
  strListEmptyBoxes = strListEmptyBoxes & "First Name " & ControlChars.CrLf
End If
If txtLname.Text.Length = 0 Then
  strListEmptyBoxes = strListEmptyBoxes & "Last Name " & ControlChars.CrLf
End If
If txtAddr.Text.Length = 0 Then
  strListEmptyBoxes = strListEmptyBoxes & "Address " & ControlChars.CrLf
End If
If txtCity.Text.Length = 0 Then
  strListEmptyBoxes = strListEmptyBoxes & "City " & ControlChars.CrLf
End If
If txtState.Text.Length = 0 Then
  strListEmptyBoxes = strListEmptyBoxes & "State " & ControlChars.CrLf
End If
If txtZip.Text.Length = 0 Then
  strListEmptyBoxes = strListEmptyBoxes & "Zip Code "
End If
```

Determine the effect of replacing this set of statements by the following single **If-then-ElseIf** structure:

```
If txtFname.Text.Length = 0 Then
  strListEmptyBoxes = strListEmptyBoxes & "First Name " & ControlChars.CrLf
ElseIf txtLname.Text.Length = 0 Then
  strListEmptyBoxes = strListEmptyBoxes & "Last Name " & ControlChars.CrLf
ElseIf txtAddr.Text.Length = 0 Then
  strListEmptyBoxes = strListEmptyBoxes & "Address " & ControlChars.CrLf
ElseIf txtCity.Text.Length = 0 Then
```

```
    strListEmptyBoxes = strListEmptyBoxes & "City " & ControlChars.CrLf
ElseIf txtState.Text.Length = 0 Then
    strListEmptyBoxes = strListEmptyBoxes & "State " & ControlChars.CrLf
ElseIf txtZip.Text.Length = 0 Then
    strListEmptyBoxes = strListEmptyBoxes & "Zip Code "
End If
```

7. Event Procedure 6–9 uses the following **If** statement to check that neither a first nor last name has been entered in the respective text boxes:

```
If txtFname.Text.Length = 0 AND txtLname.Text.Length = 0 Then
    txtFname.Text = "Cash"
End If
```

Determine the effect of replacing this statement with the following:

```
If (txtFname.Text.Length * txtLname.Text.Length) = 0 Then
    txtFname.Text = "Cash"
End If
```

8. (Case study) For your selected project (see project specifications at the end of Section 1.5), complete all order entry forms by adding appropriate after-the-fact data validation code to the appropriate event procedures.

6.8 Knowing About: Programming Costs

Any project that requires a computer incurs both hardware and software costs. The costs associated with the hardware consist of all costs relating to the physical components used in the system. These components include the computer itself, peripherals, and any other items, such as air conditioning, cabling, and associated equipment, required by the project. The software costs include all costs associated with initial program development and subsequent program maintenance. As illustrated in Figure 6–26, software costs represent the greatest share of most computer projects.

The reason that software costs contribute so heavily to total project costs is that these costs are labor-intensive that is, they are closely related to human productivity, while hardware costs are more directly related to manufacturing technologies. For example, microchips that cost over $500 per chip 15 years ago can now be purchased for under $1 per chip.

It is far easier, however, to dramatically increase manufacturing productivity by a thousand, with the consequent decrease in hardware costs, than it is for people to double either the quantity or the quality of their thought output. So as hardware costs have plummeted, the ratio of software costs to total system costs (hardware plus software) has increased dramatically. As was previously noted in Section 1.2 (see Figure 1–11, repeated as Figure 6–27 for convenience), maintenance of existing programs accounts for the majority of software costs.

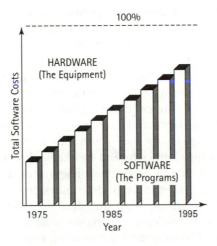

Figure 6-26 *Software is the Major Cost of Most Engineering Projects*

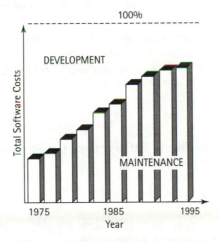

Figure 6-27 *Maintenance is the Predominant Software Cost*

How easily a program can be maintained (debugged, modified, or enhanced) is related to the ease with which the program can be read and understood, which is directly related to the modularity with which the program was constructed. Modular programs are constructed using procedures, each of which performs a clearly defined and specific task. If each procedure is clearly structured internally and the relationship between procedures is clearly specified, each procedure can be tested and modified with a minimum of disturbance or undesirable interaction with the other procedures in the program.

Just as hardware designers frequently locate the cause of a hardware problem by using test methods designed to isolate the offending hardware subsystem, modular software permits the software engineer to similarly isolate program errors to specific software units.

Once a bug has been isolated, or a new feature needs to be added, the required changes can be confined to appropriate procedures without radically affecting other procedures. Only if the procedure in question requires different input data or produces different outputs are its surrounding procedures affected. Even in this case, the changes to the surrounding procedures are clear: they must either be modified to output the data needed by the changed procedure or be changed to accept the new output data. Procedures help the programmer determine where the changes must be made, while the internal structure of the procedure itself determines how easy it will be to make the change.

Although there are no hard and fast rules for well-written procedures, specific guidelines do exist. Programming teams usually set standards that dictate the way source code should be written and formatted. Each procedure should have one entrance point and one exit point, and each control structure in the unit, such as a **Do** loop, should also contain a single entry and exit point. This makes it easy to trace the flow of data when errors are detected. All the Visual Basic selection and repetition statements that alter the normal sequential program flow conform to this single-input-single-output model.

As we have stressed throughout the text, instructions contained within a procedure should use variable names that describe the data and are self-documenting. This means that they tell what is happening without a lot of extra comments. For example, the statement

```
x = (a - b) / (c - d)
```

does not contain intelligent variable names. A more useful set of instructions, assuming that a slope is being calculated, is:

```
slope = (y2 - y1) / (x2 - x1)
```

Here, the statement itself tells what the data represents, what is being calculated, and how the calculation is being performed. Always keep in mind that the goal is to produce programs that make sense to any programmer reading them, at any time. The use of mnemonic data names makes excessive comments unnecessary. The program should contain a sufficient number of comments explaining what a procedure does and any other information that would be helpful to other programmers.

Another sign of a good program is the use of indentation to alert a reader to nested statements and indicate where one statement ends and another begins. Consider the following pseudocode listing the algorithm for determining "What to Wear":

If it is below 60 degrees
If it is snowing
wear your lined raincoat

Else

wear a topcoat

If it is below 40 degrees

wear a sweater also

If it is below 30 degrees

wear a jacket also

ElseIf it is raining

wear an unlined raincoat

Because the **If** and **Else** statement matches are not clearly indicated, the instructions are difficult to read and interpret. For example, consider what you would wear if the temperature is 35 degrees and it is raining. Now consider the following version of "What to Wear":

If it is below 60 degrees

  If it is snowing

   wear your lined raincoat

  Else

   wear a topcoat

  If it is below 40 degrees

   wear a sweater also

  If it is below 30 degrees

   wear a jacket also

  ElseIf it is raining

   wear an unlined raincoat

The second version is indented, making it clear that we are dealing with one main **If-ElseIf** statement. If it is below 60 degrees, the set of instructions indented underneath the first **If** will be executed; otherwise, the **ElseIf** condition will be checked. Although a Visual Basic program essentially ignores indention and will always pair an **ElseIf** with the closest matching **If**, indention is extremely useful in making code understandable to the programmer.

6.9 Common Programming Errors and Problems

Beginning Visual Basic programmers commonly make three errors when using repetition statements:

1. Testing for equality in repetition loops when comparing floating point or double-precision operands. For example, the condition `num = 0.01` should be replaced by a test requiring that the absolute value of `num - 0.01` be less than an acceptable

amount. The reason for this is that all numbers are stored in binary form. Using a finite number of bits, decimal numbers such as .01 have no exact binary equivalent, so that tests requiring equality with such numbers can fail.

2. Failure to have a statement within a **Do** loop that alters the tested condition in a manner that terminates the loop.

3. Modifying a **For** loop's counter variable within the loop.

6.10 Chapter Review

Key Terms

counter loop	**For/Next** loop
Do/Loop Until loop	infinite loop
Do/Loop While loop	nested loop
Do Until loop	posttest loop
Do While loop	pretest loop
Exit Do	sentinel values
fixed count loop	variable condition loop

Summary

1. A section of repeating code is referred to as a *loop*. The loop is controlled by a repetition statement that tests a condition to determine whether the code will be executed. Each pass through the loop is referred to as a *repetition* or *iteration*. The tested condition must always be explicitly set prior to its first evaluation by the repetition statement. Within the loop there must always be a statement that permits altering the condition so that the loop, once entered, can be exited.

2. There are three basic types of loops:
    a. `Do While`
    b. `For/Next`, and
    c. `Do/Loop Until`

   The `Do While` and `For/Next` loops are *pretest* or *entrance-controlled loops*. In this type of loop, the tested condition is evaluated at the beginning of the loop, requiring that the tested condition be explicitly set prior to loop entry. If the condition is **True**, loop repetitions begin; otherwise the loop is not entered. Iterations continue as long as the condition remains **True**.

   The `Do/Loop Until` loop is a *posttest* or *exit-controlled loop*, where the tested condition is evaluated at the end of the loop. This type of loop is always executed at least once. `Do/Loop Until` loops continue to execute as long as the tested condition is **False** and terminate when the condition becomes **True**.

3. Loops are also classified according to the type of tested condition. In a *fixed-count loop*, the condition is used to keep track of how many repetitions have occurred. In a *variable-condition loop*, the tested condition is based on a variable that can change interactively with each pass through the loop.

4. In Visual Basic, the most commonly used form for a **While** loop is:

```
Do While condition
    statement(s)
Loop
```

The *condition* is tested to determine if the statement or statements within the loop are executed. The condition is evaluated in exactly the same manner as a condition contained in an **If-Else** statement; the difference is how the condition is used. In a **Do While** statement, the statement(s) following the condition is(are) executed repeatedly, as long as the expression is **True**. An example of a **While** loop is:

```
count = 1                    ' initialize count
Do While count <= 10
  lstDisplay.Items.Add(count)
    count = count + 1    ' increment count
Loop
```

The first assignment statement sets count equal to 1. The Do While loop is then entered and the condition is evaluated for the first time. Since the value of count is less than or equal to 10, the condition is **True** and the statements within the loop are executed. The first statement displays the value of count. The next statement adds 1 to the value currently stored in count, making this value equal to 2. The Do While structure now loops back to retest the condition. Because count is still less than or equal to 10, the two statements within the loop are again executed. This process continues until the value of count reaches 11.

The Do While loop always checks a condition at the top of the loop. This requires that any variables in the tested expression must have values assigned before the Do While is encountered. Within the Do While loop there must be a statement that alters the value of the tested condition.

5. Sentinels are prearranged values used to signal either the start or end of a series of data items. Typically, sentinels are used to create Do While loop conditions that terminate the loop when the sentinel value is encountered.

6. The For/Next structure is extremely useful in creating loops that must be executed a fixed number of times. The initializing value, final value, and increment used by the loop are all included within the For statement. The general syntax of a For/Next loop is:

```
For counter = start value To end value Step increment value
    statement(s)
Next counter
```

7. Both Do While and For/Next loops evaluate a condition at the start of the loop. The Do/Loop Until structure is used to create an exit-controlled loop, because it checks its expression at the end of the loop. This ensures that the body of a **Do** loop is executed at least once. The syntax for this loop structure is:

```
Do
    statement(s)
Loop Until condition
```

The important concept to notice in the **Do/Loop Until** structure is that all statements within the loop are executed at least once before the condition is tested, and the loop is repeated until the condition becomes **True** (another way of viewing this is that the loop executes while the condition is **False**). Within the loop, there must be at least one statement that alters the tested expression's value.

Test Yourself—Short Answer

1. A section of repeating code is referred to as a _____.
2. A prearranged value used to signal either the start or end of a series of data items is called a _____.
3. In the **For Next** loop statement, `For X = 1 To 100 Step 5`, what is the purpose of the Step clause?
4. List the four elements required in the construction of repetitive sections of code.
5. Explain the difference between a pretest loop and a posttest loop.

Problems

Note: in all the problems listed below, output should be displayed in a **List Box** control.

1. Determine the output of the following program segment, assuming that all variables have been declared as `single`.

```
sngNum = 1734527
sngComputedValue = 0
sngCounter = 0

Do While sngComputedValue < 20
    sngSmallNum = sngNum / 10
    sngLargeNum = Int(sngSmallNum)
    sngDigit = sngNum - sngLargeNum * 10
    sngComputedValue = sngComputedValue + sngDigit
    sngNum = sngLargeNum

    lstOutput.Items.Add("sngCounter = " & sngCounter)
    lstOutput.Items.Add("sngComputedValue  = " & _
        sngComputedValue)
    sngCounter = sngCounter + 1
Loop
```

2. Write a loop that displays the numbers 1 to 10 on two lines.
3. Write a loop that displays the even numbers from 2 to 20 on two lines.
4. Write a loop that displays the first 50 numbers in the following sequence: 1, 2, 4, 7, 11, 16, 33, ...
5. Write a loop that displays all integers less than 1000 whose square roots are integers (i.e., 1, 4, 16, 25, . . .).

6. Write a loop that displays the following table:

```
1 2 3 4
2 3 4 5
3 4 5 6
4 5 6 7
5 6 7 8
6 7 8 9
7 8 9 10
```

7. Write a loop that displays the following table:

```
1 2 3 4 5
2 3 4 5 6
3 4 5 6 7
4 5 6 7 8
5 6 7 8 9
6 7 8 9 10
```

8. Write a loop that displays the following table:

```
1
2 4
3 6 9
4 8 12 16
5 10 15 20 25
```

9. Write a loop that displays the following:

```
     *
    * *
   * * *
  * * * *
 * * * * *
* * * * * *
```

10. Write a loop that displays the following:

```
* * * * * *
 * * * * *
  * * * *
   * * *
    * *
     *
```

Programming Projects

1. a. Create an application that determines the most efficient change to be given from a one dollar bill. The change should be given in terms of quarters, dimes, nickels, and pennies. For example, a purchase of 44 cents would require change of two quarters, a nickel, and a penny (two quarters and six pennies would not be correct). Your program should:

   i. Accept the amount of purchase in terms of the number of cents (integers, no decimals).

   ii. Calculate the change required.

   iii. Determine the number of quarters, dimes, nickels, and pennies necessary for the *most efficient* change.

   iv. Add a Clear button to clear all the quarters, dimes, nickels, and pennies and set the focus to the input text box.

   A suggested form is shown in Figure 6–28.

   b. Change your code so that if the amount of purchase is over one dollar or less than 0, an error message is given and the input text box receives the focus.

2. Credit scoring is a common practice for businesses that offer credit to their customers. Some of the factors that are generally used in credit scoring include whether the customer owns a home, has a telephone in their own name, has a savings or checking account, the years employed at their present job, and so on. In this project you are to construct a program that determines a credit score. The credit scoring algorithm used by the company requesting the program is as follows:

   i. Add 5 points for each of the following: phone (in customer's name), owns home, has a savings or checking account.

   ii. If the customer has been at the same job for less than two years, add no points; if they have been at the same job for two years but less than four years, add 3 points, and if they have been at the same job for four or

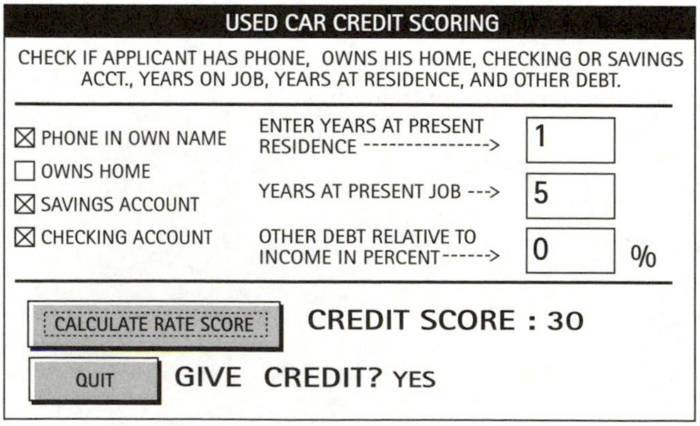

Figure 6–28 *Form for Project 1a*

more years, add 5 points. For example, for three years at the same job, add 3 points.

iii. If the customer has been at the same residence for less than two years, add no points; if they have been at the same residence for two years but less than four years, add 3 points; and if they have been at the same residence for four or more years, add 5 points. For example, for three years at the same residence, add 3 points.

iv. If the customer has other debt, the percent of this debt relative to total income is evaluated as follows:

no debt, add 10 points

up to 5% of income, add 5 points

5% to <25% of income, no points

25% or more of income, subtract 10 points

Your program should permit a user to enter all the above information. It should then display the credit score (number of points) based on the entered data. A form for this application is shown in Figure 6–29.

3. Wind chill is calculated by subtracting wind speed times 1.5 from the current temperature. For example, if the current temperature is 40 degrees and the wind speed is 10 miles per hours, then Wind Chill = 40 − 1.5 * 10 = 25 degrees. For this project, the input for your program should include current temperature and a minimum value for wind speed (value should be at least 0). Your program should display a table of 10 values for wind speed and corresponding wind chill, starting with the input value for wind speed. For each pair of values, increment wind speed by 2. Use a **Do While-Loop** structure to handle the repetition. Output the pairs of values in a list box in a second form. Express wind chill as an integer value. Figure 6–30 illustrates the input form you should construct for this project.

For the form shown, the <u>D</u>isplay button should display a second form with the table values. The <u>C</u>lear button should clear all input entries on the input

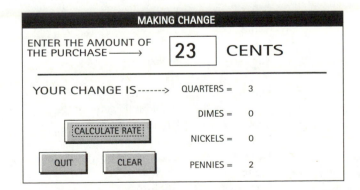

Figure 6–29   *Form for Project 2*

Figure 6–30   *Form for Project 3*

form, and the E<u>x</u>it button should end the program. The second form should have a <u>R</u>eturn that hides the form and redisplays the input form. For this project, use the following properties table.

Property Table for Project 3

Object	Property	Setting
Form	Name	frmWindSpeed
	Text	Wind Chill Calculator
Label	Name	lblCurrentTemp
	Text	Current Temperature
TextBox	Name	txtCurrentTemp
	Text	(blank)
Label	Name	lblMinWindSpeed
	Text	Minimum Wind Speed
TextBox	Name	txtMinWindSpeed
	Text	(blank)
Button	Name	btnDisplay
	Text	&Display
Button	Name	btnClear
	Text	&Clear
Button	Name	btnExit
	Text	E&xit
Form	Name	frmWindChill
	Text	Wind Chill Factor
Label	Name	lblCurrentTemp
	Text	For a temperature of:
ListBox	Name	lstCurrentTemp
Button	Name	btnReturn
	Text	&Return

4. Modify your solution to Project 3 to have your program display a two-way table of wind chill factors for pairs of wind speed and temperature. Input for the program should include a minimum value for temperature and a minimum value for wind speed. Output should be displayed on a separate form. All numeric values should be integers. Column headings should represent incremented values of temperature and row headings should represent incremented values of wind speed. Increase wind speed by 2 and temperature by 5.

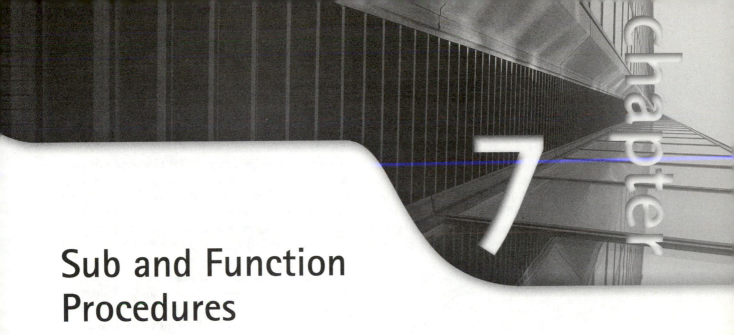

Sub and Function Procedures

Goals

As we have seen, an important element of a Visual Basic program is the Form. The basic processing units on a Form consist of event-driven procedures, which are attached to the objects placed on the Form. In addition to event procedures, Visual Basic programs also may contain any number of additional sub, function, and property procedures. To distinguish these procedure types from event procedures, these three new types of procedures are collectively referred to as *general* procedures. By definition, then, general procedures are not associated with specific events. Each Visual Basic general procedure is identified using one of three keywords: *Sub, Function,* or *Property.* In this chapter we learn how to write *Sub* and *Function* general procedures, how to pass data to these procedures, how to have the procedures process the passed data, and how they can be used to return a result.

Professional programs are designed, coded, and tested very much like hardware, as a set of modules that are integrated to perform a completed whole. A good analogy of this is an automobile, where one major module is the engine, another is the transmission, a third the braking system, a fourth the body, and so on. Each of these modules is linked together and ultimately placed under the control of the driver, who can be compared to a supervisor or main program module. The whole now operates as a complete unit that is able to do useful work, such as driving to the store. During the assembly process, each module is individually constructed, tested, and freed of defects (bugs) before it is installed in the final product.

Now consider what you might do if you wanted to improve your car's performance. You might have the existing engine altered or removed altogether and replaced with a new engine. Similarly, you might change the transmission, tires, or shock absorbers as your budget allows.

In this analogy, each of the major components of a car can be compared to a procedure that is designed to perform a specific task. For example, the driver calls on the engine when the gas pedal is pressed. The engine accepts inputs of fuel, air, and electricity to turn the driver's request into a useful product—power—and then sends this output to the transmission for further processing. The transmission receives the output of the engine and converts it to a form that can be used by the drive axle. An additional input to the transmission is the driver's selection of gears (e.g., drive, reverse, or neutral).

In each case, the engine, transmission, and other modules only "know" the universe bounded by their inputs and outputs. The driver need know nothing of the internal operation of the engine, transmission, drive axle, and other modules that are being controlled. The driver simply "calls" on a module, such as the engine, brakes, air conditioning, or steering, when that module's output is required. Communication between modules is restricted to passing needed inputs to each module as it is called upon to perform its task, and each module operates internally in a relatively independent manner. This same modular approach is used by programmers to create and maintain reliable Visual Basic applications, using general procedures in addition to event-specific procedures.

7.1 Sub Procedures

The first type of *general procedure* that we examine is the **Sub** procedure. In previous examples and exercises, *event procedures* were called into action by a specific event. *Sub procedures*, by contrast, are called into action by the application code.

Event procedures use the same **Sub** procedure structure; however, the keyword `Handles` found at the end of the declaration is used to easily identify the fact that it is an *event procedure* and identifies the event to which the procedure responds. For example, as illustrated in Figure 7–1, an application might have three Text boxes, each of which is meant to receive numeric input from a user. For each Text box's **Leave** event, we could include a check that a valid number was entered. Instead of repeating the same code, however, a more efficient strategy would be to create a **Sub** procedure that accepts a string and determines whether the entered string represents a numeric value. Assuming such a procedure was written, each Test box's **Leave** event could then activate this same block of code. Figure 7–2 illustrates the connection between the **Sub** procedure and its three invoking event procedures. It is important to notice that when the **Sub** procedure has completed execution, control is returned to the calling code.

As illustrated in Figure 7–2, a **Sub** procedure is a distinct procedure in its own right, very similar to an event **Sub** procedure. Its purpose is to operate and manipulate as many pieces of data and values as required. Although Figure 7–2 shows the **Sub** procedure being invoked by an event procedure, this is not a requirement. Any one of the three types of general procedures can be invoked by either an event procedure or by other general procedures. These multipurpose blocks of code can be written and stored in a specific form, in a standard code module, or in a class.

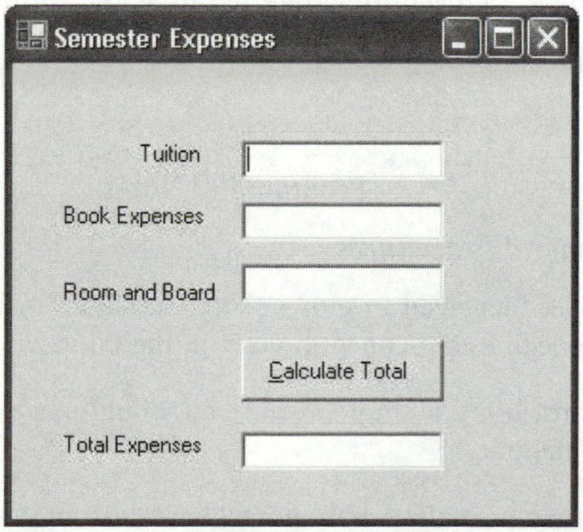

Figure 7–1   *An Application that Requires the Input of Three Numbers*

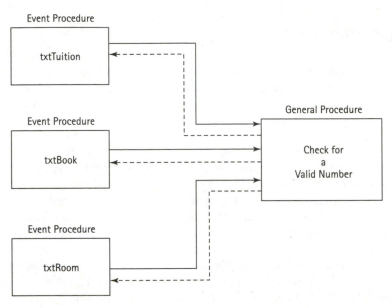

Figure 7–2 *Using a Single General Procedure to Validate Numeric Input*

A general procedure is called into action (invoked) simply by using its defined name. For example, the statement

```
Message()
```

initiates the execution of a **Sub** procedure named `Message`. This statement is used in Program 7-1 to call a **Sub** procedure that displays the message `Hello World`. The statement that invokes a procedure is referred to as the *calling* statement. Figure 7–3 shows the interface for Program 7–1.

Programmer Notes

Where To Place General Procedures

General procedures can be placed in either Form, standard, or class modules. In all of these cases, the general procedures are coded directly in the Code window.

For simple applications, using a single Form, you would place all of the general procedures in the existing Form module.

In the case where your procedure has more generality and can be used by a number of applications, you would open a standard module by selection the Add Module option from the Project menu and code the procedure in the Code window. Standard modules, by definition, contain only Visual Basic code and typically are used to construct Program Libraries. In its simplest configuration a Program Library consists of one or more standard modules containing well-tested and efficient procedures guaranteed to perform without error if the arguments supplied to the procedure are correct.

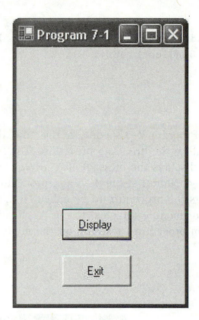

Figure 7–3 *Program 7–1's Interface*

Table 7–1   Program 7–1's Properties Table

Object	Property	Setting
Form	Name	frmMain
	Text	Program 7–1
Label	Name	lblDisplay
	Text	(blank)
Button	Name	btnDisplay
	Text	&Display
Button	Name	btnExit
	Text	E&xit

Program 7–1's Event and General Procedure Code

```
Private Sub btnDisplay_Click(ByVal sender As Object, ByVal e As _
    System.EventArgs) Handles btnDisplay.Click
  Message()
End Sub

Public Sub Message()
  lblDisplay.Text = "Hello World"
End Sub

Private Sub btnExit_Click(ByVal sender As Object, ByVal e As _
    System.EventArgs) Handles btnExit.Click
  Beep()
  End
End Sub
```

In reviewing Program 7–1's code, notice that the **Click** event for the btnDisplay Button makes a call to the `Message` procedure. The `Message` procedure, which is a **Sub** procedure, simply displays the message `Hello World` in the label on the Form as illustrated on Figure 7–4. Note that the `Message` procedure has been declared as **Public**. This designation permits the procedure to be called from any procedure and function residing on any Form or module attached to the Application. A **Private** declaration restricts it to be called from procedures residing on the module containing the procedure. These

Figure 7–4   *The Output Created by Pressing Program 7–1's Display Button*

keywords—**Public** and **Private**—are used to control access to blocks of code. For more information see Section 7.4, Variable Scope.

As written, Program 7–1 makes no provision for either passing data into the **Sub** procedure or for transmitting data back from it. The program does, however, clearly illustrate the connection when one procedure makes a call to another procedure. Before seeing how data can be exchanged between two procedures, let's see how to create the procedure used in Program 7–1.

Creating a General Sub Procedure

The steps necessary for creating a general **Sub** procedure on a form are as follows:
Ensure that the Code window is activated by:

- Double clicking on a Form, or
- Pressing the F7 function key, or
- Selecting the Code item from the View menu

Once the Code window is active, type a procedure declaration directly into the Code window. This typically is entered after the `End Sub` of the last procedure. This line should have the form:

```
Public Sub procedure-name()
```

Visual Basic will complete the template for the new procedure when you have entered the declaration. If you omit the **Public** keyword, the procedure will become **Public** by default. After Visual Basic has created the procedure stub, type in the required code in the same manner as you would for an event procedure. Once you have created a **Sub** procedure you can always view or edit it by searching through the code screen or by finding it in the Method Name list with the correct Form displayed in the Class Name drop-down list.

Exchanging Data with a General Procedure

In exchanging data with a general procedure, we must be concerned with both the sending and receiving sides of the data exchange. We first look at the sending of data into a **Sub** procedure.

In its most general syntax, a **Sub** procedure is called into action using a statement having the form:

```
procedure-name(argument list)
```

Except for the addition of the argument list, this is identical to the statement used in Program 7–1 to invoke the Message procedure. The **Sub** procedure name, as illustrated in Figure 7–5, identifies which procedure is to be executed; the argument list is used to provide data to the **Sub** procedure that has been called.

The arguments in a **Calling Statement** can consist of constants, variables, or expressions that can be evaluated to yield a value at the time of the call. For example, the statement:

```
Circumference(3.5)
```

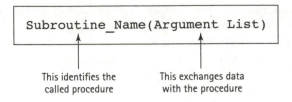

Figure 7–5 *Calling a Sub Procedure*

both calls a **Sub** procedure named `Circumference` and makes the number 3.5 available to it. Here the argument list consists of a single argument: the constant 3.5. Similarly, the statement:

`Display(2.67, 8)`

calls a **Sub** procedure named `Display` and makes two arguments—the real constant 2.67 and the integer constant 8—available to the called **Sub** procedure. In the following statement:

`Area(radius)`

the **Sub** procedure `Area` is called using a variable named `radius` as an argument. To illustrate the calling of a **Sub** procedure, consider Program 7–2. Included within it is a **Sub** procedure named `Area` to receive the transmitted data. Figure 7–6 shows the interface for Program 7–2, and Table 7–2 lists the objects and properties for this program.

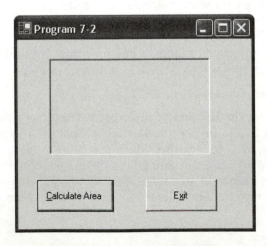

Figure 7–6 *Program 7–2's Interface*

Table 7–2   Program 7–2's Properties Table

Object	Property	Setting
Form	Name	frmMain
	Text	Program 7–2
Textbox	Name	txtDisplay
	Text	(blank)
Button	Name	btnRun
	Text	&Calculate Area
Button	Name	btnExit
	Text	E&xit

Programmer Notes

Viewing and Editing a General Procedure

To view and edit an existing general procedure on a form:

1. Ensure that the Code window is activated by either:
   - Double clicking on a Form, or
   - Pressing the F7 function key, or
   - Selecting the Code item from the <u>V</u>iew menu
2. Select the Form from the Class Name selection box.
3. Select the procedure's name from the Method Name selection box.

Program 7–2's Event and Sub Procedure Code

```
Private Sub btnRun_Click(ByVal sender As Object, ByVal e As _
    System.EventArgs) Handles btnRun.Click
  Dim radius As Single

  radius = Val(InputBox("Enter the radius", "Input Request", "0"))
  Area(radius)
End Sub

Public Sub Area(ByVal rad As Single)
  Const PI As Single = 3.1416

  txtDisplay.Clear()
  txtDisplay.AppendText("For a circle with radius " & rad & _
      ControlChars.CrLf)
  txtDisplay.AppendText("The area is " & Format(PI * rad ^ 2, ".0000"))
```

```
End Sub

Private Sub btnExit_Click(ByVal sender As Object, ByVal e As _
    System.EventArgs) Handles btnExit.Click
  Beep()
  End
End Sub
```

In reviewing Program 7–2's code, note that the **Procedure Calling Statement** in the `btnCalculate` click procedure both calls the `Area` **Sub** procedure into action and makes one argument available to it. Let's now see how the **Sub** procedure `Area` has been constructed to correctly receive this argument.

Like all general procedures, a **Sub** procedure begins with a declaration and ends with an `End Sub` line, as illustrated in Figure 7–7. In addition to naming the procedure, the declaration is used to pass data between the **Sub** and its calling procedure. The purpose of the statements after the declaration is to process the passed data.

The general **Sub** procedure declaration must include the keyword **Sub**, the name of the general procedure, and the names of any parameters that will be used by it. Here, we have retained the convention that a *parameter* refers to the procedure's declaration of what data it will accept, whereas an *argument* refers to the data sent by the calling function. (Another name for a parameter is a *formal argument*, whereas the data sent by the calling procedure is sometimes referred to as *actual arguments*.) For example, the declaration of the general procedure in Program 7–2:

```
Public Sub Area(ByVal rad As Single)
```

contains a single parameter named `rad`. The names of parameters are selected by the programmer according to the same rules used to select variable names. It should be noted that the names selected for parameters may, but do not have to, be the same as the argument names used in the calling statement. The keyword `ByVal` will be discussed in Section 7.2.

The purpose of the parameters in a general procedure header is to provide names by which the general procedure can access values transmitted through the **Calling Statement**. Thus, the argument name `r` is used within the general procedure to refer to the value transmitted by the **Calling Statement**. In this regard, it is extremely useful to

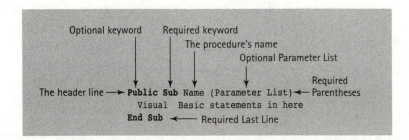

Figure 7–7   *The Structure of a General Sub Procedure*

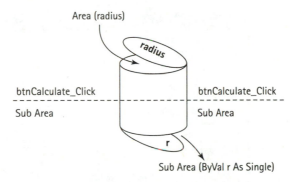

Figure 7–8 *Exchanging Data with a Sub Procedure*

visualize arguments and parameters as containers or pipelines through which values can be transmitted between called and calling program units. As illustrated in Figure 7–8, the parameter named r effectively opens one side of the container through which values will be passed between the btnCalculate_Click and Area procedures. Within the btnCalculate_Click event procedure, the same container is known as the argument named radius, which is also a variable of this event procedure.

It is important to note that **Sub** procedures do not know where the values made available to them come from. As far as the Area general procedure is concerned, the parameter r can be treated as a variable that has been initialized externally. However, parameters still must be declared. Once declared, a parameter can be used anywhere within the general procedure the same way a variable can be used. Also, as illustrated in Program 7–2, named constants used by the general procedure (in this case the constant PI) as well as variables internal to the procedure also must be declared.

In addition, the individual data types of each argument and its corresponding parameter must be the same. Thus, if a general procedure's first parameter is declared as an integer, then an integer variable, integer constant, or integer expression must be used as an argument when the procedure is called. If the general procedure's second parameter has been declared as **Single**, then the second argument in the **Calling Statement** must also be a **Single**.

Argument and parameter data type mismatches will result in an argument type mismatch error message when the program is run.

Programmer Note

Caution

Because an argument and its corresponding parameter both reference the same memory locations (see Figure 7–8), the rule concerning the correspondence between numbers and data types of arguments and parameters is simple: They must MATCH! If there are two arguments in a general procedure call, there must be two parameters in the general procedure's parameter list. The first argument becomes the first parameter, and the second argument becomes the second parameter.

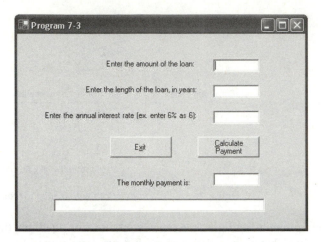

Figure 7–9 *Program 7–3's Interface*

A Practical Application Illustrating Input Data Validation

The examples presented so far have been useful in illustrating how to construct and call **Sub** procedures. Clearly, however, the **Sub** procedure calls were not necessary because the code in these general procedures could have been included directly in the event procedures making the calls. We now present an application that uses **Sub** procedures in a more useful and practical way.

Consider Figure 7–9, illustrating the interface for a loan payment program. The program calculates the monthly payment due on a loan after the user enters the amount of the loan, the time in years, and the annual interest rate for the loan. The program uses the standard convention that payments must be made monthly and that the interest is calculated as a monthly compounded rate.

In addition to the three text boxes shown on Figure 7–9 that will be used for data entry, the Form contains two more Text boxes that will be used for output. The Text box that is named txtPay will be used to display the calculated monthly payment for the loan. The Text box at the bottom of the Form, named txtError, is used to display error messages. Table 7–3 lists the properties table for this interface.

As a practical matter, only positive numbers should be accepted for the user-entered data. Rather than including individual input validation code for each of the three text boxes, a single data entry validation **Sub** procedure, named CheckVal, will be constructed. This procedure is called from each Text box when the user signals completion of data entry in the box. This will be done using the Text box's **KeyPress** event. For each text box we "capture" the key press and determine when the Enter key was pressed (see Section 4.3 for a review of this). Once this key has been detected, the CheckVal data validation procedure is called. The algorithm used in CheckVal is:

Clear all text boxes of text

If the entered text does not represent a valid number

Print the message "Please enter a valid number"

Table 7–3 Program 7–3's Properties Table

Object	Property	Setting
Form	Name	frmMain
	Text	Program 7–3
Label	Name	lblAmt
	Text	Enter the amount of the loan:
Text box	Name	txtAmt
	Text	(blank)
Label	Name	lblTime
	Text	Enter the length of the loan, in years:
Text box	Name	txtTime
	Text	(blank)
Label	Name	lblRate
	Text	Enter the annual interest rate (ex. Enter 6% as 6):
Text box	Name	txtRate
	Text	(blank)
Label	Name	lblPay
	Text	The monthly payment is:
Text box	Name	txtPay
	TabStop	False
Text box	Name	txtError
	TabStop	False
Button	Name	btnPay
	Text	&Calculate Payment
Button	Name	btnExit
	Text	E&xit

 in the Error text box
Else if the entered text does not represent a positive number
 Print the message "The entered value must be positive"
 in the Error text box
Else
 Set focus to the next control
Endif

Following is the complete event and general procedure code used in Program 7–3:

Program 7–3's Event and General Procedure Code

```
' These named constants are entered in
' the (General) object declarations section
```

```
' As such, they can be used by any procedure on the form
Const ENTERKEY = Chr(13)
Const FromAmt As Integer = 1
Const FromTime As Integer = 2
Const FromRate As Integer = 3

' These three event procedures clear the pay and error Text boxes
' whenever the other three text boxes receive focus

Private Sub txtAmt_Enter(ByVal sender As Object, _
    ByVal e As System.EventArgs) Handles txtAmt.Enter
  Clear()
End Sub

Private Sub txtRate_Enter(ByVal sender As Object, _
    ByVal e As System.EventArgs) Handles txtRate.Enter
  Clear()
End Sub

Private Sub txtTime_Enter(ByVal sender As Object, _
    ByVal e As System.EventArgs) Handles txtTime.Enter
  Clear()
End Sub

Private Sub txtAmt_KeyPress(ByVal sender As Object, ByVal e _
    As System.Windows.Forms.KeyPressEventArgs) Handles txtAmt.KeyPress
  If e.KeyChar = ENTERKEY Then
    CheckVal(txtAmt.Text, FromAmt)
  End If
End Sub

Private Sub txtTime_KeyPress(ByVal sender As Object, ByVal e _
    As System.Windows.Forms.KeyPressEventArgs) Handles txtTime.KeyPress
  If e.KeyChar = ENTERKEY Then
    CheckVal(txtTime.Text, FromTime)
  End If
End Sub

Private Sub txtRate_KeyPress(ByVal sender As Object, ByVal e _
    As System.Windows.Forms.KeyPressEventArgs) Handles txtRate.KeyPress
  If e.KeyChar = ENTERKEY Then
    CheckVal(txtRate.Text, FromRate)
```

```
      End If
   End Sub

   ' This is the event procedure that calculates the payment

   Private Sub btnPay_Click(ByVal sender As Object, _
       ByVal e As System.EventArgs) Handles btnPay.Click
      Dim amt, time, rate, payment As Single

      amt = Val(txtAmt.Text)
      time = Val(txtTime.Text) * 12 ' converted years to months
      rate = Val(txtRate.Text) / 1200 ' converted to monthly rate
      If amt * time * rate <> 0 Then
         payment = (amt * rate) / (1 - (1 + rate) ^ -time)
         txtPay.Text = FormatCurrency(payment)
      Else
         txtError.Text = ("Please check all of the input data")
      End If
   End Sub

   ' This is the input data validation general Sub procedure
   Private Sub CheckVal(ByVal s1 As String, ByVal fromwhere As Integer)
      Clear()
      If Not (IsNumeric(s1)) Then
         txtError.Text = ("Please enter a valid number")
      ElseIf Val(s1) <= 0 Then
         txtError.Text = ("The entered value must be positive")
      Else ' a valid data was entered, so we shift the focus
         Select Case fromwhere
            Case FromAmt
               txtTime.Focus()
            Case FromTime
               txtRate.Focus()
            Case FromRate
               btnPay.Focus()
         End Select
      End If
   End Sub

   ' This is a general Sub procedure used to clear the pay & error Text boxes
   Private Sub Clear()
      txtPay.Clear()
      txtError.Clear()
   End Sub
```

```
Private Sub btnExit_Click(ByVal sender As System.Object, _
    ByVal e As System.EventArgs) Handles btnExit.Click
  Beep()
  End
End Sub
```

In reviewing Program 7–3's code, first note that the Enter Event procedures for each Text box call the Clear **Sub** procedure. This procedure simply clears the Pay and Error Text boxes. The reason for this is that the other three Text boxes are used in this application for data entry. The rationale is that once an input area receives the focus, all output messages and any calculations from prior data should be cleared.

Now concentrate on the KeyPress **Event** procedures and note that each of these procedures calls the CheckVal **Sub** procedure when the Enter key has been pressed. The value for the Enter key has been set as a named constant. This constant declaration is outside of any procedure and is therefore available to any procedure within the form.

The CheckVal **Sub** procedure uses two parameters: a string and an integer. The string represents the text value from either the Amount, Time, or Rate text boxes, while the integer is used to communicate which text box event made the call. In addition, we have used three named constants for the integer arguments used in the **Calling Statement**. Note that FromAmt, FromTime and FromRate are also constants.

The first task accomplished by the CheckVal procedure is to call the procedure Clear, which clears any prior text in the Pay and Error Text boxes. Then, the procedure either produces an error message and keeps focus in the current text box, or moves focus to the next control in the tab sequence. (See Table 7–5 on page 380 for a description of the IsNumeric function.)

Finally, take a look at the btnPay_Click procedure. This event procedure uses a common programming "trick" to determine when to make its calculation. If any of the text box values are zero, a valid payment cannot be calculated. Rather than checking each text box for a zero value, however, we can check all boxes at once by checking the value of Val(txtAmt.Text) * Val(txtTime.text) * Val(txtRate.Text). If any of the individual values are zero, the product of all three values also will be zero. Thus, we only make the payment calculation if all three boxes have a nonzero value. The calculation of the payment is made using the formula:

$$\text{Monthly Payment} = \frac{(\text{Loan Amount}) * (\text{Time of Loan in Months})}{1 - (1 + \text{Monthly Interest Rate})^{-\text{Time of Loan in Months}}}$$

Because the input of interest rate is an annual percentage rate, and the time is in years, the entered rate is first divided by 1200 to convert it to a monthly decimal rate, and the number of years is multiplied by 12 to convert it to a time in months. Figure 7–10 illustrates a sample run using Program 7–3 once valid input data has been entered.

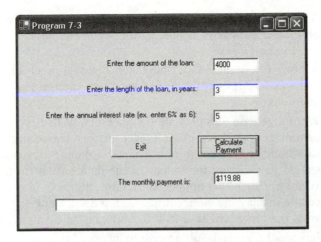

Figure 7–10   *A Sample Run Using Program 7–3*

Exercises 7.1

1. For the following general **Sub** procedure headers, determine the number, type, and order (sequence) of the arguments that must be passed to the procedure.[1]

   a. `Public Sub Factorial(n As Integer)`

   b. `Public Sub Price(type As Integer, yield As Single, maturity As Single)`

   c. `Public Sub Yield(type As Integer, price As Double, maturity As Double)`

   d. `Public Sub Interest(flag As Boolean, price As Double, time As Double)`

   e. `Public Sub Total(amount As Single, rate As Single)`

   f. `Public Sub Roi(a As Integer, b As Integer, c As String, d As String, e As Single)`

   g. `Public Sub Get_val(item As Integer, iter As Integer, decflag As Boolean, delim As Boolean)`

2. Write **Sub** procedure declarations and **Calling Statements** for the following:

   a. A procedure named `Test` having a single precision parameter named `exper`. The corresponding argument used in calling `Test` is named `value`.

   b. A procedure named `Minute` having an integer parameter named `time`. The corresponding argument used in calling `Minute` is named `second`.

   c. A procedure named `Key` having a boolean parameter named `codeflag`. The corresponding argument used in calling `Key` is also named `codeflag`.

---

[1]The keywords `ByVal` and `ByRef` have been left out for simplicity.

d. A procedure named `Yield` having a single precision parameter named `rate` and an integer parameter named n. The arguments used in calling `Yield` are named `coupon` and `years`.

e. A procedure named `Rand` having two single precision parameters named `seed` and `randno`, respectively. The arguments used in calling `Rand` are named `Seed` and `Rval`.

3. a. Write a general **Sub** procedure named `Check` that has three parameters. The first parameter should accept an integer number, the second parameter a single precision number, and the third parameter a double precision number. The procedure should just display the values of the data passed to it when it is called. (**Note:** When tracing errors in general **Sub** procedures, it is very helpful to have the procedure display the values it has been passed. Quite frequently, the error is not in what the procedure does with the data, but in the data received and stored.)

b. Include the general **Sub** procedure in Exercise 3a in a working program. Test the procedure by passing various data to it. For example, when the procedure is invoked by the statement `Check(5, 6.27, -18.98765432)` it should display the values 5, 6.27, and -18.98765432.

4. a. Write a general **Sub** procedure named `Find_abs` that accepts a double precision number passed to it, computes its absolute value, and displays the absolute value. The absolute value of a number is the number itself if the number is positive, and the negative of the number if the number is negative.

b. Include the general **Sub** procedure in Exercise 4a in a working program. Test the procedure by passing various data to it.

5. a. Write a general **Sub** procedure named `Mult` that accepts two single precision numbers as parameters, multiplies these two numbers, and displays the result.

b. Include the general **Sub** procedure in Exercise 5a in a working program. Test the procedure by passing various data to it.

6. a. Write a general **Sub** procedure named `SquareIt` that computes the square of the value passed to it and displays the result. The procedure should be capable of squaring numbers with decimal points.

b. Include the general **Sub** procedure in Exercise 6a in a working program. Test the procedure by passing various data to it.

7. a. Write a general **Sub** procedure named `RectangleArea` that accepts two parameters named `width` and `length` as **Single** data. The procedure should calculate the area of a rectangle by multiplying the passed data, and then display the calculated area.

b. Include the `Area` general procedure in Exercise 7a in a working program. The calling procedure should correctly call and pass the values 4.4 and 2.0 to `Area`. Do a hand calculation to verify the result displayed by your program.

7.2 Passing Arguments By Value and By Reference

In addition to receiving inputs when called, every **Sub** procedure has the capability of returning one or more values to its calling routine. The mechanism for doing this relies on the correspondence between arguments used in the **Calling Statement** and the parameters used in the general procedure header.

As described earlier, arguments may be passed to a procedure either by value (**ByVal**) or by reference (**ByRef**). In Visual Basic the default is **ByVal**, which means that only a copy of the argument is passed to the procedure. By doing so, the procedure cannot make changes to the original argument. If, however, you want the procedure to be able to change the original argument, then you would pass the argument by reference. This section describes in detail the uses of **ByVal** and **ByRef**.

In some procedure calls, the called procedure receives direct access to the variables of the calling procedure that were used as arguments. As we have seen, this forms the basis for returning values to the calling procedure and is referred to as a *pass by reference*, or **ByRef** for short. To be clear, if the called procedure has declared an argument to be passed **ByRef**, then any change to the variable in the called procedure will have the effect of changing the value of the variable in the calling procedure. In some cases you may not wish to provide the called procedure this access.

To prevent a called procedure from having access to the calling procedure's arguments, a *pass by value* call can be made. In a pass by value, the called procedure is provided numeric values that cannot be altered. We have already seen one method of doing this. For example, the statement `Calc (10, 20, 30, sum, prod)` calls the `Calc` procedure with three arguments that are values. Regardless of what the receiving parameter names are, changing these parameters' values will not alter the constants 10, 20, and 30 in the calling statement. In a similar manner, *the values of variables used as arguments can also be transmitted to a called procedure by enclosing the variable names within parentheses.* For example, the statement `Calc((firnum), (secnum), (thirdnum), sum, prod)` passes the first three arguments by value and the last two by reference. This is because the parentheses around each of the first three arguments cause Visual Basic to evaluate the expressions within the parentheses. The evaluation of an expression, even one consisting of a single variable, is a value. It is the value that is then transmitted to the called procedure. Even if any or all of the first three parameters are declared as **ByRef**, using the parentheses ensures that the arguments are passed by value and the values of the arguments are not changed by Calc.

Finally, in writing a general procedure, you can ensure that only a value is to be received. This is accomplished by placing the keyword **ByVal** in front of the parameter's name when the parameter is declared. You should avoid the method in the previous paragraph and instead ensure that the parameters are declared as **ByVal** instead of **ByRef**. For example, the declaration

```
Public Sub Calc(ByVal x As Single, ByVal y As Single, ByVal Z As Single, _
    ByRef total As Single, ByRef product As Single)
```

ensures that any changes in value made by `Calc` to parameters x, y, and z will not be reflected in the associated variables in the procedures that called `Calc`. In Visual Basic .NET, the default declaration for parameters is pass by value. If you do not specify **ByRef** or **ByVal** in your procedure declaration, Visual Basic will complete the declaration for you and insert **ByVal** for each undeclared parameter.

To illustrate how a general **Sub** procedure can return values to a calling procedure, consider Procedure Code 7–1.

Procedure Code 7–1

```
Private Sub frmMain_Click(ByVal sender As Object, _
    ByVal e As System.EventArgs) Handles MyBase.Click
  Dim firnum, secnum As Single

  firnum = Val(InputBox("Enter a number", "Input Request", "0"))
  secnum = Val(InputBox("Enter a number", "Input Request", "0"))
  lstDisplay.Items.Add("The value entered for firnum was: " & firnum)
  lstDisplay.Items.Add("The value entered for secnum was: " & secnum)

  Newval(firnum, secnum)
  lstDisplay.Items.Add(" ")
  lstDisplay.Items.Add("After the call to Newval:")
  lstDisplay.Items.Add("The value in firnum is now " & firnum)
  lstDisplay.Items.Add("The value in secnum is now " & secnum)
End Sub

' Here is the called procedure
Public Sub Newval(ByRef xnum As Single, ByRef ynum As Single)
  xnum = 86.5
  ynum = 96.5
End Sub
```

In calling the `Newval` **Sub** procedure within Procedure Code 7–1, it is extremely important to understand the connection between the arguments used in the **Calling Statement** and the parameters used in the general procedure header. *Both reference the same data items because they are declared ByRef*. The significance of this is that the value in the calling argument can be altered by the general procedure providing a basis for returning values from a general procedure. Thus, the parameters `xnum` and `ynum` do not store copies of the values in `firnum` and `secnum`, but directly access the locations in memory set aside for these two arguments. This type of general procedure call, where a general procedure's parameters reference the same memory locations as the arguments of the calling procedure, is formally referred to as a *pass by reference*, which in Visual Basic is referred to as a **ByRef** call. The equivalence between argument and parameter names used in Procedure Code 7–1 is illustrated in Figure 7–11. It is easier to consider both argument and parameter names as different names referring to the same value. The calling procedure refers to the value using an argument name, while the general procedure refers to the same value using its parameter name.

A sample output that is produced by Procedure Code 7–1 is:

```
The value entered for firnum was: 10
The value entered for secnum was: 20
```

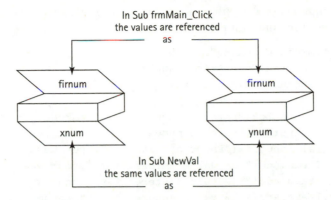

In Sub frmMain_Click
the values are referenced
as

firnum

xnum

firnum

ynum

In Sub NewVal
the same values are referenced
as

Figure 7–11   *The Equivalence of Arguments and Parameters in Procedure Code 7–1*

```
After the call to Newval:
The value in firnum is now 86.5
The value in secnum is now 96.5
```

In reviewing this output, note that the values displayed for the variables `firnum` and `secnum` have been changed immediately after the call to the `Newval` general procedure. This is because these two variables were used as arguments in the calling statement, which gives `Newval` access to them. Within `Newval`, these arguments are known as the parameters `xnum` and `ynum`, respectively. As illustrated by the final displayed values, the assignment of values to `xnum` and `ynum` within `Newval` is reflected in the calling procedure as the altering of `firnum`'s and `secnum`'s values.

The equivalence between calling arguments and a **Sub** procedure's parameters, illustrated in Procedure Code 7–1, provides the basis for returning any number of values from a **Sub** procedure. For example, assume that a **Sub** procedure is required to accept three values, compute these values' sum and product, and return the computed results to the calling routine. Naming the **Sub** procedure `Calc` and providing five parameters (three for the input data and two for the returned values), the following general procedure can be used.

```
Public Sub Calc(ByVal x As Single, ByVal y As Single, ByVal z As Single, _
    ByRef total As Single, ByRef product As Single)
  total = x + y + z
  product = x * y * z
End Sub
```

This general procedure has five parameters, named `x`, `y`, `z`, `total`, and `product`, all declared as **Single** arguments. Within the general procedure, only the last two arguments are altered. The value of the fourth argument, `total`, is calculated as the sum of the first three arguments, and the last argument, `product`, is calculated as the product of the arguments x, y, and z. Procedure Code 7–2 shows how this **Sub** procedure could be called from an event procedure.

```
Private Sub frmMain_Click(ByVal sender As Object, _
    ByVal e As System.EventArgs) Handles MyBase.Click
  Dim firnum, secnum, thirdnum, sum, prod As Single

  firnum = Val(InputBox("Enter a number", "Input Request", "0"))
  secnum = Val(InputBox("Enter a number", "Input Request", "0"))
  thirdnum = Val(InputBox("Enter a number", "Input Request", "0"))
  lstDisplay.Items.Add("The value entered for firnum was: " & firnum)
  lstDisplay.Items.Add("The value entered for secnum was: " & secnum)
  lstDisplay.Items.Add("The value entered for thirdnum was: " & thirdnum)

  Calc(firnum, secnum, thirdnum, sum, prod)
  lstDisplay.Items.Add(" ")
  lstDisplay.Items.Add("The sum of these numbers is: " & sum)
  lstDisplay.Items.Add("The product of these numbers is: " & prod)
End Sub


'  Here is the called procedure
Public Sub Calc(ByVal x As Single, ByVal y As Single, ByVal z As Single, _
    ByRef total As Single, ByRef product As Single)
  total = x + y + z
  product = x * y * z
End Sub
```

Within the calling event procedure, the Calc general procedure is called, using the five arguments firnum, secnum, thirdnum, sum, and prod. As required, these arguments agree in number and data type with the parameters declared by general procedure Calc. Of the five arguments passed, only firnum, secnum, and thirdnum have been assigned values when the call to Calc is made. The remaining two arguments have not been initialized and will be used to receive values back from Calc. Note that the last two parameters in the Calc procedure are declared as **ByRef** while the first three are **ByVal**. Figure 7–12 illustrates the relationship between argument and parameter names, and the values they contain after the return from Calc, for the following sample run using this procedure code:

```
The value entered for firnum was: 2.5
The value entered for secnum was: 6
The value entered for thirdnum was: 10

The sum of these numbers is: 16.5
The product of these numbers is: 150
```

Once Calc is called, it uses its first three parameters x, y, and z to calculate values for total and product and then returns control to the calling program. Because of the

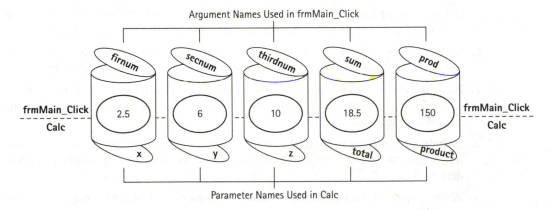

Figure 7–12   *Relationship Between Arguments and Parameters for Procedure Code 7–2*

order of its calling arguments, the calling procedure knows the values calculated by Calc as sum and prod, which are then displayed. Although all of the examples we have used have illustrated calling a general procedure from an event procedure, this is not required in Visual Basic. A general procedure can be called by any procedure, including another general procedure, including itself (as described in Section 7.5).

In general, the arguments used in calling a general procedure can be variables (as illustrated in Procedure Code 7–2), single constants, or more complex expressions yielding the correct argument data type. For example, a valid call to Calc is:

```
Calc(2.0,3.0,6.2,sum,product)
```

When an argument is either a constant value or an expression that yields a constant value, the corresponding parameter in the called general procedure must never be used on the left-hand side of an assignment statement. To do so would be an attempt to change the value of a constant within the calling procedure.

In addition to its parameters, a general procedure may declare as many variables as needed to complete its task. These variable declarations are made in the same manner as variable declarations for event procedures. For example, if i, j, and k are integer parameters and count and maxval are integer variables within a **Sub** procedure named Findmax, a valid general procedure heading and declaration statement is:

```
Public Sub Findmax(ByRef i As Integer, ByRef j As Integer, ByRef k As Integer)
  Dim count, maxval As Integer
```

Depending on what the procedure does, the parameters may be declared **ByVal** instead of **ByRef**.

Exercises 7.2

1. a. Write a general **Sub** procedure, named Find_abs, that accepts a double precision number passed to it, computes its absolute value, and returns the absolute value

to the calling function. The absolute value of a number is the number itself if the number is positive, and the negative of the number if the number is negative.

b. Include the function in Exercise 1a in a working program. Have the calling procedure display the returned value. Test the function by passing various data to it.

2. a. Write a general **Sub** procedure, named `Mult`, that accepts two double precision numbers as parameters, multiplies these two numbers, and returns the result to the calling function.

b. Include the function written in Exercise 2a in a working program. Have the calling procedure display the returned value. Test the function by passing various data to it.

3. a. Write a general **Sub** procedure, named `Findmax`, that accepts two parameters named `firnum` and `secnum` as single precision values and returns the largest of these parameters in a third parameter named `max`.

b. Include the `Findmax` general procedure written for Exercise 3a in a working program.

4. a. Write a general **Sub** procedure, named `RightTriangle`, that accepts the lengths of two sides of a right triangle and one of the angles as the parameters `a`, `b`, and `angle`, respectively. All of these parameters should be declared as **Singles**. The general procedure should determine and return both the hypotenuse and the remaining angle of the triangle (*Hint:* Use the Pythagorean Theorem that $c^2 = a^2 + b^2$).

b. Include the `RightTriangle` procedure for Exercise 4a in a working program.

5. a. The time in hours, minutes, and seconds is to be passed to a general **Sub** procedure named `Totsec`. Write `Totsec` to accept the input data, determine the total number of seconds in the passed data, and display the calculated value.

b. Include the `Totsec` procedure for Exercise 5a in a working program. Use the following test data to verify your program's operation: hours = 10, minutes = 36, and seconds = 54. Do a hand calculation to verify the result displayed by your program.

6. a. Write a general **Sub** procedure named `Time` that accepts an integer number of seconds in the parameter named `Totsec` and returns the number of hours, minutes, and seconds corresponding to the total seconds in the three parameters named `hours`, `mins`, and `secs`.

b. Include the `Time` procedure for Exercise 6a in a working program.

7. Write a general **Sub** procedure named `Daycount` that accepts a month, day, and year as integer parameters, and estimates the total number of days from the turn of the century corresponding to the passed date, and returns the estimate, as a long integer, to the calling procedure. For this problem assume that each year has 365 days and each month has 30 days. Test your general procedure by verifying that the date 1/1/00 returns a day count of one.

8. Write a general **Sub** procedure named `Liquid` to be called using the statement `Liquid(cups, gallons, quarts, pints)`. The procedure is to determine the number of gallons, quarts, pints, and cups in the passed value named `cups`, and directly alter the respective arguments in the calling general procedure. Use the relationships of two cups to a pint, four cups to a quart, and 16 cups to a gallon.

9. a. A clever and simple method of preparing to sort dates into either ascending (increasing) or descending (decreasing) order is to first convert a date having the form month/day/yr into an integer number using the formula date = year * 10000 + month * 100 + day. For example, using this formula the date 12/6/88 converts to the integer 881206 and the date 2/28/90 converts to the integer 900228. Sorting the resulting integer numbers automatically puts the dates into the correct order. Using this formula, write a general **Sub** procedure named `Convert` that accepts a month, day, and year, converts the passed data into a single date integer, and returns the integer to the calling procedure.

   b. Include the `Convert` procedure for Exercise 9a in a working program. The main procedure should correctly call `Convert` and display the integer returned by the general procedure.

10. a. Write a general **Sub** procedure named `Date` that accepts an integer of the form described in Exercise 9a, determines the corresponding month, day, and year, and returns these three values to the calling procedure. For example, if `Date` is called using the statement:

   `Date(19901116, month, day, year)`

   the number 11 should be returned in month, the number 16 in day, and the number 90 in year.

   b. Include the `Date` procedure written for Exercise 10a in a working program.

7.3 Function Procedures

Visual Basic provides two types of functions: intrinsic and user-defined. We already are familiar with intrinsic functions, such as `Abs`, `Sqrt`, `Exp`, and so on (see Section 3.4), which are provided as an intrinsic part of the Visual Basic language in its Math library. User-defined functions perform in a manner identical to intrinsic functions, except that they are user-written. A function, like a **Sub** procedure, is a distinct procedure containing multiple statements. The key difference between **Sub** procedures and functions, however, is that functions are intended to directly return a single value to its calling procedure (see Figure 7–13).

   Figure 7–14 illustrates the general form of a function. As with **Sub** procedures, the purpose of the function header is to provide the function with a name, and specify the number and order of parameters expected by the function. In addition, the header identifies the data type of the value returned by the function. The statements after the declaration are used to operate on the passed parameters and return a single value back to the calling function.

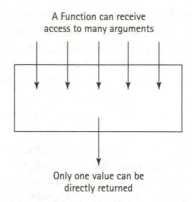

Figure 7–13 *A Function Directly Returns a Single Value*

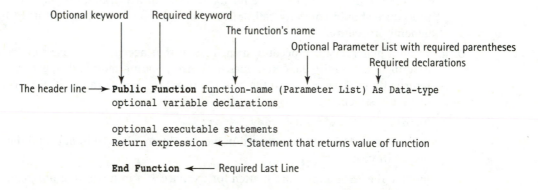

Figure 7–14 *The Structure of a Function Procedure*

Note that a function's declaration includes a declaration of the data type of the value returned by the function. This can be any of Visual Basic's data types. The parameters in the declaration are intended for passing data into the function. For example, the following function declaration can be used for a function named `Fmax` that receives two values and returns a single-precision value:

```
Public Function Fmax(ByVal x As Single, ByVal y As Single) As Single
```

The names of the arguments in the function declaration, in this case `x` and `y`, are chosen by the programmer. Because the header declaration for `Fmax` includes two parameters, this function expects to receive two data items when it is called. Instead of the parameter names `x` and `y`, any two valid variable names could have been used to refer to the data passed to the function. Even if the function does not have any parameters, which is an extremely rare occurrence, the parentheses following the function name must always be included. In the above example, the parameters are passed by value. One could also declare parameters as pass by reference. As a specific application, consider the function `Celsius` that converts a Fahrenheit temperature into its equivalent Celsius value.

```
Public Function Celsius(ByVal fahrentemp As Single) As Single
    Return 5 / 9 * (fahrentemp - 32)
End Function
```

The `Celsius` function is simple in that its only statement returns the value computed. The function is then completed with the `End Function` statement. Instead of the **Return** *expression* statement, you could have a statement `Celsius = 5 / 9 * (fahrentemp - 32)` also returning the same value when the function `Celsius` is called (i.e., *Function_name = expression*).

Note that the `Celsius` function is declared as returning a single-precision value and has one parameter, named `fahrentemp`. Within the function declaration `fahrentemp` is declared as a single-precision parameter. As written, `Celsius` expects to receive one single-precision argument. From a programming viewpoint, parameters can be considered as variables whose values are assigned outside of the function and passed to the function when it is called.

Programmer Notes

Functions versus Sub Procedures

Students often ask "When creating a general procedure, should I create a **Function** or a **Sub** Procedure?"

The answer to this question is fairly straightforward. Because functions are designed to return a single value, use a function whenever the result of a processing operation is a single value; otherwise, use a **Sub** procedure. However, if the required procedure must return more than one value, use a **Sub** procedure and return the values through the parameter list, declaring those parameters as **ByRef**. Similarly, if the procedure returns no value and is used either to display data, request input from a user, or alter the graphical user interface, construct the procedure as a **Sub** procedure.

Calling a Function Procedure

Having written a function named `Celsius`, we now turn our attention to how this function can be called by other procedures. User-written functions are called in the same way intrinsic functions are called—by giving the function's name and passing any data to it in the parentheses following the function name (see Figure 7–15). At the same time the function is called, attention must be given to using its calculated value correctly.

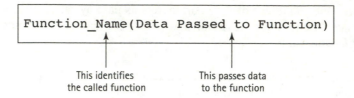

Figure 7–15   *Calling and Passing Data to a Function*

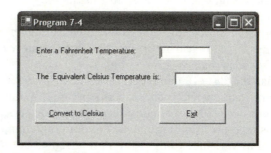

Figure 7–16   *Program 7–4's Interface*

To clarify the process of sending data to a function and using its returned value, consider Program 7-4 that calls the function Celsius. Figure 7–16 shows the interface for Program 7–4 and Table 7–4 lists the objects and properties for this program.

Program 7–4's Event and General Procedure Code

```
' This event procedure clears the output text box
' whenever the input text box gets focus
Private Sub txtFahr_Enter(ByVal sender As Object, ByVal e As _
    System.EventArgs) Handles txtFahr.Enter
  txtCelsius.Clear()
End Sub


Private Sub btnConvert_Click(ByVal sender As Object, ByVal e As _
    System.EventArgs) Handles btnConvert.Click
  Dim fahrenheit As Single

  fahrenheit = Val(txtFahr.Text)
  txtCelsius.Text = Celsius(fahrenheit)
End Sub


' This Function converts a Fahrenheit temperature to Celsius
Public Function Celsius(ByRef fahrentemp As Single) As Single
  Return 5 / 9 * (fahrentemp - 32)
```

Table 7–4   Program 7–4's Properties Table

Object	Property	Setting
Form	Name	frmMain
	Text	Program 7–4
Label	Name	lblFahr
	Text	Enter a Fahrenheit Temperature:
Label	Name	lblCelsius
	Text	The Equivalent Celsius Temperature is:
Text box	Name	txtFahr
	Text	(blank)
Text box	Name	txtCelsius
	TabStop	False
Button	Name	btnConvert
	Text	&Convert to Celsius
Button	Name	btnExit
	Text	E&xit

```
End Function

' This is the Exit event procedure
Private Sub btnExit_Click(ByVal sender As Object, ByVal e As _
    System.EventArgs) Handles btnExit.Click
  Beep()
  End
End Sub
```

As illustrated in Program 7–4, calling a function is rather trivial. It requires only that the name of the function be used and that any data passed to the function be enclosed within the parentheses following the function name. The items enclosed within the parentheses are called *arguments* of the called function. As illustrated in Figure 7–17, the parameter `fahrentemp` within `Celsius` references the argument `fahrenheit`

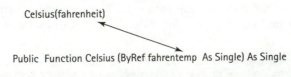

Figure 7–17   *Assigning Arguments to Parameters*

in the `btnConvert_Click` event procedure.[2] The function itself does not know which procedure made the function call. The calling procedure must, however, provide arguments that match in number, order, and data type to the parameters declared by the function. As with general procedures, no data type conversions are made between argument and parameters.

At the time a function is called, the program must also have a way to use the value provided by the function. We must either provide a variable to store the value or use the value directly in an expression, as was done in Program 7–4. Storing the returned value in a variable is accomplished using a standard assignment statement. For example, the assignment statement:

```
thistemp = Celsius(fahrenheit)
```

assigns `Celsius`' returned value in the variable named `thistemp`. This assignment statement does two things. First, the right-hand side calls `Celsius` and the result returned by the `Celsius` function is stored in the variable `thistemp`. Because the value returned by `Celsius` is single-precision, the variable `thistemp` must also be declared as a **Single** data-typed variable within the calling procedure's variable declarations.

CAUTION

It is important to know that when a parameter is declared as **ByRef**, the function receives direct access to the variable. This is because the call is by reference in the same manner as a call to a **Sub** procedure. Thus, the function can alter a calling procedure's variable by returning a value through the parameter list. For example, the calling statement `Celsius(fahrenheit)` in Program 7–4 gives `Celsius` access to variable `fahrenheit`, even though this variable is "known" as `fahrentemp` within `Celsius`. Thus, if the assignment statement `fahrentemp = 22.5` is contained in the function, both the value in `fahrentemp` and the value in `fahrenheit`, within the calling procedure, are changed. The reason for this, as illustrated in Figure 7–18, is that both `fahrenheit` and `fahrentemp` *refer to the same storage location and are simply different names for the same variable*. Because of this equivalence, it is important that functions never assign values to their parameters.

As with **Sub** procedures, you can pass data to functions by value by placing the keyword **ByVal** in front of the parameter's name when the parameter is declared. For example, the declaration:

```
Public Function Celsius(ByVal fahrentemp As Single) As Single
```

ensures that the `fahrentemp` parameter is effectively a named constant for the values being transmitted. As such, the value in `fahrentemp` cannot be altered from within

---

[2]The argument named `fahrenheit` was used here to illustrate the equivalence between arguments and parameters. Thus, the `btnConvert_Click` event could just have easily been written using the single statement `txtCelsius.Text = Celsius(Val(txtFahr.Text))`.

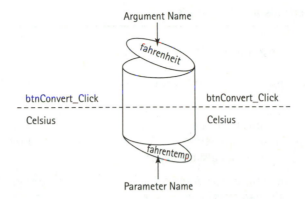

Figure 7–18 *The Relationship Between Argument and Parameters*

`Celsius`. In Visual Basic .NET, the declaration **ByVal** or **ByRef** is always specified and the default for a parameter is **ByVal**.

Creating Functions that Manipulate Strings

User-written functions that return a string value are written in the same manner as any other function procedures except that the return data type must be declared as a string. For example, the declaration:

```
Public Function Addchar(ByVal string1 As String) As String
```

declares that the `Addchar` function accepts a string parameter named `string1` and returns a string. In general, functions that return strings are not often needed, because Visual Basic provides an extremely extensive set of intrinsic string methods and functions. However, these methods and functions may be used in the user-defined functions. The more commonly used of these are listed in Table 7–5. Other older intrinsic string functions that have been referenced earlier in the book are `Left`, `Right`, `Mid`, and `Instr`. These will not be discussed here.

With the following string methods, the position (index) of characters in a string starts at 0. So, for example, the position or index of the letter "b" in the string "abc" is 1.[3] It is also important to note that string methods and functions do not alter the initial string.

In addition to the string methods and functions listed in Table 7–5, strings can be compared using Visual Basic's relational operators. Each character in a string is stored

---

[3]There are also older string functions that are equivalent to these string methods. When using the functions, note that the position of the first character in a string is usually 1.

Table 7–5   Intrinsic String Methods and Functions

Name	Description	Example
`str.Length`	Returns the number of characters in a string.	`"abcde".Length` returns 5
`str.IndexOf(str2)`	Returns the beginning position of string str2 in str; -1 is returned if str2 is not a substring of str	`"abcde".IndexOf(cd)` returns 2
`str.ToUpper`	Returns a copy of the string with all characters in upper case.	`"AbcDe".ToUpper` returns `"ABCDE"`
`str.ToLower`	Returns a copy of the string with all characters in lower case.	`"AbcDe".ToLower` returns `"abcde"`
`str.Substring(m[, n])`	If n is specified, returns a string starting at position m for n characters. If n is not specified, returns a string starting at m to the end of str.	`"abcde".Substring(3)` returns `"de"` `"abcde".Substring(2,2)` returns `"cd"`
`str.TrimStart`	Returns a copy of the string with all leading spaces removed.	`"   ab cde   ".TrimStart` returns `"ab cde   "`
`str.TrimEnd`	Returns a copy of the string with all trailing spaces removed.	`"   abc de   ".TrimEnd` returns `"   abc de"`
`str.Trim`	Returns a copy of the string with all leading and trailing spaces removed.	`"   abc de   ".Trim` returns `"abc de"`
`IsNumeric(str)`	Returns a Boolean value (True or False) indicating whether the string can be evaluated as a number.	`IsNumeric("12.4")` returns `True`

in binary, using the ANSI code. In the ANSI code, a blank precedes (is less than) all letters and numbers; the digits are stored in order from 0 to 9; and the letters of the alphabet are stored in order from A to Z. It is also important to note that, in ANSI, the digits come before, or are less than, the letters, and that uppercase letters come before lowercase letters.

Typically, Visual Basic's intrinsic string methods and functions are used to create useful string manipulation **Sub** procedures. For example, consider Program 7–5, that

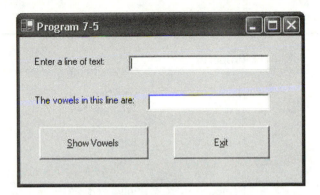

Figure 7–19 *Program 7–5's Interface*

processes a string to determine the number of vowels it contains. Figure 7–19 shows the interface to Program 7–5 and Table 7–6 lists the objects and properties for this program.

Program 7–5's Event and General Procedure Code

```
' This event procedure clears the Vowels Text box
' whenever the Input text box gets focus
Private Sub txtInput_Enter(ByVal sender As Object, _
    ByVal e As System.EventArgs) Handles txtInput.Enter
  txtVowels.Clear()
End Sub

' This event procedure calls the Procedure
Private Sub btnShow_Click(ByVal sender As Object, _
    ByVal e As System.EventArgs) Handles btnShow.Click
  ShowVowels(txtInput.Text)
End Sub

' This Procedure displays the vowels
Public Sub ShowVowels(ByVal s1 As String)
  Dim length, position As Integer
  Dim str1, strlower, out As String

  out = ""
  length = s1.Length  ' find the string's length
  For position = 0 To length - 1
    str1 = s1.Substring(position, 1) ' extract next character
    strlower = str1.ToLower
    Select Case strlower
      Case "a", "e", "i", "o", "u"
        out = out & str1
```

Table 7-6   The Properties Table for Program 7-5

Object	Property	Setting
Form	Name	frmMain
	Text	Program 7-5
Label	Name	lblInput
	Text	Enter a line of text:
Label	Name	lblVowels
	Text	The vowels in this line are:
Text box	Name	txtInput
	Text	(blank)
Text box	Name	txtVowels
	TabStop	False
Button	Name	btnShow
	Text	&Show Vowels
Button	Name	btnExit
	Text	E&xit

```
      End Select
    Next position
    txtVowels.Text = out
End Sub


' This is the Exit event procedure
Private Sub btnExit_Click(ByVal sender As Object, ByVal e As _
    System.EventArgs) Handles btnExit.Click
    Beep()
    End
End Sub
```

In reviewing the Showvowels **Sub** procedure, note that the length of the string is used to determine the terminating value for the **For** loop. In this loop, each character is "stripped off" using the Substring method and converted to its lowercase form. This is done so that both uppercase and lowercase vowels can be recognized by comparing all letters to the lowercase forms of the vowels. The converted character is then compared to the lowercase characters a, e, i, o, and u. If there is a match to one of these charac-

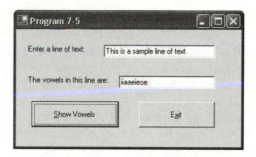

Figure 7–20 *A Sample Output Produced by Program 7–5*

ters, the original character is appended to the output string. After each character in the string has been examined, the output string is displayed in the second Text box. Figure 7–20 illustrates a sample output produced by Program 7–5.

Exercises 7.3

1. For the following function declarations, determine the number, type, and order (sequence) of the values that must be passed to the function and the type of value returned by the function:

   a. `Public Function IntToSingle(ByVal n As Integer) As Single`

   b. `Public Function Volts(ByVal res As Single, ByVal amp As _`
      `Single) As Single`

   c. `Public Function Power(ByVal type As Boolean, ByVal cap As _`
      `Single) As Double`

   d. `Public Function Flag(ByVal type As Boolean, ByVal time As _`
      `Double) As Boolean`

   e. `Public Function Energy(ByVal pow As Double, ByVal time As _`
      `Double) As Double`

   f. `Public Function Roi(ByVal a As Single, ByVal b As Single, _`
      `ByVal c As Single, ByVal d As Integer) As Single`

   g. `Public Function Getval(ByVal item As Integer, ByVal delim As _`
      `String) As Double`

   h. `Function Locase(ByVal c As String) As String`

2. a. Write a function named `Check` that has three parameters. The first parameter should accept an integer number, the second parameter a single precision number, and the third parameter a string. The function should display the values of the data passed to the function when it is called, and return a value of 1. (**Note:** When tracing errors in functions, it is very helpful to have the function display the values it has been passed. Quite frequently, the error is not in what the function does with the data, but in the data it receives and stores.)

b. Include the function in Exercise 2a in a working program.

3. Write a function named `CelToFahr` that converts a Celsius temperature to a Fahrenheit temperature according to the formula *Fahrenheit = 9/5(Celsius) + 32.*

4. Write a function named `Hyptns` that accepts the lengths of two sides of a right triangle and determines the triangle's hypotenuse. (The hypotenuse of a right triangle is equal to the square root of the sum of the squares of the other two sides.) Include `Hyptns` in a working program and verify that it works properly by passing various values to it, displaying the returned value, and checking that the displayed value is correct.

5. Write a function that has the declaration `Public Function Absdif(ByVal x As Single, ByVal y As Single)` that returns the absolute value of the difference between two real numbers. For example, the function calls `Absdif(2,10)`, `Absdif(-1,-10)`, and `Absdif(-2,10)` should return the values, 8, 9, and 12, respectively. Include the function `Absdif` in a program and test the function by passing various numbers to it, displaying the returned value, and checking that the displayed value is correct.

6. Write and execute a function that accepts an integer parameter and determines whether the passed integer is even or odd. (*Hint:* use the **Mod** operator.)

7. a. Write a function named `Round` that rounds any single precision value to two decimal places. Rounding to two decimal places is obtained using the following steps:

   Step 1: Multiply the passed number by 100

   Step 2: Add 0.5 to the number obtained in Step 1

   Step 3: Take the integer part of the number obtained in Step 2

   Step 4: Divide the result of Step 3 by 100

   b. Include the function written in Exercise 7a in a working program. Test the function by passing various data to it and verifying the displayed value.

8. Modify the `Vowels` procedure in Program 7–5 to count and display the total number of vowels contained in the string passed to it.

9. Modify the `Vowels` procedure in Program 7–5 to count and display the numbers of each individual vowel contained in the string. That is, the function should display the total number of a's, e's, and so forth.

10. a. Write a function to count the total number of non-blank characters contained in a string. For example, the number of non-blank characters in the string " abc def " is six.

    b. Include the function for Exercise 10a in a complete working program.

11. Write and test a procedure that reverses the characters in a string.

7.4 Variable Scope

By their very nature, procedures are constructed to be independent modules. This implies that variables declared in one procedure, be it an event or general procedure,

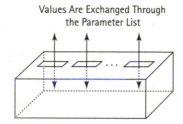

Values Are Exchanged Through
the Parameter List

Figure 7–21   *A Procedure Can Be Considered a Closed Box*

cannot be accessed by another procedure, unless specific provisions are made to allow such access. As we have seen, one such access is provided through a procedure's parameter list (see Figure 7–21). Given this fact, both event and general procedures may be compared to a closed box, with slots at the top through which values may be exchanged with the calling procedure.

The metaphor of a closed box is useful because it emphasizes the fact that what goes on inside the procedure, except for the altering of an parameter's value, is hidden from all other procedures. This includes any variables declared within the procedure. These internally declared variables, available only to the procedure itself, are said to be "local to the procedure," and are called *procedure-level* or *local variables*. This term refers to the *scope* of a variable, where scope is defined as the section of the program where the variable is valid, visible, or "known." A variable can have either a local, form-level, or global scope. A variable with a local scope is simply one that has had storage locations set aside for it by a declaration statement made within a procedure. Local variables are meaningful only when used in expressions or statements inside the procedure that declared them. This means that the same variable name can be declared and used in more than one procedure. For each procedure that declares the variable, a separate and distinct variable is created.

By definition, all variables that are declared within a procedure using the **Dim** keyword are local variables. Visual Basic does, however, provide two different means of extending the scope of a variable from one procedure into another. One way is to use a variable as an argument in a calling statement and to declare the parameter **ByRef**, which gives the called procedure access to the variable. The second method is to use module-level variables. *Module-level variables*, said to have *module-level scope,* are variables that are not declared in the procedure. Such variables must be declared as either **Private** or **Public** (declaring a module-level variable with the **Dim** keyword is the same as making it **Private**). Module level variables that have been declared as **Private** are accessible only to procedures in the module, and are referred to as *form-level* variables. **Public** module-level variables are available and shared between all modules in a project and their procedures, and are referred to as *global* and *project-level* variables. Table 7–7 lists the scope of variables in Visual Basic. It should be noted that procedures share the same scope rules as module-level variables. That is, a **Public** procedure can be called from any module in an application, while a **Private** procedure can only be called by other procedures residing on the same module.

Table 7–7 Variable Scope

Scope	Private or Dim	Public
Procedure-Level (Local Variables)	Variables are private to the procedure in which they are declared.	Not applicable. Local variables cannot be declared as Public.
Module-Level (Form-level and global variables)	Variables are private within the module in which they are declared, and are referred to as form-level variables. They are shared and can be accessed by every procedure in the module.	Variables are available to all modules, and are referred to as global variables. They are shared and can be accessed by any procedure in the project, no matter where the procedure is located.

As discussed later in this chapter, global variables should be used with great care because they make debugging very difficult.

To illustrate the scope of both local and module-level variables, consider Procedure Code 7–3.

Procedure Code 7–3

```
Private firstnum As Integer ' create a module-level variable named firstnum

Private Sub frmMain_Click(ByVal sender As Object, _
    ByVal e As System.EventArgs) Handles MyBase.Click
  First()
End Sub

Public Sub First()
  Dim secnum As Integer

  firstnum = 10 ' store a value into the module-level variable
  secnum = 20   ' store a value into the local variable
  lstDisplay.Items.Clear()
  lstDisplay.Items.Add("From First: firstnum = " & firstnum)
  lstDisplay.Items.Add("From First: secnum = " & secnum)

  Second()

  lstDisplay.Items.Add("")
  lstDisplay.Items.Add("From First again: firstnum = " & firstnum)
  lstDisplay.Items.Add("From First again: secnum = " & secnum)
End Sub
```

```
Private Sub Second()
  Dim secnum As Integer ' create a second local variable named secnum

  secnum = 30  ' this only affects this local variable's value

  lstDisplay.Items.Add("")
  lstDisplay.Items.Add("From Second: firstnum = " & firstnum)
  lstDisplay.Items.Add("From Second: secnum = " & secnum)

  firstnum = 40   ' this changes firstnum for both procedures
End Sub
```

The variable firstnum in Procedure Code 7–3 is a module-level variable because its storage is created by a declaration statement located outside a procedure. Because both procedures, First and Second, are located on the form module in which firstnum is declared, both of these procedures can use this global variable with no further declaration needed.

Procedure Code 7–3 also contains two separate local variables, both named secnum. Storage for the secnum variable named in First is created by the declaration statement located in First. A different storage area for the secnum variable in Second is created by the declaration statement located in the Second procedure. Figure 7–22 illustrates the three distinct storage areas reserved by the three declaration statements used in Procedure Code 7–3.

Each of the variables named secnum are local to the procedure in which their storage is created, and each of these variables can only be used from within the appropriate procedure. Thus, when secnum is used in First, the storage area reserved by First for its secnum variable is accessed, and when secnum is used in Second, the storage area reserved by Second for its secnum variable is accessed. The following output is produced when the frmMain_Click event in Procedure Code 7–3 is activated:

```
From First: firstnum = 10
From First: secnum = 20

From Second: firstnum = 10
From Second: secnum = 30

From First again: firstnum = 40
From First again: secnum = 20
```

Let us analyze the output produced by Procedure Code 7–3. Since firstnum is a global variable, both the First and Second procedures can use and change its value. Initially, both procedures print the value of 10 that First stored in firstnum. Before returning, Second changes the value of firstnum to 40, the value displayed when the variable firstnum is next displayed from within First.

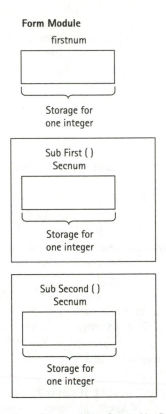

Figure 7–22   *The Three Storage Areas Created by Procedure Code 7–3*

Because each procedure only "knows" its own local variables, First can only display the value of its secnum and Second can only display the value of its secnum variable. Thus, whenever secnum is printed from First, the value of 20 is displayed, and whenever secnum is printed from Second, the value 30 is displayed.

Visual Basic does not confuse these two secnum variables because only one procedure can execute at a given moment. While a procedure is executing, only those variables that "are in scope" for that procedure (module-level and local) can be accessed.

The scope of a variable in no way influences or restricts the data type of the variable. Local variables can be a character, integer, single, double, or any of the other data types (long, boolean, and so on) we have introduced, as can module-level variables. The scope of a variable is determined by the placement of the declaration statement that reserves storage for it. Finally, if both a module-level and local variable have the same name, the local variable will be accessed by the procedure in which that local variable is declared.

Using Module-Level Variables

Module-level variables are useful if a variable must be shared between many procedures. Rather than passing the same variable to each procedure, it is easier to define the variable once as module-level. Doing so also alerts anyone reading the program that many procedures use the variable. Most large programs make use of a few module-level variables, and the majority of these variables should be named constants. Such named constants can then be shared by all procedures as "read-only" variables, which restrict any one procedure from altering the constant's value. Smaller programs containing a few procedures, however, should rarely contain module-level variables, though they may contain module-level named constants. The reason for this is that module-level variables allow the programmer to "jump around" the normal safeguards provided by procedures. By indiscriminately making variables module-level, you destroy the safeguards Visual Basic provides to make procedures independent and insulated from each other, including the necessity of carefully designating the type of parameters needed by a procedure, the variables used in the procedure, and the values returned.

By their very nature, module-level variables provide all procedures with the ability to access and change the value of the variable. Because no single procedure has exclusive use of such a variable, it is often difficult to determine which procedure actually accessed and changed a given variable's value. This makes debugging and maintaining code much more difficult. Therefore, module-level variables should be used with great care.

Static Variables

The scope of a variable defines the location within a program where that variable can be used. Given a program, you could take a pencil and draw a box around the section of the program where each variable is valid. The space inside the box would represent the scope of a variable. From this viewpoint, the scope of a variable can be thought of as the space within the program where the variable is valid.

In addition to the space dimension represented by its scope, variables also have a time dimension. The time dimension refers to the length of time that storage locations are reserved for a variable. This time dimension is referred to as the variable's "lifetime." For example, all local variable storage locations are released back to the computer when a procedure is finished running. Consider Procedure Code 7–4, where the **Sub** procedure Test is called four times when the Form_Click event is activated.

Procedure Code 7–4

```
Private Sub Form_Click(ByVal sender As Object, _
    ByVal e As System.EventArgs) Handles MyBase.Click
  Dim count As Integer

  lstDisplay.Items.Clear()
  count = 1
  For count = 1 To 4
    Test
  Next count
End Sub

Private Sub Test()
  Dim num As Integer
```

```
lstDisplay.Items.Add("The value of num is " & num)
    num = num + 1
End Sub
```

When the `Form_Click` procedure in this code is executed, the display produced is:

```
The value of num is 0
The value of num is 0
The value of num is 0
The value of num is 0
```

This output is produced because each time `Test` is called, the local variable `num` is created and initialized to zero. When the **Sub** procedure returns control to the event procedure `Form_Click`, the variable `num` is destroyed along with any value stored in it. Thus, the effect of incrementing `num` in `Test` is lost.

The initialization used in `Test` is called a runtime initialization because it occurs each time the **Sub** procedure containing the variable is called. There are cases, however, where we would like a subroutine to preserve the value of its local variables between calls. This can be accomplished by declaring a variable inside a procedure using the `Static` keyword, rather than `Dim` keyword. For example, consider Procedure Code 7–5, which is identical to Procedure Code 7–4, except that local variable `num` in the `Test` **Sub** procedure has been declared as `Static`.

Procedure Code 7–5

```
Private Sub Form_Click(ByVal sender As Object, _
    ByVal e As System.EventArgs) Handles MyBase.Click
  Dim count As Integer

  lstDisplay.Items.Clear()
  count = 1
  For count = 1 To 4
    Test
  Next count
End Sub

Private Sub Test()
  Static num As Integer

  lstDisplay.Items.Add("The value of num is " & num)
  num = num + 1
End Sub
```

The output produced by the activation of this code is:

```
The value of num is 0
The value of num is 1
The value of num is 2
The value of num is 3
```

As illustrated by this output, the variable num is set to zero only once. The **Sub** procedure Test then increments this variable, just before relinquishing control back to its calling procedure. The value that num has when Test is finished executing is retained and displayed when Test next called. The reason for this is that local static variables are not created and destroyed each time the procedure declaring the static variable is called. Once created, they remain in existence for the life of the program.

Because local static variables retain their values, they are not initialized in the same way as variables declared as Dim. Their initialization is done only once, when the program is translated into executable form. At translation time all **Static** numeric variables are created and initialized to zero.[4] Thereafter, the value in the variable is retained each time the function is called. If you want the static variable to be initialized to a value other than zero, you would set its initial value as in the following:

```
Static num As Integer = 3
```

Exercises 7.4

1. Describe what is meant by the word *scope*, as it is applied to variables.

2. What do you think is the scope of a procedure's parameters?

3. a. What is the scope of module-level variables that are declared as **Private**?

   b. What is the scope of module-level procedures that are declared as **Private**?

4. a. What is the scope of module-level variables that are declared as **Public**?

   b. What is the scope of module-level procedures that are declared as **Public**?

5. a. The following procedures use the same variable and parameter names, n and sum, in both the calling and called procedure. Determine if this causes any problem for the program.

```
Private Sub Form_Click(ByVal sender As Object, _
        ByVal e As System.EventArgs) Handles MyBase.Click
  Dim count As Integer
  Dim n, sum As Single

  For count = 1 To 4
    n = Val(InputBox("Enter a number", "Input Request", "0"))
    lstDisplay.Items.Add("The number just entered is " & n)
    sum = Accumulate(n)
```

---

[4]String variables are initialized to zero-length strings.

```
   Next count
   lstDisplay.Items.Add("The sum of the numbers entered is " & sum)
End Sub

Private Function Accumulate(n As Single) As Single
   Dim sum As Single

   sum = sum + n
   Return sum
End Function
```

    b. Assume that the numbers 10, 20, 30, and 40 were entered by a user, in response to the event click procedure in Exercise 5a. Determine the output of the program for these inputs.

    c. What change in the function procedure will cause it to produce the correct sum?

7.5   Recursion[5]

Because Visual Basic allocates new memory locations for parameters and local variables each time a function is called, it is possible for all general procedures to call themselves. Procedures that do so, which can be both **Sub** and **Function** procedures, are referred to as *self-referential* or *recursive* procedures. When a procedure invokes itself, the process is called *direct recursion*. Similarly, a procedure can invoke a second procedure, which in turn invokes the first procedure. This type of recursion is referred to as *indirect* or *mutual recursion*.

Mathematical Recursion

The recursive concept is that a solution to a problem can be stated in terms of "simple" versions of itself. Some problems can be solved using an algebraic formula that shows recursion explicitly. For example, consider finding the factorial of a number n, denoted as $n!$, where n is a positive integer. This is defined as:

$$1! = 1$$
$$2! = 2 * 1 = 2 * 1!$$
$$3! = 3 * 2 * 1 = 3 * 2!$$
$$4! = 4 * 3 * 2 * 1 = 4 * 3!$$

and so on.

---

[5]This topic may be omitted on first reading with no loss of subject continuity.

The definition for $n!$ can be summarized by the following statements:

$1! = 1$

$n! = n * (n - 1)!$ for $n > 1$

This definition illustrates the general considerations that must be specified in constructing a recursive algorithm:

1. What is the first case?
2. How is the nth case related to the $(n - 1)$ case?

Although the definition seems to define a factorial in terms of a factorial, the definition is valid because it can always be computed. For example, using the definition, 3! is first computed as:

$3! = 3 * 2!$

The value of 3! is determined from the definition as:

$2! = 2 * 1!$

Substituting this expression for 2! in the determination of 3! yields:

$3! = 3 * 2 * 1!$

1! is not defined in terms of the recursive formula, but is simply defined as being equal to 1. Substituting this value into the expression for 3! gives us

$3! = 3 * 2 * 1 = 6$

To see how a recursive procedure is defined in Visual Basic, we construct the function Factorial. In pseudocode, the processing required of this function is:

If n = 1
  Factorial = n
Else
  *Factorial = n * Factorial(n − 1)*

Note that this algorithm is simply a restatement of the recursive definition previously given. In Visual Basic, this can be written as:

```
Public Function Factorial(ByVal n As Long) As Long
  If n = 1 Then
    Return 1
  Else
```

```
      Return n * Factorial(n - 1)
   End If
End Function
```

In the program, *n* has been declared as a long integer. This is because the factorial can easily exceed the bounds of an integer, which has a valid range from −32,768 to +32,767. (For example, the factorial of 8 is 40,320). Program 7–6 illustrates the `Factorial` function within the context of a complete program. Figure 7–23 shows the interface for Program 7–6 and Table 7–8 lists the objects and properties for this program. Note that the **Return** keyword is used within the function.

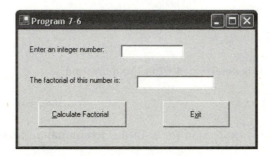

Figure 7–23 *Program 7–6's Interface*

Table 7–8   The Properties Table for Program 7–6

Object	Property	Setting
Form	Name	frmMain
	Text	Program 7–6
Label	Name	lblInput
	Text	Enter an integer number:
Label	Name	lblFactorial
	Text	The factorial of this number is:
Text box	Name	txtInput
	Text	(blank)
Text box	Name	txtFactorial
	TabStop	False
Button	Name	btnFactorial
	Text	&Calculate Factorial
Button	Name	btnExit
	Text	E&xit

Program 7–6's Event and General Procedure Code

```
' This event procedure clears the txtFactorial output Text box
' whenever the txtInput box gets focus
Private Sub txtInput_Enter(ByVal sender As Object, _
    ByVal e As System.EventArgs) Handles txtInput.Enter
  txtFactorial.Text = ""
End Sub


' This event procedure calls the Factorial Function
Private Sub btnFactorial_Click(ByVal sender As Object, _
    ByVal e As System.EventArgs) Handles btnFactorial.Click
  Dim number, fact As Long

  number = Int(Val(txtInput.Text))
  fact = Factorial(number)
  txtFactorial.Text = fact
End Sub


' This function calculates the factorial recursively
Public Function Factorial(ByVal n As Long) As Long
  If n = 1 Then
    Return 1
  Else
    Return n * Factorial(n - 1)
  End If
End Function


' This is the Exit event procedure
Private Sub btnExit_Click(ByVal sender As Object, _
    ByVal e As System.EventArgs) Handles btnExit.Click
  Beep()
  End
End Sub
```

Figure 7–24 illustrates a sample run of Program 7–6.

How the Computation is Performed

The sample run of Program 7-6 initially invoked Factorial with a value of 3, using the call

```
fact = Factorial(n)
```

Let's see how the computer actually performs the computation. The mechanism that makes it possible for a Visual Basic procedure to call itself is that Visual Basic allocates

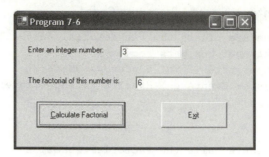

Figure 7–24 *A Sample Output of Program 7–6*

new memory locations for all procedure parameters as each procedure is called. This allocation is made dynamically, as a program is executed, in a memory area referred to as the *stack*.

A *stack* is simply an area of memory used for rapidly storing and retrieving data. It is conceptually similar to a stack of trays in a cafeteria, where the last tray placed on top of the stack is the first tray removed. This last-in/first-out mechanism provides the means for storing information in order of occurrence. Each procedure call simply reserves memory locations on the stack for its parameters, its local variables, a return value, and the address where execution is to resume in the calling procedure when the called procedure has completed execution. Thus, when the procedure call `Factorial(n)` is made, the stack is initially used to store the address of the instruction being executed (`fact = Factorial(n)`), the parameter value for n, which is 3, and a space for the value to be returned by the `Factorial` procedure. At this stage, the stack can be envisioned as shown in Figure 7–25. From a program execution standpoint, the procedure that made the call to `Factorial`, in this case the `btnFactorial_Click` event, is suspended and the code for the `Factorial` procedure starts executing.

Within the `Factorial` function itself, another procedure call is made. That this call is to `Factorial` is irrelevant as far as Visual Basic is concerned. The call simply is another request for stack space. In this case, the stack stores the address of the instruction being executed in `Factorial`, the number 2, and a space for the value to be returned by the function. The stack can now be envisioned as shown in Figure 7–26. At

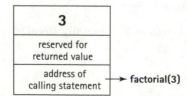

Figure 7–25 *The Stack for the First Call to Factorial*

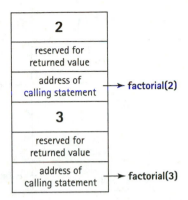

Figure 7–26 *The Stack for the Second Call to Factorial*

this point, a second version of the code for `Factorial` begins execution, while the first version is temporarily suspended.

Once again, the currently executing code, the second invocation of `Factorial`, makes a function call. That this call is to itself is irrelevant in Visual Basic. The call is once again handled in the same manner as any procedure invocation and begins with allocation of the stack's memory space. Here the stack stores the address of the instruction being executed in the calling procedure, which happens to be `Factorial`, the number 1, and a space for the value to be returned by the function. The stack can now be envisioned as shown in Figure 7–27. At this point the third and final version of the code for `Factorial` begins execution, while the second version is temporarily suspended.

This third call to `Factorial` results in a returned value of 1 being placed on the stack. This completes the set of recursive calls and permits the suspended calling procedures to resume execution and be completed in reverse order. The value of 1 is used by the second invocation of `Factorial` to complete its operation and place a return value of 2 on the stack. This value is then used by the first invocation of `Factorial` to complete its operation and place a return value of 6 on the stack, with execution now returning to the `btnFactorial_Click` event procedure. The original calling statement within this procedure stores the return value of its invocation of `Factorial` into the variable fact.

Recursion Versus Iteration

The recursive method can be applied to any problem in which the solution is represented in terms of solutions to simpler versions of the same problem. The most difficult tasks in implementing recursion, however, are deciding how to create the process and visualizing what happens at each successive invocation.

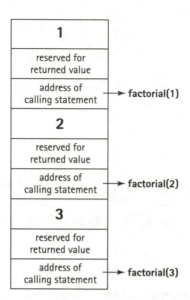

Figure 7–27 *The Stack for the Third Call to Factorial*

Any recursive procedure can always be written in a nonrecursive manner using an iterative solution. For example, the factorial procedure can be written using an iteration algorithm as:

```
Public Function Factorial(ByVal n As Long) As Long
  Dim fact As Long

  fact = 1
  Do
    fact = fact * n
    n = n - 1
  Loop While n > 0
  Return fact
End Function
```

Because recursion is usually a difficult concept for beginning programmers, under what conditions would you use it in preference to a repetitive solution? The answer is rather simple.

If a problem solution can be expressed repetitively or recursively with equal ease, the repetitive solution is preferable because it executes faster (there are no additional procedure calls that consume processing time) and uses less memory (the stack is not used for the multiple procedure calls needed in recursion). There are times, however, when recursive solutions are preferable.

First, some problems are simply easier to visualize using a recursive algorithm than a repetitive one. A second reason for using recursion is that it sometimes provides a much simpler solution. In these situations, obtaining the same result using repetition would require extremely complicated coding that can be avoided using recursion. An example of this is an advanced sorting algorithm known as the *Quicksort*.

Exercises 7.5

1. The Fibonacci sequence is 0, 1, 1, 2, 3, 5, 8, 13, . . . such that the first two terms are 0 and 1, and each term thereafter is defined recursively as the sum of the two preceding terms; that is,

   $Fib(n) = Fib(n - 1) + Fib(n - 2)$

   Write a recursive procedure that returns the nth number in a Fibonacci sequence, when n is passed to the procedure as an argument. For example, when $n = 8$, the procedure returns the 8th number in the sequence, which is 13.

2. The sum of a series of consecutive numbers from 1 to n can be defined recursively as:

   $sum(1) = 1;$

   $sum(n) = n + sum(n - 1)$

   Write a recursive Visual Basic procedure that accepts n as an argument and calculates the sum of the numbers from 1 to n.

3. a. The value of x^n can be defined recursively as:

   $x^0 = 1$

   $x^n = x * x^{n-1}$

   Write a recursive procedure that computes and returns the value of x^n.

   b. Rewrite the procedure for Exercise 3a so that it uses a repetitive algorithm for calculating the value of x^n.

4. a. Write a procedure that recursively determines the value of the nth term of a geometric sequence defined by the terms

   $a, ar, ar^2, ar^3, . . . ar^{n-1}$

   The argument to the procedure should be the first term, a, the common ratio, r, and the value of n.

   b. Modify the procedure for Exercise 4a so that the sum of the first n terms of the sequence is returned.

5. a. Write a procedure that recursively determines the value of the nth term of an arithmetic sequence defined by the terms

   $a, a + d, a + 2d, a + 3d, . . . a + (n - 1)d$

   The argument to the procedure should be the first term, a, the common difference, d, and the value of n.

   b. Modify the procedure for Exercise 5a so that the sum of the first n terms of the sequence is returned. (*Hint:* This is a more general form of Exercise 2.)

Figure 7–28   *Rotech's Main Menu Form*

7.6 Focus on Program Design and Implementation: A General Procedure Menu System[6]

Figure 7–28 illustrates Rotech's Main Menu Form as it was developed in Section 2.6 and has been used throughout subsequent Focus sections. As shown, this form has five Buttons.

As currently implemented, each Button shown in Figure 7–28, except for the E**x**it button, uses its individual **Click** event to hide the Main Menu Form and display an appropriate second Form. Figure 7–29 illustrates the underlying structure of this relationship. Note that, except for the Form's name, each Button repeats the same three lines of code. As a specific example of this code, Procedure Code 7–6 lists the code triggered by clicking the W̲alk Ins Button.

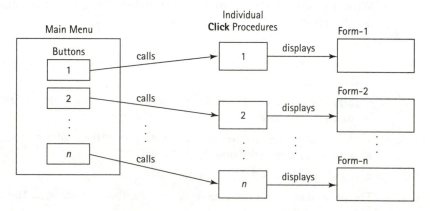

Figure 7–29   *Disbursed Display Controls*

---

[6]The Rotech project, as it should exist at the start of this section (which includes all of the capabilities built into it through the end of Section 6.7) can be found at http://computerscience.jbpub.com/bronsonvbnet in the ROTECH6 folder as project rotech6.

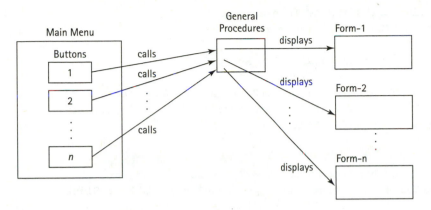

Figure 7–30   *Centralized Display Control*

Procedure Code 7–6

```
Private Sub btnWalkins_Click(ByVal sender As System.Object, _
    ByVal e As System.EventArgs) Handles btnWalkins.Click
  Dim frmWalkRef as New frmWalkIn()
  frmWalkRef.KeyPreview() = True
  Me.Hide
  frmWalkRef.Show()
End Sub
```

The structure shown in Figure 7–29 is an example of one type of programming style, called *disbursed programming*, where each event code sets its own preconditions, such as hiding the current Form and setting the KeyPreview property, and is responsible for determining the next displayed Form. A second programming style, called *centralized programming*, gathers similar tasks together into a single general procedure and requires that the appropriate event codes simply make a single call to this single procedure. The structure of this approach, as it applies to a Main Menu, is illustrated in Figure 7–30. Although this second approach requires the addition of a new general procedure, it does have the advantage of centralizing the code for what is essentially the single task of hiding the current Form and displaying a second one. The new general procedure is usually placed on the same Form as the Buttons.

Procedure Code 7–7 illustrates how the call to the general procedure would be made within each Button's **Click** event, for Rotech's Main Menu. Note that each call uses a single named constant argument to identify which Button was pressed.

Procedure Code 7–7

```
' Declarations Section Code

' These constants are used to identify which button was pressed
Const intMAILBUTTON As Integer = 1
Const intWALKBUTTON As Integer = 2
```

```
Const intEXITBUTTON As Integer = 6
Const intSTUB As Integer = 99


' Here are the Buttons' Click Event Code

Private Sub btnMailins_Click(ByVal sender As Object, _
    ByVal e As System.EventArgs) Handles btnMailins.Click
  mainmenu(intMAILBUTTON)
End Sub


Private Sub btnWalkins_Click(ByVal sender As Object, _
    ByVal e As System.EventArgs) Handles btnWalkins.Click
  mainmenu(intWALKBUTTON)
End Sub


Private Sub btnInvRec_Click(ByVal sender As Object, _
    ByVal e As System.EventArgs) Handles btnInvRec.Click
  mainmenu(intSTUB)
End Sub


Private Sub btnReports_Click(ByVal sender As Object, _
    ByVal e As System.EventArgs) Handles btnReports.Click
  mainmenu(intSTUB)
End Sub


Private Sub btnExit_Click(ByVal sender As Object, _
    ByVal e As System.EventArgs) Handles btnExit.Click
  mainmenu(intEXITBUTTON)
End Sub
```

Note that each Click event in Event Procedure 7–7 is a call to the same general procedure, which we have named mainmenu, with a single argument that clearly identifies the clicked Button. At this stage there are five Buttons; thus we have assigned the last, or Exit button, the number 5. We also have assigned the intSTUB constant the number 99, which is much higher than the number of actual Buttons that will ever be placed on the Main Menu Form. Then, as we develop a specific Form and use one of the existing Button Event codes to trigger the Form's display in place of the Stub Form, we will assign the numbers 3 and 4 to two new named constants. If we add a new Button to the Main Menu (as we do in the next Focus section), we will use the number 6, and so on, for each added Button.

Procedure Code 7–8 shows the code for the new mainmenu general procedure.

Procedure Code 7–8

```
Public Sub mainmenu(intFromButton As Integer)
  Dim frmMailRef as New frmMailIn()
```

```
   Dim frmWalkRef as New frmWalkIn()
   Dim frmStubRef as New frmStub()
   Me.Hide
   Select Case intFromButton
     Case intMAILBUTTON
       frmMailRef.KeyPreview = True
       frmMailRef.Show()
       frmMailRef.Refresh()
     Case intWALKBUTTON
       frmWalkRef.KeyPreview = True
       frmWalkRef.Show()
       frmWalkRef.Refresh()
     Case intSTUB
       frmStub.Show()
       frmStub.Refresh()
     Case intEXITBUTTON
       Beep()
       End
   End Select
End Sub
```

In reviewing this `mainmenu` procedure, note that the first statement in the procedure hides the current main menu form.[7] This statement is only made once, as opposed to being included within each **Click** event's code. A `Select Case` statement is then used to determine the action to take, depending on the value of the passed parameter. In each case, except when the Exit button is pressed, a second Form is displayed. The reason for using both a `Show` and `Refresh` method in the `mainmenu` procedure is that, although the `Show` method automatically performs a load of the designated window, if the Form's **AutoRefresh** property is set to **False** all graphical elements on the Form may not be displayed. Calling the `Refresh` method forces a redraw of all graphical elements on the Form, which ensures a correct display. Now, as a new Form is added to replace the Stub Form, we only need to add a new named constant, replace the `intSTUB` constant in the appropriate event procedure calling statement, and add an appropriate `Case` statement within the `Select Case` statement. We will do this in Section 8.5, when we add an About Box to our program.

Although the centralized approach may initially appear more complicated than the disbursed approach, in practice it is very convenient to have the names of all displayed Forms and all of the display code located together in a single place. In either case, you will encounter both approaches in your programming work. Which one you adopt is a matter of both programming style and required policy.

Exercises 7.6

(Note: The Rotech Systems project, at the stage of development begun in this section, can be found at http://computerscience.jbpub.com/bronsonvbnet in the ROTECH6 folder as

---

[7]An alternative is to use the statement `frmMain.Hide`, which explicitly names the main menu form.

project rotech6. *The project, as it exists at the end of this section, can be found in the ROTECH7 folder as project* rotech7.*)*

1. a. Make the changes to the Main Menu Form described in this section or locate and load the project from http://computerscience.jbpub.com/bronsonvbnet.

   b. Test that all Buttons on the Main Menu form work correctly after you have made the changes for Exercise 1a.

2. Add a new Button named btnAbout to the Main Menu Form. The button text should be set to <u>A</u>bout. When this new button is clicked the Stub Form should be displayed.

3. (Case study) Redo the Main Menu form for your selected project (see project specifications at the end of Section 1.5) to conform to the centralized programming style described in this section.

7.7 Knowing About Debugging

Debugging refers to the process of finding errors, or "bugs," in program code and correcting them. Visual Basic provides a number of debugging tools that can help in this process. Specifically, these tools let us analyze program execution and permit us to look inside application code as it is running. This is accomplished by setting *breakpoints* in your code, which stop a program in Break mode when they are reached; or running your code in *single-step* mode, which executes one instruction at a time. To accomplish this, and other useful debugging tasks, there are three distinct debugging windows, shown in Figures 7–31a, –b, and –c. Table 7–9 describes the different debugging windows you will use to analyze and fix errors in your programs.

The Immediate and Locals windows can be activated in Break mode from the Debug Menu, shown in Figure 7–32. If the Debug toolbar (Figure 7–33) is not visible, you can

Figure 7–31a   *The Immediate Debug Window*

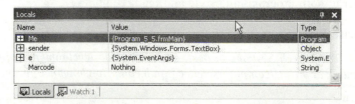

Figure 7–31b   *The Locals Debug Window*

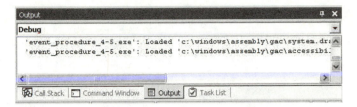

Figure 7–31c   *The Output Window*

Table 7–9   The Debug Windows

Name	Use
Immediate window	Displays information resulting from statements typed directly into this window. Useful for immediately determining the effect of a single-line statement. (Cannot accommodate multiline statements.) It is automatically opened in Break mode. Code can be dragged, copied, and pasted between the Code and Immediate windows, but code cannot be saved in the Immediate window.
Locals window	Automatically displays all of the declared variables and their values in the current procedure. The Locals window is automatically updated whenever a variable's value changes.
Output window	Displays the output from the Debug.WriteLine (*parameter*) method. This method call can be placed anywhere in a program. The parameter to this method can be a string or a variable.

make it so using the <u>T</u>oolbars option from the <u>V</u>iew menu, as shown in Figure 7–34. The Output window can be activated in Break mode from the <u>V</u>iew menu and then the Oth<u>e</u>r Windows option.

The Immediate, Output, and Locals windows are used in Break mode. In this mode a program's execution is temporarily suspended and the various Debug windows are used to gain a "snapshot" view of the values of variables and expressions at the point in your code where execution has been temporarily suspended. Once in a debug window, you can change the value of variables and properties to see how the changes affect the application.

Break mode can only be reached from Run time mode. In Break mode, program execution is suspended, giving you an opportunity to both view and edit code. You can always determine the mode you are in by examining the Visual Basic title bar. Figures 7–35a, –b, and –c show how the title bar looks in each of the three modes: Design, Run and Break.

The characteristics of each of the Visual Basic three operating modes, as they relate to the Visual Basic debugging facilities, are listed Table 7–10.

Figure 7–32 *Activating the Debug Windows from the Menu Bar*

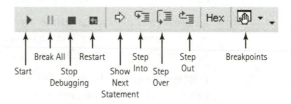

Figure 7–33 *The Debug Toolbar's Buttons*

Switching from one mode to another can be accomplished using the Menu option, Function keys, or Toolbar Buttons. For example, you already know how to switch from Design mode to Run mode by using either the <u>D</u>ebug menu option, then <u>S</u>tart, or pressing the F5 function key. Additionally, you can use one of the three Standard Toolbar functions illustrated in Figure 7–36 to switch between modes. Table 7–11 lists the Buttons that are active in each mode. Note that when in Break mode, the Start button becomes a Continue Button.

Breakpoints

A *breakpoint* is a designated statement at which program execution automatically stops and the mode switches from run to break. Once in break mode the Immediate or Local Debug window can be activated and either window used to both examine and alter one or more variable's value. The program can then be continued in single-step, step-over, or run mode.

Breakpoint statements are designated in either design or break mode in the Code window. This is accomplished by first placing the cursor on the designated line and either:

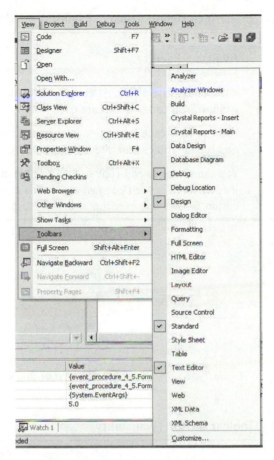

Figure 7–34   *Making the Debug Toolbar Visible*

Figure 7–35a   *Identifying the Current Mode—Design Mode*

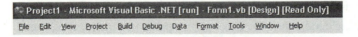

Figure 7–35b   *Identifying the Current Mode—Run Mode*

Figure 7–35c   *Identifying the Current Mode—Break Mode*

Table 7–10 Predefined Debug Window Facilities by Mode

Mode	Available Facility
Design	You can activate all three Debug windows and set breakpoints in the Code window. You can only execute code from within the Immediate window.
Run	You can view code by running in either single-step mode or by having set a breakpoint. You cannot directly access any of the Debug windows.
Break	You can view and edit code in the Code window. You can examine and modify data in all of the Debug windows. You can restart the program, end execution, or continue execution from the suspended point.

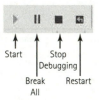

Figure 7–36 *The Standard Toolbar's Start, Break, and End Buttons*

Table 7–11 Toolbar Button Availability

Mode	Available Mode Buttons and Access Keys
Design	Start (F5 key)
Run	Break (Ctrl + Break Keys) and End
Break	Continue (F5 Key) and End

1. Pressing the F9 key, or

2. Right mouse clicking and selecting "Insert Breakpoint," or

3. Selecting the New Breakpoint option from the Debug menu

Once a statement has been designated as a breakpoint statement, it will be both highlighted in the Code window and bulleted in Code window's left-side margin. As an example of setting breakpoints, consider the event code illustrated in the Code window shown in Figure 7–37.

Note in Figure 7–37 that two statements are highlighted and each of these statements has a bullet mark in the Code window's left-side margin. The highlighting and

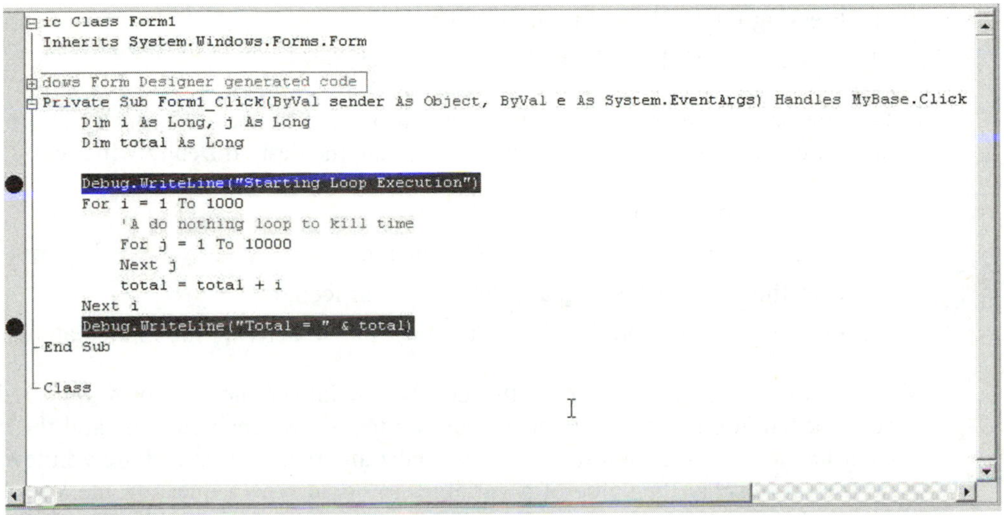

```
ic Class Form1
  Inherits System.Windows.Forms.Form

dows Form Designer generated code
Private Sub Form1_Click(ByVal sender As Object, ByVal e As System.EventArgs) Handles MyBase.Click
    Dim i As Long, j As Long
    Dim total As Long

    Debug.WriteLine("Starting Loop Execution")
    For i = 1 To 1000
        'A do nothing loop to kill time
        For j = 1 To 10000
        Next j
        total = total + i
    Next i
    Debug.WriteLine("Total = " & total)
End Sub

Class
```

Figure 7–37   *Event Code with Two Breakpoint Statements*

bulleting indicate that these two statements are breakpoint statements. This means that execution during run time will stop just prior to each statement being executed. When this occurs an appropriate Debug window can be activated for examining and modifying all program variables. Run time mode can then be restarted by pressing either the Run toolbar button (or the F5 key), the Step Into toolbar button (or the F11 key) for single-step execution, or the Step Over toolbar button (or the F10 key) if execution was suspended at a line that called either a **Sub** or **Function** procedure. (The Debug toolbar is shown in Figure 7–33.)

To explicitly clear breakpoints you must also be in either Design or Break mode. For specific breakpoints, place the cursor on the desired statement in the Code window and repeat one of the steps used to set the breakpoint. For example, if the breakpoint is on, the F9 key will toggle it off. To explicitly clear all breakpoints in a program, either:

1. Press the Ctrl +Shift+F9 keys at the same time
2. Select the Clear All Breakpoints option from the Debug menu

Note that breakpoints are saved when the file containing the code is saved.

To illustrate how breakpoints work, create and execute the program containing the code previously shown in Figure 7–37. Note that when the Form_Click event is activated the program suspends execution at the first breakpoint statement and opens up a Code window. Press the step-into toolbar button or F11. This will execute the Debug.Writeline ("Starting Loop Execution") method. Bring up the Output window. Note that the Starting Loop Execution line appears as the last entry on the window. Any subsequent use of the Writeline method will continue to generate output in this window. Now press the continue toolbar button to restart program execution. Note that the code contains a nested **For** loop that uses the inner loop simply to waste time. This gives you sufficient time to experiment moving into break mode by either:

1. Pressing the Break toolbar button, or
2. Pressing the Ctrl and Break keys at the same time

Try one or both of these methods to switch back to break mode once the program has been restarted. Once in break mode you activate the desired Debug window by

1. Clicking on the window, if it is visible,
2. Selecting the window from the View menu,
3. Selecting the window using a Debug toolbar icon, or
4. Pressing the Ctrl and G keys at the same time to activate the Immediate window.

Figure 7–38 illustrates how the Locals and Immediate windows appeared for one such switch into break mode. The Locals window shows each variable and the value that each has at the time the breakpoint was encountered. The Immediate window can also be used to display the value of a variable. To do so type a question mark and then the name of the variable. You can also change the value of a variable. Figure 7–38 shows how to display the value of the variable total and set it equal to 14. Clearly, the Locals window is easier to use because you don't have to enter a question mark to display the variable's value, as is required with the Immediate window. After you restart the program note that the program automatically switches back to Break mode once again just prior to executing the Debug statement located after the nested loop. This is because this statement is a **Breakpoint** statement.

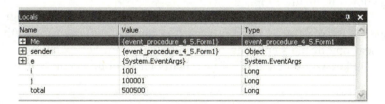

Figure 7–38a *The Locals Window*

Figure 7–38b *The Immediate Window*

> **Programmer Notes**
>
> *Creating and Clearing Breakpoint Statements:*
>
> **Breakpoint** statements are created and cleared using the same steps. In both cases you must either be in Design or Break mode. When you are on the desired line of code, either
>
> 1. Move the cursor to the gray margin to the left of the line of code and click,
> 2. Do a right mouse click and select "Insert Breakpoint," or
> 3. Press the F9 key.
>
> Each of these steps is a toggle that both selects and deselects a statement as a breakpoint. To clear all breakpoints in either Design or Break mode do one of the following:
>
> 1. Press the Ctrl +Shift+F9 keys at the same time
> 2. Select the Clear All Breakpoints option from the Debug menu
>
> Breakpoints are saved when the code containing the breakpoint is saved.

Step-Over Execution

A very useful debugging procedure in conjunction with single-stepping through a section of code is to use the Step Over toolbar Button whenever a call to a **Sub** procedure or function is encountered. The Step Over Button causes execution of the complete called procedure rather than stepping into it, but puts the program back into Break mode when the called procedure has completed execution. Thus, when you encounter a call to a general procedure and are interested in single stepping through the called procedure use the Step Into toolbar button; otherwise use the Step Over toolbar Button to complete the called procedure execution and move to the next executable statement in the calling procedure code.

7.8   Common Programming Errors

The common errors associated with general procedures are:

1. Forgetting to use the word **Sub** or **Function** on the declaration before the general procedure name.
2. Using an argument list that does not match with the general procedure parameter list. These errors fall into the following categories:
   a. The number of arguments is not the same as the number of parameters.
   b. The order of arguments and corresponding parameters do not match.
   c. The data types of arguments and corresponding parameters do not match.
3. Attempting to alter the value of a passed constant, expression, or function result. For example, assume that a general procedure named Area has the declaration:

```
Public Sub Area(ByRef radius As Single)
```

and is called using the statement:

```
Area(Rad)
```

Here, the value in `Rad` is referenced within the general procedure as the parameter `radius`. If the general procedure subsequently alters the value of radius, the value of `Rad` also is changed. This is a consequence of the fact that both `Rad` and `radius` reference the exact same storage location area.

Now assume that the general procedure is called using the following statement:

```
Area(3.62)
```

Here the value in `radius` cannot be changed within `Area`. An attempt to do so is essentially an attempt to redefine the value of the constant 3.62, usually causing a run-time error.

4. Inadvertently changing the value of a parameter inside a general procedure when the calling unit did not expect the change. This is an unwanted side effect that can be avoided by passing argument values by value, rather than by reference.

7.9 Chapter Review

Key Terms

arguments	global variables
ByRef	local scope
ByVal	local variables
call by reference	module-level variables
call by value	parameters
called procedure	recursive procedures
calling procedure	scope
form-level variables	stack
formal argument	**Static**
function procedure	static variables
general procedure	**Sub** procedure

Summary

1. The most commonly used syntax for a general **Sub** procedure is:

   Public Sub *Name(Parameter List)*
       Visual Basic statements in here
   End Sub

   Even if the **Sub** procedure has no parameter list, the parentheses must be present.
2. A general **Sub** procedure is called using a Calling statement having the form:

   procedure-name(argument list)

The arguments in the calling statement may be constants, variables, or expressions using combinations of constants and variables. The data type, number, and order of the arguments used in the calling statement must agree with the data type, number, and order of the corresponding parameters in the general procedure argument list.

3. Except for constants, arguments may be passed by reference or by value. When passed by value (**ByVal**), the called procedure is passed a copy of the argument variable and cannot change the original value. When passed by reference (**ByRef**), the called procedure can change the argument value. For example, the declaration:

```
Public Sub Test(ByVal radius As Single)
```

declares that the radius parameter is passed by value. If the called procedure is returning a value in the variable, the parameter should be declared **ByRef**. Otherwise, it is safer to use **ByVal** so you don't mistakenly change the argument value.

4. All functions (intrinsic and user-written) calculate and directly return a single value. The most commonly used syntax for a user-written function is:

```
Public Function function-name(Parameter List) As Data-type
    optional variable declarations

    optional executable statements
    Return value
  End Function
```

5. A function is called by using its name and passing any data to it in the parentheses following the name.

6. The arguments passed to a function must agree in type, order, and number with the function parameters.

7. Every variable used in a procedure has a *scope*, determining where in the program the variable can be used. The scope of a variable is either *local* or *module-level* and is determined by where the variable definition statement is placed. A local variable is defined within a procedure and can only be used within its defining procedure. A module-level variable is defined outside a procedure. If the module-level variable is declared as **Private**, it can be used by any procedure located on the same module in which it is declared. If it is declared as **Public**, it can be used by every procedure on any module in the project. Global variables are also referred to as *module-level* variables.

8. Global variables are in scope for the life of the application. Local variables are effectively destroyed when they go out of scope. To keep a local variable's value from being destroyed, the variable can be declared as `Static`.

9. Procedures also have scope. **Private** procedures can only be called from procedures residing on the same module as the **Private** procedure, while **Public** procedures can be called by every procedure in the application, regardless of the module containing the calling procedure.

10. A recursive solution is one in which the solution can be expressed in terms of a "simpler" version of itself. A recursive algorithm must always specify:
    a. The first case or cases
    b. How the *n*th case is related to the (*n* − 1) case
11. If a problem solution can be expressed repetitively or recursively with equal ease, the repetitive solution is preferable because it executes faster and uses less memory. In many advanced applications, recursion is simpler to visualize and the only practical means of implementing a solution.

Test Yourself—Short Answer

1. General Procedures can be placed in any of three different places: (a) _____, (b) _____, and (c) _____ modules.
2. Explain the difference between a **Sub** procedure designated as **Public** and one designated as **Private**.
3. Data can be exchanged between the calling procedure and the procedure being called through the use of the _____.
4. Consider the statement XYZ(x, y, z) and the procedure declaration

   ```
   Public Sub XYZ(ByRef x As integer, ByVal y As integer, ByRef z
   As integer)
   ```

   Will the procedure XYZ be able to make changes to any of the values of **x** or **y** or **z**?_____. Why or why not?_____

5. Explain the difference between passing arguments by value and passing arguments by reference.
6. Determine what characters are assigned to strMessage for the statement

   ```
   strMessage = "The Cat in the Hat".Substring(2,1)
   ```

7. Determine what value is assigned to strindex for the statement

   ```
   strindex = "The Cat in the Hat".IndexOf("t")
   ```

8. Determine what characters are assigned to strMessage for the statement

   ```
   strMessage =  "  The Cat in the Hat ".Trim
   ```

9. Write a **Calling** statement that could be used to call the **Sub** procedure having the declaration

   ```
   Public Sub Message(ByVal x As string, ByVal y As integer)
   ```

10. Write a **Sub** procedure declaration and a **Calling** statement for a procedure called Mine having a single precision parameter named price. The corresponding argument used in calling Mine is named dollar.

Programming Projects

1. Qualification for a loan from a local bank is based upon criteria with respect to employment, home ownership, major credit cards, and assets. Points are awarded or taken away based upon responses to questions about the above categories.

   Loan Criteria:

   With respect to employment, if the applicant has full-time employment, award one point and display a text box to input number of years at present employer. If the applicant has been employed at least three years, award an additional point; at least six years, award an additional two points; more than 10 years, award an additional three points. (Applicant can receive 1, 2, 3, or 4 points for full-time employment.)

   With respect to home ownership, award two points if applicant owns home, zero points otherwise.

   With respect to major credit cards, these conditions apply for EACH credit card (MasterCard, VISA, AMEX): award one point with credit balance less than $500; deduct one point for credit balance at least $500; deduct two points for credit balance at least $3000; deduct three points for credit balance at least $5000. The applicant receives either $+1$, -1, -2, or 3 points depending upon the credit balance of the credit card. Display a text box to input credit balance for each check box that is selected.

   With respect to financial assets, these conditions apply for EACH instance: award one point if asset is at least 20% of loan amount; award two points is asset is at least 50% of loan amount; award three points if asset is at least 100% of loan amount. Display a text box to input asset amount for each check box that is selected. The applicant gets either 0, 1, 2, or 3 points depending upon the size of the asset with respect to the amount of the loan.

   The applicant will qualify for a loan if the number of points awarded totals at least eight. Use a text box to display an appropriate message that the applicant has either qualified or not qualified for a loan. Figure 7–39 shows the interface for this project.

   Program Requirements:

   The user should be able to check/uncheck choices in any order so that if a change is made, the appropriate category points are recalculated. (*Hint:* This can be done in the CheckBox and Radio Button **Click** event procedures.)

   Use **Sub** functions to calculate points for credit card and asset balances. The same Sub function should be called to calculate the appropriate number of points for each credit card account that is listed on the application form. For each asset listed by the applicant, the same **Sub** function should be called to calculate the appropriate number of points. These **Sub** functions should be placed in a standard module.

2. The Texas Fence Company has asked you to write a program that will calculate the amount of materials needed for a fence given its length and width. (See Figure 7–40.)

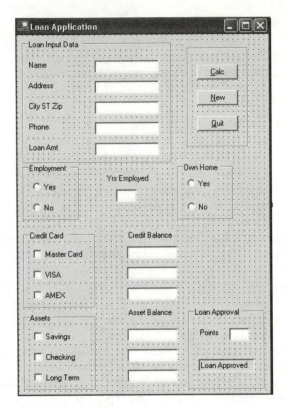

Figure 7–39 *Form for Programming Project 1*

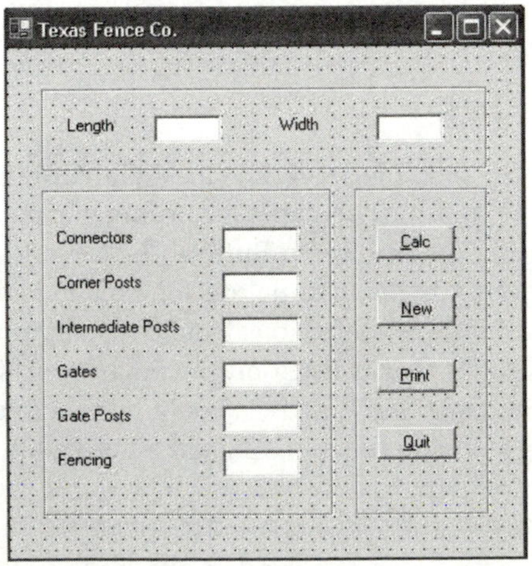

Figure 7–40 *Form for Programming Project 2*

Project Property Table

Object	Property	Setting
Form	Name	frmFence
	Text	Texas Fence Co.
GroupBox	Name	grpInput
Label	Name	lblLength
	Text	Length
TextBox	Name	txtLength
	Text	(blank)
Label	Name	lblWidth
	Text	Width
TextBox	Name	txWidth
	Text	(blank)
GroupBox	Name	grpOutput
Label	Name	lblConnectors
	Text	Connectors
TextBox	Name	txtConnectors
	Text	(blank)
Label	Name	lblCornerPosts
	Text	Corner Posts
TextBox	Name	txtCornerPosts
	Text	(blank)
Label	Name	lblIntermediatePosts
	Text	Intermediate Posts
TextBox	Name	txtIntermediatePosts
	Text	(blank)
Label	Name	lblGates
	Text	Gates
TextBox	Name	txtGates
	Text	(blank)
Label	Name	lblGatePosts
	Text	Gate Posts
TextBox	Name	txtGatePosts
	Text	(blank)
Label	Name	lblFencing
	Text	Fencing
TextBox	Name	txtFencing
	Text	(blank)
GroupBox	Name	grpCommands
Button	Name	btnCalc
	Text	&Calc
Button	Name	btnNew
	Text	&New
Button	Name	btnPrint
	Text	&Print
Button	Name	btnQuit
	Text	&Quit

Figure 7–40 *(continued)*

Requirements:

All fences are rectangular and the gate (only one) is always placed on the longer side. The gate occupies four linear feet. Every fence contains four corner fence posts, two gate posts, and one gate.

Fence posts that are neither corner posts nor gate posts are called intermediate posts. The fence may contain intermediate fence posts depending upon the length of fencing required. The maximum distance between any two fence posts (corner, intermediate, and gate) is 10 feet. Therefore, if the length of a side is 10 feet or less, no intermediate fence post is required for that side.

Three connectors are required at each intermediate fence post, three connectors are required at each gate post, and six connectors are required at each corner fence post.

Your output should display the number of connectors, corner posts, intermediate posts, corner posts, gate posts, gates (only one for this problem) and fencing. You may assume that the length and width are sufficient to include a four-foot gate. Declare global variables to hold values of length, width, number of connectors, number of corner posts, number of intermediate posts, number of gate posts, and amount of fencing.

Because specifications for constructing a fence may change in the future, use constants to represent the number of connectors needed for each type of fence post. Perform all calculations in a **Sub** procedure. Store the **Sub** procedure in a standard module.

3. This assignment is a modification to Project 2. In addition to computing the number of fence components needed for a given job, your program should also compute the corresponding cost for each component. Use the following unit costs in your program.

Material Cost per Unit:

Connector	$ .75
Corner post	$6.50
Intermediate post	$5.00
Gatepost	$7.50
Gate	$35.00
Fencing	$1.00 per linear foot

Your program should permit at most two gates; if two gates are required, they should not be placed between the same pair of corner posts. Because cost of materials will certainly change in the future, you should use constants to represent the unit costs for fence materials, and perform all calculations in a **Sub** procedure. (See Figure 7–41.)

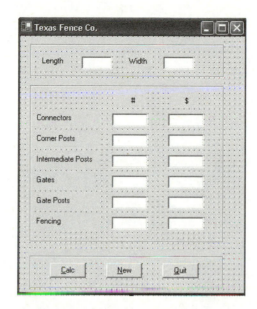

Figure 7–41 *Form for Programming Project 3*

Structured Data

The variables that we have used so far have all had a common characteristic: each could store only one value at a time. For example, although the variables key, count, and grade declared in the statements

```
Dim key As String
Dim count As Integer
Dim grade As Single
```

are of different data types, each variable can store only one value of the declared data type. These types of variables are called atomic *or* scalar *variables. An atomic variable is a variable whose value cannot be further subdivided or separated into a legitimate data type.*

Another method of storing and retrieving data is to use a data structure. A data structure *is a data type whose values can be decomposed into individual data elements, each of which is either atomic or another data structure, and provides an access scheme for locating individual data elements within the structure. One of the simplest and most widely used data structures, an* array, *consists of a set of logically related individual items, all of which have the same data type. Table 8–1 illustrates three groups of items. The first group is a list of five single precision temperatures, the second group is a list of four character codes, and the last group is a list of six integer grades.*

In this chapter we describe how arrays are declared, initialized, stored inside a computer, and used. We also introduce structures. A structure *is a user-defined data type whose elements need not all be of the same data type. Both arrays and structures require the Visual Basic built-in procedural operations for individual element access and manipulation. In Chapter 12 we present an advanced data structure, referred to as a* Class, *that requires the programmer to define both the type of data and the operations that can be used on the individual elements in the data structure.*

8.1 One-Dimensional Arrays

A *one-dimensional* array, also referred to as either a *single-dimensional* array or a vector, is a list of related values with the same data type stored using a single group

Table 8–1 Three Individual Lists

Temperatures	Codes	Grades
95.75	Z	98
83.0	C	87
97.625	K	92
72.5	L	79
86.25		85
		72

Table 8–2   A List of Grades

Grades
98
87
92
79
85
72

name.[1] In Visual Basic, as in other computer languages, the group name is referred to as the array name. Consider the list of grades illustrated in Table 8–2.

All the grades in this list are integer numbers and must be declared as such. However, the individual items in the list do not have to be declared separately. The items in the list can be declared as a single unit and stored under a common variable name called the array name. For convenience, we choose `grades` as the name for the list shown in Table 8–2.

Each item in an array is called an *element* of the array. The individual elements stored in the array illustrated in Figure 8–1 are stored sequentially, with the first array element stored in the first reserved location, the second element stored in the second reserved location, and so on, until the last element is stored in the last reserved location. This sequential storage allocation for the list is a key feature of arrays because it provides a simple mechanism for easily locating any single element in the list. Because elements in the array are stored sequentially, any individual element can be accessed by giving the name of the array and the element's position. This position is called the element's *index* or *index value* (the two terms are synonymous).

The general syntax for declaring a one-dimensional array is:

```
Dim arrayname(upper-index) As data-type
```

For example, the declaration

```
Dim grades(5) As Integer
```

specifies that `grades` is to store six individual integer values, with array indices 0 through 5. Note that this **Declaration** statement gives the array name, the data type of the items in the array, and the value of the largest index. Figure 8–1 illustrates the `grades` array in memory with the correct designation for each array element. Note that the number of elements in the array is `upper-index` + 1.

The first element of the `grades` array has an index of 0, the second element has an index of 1, and so on.

---

[1]Note that lists can be implemented in a variety of ways. An array is simply one implementation of a list in which all of the list elements are of the same type and each element is stored consecutively in a set of contiguous memory locations.

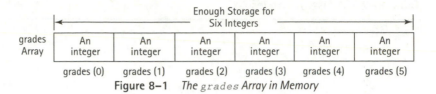

Figure 8–1   *The* `grades` *Array in Memory*

Programmer Notes

Structured Data Types

In contrast to atomic types, such as integer and single precision data, there are structured types. A *structured type,* which is sometimes referred to as a *data structure,* is any type whose values can be decomposed and are related by some defined structure. Additionally, operations must be available for retrieving and updating individual values in the data structure.

Single-dimensional arrays are examples of a structured type. In a single-dimensional array, such as an array of integers, the array is composed of individual integer values, where integers are related by their position in the list. Indexed variables provide the means of accessing and modifying values in the array.

In Visual Basic, the array name and index of the desired element are combined by listing the index in parentheses after the array name. For example, given the declaration

```
Dim grades(5) As Integer
```

grades(0) refers to the first grade stored in the grades array,
grades(1) refers to the second grade stored in the grades array,
grades(2) refers to the third grade stored in the grades array,
grades(3) refers to the fourth grade stored in the grades array,
grades(4) refers to the fifth grade stored in the grades array,
grades(5) refers to the sixth grade stored in the grades array.

The indexed variable, grades(0), is read as "grades sub zero." This is a shortened way of saying "the grades array indexed by zero," and distinguishes the first element in an array from an atomic variable that could be declared as grades0. Similarly, grades(1) is read as "grades sub one," grades(2) is read as "grades sub two," grades(3) as "grades sub three," and so on. In some programs, it may make more sense to ignore the first element of the array (e.g., grades(0)) and just use grades(1) through grades(5) when five grades need to be processed.

Where To Declare Arrays

Arrays may be declared at the same places and have the same scope as scalar variables. An array declared within a procedure is local to the procedure and can be accessed only from within the procedure unless it is passed as an argument to another procedure. An array declared outside of a procedure will have either module or project scope, depending on the keyword used to declare the array. If the `Dim` keyword is used, the array will have module scope (that is, it can be accessed from any procedure in the module); otherwise, if the `Public` keyword is used, the array will have *project scope* (that is, it can be accessed from *any* procedure in any module attached to the project). Additionally, to create a local static array (one that will retain the values of its elements between procedure calls) the array can be declared as **Static** within a procedure. Table 8–3 summarizes this information.

All of our programs will declare arrays at either the Procedure or Module level.

Using Indexed Variables

Array variables can be used anywhere that scalar variables are valid. Examples using the elements of the grades array are:

```
grades(0) = 98
grades(1) = grades(1) - 11
grades(2) = grades(2)/2
grades(3) = 79
grades(3) = (grades(0) + grades(1) + grades(2)) / 2.2
sum = grades(0) + grades(1) + grades(2) + grades(3)
```

The index contained within parentheses need not be an integer constant; any expression that evaluates to an integer may be used as an index. In each case the value of the expression must be within the valid index range defined when the array is declared. For example, assuming that i and j are integer variables, the following indexed variables are valid:

```
grades(i)
grades(2*i)
grades(j-i)
```

If an array `grades` is declared with an upper bound of 5 and the program tries to access `grades (6)`, a run-time error will occur that indicates the index is outside the bounds of the array.

Table 8–3 Declaring Arrays

Placement	Keyword	Scope
Within a Procedure	`Dim`	Procedure Level
Within a Procedure	`Static`	Procedure Level but retains values
Declaration section of the General code object	`Dim`	Module Level
Declaration section of the General code object	`Public`	Project Level

One extremely important advantage of using integer expressions as indices is that it allows sequencing through an array by using a loop. This makes statements such as

```
sum = grades(0) + grades(1) + grades(2) + grades(3) + grades(4) + grades(5)
```

unnecessary. The index values in this statement can be replaced by a **For** loop counter to access each element in the array sequentially. For example, the code

```
sum = 0                      ' initialize the sum to zero
For  i = 0 To 5
  sum = sum + grades(i)      ' add in a grade value
Next i
```

sequentially retrieves each array element and adds the element to sum. Here the variable i is used both as the counter in the For loop and as an index. As i increases by one each time through the loop, the next element in the array is referenced. The procedure for adding the array elements within the For loop is similar to the accumulation procedure we have used many times before.

The advantage of using a For loop to sequence through an array becomes apparent when working with larger arrays. For example, if the grades array contained 100 values rather than just six, simply changing the number 5 to 99 in the For statement is sufficient to sequence through the 100 elements and add each grade value to the sum.

As another example of using a For loop to sequence through an array, assume that we want to locate the maximum value in an array of 1000 elements named grades. The procedure we will use to locate the maximum value is to assume initially that the first element in the array is the largest number. Then, as we sequence through the array, the maximum is compared to each element. When an element with a higher value is located, that element becomes the new maximum. The following code does the job.

```
maximum = grades(0)               ' set the maximum to element one
For  i = 1 To 999                 ' cycle through the rest of the array
  If grades(i) > maximum   Then   ' compare each element to the maximum
    maximum = grades(i)           ' capture the new high value
  End If
Next i
```

In this code, the For statement consists of one If statement. The first element in the array (grades(0)) is set to the maximum so the For loop starts with i equal to 1 instead of 0. The search for a new maximum value starts with the second element of the array and continues through the last element. Each element is compared to the current maximum, and when a higher value is encountered, it becomes the new maximum.

Input and Output of Array Values

Individual array values can be assigned values and have their values displayed in the same manner used for scalar variables. Examples of individual **Data** assignment statements include:

```
grades(0) = Val(InputBox("Enter a value for grade 0", "Input request", "0"))
grades(1) =   96.5
grades(2) = grades(1) * 1.2
```

In the first statement a single value will be read and stored in the indexed variable named `grades(0)`. The second statement causes the value 96.5 to be in the indexed variable `grades(1)`, while the last statement multiplies `grades(1)` by 1.2 and assigns the value of this computation to `grades(2)`.

Typically, for interactive data input, a loop is used to cycle through the array, and each pass through the loop is used to assign a value to an array element. For example, the code

```
message = "Enter a grade"
For i = 0 To 5
   grades(i) = Val(InputBox(message, "Input Dialog", "0"))
Next i
```

prompts the user for six grades. The first value entered is stored in `grades(0)`, the second value entered in `grades(1)`, and so on until six grades have been input.

During output, individual array elements can be displayed in a ListBox control and complete sections of the array can be displayed by including a *listboxname*. `Items.Add` method within a loop. With a list box named `lstDisplay`, examples of this are:

```
lstDisplay.Items.Add(grades(2))
```

and

```
lstDisplay.Items.Add("The value of element " & i  & " is " & grades(i))
```

and

```
Dim amount(19) as Integer, k as Integer

For k = 5 To 19
   lstDisplay.Items.Add(k & "   "  & amount(k))
Next k
```

The first statement displays the value of the indexed variable `grades(2)`. The second statement displays the value of the index `i` and the value of `grades(i)`. Before this statement can be executed, `i` would have to have an assigned value. Finally, the last statement includes an `Add` method within a `For` loop. Both the value of the index and the value of the elements from 5 to 19 are displayed.

Program 8-1 illustrates these input and output techniques, using an array named `grades` that is defined to store six integer numbers. Included in the program are two

Figure 8–2 *Program 8–1's Interface*

Table 8–4   Program 8–1's Properties Table

Object	Property	Setting
Form	Name	frmMain
	Text	Program 8–1
ListBox	Name	lstDisplay
Button	Name	btnExecute
	Text	&Execute
Button	Name	btnExit
	Text	E&xit

For loops. The first For loop is used to cycle through each array element and allows the user to input individual array values. After six values have been entered, the second **For** loop is used to display the stored values. Figure 8–2 shows the interface for Program 8–1 and Table 8–4 lists the objects and properties for this program.

Program 8–1's Event Code

```
Const MAXGRADES As Integer = 5
Dim grades(MAXGRADES) as Integer

Private Sub btnExecute_Click(ByVal sender As Object, _
    ByVal e As System.EventArgs) Handles btnExecute.Click
  ' preconditions - MAXGRADES and grades() set at the module level
```

```
   Dim i As Integer

   For i = 0 To MAXGRADES ' Enter the grades
      grades(i) = Val(InputBox("Enter a grade", "Input Dialog", "0"))
   Next i

   For i = 0 To MAXGRADES  ' Print the grades
      lstDisplay.Items.Add("grades(" & i & ") is " & grades(i))
   Next i
End Sub

Private Sub btnExit_Click(ByVal sender As Object,_
     ByVal e As System.EventArgs) Handles btnExit.Click
   Beep()
   End
End Sub
```

A sample run of Program 8–1 produced the output illustrated in Figure 8–3.

In reviewing the output produced by Program 8-1, pay particular attention to the difference between the index value displayed and the numerical value stored in the corresponding array element. The index value refers to the location of the element in the array, while the indexed variable refers to the value stored in the designated location.

In addition to simply displaying the values stored in each array element, the elements can also be processed by appropriately referencing the desired element. For

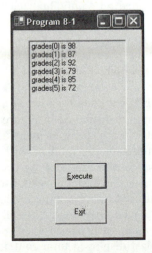

Figure 8–3   *A Sample Output Using Program 8–1*

example, assume that the `btnExecute_Click` event procedure in Program 8–1 is modified to Procedure Code 8–1 as follows:

Procedure Code 8–1

```
Private Sub btnExecute_Click(ByVal sender As Object, _
    ByVal e As System.EventArgs) Handles btnExecute.Click
  ' preconditions - MAXGRADES and grades() set at the module level
  Dim i, total As Integer
  Dim basestring, message As String

  basestring = "Enter grade"
  For i = 0 To MAXGRADES   ' Enter the grades
    message = basestring + "(" + Str(i) + ")"
    grades(i) = Val(InputBox(message, "Input Dialog", "0"))
  Next i

  lstDisplay.Items.Clear()
  lstDisplay.Items.Add("The total of the grades")
  For i = 0 To MAXGRADES    ' Print the grades
    lstDisplay.Items.Add(grades(i))
    total = total + grades(i)
  Next i
  lstDisplay.Items.Add("is " & total)
End Sub
```

In this modified code the value of each element is accumulated in a total, displayed upon completion of the individual display of each array element. Also note in this event code that we have included an "individualized" message within the `InputBox` function by concatenating the string version of the index i plus one to the output message. Thus, the message displayed in the first `InputBox` will be `Enter grade(0)`, the message displayed in the second input request will be `Enter grade(1)`, and so on. This event code is used in Program 8–2, which is identical in all respects to Program 8–1, except for the form's caption and the new `btnExecute_Click` event procedure. A sample output produced by executing this event code is shown in Figure 8–4.

Note that in the output displayed in Figure 8–4, unlike that shown in Figure 8–3, only the values stored in each array element are displayed. Although the second `For` loop was used to accumulate the total of each element, the accumulation also could have been accomplished in the first loop by placing the statement `total = total + grade(i)` after the `InputBox` function was used to enter a value. Also note that the `lstDisplay` statement used to display the total is made outside of the second `For` loop, so that the total is displayed only once, after all values have been added to the total. If this `lstDisplay` statement were placed inside of the `For` loop, six totals would be displayed, with only the last displayed total containing the sum of all of the array values. In all the programs using the grades array, because the array is declared as Integer and

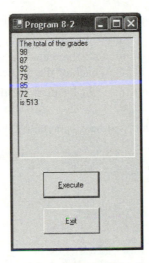

Figure 8–4 *A Sample Output Using Program 8–2*

the `Inputbox` function returns a string, the `Val` function is used to convert the string to a numerical value.

Exercises 8.1

1. Using the `Dim` keyword, write array declarations for the following:
   a. a list of 100 single-precision grades
   b. a list of 50 single-precision temperatures
   c. a list of 30 characters, each representing a code
   d. a list of 100 integer years
   e. a list of 32 single-precision velocities
   f. a list of 1000 single-precision distances
   g. a list of 6 integer code numbers

2. Write appropriate notation for the first, third, and seventh elements of the following arrays:
   a. `Dim grade(20) As Integer`
   b. `Dim grade(10) As Single`
   c. `Dim amps(16) As Single`
   d. `Dim distance(15) As Integer`
   e. `Dim velocity(25) As Single`
   f. `Dim time(100) As Single`

3. a. Write individual `InputBox` function calls that can be used to enter values into the first, third, and seventh elements of each of the arrays in Exercises 2a through 2f.

b. Write a `For` loop that can be used to enter values for the complete array in Exercise 2a.

4. a. Write individual statements that can be used to print the values from the first, third, and seventh elements of each of the arrays in Exercises 2a through 2f.

b. Write a `For` loop that can be used to display values for the complete array in Exercise 2a.

5. List the elements that will be displayed by the following sections of code:

a.
```
For m = 0 To 4
    lstDisplay.Items.Add(a(m))
Next m
```

b.
```
For  k = 0 To 4 Step 2
   lstDisplay.Items.Add(a(k))
Next k
```

c.
```
For j = 3 To 10 Step 1
   lstDisplay.Items.Add(b(j))
Next j
```

d.
```
For  k = 3 To 12  Step 3
   lstDisplay.Items.Add(b(k))
Next k
```

e.
```
For i = 2 To 11 Step 2
    lstDisplay.Items.Add(c(i))
Next i
```

Note to Students: For Exercises 6–12, display the output in a ListBox control.

6. a. Write a program to input the following values into an array named `prices`: 10.95, 16.32, 12.15, 8.22, 15.98, 26.22, 13.54, 6.45, 17.59. After the data has been entered, have your program output the values.

b. Repeat Exercise 6a, but after the data has been entered, have your program display it in the following form:

10.95 16.32 12.15

8.22 15.98 26.22

13.54 6.45 17.59

7. Write a program to input eight integer numbers into an array named `temp`. As each number is input, add the numbers into a total. After all numbers are input, display the numbers and their average.

8. a. Write a program to input 10 integer numbers into an array named `fmax` and determine the maximum value entered. Your program should contain only one loop and the maximum should be determined as array element values are being input. (*Hint:* Set the maximum equal to the first array element, which should be input before the loop used to input the remaining array values.)

b. Repeat Exercise 8a, keeping track of both the maximum element in the array and the index number for the maximum. After displaying the numbers, print these two messages

```
The maximum value is: ____
```

```
This is element number ____ in the list of numbers
```

Have your program display the correct values in place of the underlines in the messages.

c. Repeat Exercise 8b, but have your program locate the minimum of the data entered.

9. a. Write a program to input the following integer numbers into an array named grades: 89, 95, 72, 83, 99. As each number is input, add the numbers to a total. After all numbers are input and the total is obtained, calculate the average of the numbers and use the average to determine the deviation of each value from the average. Store each deviation in an array named deviation. Each deviation is obtained as the element value less the average of all the data. Have your program display each deviation alongside its corresponding element from the grades array.

b. Calculate the variance of the data used in Exercise 9a. The variance is obtained by squaring each individual deviation and dividing the sum of the squared deviations by the number of deviations.

10. Write a program that stores the following prices in an array named prices: 9.92, 6.32, 12.63, 5.95, 10.29. Your program should also create two arrays named units and amounts, each capable of storing five double precision numbers. Using a **For** loop and an InputBox function call, have your program accept five user-input numbers into the units array when the program is run. Your program should store the product of the corresponding values in the prices and units arrays in the amounts array (for example, amounts(1) = prices(1) * units(1)) and display the following output (fill in the table appropriately):

Price	Units	Amount
9.92	.	.
6.32	.	.
12.63	.	.
5.95	.	.
10.29	.	.

Total: .

11. Write a program that specifies three one-dimensional arrays named prices, quantity, and amount. Each array should be capable of holding 10 elements. Using a **For** loop, input values for the prices and quantity arrays. The entries in the amount array should be the product of the corresponding values in the prices and

quantity arrays (thus, `amount(i) = price(i) * quantity(i)`). After all of the data has been entered, display the following output:

```
Price           Quantity        Amount

-----           --------        ------
```

Under each column heading, display the appropriate value.

12. a. Write a program that inputs 10 float numbers into an array named `raw`. After 10 user-input numbers are entered into the array, your program should cycle through raw 10 times. During each pass through the array, your program should select the lowest value in `raw` and place the selected value in the next available slot in an array named `sorted`. Thus, when your program is complete, the sorted array should contain the numbers in `raw` in sorted order from lowest to highest. (*Hint:* Make sure to reset the lowest value selected during each pass to a very high number so that it is not selected again. You will need a second **For** loop within the first **For** loop to locate the minimum value for each pass.)

   b. The method used in Exercise 12a to sort the values in the array is very inefficient. Can you determine why? What might be a better method of sorting the numbers in an array?

8.2   Additional Array Capabilities

The sizes of all the arrays we have considered have been declared at design time. There are times, however, when you might want to set the array size during run time based on user input, rather than at design time. How this is done is described in this section. Also described is the method for passing local arrays into procedures as arguments. Finally, additional array processing techniques are presented, including the declaration and processing of multidimensional arrays.

Dynamic Arrays

There are times when you, as a designer, will not know how large an array must be. Fortunately, Visual Basic provides a means of changing an array size at run time. Such arrays are referred to as *dynamic arrays*. A dynamic array can be resized at any time during program execution. For example, you might need a very large array for a short period of time. Rather than allocate a fixed array size that will remain in effect throughout the program execution, you can create a dynamic array. Then, when you no longer need the array, you can redimension it to a smaller size.

The method for creating a dynamic array is fairly simple. First, declare the array as either global or local. The difference in creating a dynamic array is to give it an empty dimension value. For example, the declaration

```
Dim Dynar() As Integer, n As Integer
```

creates a dynamic integer array named `Dynar`. To actually set the size of the array you must use the `ReDim` statement, which can only appear within a procedure. The `ReDim` statement is an executable statement that redimensions the size of the array at run time. For example, the statements:

```
n = Val(InputBox("Enter the number of grades", "Input Dialog", "0"))
ReDim Dynar(n)
```

will cause the `Dynar` array to have the number of elements entered by the user in response to the input dialog request. Similarly, the statement:

```
ReDim Dynar(10)
```

causes the `Dynar` array to be redimensioned to accommodate 10 integers.

UBound is a function provided by Visual Basic for determining the largest available index value of an array. The function name is derived from Upper Bound. For example, if the array `test` is declared using the declaration statement:

```
Dim test(10) As Integer
```

then `UBound(test)` will return a value of 10. This function is useful with dynamic arrays. Arrays also have a **Length** property that returns the size of the array, which is the number of elements in the array. Given the `test` array, `test.Length` returns 11, or `UBound(test)+1`.

Unless specific steps are taken to preserve the values in a dynamic array, these values will be lost when the array is redimensioned. If you want to resize an array without losing the existing element values, use the `Preserve` keyword. Thus, the statement

```
ReDim Preserve Dynar(UBound(Dynar) + 15)
```

enlarges the `Dynar` array by 15 elements without losing the existing element values.

Arrays as Arguments

An individual array element can be passed to a general procedure (**Sub** and **Function**) in the same manner as any scalar variable. For a single array element this is done by including the element as an indexed variable in a procedure call statement's argument list. For example, the procedure call

```
Fmax(temp(2),temp(4))
```

makes the individual array elements `temp(2)` and `temp(4)` available to the **Fmax** procedure.

Passing a complete array to a procedure is, in many respects, an easier operation than passing individual elements. For example, if `temp` is an array, the statement `Fmax(temp)` makes the complete `temp` array available to the **Fmax** procedure.

On the receiving side, the called procedure must be alerted that an array is being made available. For example, assuming `temp` was declared as `Dim temp(4) As Integer`, a suitable procedure heading and parameter declaration for the **Fmax** procedure is:

```
Public Sub Fmax(ByVal vals() As Integer)
```

In this procedure heading, the parameter name `vals` is local to the procedure. However, `vals` refers to the original array created outside the procedure. This is made clear in Procedure Code 8-2, where the `temp` array that is declared local to the `frmMain_Click` event procedure is passed to the `Fmax` procedure.

Procedure Code 8-2

```
Private Sub frmMain_Click(ByVal sender As Object, _
    ByVal e As System.EventArgs) Handles MyBase.Click
  Dim temp() As Integer = {2, 18, 1, 27, 6}

  Fmax(temp)
End Sub

Public Sub Fmax(ByVal vals() As Integer)
  Dim i, max As Integer

  max = vals(0)
  For i = 1 To 4
    If max < vals(i) Then max = vals(i)
  Next i
  lstDisplay.Items.Add("The maximum value is " & max)
End Sub
```

Only one array is created in Procedure Code 8-2. In the `frmMain_Click` procedure this array is known as `temp`, and in `Fmax`, the array is known as `vals`. As illustrated in Figure 8-5, both names refer to the same array. Thus, in Figure 8-5 `vals(3)` is the

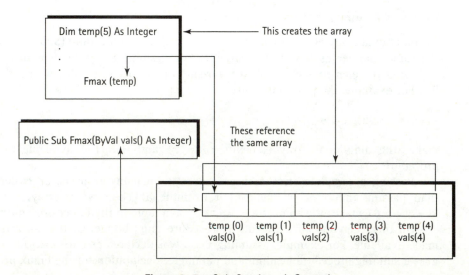

Figure 8-5 *Only One Array Is Created*

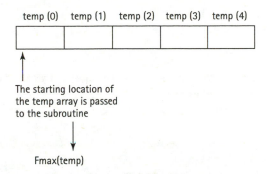

temp (0) temp (1) temp (2) temp (3) temp (4)

The starting location of
the temp array is passed
to the subroutine

Fmax(temp)

Figure 8–6 *The Starting Location of the Array Is Passed*

same element as `temp(3)`. So when an array is passed as a parameter to a procedure, declaring it as **ByVal** does not restrict the procedure from modifying the passed array elements. The called procedure can change any or all of the elements of the array. In the **Fmax** procedure above, if there was a statement

```
vals(4) = 0
```

the value of `temp(4)` would be changed to 0.

Note that the array declaration statement for `temp` and the five statements used to initialize the array elements can be replaced by the following statement which uses { } (curly brackets) instead of parentheses and does not specify the length of the array:

```
Dim temp() = {2,18,1,27,6}
```

Note that the parameter declaration for `vals` in `Fmax` does not contain the number of elements in the array. This makes sense when you realize that only one item is actually passed to `Fmax` when the procedure is called. As you might have suspected, the item passed is the starting location of the `temp` array. This is illustrated in Figure8–6.

Now let us generalize `Fmax` to find and return the maximum value of an integer array of arbitrary size. Consider Procedure Code 8–3.

Procedure Code 8–3

```
Private Sub frmMain_Click(ByVal sender As Object, _
    ByVal e As System.EventArgs) Handles MyBase.Click
  Dim temp(4), maximum As Integer

  temp(0) = 2
  temp(1) = 18
  temp(2) = 1
  temp(3) = 27
  temp(4) = 6
```

```
    Fmax(temp, 5, maximum)
    lstDisplay.Items.Add("The maximum value is " & maximum)
End Sub

Public Sub Fmax(ByVal vals() As Integer, ByVal final As Integer, _
    ByRef max As Integer)
  Dim i As Integer

  max = vals(0)
  For i = 1 To final - 1
    If max < vals(i) Then max = vals(i)
  Next i
End Sub
```

The more general form of Fmax listed in Procedure Code 8–3 returns the maximum value in any single-dimensioned integer array passed to it. The procedure expects that an integer array and the number of elements in the array will be passed into it as arguments. Then, using the number of elements as the boundary for its search, the procedure's For loop causes each array element to be examined in sequential order to locate the maximum value. This value is passed back to the calling routine through the third argument in the function call. The output displayed when the code is executed is:

```
The maximum value is 27
```

max must be passed by reference (ByRef) because the calculated value stored in max is used by the calling procedure. In this example, the other parameters were declared as ByVal but could have also been declared as ByRef.

Multidimensional Arrays

In addition to one-dimensional arrays, Visual Basic provides the capability of defining and using larger array sizes.

A *two-dimensional* array consists of both rows and columns of elements. For example, the array of numbers:

```
    8   16    9   52
    3   15   27    6
   14   25    2   10
```

is called a two-dimensional array of integers. This array consists of three rows and four columns. To reserve storage for this array, both the number of rows and the number of columns must be included in the array's declaration. For example, the declaration

```
Dim vals(2, 3) As Integer
```

specifies that vals is a two-dimensional array having 3 rows and 4 columns. Similarly, the declarations:

```
Dim volts (10,5) As Single
Dim code (6,26) As String
```

specify that the array volts consists of 11 rows (indices 0 to 10) and 6 columns (indices 0 to 5) of single-precision numbers and that the array code consists of 7 rows and 27 columns, with each element capable of holding a string.

To make it possible to locate an element in a two dimensional array, each element is identified by its position in the array. As illustrated in Figure 8–7, the term vals(1,3) uniquely identifies the element in row 1, column 3. As with one-dimensional array variables, two-dimensional array variables can be used anywhere that scalar variables are valid. Examples using elements of the vals array are:

```
watts = vals(2,3)
vals(1,1) = 62
newnum = 4 * (vals(2,1) - 5)
sumrow1 = vals(1,0) + vals(1,1) + vals(1,2) + vals(1,3)
```

The last statement causes the values of the four elements in row 1 to be added and the sum to be stored in the scalar variable sumrow1.

As with one-dimensional arrays, two-dimensional arrays can be declared either at the project, module, or procedure level. Additionally, as with one-dimensional arrays, two-dimensional array elements are processed and displayed using individual element notation, as illustrated in Procedure Code 8–4.

Procedure Code 8–4

```
Const ROWS As Integer = 2
Const COLS As Integer = 3
Dim vals(ROWS, COLS) As Integer
```

```
' This is a sub procedure used to initialize the array
```

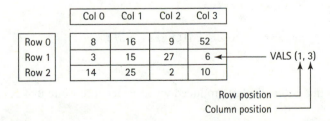

Figure 8–7   *Array Declared as* vals (1, 3). *Each Array Element is Identified by Its Row and Column Position*

```
Private Sub setvals()
   vals(0, 0) = 10
   vals(0, 1) = 20
   vals(0, 2) = 30
   vals(0, 3) = 40
   vals(1, 0) = 15
   vals(1, 1) = 25
   vals(1, 2) = 35
   vals(1, 3) = 45
   vals(2, 0) = 50
   vals(2, 1) = 60
   vals(2, 2) = 70
   vals(2, 3) = 80
End Sub

Private Sub frmMain_Click(ByVal sender As Object, _
      ByVal e As System.EventArgs) Handles MyBase.Click
   Dim i, j As Integer

   setvals()
   txtDisplay.Clear()
   ' Display by explicit element
   txtDisplay.AppendText("Display of vals() by explicit element" & _
      ControlChars.CrLf)
   txtDisplay.AppendText(vals(0, 0) & " " & vals(0, 1) & " " & vals(0, 2) _
      & " " & vals(0, 3) & ControlChars.CrLf)
   txtDisplay.AppendText(vals(1, 0) & " " & vals(1, 1) & " " & vals(1, 2) _
      & " " & vals(1, 3) & ControlChars.CrLf)
   txtDisplay.AppendText(vals(2, 0) & " " & vals(2, 1) & " " & vals(2, 2) _
      & " " & vals(2, 3) & ControlChars.CrLf)
   ' Display using a nested loop
   txtDisplay.AppendText("Display of vals() using a nested loop" & _
      ControlChars.CrLf)
   For i = 0 To ROWS
     For j = 0 To COLS
       txtDisplay.AppendText(vals(i, j) & " ")
     Next j
     txtDisplay.AppendText(ControlChars.CrLf)
   Next i
End Sub
```

Following is the display produced when Procedure Code 8–4 is executed:

```
Display of vals() by explicit element
   10   20   30   40
   15   25   35   45
   50   60   70   80


Display of vals() using a nested loop
   10   20   30   40
   15   25   35   45
   50   60   70   80
```

The first display of the `vals` array produced by Procedure Code 8–4 is constructed by explicitly designating each array element. The second display of array element values, which is identical to the first, is produced using a nested `For` loop. Nested loops are especially useful when dealing with two-dimensional arrays because they allow the programmer to easily designate and cycle through each element. A multiline TextBox control is used for the display of the array. The `AppendText` method does not automatically place output on a new line, so the control character `CrLf` (or NewLine) must be output whenever a new line is required. In Procedure Code 8–4, the variable `i` controls the outer loop and the variable `j` controls the inner loop. Each pass through the outer loop corresponds to a single row, with the inner loop supplying the appropriate column elements. After a complete column is printed, a new line is started for the next row. The effect is a display of the array in a row-by-row fashion.

Once two-dimensional array elements have been assigned to an array, processing can begin. Typically, **For** loops are used to process two-dimensional arrays because, as was previously noted, they allow the programmer to easily designate and cycle through each array element. For example, the nested **For** loop in the following code is used to multiply each element in the `vals` array by the number 10.

```
For i = 0 To ROWS
  For j = 0 To COLS
    vals(i,j) = 10 * vals(i,j)
  Next j
Next i
```

Although arrays with more than two dimensions are not commonly used, Visual Basic does allow larger arrays to be declared. This can be done by specifying the maximum index of all indices for the array. For example, the declaration `response(4, 10, 6)` specifies a three-dimensional array. Conceptually, as illustrated in Figure 8–8, a three-dimensional array can be viewed as a book of data tables. Using this visualization, the first index can be thought of as the location of the desired row in a table, the second index value as the desired column, and the third index value as the page number of the selected table.

Conceptually, a four-dimensional array can be represented as a shelf of books, where the fourth dimension is used to specify a desired book on the shelf, and a five-dimensional array can be viewed as a bookcase filled with books where the fifth dimension refers to a selected shelf in the bookcase. Using the same analogy, a

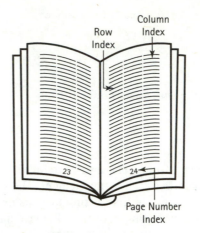

Figure 8-8 *Representation of a Three-Dimensional Array*

six-dimensional array can be considered as a single row of bookcases where the sixth dimension references the desired bookcase in the row. Finally, a seven-dimensional array can be considered as multiple rows of bookcases where the seventh dimension references the desired row. Alternatively, three-, four-, five-, six-, and seven-dimensional arrays can be viewed as mathematical *n*-tuples of order three, four, five, six, and seven, respectively.

Passing Multidimensional Arrays

Multidimensional arrays are passed as arguments in a process similar to passing one-dimensional arrays. However, the declaration for the array parameter in the procedure must include one or more commas to indicate that the array is multidimensional. The called procedure receives access to the entire array. For example, consider Procedure Code 8-5.

Procedure Code 8-5

```
Private Sub frmMain_Click(ByVal sender As Object, ByVal e As _
    System.EventArgs) Handles MyBase.Click
  Dim vals(1, 1) As Integer
  vals(0, 0) = 10
  vals(0, 1) = 20
  vals(1, 0) = 30
  vals(1, 1) = 40

  Display(vals)
End Sub
```

```
Private Sub Display(ByVal nums(,) As Integer)

   lstDisplay.Items.Add(nums(0, 0))
   lstDisplay.Items.Add(nums(0, 1))
   lstDisplay.Items.Add(nums(1, 0))
   lstDisplay.Items.Add(nums(1, 1))
End Sub
```

Only one array is created in Procedure Code 8-5. This array is known as `vals` in the Calling procedure and as `nums` in the Display procedure. Thus, `vals(0,1)` refers to the same element as `nums(0,1)`. The display produced when this procedure code is executed is:

10

20

30

40

Arrays and Strings

Arrays and strings frequently are used together in many programming situations. Assume that we need to develop a function that returns the day of the week corresponding to its ordinal number. As a first attempt at solving this problem, consider Procedure Code 8-6.

Procedure Code 8–6

```
Private Sub frmMain_Click(ByVal sender As Object, ByVal e As _
   System.EventArgs) Handles MyBase.Click
  Dim thisday As String
  Dim daynumber As Integer

  daynumber = Val(InputBox("Enter a day from 1 to 7 (ex. 1 for Sunday)"))
  thisday = Dayname(daynumber)
  txtDisplay.Text = "This corresponds to " & thisday
End Sub


Public Function Dayname(dayint) As String
  Dim days() As String = {"Sun", "Mon", "Tue", "Wed", "Thu", "Fri", "Sat"}

  Return days(dayint - 1)
End Function
```

The function `Dayname` listed in Procedure Code 8-6 uses an array of strings to store the seven day names, and selects the correct day, using the day's ordinal value minus one as an index into the `days` array. It is important to subtract one to determine the index because `days(0)` corresponds to Sunday, `days(1)` is Monday, and so on. Although this solution works, we actually can do much better by considering the string data as a single array of characters. Using this conceptualization, the `Day-name` data is incorporated into a single `days` string as follows:

```
days ="SunMonTueWedThuFriSat"
```

In this string each group of three characters constitutes a day name and the complete string is simply a convenient way of holding seven individual pieces of data. To extract any single name requires knowing the starting index position of the beginning letter and then extracting three characters from this position. For example, the expression `Mid(days,4,3)` extracts the three characters `Mon`, starting from position 4 in the `days` string. Procedure Code 8–7 illustrates how this expression can be used within the `Day-name` function to locate and return the correct day.

Procedure Code 8–7

```
Private Sub frmMain_Click(ByVal sender As Object, ByVal e As _
    System.EventArgs) Handles MyBase.Click
  Dim thisday As String
  Dim daynumber As Integer

  daynumber = Val(InputBox("Enter a day from 1 to 7 (ex. 1 for Sunday)"))
  thisday = Dayname(daynumber)
  txtDisplay.Text = "This corresponds to " & thisday
End Sub

Public Function Dayname(dayint) As String
  Const DAYLENGTH As Integer = 3
  Dim days As String

  days = "SunMonTueWedThuFriSat"
  Return days.Substring(DAYLENGTH * (dayint - 1), DAYLENGTH)
 End Function
```

Note that the starting index value into the string is determined by the expression `DAYLENGTH * (dayint - 1)`, where `DAYLENGTH` is a named constant having a value of 3 and is the length of each day's name. Once the starting position is located, the next three characters are extracted. Using strings in this manner, the trick is always to determine an expression that correctly locates the effective starting index value. To really make these programs robust, they should check that the value input is between 1 and 7; this is left as an exercise for the reader.

Exercises 8.2

For the following exercises use a multiline TextBox control to display the answers.

1. Modify the `Fmax` procedure in Procedure Code 8–3 to locate and return the minimum value of the passed array.

2. Write a program that stores the following numbers into a local array named `grades`: 65.3, 72.5, 75.0, 83.2, 86.5, 94.0, 96.0, 98.8, 100. There should be a procedure call to `show` that accepts the `grades` array as a parameter argument named `grades` and then displays the numbers in the array.

3. Write a program declaring three one-dimensional arrays named `price`, `quantity`, and `amount`. Each array should be capable of holding 5 single precision numbers. The numbers that should be stored in `price` are 10.62, 14.89, 13.21, 16.55, 18.62. The numbers that should be stored in `quantity` are 4, 8.5, 6, 7.35, 9. Your program should pass these three arrays to a procedure called `extend`, which should calculate the elements in the `amount` array as the product of the equivalent elements in the `price` and `quantity` arrays. (For example, `amount(1)` = `price(1)` * `quantity(1)`.) After `extend` has put values into the amount array, the values in the array should be displayed from within the procedure that called `extend`.

4. Write a program that includes two functions named `average` and `variance`. The `average` function should calculate and return the average of the values stored in an array named `testvals`. The `testvals` array should be declared as a local array and include the values 89, 95, 72, 83, 99, 86. The `variance` function should calculate and return the variance of the data. The variance is obtained by subtracting the average from each value in `testvals`, squaring the values obtained, adding them, and dividing by the number of elements in `testvals`. The values returned from `average` and `variance` should be displayed from within the procedure that called these functions.

5. Write appropriate declaration statements for:
   a. an array of integers with 6 rows and 10 columns named `nums`
   b. an array of integers with 2 rows and 5 columns named `nums`
   c. an array of single characters with 7 rows and 12 columns named `codes`
   d. an array of single characters with 15 rows and 7 columns named `codes`
   e. an array of single precision numbers with 10 rows and 25 columns named `vals`
   f. an array of single precision numbers with 16 rows and 8 columns named `vals`

6. Write a Visual Basic function that can be used to add the values of all elements in the `vals` array used in Exercise 5a and returns the total.

7. Write a Visual Basic program that adds equivalent elements of the two-dimensional arrays named `first` and `second`. Both arrays should have two rows and three columns. For example, element (1, 2) of the resulting array should be the sum of `first(1,2)` and `second(1,2)`. The `first` and `second` arrays should be initialized as follows:

```
   first                    second

------------             ------------

16    18    23           24    52    77

54    91    11           16    19    59
```

8. a. Write a Visual Basic program that finds and displays the maximum value in a two-dimensional array of integers. The array should be declared as a two-by-three array of integers and initialized with the following numbers: 16, 22, 99, 4, 18, −258.

   b. Modify the program in Exercise 8a so that it also displays the maximum value's row and column index values.

9. Write a procedure that multiplies each element of a three-row-by-four-column array by a scalar number. Both the array name and the number by which each element is to be multiplied are to be passed into the procedure as arguments.

10. Modify Procedure Code 8–7 so that the complete name of each day is returned. (*Hint:* You will have to make DAYLENGTH equal to the length of the longest day.)

11. Write a function named `Moname` that returns a month name corresponding to the integer that represents the month. Use the string

    `months = "JanFebMarAprMayJunJulAugSepOctNovDec"` in your function.

12. a. Write a function named Seasons that returns a season name corresponding to the integer representing the season. Use the relationship that the numbers 1, 2, 3, and 4 correspond to the seasons Winter, Spring, Summer, and Autumn, respectively.

    b. Modify the function for Exercise 12a so that it returns the season corresponding to each month. Use the following assignments:

Months	Season
Dec, Jan, Feb	Winter
Mar, Apr, May	Spring
Jun, Jul, Aug	Summer
Sep, Oct, Nov	Autumn

    Hint: Convert the month to an equivalent season using the expression
    `(m Mod 12) / 3 + 1`.

8.3   Structures

An array allows access to a list or table of data of the same data type, using a single variable name. At times, however, we may want to store information of varying types, such as a string name, an integer part number, and a real price, together in one structure. A data structure that stores different types of data under a single variable name is called a *record*.

Name:

Type:

Location in Dungeon:

Strength Factor:

Intelligence Factor:

Type of Armor:

Figure 8–9 *Typical Components of a Video Game Character*

Name: Golgar

Type: Monster

Location in Dungeon: G7

Strength Factor: 78

Intelligence Factor: 15

Type of Armor: Chain Mail

Figure 8–10 *The Form and Contents of a Record*

To make the discussion more tangible, consider data items that might be stored for a video game character, as illustrated in Figure 8–9.

Each of the individual data items listed in Figure 8–9 is an entity by itself, referred to as a *data field*. Taken together, all the data fields form a single unit that is referred to as a *structure* in Visual Basic .NET.

Although there could be hundreds of characters in a video game, the form of each character's record is identical. In dealing with records, it is important to distinguish between a record's form and its contents.

A record's *form* consists of the symbolic names, data types, and arrangement of individual data fields in the record. The record's *contents* consist of the actual data stored in the symbolic names. Figure 8–10 shows acceptable contents for the record form illustrated in Figure 8–9.

Using a structure requires that the record must be created and variables declared to be of the new structure type. Then specific values can be assigned to individual variable elements. Creating a structure requires listing the data types, data names, and arrangement of data items. For example, a record for a birthdate could be:

Month:

Day:

Year:

and the declaration

```
Structure Birthdate
   Dim month As Integer
   Dim day As Integer
   Dim year As Integer
End Structure
```

creates a structure named `Birthdate` that consists of three data items or fields that are called members of the structure.

The term `Birthdate` is a structure type name: it creates a new data type that is a data structure of the declared form. By convention the first letter of a user-selected data type name is uppercase, as in the name `Birthdate`, which helps to identify it when it is used in subsequent declaration statements. Here, the declaration for the `Birthdate` structure creates a new data type and describes how individual data items are arranged within the structure. To use a structure, you must declare variables of that type. For example, the declaration statement

```
Dim mybirthday As Birthdate
```

declares the variable `mybirthday` to be of type `Birthdate`. Assigning actual data values to the data items of a structure is called *populating the structure,* and is a relatively straightforward procedure. Each member of a structure is accessed by giving both the variable name and individual data item name, separated by a period. Thus, `mybirthday.month` refers to the first member of the `mybirthday` structure, `mybirthday.day` refers to the second member of the structure, and `mybirthday.year` refers to the third member.

Table 8–5 lists where structures may be created and the scoping rules for their declaring variables of a structure type. A structure definition cannot go inside a procedure. Typically, the **Structure** statement is placed at the top of a file with the module-level declarations. By default, a structure is **Public** but you can declare it to be **Private**.

Table 8–5   Structure Creation and Declaration Scope

Procedure/Module	Creation of a Structure	Variable Declarations
Procedure	Not Permitted	Local only
Form Module	Private only	Private only
Standard Module	Private or Public	Private or Public
Class Module	Private only	Private only

The individual members of a structure are not restricted to integer data types, as illustrated by the `Birthdate` structure. Any valid Visual Basic data type can be used. For example, consider an employee record consisting of the following data items:

Name:

Identification Number:

Regular Pay Rate:

Overtime Pay Rate:

Programmer Notes

Homogeneous and Heterogeneous Data Structures

Both arrays and records are structured data types. The difference between these two data structures is the types of elements they contain. An array is a *homogeneous* data structure, meaning that each of its components must be of the same type. A record is a *heterogeneous* data structure, meaning that each of its components can be of different data types. Thus, an array of records would be a homogeneous data structure elements of the same heterogeneous type.

A suitable structure for these data items is:

```
Structure Payrec
   Dim name As String
   Dim idnum As Long
   Dim regrate As Single
   Dim otrate() As Single
End Structure
```

Before leaving single structures, it is worth noting that the individual members of a structure can be any valid Visual Basic data type, including both arrays and structures. For example, the `otrate` member of `Payrec` consists of an array. However, Visual Basic does not allow you to declare the number of elements in the array within the structure declaration. You must use the `ReDim` statement inside a procedure to specify the size of the array. Accessing an element of a member array requires giving the structure's variable name, followed by a period, followed by the array designation. For example, if `employee` is of type `Payrec`, then `employee.otrate(2)` refers to the third value in the `employee.otrate` array.

Declaring an array of structures is the same as declaring an array of any other variable type. For example, an array of eleven `Payrec` structures can be declared using the statement:

```
Dim employee(10) As Payrec
```

This declaration statement constructs an array named `employee` consisting of 11 elements, each of which is a structure of the data type `Payrec`. Note that the creation of an array of eleven structures has the same form as the creation of any other array. For example, creating an array of eleven integers named `employee` requires the declaration:

```
Dim employee(10) As Integer
```

In this declaration the data type is `integer`, whereas in the former declaration for `employee` the data type is `Payrec`. Once an array of structures is declared, a particular data item is referenced by giving the position of the desired structure in the array followed by a period and the appropriate structure member. For example, the variable `employee(2).idnum` references the `idnum` member of the third `employee` structure in the `employee` array.

Exercises 8.3

1. Declare a structure data type for each of the following records:

   a. a student record consisting of a student identification number, number of credits completed, and cumulative grade point average

   b. a student record consisting of a student's name, birthdate, number of credits completed, and cumulative grade point average

   c. a mailing list consisting of a first name, last name, street address, city, state, and zip code

   d. a stock record consisting of the stock name, the price of the stock, and the birthdate of purchase

   e. an inventory record consisting of an integer part number, part description, number of parts in inventory, and an integer reorder number

2. For the individual data types in Exercise 1, define a suitable structure variable name, and initialize each structure with the appropriate following data:

   a. Identification Number: 4672

      Number of Credits Completed: 68

      Grade Point Average: 3.01

   b. Name: Rhona Karp

      Birthdate: 8/4/60

      Number of Credits Completed: 96

      Grade Point Average: 3.89

   c. Name: Kay Kingsley

      Street Address: 614 Freeman Street

      City: Indianapolis

      State: IN

      Zip Code: 07030

    d. Stock: IBM

       Price Purchased: 134.5

       Birthdate Purchased: 10/1/86

    e. Part Number: 16879

       Description: Battery

       Number in Stock: 10

       Reorder Number: 3

3. a. Write a Visual Basic program that prompts a user to input the current month, day, and year. Store the data entered in a suitably defined record and display the birthdate in an appropriate manner.

   b. Modify the program in Exercise 3a to use a record that accepts the current time in hours and minutes.

4. Write a Visual Basic program that uses a structure for storing the name of a stock, its estimated earnings per share, and its estimated price-to-earnings ratio. Have the program prompt the user to enter these items for five different stocks, each time using the same structure to store the entered data. When the data has been entered for a particular stock, have the program compute and display the anticipated stock price based on the entered earnings and price-per-earnings values. For example, if a user entered the data XYZ 1.56 12, the anticipated price for a share of XYZ stock is $(1.56)*(12) = \$18.72$.

5. Write a Visual Basic program that accepts a user-entered time in hours and minutes. Have the program calculate and display the time one minute later.

6. a. Write a Visual Basic program that accepts a user-entered birthdate. Have the program calculate and display the birthdate of the next day. For purposes of this exercise, assume that all months consist of 30 days.

   b. Modify the program in Exercise 6a to account for the actual number of days in each month.

7. Define arrays of 100 structures for each of the data types in Exercise 1 of this section.

8.4   Searching and Sorting

Most programmers encounter the need to both sort and search a list of data items at some time in their programming careers. For example, numerical data might have to be arranged in either increasing (ascending) or decreasing (descending) order for statistical analysis, lists of names may have to be sorted in alphabetical order, or a list of dates may have to be rearranged in ascending date order. Similarly, a list of names may have to be searched to find a particular name in the list, or a list of dates may have to be searched to locate a particular date. In this section we introduce the fundamentals of both sorting and searching lists. Note that it is not necessary to sort a list before searching it, although, as we shall see, much faster searches are possible if the list is in sorted order.

Search Algorithms

A common requirement of many programs is to search a list for a given element. For example, in a list of names and telephone numbers, we might search for a specific name so that the corresponding telephone number can be printed, or we might wish to search the list simply to determine if a name is there. The two most common methods of performing such searches, though they may not be the fastest, are the linear and binary search algorithms.

Linear Search   In a *linear search*, also known as a *sequential search*, each item in the list is examined in the order in which it occurs in the list until the desired item is found or the end of the list is reached. This is analogous to looking at every name in the phone directory, beginning with Aardvark, Aaron, until you find the one you want or until you reach Zzxgy, Zora. Obviously, this is not the most efficient way to search a long alphabetized list. However, a linear search has these advantages:

1. The algorithm is simple.
2. The list need not be in any particular order.

In a linear search, the search begins at the first item in the list and continues sequentially, item by item, through the list. The pseudocode for a function performing a linear search is:

For all the items in the list

  Compare the item with the desired item

  If the item was found

    Return the index value of the current item

  Endif

EndFor

Return -1 to indicate the item was not found

Note that the return value indicates whether the item was found or not. If the return value is −1, the item was not in the list. Otherwise, the return value within the **For** loop provides the index of where the item is located within the list. The function `linearSearch()`, included in Program 8-4 procedure code, implements this linear search algorithm as a Visual Basic function. Note that the elements in the array `nums` are initialized in its declaration statement.

Program 8–4's Event and General Procedure Code

```
'  This function returns the index of key in the list
'  -1 is returned if the value is not found
Public Function linearSearch(ByVal list() As Integer, ByVal size As Integer, _
   ByVal key As Integer) As Integer
```

```
   Dim index As Integer

   For index = 0 To size
     If list(index) = key Then
        return index
     End If
   Next index
   return -1
End Function

Private Sub btnSearch_Click(ByVal sender As Object, ByVal e As _
    System.EventArgs) Handles btnSearch.Click
   Dim nums() As Integer = {5, 10, 22, 32, 45, 67, 73, 98, 99, 101}
   Dim item, location As Integer

   item = Val(txtSearch.Text)
   location = linearSearch(nums, 9, item)

   If location > -1 Then
     txtDisplay.Text = "The item was found at index location " & location
   Else
     txtDisplay.Text = "The item was not found in the list"
   End If

End Sub

Private Sub txtSearch_Enter(ByVal sender As Object, ByVal e As _
    System.EventArgs) Handles txtSearch.Enter
   txtDisplay.Text = ""
End Sub

Private Sub btnExit_Click(ByVal sender As Object, ByVal e As _
    System.EventArgs) Handles btnExit.Click
   Beep()
   End
End Sub
```

In reviewing `linearSearch`, note that the `For` loop is simply used to access each element in the list, from first element to last, until a match is found with the desired item. If the desired item is located, the index value of the current item is returned, causing the loop to terminate; otherwise, the search continues until the end of the list is encountered. Two sample runs of Program 8–4 are illustrated in Figures 8–11 and 8–12, respectively.

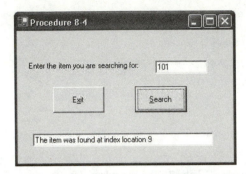

Figure 8-11 *First Sample Run of Program 8-4*

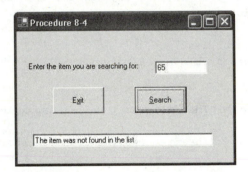

Figure 8-12 *Second Sample Run of Program 8-4*

As has already been pointed out, an advantage of linear searches is that the list does not have to be in sorted order to perform the search. Another advantage is that if the desired item is toward the front of the list, only a small number of comparisons will be done. The worst case, of course, occurs when the desired item is at the end of the list. On average, however, and assuming that the desired item is equally likely to be anywhere within the list, the number of required comparisons will be $N/2$, where N is the list's size. Thus, for a 10-element list, the average number of comparisons needed for a linear search is 5, and for a 10,000 element list, the average number of comparisons needed is 5000. As we show next, this number can be significantly reduced using a binary search algorithm.

Binary Search   In a *binary search*, the list must be in sorted order. Starting with an ordered list, the desired item is first compared to the element in the middle of the list. (For lists with an even number of elements, either of the two middle elements can be used). Three possibilities present themselves once the comparison is made: the desired item may be equal to the middle element, it may be greater than the middle element, or it may be less than the middle element.

In the first case, the search has been successful, and no further searches are required. In the second case, since the desired item is greater than the middle element, if it is found at all, it must be in the upper part of the list. This means that the lower part of the list consisting of all elements from the first to the midpoint element can be discarded from any further search. In the third case, because the desired item is less than the middle element, if it is found at all, it must be found in the lower part of the list. For this case, the upper part of the list containing all elements from the midpoint element to the last element can be discarded from any further search.

The algorithm for implementing this search strategy is illustrated in Figure 8–11 and defined by the following pseudocode:

Set the lower index to 0

Set the upper index to one less than the size of the list

Begin with the first item in the list

Do While the lower index is less than or equal to the upper index

   Set the midpoint index to the integer average of the lower and upper index values

   Compare the desired item to the midpoint element

   If the desired element equals the midpoint element

      Return the index value of the current item

   Else If the desired element is greater than the midpoint element

      Set the lower index value to the midpoint value plus 1

   Else if the desired element is less than the midpoint element

      Set the upper index value to the midpoint value less 1

   Endif

 End Do

Return –1 because the item was not found

As illustrated by both the pseudocode and the flowchart of Figure 8–13, a **Do while** loop is used to control the search. The initial list is defined by setting the lower index value to 0 and the upper index value to one less than the number of elements in the list. The midpoint element is then taken as the integerized average of the lower and upper values. Once the comparison to the midpoint element is made, the search is subsequently restricted by moving either the lower index to one integer value above the midpoint, or by moving the upper index one integer value below the midpoint. This process is continued until the desired element is found or the lower and upper index values become equal. The function `binarySearch()` presents the Visual Basic version of this algorithm.

```
' This function returns the location of key in the list
' a -1 is returned if the value is not found
Public Function binarySearch(ByVal list() As Integer, ByVal size _
    As Integer, ByVal key As Integer) As Integer
  Dim left, right, midpt As Integer
```

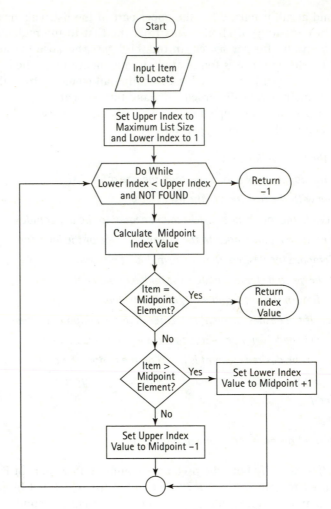

Figure 8–13 *The Binary Search Algorithm*

```
left = 0
right = size - 1

Do While left <= right
   midpt = Int((left + right) / 2)
   If key = list(midpt) Then
     Return midpt
   ElseIf key > list(midpt) Then
     left = midpt + 1
   Else
     right = midpt - 1
   End If
```

```
Loop
   Return -1
End Function
```

The value of using a binary search algorithm is that the number of elements that must be searched is cut in half each time through the **While** loop. Thus, the first time through the loop, N elements must be searched, the second time through the loop, $N/2$ of the elements have been eliminated and only $N/2$ remain. The third time through the loop, another half of the remaining elements have been eliminated, and so on.

In general, after p passes through the loop, the number of values remaining to be searched is $N/(2^p)$. In the worst case, the search continues until there is less than or equal to 1 element remaining to be searched. Mathematically, this can be expressed as $N/(2^p)$ # 1. Alternatively, this may be rephrased as p is the smallest integer such that 2^p <= N. For example, for a 1000-element array, N is 1000 and the maximum number of passes, p, required for a binary search is 10. Table 8-6 compares the number of loop passes needed for a linear and binary search for various list sizes.

As illustrated, the maximum number of loop passes for a 50-item list is almost 10 times more for a linear search than for binary search, and is even more spectacular for larger lists. As a rule of thumb, 50 elements are usually taken as the switchover point: for lists smaller than 50 elements linear searches are acceptable, but for larger lists a binary search algorithm should be used.

Big O Notation

On average, over a large number of linear searches with N items in a list, we would expect to examine half ($N/2$) of the items before locating the desired item. In a binary search the maximum number of passes, p, occurs when $(N/2)^p = 1$. This relationship can be algebraically manipulated to $2^p = N$, which yields $p = \log_2 N$, which approximately equals $3.33 \log_{10} N$.

For example, finding a particular name in an alphabetical directory with $N = 1000$ names would require an average of 500 ($N/2$) comparisons using a linear search. With a binary search, only about 10 (= $3.33 * \log_{10} 1000$) comparisons would be required.

A common way to express the number of comparisons required in any search algorithm using a list of N items is to give the order of magnitude of the number of comparisons required, on average, to locate a desired item. Thus, the linear search is said to be of order N and the binary search of order $\log_2 N$. Notationally, this is expressed as $O(N)$ and $O(\log_2 N)$, where the O is read as "the order of."

Table 8-6 A Comparison of Do While Loop Passes for Linear and Binary Searches

Array Size	10	50	500	5,000	50,000	500,000	5,000,000
Average Linear Search Passes	5	25	250	2,500	25,000	250,000	2,500,000
Maximum Linear Search Passes	10	50	500	5,000	50,000	500,000	5,000,000
Maximum Binary Search Passes	4	6	9	13	16	19	23

Sort Algorithms

For sorting data, two major categories of sorting techniques exist, called internal and external sorts, respectively. *Internal sorts* are used when the data list is not too large and the complete list can be stored within the computer's memory, usually in an array. *External sorts* are used for much larger data sets that are stored in large external disk or tape files and cannot be accommodated within the computer memory as a complete unit.

Here we present two internal sort algorithms that are commonly used when sorting lists with less than approximately 50 elements. For larger lists, more sophisticated sorting algorithms are typically employed. The following sections are only meant to illustrate programming techniques. Visual Basic .NET provides the array method `Array.Sort(arrayname)`, which can be called to sort an array named `arrayname`.

Selection Sort   One of the simplest sorting techniques is the selection sort. In a *selection sort*, the smallest value is initially selected from the complete list of data and exchanged with the first element in the list. After this first selection and exchange, the next smallest element in the revised list is selected and exchanged with the second element in the list. Because the smallest element is already in the first position in the list, this second pass need only consider the second through last elements. For a list consisting of N elements, this process is repeated $N - 1$ times, with each pass through the list requiring one less comparison than the previous pass.

For example, consider the list of numbers illustrated in Figure 8–14. The first pass through the initial list results in the number 32 being selected and exchanged with the first element in the list. The second pass, made on the reordered list, results in the number 155 being selected from the second through fifth elements. This value is then exchanged with the second element in the list. The third pass selects the number 307 from the third through fifth elements in the list and exchanges this value with the third element. Finally, the fourth and last pass through the list selects the remaining minimum value and exchanges it with the fourth list element. Although each pass in this example resulted in an exchange, no exchange would have been made in a pass if the smallest value were already in the correct location.

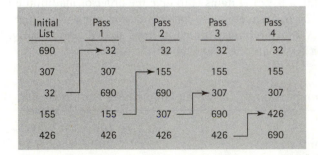

Figure 8–14   *Sample Selection Sort*

In pseudocode, the selection sort is described as:

> *Set interchange count to zero (not required, but done just to keep track of the interchanges)*
> *For each element in the list from first to next-to-last*
>> *Find the smallest element from the current element being referenced to the last element by:*
>>> *Setting the minimum value equal to the current element*
>>> *Saving (storing) the index of the current element*
>>> *For each element in the list from the current element + 1 to the last element in the list*
>>>> *If element(inner loop index) < minimum value*
>>>>> *Set the minimum value = element(inner loop index)*
>>>>> *Save the index of the new found minimum value*
>>>> *Endif*
>>> *EndFor*
>>> *Swap the current value with the new minimum value*
>>> *Increment the interchange count*
>> *EndFor*
> *Return the interchange count*

The function selectionSort incorporates this algorithm into a Visual Basic function.

```
Public Function selectionSort(ByRef num() As Integer, ByVal maxsub _
    As Integer) As Integer
  Dim i, j, min, minidx, temp, moves As Integer

  moves = 0
  For i = 0 To maxsub - 1
    min = num(i)         ' assume minimum is the first array element
    minidx = i           ' index of minimum element
    For j = i + 1 To maxsub
      If num(j) < min Then    ' if we've located a lower value
          min = num(j)                        ' capture it
          minidx = j
      End If
    Next j
    If min < num(i) Then      ' check if we have a new minimum
      temp = num(i)           ' and if we do, swap values
      num(i) = min
      num(minidx) = temp
      moves = moves + 1
```

```
    End If
  Next i
  Return moves   ' return the number of moves
End Function
```

The selectionSort function expects two parameters: the list to be sorted and the maximum index of the array (number of elements minus 1). As specified by the pseudocode, a nested set of **For** loops performs the sort. The outer For loop causes one pass through the list. For each pass, the variable min is initially assigned the value num(i), where i is the outer **For** loop's counter variable. Because i begins at 0 and ends at maxsub - 1, each element in the list except the last is successively designated as the current element.

The inner loop is used in the function cycles through the elements below the current element to select the next smallest value. Thus, this loop begins at the index value i+1 and continues through the end of the list. When a new minimum is found, its value and position in the list are stored in the variables named min and minidx, respectively. Upon completion of the inner loop, an exchange is made only if a value less than that in the current position was found.

Program 8–5 was constructed to test selectionSort. This program implements a selection sort for the same list of 10 numbers previously used to test our search algorithms. For later comparison to the other sorting algorithms, the number of actual moves made by the program to put the data into sorted order is counted and displayed. For convenience, only the event code contained within Program 8–5 that calls the selection sort function is listed.

Program 8–5's Event Procedure Code

```
Private Sub frmMain_Click(ByVal sender As Object, ByVal e As _
    System.EventArgs) Handles MyBase.Click
  Const maxsub As Integer = 9
  Dim nums() As Integer = {22, 5, 67, 98, 45, 32, 101, 99, 73, 10}
  Dim i, moves As Integer

  moves = selectionSort(nums, maxsub)
  txtDisplay.Clear()
  txtDisplay.AppendText("The sorted list, in ascending order, is:" & _
    ControlChars.CrLf)
  For i = 0 To maxsub
    txtDisplay.AppendText("   " & nums(i))
    Next i
    txtDisplay.AppendText(ControlChars.CrLf & moves & _
      " moves were made to sort this list")
    End Sub
```

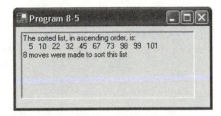

Figure 8–15   *The Output Produced by Program 8–5*

The output produced by Program 8–5 is shown in Figure 8–15.

Clearly, the number of moves displayed depends on the initial order of the values in the list. An advantage of the selection sort is that the maximum number of moves that must be made is $N - 1$, where N is the number of items in the list. Further, each move is a final move that results in an element residing in its final location in the sorted list.

A disadvantage of the selection sort is that $N(N - 1)/2$ comparisons are always required, regardless of the initial arrangement of the data. This number of comparisons is obtained as follows: the last pass always requires one comparison, the next-to-last pass requires two comparisons, and so on, to the first pass, which requires $N - 1$ comparisons. Thus, the total number of comparisons is:

$$1 + 2 + 3 + \ldots + N - 1 = N(N - 1)/2 = N^2/2 - N/2.$$

For large values of N, the N^2 dominates, and the order of the selection sort is $O(N^2)$.

Exchange ("Bubble") Sort   In an *exchange sort*, elements of the list are exchanged with one another in such a manner that the list becomes sorted. In a *bubble sort,* which is a type of exchange sort, successive values in the list are compared, beginning with the first two elements. If the list is to be sorted in ascending (from smallest to largest) order, the smaller value of the two being compared is always placed before the larger value. For lists sorted in descending (from largest to smallest) order, the smaller of the two values being compared is always placed after the larger value.

For example, assuming that a list of values is to be sorted in ascending order, if the first element in the list is larger than the second, the two elements are interchanged. Then the second and third elements are compared. Again, if the second element is larger than the third, these two elements are interchanged. This process continues until the last two elements have been compared and exchanged, if necessary. If no exchanges were made during this initial pass through the data, the data is in the correct order and the process is finished; otherwise, a second pass is made through the data, starting from the first element and stopping at the next-to-last element. The reason for stopping at the next-to-last element on the second pass is that the first pass always results in the most positive value "sinking" to the bottom of the list.

As a specific example of this process, consider the list of numbers illustrated in Figure 8–16. The first comparison results in the interchange of the first two element values,

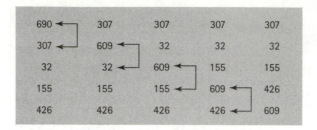

Figure 8–16   *The First Pass of an Exchange Sort*

690 and 307. The next comparison, between elements two and three in the revised list, results in the interchange of values between the second and third elements, 690 and 32. This comparison and possible switching of adjacent values is continued until the last two elements have been compared and possibly switched. This process completes the first pass through the data and results in the largest number moving to the bottom of the list. As the largest value sinks to its resting place at the bottom of the list, the smaller elements slowly rise, or "bubble," to the top of the list. This bubbling effect of the smaller elements is what gave rise to the name "bubble" sort for this sorting algorithm.

Because the first pass through the list ensures that the largest value always moves to the bottom of the list, the second pass stops at the next-to-last element. This process continues, with each pass stopping at one higher element than the previous pass, until either $N - 1$ passes through the list have been completed or no exchanges are necessary in any single pass. In both cases the resulting list is in sorted order. The pseudocode describing this sort is:

Set interchange count to zero (not required, but done just to keep track of the interchanges)
For the first element in the list to one less than the last element (i index)
  For the second element in the list to the last element (j index)
    If num(j) < num(j − 1)
      Swap num(j) with num(j − 1)
      Increment interchange count
    End If
  End For
End For
Return interchange count

This sort algorithm is coded in Visual Basic as the function bubbleSort, which is included within Program 8–6 for testing purposes. This program tests bubbleSort with the same list of 10 numbers used in Program 8–5. For comparison to the earlier selec-tion sort, the number of adjacent moves (exchanges) made by bubbleSort is also counted and displayed.

Program 8–6's Event and General Procedure Code

```
Public Function bubbleSort(ByRef num() As Integer, ByVal maxsub _
    As Integer) As Integer
  Dim i, j, temp, moves As Integer

  moves = 0
  For i = 0 To (maxsub - 1)
    For j = 2 To maxsub
      If num(j) < num(j - 1) Then
        temp = num(j)
        num(j) = num(j - 1)
        num(j - 1) = temp
        moves = moves + 1
      End If
    Next j
  Next i
  Return moves
End Function


Private Sub frmMain_Click(ByVal sender As Object, ByVal e As _
    System.EventArgs) Handles MyBase.Click
  Const maxsub As Integer = 9
  Dim nums() As Integer = {22, 5, 67, 98, 45, 32, 101, 99, 73, 10}
  Dim i, moves As Integer

  moves = bubbleSort(nums, maxsub)
  txtDisplay.Clear()
  txtDisplay.AppendText("The sorted list, in ascending order, is: " & _
      ControlChars.CrLf)
  For i = 0 To maxsub
    txtDisplay.AppendText("   " & nums(i))
  Next i
  txtDisplay.AppendText(ControlChars.CrLf & moves & _
    " moves were made to sort this list")
End Sub
```

Figure 8–17 illustrates the output produced by Program 8–6.

As with the selection sort, the number of comparisons using a bubble sort is $O(N^2)$ and the number of required moves depends on the initial order of the values in the list. In the worst case, when the data is in reverse sorted order, the selection sort performs

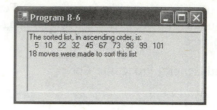

Figure 8–17 *The Output Produced by Program 8–6*

better than the bubble sort. Here both sorts require $N(N - 1)/2$ comparisons, but the selection sort needs only $N - 1$ moves, while the bubble sort needs $N(N - 1)/2$ moves. The additional moves required by the bubble sort result from the intermediate exchanges between adjacent elements to "settle" each element into its final position. In this regard, the selection sort is superior because no intermediate moves are necessary. For random data, such as that used in Programs 8–5 and 8–6, the selection sort generally performs equal to or better than the bubble sort. A modification to the bubble sort, which causes the sort to terminate when the list is in order regardless of the number of passes made, can make the bubble sort operate as an $O(N)$ sort in specialized cases.

Exercises 8.4

For the following problems use a ListBox control to display your answers.

1. a. Modify Program 8–5 to use a list of 100 randomly generated numbers and determine the number of moves required to put the list in order using a selection sort. Display both the initial list and the reordered list.

   b. Redo Exercise 1a using a bubble sort.

2. For the functions selectionSort and bubbleSort, a simple modification can allow the sorting to be done in decreasing order. In each case, identify the required changes and then rewrite each function to accept a parameter indicating whether the sort should be in increasing or decreasing order. Modify each function to correctly receive and use this parameter.

3. The selection and bubble sort both use the same technique for swapping list elements. Replace the code in these two functions that performs the swap, by a call to a procedure named `swap`.

4. a. Modify Program 8–6 to use a larger test list consisting of 20 numbers.

   b. Modify Program 8–6 to use a list of 100 randomly selected numbers.

5. A company currently maintains two lists of part numbers, where each part number is an integer. Write a Visual Basic program that compares these lists of numbers and displays the numbers, if any, that are common to both. (*Hint:* Sort each list prior to making the comparison.)

6. Redo Exercise 5, but display a list of part numbers that are only on one list, but not both.

7. Rewrite the binary search algorithm to use recursion rather than iteration.

8.5 Focus on Program Design and Implementation: About Dialog Boxes and Splash Screens

In addition to operational forms, such as the Rotech order entry form, most applications include informational About boxes and a Splash screen. Both of these are forms that are added into a project using the techniques you have learned, but are displayed in very different ways. In this Focus section we describe these forms, how they are created, and how their display is triggered within an application.

Adding an About Dialog Box

An *About box* is an informational screen that provides general information about an application, such as its name, version number, programming company, and/or programmer. In addition, About boxes can also be used to provide help information. From a design viewpoint an About box is just another form that is added into a project. As such, an application can have as many About boxes as needed, with the first one usually providing general information about the program, such as that shown in Figure 8–18, and with additional ones acting as help screens.

While an About box may look different from other screens we have seen, it is really just a form. Therefore adding an About box to an application is accomplished by adding a form. From the Project menu, select Add Windows Form and name the new form frmAbout.

Once an About box has been added into a project it must be linked in operationally, so that it can be displayed under user control. This usually is done using two buttons: one on your application's first Form that triggers the About box display, and the second, the OK Button on the About box that causes your application's initial Form to be redisplayed. Figure 8–19 illustrates this relationship.

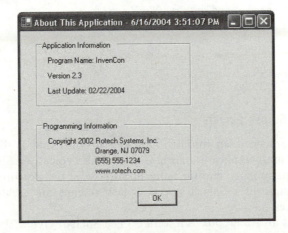

Figure 8–18 *A Sample About Box*

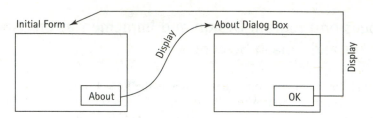

Figure 8-19 *Displaying an About Box and Returning*

Assuming that the button used to display the About box has been named btnAbout, its **Click** event is coded as listed in Event Procedure 8-1.

Event Procedure 8-1

```
Private Sub btnAbout_Click(ByVal sender As System.Object, ByVal e As _
    System.EventArgs) Handles btnAbout.Click
  Dim frmAboutRef As New frmAbout()

  Me.Hide
  frmAboutRef.Show()
End Sub
```

This procedure first hides the currently displayed form and then displays the About box. On the return side, the OK button in the About box would use the code listed in Event Procedure 8-2 to redisplay the frmMain Form. The body of this event code is a copy of Event Procedure 8-1, with a name change for the form to be displayed.

Event Procedure 8-2

```
Private Sub btnOK_Click(ByVal sender As System.Object, ByVal e As _
    System.EventArgs) Handles btnOK.Click
  Dim frmMainRef As New frmMain()

  Me.Hide
  frmMainRef.Show()
End Sub
```

Adding a Splash Screen

A *Splash screen* is an initial informational Form that is displayed for a few seconds before the main application Form is presented. Typically a Splash screen is used to present a company name and the name or purpose of the executing application. Figure 8-20 is an example of a Splash screen. Splash screens are created in the same manner as About boxes.

Just as an About box is a form, so is a Splash screen. The difference between a regular Form and a Splash screen Form is:

Figure 8–20   *A Sample Splash Screen*

a. a Splash screen has no user controls on it

b. a Splash screen appears automatically when the program is first executed

c. a Splash screen disappears in a few seconds and then brings up the main menu Form

Most Splash screens include some graphics that, for example, display a company logo or an image that a company associates itself with. The Picture box is a standard Visual Basic control that allows graphics to be displayed. A Picture box control is placed on a Form in the same manner as all other controls—by selecting the control from the Toolbox and placing it on the Form. The Picture box so placed, however, will contain no image. The types of images that can be placed within a Picture box include bitmaps (files stored with either a .bmp or .dib extension), icons (files stored with a .ico extension), and metafiles (files stored with either a .wmf or .emf extension). To place an image within a Picture box you must select the Image property and then click on the ellipses box shown. Doing so produces the file dialog box asking for the file name of the image. It is from this dialog box that you select the location and image to be set as the Image property; it is this image that is then displayed.

To make the Splash screen look more professional, we use a Group box control to create a border around the Form. This is done for appearance purposes as we have removed the Form's normal border (see FormBorderStyle discussion below).

Table 8–7 displays the properties table for the Figure 8–20 Splash screen. There are some properties used that we have not seen before. The following identifies them and describes what they do.

FormBorderStyle   This **Form** property controls what type of border the Form will have. Normally we don't change this property using the default value of Sizable. For the Splash screen, we use a value of None, causing no border to be displayed.

X   This property controls the horizontal or left coordinate of the control on the Form. Normally we set the X property by dragging a control on the Form to the position desired. For a more precise position, we can set it explicitly by entering a coordinate in the X property. The property is accessed by expanding (press the +) the **Location** property.

Y   This is the same as the X property but controls the vertical coordinate.

Width   This property controls the width of the control on the Form. Normally we set the X property by dragging a control sizing handle to the desired width. For a more precise sizing, we can set it explicitly by entering a value in the **Width** property. The property is accessed by expanding (pressing the +) the **Size** property.

Height   This is the same as the **Width** property but controls the height of the control.

SizeMode   This **Picture** box property controls how the image is displayed. The StretchImage value causes the image to be expanded or shrunk to fit the size of the Picture box.

The trick now is to display the Splash screen for a few seconds as the initial screen when an application is first executed, immediately followed by the frmMain screen, which becomes the application's second screen. There are times, however, when you might want a form other than frmMain to be initially loaded and displayed, as is the case with a Splash screen. There are two solutions to this problem: either designate the Splash screen as the first Form to be loaded, and have the Splash screen display the frmMain screen, or designate a separate procedure to begin processing before any form is loaded, and have this procedure load the appropriate forms in sequence. Although the second solution is the preferred one, for reasons which will become apparent, we consider each of these solutions in turn, as they both yield insight into moving from one form to another within a single application.

To explicitly designate the frmSplash screen as the initial Form to be loaded, right mouse click on the project and select the last option—Properties (see Figure 8–21). When this option is selected, a dialog box similar to the one shown in Figure 8–22 is displayed. As illustrated, we have selected the frmSplash Form from the drop-down list as the Startup Object, rather than frmMain Form. Pressing the OK Button causes this selection to take effect and to become the startup Form. Although this will cause the splash screen to be displayed, we are still left with the problem of unloading this screen and loading the frmMain Form when we want the "working" part of the program to begin.

One method of switching from the Splash screen to the Main Menu Form (frmMain) is to use a button on the Splash screen, and have its **Click** event trigger the display of the Main Menu Form. Assuming we have named this control btnContinue, its **Click** event would be coded as listed in Event Procedure 8–3.

Event Procedure 8–3

```
Private Sub btnContinue_Click(ByVal sender As System.Object, ByVal e As _
    System.EventArgs) Handles btnContinue.Click
  Dim frmMainRef As New frmMain()

  Me.Close()
  frmMainRef.Show()
End Sub
```

Table 8-7   Figure 8-20's Properties Table

Object	Property	Setting
Form	Name	frmSplash
	FormBorderStyle	None
	Location	
	X	0
	Y	0
	Size	
	Width	456
	Height	256
GroupBox	Name	grpBox1
	Location	
	X	5
	Y	5
	Size	
	Width	443
	Height	252
Label	Name	lblProduct
	Text	Disk Promotion Program
Label	Name	lblCompany
	Text	Rotech Systems, Inc.
Label	Name	lblVersion
	Text	Version 2.15
Label	Name	lblCopyright
	Text	Copyright 1999
Label	Name	lblCompany2
	Text	Rotech Systems, Inc.
PictureBox	Name	picRotech
	Image	Sinewave.ico[2]
	Location	
	X	16
	Y	24
	Size	
	Width	152
	Height	224
	SizeMode	StretchImage
Timer	Name	tmrSplash
	Enabled	False
	Interval	4000

[2]This file actually comes standard with Visual Studio .Net. It is located in \Program Files\Microsoft Visual Studio .Net\Common7\Graphics\icons\Industry\SINEWAVE.ICO.)

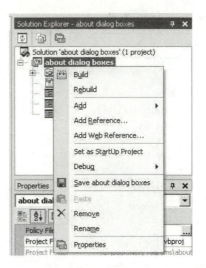

Figure 8–21 *Changing a Project's Properties*

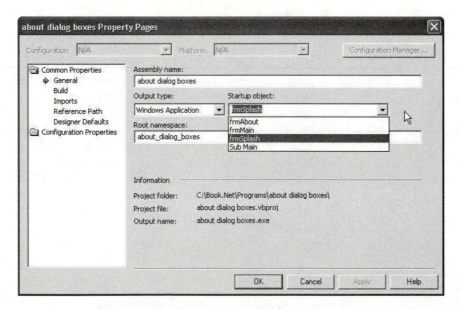

Figure 8–22 *Selecting an Alternative Startup Form*

The code listed in Event Procedure 8–3 is code that is familiar to us. It is similar to Event Procedure 8–2, used extensively within the Rotech project except that it has a call to close the form instead of hiding it. However, the more conventional method for displaying a Splash screen is to start the application with a procedure containing a **Timing** loop.

Figure 8–23   *Timer Control in the Toolbox*

Controlling events based on time is accomplished in Visual Basic via the **Timer** control, a standard control in the Windows Forms tab of the Toolbox (Figure 8–23). The Timer is a stopwatch. It starts counting time when its **Enabled** property is set to **True**. It stops counting when **Enabled** is set to **False**. The Timer control tells our program when a period of time has elapsed by causing its **Tick** event to fire. The period of time is set in the **Timer Interval** property. See the last entry in Table 8–7. Note that the Interval unit is milliseconds. In our program we want the Splash screen to appear for 4 seconds, so we set the **Interval** property to 4000. Note that when you add the Timer control to your program, it will appear in the system tray as it does not get displayed when the program executes.

This may sound confusing, but following our Splash screen example will make it clearer. See Procedure Code 8–11, which is the code for the Splash screen Form frmSplash. It consists of code for two events: the initial Form Load and the **Tick** event of the Timer. When the project starts, the frmSplash Form will be executed first. Remember to set this up in the Properties section of the Project as was previously discussed. When the Form is loaded, the Splash screen will appear. It is at this point we want to start the stopwatch or Timer control. This is done by setting its **Enabled** property to True. After 4 seconds (4000 milliseconds), the Timer **Tick** event will fire. At this point we want to turn off the Timer by setting its **Enabled** property to **False**, hide the Splash screen and display the Main Menu Form. This is done in the **Tick** event procedure.

Procedure Code 8–11

```
Private Sub tmrSplash_Tick(ByVal sender As Object, ByVal e As _
    System.EventArgs) Handles tmrSplash.Tick
  Dim frmMainRef As New frmMain()

  tmrSplash.Enabled = False
  Me.Close()
  frmMainRef.Show()
End Sub

Private Sub frmSplash_Load(ByVal sender As Object, ByVal e As _
    System.EventArgs) Handles MyBase.Load

  tmrSplash.Enabled = True
End Sub
```

Exercises 8.5

(Note: The Rotech Systems project, at the stage of development begun in this section, can be found at http://computerscience.jbpub.com/bronsonvbnet in the ROTECH folder. The project, as it exists at the end of this section, can be found in the ROTECH8 *folder as project* rotech8. *If you are developing the system yourself, following the procedures given in this section, we suggest that you first copy all of the files in the ROTECH7 folder onto your system, and then work out of this latter folder. When you have finished your changes you can compare your results to the files in the ROTECH8 folder.)*

1. a. Add the About box shown in Figure 8–18 to the Rotech project. Add a Button named btnAbout to the project Main Menu and use Event Procedure 8–1 to display the box. Event Procedure 8–2 should be used with the OK button in the About box to redisplay the Main Menu Form.

   b. Test the About box constructed in Exercise 1a to ensure that it can be displayed from the Main Menu and that it, in turn, can be used to redisplay the Main Menu.

2. a. Add the Splash screen shown in Figure 8–20 to the Rotech project. Use Procedure Code 8–11 to display this screen.

   b. Test that the project initially displays the Splash screen and then displays the Main Menu Form when the application is executed.

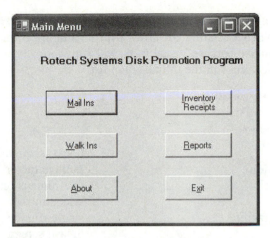

Figure 8–24 *New Main Menu Form with About Box*

3. Add a Button to the Splash screen constructed in Exercise 2a. The Button should have the caption OK, and if it is pressed the Splash screen should hide itself immediately and display the Main Menu Form. This Button should be in addition to the normal operation provided by Procedure code 8–11.

4. a. (Case study) Add an About box to your selected project (see project specifications at the end of Section 1.5).

   b. Add a Splash screen to your selected project.

8.6 Common Programming Errors

Five common errors are associated with using arrays:

1. *Using an index that references a nonexistent array element.* For example, declaring the array to be of size 20 and using an index value of 25. This error results in a runtime error and message that the `Index was outside the bounds of the array`.

2. *Forgetting to declare the array.* This error results in a compiler error each time an indexed variable attempting to access the array is encountered.

3. *Forgetting that the indices of an array go from 0 to N where N is the upper index of the array and that there are $N + 1$ elements in the array.* When using a **For** loop within a program of the form `For i = 0 To n`, it is important to use the correct starting and ending values for `i`.

4. *Forgetting to initialize the array.* Although Visual Basic automatically sets all elements of numerical arrays to zero and all elements of string arrays to zero-length, it is up to the programmer to ensure that each array is correctly initialized before processing of array elements begins.

5. *Including the upper index of the array when initializing an array with its declaration.* When declaring an array with an initialization list, you do not include the upper index because Visual Basic will automatically make the array large enough to hold the values in the initialization list.

8.7 Chapter Review

Key Terms

About box	linear (sequential) search
Big O notation	null character ('\0')
binary search	one-dimensional array
bubble sort	selection sort
control character	single-dimensional array
index	Splash screen
indexed variable	two-dimensional array

Summary

1. A single-dimensional array is a data structure that can be used to store a list of values of the same data type. Such arrays must be declared by giving the data type of the values that are stored in the array and the value of the largest index. For example, the declaration

```
Dim num(99) As Integer
```

creates an array of 100 integers, with indices from 0 to 99 (num(0), num(1), ... num(99)). Array indices always start with 0.

2. Array elements are referenced using the array name and an index, for example, num(22). Any integer valued expression can be used as an index.

3. An array can be initialized using a single statement such as

```
Dim grades() = {92, 78, 85, 100}
```

The length of the array is not specified.

4. The ReDim statement is an executable statement that resizes an array at run time.

5. A two dimensional array is declared by listing both a row and a column upper index with the data type and name of the array. For example, the statements

```
Const ROWS As Integer = 5
Const COLS As Integer = 7
Dim vals(ROWS, COLS) As Integer
```

create a two-dimensional array consisting of six rows (0 through 5) and eight columns (0 through 7) of integer values.

6. Visual Basic permits the declaration of arrays with a maximum of 32 dimensions.

7. Arrays are passed to procedures by using the name of the array as an argument. Within the procedure, a parameter must be specified for the passed array name and the length of the array parameter is not specified.

8. The linear search is an $O(N)$ search. It examines each item in a list until the searched item is found or until it is determined that the item is not in the list.

9. The binary search is an $O(\log_2 N)$ search. It requires that a list be in sorted order before it can be applied.

10. The selection and exchange sort algorithms require an order of magnitude of N^2 comparisons for sorting a list of N items.

11. A Splash screen is an initial informational Form that is displayed for a few seconds before the main application Form is presented.

12. Controlling events based on time is accomplished in Visual Basic via the **Timer** control. At design time, this control is displayed in the component tray below the form and at run time it is invisible. The Timer is a stopwatch; it starts counting time when its **Enabled** property is set to **True** and stops counting when **Enabled** is set to **False**. The Timer control tells a program when a period of time has elapsed by causing its **Tick** event to fire.

Test Yourself—Short Answer

1. A one-dimensional array requires one _____ to identify which element is being referred to in a statement.

2. What is the difference between a fixed array and a dynamic array?

3. Write a **Declaration** statement for an array named `aintQuantities` that holds 10 integer numbers.

4. Write a **Declaration** statement for an array named `afltPrices` that holds 10 floating point numbers.

5. Declare an array named `astrMessages` that holds 10 strings.

6. Declare a two-dimensional array named `aintPartNums` capable of holding 4 rows and 5 columns of integers.

7. The _____ function will return an array's upper limit.

8. The _____ method and the _____ character allows a **TextBox** control to display more than one line.

9. Declare a structure name Stock that is composed of a string field called `symbol` and a floating point field called `price`.

10. What is the difference between an array and a structure?

Programming Projects

1. For this project you will create three integer arrays. The elements in the third array will be obtained by multiplying corresponding elements in the first two arrays. Finally, the sum and average of each array's elements will be computed and displayed.

   Specifically, write a Visual Basic program that stores the odd numbers from 1 to 20 in one array and the even numbers from 1 to 20 in another array. The program should then multiply the first element of the first array by the first element in the second array and store the product into a third array. The cross-multiplication of corresponding elements in the first two arrays should continue until the product of the 10th element in each of the first two arrays is stored in the 10th element of the third array. Your program must then calculate and display the sum and average of the numbers in each of the three arrays.

First array	Second array	Third Array
1	2	2
3	4	12
5	6	30
.	.	.
.	.	.
19	20	3800

2. Write a Visual Basic program that accepts two numbers from the user (in text boxes) representing the rows and columns of a table. Using this input, display a multiplication table with the number of input rows and columns in a multiline text box, such as that shown in Figure 8–25. The maximum number of rows is 15 and the maximum number of columns is 10. An executable example of this calculator can be found at http://computerscience.jbpub.com/bronsonvbnet in the folder "Final Programs." (*Hint:* Set the font of the text box on the form to Courier New. To have the output display in equal width columns, for each value that is displayed, use the method `String.Format("{0,4}", value)` so each value is displayed in a field that is 4 characters wide).

In constructing your program be sure to:

—Comment your program.
—Use proper formatting, indenting, and so forth.

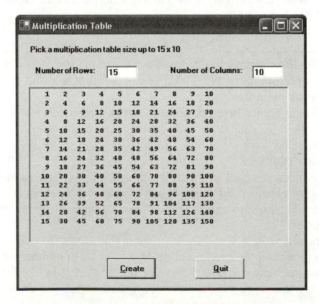

Figure 8–25 *Form for Programming Project 2*

3. The LoCal Ice Cream Shoppe sells ice cream to its customers in either a cup or a cone. The charges for number of scoops and topping are as follows:

Scoops	Charge	Toppings	Charge
1	$1.25	0	$0.00
2	$1.85	1	$0.40
3	$2.35	2	$0.80
		3	$1.10

For a cone, the customer is charged an additional $0.25. Using this information, write a Visual Basic program to calculate the total charge for each order. Use one set of radio Buttons for the "Number of Scoops" and a second set for the "Number of Toppings." Additionally, supply the application with a check box for the choice of a cone or cup of ice cream. Your project should also use an array of type Single to store the charge for 1 to 3 scoops, as well as a second Single array for the 0 to 3 toppings charge. The total charge for each order should be displayed, in currency format, in a text box.

4. After performing a cost study on the price of toppings, the LoCal Ice Cream Shoppe plans to change the way in which they charge for toppings. Their new price structure will reflect the type of topping. The charge for number of scoops and an additional charge for cones will stay the same (as defined in Exercise 3).

Toppings	Charge
Chocolate sprinkles	$0.45
Chocolate sauce	$0.45
Shredded coconut	$0.40
Cherries	$0.35
Chopped nuts	$0.50
Butterscotch sauce	$0.40

Either modify the program for Exercise 3 or write a new Visual Basic program that incorporates these additional prices in the customer's final bill. Use an array of type Single to store the corresponding charges for the toppings. The total charge should be displayed using a currency format.

Accessing Databases

A growing area of importance for Visual Basic is the construction of database applications, which includes both the maintenance of existing data and the rapid retrieval and display of information stored in the data base. In Section 9.1 we introduce the terminology and fundamental structures used in database design. The remaining sections present the controls, methods, and events that permit construction of Visual Basic database applications.

9.1 Introduction to Databases

A *database* is defined as any collection of related data used by an organization. In this context, *organization* is a generic term that refers to any self-contained social unit such as a company, university, hospital, or family. Such organizations may wish to use the following in a database:

- Student data
- Patient data
- Employee data
- Customer data
- Expense data
- Product data
- Sales data

The data in a database always consist of two types:

1. *Entities* about which the organization needs to store information, such as employees, customers, suppliers, and products.

2. R*elationships* that link the entities together and express the associations between them.

As a specific example illustrating these concepts, consider that Rotech Systems, Inc. is a small corporation that operates from two office locations. Assume that the company currently employs 20 people, each assigned to one of the two offices. In addition, the company employs 10 salespeople working out of their homes and reporting to one of the two offices. The relevant data for these employees is listed in Tables 9–1 through 9–3.

Before examining the relationships between each of the tables illustrated in Tables 9–1 through 9–3, we take a moment to concentrate on the tables themselves.

First, note that the data stored in each table is relevant to a specific entity. For our example there are three tables that correspond to three entities: internal employee phone numbers, external sales force addresses, and office locations. Individually, each table is constructed to be a logical grouping of related information arranged in rows and columns. Mathematically, such a two-dimensional table is referred to as a *relation* if the following conditions hold:

1. Each location in the table can contain a single value.

2. Each column in the table has a unique identifying name.

3. All values in a column have the same data type.

Table 9–1   Internal Employee Telephone Directory (Table name is PhoneBook and the primary key is the ID field)

ID	Name	Ext	Office
1	Bronson, Bill	321	HM
2	Engle, Alan	234	HM
3	Dieter, Frank	289	F1
4	Dreskin, James	367	HM
5	Farrell, Mike	564	F1
7	Ford, Sue	641	F1
9	Gent, Hillary	325	HM
10	Grill, John	495	F1
11	Jones, Kay	464	F1
12	Jones, Mary	790	HM
14	Macleod, Jim	761	HM
15	Miller, Harriet	379	HM
21	O'Neil, Pat	856	F1
22	Schet, David	485	F1
23	Smith, Bill	251	F1
24	Smith, Dave	893	HM
26	Swan, Kurt	168	HM
27	Ward, Ann	726	F1
28	Williams, John	673	HM
30	Bass, Harriet	893	HM

Table 9–2   Sales Representatives Mailing Addresses (Table name is SalesRep and the primary key is the ID field)

ID	Office	FName	MI	LName	Addr1	Addr2	City	State	Zip
1	HM	Mary	A	Gerardo	614 Tremont Ave.		Hoboken	NJ	07030
2	HM	Bill	J	Bottlecheck	892 Freeman St.		Orange	NJ	07050
3	HM	Jayne		Scott	Apt. 12	56 Lyons Ave.	Bloomfield	NJ	07060
4	HM	Melissa	V	Smyth	78 Barnstable Rd.		Summit	NJ	07045
5	HM	Brian		Russell	93 Fairmont Ter.		Mountainside	NJ	07036
6	HM	Sara		Blitnick	832 Addison Drive		Maplewood	NJ	07085
7	F1	Blake		DiLorenzo	642 Schuller Dr.		Cherry Hill	NJ	07961
8	F1	Helen		Thomas	745 SkyLine Dr.		Camden	NJ	07920
9	F1	Mark		Somers	Apt. 3B	17 Turney St.	Trenton	NJ	07936
10	F1	Scott		Edwards	Apt. 46	932 Coleridge Rd.	Atlantic City	NJ	07018

Table 9–3 Office Location List (Table name is Offices and the primary key is the ID field)

ID	Office	Address	City	State	Zip
1	HM	33 Freeman St.	Orange	NJ	07050
2	F1	614 Tremont Ave.	Trenton	NJ	07936

4. The data in each row is distinct (that is, no two rows have the same data).

5. No information is lost by reordering columns.

6. No information is lost by reordering rows.

A *relational database* is defined as a collection of relations. As a practical matter, then, a relational database is simply any database that stores all of its data in table form. Because Visual Basic and most of the currently popular database programs, such as Access, Paradox, and dBase, deal with relational databases, this is the only type of database we will consider.

Each column in a table is designated by a heading, referred to as both a *field name* and an *attribute name* (the two terms are synonymous). For example, the four columns in Table 9–1 have the field names ID, Name, Ext, and Office, respectively. In a similar manner, each row in a table is referred to as a *record*. Thus, Table 9–1 has 20 records, Table 9–2 has 10 records, and Table 9–3 has two records.

In addition to storing information about each entity, a database must also provide information as to how the entities are related. Relationships between entities are typically signified by phrases such as "is related to," "is associated with," "consists of," "is employed by," "works for," and so on. Such relationships between entities are conveniently expressed using an entity-relationship diagram (ERD), in which a straight line connects two or more entities. The exact relationship between entities is marked on the line using the symbols illustrated in Figure 9–1.

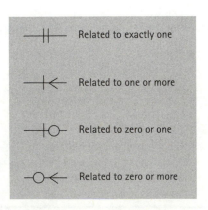

Figure 9–1 *ERD Symbols*

For example, Figure 9–2 illustrates the relationship between an employee and a company. ERD diagrams are always meant to be read from left-to-right and then from right-to-left. When reading from one entity to another, the ERD symbol attached to the starting entry is ignored. Thus, reading Figure 9–2 from left to right, and ignoring the symbol closest to the company entity, we see that a company employs zero or more employees. Reading from the right entity to the left entity, and again ignoring the symbol closest to the starting entity, we see that an employee is "employed by" exactly one company. The designation of "zero or more" or "exactly one" is termed the *cardinality* of the relationship and refers to the number of one entity that is related to another entity.

Figure 9–3 is the ERD diagram for the Rotech Company database. As illustrated in this diagram, the database consists of three entities. Reading from the Office entity to the Internal Employees entity, we see that an office consists of one or more employees, and reading from the Office entity to the Sales Force entity, we see that an office consists of one or more sales representatives. Similarly, reading the ERD diagram from right-to-left, we see that an internal employee is related to exactly one office, as are the sales representatives.

The relationships illustrated in Figure 9–3 are both examples of *one-to-many* relationships. That is, one office may consist of many internal employees but each internal employee can only be associated with one office. This same one-to-many relationship exists for the sales force.

In addition to a one-to-many relationship there is a many-to-many relationship. Such a relationship is illustrated in Figure 9–4, which relates authors to the books they write. As seen in this figure, an individual author can be associated with one or more titles, while an individual title can have more than one author.

Figure 9–2   *A Relationship Between Entities*

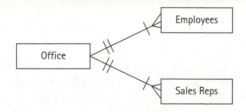

Figure 9–3   *The Rotech Company ERD Diagram*

Figure 9–4   *A Many-to-Many Relationship*

Stored and Index Ordering

As each record is added to a table it is typically appended to the end of the existing set of records. This ordering of records is referred to as the table's original, or *stored*, order. For example, note the ordering of the telephone records illustrated in Table 9–1. The ordering of these records is in stored order—the order in which records were added to the table.

Frequently, it is convenient to have a table's records ordered either alphabetically, numerically, or chronologically. Rather than resorting all of the records, which can be time-consuming for large databases, indexes are used. An *index* is a separate table of record positions, called *pointers*, which lists the positions of the table's records in the desired order. For example, if we frequently wanted to access Table 9–1 in alphabetical name order, we would create an index based on the Name field. The first entry in the Name index table would be record number 30, followed by record number 1, followed by record numbers 3 and 4, and so. Reading the telephone table in Name index order would then provide us with an alphabetical list of names and their respective extensions.

Each index created for a table relies on one or more fields. The field on which a table's records are ordered is referred to as a *key field*. Thus, if the records in Table 9–1 are ordered by the Name field, the key field for this ordering is the Name field. A *compound key* is one in which two or more fields are used to create the index. For example, you might wish a table of employees to be listed in departmental order and then in alphabetical last name order. Creating a compound key consisting of department name followed by last name, and then indexing the table based on this key, would produce the desired result.

In constructing a database table, it is advisable that each record have at least one key field that can be used to uniquely identify each record in a table. When a key field is used in this manner it is referred to as a *primary key*. Typically, in the absence of any other key field, the record number is taken to be the primary key. The record number is assigned sequentially, starting from 1, to each new record that is added to a table. If a record is deleted from the table, the record number is also deleted and not used again. In all of our tables we will assume that the record number is the primary key. Thus, displaying a table in record number order is the same as displaying it in what we previously referred to as its stored order.

Structured Queries

In addition to ordering a table's records in either stored or index order, you will encounter situations that require either listing a single table's records in a manner that is different from an existing index order, combining records from one or more tables, or asking and answering specific questions about the data. For example, you might need to determine how many customers have a balance outstanding over sixty days, or how many customers have exceeded their credit limit. In almost all of these situations you could construct a new index (for example, based on outstanding days or outstanding amounts), use the data in the new indexed order, and then delete the index when you have completed the task at hand. An alternative is to use a structured query. A *structured query* is a statement, written according to the rules of a language called Structured

Query Language (SQL), that uniquely identifies a set of records from one or more tables. For example, a requirement such as

> *SELECT all of the internal employee names from the PhoneBook table (Table 9–1) who are assigned to the Office designated as HM*

should result in all of the names being listed for those employees in Table 9–1 who are assigned to the home office. When this statement is written as an **SQL** structured statement, it becomes

```
SELECT Names FROM PhoneBook WHERE Office = "HM"
```

In Section 9.4 we present structured queries in detail, show how to construct such statements, and incorporate them within Visual Basic to create a desired subset of records from one or more tables.[1]

Exercises 9.1

1. Define the following terms and identify how they are related:
   a. table
   b. record
   c. field
2. Define the following terms:
   a. ERD diagram
   b. cardinality
   c. index
   d. stored order
   e. key field
   f. primary key
   g. relational database
3. a. List the fifth record that will be printed if Table 9–1 is displayed in stored order.
   b. List the fifth record that will be printed if Table 9–1 is displayed in name index order.
   c. List the fifth record that will be printed if Table 9–1 is displayed in extension index order.
   d. For your answers to Exercises 3a and 3b, what specific order did you assume for the index?
4. a. List the sixth record that will be printed if Table 9–2 is displayed in stored order.
   b. List the sixth record that will be printed if Table 9–2 is displayed in last name index order.

---

[1]The set of records can be empty; i.e., no records meet the criteria.

    c. List the sixth record that will be printed if Table 9–2 is displayed in city index order.

    d. List the sixth record that will be printed if Table 9–2 is displayed in zip code order.

    d. For your answers to Exercises 4a, 4b, and 4c, what specific order did you assume for the index?

5. Download[2] the Biblio database, which contains tables for authors, book titles, and publishers. The figure that follows illustrates the ERD diagram for these tables. Using this diagram, describe the relationships between the various entities.

The ERD Diagram for the Biblio Database

6. For the following queries, determine the record that will be displayed:

    a. SELECT all of the internal employee names from the PhoneBook table (Table 9–1) whose extensions are between 100 and 200.

    b. SELECT all of the internal employee name from the PhoneBook table (Table 9–1) whose last name begins with B.

    c. SELECT all of the sales representatives from the SalesRep table (Table 9–2) who are assigned to office HM.

    d. SELECT all of the sales representatives from the SalesRep table (Table 9–2) who live in Orange, New Jersey.

    e. SELECT all of the sales representatives from the SalesRep table (Table 9–2) who have a middle initial.

9.2 Using ADO.NET with Visual Basic

Visual Basic .NET supports Microsoft's newest generation of database interface technology known as ADO.NET, based on Microsoft's previous version called ADO (ActiveX Data Objects). ADO.NET is an extremely powerful data access component that allows you to access database data in many formats. (ADO.NET is a very complex technology; covering all aspects of the technology is beyond the scope of this text.) This chapter will cover the basics of ADO.NET, specifically showing how to access and manipulate Microsoft Access databases within Visual Basic.

    The basic idea behind using databases in Visual Basic is to

a. create a link or connection between the database, known as the data source, and the Visual Basic application;

b. retrieve fields from tables in the database and display them on a Form; and

---

[2]This database is a Microsoft product that accompanied a prior version of Visual Basic. It can be downloaded at http://computerscience.jbpub.com/bronsonvbnet.

c. store values on the Form in the database.

In order to get this functionality, your application must perform the following required steps:

- Set up a connection to a data source.
- Create a data adapter to handle the transfer of data to and from the data source and your application.
- Create a dataset to hold the data in memory while your application works with it.
- Add controls to your form and set their properties to bind the controls to the fields in the dataset.

Although Visual Basic provides enormous flexibility in how to interact with databases, this text will concentrate on a few specific ways. Figure 9–5 shows the key components that will be described. Learning the techniques described will provided the foundation for using the more advanced aspects of ADO.

Setting Up a Data Connection

In order to access any database from within Visual Basic a connection to the database must be established. The most convenient database to connect to is Microsoft Access. However, any database can be used as long as it is ODBC (Open DataBase Connectivity) compliant. ODBC is a standard that allows for database access by almost any programming language or personal productivity tool (e.g., Excel).

We demonstrate the steps involved in accessing a database via a program that allows the user to navigate through records in a phonebook database. By 'navigate' we mean being able to look at the first, last, next, and previous records in the database. The database is called COMPANY[3] and it consists of three tables. This exercise will use the PhoneBook table, which has the following structure:

Field Name	Data Type
ID	AutoNumber
Name	Text
Ext	Number
Office	Text

The interface for this program, Program 9–1, is displayed in Figure 9–6. To start the program create a blank Form and name the project Program 9–1.

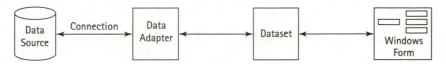

Figure 9–5 *Setting up Data Access in Visual Basic*

---

[3]The COMPANY.MDB database can be downloaded from the Databases folder at http://computerscience.jbpub.com/bronsonvbnet.

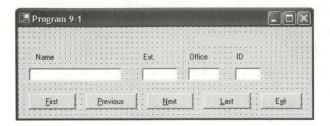

Figure 9–6   *Program 9–1's Interface*

Figure 9–7   *Data Controls in the Toolbox*

Using a database in Visual Basic involves understanding a new set of objects called *Data Controls*. Data Controls are accessed by clicking on the Data Button in the Toolbox, as shown in Figure 9–7.

As a general rule, the objects that start with OLE deal with Microsoft Access and the ones that start with SQL relate to other databases. To establish a connection to an Access database we select the OleDbConnection object. Drag an OleDbConnection control from the Toolbox to the Form. Note that the control does not appear on the Form but in the component tray below the Form. From the Properties window, select **ConnectionString** and click on **New Connection**. Figure 9–8 shows the Properties window for

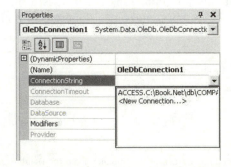

Figure 9–8   *Creating a Connection Using the ConnectionString Property*

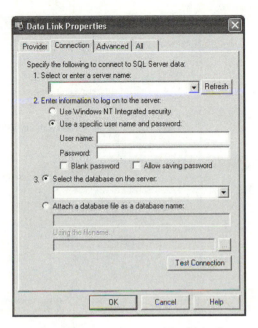

Figure 9–9   *Data Link Properties Dialog Box*

OleDbConnection1 and the **ConnectionString** property. Figure 9–9 displays the Data Link Properties dialog box.

Clicking on the Provider tab will bring up the dialog box shown in Figure 9–10.

Because we are working with an Access database, select the *Microsoft Jet 4.0 OLE DB Provider* and click on *Next*. The Connection Tab appears as shown in Figure 9–11.

Under the heading "1. SELECT or enter a <u>d</u>atabase name:", click on the button with the ellipses (...) and browse to the actual database file. In our example, the database file name is COMPANY.MDB. You can click on the Test Connection Button to ensure that the connection has been set up properly. You should then see a message box that displays "Test connection succeeded." Click the OK Button to dismiss the message box.

Visual Basic provides a window, the Server Explorer, that displays databases connected to programs. This window is useful for determining the existence of connections and other databases properties. The Server Explorer window can be viewed by clicking on View and choosing Server Explorer. The Server Explorer is displayed between the Toolbox and Form Designer. Expand the Data Connections tree for the COMPANY.MDB by clicking on the + sign to the left of the string that starts with ACCESS. This enables you to view the tables and fields in the database. In our example there are three tables, as shown in Figure 9–12.

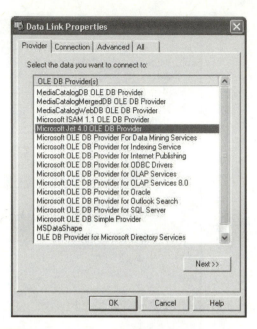

Figure 9–10   *Provider Tab*

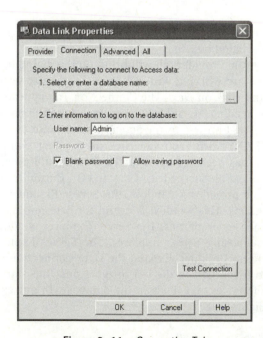

Figure 9–11   *Connection Tab*

Figure 9–12 *Expanded Tree of the Server Explorer*

Programmer Notes

Setting up Database Access

Visual Basic provides a set of Data controls in the Toolbox that are used to set up database access. Setting up your application to work with a database requires several steps:

- Set up a connection to a data source.
- Create a data adapter to handle the transfer of data to and from the data source and your application.
- Create a dataset to hold the data in memory while your application works with it.
- Add controls to your form and set their properties to bind the controls to the fields in the dataset.

When using a Microsoft Access Database, use the OleDbConnection and OleDbDataAdapter controls, which appear in the component tray below the Form design after they are dragged to the Form. Visual Basic provides a Data Adapter Configuration Wizard to help you specify the connection and database commands that are used to select database records.

Setting up a Data Adapter

After a connection has been established, the next step is to set up the data adapter. The data adapter passes data back and forth between a data source and a program. The data adapter, like the data connection, is created via an object in the Data Toolbox. Because this is a Microsoft Access database, the OleDbDataAdapter control is used. Drag an OleDbDataAdapter control from the Data tools in the Toolbox to the Form. The control will appear in the tray below the Form and the Data Adapter Configuration Wizard (Figure 9–13) will automatically open.

The Data Adapter Configuration Wizard simplifies the task of using a database table. In our program we use it to select the fields in the table that are needed in the program.

Figure 9–13   *First Screen of the Data Adapter Configuration Wizard*

Click on the Next Button to bring up the second screen that's shown in Figure 9–14. This screen allows for the linkage of the data adapter to a data connection. This is needed because a program could have multiple connections open. As we have only one connection set up, the one to the COMPANY.MDB, it appears in the text box. If there were others, they would appear in the drop-down list. Click on the Next Button to proceed.

On the next screen (Figure 9–15) you have only one choice available for Query types, which is "Use SQL statements." Click on Next to bring up the next screen, which is for Generating the SQL statements.

The purpose of this screen is to allow for the selection of fields and records to be retrieved by the Data Adapter. The specification of what to retrieve is achieved via structured query or an **SQL** statement. As it is not assumed that everyone knows SQL syntax, the wizard automatically creates the **SQL** statement for us. However, in order to do so we will need to specify what fields we require. This can be done by clicking on the Query Builder Button. This brings up a dialog box similar to Figure 9–16. Choose the table you want to use, which will be Phonebook in our example, click on Add and then Close.

Next, choose the fields that you want (Figure 9–17) and the Query Builder generates the necessary **SQL** statements. In this example, all fields of the Phonebook table were chosen. Click OK to complete the task, and Figure 9–18 is displayed.

Click on Next and you'll see the final screen, which displays the results of the Data Adapter configuration. Click on Finish to end the process. (See Figure 9–19.)

Before moving to the next step, it is time to change the names of the connection and data adapter controls (Figure 9–20) to conform to the standard naming conven-

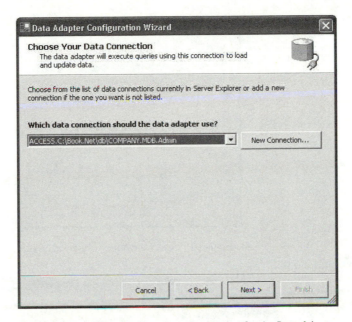

Figure 9–14   *Choosing Your Data Connection for the Data Adapter*

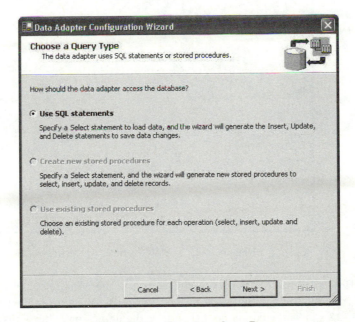

Figure 9–15   *Choosing a Query Type*

tions. Click on the OleDbConnection control in the component tray to bring up its property window. Change the **Name** property from OleDbConnection1 to conPhonebook (Figure 9–21).

Figure 9–16 *Select the table(s) you want included*

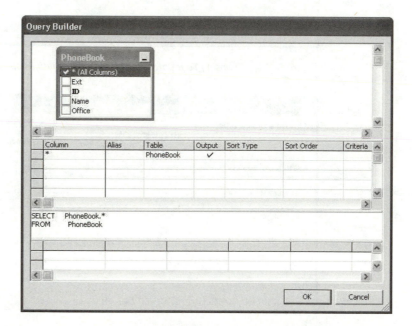

Figure 9–17 *Select the Fields you want included*

Now click on the OleDbAdapter control in the component tray to bring up its property window. Change the Name property from OleDbDataAdapter1 to daPhonebook. Figure 9–22 shows the component tray after the names have been changed.

Creating a Dataset

The third step in the process is the creation of a dataset. A *dataset* is a copy of the data that is retrieved from the database and then inserted into memory. An application does

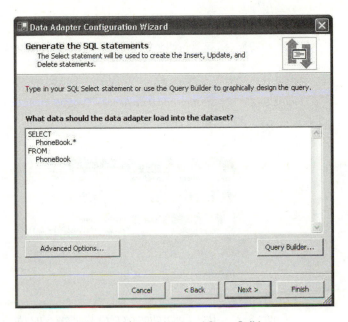

Figure 9–18   *Completed Query Builder*

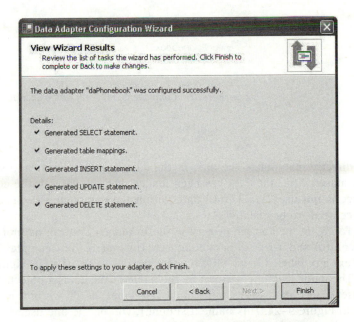

Figure 9–19   *Final Data Adapter Configuration Screen*

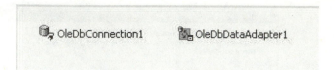

Figure 9–20 *Connection and Data Adapter Controls in the Component Tray*

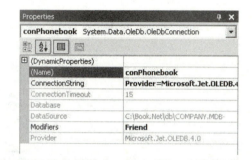

Figure 9–21 *Data Connection Property Window After Name Change*

Figure 9–22 *Component Tray After Name Change*

not directly manipulate the data in the data source but instead uses the data copied to the dataset. After the data has been loaded into the dataset, the connection to the data source is not used again until data within the dataset has been modified and the data source needs to be updated.

To create the dataset, select the OleDbAdapter control, daPhonebook, right-click on the control and select Generate dataset. This opens the Generate dataset dialog box. In the text box labeled New, enter a name such as dsPhone as in Figure 9–23.

The name dsPhone will not be the name of the dataset object. Visual Basic creates a dataset object and assigns it the name DsPhone1, as shown in the completed component tray in Figure 9–24. This name, DsPhone1, will be the one used to reference the dataset object in the program. The reason for complexity in names is beyond the scope of this book. For now simply use the name created by Visual Basic.

After clicking OK to dismiss the Generate dataset dialog box, we have completed the configuration of the connection to our Microsoft Access Database. The next step is

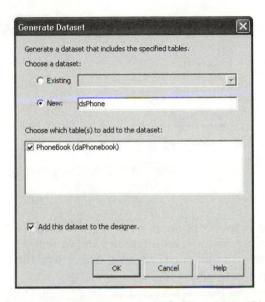

Figure 9–23   *Naming the Dataset in the Generate Dataset Dialog Box*

Figure 9–24   *Completed Component Tray*

to bind the control on the form to the ADO.NET DsPhone1 dataset and then write code to fill the dataset at run-time.

Binding Data to Controls

Data binding is the process of connecting a control to one or more data elements. A *data-aware control* is one that is capable of automatically displaying data from a field(s) in a dataset. To bind a data-aware control to a dataset, you must have set up the connection, data adapter, and dataset as we have done so far.

ADO.NET supports two types of binding: simple binding and complex binding.

- *Simple binding* connects one control to one data element. In our examples, the Text property of a text box will be associated with a field in a table.
- *Complex binding* is used when more than one data element is bound to a control, such as displaying data from multiple rows of a dataset. This type of binding is used for DataGrid controls, described later in this chapter.

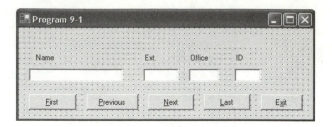

Figure 9–25 *Program 9–1's Interface*

We need to add controls to our Form for Program 9–1 before doing the binding. The interface for this program is repeated in Figure 9–25. There are four text boxes used to display the data in a current record: Name, Ext, Office field, and ID. Each text box has a corresponding label.

There are also five buttons: one to show the previous record, one to show the next record, one to show the first record, one to show the last record, and an exit button.

To bind the TextBox controls on the Form to the DsPhone1 dataset, the **Databind-ings.Text** property of each needs to be set. First, select the txtName text box and click the plus sign next to the **DataBindings** property in the Properties window to expand its contents. The **DataBindings** property has three subproperties: (**Advanced**), **Tag**, and **Text**. Select the **Text** subproperty and click the down arrow. You will see a drop-down box that displays an entry for the DsPhone1 dataset (refer to Figure 9–26).

Click the plus sign to the left of DsPhone1 and then click the plus sign to the left of Phonebook. This displays all the fields of the dataset, in this case all the fields of the PhoneBook table. Because we had selected the txtName text box, click Name to set the

Figure 9–26 *Databindings.Text Property*

binding. Repeat this process for the txtOffice text box (bind to the Office field) and the txtExt text box (bind to the Ext field).

Table 9–4 lists the property settings for Program 9–1's controls.

Filling the Dataset

What we have done so far creates all the connections and linkages to propagate the data from the tables to the controls. However code needs to be written to *fill* the dataset at run-time. This is accomplished with the data adapter's `Fill` method. The general format of the `Fill` method is:

```
DataAdaptername.Fill(DataSetName)
```

DataAdaptername is the name of a data adapter object (in our case daPhoneBook) and `DataSetName` is the name of the dataset object (DsPhone1) to fill. After this method is executed, the dataset object contains data from all the fields specified when the dataset object was set up. A call to this method is generally added to the Load event of the Form as shown in the following example:

```
Private Sub frmMain_Load(ByVal sender As System.Object, ByVal e As _
    System.EventArgs) Handles MyBase.Load
  daPhonebook.Fill(DsPhone1)
End Sub
```

When the method daPhonebook.Fill(DsPhone1)is executed, the dataset DsPhone1 is filled with the contents of the Phonebook Access database. In our example, it contains records with the names, offices, extensions, and IDs of 20 people. Note that the database is filled in ascending order of the ID field. In the next section, we will show how to fill the database in alphabetical order using the Name field.

Navigating through the Dataset

All Windows Forms in Visual Basic have two built-in objects that are created when you bind controls to a dataset: BindingContext and CurrencyManager. The *BindingContext* object manages all of the data bindings for the controls on the form. The *CurrencyManager* gives you a simple way to navigate among the rows in a dataset. These objects keep the control instances synchronized with the data in the dataset so that they always display data from the same record.

Program 9–1 is shown below. The four Button event procedures are used to display the first, previous, next, and last record. When using bound data on a Form, use the properties of the Forms' `BindingContext`. When retrieving records from a database, it is usual to retrieve more than one. However, at any time, the program will be pointing to only one of the set of records. The position of this record in the dataset that has focus (also referred to as the current record) is stored in the Position property; this property is zero-based, meaning the first record is at position 0. To display the next record, add one to the position. To display the previous record, subtract one from the position. Consider the code:

```
Me.BindingContext(DsPhone1, "Phonebook").Position -= 1
```

Table 9–4 Program 9–1's Properties Table

Object	Property	Setting
Form	Name	frmMain
	Text	Program 9-1
Label	Name	lblName
	Text	Name
TextBox	Name	txtName
	Text	(blank)
	Databindings.Text	Phonebook.Name
Label	Name	lblExt
	Text	Ext.
TextBox	Name	txtExt
	Text	(blank)
	Databindings.Text	Phonebook.Ext
Label	Name	lblOffice
	Text	Office
TextBox	Name	txtOffice
	Text	(blank)
	Databindings.Text	Phonebook.Office
Label	Name	lblID
	Text	ID
TextBox	Name	txtID
	Text	(blank)
	Databindings.Text	Phonebook.ID
Label	Name	lblPosition
	Text	(blank)
Button	Name	btnPrevious
	Text	&Previous
Button	Name	btnNext
	Text	&Next
Button	Name	btnFirst
	Text	&First
Button	Name	btnLast
	Text	&Last
Button	Name	btnExit
	Text	E&xit

DsPhone1 is the name of the dataset and Phonebook is the name of the table. This statement subtracts one from the **Position** property and moves to the previous record. Similarly, the code

```
Me.BindingContext(DsPhone1, "Phonebook").Position += 1
```

moves to the next record.

The Currency Manager is another mechanism that also can be used for doing this navigating. Consider the following code:

```
Dim currManager As CurrencyManager

currManager = Me.BindingContext(DsPhone1, "Phonebook")
currManager.Position += 1
```

The **Position** property of the CurrencyManager can be used to navigate among the rows in the table. The **Count** property

```
currManager.Count
```

can be used to determine the number of records (rows) in the table.

Program 9–1

```
Dim currManager As CurrencyManager

Private Sub frmMain_Load(ByVal sender As System.Object, ByVal e As _
    System.EventArgs) Handles MyBase.Load
  'Fill in the dataset
  daPhonebook.Fill(DsPhone1)
  currManager = Me.BindingContext(DsPhone1, "Phonebook")
  ShowPosition()
End Sub

Private Sub btnPrevious_Click(ByVal sender As System.Object, ByVal e As _
    System.EventArgs) Handles btnPrevious.Click
  currManager.Position -= 1
  ShowPosition()
End Sub

Private Sub btnNext_Click(ByVal sender As System.Object, ByVal e As _
    System.EventArgs) Handles btnNext.Click
  currManager.Position += 1
  ShowPosition()
```

```
End Sub

Private Sub btnFirst_Click(ByVal sender As System.Object, ByVal e As _
    System.EventArgs) Handles btnFirst.Click
  currManager.Position = 0
  ShowPosition()
End Sub

Private Sub btnLast_Click(ByVal sender As System.Object, ByVal e As _
    System.EventArgs) Handles btnLast.Click
  currManager.Position = currManager.Count - 1
  ShowPosition()
End Sub

Private Sub ShowPosition()
  lblPosition.Text = "Record " & currManager.Position + 1 & " of " _
      & currManager.Count
End Sub

Private Sub btnExit_Click(ByVal sender As System.Object, ByVal e As _
    System.EventArgs) Handles btnExit.Click
  Beep()
  End
End Sub
```

The ShowPosition procedure displays the number of records in the table (count) and the current record number, which is the current record **Position** plus 1. Figure 9–27 shows the Form after the Next Record Button has been clicked. This action displays the second record of the database.

Note that if you're at the last record in the dataset and click on the Next Button, you still remain on the last record and do not generate an error. Similarly, if you're on the first record in the dataset and click on the Previous Button, you remain on the first record. The value of currManager.Position will not go below zero or above the number of records minus one.

Figure 9–27   *Record 2 of the Phonebook Database*

When designing the user interface, it may be helpful to see all the data in the database. This can be done by using the Data Adapter Preview Dialog. To bring up this dialog box, select the data adapter control in the design window (daPhonebook in our example), right-click on it, and select `Preview Data`. In the Data Adapter Preview Dialog, make sure that the data adapter name is displayed in the Data adapters list in the upper left. Then click on `Fill dataset`. You can also view the data by clicking on Preview Data ... below the Properties Window. Refer to Figure 9–28 to see the Phonebook dataset.

The data being previewed shows the original order of the records in the database; in this example, the records are in ascending order of ID rather than alphabetical order by Name. It may be useful to have the records sorted by Name, which can be done in several ways. Section 9.3 will discuss writing **SQL** statements to accomplish this. A simple way is to use a facility in the Query Builder available in the Data Adapter Configuration Wizard.

Figure 9–17 shows the screen that is displayed when choosing fields in the Table. Instead of choosing all the fields by checking the All Columns box, checking each individual field brings up each field in the grid below. Select the box corresponding to the `Name` row and the `Sort Type` Column and click on the down arrow to select

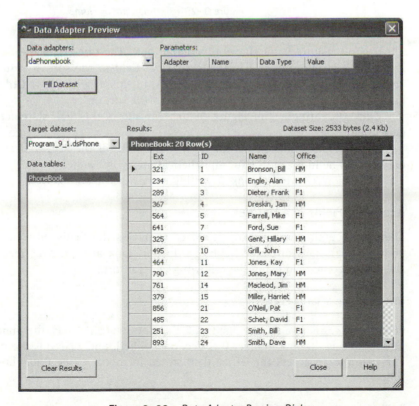

Figure 9–28   *Data Adapter Preview Dialog*

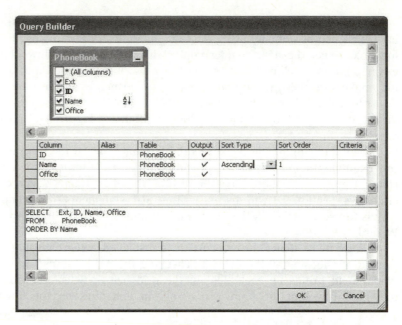

Figure 9–29 *Sorting Data by Name*

ASCending. Figure 9–29 shows this dialog box. The one (1) in the Sort Order column indicates it is the first, and in this case, only field in the sort. It would be possible to create a sort that consists of multiple fields. In this case the Sort Order column would have a number to indicate the field's place in the sort order.

Click OK, bringing up Figure 9–30. This shows the **SQL** statement that has been generated.

Note the line PhoneBook ORDER BY Name. This is the **SQL** clause that indicates the data should be in ascending (or alphabetical) order by Name.

In Section 9.4 we will look at writing our own **SQL** statements.

Accessing Fields in a Dataset

There will be situations where you need to access the fields in a dataset and perhaps perform operations on these fields. To do this, look at each row (record) of a table to access a specific field using the following general form

Datasetname.table(rownumber).field

where *Datasetname* is the name of the dataset, *table* is the name of the table, *rownumber* is the row number (i.e., record number), and *field* is the name of the field. For example, to access the Office field stored in row 5 of the Phonebook table, use the following expression:

DsPhone1.Phonebook(5).Office

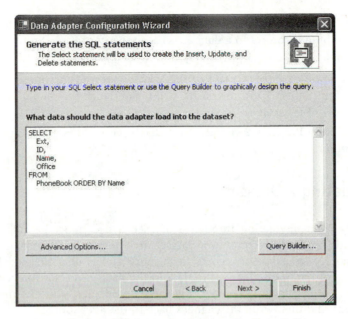

Figure 9-30 *SQL Statements Generated by Query Builder*

It is important to remember that the first row number is 0, and row number 5 is actually the sixth row in the table.

Every table has a **Count** property holding the number of rows in the table. To access this value, use the general form:

*Datasetname.table.*Count

To determine how many records in the Phonebook table have an Office field of 'HM', use the following code:

```
Dim hmoffices, i As Integer

hmoffices = 0
For i = 0 to DsPhone1.Phonebook.Count -1
  If DsPhone1.Phonebook(i).Office = "HM" Then
    hmoffices = hmoffices  + 1
  End If
Next i
MessageBox.Show("Number of HM offices is " & hmoffices)
```

Exercises 9.2

1. List the three main steps required to set up database access.

2. Describe the purpose of a data adapter.

3. How is a dataset different from a database table?

4. To bind a control to a dataset, what property of each control needs to be set?

5. Enter and execute Program 9–1 on your computer.

6. Modify Program 9–1 so that the displayed records are presented in reverse order; i.e., from highest ID to lowest ID. (*Hint:* Configure the data adapter again by using the Query Builder.)

7. Modify Program 9–1 so that the displayed records are presented in extension value order.

9.3 Updating a Dataset

Aside from navigating through a dataset, a user must be able to add records, delete records, and edit records in a dataset. It is important to remember that a dataset is a temporary snapshot of records in memory and is disconnected from the original data source or database. Changes to data in the dataset do not affect the database unless an explicit operation is executed. Via the data adapter, you can make the changes in the dataset and then write the changes back to the data source.

Figure 9-31 shows the interface for Program 9-2. In addition to the controls that are in Program 9-1, this interface includes buttons for adding, deleting, and editing records. The Save Button is used only during Edit mode.

Figure 9-32 shows the Form that is displayed when the program is run. This displays the fifth record of the table, after the Next Button has been clicked four times. Note that the text boxes are locked and the Save Button is grayed out. The only time the Save Button is available and the text boxes may be changed is after the Edit Button is

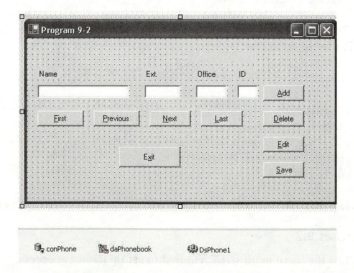

Figure 9–31 *Program 9–2's Interface*

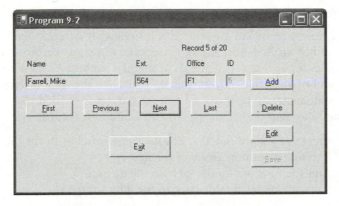

Figure 9–32   *Program 9–2's Initial Form*

clicked. The ID field is automatically created when a record is added, and its value cannot be set or changed by the user.

Initialization Code

There is code that must be run when the program starts and the form is loaded. This code fills in the dataset, locks the text boxes so they cannot be changed, and sets some variables. The global variable edit is set to **True** only when the user has selected the Edit Button so its value is initialized to **False**. Event Code 9–1 shows the initialization of the global variables and the `frmMain_Load` procedure.

Event Code 9–1

```
Dim currManager As CurrencyManager
Dim edit As Boolean
Dim Mboxmessage As String
Dim Savename, Saveoffice, SaveExt As String

Private Sub frmMain_Load(ByVal sender As System.Object, ByVal e As _
    System.EventArgs) Handles MyBase.Load
  currManager = Me.BindingContext(DsPhone1, "Phonebook")
  'Fill in the dataset
  daPhonebook.Fill(DsPhone1)
  'lock the text boxes so they can't be changed
  txtName.ReadOnly = True
  txtExt.ReadOnly = True
  txtOffice.ReadOnly = True
  txtID.ReadOnly = True
  btnSave.Enabled = False
  edit = False
End Sub
```

Adding a Record

Adding a new record to a database is a somewhat complicated process. At a high level, the Form has an Add Button that a user clicks to start the process. The program prompts the user to input text for the fields of the new record. All new records are always added to the end of the table. If you want to rearrange the data after adding records, the **SQL Select** statement can be modified and the dataset is refilled.

The following steps must be done to add a new record:

- Create an empty row that has the same fields as in the table to be modified.
- Enter data into the fields of the new row.
- Add the new row to the table in the dataset.
- Save the updated table back to the data source.

Now we will look at each step in detail.

Creating a New Empty Row   To create an empty row you must declare an object variable that can reference the row. With *newrow* as the name of the object variable, an example of this declaration is:

```
Dim newrow as System.Data.DataRow
```

Now create the row using the object variable *newrow* set equal to *DataSet.Table*.NewRow as in this example:

```
newrow = DsPhone1.Phonebook.NewRow
```

After this statement has executed, *newrow* references a new empty row that has the same layout as the PhoneBook table. Note that this new row is not yet part of the DsPhone1 dataset.

Entering Data into the New Row   The next step entails using the row's Item method to assign a value to a field. With *newvar* as the name of the object variable, the general form is:

```
newvar.Item(Fieldname) = value
```

Assign a value to each field in the table's row. In the Phonebook Table, the field names are Name, Ext, Office, and ID. Use InputBox to get the user data or the user can enter the data into the text boxes on the Form. The following statements could be included in the procedure:

```
newrow.Item("Name") = InputBox("Enter the Name - Last, First")
newrow.Item("Ext") = InputBox("Enter the Extension")
newrow.Item("Office") = InputBox("Enter an Office Code (HM or F1)")
```

It is not necessary to enter an ID as that is automatically assigned.

Adding the New Row to the Table   After the new values have been stored in the fields of the new row, add the new row to the table. This is done using the Add method, which has the general form:

```
dataset.Table.Rows.Add(newvar)
```

In our example, this becomes:

```
DsPhone1.Phonebook.Rows.Add(newrow)
```

Saving the Updated Table   To make the new row a part of the database (only the dataset has been updated so far), use the data adapter's Update method. The general form of this is

```
DataAdapter.Update(dataset)
```

which in our example becomes

```
daPhonebook.Update(DsPhone1)
```

After this statement has been executed, the entire dataset is saved back to the data adapter's data source, which is the Phonebook database. After the update has occurred, the call to the Refresh method forces the contents of the data-bound controls to be refreshed. A call to the ShowPosition procedure from Program 9–1 causes the record number and count to be refreshed. Event Code 9–2 shows the code that can be used to add a row to the database table.

Event Code 9–2 btnAdd_Click Procedure

```
Private Sub btnAdd_Click(ByVal sender As System.Object, ByVal e As _
    System.EventArgs) Handles btnAdd.Click

    Dim newrow As System.Data.DataRow

    ' add new row
    newrow = DsPhone1.PhoneBook.NewRow
    ' enter data in each field
    Try
        newrow.Item("Name") = InputBox("Enter the Name - Last, First")
        newrow.Item("Ext") = InputBox("Enter the Ext - 3 digits")
        newrow.Item("Office") = InputBox("Enter an Office Code (HM or F1)")
        DsPhone1.PhoneBook.Rows.Add(newrow)
        daPhonebook.Update(DsPhone1)
        'Move to display added record which is at end
        currManager.Position = currManager.Count - 1
        currManager.Refresh()
```

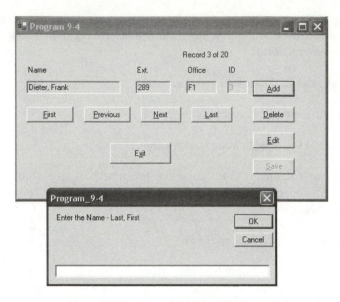

Figure 9–33   *Input Dialog to Add a Record*

```
      ShowPosition()
   Catch
      'If cancel is clicked during InputBox or other errors occur
       MessageBox.Show("Canceling Add Operation")
   End Try
End Sub
```

Note the `Try-Catch` block in the procedure. This is a **Visual Basic** statement that will catch any run-time exceptions or errors that occur between the statements **Try and Catch**. For example, if the user clicks Cancel during the InputBox dialog, the Catch block will cause the message "`Canceling Add Operation`" to be displayed. The Try-Catch block is more fully discussed in Chapter 10.

Figure 9–33 shows the Form and the Input dialog box that first appear when the Add Button is clicked.

Deleting a Record

Deleting a record from a dataset is a simpler process than adding a record. To delete a record, call the `RemoveAt` method that pertains to the CurrencyManager

```
cmvar.RemoveAt(rowindex)
```

where `cmvar` is the object variable that references the Currency Manager object and `rowindex` is the position of the row that is to be removed. If `currManager` is the object variable, the following statement can be used to remove the current record:

```
currManager.RemoveAt(currManager.Position)
```

In using this statement, however, we must provide for a contingency. Because all information in a deleted record is lost, we should build in a safety mechanism to protect against a user inadvertently activating the Delete Button. Before deleting a record, we first want to ensure that the user really wants to proceed with the deletion. This "safety check" can be handled with a message box similar to the one shown in Figure 9–34. As illustrated, the message box consists of a critical icon and two push buttons, with the default being the second, or cancel, button. Thus, if a user accidentally presses the Enter key, the deletion will not take place, and only a positive action on the part of the user will cause the deletion to occur. The appropriate message box can be created using the following code:

```
Dim msgresult as Integer

msgresult = MessageBox.Show("Press OK to Delete", "Program 9-4", _
    MessageBoxButtons.OKCancel, MessageBoxIcon.Exclamation, _
    MessageBoxDefaultButton.Button2)

If msgresult = DialogResult.OK Then
    . . .
```

Program 9–2's btnDelete control's **Click** event is listed as Event Code 9–3. Assume that the variable `currManager` has already been declared as a global variable and its position is set to the record that is to be deleted.

Event Code 9–3 btnDelete_Click Procedure

```
Private Sub btnDelete_Click(ByVal sender As System.Object, ByVal e As _
    System.EventArgs) Handles btnDelete.Click
  Dim MboxType As Integer

  Mboxmessage = "Press OK to Delete"
  If MessageBox.Show(Mboxmessage, "Program 9-4", MessageBoxButtons.OKCancel, _
```

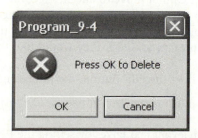

Figure 9–34   *The Delete Warning Message Box*

```
      MessageBoxIcon.Exclamation, MessageBoxDefaultButton.Button2) = _
        DialogResult.OK Then
      MessageBox.Show("Deleting record " & currManager.Position + 1)
      currManager.RemoveAt(currManager.Position)
      daPhonebook.Update(DsPhone1)
      currManager.Refresh()
      ShowPosition()
    End If
  End Sub
```

After the record is deleted from the dataset, a call to the Update method is made to update the database. After that, the data-bound controls are refreshed and the record position and count is updated on the form.

Editing a Record

An existing record's fields can be edited by modifying the desired field in the current record and then saved to the database by a call to the Update method. However, because there are so many safeguards that must be taken to ensure the process works correctly, the user must first click the Edit Button before being able to change the value of the fields. The following steps are taken by the user to edit a record:

1. Make the desired record the current record (move to the record by using one of the four positioning buttons).
2. Click the Edit Button to begin the editing process.
3. Assign new values to the desired fields.
4. Click either Save to save the changes to the database or Cancel to undo the operation.

To ensure that a user does not mistakenly type a new value in a text box that is bound to a field of a record, the **ReadOnly** properties of the text boxes are set to **True**, locking those text boxes. Only when the user clicks the Edit Button are the text boxes unlocked. At that time, the user may type in new values to those fields that can be changed. In our example, the value of the Name, Office, and Ext fields may be edited. The ID cannot be changed, and its text box remains locked. When the editing process begins, the Add Button is changed to become a Cancel Button and all other buttons are disabled so the user cannot move to another record.

After the user completes the editing of one record, either the Save Button or the Cancel Button should be clicked. If, however, the user clicks Exit or Closes the Form instead, there is a prompt asking if they would like the edited record changed before the Form is closed.

When a user clicks the Edit Button, the following is done in the code:

- Save the values of the Text property of the text boxes in case the user cancels the operation.
- Unlock the relevant text boxes by setting the **ReadOnly** property of each to **False**.
- Disable the navigation buttons.

- Enable the <u>S</u>ave Button.
- Change the Text property of the <u>A</u>dd Button to "<u>C</u>ancel." (See the additional code below that must be added to the `btnAdd_Click` procedure.)
- Set a flag indicating an edit is in progress. (A Boolean variable edit is used.)

The code for the `btnEdit_Click` procedure is shown in Event Code 9–4.

Event Code 9–4 btnEdit_Click Procedure

```
Private Sub btnEdit_Click(ByVal sender As System.Object, ByVal e As _
    System.EventArgs) Handles btnEdit.Click
    'Save the initial values in case the user cancels the operation
    Savename = txtName.Text
    Saveoffice = txtOffice.Text
    SaveExt = txtExt.Text
    'Unlock the text boxes so they can be changed
    txtExt.ReadOnly = False
    txtOffice.ReadOnly = False
    txtName.ReadOnly = False
    'Disable navigation
    btnNext.Enabled = False
    btnPrevious.Enabled = False
    btnFirst.Enabled = False
    btnLast.Enabled = False
    btnDelete.Enabled = False
    'Enable Save button
    btnSave.Enabled = True
    'Change Add button to become Cancel
    btnAdd.Text = "&Cancel"
    edit = True
End Sub
```

Figure 9–35 illustrates the Form after the <u>E</u>dit Button has been clicked. Note that the <u>A</u>dd Button is now a <u>C</u>ancel Button and the navigation buttons have been disabled (grayed out). Also note that the text boxes for Name, Office, and Ext are now white, indicating that they can be changed.

After the user has completed the editing changes, the <u>S</u>ave Button is clicked to save the changed fields to the dataset, as well as to update the database. The following is the algorithm for the Save:

- Check that the user really wants to save the edited record
- If not, call a cancel procedure (see below)
- Otherwise, move off the current record so the edited record becomes part of the dataset
- Call the restore procedure, which does the following:
  - Locks the text boxes
  - Enables the navigation buttons

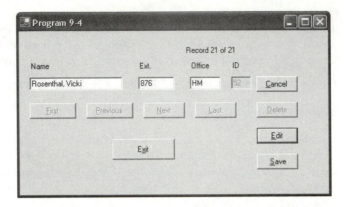

Figure 9–35 *Form after the Edit Button is Clicked*

- Disables the Save Button
- Changes the **Text** property of the Add button back to "Add"
- Turns off the edit flag to indicate the edit is no longer in progress
- Updates the database
- Refreshes the data-bound controls

When the user clicks the Save Button, a prompt appears to make sure the user wants to save the record that was just changed. In Figure 9–36, a record was previously added to the database and now the user has clicked edit to change the extension (Ext) from 876 to 987.

Because the Add Button has become a Cancel Button while an edit is in progress, the user also can click on the Cancel Button to cancel the edit operation. The code that

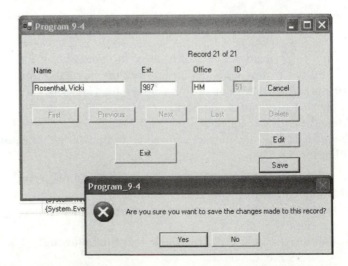

Figure 9–36 *Prompt after Clicking the Save Button When Editing a Record*

must be added to the beginning of the `btnAdd_Click` procedure (see Event Code 9–2) is the following:

```
If btnAdd.Text = "&Cancel" Then
  cancel()
Else
(code above in Event Procedure 9-1)
End If
```

so the cancel procedure may be called from `btnAdd_Click` or from within the `btnSave_Click` procedure. The algorithm for the cancel procedure is:

- Restore the saved values of the text boxes
- Call the restore procedure which does the following:
  - Locks the text boxes
  - Enables the navigation buttons
  - Disables the Save Button
  - Changes the Text property of the Add Button back to "Add"
  - Turns off the edit flag to indicate the edit is no longer in progress

Note that in the following code, variables `MboxType`, `Mboxmessage`, and `Edit` are declared as global variables.

Event Code 9–5 btnSave_Click Procedure

```
Private Sub btnSave_Click(ByVal sender As System.Object, ByVal e As _
    System.EventArgs) Handles btnSave.Click
  Mboxmessage = "Are you sure you want to save the changes made to this" & _
    "record?"
  If MessageBox.Show(Mboxmessage, "Program 9-4", MessageBoxButtons.YesNo, _
    MessageBoxIcon.Exclamation) = DialogResult.Yes Then
    currManager.Position += 1
    restore()
    daPhonebook.Update(DsPhone1)
    currManager.Refresh()
  Else
    cancel()
  End If
End Sub

Private Sub restore()
  'Lock the text boxes so they can't be changed
  txtName.ReadOnly = True
  txtExt.ReadOnly = True
  txtOffice.ReadOnly = True
```

```
    txtID.ReadOnly = True
    'Enable navigation
    btnNext.Enabled = True
    btnPrevious.Enabled = True
    btnFirst.Enabled = True
    btnLast.Enabled = True
    btnDelete.Enabled = True
    'Disable save button
    btnSave.Enabled = False
    'Change from Cancel back to Add
    btnAdd.Text = "&Add"
    edit = False
End Sub

Private Sub cancel()
    'Restore saved values since canceling edit operation
    txtName.Text = Savename
    txtOffice.Text = Saveoffice
    txtExt.Text = SaveExt
    restore()
End Sub
```

Code also must be included in the btnExit_Click and the Form Closing procedures, in case the user was in the middle of an edit and does want to save the changed record. The code displays a MessageBox with a prompt asking if the user wants to save the record. If so, the Update method is called and the Form is then closed.

```
Private Sub btnExit_Click(ByVal sender As System.Object, ByVal e As _
    System.EventArgs) Handles btnExit.Click
  If edit Then
    Mboxmessage = "Do you want to save the changes made to the last record?"
    If MessageBox.Show(Mboxmessage, "Program 9-4", MessageBoxButtons.YesNo, _
        MessageBoxIcon.Exclamation) = DialogResult.Yes Then
      currManager.Position += 1
      daPhonebook.Update(DsPhone1)
    End If
  End If
  Beep()
  End
End Sub
```

Exercises 9.3

1. Program 9–2 provides Buttons for adding, deleting and editing records. When is the **ReadOnly** property of a bound text box set to True, and why?

2. Event Code 9-2 contains the code for adding a record. Why is it important to include a Try-Catch block in this code?

3. What method is used to delete a record from a dataset? Does this method remove the record from the database?

4. Program 9-2 enables you to add a new row to a table by using InputBoxes to enter the new data. What other techniques could be used to enter new data for the fields of the record?

9.4   Creating Datasets Using SQL

There are many different ways to view the records in a dataset. There will be times when you will need to create a set of records that is constructed from more than one table, or view a subset of records that meets one or more criteria. For example, you might need to create a list of people whose outstanding balance is over sixty days old, or create a list of people who owe more than $500, or possibly cross-check two tables to determine names that appear in both. For situations such as these, you will need to build your own structured queries instead of relying on the one created by the Data Adapter Configuration Wizard.

Reviewing Program 9-1, the data source was set to the entire PhoneBook at design time, causing the Jet engine to create a dataset consisting of all records in stored order. Looking at Figure 9-18, the SQL statement that was initially generated by the Query Builder was

```
SELECT Phonebook.* FROM PhoneBook
```

However, this statement was expanded to list all the fields as in the following statement

```
SELECT Ext, ID, Name, Office FROM PhoneBook
```

when the statement was stored. These two SQL statements are also equivalent to

```
SELECT * FROM PhoneBook
```

This statement is rather easy to read, once you understand that the * is a shortcut meaning all fields are to be listed in the order they appear in the table. Thus, this statement is read "*select* all fields *from the* PhoneBook table." Because no further constraints are placed on the table, the default is to select all of the table records.

Figure 9-37 shows the properties for the data adapter daPhonebook. The SQL statement is stored in the **SelectCommand.CommandText** property. Like any other property of a control, any element of the SQL statement can be changed. As you will see from the text that follows, the basics of SQL are straightforward.

There are four ways to create the SQL statement for the data adapter:

- Use the Query Builder in the Data Adapter Configuration Wizard to generate the SQL statement

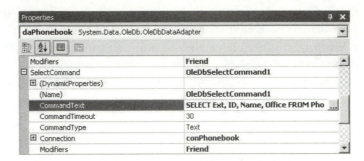

Figure 9–37   *Data Adapter SelectCommand.CommandText Property*

- Use the Data Adapter Configuration Wizard, but type in the **SQL** statement instead of using the Query Builder
- Type the **SQL** statement directly into the **SelectCommand.CommandText** property of the Data Adapter at design time
- Use code to set the value of the **SelectCommand.CommandText** property of the Data Adapter at run-time

As defined in Section 9.1, a *structured query* is a statement written according to the rules of a language called Structured Query Language (SQL), that uniquely identifies a set of records from one or more tables. Structured queries provide much more flexibility to create and order individualized sets of records and can be entered either at design time or set at run-time. However, we must become familiar with the components of the **SELECT** statement.

SQL was developed by IBM in the 1970s and became the foundation of its data management software. In 1986, an American National Standards Institute (ANSI) standard was approved for this language, and since that time many commercial DBMS products, including Microsoft's Jet engine, support it as an extremely powerful technique for extracting data from database tables.

The basic syntax of an SQL SELECT command, referred to as a structured query, is:

```
SELECT field(s) FROM table(s) [WHERE condition(s)] [ORDER BY field(s)]
```

Formally, this statement consists of four clauses: a **SELECT** clause, a **FROM** clause, an optional **WHERE** clause, and an optional **ORDER BY** clause. The words **SELECT**, **FROM**, **WHERE**, and **ORDER BY** are all SQL keywords.

At a minimum, a structured query must contain both a **SELECT** and a **FROM** clause; the **SELECT** clause specifies the field values that will be returned by the query, while the **FROM** clause specifies the table or tables where records will be searched. Additionally, if any restrictions are placed on the data to be selected, or the selected information is to be presented in a specified order, the **WHERE** and **ORDER BY** clauses must be included, respectively. Let's examine the following SQL statement:

```
SELECT * FROM PhoneBook ORDER BY Ext
```

- the **SELECT** * clause specifies that all fields are to be obtained
- the **FROM** clause specifies that the fields are to come from the PhoneBook table
- the **ORDER BY** clause specifies that the dataset is to be constructed in increasing (i.e., ascending) order based on the values in the Ext field. If descending order is desired (that is, from highest to lowest extension values) the **SQL** keyword **DESC** must be placed after the field name in the **ORDER BY** clauses. Thus, the SQL statement `SELECT * FROM PhoneBook ORDER BY Ext DESC` performs the same function as the previous **SQL** statement, but returns the data in descending extension number order.

Because structured queries are so versatile and can be used to construct datasets that contain records constructed from more than one table, they are used extensively for many Visual Basic database applications.

Finding Specific Data in a Dataset

To illustrate the usefulness of creating datasets using structured queries, we present a number of examples using the SQL **SELECT** statement. In the first two examples we use the Company database, whose tables were previously listed as Tables 9–1 through 9–3. We then construct datasets with records derived from two tables. For these latter examples we will use the Biblio database.

Example 1: Using the PhoneBook table, create a dataset consisting of all fields for employees in the home office.
    The structured query for this example is:

```
SELECT * FROM PhoneBook WHERE Office = 'HM'
```

Here we have used a **WHERE** clause, creating a set of records where each record must meet the specified condition to be included in the final dataset. The resulting set of records is frequently referred to as a *filtered set*, and the **WHERE** clause itself is commonly referred to as a *filter*. In reviewing this clause, note that the value being searched for—HM—is enclosed in single quotes. This is required in SQL when the field type of the desired item is a string type. If the field type were numeric, the value in the SQL **WHERE** clause would not be enclosed in single quotes. As always, the asterisk (*) in the query results in all fields in the selected records being included in the dataset, in the order in which they exist in the underlying table. To change this order, individually list the fields in the desired order. For example, the structured query:

```
SELECT Office, Name, Ext, ID FROM PhoneBook WHERE Office = 'HM'
```

extracts the same data as the prior query, but creates a dataset in which each record has the field order listed in the **SELECT** statement. This ordering makes no difference to an application, as long as the fields required by the bound controls are included in the query. Each bound control will subsequently extract its required field from the resulting dataset no matter where the field is physically located within a record.

Finally, note that when explicit fields are listed within a **SELECT** clause, the individual field names are separated by commas.

Looking back at Program 9–1, the **SQL** query was created at design time and the dataset was subsequently filled at design time. If you want to change the dataset at runtime, insert the following statements in your program to include only those employees in the home office:

```
Dim SQ As String
SQ = "SELECT Office, Name, Ext, ID FROM PhoneBook WHERE Office = 'HM'"
daPhonebook.SelectCommand.CommandText = SQ
daPhonebook.Fill(DsPhone1)
```

Example 2: Using the SalesRep table, create a dataset consisting of all fields for employees living in Orange.

The structured query for this example is:

```
SELECT * FROM SalesRep WHERE City = 'Orange'
```

In reviewing this query, note that once again, because the City is a string field, we have enclosed the value being searched for within single quotes. As always, the query defines both the fields to be included in the dataset and the table from which these fields are to be taken. Additionally, the **WHERE** clause creates a filtered record set, where each selected record meets the stated requirement.

Although both of the preceding two examples have used a simple relational expression in the **WHERE** clause, compound expressions using the **And** and **Or** keywords are valid. For example, the structured query

```
SELECT Name FROM PhoneBook WHERE Ext < 300 OR Ext > 900
```

produces a set of records consisting of the Name field only for those individuals having an extension number either less than 300 or greater than 900. Note that because the Ext field is defined as a numeric field, the values within the relational expression have not been enclosed in single quotes.

Accessing All Records in a Dataset

Finally, often all records from a dataset have to be processed. The following code, using the Currency Manager, illustrates how this can be done. The purpose of this code is to delete every record in the PhoneBook table whose Office field is equal to 'HM.'

```
Dim SQ As String
currManager = Me.BindingContext(DsPhone1, "Phonebook")

SQ = "SELECT * FROM PhoneBook WHERE Office = 'HM'"
daPhonebook.SelectCommand.CommandText = SQ
```

```
daPhonebook.Fill(DsPhone1)

currManager.Position = 0
Do While currManager.Count > 0
    currManager.RemoveAt(currManager.Position)
Loop
```

In this code, the dataset is constructed using the **SQL** statement that finds all records with the Office field equal to 'HM.' By setting the **Position** property of the CurrencyManager to 0, the current record is set to the first record in the dataset. When the loop is executed, the first record in the dataset is deleted using the **RemoveAt** method. The loop uses the number of records in the dataset as its test. When there are no records left, the loop is exited.

DataGrid Control

The **DataGrid** control is a powerful tool used to display and modify one or more database tables. It displays data from a database table as a series of rows and columns, and enables you to see the entire dataset by scrolling down the DataGrid (similar to the Preview dataset option). By setting several properties of the control, you can associate it with the records in a dataset. Each row of the dataGrid corresponds to a record in a dataset and each column references the corresponding field. The DataGrid references the dataset directly and does not contain a copy of the data. Any changes made to the fields of the DataGrid are reflected in the dataset. However, the changes are not made to the data source until the data adapter's `Update` method is called.

To create a DataGrid on a form, click on the DataGrid control in the toolbox and then draw it on the Form, or double-click on the tool and resize it on the Form. Figure 9–38 shows the DataGrid in the toolbox. Figure 9–39 shows what the DataGrid first

Figure 9–38   *DataGrid in the Toolbox*

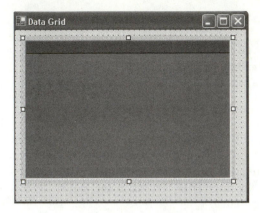

Figure 9–39 *DataGrid Control Initially placed on a Form*

looks like when it is drawn on the Form. The DataGrid control is associated with a table in an existing dataset by setting its **DataSource** property to the name of the table you want to display.

The DataGrid control has a number of properties and methods that are described in Table 9–5. Note that this is just a small subset of the entire set of properties and methods.

The following illustrates how a DataGrid can be used. Using the Phonebook table in the Offices database, set up a data connection and data adapter as you did for Program 9–1 in the section *Navigating through Datasets* (page 525). However, for this program we want the columns in a specific order, which can be done in one of several ways. In the Query Builder of the Data Adapter Configuration Wizard, select the Phonebook table and then choose the fields in the following order: ID, Name, Ext, and Office. Instead of setting the query at design time, you can set it at run-time. In the frmMain_Load procedure, you can set the **SelectCommand.CommandText** property of the daPhonebook data adapter to the following SQL statement:

```
daPhonebook.SelectCommand.CommandText = _
    "SELECT ID, Name, Ext, Office FROM Phonebook"
```

Select the DataGrid on the Form and find its **DataSource** property in the Properties Window. Select this property, click the down-arrow and select `DsPhone1.Phonebook` in the drop-down window. This sets up the connection from the dataset to the DataGrid. The field names of the Phonebook are now shown as column headings on the DataGrid, as seen in Figure 9–40.

To populate the DataGrid with the selected fields of the Phonebook table, the `frmMain_Load` procedure is the following:

```
Private Sub frmMain_Load(ByVal sender As System.Object, ByVal e As _
    System.EventArgs) Handles MyBase.Load
```

Table 9–5   Some Important DataGrid Properties and Methods

Property	Description
AllowSorting	Returns or sets the value indicating whether the grid can be sorted by clicking the column header.
CaptionText	Returns or sets the text that appears in the title bar at the top of the grid.
CaptionVisible	Returns or sets the value indicating whether the caption in the title bar is visible.
DataMember	Returns or sets the specific table in the DataSource for which the control displays a grid.
DataSource	Returns or sets the data source that is bound to the DataGrid.
Enabled	Returns or sets the grid's user interactivity status. When set to **True**, the user may interact with the grid.
ReadOnly	When set to **True**, the user cannot update the contents of the grid. When set to **False**, the user can edit, delete, and add records to the grid, which are then reflected in the underlying dataset.

Method	Description
Focus	Sets the focus and activates the DataGrid.
Refresh	Repaints the DataGrid.
ResetBindings	Refreshes the data derived from the data source.
SetDataBinding	Sets the DataSource and DataMember properties at run-time.

```
DsPhone1.Clear()
daPhonebook.SelectCommand.CommandText = _
  "SELECT ID, Name, Ext, Office FROM Phonebook"
daPhonebook.Fill(DsPhone1)
End Sub
```

When the program is run and the Form is loaded, the dataset is first cleared of all data, the SQL statement is set, and the dataset is then filled using the Fill method of the data adapter. The DataGrid contains the data as shown in Figure 9–41. Note that the widths of the columns can be changed by moving to the column headings, clicking on the right/left arrow, and moving either left or right to make a column wider or smaller (Figure 9–42).

In this program the only button is an Exit Button, which does not include a call to the data adapter's Update method. Without that, any changes that may have been made to the fields in the DataGrid will not be saved back to the data source. However, this code can easily be added.

To extend this example, suppose you want to find only those people in the Phonebook whose offices are equal to 'HM.' The SQL statement above can be changed to

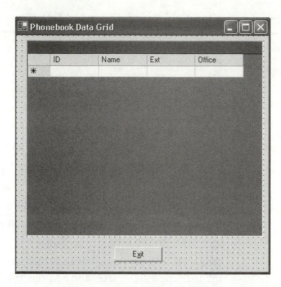

Figure 9–40 *DataGrid Control with Field Names as Column Headings*

Figure 9–41 *Phonebook Fields Displayed in a DataGrid*

```
daPhonebook.SelectCommand.CommandText = _
    "SELECT ID, Name, Ext, Office FROM Phonebook WHERE Office = 'HM'"
```

The DataGrid displayed when the program is run is shown in Figure 9–43.

Relationships Reconsidered

The Company database that we have used consists of three tables that, in practice, would be used independently of each other. That is, we could easily construct three

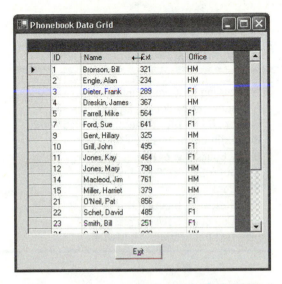

Figure 9–42   *Changing the Width of a Column*

Figure 9–43   *Finding Only People in HM Office*

forms, each of which uses its own **Data** controls to assess and display data from each of the three tables individually.

It is not unusual to encounter databases with tables that are related in a more significant manner. As an example, consider the Biblio database. This database consists of tables containing information about publishers, titles, and authors of current computer science text books. Tables 9–6 through 9–9 list the names and the first ten records of each of the four tables that comprise the Biblio database. The relationship between the Publishers, Titles, and Authors tables is shown by the ERD diagram illustrated in Figure 9–44.

Table 9–6 Publishers

PubID	Name	Company Name	Address
1	ACM	Association for Computing Machinery	11 W. 42nd St., 3rd flr.
2	Addison-Wesley	Addison-Wesley Publishing Co Inc.	Rte. 128
3	Bantam Books	Bantam Books Div of Bantam Doubleday Dell	666 Fifth Ave.
4	Benjamin/Cummings	Benjamin Cummings Publishing Company Subs.	390 Bridge Pkwy.
5	Brady Pub.	Brady Books Div. of Prentice Hall Pr.	15 Columbus Cir.
6	Computer Science Press	Computer Science Press Inc Imprint	41 Madison Ave.
7.	ETN Corporation	ETN Corp.	RD 4, Box 659
8	Gale	Gale Research, Incorporated	835 Penobscot Bldg.
9	IEEE	IEEE Computer Society Press	10662 Los Vaqueros
10	Intertext	Intertext Publications/Multiscience	2633 E. 17th Ave.

As shown in Figure 9–44, and reading from left-to-right, a publisher can be associated with zero or more titles, and a title can have one or more authors. Similarly, reading from right-to-left, an author can be associated with one or more titles, while a title can only be associated with a single publisher. Using Tables 9–6 through 9–7 we can easily establish datasets for any of the one-to-many relationships shown in Figure 9–44. This is accomplished by matching a desired field value in the appropriate table. For example, if we needed to locate all titles associated with the publisher ETN, the following structured query could be entered as a **SelectCommand.CommandText** property value:

```
SELECT * FROM Titles WHERE PubID = 7
```

This type of query, which is a straightforward lookup in a single table, is typical of that used for a one-to-many relationship. The standard practice here is simply to locate all records in the table on the many side of the relationship that have a matching field value for the single entity on the one side of the relationship. Unfortunately, no such simple lookup generally exists for locating matching entries corresponding to a many-to-many relationship.

For example, assume that we need to locate all authors associated with a single title. Because the titles-to-authors relationship is a many-to-many relationship, each title can have one or more associated authors and each author can be associated with one or more titles. To handle such relationships, tables referred to as both *cross-reference*, *correlation*, and *intersection* tables (all three terms are synonymous) are used. An example of a correlation table is illustrated by Table 9–9. Here, all authors associated with a particular ISBN number can be identified by locating all occurrences of the same

City	State	Zip	Telephone	Fax	Comments
New York	NY	10036	212-869-7440		
Reading	MA	01867	617-944-3700	617-964-9460	
New York	NY	10103	800-223-6834	212-765-3869	GENERAL TRA
Redwood City	CA	94065	800-950-2665	415-594-4409	
New York	NY	10023	212-373-8093	212-373-8292	
New York	NY	10010	212-576-9400	212-689-2383	Introductory
Montoursville	PA	17754-9433	717-435-2202	717-435-2802	Technical Book
Detroit	MI	48226-4094	313-961-2242	313-961-6083	
Los Altamitos	CA	90720	800-272-6657	714-821-4010	PROFESSION
Anchorage	AK	99508			

ISBN number in the first column. Similarly, all books written by a single author can be identified by locating all occurrences of the author's ID number in the second column. Thus, if we needed to locate all of the authors associated with the book entitled *Guide to ORACLE*, which has an ISBN number of 0-0702063-1-7 (see the fifth record in Table 9–7), we could use the following structured query:

```
SELECT * FROM TitleAuthor WHERE ISBN = '0-0702063-1-7'
```

Similarly, if we needed to identify all books associated with the author named Virginia Andersen (the fourth author listed in Table 9–8), who has the author identification number 4, we could use the following structured query:

```
SELECT * FROM TitleAuthor WHERE Au_ID = 4
```

Note that in the first query the "looked for" value has been enclosed in single quotes, while in the second query no quotes are used. This is because the ISBN field is defined as a string field, while the Au_ID field is defined as a numeric field in the TitleAuthor table.

Creating Multitable Datasets

In addition to using structured queries to either filter or order data from a single table, they can be used to create sets of records derived from two or more tables. To illustrate this use of structured queries, we will again use the Biblio database (see Tables 9–6 through 9–9).

Table 9–7   Titles

Title	Year Published	ISBN	PubID	Description/Notes	Subject
Database management; developing application	1989	0-0131985-2-1	17	xx, 441 p. : il	
SELECT– SQL ; the relational database language	1992	0-0238669-4-2	12	xv, 446 p.	
dBase IV programming	1994	0-0280042-4-8	73		
Step-by-step dBase IV	1995	0-0280095-2-5	52		
Guide to ORACLE	1990	0-0702063-1-7	13	xii, 354 p. : ill/Includes I	ORACLE
The database experts' guide to SQL 00703	1988 10	0-0703900-6-1			
Oracle/SQL; a professional programmer's guide	1992	0-0704077-5-4	13	xx, 543 p. : il	
SQL 400: A Professional Programmer's Guide	1994	0-0704079-9-1	52		
Database system concepts	1986	0-0704475-2-7	13		
Microsoft FoxPro 2.5 applications programming	1993	0-0705015-3-X	61	xiii, 412 p. : i	

Table 9–8   Authors

Au_ID	Author	Year Born
1	Adams, Pat	
2	Adrian, Merv	
3	Ageloff, Roy	1943
4	Andersen, Virginia	
5	Antonovich, Michael P.	
6	Arnott, Steven E.	
7	Arntson, L. Joyce	
8	Ault, Michael R.	
9	Avison, D. E.	
10	Bard, Dick	1941

Table 9–9   TitleAuthor

ISBN	Au_ID
0-0131985-2-1	13
0-0238669-4-2	113
0-0280042-4-8	11
0-0280042-4-8	120
0-0280095-2-5	171
0-0702063-1-7	26
0-0702063-1-7	65
0-0702063-1-7	104
0-0703900-6-1	96
0-0704077-5-4	59

Figure 9–44   *The ERD Diagram for the Biblio.mdb Database*

As a specific example, assume that we want to create a set of records that consist of a book's title and its publisher. Additionally, we want the final list of records to be in alphabetical order by publisher. To create this record set we would use the Titles table to locate all of the titles, and the Publishers table to locate all of the publishers. When using two tables, the general format of the SELECT statement is:

```
SELECT Titles.Title, Publishers.Name
FROM Titles, Publishers
```

```
WHERE Titles.PubID = Publishers.PubID
ORDER by Publishers.Name
```

For clarity we have written the query across three lines to easily identify each of the individual clauses. In practice, this single statement can be written as a single line as a data adapter's **SelectCommand.CommandText** property.

In reviewing this query you should note two items: The first is that the **FROM** clause identifies two tables. As with the **SELECT** clause, where multiple fields can be identified, the **FROM** clause can include multiple table names. When this is done, individual table names must be separated by commas. The second item to note is the manner in which the field names have been identified throughout the query. Because we are dealing with two tables—both of which use the same field names—we must clearly establish which field is being referenced. This is accomplished using standard dot notation by listing the table name before the field name, and separating the two with a period. Thus, the name Titles.PubID refers to the PubID field in the Titles table, and Publishers.PubID refers to the PubID in the Publishers table. This notation can be used wherever a field name is required, but if there is no ambiguity about which table is being used the table name can always be omitted. Thus, the field name Titles.Title in the **SELECT** clause can be written simply as Title, because this field only exists in one of the tables referenced in the **FROM** clause.

Run-time Structured Queries

As we have already seen, a structured query can be entered as a data adapter **Select-Command.CommandText** property value at design time. For large queries, however, this can become error prone and provide queries that are cumbersome to debug. For example, a query such as

```
SELECT Titles.Title, Publishers.Name
FROM Titles, Publishers
WHERE Titles.PubID = Publishers.PubID
ORDER by Publishers.Name
```

is really too long to be conveniently entered as a **SelectCommand.CommandText** value. As we have seen, an alternative to entering such queries at design time is to set them at run-time. For example, consider Event Procedure 9–5, which uses the Form load event to set and fill the dataset whose data adapter is named daPubs. For this program, we will use a DataGrid to display the dataset.

Event Procedure 9–5

```
Private Sub Form1_Load(ByVal sender As System.Object, ByVal e As _
    System.EventArgs) Handles MyBase.Load
  Dim Sel, Frm, Whr, Ord, SQ As String
```

```
Sel = "SELECT Titles.Title, Publishers.Name"
Frm = " FROM Titles, Publishers"
Whr = " WHERE Titles.PubID = Publishers.PubID"
Ord = " ORDER By Publishers.Name"

SQ = Sel & Frm & Whr & Ord
daPubs.SelectCommand.CommandText = SQ
DsPubs1.Clear()
daPubs.Fill(DsPub1)

End Sub
```

The new feature illustrated by this event procedure is the construction of a string named SQ and the assignment of this string to daPubs.SelectCommand.Command Text. Although we have constructed the SQ string from four strings, each of which highlights an individual SQL clause, this was done for the convenience of making each line a manageable size.

Note that the final daPubs.SelectCommand.CommandText setting is identical to that which could have been entered as the daPubs.SelectCommand.CommandText at design time. Event Procedure 9–5 is used in Program 9–3, whose interface is shown in Figure 9–45.

After the connection, data adapter, and dataset have been set up, add a DataGrid to the form. Table 9–10 shows the properties Table for this Form. In the DataGrid's properties window, set its **DataSource** property to DsPubs1 and its **DataMember** property to Publishers. To ensure that the user cannot change any of the records, set the **ReadOnly** property to **True**.

When Program 9–3 is executed, the Form Load event causes the Jet engine to create a dataset consisting of records constructed from both the Titles and Publishers tables. Each record in the set will consist of two fields: a Titles field, whose values come from the Titles table, and a Name field, whose values come from the Publishers table. Additionally, the records in the set will be in alphabetical order, by publisher's name. The screen that appears when this program is first run is shown in Figure 9–46. Note that the rows have alternating colors; this is done by setting the **AlternatingBackColor** property to ControlLight.

Exercises 9.4

1. a. List the four clauses that can be present in a structured query.

   b. What are the two clauses that must be present in a structured query?

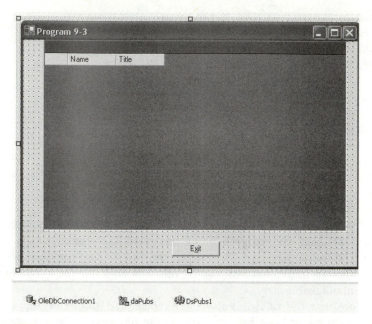

Figure 9–45 *Program 9–3's Interface*

Table 9–10   Program 9–3's Properties Table

Object	Property	Setting
Form	Name	frmMain
	Text	Program 9-3
DataGrid	Name	dgPubs
	DataMember	Publishers
	DataSource	DsPubs1
	ReadOnly	True
	AlternatingBackColor	ControlLight
Button	Name	btnExit
	Text	E&xit

2. Using the Company database (Tables 9–1 through 9–3), write a structured query to create a dataset consisting of all fields for the following criteria:

   a. All records from the SalesRep table (Table 9–2) whose representatives are assigned to office HM.

   b. All records from the SalesRep table (Table 9–2) whose representatives live in Orange, New Jersey.

   c. All records from the SalesRep table (Table 9–2) whose representatives have a middle initial.

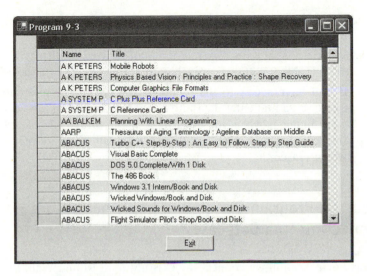

Figure 9–46   *The Output from Program 9–3*

   d. All records from the PhoneBook table (Table 9–1) for employees whose last name begins with B.

   e. All records from the PhoneBook table (Table 9–1d) whose employees have an extension number between 100 and 200.

3. Using the Publishers Table (Table 9–6), write a structured query to create a dataset consisting of all fields for the following criteria:

   a. All records with a New York City field value.

   b. All records with a New York State field value.

   c. All records with both a New York City and New York State field value.

   d. All records with a name field value beginning with the letter A.

   e. All records with a zip code between 07000 and 07999.

4. Using the Authors Table (Table 9–8), write a structured query to create a dataset consisting of the indicated fields for the following criteria:

   a. All author names for authors born before 1943.

   b. All Au_ID and author fields for authors whose birth date field is blank.

   c. All Au_ID fields for authors whose name begins with the letter C.

5. Enter and run Program 9–3 on your computer.

6. a. Write a Visual Basic Program that can be used to display all titles, ISBN numbers, and year published from the Titles table (Table 9–7) in year published order.

   b. If you have access to the Biblio database, run the program that you wrote for Exercise 6a.

7. a. Modify the program for Exercise 6a so that only texts published between 1989 and 1992 are accessed by your program.

b. If you have access to the Biblio database, run the program that you wrote for Exercise 7a.

8. a. Write a Visual Basic Program that can be used to display all fields of the Author table (Table 9–8) for records that do not have any data in their year born field.

b. If you have access to the Biblio database, run the program that you wrote for Exercise 8a and enter data into a text box bound to the year born field. Describe what happens when you enter data, move to another record, and return back to the record for which you entered a date. Did the date remain with the record or was it erased?

9.5 Focus on Program Design and Implementation: Connecting to a Database

In this Focus section we connect the existing Mail In and Walk In Forms to a database for storage of all transactions entered using these two order-entry screens. We then add an operational form for entering and storing disk package receipts into inventory. All three of these forms will require data controls to provide access to the required data table; we will not, however, make any of the existing form controls data-aware by binding them to the dataset. In this manner the forms are strictly used for input, and not for viewing or changing existing records. The actual writing of the entered data items into the data table is accomplished in software.

Before connecting the application to a data table, however, we must clearly understand the record structure that we will be interfacing with. This item is considered first.

The Data Table The data table we will use to store all inventory receipts and disbursements, which is named `RecDis`, is a Microsoft Access table and can be found in the `Disktran.mdb` database. The table's record structure, which consists of its field names and specifications, is listed in Table 9–11. Currently, the `RecDis` table contains 20 records, of which the relevant fields for our immediate purpose are listed in Table 9–12.

Tips from the Pros

The Text Data Type

Beginning programmers frequently make the mistake of assuming that a data value that appears to be a number should be stored as a numerical data type. Doing this can cause real problems, as illustrated by the following example. Consider the zip code values 92034, 47390, 07078, and 91843, as well as the phone extensions 7604, 5419, 2834, and 0365. If these zip codes are stored as numbers, the leading zero in the 07078 zip code will not displayed when it is printed. The same is true for the phone extension 0365 if the extension numbers are stored

Table 9–11 The RecDis Field Specifications

Field Name	Data Type	Field Width	Usage
ID	Autonumber	Not applicable	Unique record identification number
Fname	Text	15 characters	Store first name
Lname	Text	20 characters	Store last name
Addr	Text	20 characters	Store address
City	Text	20 characters	Store city
St	Text	2 characters	Store state
Zip	Text	10 characters	Store zip code
Quantity	Number	Not applicable	Store quantity
RDCode	Text	1 character	Store a receipt/delivery code
RDDate	Date	Not applicable	Store date of receipt/delivery
RetCode	Text	1 character	Store a return code
RetDate	Date	Not applicable	Store a return date

in number fields. The reason for this is that the default in all database programs is to suppress all leading zeros for any printed number value.

The correct rule to follow when assigning data types is the following: *Unless the normal mathematical operations of addition, subtraction, averaging, and so forth make sense for values that appear as numbers, store the values as text.* Doing so ensures that when the values are printed, all leading zeros will be displayed.[4]

In reviewing the current records in the RecDis file, first note the last two columns, listing the RDCode and RDDate fields (the RD refers to Receipt and Disbursement). Valid codes for this field are listed in Table 9–13. These codes are used in the next Focus section to provide detailed reports on the exact disposition of inventory, including how many Mail In orders were filled, how many Walk In orders were filled, and how inventory was received and returned to the manufacturer.

In addition to the RDCodes, the last field listed in Table 9–11 provides the date of each transaction. It is extremely important to always add a date (and possibly time) stamp to each stored transaction. The reason for this is that, inevitably, in addition to asking you *if* a transaction took place, you will be asked to provide information about *when* it took place. For example, imagine that in six months a Mail In customer sends a

---

[4]The author was once called in to determine the problem with an existing program that had printed 10,000 mailing labels for New Jersey, in which all of the zip codes appeared as 4-digit rather than 5-digit numbers. Except for the expense and time in printing the original labels, the problem was easily fixed by changing the zip code field type from number to text, ensuring that the leading 0 in the New Jersey zip codes was printed. An alternative fix would have been to use the Format function to explicitly force the display of all leading zeros.

Table 9–12   The RecDis Data

ID	Fname	Lname	Addr	City	St	Zip	Qnt.	Code	RDDate
1	Receipt	of Inventory					3000	r	4/1/99
2	Susan	Fortunato	2 Addison Rd.	Stockton	CA	95208	1	m	4/15/99
3	Bill	Jones	8 Feather Lane	W. Orange	NJ	07052	1	m	4/15/99
4	Diane	Smith	62 Oaklawn Rd.	Hewlett	NY	11557	2	m	4/15/99
5	Greg	Minor	818 Freemont Tr.	Florence	AZ	85232	1	m	4/15/99
6	Donna	Ende	16 Millhouse Rd.	Geneva	FA	32732	1	m	4/15/99
7	Jim	Bamson	22 Yale St.	Ann Arbor	MI	48106	3	m	4/15/99
8	Steve	Crowley	16 Maple St	Springfield	MA	01101	1	m	4/15/99
9	Rhonda	Harrison	3 Chestnut St.	Harrison	NJ	07029	1	m	4/15/99
10	Rochelle	Brown	10 Tivoli Pl.	Springfield	OH	45501	1	m	4/15/99
11	Returned	to Vendor					300	t	4/17/99
12	Damaged	Inventory					125	d	4/17/99
13	Julia	McDonald	25 South St	Hillsdale	NY	12529	1	m	4/17/99
14	Adjustment	to Inventory					30	o	4/17/99
15	Ronald	Dimol	18 Newman St.	Miami Beach	FL	33139	2	m	4/17/99
16	Loretta	Hartman	1 Ridgedale Ave.	St. Paul	MN	55101	2	m	4/17/99
17	Douglas	Evans	10 Pitman Pl.	Gunlock	UT	84733	1	m	4/17/99
18	Roberta	Lopez	18 2nd St.	Madison	NJ	07940	5	w	4/17/99
19	Joe	Lesser	25 E. Palidino St.	Hollywood	FL	33022	1	m	4/17/99
20	Cash						1	w	4/17/99

Table 9–13   Valid RDCodes

Code	Meaning
m	A disbursement from inventory due to a mail-in order
w	A disbursement from inventory due to a walk-in order
r	A receipt into inventory from the disk manufacturer
t	A return to the vendor from inventory
d	Damaged inventory
o	Other inventory adjustment

letter to the manufacturer asking about the free disk package they requested but never received. You subsequently receive a call from the disk manufacturer requesting information about this. You then confidently look up the person's name and address, and report to the manufacturer that this request was filled. The next question, of course, is "When did you fill it?" If you cannot answer this question, your credibility as a programmer can come into question. This is typical of the type of inquiries you must anticipate if you are to successfully program commercial applications. As a general rule, always mark each transaction with the date that it occurred.

With this preliminary understanding of the data that is stored for each transaction, we can now use the information presented in this chapter to connect our Rotech application to the Disktran database.

Connecting the Order-Entry Forms to a Database

The application's two order entry forms are the Mail In and Walk In Forms. We will work with one form at a time, starting with the current Mail In Form, shown in Figure 9–47. The first and only obvious change to this run-time Form is to make it look like Figure 9–48, where we have added a **Label** and TextBox control for a date field.

As shown in Figure 9–48, the new text box will contain a date when viewed by the user; the date presented will be the current ("today's") date. In addition to the two new run-time controls shown in this figure, we will set up a data connection to the data source (RecDis database), and set up the data adapter and the dataset. Figure 9–49 shows how the Mail In Form looks at design time, with the data controls in the component tray below the form. The relevant properties for the new controls are listed in Table 9–14.

Normally, after adding a data adapter to a form, a number of **TextBox** controls are bound to the dataset using each text box's **DataBindings.Text** property. In this particular case, however, we want only to use the text boxes as input controls, and not view and change data within existing transaction records. As such, we will not bind them to fields in the dataset. In this manner, to the only purpose for the data controls is to make the database table RecDis available to code on the Form. It is in the code that we will capture the input data and write it to the database. Procedure Code 9–1 lists the total additional code required, both to initialize the current date into the added text box and

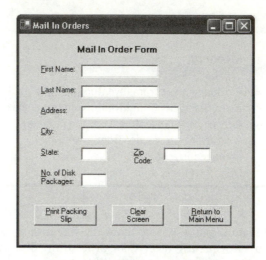

Figure 9–47 *The Current Mail In Form*

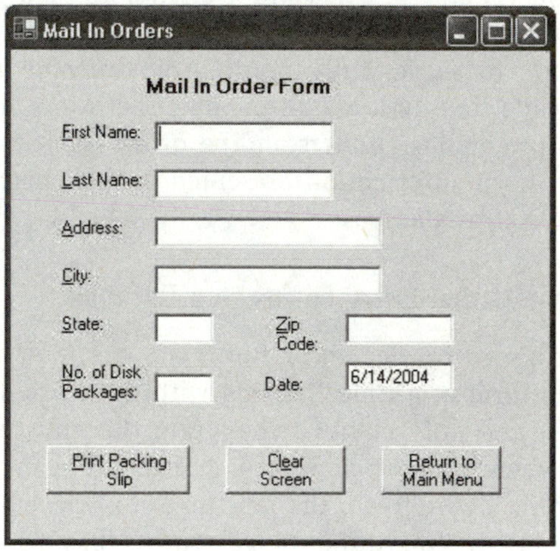

Figure 9–48 *Adding a Date Input Capability*

to write the transaction into the existing database table. Refer back to Chapter 6 and Event Procedure 6–8 for the original btnPrint_Click procedure.

Procedure Code 9–1

```
'Form-Level code to set the current date into txtDate
Private Sub frmMailIn_Load(ByVal sender As System.Object, ByVal e As _
    System.EventArgs) Handles MyBase.Load
  txtDate.Text = FormatDateTime(Now, DateFormat.ShortDate)
End Sub
```

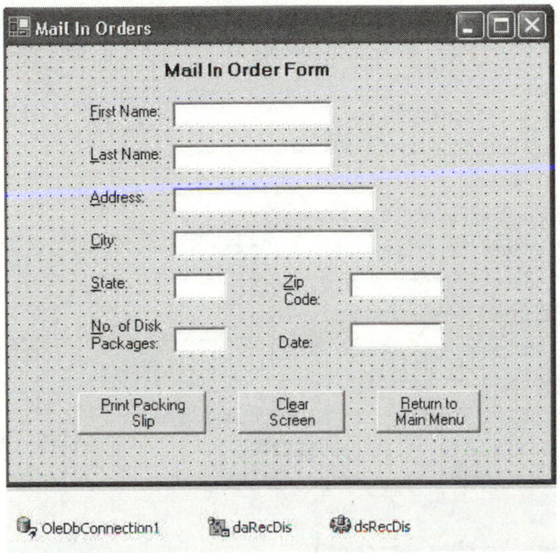

Figure 9–49   *The Mail In Form at Design Time*

Table 9–14   Additional Mail In Form Controls

Object	Property	Setting
Label	Name	lblDate
TextBox	Name	txtDate
	Text	(blank)

```
Private Sub btnPrint_Click(ByVal sender As System.Object, ByVal e As _
    System.EventArgs) Handles btnPrint.Click

  'Add the following named constant at the top of the event code
  'it provides the code for a mail-in disbursement from inventory

  Const strMAILINS As String = "m"

  Dim newrow As System.Data.DataRow

  'Continue with the existing code from Event Procedure 6-9
  .
  .
  .
  .
```

```
'Add the following section of code at the end of the event
'procedure, immediately after the Print and before the End If statement

    'set up new row (record)
    newrow = dsRecDis.RecDis.NewRow
    'enter data in each field
    newrow.Item("Fname") = txtFname.Text
    newrow.Item("Lname") = txtLname.Text
    newrow.Item("Addr") = txtAddr.Text
    newrow.Item("City") = txtCity.Text
    newrow.Item("St") = txtState.Text
    newrow.Item("Zip") = txtZip.Text
    newrow.Item("Quantity") = txtQuantity.Text
    newrow.Item("RDCode") = strMAILINS
    newrow.Item("RDDATE") = txtDate.Text

    'Update dataset with new record
    dsRecDis.RecDis.Rows.Add(newrow)
    'Write the record to the database
    daRecDis.Update(dsRecDis)
  End If

End Sub
```

In reviewing Procedure Code 9–1, note that not much has been added to the existing code. The FrmMailIn_Load event is used to initialize the added text box with the current date. The code attached to the end of the existing btnPrint button Click event procedure simply sets the field values to those in the text boxes, and then writes the data out using the Update method of the data adapter. The new code will not be executed unless the entire form is filled out correctly. Placing this code after the packing slip has been printed is the correct location, because it is at this point that all data has been validated and that the user has committed to having it printed. We are simply storing away data that has already been committed to a hard copy packing-slip printout.

Except for a few minor alterations, the same changes that we have made to the Mail In Form must also be made to the Walk In Form. Figure 9–50 shows the current Walk In Form, while Figure 9–51 shows the new form as it will look at design time.

The three additional controls that we have added to the Walk In Form have the properties listed in Table 9–15. Note that these are the exact same properties as previously listed for the Mail In Form in Table 9–14.

Again, as with the Mail In Form, we want to only use the text boxes as input controls, and not for viewing or changing data in existing records. As such, we do not bind them to the controls, but once again modify the program to store transaction records into the RecDis table. Procedure Code 9–2 lists the additional code required.

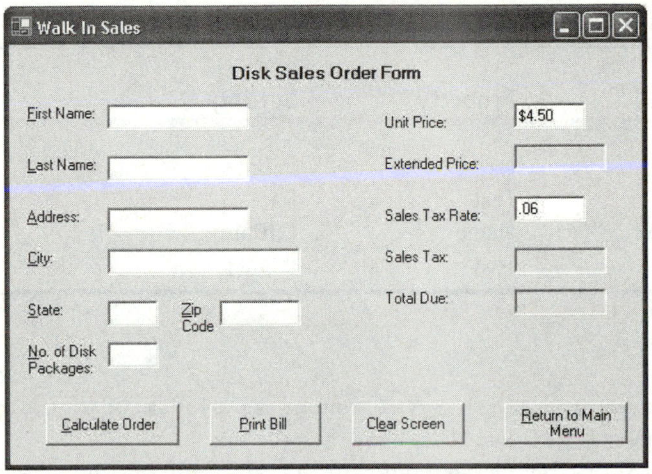

Figure 9–50   *The Current Walk In Form*

Figure 9–51   *The Walk In Form at Design Time*

Procedure Code 9–2

```
' Form-Level code to set the current date into txtDate
Private Sub frmWalkIn_Load(ByVal sender As System.Object, ByVal e As _
    System.EventArgs) Handles MyBase.Load
  txtDate.Text = FormatDateTime(Now, DateFormat.ShortDate)
End Sub
```

Table 9–15 Additional Walk In Form Controls

Object	Property	Setting
Label	Name	lblDate
	Text	Date:
Text Box	Name	txtDate
	Text	(blank)

```
Private Sub btnPrint_Click(ByVal sender As System.Object, ByVal e As _
    System.EventArgs) Handles btnPrint.Click
  ' Add the following named constant at the top of the event code
  ' it provides the code for a walk-in disbursement from inventory

  Const strWALKINS As String = "w"
  Dim newrow As System.Data.DataRow

  ' Continue with the existing code
      .
      .
      .


  'Add the following section of code at the end of
  'the event procedure, immediately after the call to Print
  ' and before the End If statement

  'set up new row (record)
  newrow = dsRecDis.RecDis.NewRow
  'enter data in each field
  'Load up the buffer
  If txtFname.Text.Length > 0 Then
    newrow.Item("Fname") = txtFname.Text
  End If
  If txtLname.Text.Length > 0 Then
    newrow.Item("Lname") = txtLname.Text
  End If
  If txtAddr.Text.Length > 0 Then
    newrow.Item("Addr") = txtAddr.Text
  End If
  If txtCity.Text.Length > 0 Then
    newrow.Item("City") = txtCity.Text
    End If
```

```
If txtState.Text.Length > 0 Then
  newrow.Item("St") = txtState.Text
End If
If txtZip.Text.Length > 0 Then
  newrow.Item("Zip") = txtZip.Text
End If
newrow.Item("Quantity") = txtQuantity.Text
newrow.Item("RDCode") = strWALKINS
newrow.Item("RDDATE") = txtDate.Text
'Update dataset with new record
dsRecDis.RecDis.Rows.Add(newrow)
'Write the record to the database
daRecDis.Update(dsRecDis)

End Sub
```

Refer back to Chapter 6 and Event Procedure 6–8 for the original `btnPrint_Click` procedure. The only difference between Procedure Code 9–2 and that listed in Procedure Code 9–1 is the set of If statements to detect that we are not attempting to write out a zero-length string. Although this type of validation had been part of the Mail In Form before we added the "store-to-table" code, no such validation existed in the Walk In Form. It needs to be made now because an attempt to write a zero-length string into a database field results in a run-time error.

Auditing

The reason for not binding the TextBox controls on both the Mail In and Walk In Data Entry Forms concerns auditing. An *audit* is an official examination and verification of accounts to ensure that they are in order. A general rule of auditing is that each and every transaction must be accounted for. Thus, once a transaction is made, it should never be deleted, and only altered when the alteration itself can be accounted for. Frequently, a second transaction is made that corrects the original record or the original record has extra fields that can be used to document the change. In this manner, a trail is always provided that can be followed to determine exactly what has happened and when it occurred.

For example, imagine that a dishonest employee sends free disks to friends using the Mail In Form, and then goes in and deletes each record after the packing slip is printed. Permitting the same employee to delete records effectively erases all traces of the illegal transactions. It is for this reason that most commercial systems do not permit deleting any transaction that has been posted (stored) into a transactions database.

Clearly, the degree of transactions control provided for each system depends on the level of security required by both the user and the application itself. For smaller systems and companies with few employees, security is usually not a prime concern. For our Rotech application we will provide an additional Form that will allow a user to review and locate all past transactions, but not to delete any transactions. Of course, any record can still be altered if the user understands how to use Microsoft's Access database and the records have not been locked at the database level. Thus, the ultimate security for each database record depends on the security imposed on the database itself and the means of access to the data.

Adding an Inventory Receipt Form   Connecting the existing Mail In and Walk In Forms to our Disktran database permits us to store all disbursements from inventory. To record all deliveries into inventory we create and add a new Inventory Receipt Form to the project. Because we have added new Forms in our two previous Focus sections, rather than once again listing the details of this procedure, we briefly review the necessary steps for adding a new form in this section's Programmers' Notes box. Following this procedure you should add a Form named `Inventory`. When this is done the Rotech Project Explorer Window will appear, as shown in Figure 9–52.

Programmers Notes

Adding a New Form:

To add a new form to an existing project, do the following:

1. Select the Add Windows Form item from the Project menu.
2. Double click on the Windows Form icon.
3. Enter a name for the form.

This procedure displays a new form and adds this new form to the Project Explorer Window. To switch between forms, simply click on the desired form in the Project Explorer Window.

The form that we want to provide is shown in Figure 9–53. The relevant property values for this new form and its Trigger Task List (TTL) are given in Tables 9–16 and 9–17, respectively.

Procedure Code 9–3 provides the four event procedures that must be written, which correspond to the last four tasks listed in the form's TTL Table.

Procedure Code 9–3

```
Const strRECEIVE As String = "r"  ' code for receipt of inventory
Const strRETURNED As String = "t" ' code for returns to vendor
```

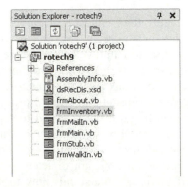

Figure 9–52   *The Rotech Project Explorer Window*

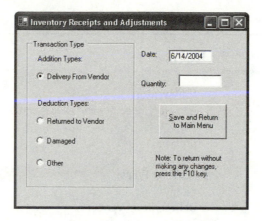

Figure 9-53   *The Inventory Form*

```
Const strDAMAGED As String = "d"   ' code for damaged inventory
Const strOTHER As String = "o"      ' code for other adjustments
Dim frmMainRef As New frmMain()
Dim newrow As System.Data.DataRow


Private Sub frmInventory_Load(ByVal sender As System.Object, ByVal e _
    As System.EventArgs) Handles MyBase.Load
  txtDate.Text = FormatDateTime(Now, DateFormat.ShortDate)
  'set up new row (record)
  newrow = dsRecDis.RecDis.NewRow
End Sub


Private Sub frmInventory_KeyDown(ByVal sender As Object, ByVal e As _
    System.Windows.Forms.KeyEventArgs) Handles MyBase.KeyDown
  If e.KeyCode = System.Windows.Forms.Keys.F10 Then 'check for F10 key
    e.Handled = True
    Me.Hide()
    frmMainRef.Show()
  End If
End Sub
Private Sub txtQuantity_KeyPress(ByVal sender As System.Object, _
    ByVal e As System.Windows.Forms.KeyPressEventArgs) Handles _
    txtQuantity.KeyPress
  Const ENTER = Chr(13) ' the ANSI value of the Enter key

  If e.KeyChar = ENTER Then
    btnReturn.Focus()
  Else
    If Asc(e.KeyChar) < Asc("0") Or Asc(e.KeyChar) > Asc("9") Then
```

Table 9–16   The Inventory Form's Property Table

Object	Property	Setting
Form	Name	frmInventory
	Text	Inventory Receipts and Adjustments
	KeyPreview	True
GroupBox	Name	grpType
Label	Name	lblAddition
	Text	Addition Types:
Radio Button	Name	radInv1
	Text	Delivery from Vendor
	Value	True
Label	Name	lblDeduction
	Text	Deduction Types:
Radio Button	Name	radInv2
	Text	Returned to Vendor
Radio Button	Name	radInv3
	Text	Damaged
Radio Button	Name	radInv4
	Text	Other
Label	Name	lblDate
	Text	Date:
TextBox	Name	txtDate
	Text	(blank)
Label	Name	lblQuantity
	Text	Quantity
TextBox	Name	txtQuantity
	Text	(blank)
	TabIndex	0
Label	Name	lblNote
	Text	Note: to return without making any changes, press the F10 key.
Button	Name	btnSave
	Text	&Save and Return to Main Menu

```
        e.Handled = True
        Beep()
        MessageBox.Show("You can only enter a number here.", _
            "Data Entry Error", MessageBoxButtons.OK, _
            MessageBoxIcon.Error)
    End If
End If
```

Table 9–17   The Inventory Receipt Form's TTL Table

Form: Inventory	Trigger	
Task	Object	Event
Obtain current date	txtDate	default or user entry
Obtain quantity	txtQuantity	user entry
Initialize date	Form	Load
Detect F10 key	Form	KeyDown
Validate quantity	txtQuantity	KeyPress
Write to database and return to Main Menu	btnReturn	Click

```
End Sub

Private Sub btnReturn_Click(ByVal sender As System.Object, ByVal e As _
    System.EventArgs) Handles btnReturn.Click
  newrow.Item("Quantity") = txtQuantity.Text
  newrow.Item("RDDate") = txtDate.Text

  'Update dataset with new record
  dsRecDis.RecDis.Rows.Add(newrow)
  'Write the record to the database
  daRecDis.Update(dsRecDis)
  Me.Close()
  frmMainRef.Show()
End Sub

Private Sub radInv1_Click(ByVal sender As System.Object, ByVal e As _
    System.EventArgs) Handles radInv1.Click
  newrow.Item("Fname") = "Receipt"
  newrow.Item("Lname") = "of Inventory"
  newrow.Item("RDCode") = strRECEIVE
End Sub

Private Sub radInv2_Click(ByVal sender As Object, ByVal e As _
    System.EventArgs) Handles radInv2.Click
  newrow.Item("Fname") = "Returned"
  newrow.Item("Lname") = "to Vendor"
  newrow.Item("RDCode") = strRETURNED
End Sub
```

```
Private Sub radInv3_Click(ByVal sender As System.Object, ByVal e As _
    System.EventArgs) Handles radInv3.Click
  newrow.Item("Fname") = "Damaged"
  newrow.Item("Lname") = "Inventory"
  newrow.Item("RDCode") = strDAMAGED
End Sub

Private Sub radInv4_Click(ByVal sender As System.Object, ByVal e As _
    System.EventArgs) Handles radInv4.Click
  newrow.Item("Fname") = "Adjustment"
  newrow.Item("Lname") = "to Inventory"
  newrow.Item("RDCode") = strOTHER
End Sub
```

The first three event codes listed in Procedure 3–1 have been used extensively within the Rotech project, and will not be commented upon. The last procedure is the one that is used to actually store the form's data into the `Disktran` database. The first task accomplished by this procedure is to assign the relevant codes (see Table 9–13) to named constants. Next, the code uses Button Click procedures to determine which Radio Button has been checked. It is in these procedures where the values for the Fname, Lname, and RDCode fields are set. In the `btnReturn_Click` procedure, the Date and Quantity values are assigned to data fields and the complete record is written to the database table. At the end of the procedure the Inventory Form is hidden and the Main Menu Form redisplayed. Because this new form is not intended to be used as extensively as the Order Entry Forms, this choice of saving and returning to the Main Menu makes sense. If we were to stay on this form after each quantity was entered, we would have to provide a separate Clear Button, a separate Save Button, and a separate Return Button. We would also have to check each time that the Return Button was pressed that the user actually wanted to directly return, without first saving the last entered values. All of this is rather unnecessary because of the form's intended usage, which is to enter an occasional receipt of inventory and return back to the Main Menu.

As the single Return Button is used for both saving and returning, however, we do have to provide a means of return in case the user inadvertently displays this form and wants to get back to the main part of the system without saving any data. Here we can use the F10 key that has been provided for each form. The general instruction to all users is, "You can always get out of trouble by pressing the F10 key." Because this key is available, we simply make note of its use on the form. Even if you should want to provide a Return Without Saving key, you must be aware that a user could press this key by accident. Thus, the general rule for such keys is that if any saving of data might be required, you must provide a Return key with the type of "safety" code previously listed as Event Code 9–4 and the message previously shown in Figure 9–36. Pressing the F10 key will not be done accidentally, and so its use here makes good programming sense.

Exercises 9.5

(Note: The Rotech Systems project, at the stage of development begun in this section, can be found at http://computerscience.jbpub.com/bronsonvbnet in the ROTECH8 folder as project rotech8. The project, as it exists at the end of this section, can be found in the ROTECH9 folder as project rotech9. If you are developing the system yourself, following the procedures given in this section, we suggest that you first copy all of the files in the ROTECH8 folder onto your system, and then work out of this latter folder. When you have finished your changes you can compare your results to the files in the ROTECH9 folder.)

1. a. Add the modifications to the Mail In Form developed in this section to make your form look like Figure 9–47. Make sure to add the additional event code listed in Procedure Code 9–1.

   b. Test the modifications made in Exercise 1a to ensure that the modifications perform correctly.

2. a. Add the modifications to the Walk In Form developed in this section so that the form looks like Figure 9–50. Make sure to add the additional event code listed in Procedure Code 9–2.

   b. Test the modifications made in Exercise 2a to ensure that the program performs correctly.

3. a. Add a new form to the Rotech project and provide it with the properties listed in Table 9–16 and the event code listed in Procedure Code 9–3.

   b. Test the form in Exercise3a to ensure that all event codes operate correctly.

4. The current Rotech system has no means for either locating an existing record within the `RecDis` table or for browsing through the complete list of records. Rectify this by adding a new form to the project, that permits locating records using a combination of a person's last name and city. Do not permit a user to alter any existing records from within your new form. Your new form should be accessed from the existing Mail In Form and redisplay the Mail In Form when the user is finished locating an existing record.

5. Modify the form created for Exercise 4 to permit entry of the return code value "a" for "address unknown", or "u" for refused shipment, when a disk package is returned by the postal delivery service for one of these reasons. This code should be stored in the existing record `RetCode` field (see next-to-last field name in Table 9–11). Permit the user to also enter a `RetDate` value (last field listed in Table 9–11) corresponding to when the return code was entered. If no date has been entered, the system should assign the current system (**Now**) date as the `RetDate` value.

6. a. (Case study) Make all necessary modifications to your selected project so that all of the data entry forms store each entered transaction (see project specifications at the end of Section 1.5). Additionally, add any new transaction forms that might be required by your application.

   b. Test that all modifications made to your project operate correctly.

9.6 Common Programming Errors and Problems

The common errors and problems encountered when using Visual Basic to access and update database tables are:

1. Not saving the last edit performed on a dataset. This occurs when the application is terminated before a Movement Button or **Movement** method has been activated. When working with databases, an application E<u>x</u>it Button should always have a provision for saving the last edit.

2. Forgetting that changes to the dataset are not automatically reflected in the data source. The data adapter's **Update** method must be called to make changes to the data source (database).

3. Forgetting to put quotes around the string in a WHERE clause of an **SQL** statement that is equal to a field. If a WHERE clause is used as in

   ```
   SELECT * FROM Phonebook WHERE Office = 'HM'
   ```

   the string HM must be surrounded by quotes.

4. Forgetting that the Position property starts at zero and that the first record in a dataset is at position zero, not one.

9.7 Chapter Review

Key Terms

ADO.NET
BindingContext object
bound control
browsing
cardinality
CurrencyManager object
current record
data aware
data control
database
data adapter
dataset
DBMS
entities

field
Fill method
navigating
organization
Position property
query
record
relational database
relationships
RemoveAt method
SQL
structured query
Update method

Summary

1. A *database* is defined as a collection of related data used by an organization, where an *organization* refers to any self-contained social unit such as a company, university, hospital, or family.

2. A *relational database* is a database in which data is stored in tables.

3. Each row in a database table is referred to as a *record*, and each column is designated by a heading, referred to as a *field name*.

4. When records are ordered by the value of a particular field, the field is referred to as a *key field*.

5. An *index* is a special type of table that lists the position of another table's records in a key field order.

6. A *structured query* is a statement, written according to the rules of a language called Structured Query Language (SQL), that uniquely identifies a set of records from one or more tables. The set of records can be empty, if no records meet the selected criteria.

7. The basic syntax of an SQL SELECT command is:

```
SELECT field-name(s) FROM table(s) WHERE condition(s) ORDER BY
field-name(s)
```

Formally, this statement consists of four clauses: a SELECT clause, a FROM clause, a WHERE clause and an ORDER BY clause. The words SELECT, FROM, WHERE, and ORDER BY are all SQL keywords.

At a minimum, a structured query must contain both a SELECT and FROM clause: the SELECT clause specifies the field values that will be returned by the query, whereas the FROM clause specifies the table or tables where records will be searched. Additionally, if any restrictions are placed on the data to be selected, or the selected information is to be presented in a specified order, the WHERE and Order clauses must be included, respectively. For example, in the statement

```
SELECT * FROM PhoneBook ORDER BY Ext
```

the SELECT *clause specifies that all fields are to be obtained, the FROM clause specifies that the fields are to come from the PhoneBook table, and the ORDER clause specifies that the dataset is to be constructed in increasing (i.e., ascending) order based on the values in the Ext field.

8. A *database management system* (DBMS) is a package of one or more computer programs designed to establish, maintain, and access a database.

9. ADO.NET is a very powerful data access component that allows access to database data in many formats.

10. Setting up an application to work with a database requires several steps: Setting up a connection to a data source, creating a data adapter to transfer the data between the data source and the application, and creating a dataset to hold the data in memory while the application works on it.

11. A data adapter uses an **SQL** statement to specify the data to retrieve. You can write your own **SQL** statement or use the Query Builder in the Data Adapter Configuration Wizard.

12. The **Fill** method of the data adapter is used to fill a dataset with data from the data source.

13. The *current record* is the record in a dataset that is currently accessible by a data control. Only one record can be the current record at any given time. Moving around or changing the current record is referred to as *navigating* or *browsing* through a dataset.

14. Many controls such as a TextBox, Label, ListBox, or DataGrid can be bound to a dataset. Being data-aware means that the control has access to a field value contained in the current record.

15. *Simple data binding* connects one control (e.g., text box) to one data element, while *complex data binding* is needed for DataGrids where data from multiple rows of the dataset are bound to the control.

16. To associate a DataGrid with a data source, use the **DataSource** property of the DataGrid.

17. All windows forms in Visual Basic have a built-in object named the BindingContext, which manages the data bindings for the controls on the form. A CurrencyManager object is added to a form when the form is connected to a data source. This object provides a simple way to navigate among the rows in a database table. Its **Position** property holds the number of the current row.

18. The **Update** method of the data adapter is used to save an updated table (dataset) to its data source.

Test Yourself—Short Answer

1. ADO.NET provides two types of binding: _____ and _____.

2. The _____ is used to facilitate the transfer of data between a data source and a dataset.

3. The first step in setting up database access is to set up a _____.

4. A database where all of the data is stored in table form is a _____.

5. In a database table, each row is a _____.

6. To bind a text box on a form to a field of a dataset, the _____ property of the text box needs to be set.

7. The CurrencyManager object's _____ method removes a specified row from a dataset.

8. The **Position** property of the CurrencyManager holds the number of the current row and the first row in a table is always row number _____.

9. The _____ property of the data adapter contains the **SQL** statement used to retrieve records from the database.

10. To create a new blank row that may be edited and added to a table, use the _____ method.

11. To prevent changes to your database but still allow the user to browse the database using a DataGrid control, set the _____ property of the DataGrid to **True**.

Programming Projects

Note: There is less direction given here as to the forms to be used and the way in which output is to be displayed than has been given in prior chapters. This is intentional and is meant to give you flexibility in designing your application.

1. This assignment is a modification to the Motel 8 project (Section 5.9, Exercise 7). The owner of Motel 8 has changed the pricing structure for a night's stay (described below). Additionally, he wants a daily report that categorizes and summarizes patron data for the previous night. Input to the program will be records stored in an Access database table, for which each record contains the following fields:

Room Number (integer)

Patron Name (20 characters)

Number of Adults (integer)

Number of Children (integer)

The name of the database, which is located at http://computerscience.jbpub.com/ bronsonvbnet in the Databases folder, is motel.mbd and the table is PATRONS. Charges for a room are calculated using the following criteria:

If the number of adults is no more than two, the cost per adult is $30; otherwise the cost per adult is $25.

If the number of children is no more than two, the cost per child is $12; otherwise the cost per child is $10.

If the number of adults plus number of children is at least five, there is a 5% discount on the total charge.

There is a minimum charge per room of $50.

There is no state or local tax charged on the total cost. Also, there is no discount for multiple night stays by the same patron.

Output for the program should include the input plus adult charge, child charge, and total charge (after the discount, if applicable) for each room.

Your program should accumulate the number of adults, number of children, and total charge. Note that based upon the above criteria, the total charge for a room is not necessarily the sum of the adult charge plus the child charge. Use a function procedure to calculate room charge.

After the last record, print column totals (do not print totals for room numbers, adult charges, children charges, or discounts) for adult count, child count, and total charge.

As an optional addition to this problem, create a second table in the Access database and write the detail lines of your report to that table along with the appropriate date (using either the `Date` or `Now` function).

Sample Output:

Date: 5-10-04

MOTEL 8 DAILY REVENUE REPORT

ROOM NMBR	PATRON NAME	ADULT COUNT	CHILD COUNT	ADULT CHARGE	CHILD CHARGE	TOTAL DISCOUNT	CHARGE
1234	SMITH JOHN	2	0	60.00	00.00	00.00	60.00
1330	JONES JIM	2	3	60.00	30.00	04.50	85.50
1335	WILSON JOE	1	0	30.00	00.00	00.00	50.00
1400	KELLY BRIAN	1	2	30.00	24.00	00.00	54.00
		6	5				249.50

2. This assignment is a modification to the State Utilities project (Section 5.9, Exercise 9). Using the original pricing structure, write the necessary code to produce a detail report with column totals.

Input to the program will be records stored in an Access database table for which each record contains the following fields:

```
CustomerID (integer)
CustomerName (text - 20 characters)
KWHUsed (integer)
```

The name of the database, which is located at http://computerscience.jbpub.com/bronsonvbnet, is utility.mbd and the table is ACCOUNTS. For each record read, compute:

Base, undiscounted, untaxed bill amount
Discount amount
State utility tax amount
City utility tax amount
Total amount due

Also compute accumulated totals for each of these amounts. Your output should be in the form of a report that contains the data read for each record plus its corresponding calculated values (for each detail record). Format for the report could be similar to that used in Exercise 1 in this section.

Incorporate the code used in your original project solution, that calculated the different charges into a **Sub** procedure that can be called for each record read. Your program can send the number of KWh used to the **Sub** procedure and it can return the five amounts listed above.

After reading all records and writing all detail lines, write the appropriate accumulated totals at the bottom of their respective columns.

3. This assignment is a modification to the Texas Fence Company project (Section 7.9, Exercise 2). The company has asked you to expand the capabilities of your initial programming effort and write a program that will produce a list of necessary components that will be needed for the next day's fencing job. The necessary requirements for each fencing job are stored in an Access database table with each record containing the following fields:

```
Job number (integer)
Length (integer)
Width (integer)
Gates (integer)
```

The name of the database, which is located at http://computerscience.jbpub.com/ bronsonvbnet, is fence.mbd and the table is JOBS. Output for the program should include a count for each of the following:

Connectors (integer)
Corner posts (integer)
Intermediate posts (integer)
Gate posts (integer)
Gate(s) (integer)
Fencing (integer)

Your program must read all records in the database table, compute the number of components needed for each job, and accumulate totals for each component category. The output for this program is just the totals for each component category (number of connectors, number of corner posts, and so forth).

Use a **Sub** procedure to calculate the number of components for each category for each job (record read). Additionally, you might offer the program user the chance to send the output to either the screen (with a form similar to the one used for the original project) or to the printer. You also may wish to create a second table for the database and write the fence component totals with the current date to that table.

Processing Visual Basic Data Files

Goals

Any collection of data stored together under a common name on an external storage medium, such as a disk, is referred to as a file. In the previous chapter we saw how to access database files that were under the control of a database management system. In this chapter we learn how to use files that are directly controlled by Visual Basic. The fundamentals of these files and how they can be created and maintained by a Visual Basic application are presented. All files, no matter how they are maintained, permit an application to use data without the need for a user to enter it manually each time the application is executed. In addition, files provide the basis for sharing data between programs, so that the data output by one program can be input directly to another program.

10.1 Introduction to Visual Basic's File Types

A *file* is a collection of data stored together under a common name, usually on a disk or CD-ROM. For example, the Visual Basic project and form modules that you store on disk are examples of files. Each stored file is identified by file name, also referred to as the file's *external name*. This is the name of the file as it is known by the operating system, and as it is displayed when you open or save a file using the operating system.

Each computer operating system has its own specification as to the maximum number of characters permitted for an external file name. Table 10–1 lists these specifications for the more commonly used operating systems.

When using the Windows operating systems, you should take advantage of the increased length specification to create descriptive file names within the context of a manageable length (generally considered to be no more that 12 to 14 characters). Very long file names should be avoided. Although such names can be extremely descriptive they do take more time to type and are susceptible to typing errors.

Table 10–1   Maximum Allowable File Name Characters

Operating System	Maximum Length
DOS	8 characters plus an optional period and 3 character extension
Windows 98, 2000, XP	255 characters
UNIX Early Versions	14 characters
UNIX Current Versions	255 characters

Using the current Windows convention, the following are all valid file names:

balances.data   records   info.data
report.bond   prices.data math.memo

File names should be chosen to indicate both the type of data in the file and the application for which it is used. Frequently, the initial characters are used to describe the data itself and an extension (the characters typed after a decimal point, which were limited to a maximum of three characters under DOS) are used to describe the application. For example, the Microsoft Excel spreadsheet program automatically applies an extension of .xls to all spreadsheet files, while Microsoft Word applies the extension .doc to its word processing files. When creating your own file names you should adhere to this practice. For example, the name prices.bond is appropriate in describing a file of prices used in a bond application. For text files, the suffix .txt is used.

On a fundamental level, the actual data stored in all files is nothing more than a series of related bytes. To access this data, a program must have some information as to what the bytes actually represent—characters, records, integers, and so on. Depending on the type of data, various modes of access are appropriate. Specifically, Visual Basic directly provides three types of file access:

- Sequential
- Random
- Binary

The term *sequential access* refers to the fact that each item in the file must be accessed sequentially, one after another, starting from the beginning of the file. Thus, the fourth item in a file cannot be read or written until the previous three items have been read or written. Sequential access is appropriate for text files, where each stored character represents either a text or control character, such as a carriage return, that is stored using the ANSI code. This type of storage permits such files to be read as ordinary text. This chapter will focus on sequential files.

Random access, also referred to as *direct access,* is appropriate for files that consist of a set of identical-length records. Typically, in using such files you must first create a user-defined type to define the various fields making up a single record. Then, because each record in the file is the same length, you can directly access any record in the file by skipping over the fixed number of bytes that correspond to all of the records prior to the desired one. This permits accessing any specific record within the file without the need to sequentially read through prior records. Random-access files are stored using binary codes, but because each record has a well-defined fixed-length size, individual records can be conveniently and individually accessed.

In *binary access,* no assumptions are made about either record sizes or data types. The data is simply read and written as pure binary information. The advantage to this approach is that binary files typically use less space than text files. The disadvantages, however, are that the file can no longer be visually inspected using a text-editing program, and that the programmer must know exactly how the data was written to the file in order to correctly read it.

To perform file processing in Visual Basic, the `System.IO` namespace must be referenced. This namespace includes the `StreamReader` and `StreamWriter` stream classes that are used in the next section for sequential access, as well as the `FileStream` class that is used in this chapter for random and binary access and may also be used for sequential access.

Exercises 10.1

1. a. Define the term *file*.

   b. Describe the difference between a file that is maintained by a database management system and the files directly supported in Visual Basic.

2. Describe the difference between a text and a binary file.

3. List the three types of file access provided in Visual Basic.

4. a. An easy method of constructing a text file is to use the Notepad application that is included in all versions of Windows. Notepad can be invoked by:

      i. Clicking on the Start button

      ii. Selecting Programs

      iii. Selecting Accessories

      iv. Selecting Notepad

      Notepad will save files as Text files, appending a .txt suffix.

   b. Use these steps to create a Text file called testfile.

5. List three differences between sequential and random-access files.

10.2 Sequential Access Files

In order to read and write data to a sequential access file, use *stream* objects. A *stream* transfers a series of bytes from one location to another.

Opening Sequential Files for Writing

To write data to a sequential file, use a `StreamWriter` object that is declared by the following:

```
Dim writevar as System.IO.StreamWriter
```

Next create an instance of the `StreamWriter` object and store its address in the variable. Visual Basic .NET provides two different methods for doing this, depending upon whether you are opening a file in output mode or append mode. To open a file in output mode, where a file named `filename` is created if necessary, use the following general format:

```
writevar = System.IO.File.CreateText(filename)
```

To open a file in append mode, use the following general format:

```
writevar = System.IO.File.AppendText(filename)
```

The difference between a file opened in output mode and one opened in append mode is in how existing files are used and where the data is physically stored in the file. In output mode, a new file is always created and the data is written starting at the beginning of the file. If the file already exists, its contents are erased. In append mode the data is written starting at the end of an existing file. If the file, however, does not exist to begin with, the two modes produce identical results and create a new file. Both methods return the address of a `StreamWriter` object that may be used to write data to the file.

The following is an example of how to open a file for output.

```
Dim pricefile As System.IO.StreamWriter
pricefile = System.IO.File.CreateText("pricelist.txt")
```

In this example, the first statement creates an object variable named `pricefile` and the second statement creates a file named `pricelist.txt`. If a file named `pricelist.txt` already exists, its contents will be erased. If it does not exist, the file is created. The variable `pricefile` is assigned the address of a `StreamWriter` object which may then be used to write data to the file.

The following is an example of opening a file for Append mode.

```
Dim addressfile As System.IO.StreamWriter
Dim filename As String = "C:\CustomerFiles\addresses.txt"
addressfile = System.IO.File.AppendText(filename)
```

This is similar to the first example above but uses a variable `filename` as the argument to the **AppendText** method. Note that the path is specified along with the filename. When a path is not specified, Visual Basic assumes the file location to be the same folder as the one in which the application is running (i.e., the current directory). If the file already exists, it is opened and data that is written will be appended to the end of the file. If the file does not exist, it will be created. The variable `addressfile` is assigned the address of a `StreamWriter` object, which may then be used to write data to the file.

When a file is opened for append mode, and if the file exists, the new data is written after the data that already exists in the file. If the file does not exist, it is created.

Opening Sequential Files for Reading

To read data from a sequential file, a `StreamReader` object is used and its declaration is shown in the following example:

```
Dim readvar as System.IO.StreamReader
```

Next open the file in input mode by creating an instance of the `StreamReader` object and storing its address in the variable `readvar`.

```
readvar = System.IO.File.OpenText(filename)
```

Filename specifies the name and/or path of the file to be opened. If *filename* does not exist, a run-time error occurs. This method returns the address of a `StreamReader` object that may be used to read data from the file.

The following are examples of how these methods are used to open a file for input.

```
Dim pricefile As System.IO.StreamReader
pricefile = System.IO.File.OpenText("pricelist.txt")
```

When opening a file for either input or output, good programming practice requires that you check that the connection has been established before attempting to use the file in any way. As mentioned above, if you open a file for input and the file does not exist, a run-time error occurs. To avoid this error, you should use the `System.IO.File.Exists` method to determine whether a file exists before trying to open it. The general syntax of this method is:

```
System.IO.File.Exists(filename)
```

The method returns true if the file exists and false if it does not exist. The following is an example of code that may be used to determine if a file exists:

```
If System.IO.File.Exists(filename) Then
  readfile = System.IO.File.OpenText(filename)
Else ' file is not found
  MessageBox.Show("The File was not successfully opened!", _
      "File Error Notification", MessageBoxButtons.OK, _
      MessageBoxIcon.Stop)
End If
```

Program 10–1 illustrates the statements required to open a file in input mode and includes error-checking to ensure that a successful open was obtained. A text box is used to display a message indicating whether the file was opened successfully. A button for opening the file is used in this example. The name of the file to be opened is hard-coded in this program. Figure 10–1 shows the interface for Program 10–1 and Table 10–2 lists the objects and properties for this program.

Program 10–1

```
Private Sub btnOpen_Click(ByVal sender As System.Object, ByVal e As _
    System.EventArgs) Handles btnOpen.Click
  Dim readfile As System.IO.StreamReader
  Dim filename As String = "testfile"
```

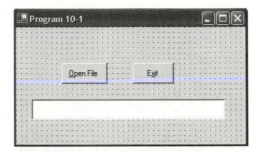

Figure 10-1 *Program 10-1's Design-Time Interface*

Table 10-2   The Properties Table for Program 10-1

Object	Property	Setting
Form	Name	frmMain
	Text	Program 10-1
Button	Name	btnOpen
	Text	&Open File
Button	Name	btnExit
	Text	E&xit
TextBox	Name	txtMessage
	Multiline	True
	Text	(blank)

```
    txtMessage.Clear()
    If System.IO.File.Exists(filename) Then
       readfile = System.IO.File.OpenText(filename)
       txtMessage.AppendText("The file " & filename & " has been _
          successfully opened")
    Else ' file is not found
       txtMessage.AppendText("The file was not successfully opened!" &  _
          ControlChars.CrLf)
       txtMessage.AppendText("Please check that the file currently exists.")
    End If
End Sub


Private Sub btnExit_Click(ByVal sender As System.Object, ByVal e As _
    System.EventArgs) Handles btnExit.Click
   Beep()
   End
End Sub
```

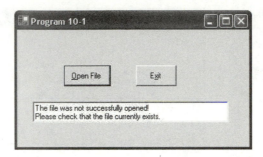

Figure 10-2　*A Sample Output Produced by Program 10-1*

Figure 10-2 illustrates a sample run using Program 10-1 that attempted to open a nonexistent file for input. Although this program can be used to open an existing file for input, it clearly lacks statements to either write, read the file data, or close the file. These topics are discussed later in this chapter.

Exception Handling

There are some situations in a program that could cause a run-time error, terminating the program abruptly. Many of these situations, or *exceptions*, could be avoided by anticipating the potential problems and including code to handle these exceptions. Intercepting errors that occur at run time is referred to as *trapping* an error, and the code that addresses the problem is called *error handling*. Visual Basic supports structured exception handling by providing Try-Catch blocks. A robust program explicitly handles exceptions via Try-Catch blocks. This allows the program to continue regardless of whether an exception occurs.

One form of a Try-Catch block is:

```
Try
     TryBlock
Catch
     CatchBlock
EndTry
```

The code in the *TryBlock* is executed. If an exception occurs, execution jumps to the code in the *CatchBlock*.

Let's look at the System.IO.File.OpenText method again. There are several conditions that would cause an exception when this method executes. Some of these are:

- The file was not found.
- The path was not found.
- The caller does not have the required permission to open the file.
- The path was Null or the value Nothing.

An example of code that could be used to catch any of these exceptions is:

```
Dim readfile As System.IO.StreamReader
Try
      readfile = System.IO.File.OpenText(filename)
Catch
      MessageBox.Show("An error has occurred when opening the file")
EndTry
```

This example will catch any exception and the same message will be displayed no matter which exception occurred. You also can specify the type of exception you want to catch by writing several Catch statements and displaying different error messages for each exception. Refer to Visual Basic Online Help Facility for OpenText to see the specific exceptions that may occur from OpenText, and Online Help for Try and Catch to see more examples of structured exception handling, including the FinallyBlock.

Note that this code would obviate the need to use the **Exists** method as shown above.

Most of the programs in this chapter include some exception handling. Please note that these examples are not meant to be complete in this area. A robust program would use exception handling (e.g., some form of a Try-Catch block) for every method that can cause an exception.

Closing a Sequential File

After you have finished using a file you must close it. Both the StreamWriter and StreamReader classes have a method for closing a file. The general form of the **Close** method is:

var.Close()

where *var* is the name of the object variable that references either a StreamWriter or StreamReader object. Because all operating systems limit the number of files that can be opened at one time, closing files that are no longer needed makes good sense. Closing a file causes all data from the stream's buffer to be written to the disk and system resources are released. A common location for the call to the Close method is in your program's Exit procedure. In the absence of a call to the Close method, all open files existing at the end of normal program execution are automatically closed by the operating system.

When a file is closed, a special end-of-file (EOF) marker is automatically placed by the operating system after the last character in the file. This EOF character has a unique numerical code that has no equivalent representation as a printable character. This special numerical value, which is system-dependent, ensures that the EOF character can never be confused with a valid character contained within the file. As we will see shortly, this character can be used as a sentinel when reading data from a file.

Writing to a Sequential File

For files opened in either output or append modes, the WriteLine and Write methods are used to write data to the file. The general form of the WriteLine method is:

```
writevar.WriteLine(data)
```

where *writevar* is the name of the `StreamWriter` object variable and `data` is the data to be written to the file. `Data` can be a constant or the name of a variable and can be a string or numeric. This method converts any numeric data to a string and writes string data to the file. The `WriteLine` method also writes a newline character immediately after the data.

The `WriteLine` method can be used to write a single newline to a file. The method is called without an argument as shown by the following:

```
writevar.WriteLine()
```

If the above is called after another call to `WriteLine`, a blank line will be created.

The general format of the `Write` method is:

```
writevar.Write(data)
```

where `var` is the name of the `StreamWriter` object variable and `data` is the data to be written to the file. `Data` can be a constant or the name of a variable and can be a string or numeric. The difference between these two methods is that the **Write** method does not write a newline after the data.

As an example, suppose you want to write a line to a file which includes the description of an item, its price, and its quantity. Program 10–2's design-time interface is shown in Figure 10–3. The program illustrates using calls to `Write` and `WriteLine` methods for writing data to an open file. The Properties Table for this program is identical to Program 10–1 except for the form's **Text** property, which is now Program 10-2, and the Text property for the btnOpen Button, which is now **W**rite to File. A `Try-Catch` block is included to handle exceptions from the `CreateText` and `Write` methods.

The following procedure will write that information to a new file named `inventory.txt`.

Program 10–2's btnOpen_Click Procedure

```
Private Sub btnOpen_Click(ByVal sender As Object, ByVal e As _
    System.EventArgs) Handles btnOpen.Click
```

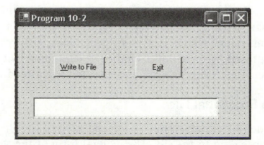

Figure 10–3 *Program 10–2's Design-Time Interface*

```
    Dim description As String = "Batteries"
    Dim price As Double = 59.95
    Dim quantity As Integer = 23

    Dim inventoryfile As System.IO.StreamWriter

    Try
        inventoryfile = System.IO.File.CreateText("inventory.txt")
        inventoryfile.Write(description)
        inventoryfile.Write("   ")
        inventoryfile.Write(price)
        inventoryfile.Write("   ")
        inventoryfile.WriteLine(quantity)
        inventoryfile.Close()
        txtMessage.AppendText("The file inventory.txt has been written")
    Catch
        MessageBox.Show("Error with file inventory.txt")
    End Try
End Sub
```

After this program is run, a file named `inventory.txt` is created with one line containing:

```
Batteries  59.95  23
```

Figure 10–4 illustrates how Program 10-2's GUI looks upon completion of the output, assuming the file was named inventory.txt. In this example we have hard-coded the name of the file. The first statement using the `Write` method writes the value of description (`Batteries`) to the file. The second statement writes two blank spaces following that. The third statement writes the value of price (59.95) to the file. The fourth statement writes two blank spaces. The fifth statement is a call to `WriteLine` instead of `Write` so that the value of quantity (23) is followed by a newline character.

Figure 10–5 illustrates the ANSI characters that are stored in the file; a code of 32 0 represents a space (blank character). Because all characters are stored using the Unicode system, the second byte for each character is a 0 when English is used.

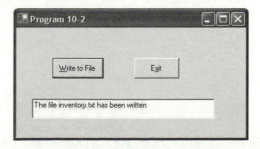

Figure 10–4   *A Sample Run using Program 10–2*

| 66 | 0 | 97 | 0 | 116 | 0 | 116 | 0 | 101 | 0 | 114 | 0 | 105 | 0 | 101 | 0 | 115 | 0 | 32 | 0 | 32 | 0 | 53 | 0 | 57 | 0 | 46 | 0 | 57 | 0 | 53 | 0 | 32 | 0 | 32 | 0 | 50 | 0 | 51 | 0 | 13 | 0 | 10 | 0 |
| B | | a | | t | | t | | e | | r | | i | | e | | s | | | | | | 5 | | 9 | | . | | 9 | | 5 | | | | | | 2 | | 3 | | CR | | LF | |

Figure 10–5 *The File Created by Program 10–2*

The following example in Event Procedure 10–1 writes the data from an array into the file pricefile.txt.

Event Procedure 10–1

```
Private Sub btnWrite_Click(ByVal sender As System.Object, _
    ByVal e As System.EventArgs) Handles btnWrite.Click
  Dim result() As Double = {.25, 17.36, 15.75, 18.47, 19.51}
  Dim i As Integer
  Dim writevar As System.IO.StreamWriter

  Try
    writevar = System.IO.File.CreateText("pricefile.txt")
    For i = 0 To 4
      writevar.Write(i)
      writevar.Write("  ")
      writevar.WriteLine(result(i))
    Next i
    writevar.Close()
  Catch
    MessageBox.Show("Error with file pricefile.txt")
  End Try
End Sub
```

When Event Procedure 10–1 is executed, the file pricefile.txt is opened for output and five lines are written to the file. The first `Write` statement writes the array index (0 through 4), the second `Write` statement writes two spaces next to the index, and the `WriteLine` statement writes the value of the corresponding array element followed by a newline. The file pricefile.txt contains the following data after this procedure has been run:

```
0   .25
1   17.36
2   15.75
3   18.47
4   19.51
```

This code uses a `Try-Catch` block to check for exceptions when opening the file and writing to the file. If, for example, the file pricefile.txt is a read-only file, the error in the `Catch` block will be displayed.

Reading From a Sequential File

Once a sequential file has been created and written to, you can read data from the file by opening it for Input using the `StreamReader` class and calling the `ReadLine` method. Reading data from a sequential file requires that the programmer know how the data was originally written to the file. This is necessary for correct "stripping" of the data from the file into appropriate variables for storage. When a file is being read, a *read position* is used to keep track of the next item to be read. When the file is opened, its read position is set to the first item in the file.

The general form for the `ReadLine` method is:

```
readvar.ReadLine()
```

readvar is the name of a `StreamReader` object variable that was returned when the file was opened for input. This method reads a line from the associated file and returns a line of data, until a newline character or EOF (end of file) is encountered.

If you know how many lines are in a file, you simply can use a **For** loop to read that number of lines from a file. This can be done by the following:

> For i = 1 to N
>   Read a line
>   Display a line
> Next i

However, there are times when the programmer does not know how much data is in the file. Another method must be used to determine when there is no more data in the file.

Checking for the End of a File   To determine when the end of a file has been reached, use the `StreamReader Peek` method. The general form of this method is:

```
readvar.Peek
```

where *readvar* is an object variable referencing a `StreamReader` object. This method looks at the next character in a file without moving the current read position and returns that character. If the current read position is at the end of the file and there are no more characters to read, the method returns -1.

Instead of using a **For** loop to read a specific number of lines, the EOF marker appended to each file can be used as a sentinel value and detected using the `Peek` method. When the EOF marker is used in this manner, the following algorithm can be used to read and display each line of the file:

> *Do Until the end-of-file has been reached*
>> *Read a line*
>> *Display a line*
> *Loop*

Using a list box `lstDisplay` to display the lines in the file, the above can be replaced by the following code:

```
Do Until readvar.Peek = -1
    input = readvar.ReadLine()
    lstDisplay.Items.Add(input)
Loop
```

Program 10-3 uses this method to open the file pricefile.txt that was created in Event Procedure 10-1 and read a line and display it until there are no more lines in the file. A list box is used to display the data that was read from the file. If the file does not exist, a message box is displayed with the error. Table 10-3 lists the objects and properties for Program 10-3.

Program 10-3

```
Private Sub btnOpen_Click(ByVal sender As System.Object, _
    ByVal e As System.EventArgs) Handles btnOpen.Click

  Dim readvar As System.IO.StreamReader
  Dim input As String
```

Table 10-3 The Properties Table for Program 10-3

Object	Property	Setting
Form	Name	frmMain
	Text	Program 10-3
Button	Name	btnOpen
	Text	&Open File
Button	Name	btnExit
	Text	E&xit
TextBox	Name	txtMessage
	Multiline	True
	Text	(blank)
ListBox	Name	lstDisplay

```
  If System.IO.File.Exists("pricefile.txt") Then
    txtMessage.Text = "File named pricefile.txt has been opened"
    readvar = System.IO.File.OpenText("pricefile.txt")
    Do Until readvar.Peek = -1
      input = readvar.ReadLine()
      lstDisplay.Items.Add(input)
    Loop
    readvar.Close()

  Else ' file is not found
    MessageBox.Show("The File was not successfully opened!", _
        "File Error Notification", MessageBoxButtons.OK, _
        MessageBoxIcon.Exclamation)
  End If
End Sub

Private Sub btnExit_Click(ByVal sender As System.Object, ByVal e As _
    System.EventArgs) Handles btnExit.Click
  Beep()
  End
End Sub
```

Figure 10–6 illustrates the output produced by Program 10–3.

There are two other **StreamReader** methods available for reading a file: the `Read` and `ReadToEnd` methods. The general form of the `Read` method is:

readvar.Read

where *readvar* is the name of a `StreamReader` object variable. This method returns only the next character from a file and returns the character code for that character. The `Chr` function can be used to convert the character code to a character.

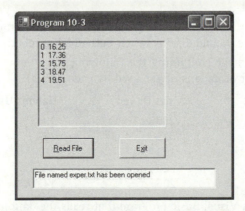

Figure 10–6   *The Output Produced by Program 10–3*

The general format of the `ReadToEnd` method is:

```
readvar.ReadToEnd
```

This method reads and returns with one statement the entire contents of a file, beginning at the current read position.

Exercises 10.2

1. a. Enter and execute Program 10–1 on your computer.

   b. Add a `Close` statement to Program 10–1 and then execute the program.

2. a. Enter and execute Program 10–2 on your computer and use it to create a file named test.txt.

   b. Substitute Event Procedure 10–1 into Program 10–2 and use it to create a file named pricefile.txt.

3. Enter and execute Program 10–3 on your computer.

4. Using the reference manuals provided with your computer's operating system, determine the maximum number of data files that can be open at the same time.

5. Would it be appropriate to call a saved Visual Basic form a file? Why or why not?

6. a. Write suitable statements to open each of the following files in output mode: out_data, prices.dat, coupons, and file_1.

   b. Write suitable statements to open each of the following files in input mode: in_date, rates.dat, distance, and file_2.

7. a. Write a Visual Basic program that stores the following numbers in a file named results.txt: .25, 18.96, 22.34, 18.94, 17.42, 22.63.

   b. Write a Visual Basic program to read the data in the results.txt file created in Exercise 7a and display the data. Additionally, the program should compute and display the sum and average of the data. Using a hand calculation, check the sum and average displayed by your program.

8. a. Write a Visual Basic program that prompts the user to enter five numbers. As each number is entered, the program should write the numbers into a file named user.txt.

   b. Write a Visual Basic program that reads the data in the user.txt file created in Exercise 8a and displays each individual number.

9. a. Create a file containing the following car numbers, number of miles driven, and number of gallons of gas used by each car:

Car No.	Miles Driven	Gallons Used
54	250	19
62	525	38
71	123	6
85	1,322	86
97	235	14

   b. Write a Visual Basic program that reads the data in the file created in Exercise 9a and displays the car number, miles driven, gallons used, and the miles per gallon for each car. The output should additionally contain the total miles driven, total gallons used, and average miles per gallon for all the cars. These totals should be displayed at the end of the output report.

10. a. Create a file with the following data containing the part number, opening balance, number of items sold, and minimum stock required:

Part Number	Initial Amount	Quantity Sold	Minimum Amount
QA310	95	47	50
CM145	320	162	200
MS514	34	20	25
EN212	163	150	160

b. Write a Visual Basic program to create an inventory report based on the data in the file created in Exercise 10a. The display should consist of the part number, current balance, and the amount that is necessary to bring the inventory to the minimum level.

11. a. Create a file containing the following data:

Identification Number	Rate	Hours
10031	6.00	40
10067	5.00	48
10083	6.50	35
10095	8.00	50

b. Write a Visual Basic program that uses the information contained in the file created in Exercise 11a to produce the following pay report for each employee:

ID No.   Rate   Hours   Regular Pay   Overtime Pay   Gross Pay

Any hours worked above 40 hours are paid at time and a half. At the end of the individual output for each employee, the program should display the totals of the regular, overtime, and gross pay columns.

12. a. Store the following data in a file:

5 96 87 78 93 21 4 92 82 85 87 6 72 69 85 75 81 73

b. Write a Visual Basic program to calculate and display the average of each group of numbers in the file created in Exercise 12a. The data should be arranged in the file so that each group of numbers is preceded by the number of data items in the group. Thus, the first number in the file, 5, indicates that the next five numbers should be grouped together. The number 4 indicates that the following four numbers are a group, and the 6 indicates that the last six numbers are a group. (*Hint:* Use a **nested** loop. The outer loop should terminate when the EOF marker is encountered.)

10.3 File Dialog Controls

Before a file can be accessed for either reading or writing, the file must be identified by name and location. In this context, location means specifying a drive, such as A:, C:, or D:, and a directory path. In some of the previous examples, the filenames have been hard-coded into the programs, which is not flexible enough for most applications. Even typing in a path and filename can be arduous and prone to errors. Most Windows users are accustomed to using a dialog box to browse their disk for a file to open or for a location to save a file. This is available from Visual Basic using the **OpenFileDialog** and **SaveFileDialog** controls.

OpenFileDialog and SaveFileDialog Controls

The **OpenFileDialog** and **SaveFileDialog** controls can be found in the toolbox (toward the bottom of the list). When you click on the control and move it to a form, it appears in a component tray at the bottom of the form. An instance of the OpenFileDialog control has a standard prefix of "ofd" and the **SaveFileDialog** control has a standard prefix of "sfd." Like other controls, they have a **Name** property, which is used to write statements that display the dialog box. Other important properties that will be described later in this chapter are **Filter**, **Title**, and **InitialDirectory**. Figure 10–7 displays a Windows Open Dialog box.

The **SaveFileDialog** control can display a standard Windows "Save As" dialog box, which is very similar to the Open Dialog box. Figure 10–8 shows a Windows Save Dialog Box.

Figure 10–7 *Windows Open Dialog Box*

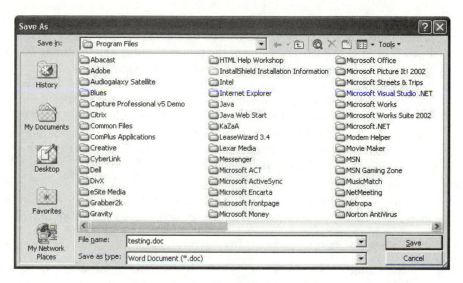

Figure 10–8   *Windows Save As Dialog Box*

As is seen in Figures 10–7 and 10–8, the Open and Save As dialog boxes are very similar, in that both provide the following components:

- Drive and Folders drop-down list box, where the user can select a drive and parent directory;
- Folder and Files list box, where the user can select a current folder and file;
- File Name text box, where the name of the selected file is displayed or where the user can enter a file name; and
- File Type list box, where the user can select the type of file to be displayed.

In addition, both dialogs provide a set of buttons for performing such functions as creating a new folder, moving up one folder level, switching between list and detail modes, processing the selected file, or canceling the dialog. Each of these functions is labeled with its corresponding button in Figure 10–8.

The following examples are for an Open Dialog box, but they also apply to a Save As Dialog box. The methods and properties are the same for both controls.

Displaying an Open Dialog Box   To display an Open Dialog box call its `ShowDialog` method. The general form of this method is:

```
DialogName.ShowDialog()
```

where *DialogName* is the name of the **OpenFileDialog** control. For example, if `ofd-Dialog` is the name of an **OpenFileDialog** control, the following statement is used to call its **ShowDialog** method.

```
ofdDialog.ShowDialog()
```

This method returns either `DialogResult.OK` or `DialogResult.Cancel` to indicate which button, OK or Cancel, was clicked by the user. When a user selects a file and the Open Button is pressed, the value of the property **ofdDialog.FileName** contains the file's full name including the drive, path, file name, and extension.

An important property to set, which affects the file names displayed, is the **Filter** property. This may be set at design time or at run-time. The **Filter** property determines what text appears in the list box "Files of type:" as well as what files will be displayed in the main part of the dialog box. A filter consists of a description, followed by a vertical bar "|", followed by the filter criteria. The general form for setting this property is:

DialogName`.Filter = "`*description1*|*filter1*|*description2*|*filter2*`. . ."`

Filters typically use the wildcard character (*) followed by a file extension. A common filter used is one that is used to display text files as shown by the following:

```
ofdDialog.Filter = "Text files (*.txt)|*.txt"
```

The string "`Text files (*.txt)`" is the description and is what is displayed in the "files of type" list box. The string to the right of the vertical bar is the actual filter.

As shown above, multiple filters may be set where each description/filter pair is separated by a vertical bar. If the user wants to display text files ending in .txt as well as Microsoft Word documents ending in .doc, the following statement may be used to set the **Filter** property:

```
ofdDialog.Filter = "Text files (*.txt)|*.txt|Word files (*.doc)|*.doc"
```

It is important to note that you should not include any spaces either before or after the symbol, |, used to separate descriptions and filter conditions.

Figure 10–9 illustrates the design-time interface for Program 10–4, which uses an **OpenFileDialog** control to obtain a user-entered file name and location, similar to the one shown in Figure 10–7.

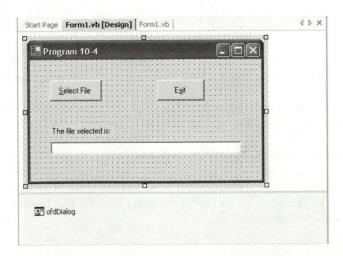

Figure 10–9 *Program 10–4's Design-Time Interface*

Table 10–4   The Properties Table for Program 10–4

Object	Property	Setting
Form	Name	frmMain
	Text	Program 10–3
Button	Name	btnSelect
	Text	&Select File
Button	Name	btnExit
	Text	E&xit
Label	Name	lblFile
	Text	The file selected is:
TextBox	Name	txtFile
	Text	(blank)
OpenFileDialog	Name	ofdDialog

Program 10–4 displays the dialog box using a filter that specifies text files and all files. Table 10–4 lists the objects and properties for this program. In reviewing the event code for Program 10–4, first note the statement ofdDialog.ShowDialog(). This is the statement that causes the **OpenFileDialog** control to display an Open Dialog box similar to the one shown in Figure 10–7. In addition, the statement immediately above the call to show the Open Dialog box is a statement that sets the **Filter** property. This property can be set either at design-time, using the Properties window, or at run-time, as is done here.

By default, the Open Dialog box displays the current directory. You may specify another directory to be initially displayed by setting the **InitialDirectory** property to that path. For example, you can use the following code to indicate that the files in directory C:\Test Files should be displayed in the Open Dialog box.

```
ofdDialog.InitialDirectory = "C:\Test Files"
ofdDialog.ShowDialog()
```

The **Title** property is another property that you may want to set in your code. By default, the string "Open" is displayed in the title bar of the Open Dialog box. This can be changed to another string by setting **Title** to that string, as shown by the following:

```
ofdDialog.Title = "Choose a File to Open"
```

Program 10–4's Event Code

```
Private Sub btnSelect_Click(ByVal sender As Object, ByVal e As _
    System.EventArgs) Handles btnSelect.Click
  ofdDialog.Filter = "Text files (*.txt)|*.txt|All files (*.*)|*.*"
  ofdDialog.ShowDialog()
  txtFile.Text = ofdDialog.FileName
End Sub
```

```
Private Sub btnExit_Click(ByVal sender As System.Object, ByVal e As _
    System.EventArgs) Handles btnExit.Click
  Beep()
  End
End Sub
```

In reviewing the output displayed by Program 10–4, it is important to note that the selected file, test.txt, has not been opened and may not even exist within the indicated folder. By pressing the Open Dialog Select File Button, the string entered into the text box is stored in the **OpenFileDialog** control **Filename** property. It is this value that is subsequently displayed in Figure 10–10. This program only selects a file and does not open or read from it.

Now let's go back to Program 10–3 and add a Select File Button on the form. Instead of hard-coding the name of the file to be opened and read, an Open Dialog box can be used to allow the user to choose the file to open. Figure 10–11 shows the inter-

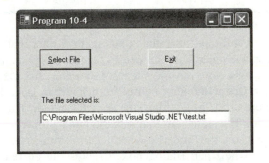

Figure 10–10   *Sample Output Produced by Program 10–4*

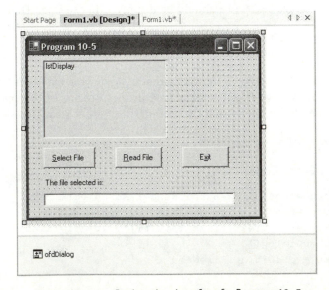

Figure 10–11   *Design-time Interface for Program 10–5*

Table 10–5   The Properties Table for Program 10–5

Object	Property	Setting
Form	Name	frmMain
	Text	Program 10–5
Button	Name	btnSelect
	Text	&Select File
Button	Name	btnRead
	Text	&Read File
Button	Name	btnExit
	Text	E&xit
Label	Name	lblFile
	Text	The file selected is:
TextBox	Name	txtFile
	Text	(blank)
ListBox	Name	lstDisplay
OpenFileDialog	Name	ofdDialog

face for this program and the code is shown in Table 10-5. Aside from the additional button to select the file, a button has been added to read the file and a list box is added to display the contents of the file.

Program 10–5

```
Private Sub btnSelect_Click(ByVal sender As System.Object, ByVal e As _
    System.EventArgs) Handles btnSelect.Click
  ofdDialog.Filter = "Text files (*.txt)|*.txt|All files (*.*)|*.*"
  ofdDialog.ShowDialog()
  txtFile.Text = ofdDialog.FileName
End Sub

Private Sub btnOpen_Click(ByVal sender As System.Object, ByVal e As _
    System.EventArgs) Handles btnOpen.Click
  Dim readvar As System.IO.StreamReader
  Dim input As String

  Try
    readvar = System.IO.File.OpenText(ofdDialog.FileName)
    Do Until readvar.Peek = -1
      input = readvar.ReadLine()
      lstDisplay.Items.Add(input)
    Loop
    readvar.Close()
  Catch
```

```
        MessageBox.Show("File could not be opened")
    End Try
End Sub

Private Sub btnExit_Click(ByVal sender As System.Object, ByVal e As _
    System.EventArgs) Handles btnExit.Click
    Beep()
    End
End Sub
```

Exercises 10.3

1. Enter and execute Program 10–3 on your computer.

2. Enter and execute Program 10–4 on your computer.

3. Write a Visual Basic program that uses an initial form to call an Open File Dialog. The call to the dialog box should be invoked from a button on the initial form. The selected filename should then be displayed in a text box contained on the initial form.

10.4 Random–Access Files[1]

The manner in which records in a file are written and retrieved is called *file access*. All of the files created thus far have used *sequential access,* which means that each item in the file is accessed sequentially, one after another. For example, the fourth item in a sequentially accessed file cannot be read without first reading the first three items in the file; the last item in the file cannot be read without first reading all of the previous items; and no item can be replaced without erasing all subsequent items. Due to the fact that items within a sequential file cannot be replaced, updating a sequential access file requires using a file update procedure in which a completely new file is created for each update. For those applications in which every record in a file must be updated, such as updating a monthly payroll file, sequential access conforms to the way the file must be updated and is not a restriction.

In some applications a direct access to each item in the file, where an individual item in the middle of the file can be retrieved, modified, and rewritten without reading or writing any other item, is preferable. *Random-access* files, which are also referred to as *direct-access* files, provide this capability. In this section we will see how to create and use such files. Note that the access method (sequential or random) refers to how data in the file are accessed and not to the codes used in storing the data. In point of fact, sequential files are stored by Visual Basic as text files, while random-access files are stored using the binary codes described in the next section.

In random-access files, the standard unit of storage is a record, where each record consists of one or more items. A record with only one field corresponds to any of Visual

---

[1]This topic may be omitted on first reading without loss of subject continuity.

Basic built-in data types, whereas a record with more than one field is declared as a structure. Due to the record structure required when using random-access files, such files typically are used only for small amounts of data and simple applications. For large amounts of data and more complicated applications, the record structure inherent in the database methods presented in Chapter 9 would be used instead.

To illustrate the use of random-access files, consider the following application. All banks and financial institutions keep a table of official banking holidays, frequently referred to as a Holiday Table. For example, Table 10–6 illustrates a typical set of banking holidays. As shown in the table, some holidays, such as New Year's Day, are always celebrated on the same day date, while others, such as President's Day, are celebrated on different days depending on the year. The importance of a Holiday Table is in computing settlement and maturity dates for financial instruments, such as stocks and bonds. Most stock and bond transactions must be settled within three working days, which excludes Saturdays, Sundays, and all holidays. Because there are algorithms for determining which dates fall on a weekend (for example Zeller's algorithm, described in Section 12.1, Exercise 10) the specific dates for each weekend need not be stored separately. This is not the case for holidays, and hence the need for a specific table listing all of the holiday dates.

A suitable user-defined structure declaration for each entry in Table 10–6 could be:

```
Structure HolidayRecord
  Public Description As String
  Public Hdate As Date
End Structure
```

The **HolidayRecord** structure provides a convenient way to organize the data into records. Using this within the context of a complete application requires opening a file for random-access, writing to and reading from the file, and closing the file. However, a problem arises when strings are stored in a random-access file such as the **Description** structure element above, because strings are variable-length. It is important to ensure

Table 10–6   A Typical Bank Holiday Table

Holiday	Month	Day
New Year' Day	1	1
President's Day	2	Depends on year
Memorial Day	5	Depends on year
Independence Day	7	4
Labor Day	9	Depends on year
Columbus Day	10	Depends on year
Veterans' Day	11	Depends on year
Christmas Day	12	25

that all records in a random-access file are the same length so all strings must have the same length. To declare a string with a fixed length, the following attribute can be added to the declaration:

```
<VBFixedString(length)>
```

where *length* is the fixed length of the string. The **HolidayRecord** structure above becomes:

```
Structure HolidayRecord
  <VBFixedString(20)> Public Description As String
  Public Hdate As Date
End Structure
```

Table 10–7 lists the four methods that Visual Basic provides for performing these operations on random-access files.

The general syntax for the FileOpen[2] method that opens a file for random-access is:

```
FileOpen(filenumber, filename, OpenMode.Random, Accessmode, _
    OpenShare.Shared, Recordlength)
```

Filenumber is an integer that is used to identify an opened random-access file. For example, the statement:

```
FileOpen(1, "Holiday.dat", OpenMode.Random, OpenAccess.ReadWrite, _
    OpenShare.Shared, Len(HolidayRecord))
```

will open a file named Holiday.dat as a random-access file as filenumber 1.

The filename used in the FileOpen statement can either be a full pathname as a string literal enclosed in double quotes or a full pathname as a string variable. If the path is omit-

Table 10–7 Random-access File Statements

Statement	Description	Example
FileOpen	Open a File	FileOpen(1, "Holiday.dat", OpenMode.Random, _ OpenAccess.ReadWrite, OpenShare.Default, Len(HolidayRecord))
FileClose	Close a File	FileClose(1)
FilePut	Write a Record	FilePut(1, LastRecord, 3)
FileGet	Read a Record	FileGet(1, LastRecord, 3)

[2]Note that you also can open sequential access files with FileOpen but with different arguments.

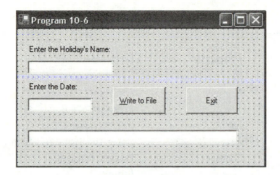

Figure 10–12   *Program 10–6's Design-Time Interface*

ted, the file is assumed to exist on the current directory. The argument `OpenMode.Random` is used to indicate the file is being opened for random-access. `Accessmode` specifies how the file will be accessed and can be set to `OpenAccess.Default`, `OpenAccess.Read-Write`, `OpenAccess.Read`, `OpenAccess.Write`. To open a file for both reading and writing, *accessmode* should be set to `OpenAccess.ReadWrite`. The argument `OpenShare.Shared` indicates that the file can be shared; that is, that other processes can use the file. The last argument is the `Recordlength` that specifies the size (i.e., length) of each stored record. Because each record is required to be of the same type, the length specification applies to all records in the file. If the specified length is less than an actual record length, a run-time error is generated; if the specified length is greater than necessary, the record is stored with additional spaces to fill out the specified length. To make the length specification agree exactly with a record size, the `Len()` function can be used in the manner shown above.

Once a file has been opened for random-access, a `FilePut` method is required to write a record to the file and a `FileGet` statement is used to read a record from the file. Program 10–6 illustrates using a `FilePut` statement to store the holiday data listed in Table 10–6. The design-time interface for this program is shown on Figure 10–12 and the objects and properties are listen in Table 10–8.

Program 10–6's Event Code

```
' Module-level Declarations

Structure Holidayrecord
  <VBFixedString(20)> Public Description As String
  Public Hdate As Date
End Structure

Dim holiday As Holidayrecord

Private Sub Form1_Load(ByVal sender As System.Object, ByVal e As _
   System.EventArgs) Handles MyBase.Load
```

Table 10–8   Program 10–6's Property Table

Object	Property	Setting
Form	Name	frmMain
	Text	Program 10-6
Label	Name	lblDescription
	Text	Enter the Holiday's Name:
TextBox	Name	txtDescription
	Text	(blank)
Label	Name	lblDate
	Text	Enter the Date:
TextBox	Name	txtDate
	Text	(blank)
Button	Name	btnWrite
	Text	&Write to File
Button	Name	btnExit
	Text	E&xit
TextBox	Name	txtMessage
	TabStop	False

```
    Const HolidayTable As String = "Holiday.dat"

    Try
      FileOpen(1, HolidayTable, OpenMode.Random, OpenAccess.ReadWrite, _
          OpenShare.Shared, Len(holiday))
    Catch
      MessageBox.Show("The file " & HolidayTable & "was not opened.", _
          "File Message", MessageBoxButtons.OK, MessageBoxIcon.Exclamation)
    End Try
  End Sub

  Private Sub btnWrite_Click(ByVal sender As System.Object, ByVal e As _
      System.EventArgs) Handles btnWrite.Click
    Static LastRecord As Integer

    holiday.Description = txtDescription.Text
    holiday.Hdate = txtDate.Text
    ' Update the record number
    LastRecord = LastRecord + 1
    ' Write the record to the file
    FilePut(1, holiday, LastRecord)
    txtMessage.Clear()
```

```
    txtMessage.Text = "The record has been written."
End Sub

Private Sub txtDate_TextChanged(ByVal sender As System.Object, _
    ByVal e As System.EventArgs) Handles txtDate.TextChanged
  txtMessage.Clear()
End Sub

Private Sub txtDescription_Enter(ByVal sender As Object, ByVal e As _
    System.EventArgs) Handles txtDescription.Enter
  txtMessage.Clear()
End Sub

Private Sub btnExit_Click(ByVal sender As System.Object, ByVal e As _
    System.EventArgs) Handles btnExit.Click
  FileClose(1)
  Beep()
  End
End Sub
```

When initially reviewing the event code in Program 10–6, look at the General Declaration section. It is here that we define the structure used by the program and declare a variable `holiday` to be an instance of this structure. Next, note that the **Form Load** event procedure is used to open the file. Finally, note the `FilePut` statement within the `btnWrite_Click` event procedure. Prior to executing this statement, the procedure assigns the field within the `Holiday` variable to the data entered into the two text boxes. This procedure also updates the record number for the next record to be written and stores this record number in the variable named `LastRecord`, where it is used to write the record into a file. Note that if a valid date is not entered, the program will fail with an Invalid Cast Exception error.

`FilePut` methods have the general syntax:

`FilePut(`*filenumber,* *recordvariable,* *recordnumber*`)`

Filenumber is the same number that was used in the FileOpen statement. *Recordvariable* contains the data that is to be written to the file referenced by *filenumber*. *Recordnumber* in the `FilePut` statement can be any integer expression that evaluates to a positive number. Because records in a random-access file are accessed by record number, applications that use random-access files must contain a means of identifying each record position in the file. If no record position is indicated, the record contents will be written at the next available position; that is, the record is appended to the file. In Program 10–6 the `LastRecord` variable is used to keep track of the current record position. The `FileClose` method is called in the exit procedure to close the file. The general syntax for this method is:

`FileClose(`*filenumber*`)`

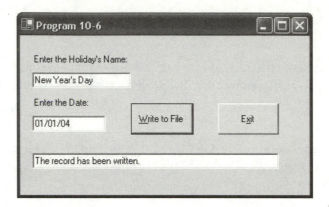

Figure 10–13 *Using Program 10–6 to Write a Record*

Figure 10–13 illustrates how this run-time interface appears after a record has been entered and written.

The counterpart to the `FilePut` is the `FileGet` statement, used to read a record from a random-access file. The general syntax of this method is:

```
FileGet(filenumber, recordvariable, recordnumber)
```

In this statement the `filenumber` is the number used in the `FileOpen` statement to open the file, `recordvariable` is the variable that is used to receive the contents of the record, and `recordnumber` is the record number of the record to be read. If no record number is indicated, the next record in the file is read. Program 10–7 uses the `FileGet` method to read the records placed in the Holiday.dat File by Program 10–6. The design-time interface for Program 10–7 is shown in Figure 10–14 and Table 10–9 lists the objects and properties for this program.

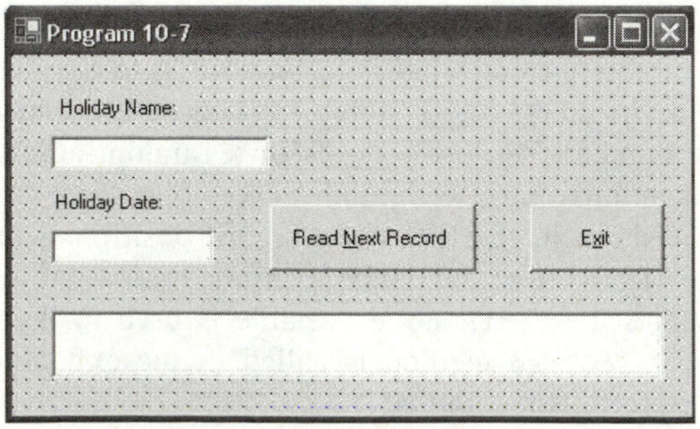

Figure 10–14 *Program 10–7's Design-Time Interface*

Table 10-9   Program 10-7's Property Table

Object	Property	Setting
Form	Name	frmMain
	Text	Program 10-7
Label	Name	lblDescription
	Text	Holiday Name:
TextBox	Name	txtDescription
	Text	(blank)
Label	Name	lblDate
	Text	Holiday Date:
TextBox	Name	txtDate
	Text	(blank)
Button	Name	btnNext
	Text	Read &Next Record
Button	Name	btnExit
	Text	E&xit
TextBox	Name	txtMessage
	TabStop	False
	Multiline	True

Programmer Notes

A Way to Clearly Identify a File Name and Location

During program development, test files usually are placed in the same directory as the program. Therefore, an expression such as Example 1 below causes no problems to the operating system. In production systems, however, it is more common for data files to reside in one directory and for program files to reside in another. For this reason it is always a good idea to include the full path name of any file opened. For example, if the Holiday.dat File resides in the directory C:/test/files, the **FileOpen** statement should include the full path name shown in Example 2 below. Then, no matter where the program originates, the operating system will know where to locate the file.

Another important convention is to list all file names at the top of a program instead of embedding the names within the **FileOpen** statement. This can easily be accomplished using a string variable to store each name, and placing this variable in the Module-level Declarations section of the opening form. For example, if a declaration such as the one shown in Example 3 below is placed within the Module-level Declarations section, it clearly lists both the name of the desired file and its location. Then, if some other file is to be tested, all that is required is a simple one-line change at the top of the program. Within a **FileOpen** statement this string variable would appear as shown in Example 4 below.

```
Example 1:  FileOpen(1, "Holiday.dat", OpenMode.Random, OpenAccess.ReadWrite, _
            OpenShare.Shared, Len(holiday))
```

Example 2:   `FileOpen(1, "C:/test/files/Holiday.dat", OpenMode.Random, _`
             `OpenAccess.ReadWrite, OpenShare.Shared, Len(holiday))`

Example 3:   `Const Filename As String = "C:\test\files\Holiday.dat"`

Example 4:   `FileOpen(1, Filename, OpenMode.Random, OpenAccess.ReadWrite, _`
             `OpenShare.Shared, Len(holiday))`

Program 10-7's Event Code

```
' Module-level Declarations

Structure Holidayrecord
  <VBFixedString(20)> Public Description As String
  Public Hdate As Date
End Structure

Dim holiday As Holidayrecord

Private Sub Form1_Load(ByVal sender As System.Object, ByVal e As _
    System.EventArgs) Handles MyBase.Load
  Const HolidayTable As String = "Holiday.dat"

  Try
    FileOpen(1, "Holiday.dat", OpenMode.Random, OpenAccess.ReadWrite, _
        OpenShare.Shared, Len(holiday))
  Catch
    MessageBox.Show("The file " & HolidayTable & "was not opened.", _
        "File Message", MessageBoxButtons.OK, MessageBoxIcon.Exclamation)
  End Try
End Sub

Private Sub btnNext_Click(ByVal sender As System.Object, ByVal e As _
    System.EventArgs) Handles btnNext.Click
  Static LastRecord As Integer
  Dim records As Integer

  records = LOF(1) / Len(holiday)
  txtMessage.Clear()
  txtMessage.AppendText("There are " & records & " records in the file.")
  txtMessage.AppendText(ControlChars.NewLine)

  ' Update the record number
  LastRecord = LastRecord + 1
  If LastRecord > records Then LastRecord = records
```

```
' Read the next record
Try
   FileGet(1, holiday, LastRecord)
   txtDescription.Text = holiday.Description
   txtDate.Text = holiday.Hdate
   txtMessage.AppendText("This is record number " & LastRecord & ".")
Catch
   MessageBox.Show("FileGet failed")
End Try
End Sub

Private Sub btnExit_Click(ByVal sender As System.Object, ByVal e As _
      System.EventArgs) Handles btnExit.Click
   FileClose(1)
   Beep()
   End
End Sub
```

In reviewing the event code in Program 10-7, only new items are contained within the btnNext_Click event code. Here the click event is used to execute a FileGet statement to retrieve the next record in the file. As with Program 10-6, a variable named LastRecord is used to store the value of the next record to be read. Also, as with Program 10-6, the user-defined record structure is declared in the Module-level Declaration section of the program, and the file itself is opened when the form is loaded. The only remaining new feature is the calculation of the number of records. This is determined by dividing the total length of the file, obtained by calling the Visual Basic function LOF, by the length of an individual record and storing the result in the variable named records. The 1 in the function call to LOF is the filenumber of the target file. A sample output displayed by Program 10-7 is shown in Figure 10-15.

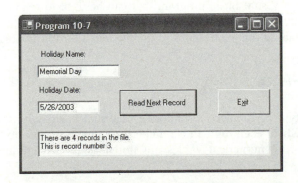

Figure 10-15 *Displaying the 3rd Record in the File*

Exercises 10.4

1. a. List the advantages of using a random-access file over a sequential file. What are the disadvantages?

   b. List two requirements in using a random-access file.

   c. Under what conditions would a database file be preferable to using a Visual Basic random-access file?

2. Enter and execute Program 10–6 on your computer.

3. Enter and execute Program 10–7 on your computer.

4. Modify Program 10–8 to include a button that can be used to read a previous record as well as the next record in the file.

5. A software distribution company is constantly opening and closing offices throughout the United States, Europe, and Asia. In its New York office it maintains a file that contains an up-to-date listing of offices and their time zones. Currently the company file contains the following data:

Paris	+1
London	0
New York	−5
Chicago	−6
Dallas	−7
San Francisco	−8
Honolulu	−10
Tokyo	+9

   The information in this file must be read each morning. It is then used by a program that automatically sends faxes to each office with the time adjusted to local time. For example, New York time is five hours behind London time and Tokyo is nine hours ahead of London time. Thus, when it is noon in London it is 7 A.M. in New York and 9 P.M. in Tokyo. Management has asked you to write a Visual Basic program that can be used to create a random-access file for the current data.

6. Write a Visual Basic program that can be used to read and display the records created by the program written for Exercise 5. Your program should include a button for reading the next record in the file and a button for reading the previous record.

10.5 Binary-Access Files[3]

The last type of file access supported in Visual Basic is binary access. Unlike a sequential file, where each digit in a number is stored using its text (ANSI) code, in a binary-access file all numerical values are stored using the computer's internal binary code.

---

[3]This topic assumes that you are familiar with the computer storage concepts presented in Section 1.7.

Assuming that the computer stores integer numbers internally using 32 bits in the two's complement format described in Section 1.7, the decimal number 8 is represented as the binary number 0000 0000 0000 0000 0000 0000 0000 1000, the decimal number 12 as 0000 0000 0000 0000 0000 0000 0000 1100, and the decimal number 497 as 0000 0000 0000 0000 0000 0001 111 1001. As hexadecimal numbers these numbers have the byte code 00 00 00 08, 00 00 00 0C, and 00 00 01 F1, respectively.

Because the external storage codes match the computer's internal storage representation, an advantage of using a binary format is that no intermediary conversions are required for storing or retrieving the data from the file. In addition, the resulting file usually requires less storage space than it would as a text file. For example, as text the number 497 requires six bytes of storage (using Unicode format) consisting of the ANSI byte code sequence 00 34 00 39 00 37 (see Appendix A for these codes). (For single digit numbers, or course, the text format, which only requires two bytes of storage, is smaller than the equivalent binary code.)

Like random-access files, the information in binary-access files also is accessed directly. The difference between the two file types, however, is that random-access files are organized as records, while binary-access files are organized by item. The same four statements used for opening, reading, writing, and closing random-access files also are used for binary-access files, with the main difference being that a byte position rather than a record position is used when reading and writing binary-access files. The general syntax for the **FileOpen** method, as it applies to a binary-access file is:

```
FileOpen(filenumber, filename, OpenMode.Binary)
```

For example, the statement

```
FileOpen(1, "bintest.dat", OpenMode.Binary)
```

will open a file named bintest.dat as a binary-access file that is assigned file number 1. Note that there is no record length argument in the `FileOpen` statement; if one is included it will be ignored. As always, the filename used in the `FileOpen` statement can either be a full path name as a literal string enclosed in double quotes, or a string variable. If the path is omitted, the file is assumed to exist on the current directory.

For writing data to a binary-access file, the `FilePut` statement must be used. As it applies to binary files, this statement has the syntax:

```
FilePut(filenumber, recordvariable, bytenumber)
```

In this statement `filenumber` is the number used in the `FileOpen` method to open the file, and `bytenumber` is any integer expression that evaluates to a positive number. If `bytenumber` is not specified, the next unused byte position in the file is used (that is, data is appended to the file).

For reading data from a binary-access file, a `FileGet` statement can be used. The general syntax of the `FileGet`, as it applies to binary-access files, is:

```
FileGet(filenumber, recordvariable, bytenumber)
```

Again, *filenumber* is the number used in the FileOpen statement to open the file, *recordvariable* is the variable that is used to receive the contents of the item that will be read, and *bytenumber* is the position of the next item to be read. If *bytenumber* is not specified, the next item in the file is read.

Program 10-8 illustrates creating a binary file and writing four items to the file. The design-time interface for this program is shown in Figure 10-16.

Program 10-8's Event Code

```
Private Sub btnSelect_Click(ByVal sender As System.Object, ByVal e As _
    System.EventArgs) Handles btnSelect.Click
  txtMessage.Clear()
  ofdDialog.Filter = "Data Files(*.dat)|*.dat|All Files (*.*)|*.*"
  ofdDialog.ShowDialog()
  txtMessage.AppendText(ofdDialog.FileName)
End Sub

Private Sub btnWrite_Click(ByVal sender As System.Object, ByVal e As _
    System.EventArgs) Handles btnWrite.Click

  Try
    FileOpen(1, ofdDialog.FileName, OpenMode.Binary)
    FilePut(1, 8)
    FilePut(1, 12)
    FilePut(1, 497)
    FilePut(1, "abcdef")
    FileClose(1)
```

Table 10-10 Program 10-8's Property Table

Object	Property	Setting
Form	Name	frmMain
	Text	Program 10-8
Open File Dialog	Name	ofdFile
Button	Name	btnSelect
	Text	&Select File
Button	Name	btnWrite
	Text	&Write to File
Button	Name	btnExit
	Text	E&xit
Text Box	Name	txtMessage
	TabStop	False
	Text	(blank)

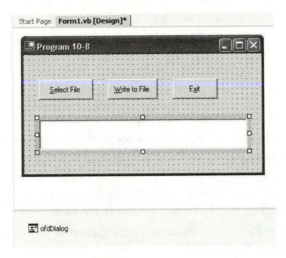

Figure 10–16 *Program 10–8's Graphical User Interface*

```
    txtMessage.Clear()
    txtMessage.AppendText("The file " & ofdDialog.FileName & " has _
        been written.")
    Catch
      txtMessage.AppendText("The file was not successfully opened")
      txtMessage.AppendText(ControlChars.NewLine & "Please check _
          that the file currently exists.")
    End Try
End Sub

Private Sub btnExit_Click(ByVal sender As System.Object, ByVal e As _
    System.EventArgs) Handles btnExit.Click
  Beep()
  End
End Sub
```

Of the three event procedures used in Program 10–8, the `btnSelect_Click` and `btnExit_Click` event codes are identical to those used in earlier programs. The only new features in this program are the `FileOpen` and `FilePut` statements in the `btnWrite_Click` event, as they relate to binary-access files. Note that for each item written to the file, a separate `FilePut` statement is required.

The binary file created by Program 10–8 is illustrated in Figure 10–17, which uses hexadecimal values to indicate the equivalent binary storage used for the file. As indicated in the figure, the file consists of eighteen bytes, where the hexadecimal values correspond to the decimal values 8, 12, 497, and the characters a, b, c, d, e, and f.

00 08 00 0C 01 F1 61 00 62 00 63 00 64 00 65 00 66 00

Figure 10–17 *The bintest.dat File as Stored by Program 10–8*

Exercises 10.5

1. List the similarities and differences between binary and random-access files.

2. Enter and execute Program 10–8 on your computer.

3. Write and execute a Visual Basic program that reads and displays the binary file created by Program 10–8.

4. a. Write and execute a Visual Basic program that writes the numbers 92.65, 88.72, 77.46, and 89.93 to a binary-access file name result.bin.

   b. Using the data in the result.bin file created in Exercise 4a, write a Visual Basic program that reads the file's data, determines the average of the four numbers read, and displays the average. Verify the output produced by your program by manually calculating the average of the four numbers.

5. a. Write and execute a Visual Basic program that creates a binary-access file named grades.dat and writes the following numbers to the file:

   100, 100, 100, 100

   100, 0, 100, 0

   86, 83, 89, 94

   78, 59, 77, 85

   89, 92, 81, 88

   b. Using the data in the grades.dat file created in Exercise 5a, write a Visual Basic program that reads the file's data, computes the average of each group of four numbers read, and displays the average.

10.6 Focus on Program Design and Implementation: Creating Screen and Printer Reports

In this last Focus section we complete the Rotech application by providing a screen and hardcopy (printer) report. At this point the procedure for adding a new form into a project and then developing the form should be familiar to you. For a review, however, the steps are:

1. a. Add a new form to the project using the procedure defined in this section.

   b. Supply the new form with a <u>R</u>eturn to Main Menu Button, whose **Click** event consists of the following three lines of code:

   ```
   Dim frmMainRef As New frmMainMenu()

   Me.Hide()
   ```

```
frmMainRef.Show()

frmMainRef.Refresh()
```

2. If the Main Menu has a button that is used to display an existing stub form, have this button display the new form; otherwise, add a button to the Main Menu to perform the display.

3. Develop the new form to perform its intended function.

Adding the New Report Form

Although we have added a number of new forms to the Rotech project, in this final Focus section we provide a last complete summary of the procedure. Specifically, to add a new form to our project select the Add Windows Form item from the Project menu, as shown in Figure 10–18. This will bring up the Add New Item dialog shown in Figure 10–19, from which you should select the Windows Form icon under the Templates. This will add the form to the Project Explorer Window. Once you have generated this new Form, configure it with the objects and properties listed in Table 10–11.

At this stage you can link this new form into the Main Menu by making a few modifications to existing code on the Main Menu Form and by adding code to the btnReturn Button's Click event. Event Procedure 10–2 presents the new return button's Click event code and Procedure Code 10–1 adds functionality to frmMain's existing code. As these are the standard types of changes we have made throughout this Focus series for adding a new form we will not comment on them further, except to note that Procedure Code 10–1 represents the final version of the mainmenu Sub procedure. Figure 10–20 shows the final Main Menu Form.

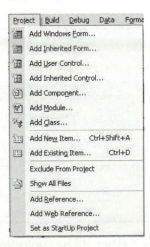

Figure 10–18　*Adding a Second Form Using the Project Menu*

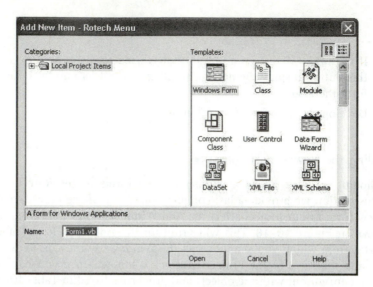

Figure 10–19 *The Add New Item Dialog Box*

Table 10–11   The Report Form's Initial Properties Table

Object	Property	Setting
Form	Name	frmReport
	Text	REPORTS SCREEN
Button	Name	btnReturn
	Text	&Return to Main Menu

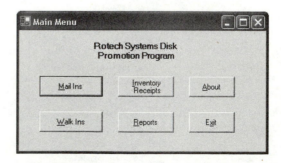

Figure 10–20 *Final Rotech Main Menu*

Event Procedure 10–2

```
Private Sub btnReturn_Click(ByVal sender As Object, _
    ByVal e As System.EventArgs) Handles btnReturn.Click
  Dim frmMainRef As New frmMain()

  Me.Hide()
  frmMainRef.Show()
End Sub
```

Procedure Code 10–1

```
Const intMAILBUTTON As Integer = 1
Const intWALKBUTTON As Integer = 2
Const intINVBUTTON As Integer = 3
Const intABOUTBUTTON As Integer = 4
Const intREPORTBUTTON As Integer = 5
Const intEXITBUTTON As Integer = 6
Const intSTUB As Integer = 99
Private Sub btnMailins_Click(ByVal sender As System.Object, ByVal e As _
    System.EventArgs) Handles btnMailins.Click
  mainmenu(intMAILBUTTON)
End Sub

Private Sub btnWalkins_Click(ByVal sender As System.Object, ByVal e As _
    System.EventArgs) Handles btnWalkins.Click
  mainmenu(intWALKBUTTON)
End Sub

Private Sub btnInvRec_Click(ByVal sender As System.Object, ByVal e As _
    System.EventArgs) Handles btnInvRec.Click
  mainmenu(intINVBUTTON)
End Sub

Private Sub btnAbout_Click(ByVal sender As System.Object, ByVal e As _
    System.EventArgs) Handles btnAbout.Click
  mainmenu(intABOUTBUTTON)
End Sub

Private Sub btnReports_Click(ByVal sender As System.Object, ByVal e As _
    System.EventArgs) Handles btnReports.Click
  mainmenu(intREPORTBUTTON)
End Sub

Private Sub btnExit_Click(ByVal sender As System.Object, ByVal e As _
```

```
      System.EventArgs) Handles btnExit.Click
    mainmenu(intEXITBUTTON)
End Sub

Public Sub mainmenu(ByVal intFromButton As Integer)
    Dim frmMailRef As New frmMailIn()
    Dim frmWalkRef As New frmWalkIn()
    Dim frmInvRef As New frmInventory()
    Dim frmReportRef As New frmReport()
    Dim frmAboutRef As New frmAbout()

    Me.Hide()
    Select Case intFromButton
      Case intMAILBUTTON
        frmMailRef.KeyPreview = True
        frmMailRef.Show()
        frmMailRef.Refresh()
      Case intWALKBUTTON
        frmWalkRef.KeyPreview = True
        frmWalkRef.Show()
        frmWalkRef.Refresh()
      Case intINVBUTTON
        frmInvRef.KeyPreview = True
        frmInvRef.Show()
        frmInvRef.Refresh()
      Case intREPORTBUTTON
        frmReportRef.KeyPreview = True
        frmReportRef.Show()
        frmReportRef.Refresh()
      Case intABOUTBUTTON
        frmAboutRef.KeyPreview = True
        frmAboutRef.Show()
        frmAboutRef.Refresh()
      Case intEXITBUTTON
        Beep()
        End
    End Select
End Sub
```

Having added a new form and linked it into the Main Menu (Steps 1 and 2), we now can develop code to have this form perform its intended function (Step 3). Figure 10–21 illustrates how we want our report form to appear. For variety, we have labeled each button with a number or letter, and used labels to identify each button's usage. An alternative and equally acceptable technique would be to make the buttons larger and use their Text property for identification purposes.

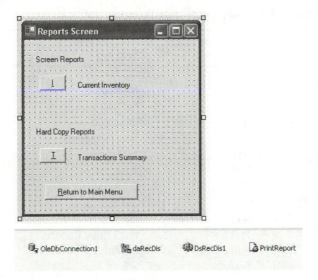

Figure 10–21   *The Completed Reports Form Interface*

Tables 10–11 and 10–12 provide the report form's properties and task list, respectively. Note that a data connection, data adapter, and dataset must be set up in order to access the database; these appear in the component tray below the form and are not visible on the form. The sole purpose of these data controls is to provide access to the Disktran database table RecDis, from which all of the reports will be constructed. We use this table to produce two reports: one for each of the first two buttons listed in the TTL table (see Table 10–13).

Creating a Screen Report

The screen report is intended to provide a quick summary of the number of disk packages available in inventory. Initially, this current inventory is determined using the following formula:

Current Inventory = Receipts

— (Returns + Damaged + Other Adjustments)

— (Mail-in Disbursals + Walk-in sales)

Figure 10–22 illustrates how this report appears for the original data provided in the Disktran's RecDis Table at http://computerscience.jbpub.com/bronsonvbnet (see Table 9–11).

The code used to produce the report shown in Figure 10–22 is listed in Procedure Code 10–2. In the Module-level Declarations section the codes used for each category of inventory transaction (previously listed in Table 9–13) are given symbolic names. The real work in producing the report is then carried out in the Click event code. Within this event code, a single loop is constructed that is used to inspect each transaction record and either add or subtract the transaction amount, as appropriate, from a running

Table 10–12   The Report Form's Property Table

Object	Property	Setting
Form	Name	frmReport
	Text	REPORTS SCREEN
Label	Name	lblScreen
	Text	Screen reports
Button	Name	btnScreen1
	Text	&I
Label	Name	lblInventory
	Text	Current Inventory
Label	Name	lblPrint
	Text	Hard Copy Reports
Button	Name	btnPrinter1
	Text	&T
Label	Name	lblSummary
	Text	Transactions Summary
Button	Name	btnReturn
	Text	&Return to Main Menu

Table 10–13   The Report Form's TTL Table

Form: Report Task	Trigger Object	Event
Prepare screen report	btnScreen1	Click
Prepare printer report	btnReport1	Click
Return to Main Menu	btnReturn	Click

total. To search through the database table, we start with rownumber zero through the count of rows minus one. Note that the dataset name should be changed from dsRecDis1 to dsRecDis. After the loop is completed, the total within the variable intTotal is concatenated to the current label lblInventory.

It should be noted that the method of calculating current inventory by cycling through each record, as is done in Procedure Code 10-2, only produces a report quickly if the number of transactions is reasonably small (typically, under a few thousand records). As the number of transactions grows to where the calculation itself takes more than two or three seconds, a better method of computing the inventory is to do the addition or subtraction as each transaction is entered, using a current inventory value that is stored in a text file. A screen report of current inventory is then produced simply

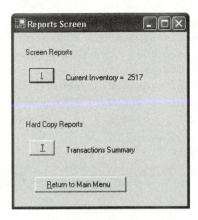

Figure 10-22   *The Screen Report*

by reading and displaying the value previously calculated and stored in the text file. This method of producing the report is left as an exercise.

Procedure Code 10-2

```
' These are the Module-level Declaration statements


Const strRECEIVE As String = "r"  ' code for receipt of inventory
Const strRETURNED As String = "t" ' code for returns to vendor
Const strDAMAGED As String = "d"  ' code for damaged inventory
Const strOTHER As String = "o"    ' code for other adjustments
Const strMAILINS As String = "m"  ' code for a mail in disbursement
Const strWALKINS As String = "w"  ' code for a walk in disbursement


Dim rownumber As Integer

Private Sub btnScreen1_Click(ByVal sender As System.Object, ByVal e As _
    System.EventArgs) Handles btnScreen1.Click
  Dim intTotal As Integer

  intTotal = 0
  rownumber = 0
  ' Move to first record and cycle through all records
  Do While rownumber < dsRecDis.RecDis.Count
    If dsRecDis.RecDis(rownumber).RDCode = strRECEIVE Then
      intTotal = intTotal + dsRecDis.RecDis(rownumber).Quantity
    ElseIf dsRecDis.RecDis(rownumber).RDCode = strRETURNED Then
      intTotal = intTotal - dsRecDis.RecDis(rownumber).Quantity
    ElseIf dsRecDis.RecDis(rownumber).RDCode = strDAMAGED Then
```

```
        intTotal = intTotal - dsRecDis.RecDis(rownumber).Quantity
   ElseIf dsRecDis.RecDis(rownumber).RDCode = strOTHER Then
        intTotal = intTotal - dsRecDis.RecDis(rownumber).Quantity
   ElseIf dsRecDis.RecDis(rownumber).RDCode = strMAILINS Then
        intTotal = intTotal - dsRecDis.RecDis(rownumber).Quantity
   ElseIf dsRecDis.RecDis(rownumber).RDCode = strWALKINS Then
        intTotal = intTotal - dsRecDis.RecDis(rownumber).Quantity
   End If
   rownumber = rownumber + 1
  Loop
  lblInventory.Text = lblInventory.Text & " = " & Str(intTotal)
End Sub
```

Creating a Printed Report

To create a printed report, we use the **PrintDocument** control as in Chapter 4. Specifically, the report that we want to produce is a detail of all transactions, a sample of which is shown in Figure 10–23. Note that the final number presented in this report is the same as that provided by the screen report shown in Figure 10–21, but that the printed report provides more detail of how this value was calculated. This relationship between corresponding printed and screen reports should always hold: a printed report,

```
Prepared: 4/17/2004      (10:24 PM)


SUMMARY OF INVENTORY TRANSACTIONS
-----------------------------------


Quantity Received :      3000
Less:
                Returned:     300
                Damaged:      125
                  Other:       30
                              -------
Net Into Inventory:      2545


Less:
                Mail-Ins:      19
                Walk-Ins:       9
                              =======

Current Inventory:       2517
```

Figure 10–23 *A Printed Report*

while providing additional information, must always tally with any screen report that provides similar summary information.

The report shown in Figure 10–23 was produced using Procedure Code 10–3. Here, a number of variables are first dimensioned within the Module-level Declarations section and subsequently used in the btnPrinter1 Button's Click event. The reason for making the declarations within the Module-level Declarations section is that this set of variables will be used for a variety of additional reports (see Exercises), and because they are not used to pass data between procedures it is safer and more efficient to make their declarations only once.

The While loop within the Click event code listed in Procedure Code 10–3 is almost the same as that used in Procedure Code 10–2, except that the If-ElseIf statement separates out each individual receipt and disbursement type, rather than simply folding them into a general total. Each of these separate values is then printed.

In reviewing the Click event code two further features should be noted. The first is the initialization of the variables that are declared in the Module-level Declaration section. This initialization must be done within any procedure that requires these variables to be initialized, as assigning values to Dimed variables cannot be done within a Module-level Declarations section.

To produce this report, the **String.Format** method is used to align the output along column boundaries and to right justify the numbers. The general form of this method is:

```
String.Format(FormatString, Arg0, Arg1 [, . . . ])
```

FormatString is a string that contains text and/or specifications for formatting and Arg0 and Arg1 are the arguments to be formatted. Note that more arguments may be used. To get the output to properly align in the columns, ensure that all the characters use the same amount of space. To do so, it is best to use a monospaced (as opposed to proportional) font such as Courier New.

As an example, suppose that we want to display the following two columns where the first column is left-justified and the second column is right-justified:

```
First number      15
Second number    255
Third number       2
```

The following code segment is used to produce this output:

```
Dim font As New Font("Courier New", 12, FontStyle.Bold Or FontStyle.Italic)
Dim number1, number2, number3 As Integer

number1 = 15
number2 = 255
number3 = 2
```

```
e.Graphics.DrawString(String.Format("{0, -18} {1, 5}", "First number", _
    number1), font, Brushes.Black, x, y)
y = y + font.GetHeight
e.Graphics.DrawString(String.Format("{0, -18} {1, 5}", "Second number", _
    number2), font, Brushes.Black, x, y)
y = y + font.GetHeight
e.Graphics.DrawString(String.Format("{0, -18} {1, 5}", "Third number", _
    number3), font, Brushes.Black, x, y)
```

The format string is "{0, -18} {1, 5}" where in the first line, 0 refers to argument 0 (the string "First number") and 1 refers to argument 1 (the variable number1). To left-justify the column output, use a negative number for the column width (-18). To right-justify the output, a positive number is used (5).

Procedure Code 10-3

```
' These are the Module-level Declaration statements

Const strRECEIVE As String = "r"   ' code for receipt of inventory
Const strRETURNED As String = "t" ' code for returns to vendor
Const strDAMAGED As String = "d"   ' code for damaged inventory
Const strOTHER As String = "o"     ' code for other adjustments
Const strMAILINS As String = "m"   ' code for a mail in disbursement
Const strWALKINS As String = "w"   ' code for a walk in disbursement

Dim rownumber As Integer
Dim intReceipts, intReturns, intDamaged, intOther As Integer
Dim intMailins, intWalkins, intTotalIn, intAmount As Integer

Private Sub btnPrinter1_Click(ByVal sender As System.Object, ByVal e As _
    System.EventArgs) Handles btnPrinter1.Click

    intReceipts = 0
    intReturns = 0
    intDamaged = 0
    intOther = 0
    intMailins = 0
    intWalkins = 0
    intTotalIn = 0
    intAmount = 0
    rownumber = 0


    ' Move to first record and cycle through all records
    Do While rownumber < dsRecDis.RecDis.Count
```

```
        If dsRecDis.RecDis(rownumber).RDCode = strRECEIVE Then
          intReceipts = intReceipts + dsRecDis.RecDis(rownumber).Quantity
        ElseIf dsRecDis.RecDis(rownumber).RDCode = strRETURNED Then
          intReturns = intReturns + dsRecDis.RecDis(rownumber).Quantity
        ElseIf dsRecDis.RecDis(rownumber).RDCode = strDAMAGED Then
          intDamaged = intDamaged + dsRecDis.RecDis(rownumber).Quantity
        ElseIf dsRecDis.RecDis(rownumber).RDCode = strOTHER Then
          intOther = intOther + dsRecDis.RecDis(rownumber).Quantity
        ElseIf dsRecDis.RecDis(rownumber).RDCode = strMAILINS Then
          intMailins = intMailins + dsRecDis.RecDis(rownumber).Quantity
        ElseIf dsRecDis.RecDis(rownumber).RDCode = strWALKINS Then
          intWalkins = intWalkins + dsRecDis.RecDis(rownumber).Quantity
        End If
        rownumber = rownumber + 1
    Loop
    PrintReport.Print()
End Sub

Private Sub PrintReport_PrintPage(ByVal sender As System.Object, ByVal e As _
    System.Drawing.Printing.PrintPageEventArgs)
    Dim font As New Font("Courier New", 12, FontStyle.Bold Or FontStyle.Italic)
    Dim x, y As Single

    intTotalIn = intReceipts - (intReturns + intDamaged + intOther)
    intAmount = intTotalIn - (intMailins + intWalkins)

    x = e.MarginBounds.Left
    y = e.MarginBounds.Top

    e.Graphics.DrawString("", Font, Brushes.Black, x, y)
    y = y + Font.GetHeight
    e.Graphics.DrawString("", Font, Brushes.Black, x, y)
    y = y + Font.GetHeight

    e.Graphics.DrawString(String.Format("{0, -20}{1, 13}", "Prepared: " &  _
        FormatDateTime(Now, DateFormat.ShortDate), FormatDateTime(Now, _
        DateFormat.LongTime)), font, Brushes.Black, x, y)
    y = y + font.GetHeight

    e.Graphics.DrawString("", font, Brushes.Black, x, y)
    y = y + font.GetHeight

    e.Graphics.DrawString("SUMMARY OF INVENTORY TRANSACTIONS", font, _
        Brushes.Black, x, y)
```

```
y = y + font.GetHeight

e.Graphics.DrawString("------------", font, Brushes.Black, _
    x, y)
y = y + font.GetHeight

e.Graphics.DrawString("", font, Brushes.Black, x, y)
y = y + font.GetHeight

e.Graphics.DrawString(String.Format("{0, -20}{1, 8}", "Quantity _
    Received:", intReceipts), font, Brushes.Black, x, y)
y = y + font.GetHeight

e.Graphics.DrawString("Less:", font, Brushes.Black, x, y)
y = y + font.GetHeight

e.Graphics.DrawString(String.Format("{0, 20}{1, 8}", "Returned:", _
    intReturns), font, Brushes.Black, x, y)
y = y + font.GetHeight

e.Graphics.DrawString(String.Format("{0, 20}{1, 8}", "Damaged:", _
    intDamaged), font, Brushes.Black, x, y)
y = y + font.GetHeight

e.Graphics.DrawString(String.Format("{0, 20}{1, 8}", "Other:", _
    intOther), font, Brushes.Black, x, y)
y = y + font.GetHeight

e.Graphics.DrawString(Space(24) & "---", font, Brushes.Black, x, y)
y = y + font.GetHeight

e.Graphics.DrawString(String.Format("{0, -20}{1, 8}", "Net Into _
    Inventory:", intTotalIn), font, Brushes.Black, x, y)
y = y + font.GetHeight

e.Graphics.DrawString("", font, Brushes.Black, x, y)
y = y + font.GetHeight

e.Graphics.DrawString("Less:", font, Brushes.Black, x, y)
y = y + font.GetHeight

e.Graphics.DrawString(String.Format("{0, 20}{1, 8}", "Mail-Ins:", _
    intMailins), font, Brushes.Black, x, y)
```

```
y = y + font.GetHeight

  e.Graphics.DrawString(String.Format("{0, 20}{1, 8}", "Walk-Ins:", _
    intWalkins), font, Brushes.Black, x, y)
y = y + font.GetHeight

e.Graphics.DrawString(Space(24) & "=====", font, Brushes.Black, x, y)
y = y + font.GetHeight

e.Graphics.DrawString(String.Format("{0, -20}{1, 8}", "Current _
    Inventory:", intAmount), font, Brushes.Black, x, y)
y = y + font.GetHeight

Beep()
Beep()

End Sub
```

Exercises 10.6

(*Note: The Rotech Systems project, at the stage of development begun in this section, can be found at http://computerscience.jbpub.com/bronsonvbnet in the ROTECH9 folder as project rotech9. The project, which includes both the screen and printer report developed in this section, can be found in the ROTECH10 folder as project rotech10. If you are developing the system yourself, following the procedures given in this section, we suggest that you first copy all of the files in the ROTECH9 folder onto your system, and then work out of this latter folder. When you have finished your changes you can compare your results to the files in the ROTECH10 folder.*)

1. a. Add the screen report developed in this section to the Rotech project located in the ROTECH9 folder.

   b. Test the screen report constructed in Exercise 1a to ensure that it correctly computes the current number of disks in inventory using the data in the RecDis table. This table is contained within the Disktran.mdb located at http://computerscience. jbpub.com/bronsonvbnet in the Databases folder.

   c. Using Rotech's Mail In form, add a number of new transactions to the RecDis table, and then re-run the screen report constructed in Exercise 1a to verify that your program correctly accounts for the new transactions.

   d. Add the printer report developed in this section to the Rotech project.

   e. Test the printer report to verify that it correlates with the screen report produced for Exercise 1c.

2. a. Add a screen report to the Rotech report screen that displays the total number of disk packages distributed due to mail-ins.

b. Modify the screen report created for Exercise 2a to permit the user to specify a state designation. If the user enters the state designation SS, the report should display the total number of disk packages distributed to all of the states combined. (This should be the same number reported in Exercise 2a.)

3. a. Add a screen report to the Rotech report screen developed in this section that displays the total number of disk packages sold to walk-ins.

4. a. The method used in producing the screen report shown in Figure 10–22 requires that each record in the transactions table be opened and inspected. Another method is to store the current inventory in a text file and then adjust this value as each transaction is entered. The screen report can then be provided simply by reading and displaying the value in this text file. For this part of the exercise, store the value 2520 into a text file (this is the current inventory amount corresponding to the records in the RecDis table), and create a screen report that opens the file, displays the number, and then closes the file.

b. Modify the Walk In, Mail In, and Inventory Receipt and Disbursement Forms so that each transaction entered into these forms correctly updates the text file created in Exercise 4a.

5. Add a screen report to the Rotech report screen that displays the net number of disk packages added to inventory. The reported number should be the sum of packages received less the number of packages returned, damaged, or otherwise adjusted.

6. Add a Printer report to the Rotech project that lists all of the inventory receipts, including returns, damaged amounts, and other adjustments, by date.

7. Add a Printer report to the Rotech project that lists all of the mail-in and walk-in disbursements by date.

8. Add a Printer report to the Rotech project that lists all of the states, in alphabetical order, to which mail-in disbursements were made, and the total mail-in disbursements made to each state. After the last state has been listed the total number of walk-in disbursements should be listed.

9. a. (Case study) Add at least one screen report to your selected project (see project specifications at the end of Section 1.5). The data for the report should be derived from a database table maintained by your application.

b. Add at least one printer report to your selected project. Again, the data for the report should be derived from a database table maintained by your application.

10.7 Common Programming Errors

These programming errors are common when using files:

1. Incorrect format of the FileOpen method used with random and binary files.

2. Failure to construct a correct full path name when appending a file name to its path for use in a `FileOpen` statement.

3. Forgetting to declare a string with a fixed length when it's part of a structure that is defining a record in a random-access file.

10.8 Chapter Review

Key Terms

AppendText method	**FilePut** method
binary-access file	**Filter** property
Close method	**OpenFileDialog** control
CreateText method	random-access file
data file	**ReadLine** method
direct-access	**SaveFileDialog** control
external file name	sequential access file
file access	**StreamReader** object
file organization	**StreamWriter** object
FileOpen method	text file
FileGet method	**WriteLine** method

Summary

1. A *data file* is any collection of data stored together under a common name.
2. The manner in which records are written to and read from a file is called the file's access *method*.
   a. In a *sequential-access file*, each record must be accessed in a sequential manner. This means that the second item in the file cannot be read until the first item has been read, the third item cannot be read until the first and second items have been read, and so on. Similarly, an item cannot be written until all previous items have been written and an item cannot be replaced without destroying all following items.
   b. In a *random-access file,* storage is by record, where each record consists of the same number of items, and any record can be read, written, or replaced without affecting any other record in the file. Each record in a random-access file is uniquely located by its position in the file.
   c. In a *binary-access file*, storage is by individual item using the computer's internal binary code.
3. Before a file can be written to or read, it must be opened.
   a. For sequential files, the syntax for opening a file depends upon whether the file is being opened for reading or writing. To open a file for writing, you must first declare a `StreamWriter` variable:

   ```
   Dim writevar as System.IO.StreamWriter
   ```

For output mode, use the `CreateText` method:

```
writevar = System.IO.File.CreateText(filename)
```

For append mode, use the `AppendText` method:

```
writevar = System.IO.File.AppendText(filename)
```

b. For random-access files, the syntax for the `FileOpen` method is:

```
FileOpen(filenumber, filename, OpenMode.Random, Accessmode, _
    OpenShare.Shared, Recordlength)
```

c. For binary-access files, the syntax for the `FileOpen` method is:

```
FileOpen(filenumber, filename, OpenMode.Binary)
```

4. a. Data is written to a sequential file using either the `WriteLine` or `Write` method. The syntax for these methods is:

```
var.WriteLine()
```

```
var.Write()
```

where `var` is the name of the object variable that references a `StreamWriter` object.

b. Data is written to a random-access file using a `FilePut` method with the syntax:

```
FilePut(filenumber, recordvariable, recordnumber)
```

If *recordnumber* is not included, the record will be placed after the current record.

c. Data is written to a binary-access file using a `FilePut` method with the syntax:

```
FilePut(filenumber, recordvariable, bytenumber)
```

If *bytenumber* is not included, the record will be placed after the current record.

5. a. Data is read from an existing sequential file using the `ReadLine` method with syntax:

```
var.ReadLine()
```

where `var` is the name of the object variable that references a `StreamReader` object.

b. Data is read from a random-access file using the `FileGet` method, having the syntax:

```
FileGet(filenumber, recordvariable, recordnumber)
```

If *recordnumber* is not included, the record that is read is the next record after the current record.

c. Data is read from a binary-access file using the `FileGet` method with the syntax:

```
FileGet(filenumber, recordvariable, bytenumber)
```

If *bytenumber* is not included, the record that is read is the next record after the current record.

6. The **Close** method is used to formally close a previously opened file.
   a. For sequential files, the general syntax of the close method is:

   ```
   var.Close()
   ```

   where `var` is the name of the object variable that references either a `StreamWriter` or `StreamReader` object.
   b. For random-access and binary-access files, the syntax is:

   ```
   FileClose(filenumber)
   ```

7. The **OpenFileDialog** control displays a standard Windows Open dialog box. The **SaveFileDialog** control displays a standard Windows Save As dialog box.
8. To display an Open dialog box, call its `ShowDialog` method.

Test Yourself—Short Answer

1. `WriteLine` and `Write` will both cause a write to a disk for a sequential file. How are they different?
2. To open a sequential file for output, use the statement `System.IO.File.` _____
3. The manner in which records are written to and read from a file is called the file's _____.
4. To write data to a file use a _____ object.
5. To determine if a file exists, you use the method _____.
6. Write the code that will open a sequential file named testdata.txt that will hold new data created during the execution of the program.
7. To determine when the end of a file has been reached, use the `StreamReader` _____ method.
8. How do you close all of the open sequential files in your program?
9. Write the code to open a sequential file named VBclass.seq so that records can be added to the end of the file.

Programming Projects

1. This assignment is a modification of the Motel 8 project (Section 9.7, Exercise 1). The owner of the motel has changed the pricing structure for a night's stay (described below). Additionally, he wants a daily report that categorizes and summarizes patron data for the previous night. Input to the program will be records stored in a BASIC sequential data file (comma delimited text file) for which each record contains the following fields:

Room Number (integer)

Patron Name (20 characters)

Number of Adults (integer)

Number of Children (integer)

The name of the file, which is located at http://computerscience.jbpub.com/bronson vbnet in the folder Text Files, is motel.txt. Charges for a room are calculated using the following criteria:

If the number of adults is no more than two, the cost per adult is $30; otherwise the cost per adult is $25.

If the number of children is no more than two, the cost per child is $12; otherwise the cost per child is $10.

If the number of adults plus the number of children is at least five, there is a 5% discount on the total charge.

There is a minimum charge per room of $50.

There is no state or local tax charged on the total cost. Also, there is no discount for multiple night stays by the same patron.

Output for the program should include the input plus adult charge, child charge, and total charge (after the discount, if applicable) for each room. Your program should accumulate the number of adults, number of children, and total charge. Note that based upon the above criteria, the total charge for a room is not necessarily the sum of the adult charge plus the child charge. Use a function procedure to calculate room charge. After the last record, print column totals (don't print totals for room numbers, adult charges, children charges, or discounts) for adult count, child count, and total charge.

As an optional addition to this problem, you might create a second sequential file and write the detail lines of your report to that file along with the appropriate date (using either the Date or Now function).

Sample Output:

Date: 5-10-04
MOTEL 8 DAILY REVENUE REPORT

ROOM NMBR	PATRON NAME	ADULT COUNT	CHILD COUNT	ADULT CHARGE	CHILD CHARGE	TOTAL DISCOUNT	CHARGE
1234	SMITH JOHN	2	0	60.00	00.00	00.00	60.00
1330	JONES JIM	2	3	60.00	30.00	04.50	85.50
1335	WILSON JOE	1	0	30.00	00.00	00.00	50.00
1400	KELLY BRIAN	1	2	30.00	24.00	00.00	54.00
		6	5				249.50

2. This assignment is a modification to the State Utilities project (Section 5.9, Project 9). Using the original pricing structure, write the necessary code to produce a detail report with column totals. Input to the program will be records stored in a sequential data file (comma delimited text file) for which each record contains the following fields:

CustomerID (integer)

CustomerName (text B 20 characters)

KWHUsed (integer)

The name of the text file is utility.txt and is available on our website. For each record, (using the criteria from Project 9), compute:

Base, undiscounted, untaxed bill amount

Discount amount

State utility tax amount

City utility tax amount

Total amount due

Also compute accumulated totals for each of these amounts. Your output should be in the form of a report that contains the data read for each record plus its corresponding calculated values (for each detail record). Format for the report could be similar to that used in Exercise 1 (of this section). Incorporate the code that you used in your original project solution that calculated the different charges into a sub procedure that can be called for each record read. Your program can send the number of KWH used to the **Sub** procedure and it can return the five amounts listed above.

   After having read all records and written all detail lines, write the appropriate accumulated totals at the bottom of the respective columns.

3. This assignment is a modification to the Texas Fence Company project (Programming Project 2 at the end of Chapter 7). The company has asked you to expand the capabilities of your initial programming effort and write a program that will produce a list of necessary components that will be needed for the next day's fencing job. The necessary requirements for each fencing job are stored in a sequential data file (comma delimited text file) with each record containing the following fields:

Job number (integer)

Length (integer)

Width (integer)

Number of gates (integer)

The name of the text file is fence.txt which is available at http://computerscience. jbpub.com/bronsonvbnet. Output for the program should include a count for each of the following:

Connectors (integer)

Corner posts (integer)

Intermediate posts (integer)

Gate posts (integer)

Gate(s) (integer)

Fencing (integer)

Your program must read all records in the data file, compute the number of components needed for each job, and accumulate totals for each component category. The output for this program is just the totals for each component category. Use a **Sub** procedure to calculate number of components for each category for each job (record read).

You might offer the program user the chance to send the output to either the screen (with a form similar to the one used for the original project) or to the printer. Additionally, you may wish to create a second file and write the fence component totals with the current date to that file.

Creating Web Applications with Visual Basic .NET

Even with decline of the hype of the new economy that was to be fueled by the Internet, it is still clear the Internet and the World Wide Web (www) have made a dramatic and lasting change in the way commerce works, the way people communicate, and the way information is delivered. Today a company is not considered legitimate unless it has a Web presence.

As a result of computer users feeling at home on the Web, many applications that formerly ran only in a traditional Windows environment have been changed to be accessible over the Internet. It is incumbent on all software developers to be able to create Web-based applications.

In the following section we will discuss some of the basic hardware and software issues involved with building Web applications. This will be followed by detailed instruction on the tools within Visual Basic .NET for writing a Web application.

11.1 Client/Server and Web Applications

The programs you have written so far run on a processor housed within the PC you are working on. In addition, Microsoft Access and the Microsoft Access programs that you read from and wrote to also resided on your PC. This should come as no surprise. However this architecture, where all the computation and storage reside on one machine, has its limitations. For one, only the person in front of the PC can run your program. For another, if you were to invoke many more programs on your PC, at some point the response time would worsen as there is only one processor to execute the instructions of all the programs it is trying to run.

An alternative to this "monolistic" approach is to split the work of executing a program with another machine which is connected on a network. This architecture, called client/server, is what most large business applications use. In a client/server architecture, processing is done at both the client or user machine and the server machine. The server machine is one that is shared by all users. In addition, all data that is to be shared is stored on the server. This includes both programs and database files. An example of a program working in this environment will clarify how this approach works and why this approach is preferred.

Assume that a company has accounting software that is used by all employees. In addition, assume each employee has a PC on his or her desk and the software is built to run in a client/server architecture. Let's trace what happens when one employee runs a program.

When the employee clicks on the icon to invoke the program, the operating system on the PC will request the server to send the executable program file to the PC. When the executable file arrives it will be loaded into the PC's RAM memory and execution of the program will begin. It is likely that the initial part of the program will be to display a form on the screen and wait for user input. The execution of displaying the form will be handled by the PC's processor.

Assume that the employee wants to retrieve a record in the database. Upon pressing the button to do so, the application will generate a query to be executed by the database management system (DBMS) program. In our applications this program was Microsoft Access. In large systems it would more likely be Oracle or Microsoft SQL-Server. Regardless of which DBMS is used, the query would be sent to the server to be executed because both the DBMS and the files the DBMS works on are located there. The DBMS executes the query and returns the resulting records back to the application. Note that the processing work of record retrieval and filtering is done by a machine other than the employee's PC. When the records return to the employee's PC, the application on the PC performs the task of properly displaying them on the form.

In this example we see that the execution of the application uses two machines: the client's machine for displaying data, and the server for database functions. The advantage of this architecture is that the DBMS and the database can be shared by multiple users and that while the server is doing its job, the processor of the employee's PC can be executing other programs. Although there are many other implications of building client/server applications, these are the two main advantages of using this architecture.

When you use the World Wide Web (www) you also are using a client/server architecture (see Figure 11–1). Assume you are at your PC and want to read the news from CNN. To do so, you invoke your Internet browser, which may be Microsoft Internet Explorer. A *browser* is a client program that allows you to send requests over the Internet, assuming you have an Internet connection (e.g., cable modem, DSL). This request, in the form of a URL (Universal Resource Locator) like *www.cnn.com* is transmitted from your PC to the Internet, which routes it to another machine to service your request. This other machine is a *server* running an application that processes these requests. The application is generally known as a Web server, and an example of this application is Microsoft's IIS (Internet Information Services). The Web server responds to the request by sending a set of statements in a language, HTML, that contains the information you requested. The HTML (HyperText Markup Language) statements are read by the browser on your PC. The browser translates the HTML into display commands that render an image on your monitor.

In the above Web example, you see again that the client PC is in charge of transmitting a request to a server; the server processes the request and then returns a result which is displayed by the client. Two different machines are tasked with processing a request by a user.

Visual Basic .NET, with Microsoft's ASP.NET(Active Server Pages) technology, allows us to develop Web-based applications. This means that instead of the application running within a Windows form, the application runs on a Web server and the results are displayed within a browser. There are thousands of applications that have been built

Figure 11–1   *Web Client/Server Architecture*

to run within a browser. Unfortunately, until .NET was developed, the task of developing a Web-based application was very difficult. While there were many tools that did part of the job (for example, Java, JavaScript, and ColdFusion) there was not an all-encompassing development environment. Visual Basic.NET provides all the elements to build a Web application in a manner that is very similar to building a Windows application.

The following three sections will develop three Web applications, each of increasing complexity. Much of what you will read will be familiar to you, as developing Web applications is not much different than developing Windows applications.

11.2 A Simple Web Application

The purpose of this first program is to allow a user to interact with a website by simply clicking on a button. While obviously simplistic, it will allow us to learn the basics of the development environment, Web controls, and Web program flow.

As previously stated, the initial steps to building a Web application are almost identical to building a Windows application. From the File menu select New and then Project. The Project dialog box now appears. From the Templates panel choose the ASP.NET Web Application icon, instead of the Windows Applications as was done in the past. When this is selected the Name fill-in box will be grayed out and the location fill-in will change to `http://localhost/WebApplication1` (Figure 11-2).

The reason `http://localhost` appears as the location is that the files that comprise the Web application will not be stored on the PC you are working on. Instead, they reside on the computer where the Web server is running. Note that the solution file that holds project information (.sln) will reside on your local PC. This is the file you need to reference when reopening an existing ASP.NET Web Project. However VB.Net will, by default, save this file in the Documents and Settings folder on the C drive.

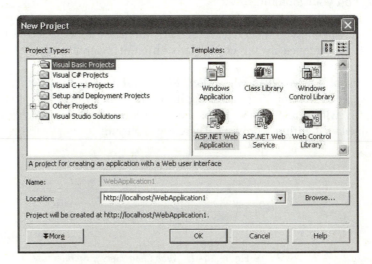

Figure 11–2   *Create a Web Application*

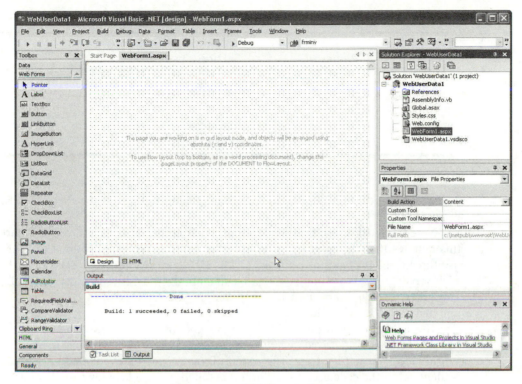

Figure 11–3   *Web Form Design Screen*

At this point you need to rename the application from WebApplication1 to WebUser-Data1. When you press the OK button the design screen will appear (Figure 11–3).

Note that this screen is similar in format to the Windows design screen, with the following exceptions:

a. The Tool box has Web Forms as the title although many of the controls are the same.

b. The design frame has a different appearance, with the two lines of text running through the middle.

c. The solutions explorer has more entries in it. The file with the .aspx extension holds the screen design and the VB code.

d. The bottom of the design frame has two tabs: Design and HTML. We will always be in Design mode, as the HTML will show the HTML generated from the VB code entered. It is possible, but not recommended, to change the generated HTML.

Although there are minimal differences in appearance, the usage of the Tool box and the design screen are exactly the same. To create the screen we want for this application, as depicted in Figure 11–3, the label and button controls were selected from the Web Form Tool box and drawn on the design form in exactly the same way as was done with a Windows application. Except for the absence of a Frame control, the screen

Table 11-1   Program 11-1's Properties Table

Object	Property	Setting
Label	ID	lblMessage
	Text	(blank)
Button	ID	btnEnter
	Text	Enter[1]

design is identical to a Windows application. Table 11-1 shows the Properties Table for Figure 11-4.

Note the small green arrow in the upper-left corner of each control in Figure 11-5; this denotes that the control is a Web server control. Web applications in VB.NET can use three different types of controls: HTML, HTML server, and Web server. Of the three, Web server controls are the most flexible and are the only ones used in our applications. The other two types are used in the situation where an existing HTML page is being updated with VB.NET code.

The behavior we want this program to exhibit is that lblMessage should display *"You have been Authorized"* when then Enter Button is clicked. This is like the "Hello World" program in Chapter 2. The code in Program 11-1's Event Code performs this. It is identical to the code used to perform this function for a Windows application.

Event Code 11-1 for Program 11-1

```
Private Sub btnDisplay_Click(ByVal sender As System.Object, ByVal e _
    As System.EventArgs) Handles btnDisplay.Click
  txtDisplay.Text = "You have been Authorized"
End Sub
```

This is all that needs to be written. Compile and run the application in the same manner as a Windows application (F5, Start from the Debug menu, and so forth). If there are no compilation errors, VB.NET will run the application by invoking the browser and passing it the URL *http://localhost/WebUserData1/WebForm1.aspx*. You might question why the URL has an .aspx suffix as opposed to an .html. It is because the .aspx suffix is the flag that this is a Web Form and therefore needs to be interpreted by the ASP.NET module on the server.

Figure 11-6 shows the result of clicking on the Enter Button. As you might expect, the text "You have been Authorized" appears. The beauty of Program 11-1 is that the logic and program flow, albeit short, are the same as the Windows application equiva-

---

[1]Accelerator keys (e.g. &Enter) cannot be used with Web applications as the browser does not recognize these keystrokes.

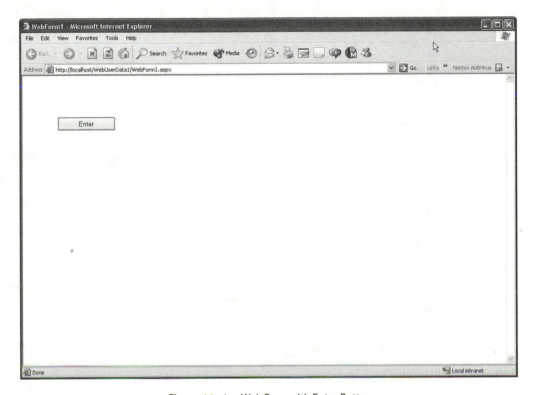

Figure 11–4 *Web Page with Enter Button*

lent. The difference is that for the Web application, the code was executed on the Web server, whereas for the Windows application the code would be executed on the client's application. However, the computer on which the program ran, for an application at this level, was of no concern to the programmer and did not impact the programming.

One difference in the interface between a Web and Windows application is the Web application does not have a Stop or End button to click to exit the program. As Web applications run within a browser, there is no specific Stop application button. When developing a Web application we need to be able to stop a program so that it can be debugged and/or modified. When the Web application is started from within the Visual Basic development, both the browser and the development environment are active. To stop the Web program, restore the development screen and click on the stop square. This will stop the browser and bring you back into the development environment, putting you back in design mode.

Finally, to prove this is really a Web application, start a new browser session and enter as the URL `http://localhost/WebUserData1/WebForm1.aspx`. Of course this is running the Web application on your computer. However, if all the files generated by VB.NET were put on a remote Web server the result would be the same.

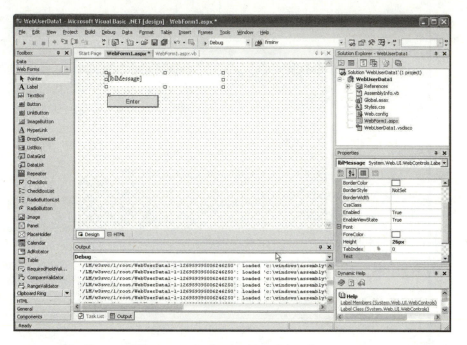

Figure 11–5 *Program 11–1's Interface*

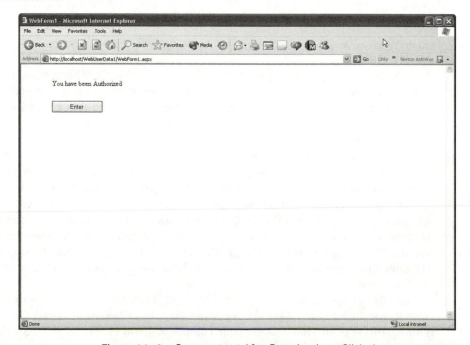

Figure 11–6 *Program 11–1 After Enter has been Clicked*

Exercises 11.2

1. What is a client/server architecture?

2. What are some key differences between a Web-based application and a Windows application?

3. Write Program 5–3 (on page 253) as a Web-based application.

11.3 A Multiform Web Application

In this section we will create an application that uses two Web forms. Though the application is very simple, the main goals of this section are to describe how multiple forms can share information and how user input is validated.

Sharing Information Among Web Forms

Many Web applications consist of multiple pages (forms) that need to share information among the pages. In the following application, we will expand the idea of the previous Web application (Program 11–1) by building an application that stores text from one form and makes it available to another. Specifically, the first Web page will request that the user enter an ID that is a valid social security number. After that is validated, the Enter Button will be replaced with a "Next Page" Button. Clicking on this button brings up a new Web page that shows the ID just typed on the first page, and also displays a Name field. Again, the purpose of this application is to show how one Web page passes information to another page, which is different from how it is accomplished with a Windows application.

In a Windows application, values stored in controls and variables in one form can be referenced by another form because they all reside in memory that remains intact when a user moves from form to form. Web Applications, however, run in a "stateless" environment. This means that when a Web server has completed formatting a page to be sent to a client (user), the Web server breaks the connection with the client and loses all references to it. That is, if the same client were to send a request to the website, it would have no knowledge of the first request because each request is treated independently. The impact on values in variables is that they are lost after the connection is terminated.

This problem of retaining state information can be solved in a number of ways.

Cookies   A *cookie* is a file that resides on the client machine and holding the state information. When the server sends back the Web page, it also sends along an additional file—the cookie. This is a technique commonly used by retail websites. Order information such as item numbers and quantities are written to a cookie after the user interacts with the website. The one potential problem with cookies is that a user can set his or her browser to disallow cookies, resulting in state information being lost.

Storing state in the URL   You will see websites return in the address portion of your browser a URL that has a normal beginning (such as `http://cgi.ebay.com`) but with many odd-looking characters at the end of the URL. These odd characters, starting with a ?, are state values. Obviously this is more limited than a cookie in terms of the amount of state data to preserve, but there is no way for the user to prevent this method.

Session objects The real problem with saving state in a Web server is that it has no way to associate a current connection with a prior one. This can be overcome if a unique identifier, a Session ID, is created on the server and assigned to the connection. Now the Web server can associate variables and any other state information with this Session ID. The Session ID is stored in the Session object and is sent back to the browser. When a subsequent request is sent by the same client, the Session ID is also sent. With this Session ID the Web server can retrieve the state from the prior request.

In our program, WebProgram2, we will use a Session object to retain session data. To store data in a Session object we use the Add method and to retrieve data we use the Item method. The general forms of the Add and Item methods are, respectively:

```
Add(ItemName, Value)
```

```
Dim var As String
var = Session.Item(ItemName)
```

where *ItemName* is a string that identifies the item being stored and *Value* is the data being stored. For example, the statement

```
Session.Add("SocSecNum", "123-45-6789")
```

stores the string "123-45-6789" in the Session object and is identified with the identifier "SocSecNum". To access the value stored in the Session object you need to specify the identifier, SocSecNum. For example,

```
Dim var As String
var = Session.Item("SocSecNum")
```

the variable *var* gets set to the string "123-45-6789".

In our program, we need to have the user's ID available for the second form. Therefore we need to store it in the Session Object.

Validating User Input

One of the most important aspects to programming is ensuring that the input entered by the user is valid. Examples of validation are:

- Disallowing negative numbers in fields that should only be greater than zero
- Ensuring that a customer ID number exists
- Making sure that debit totals equal credit totals in accounting applications

To ensure that data is valid, we typically have to write Visual Basic code. This is a tedious task that requires that the program designer think of every conceivable error a user can cause. For each error, code must be written to first detect it and then notify the user.

When writing Web applications, VB.NET simplifies this task by providing controls that can be used to validate user input. These validator controls are associated with standard input controls, such as a text box. The control is configured to test for a condition. If the test fails, the control will display an error message. Table 11–2 describes the validator controls that are available.

We will demonstrate how some of these validator controls work within sample programs. However, the other validator controls work in a similar manner. All the validator controls can be accessed from the Web Form tool box.

This application, called WebProgram2, consists of two forms. The first form consists of a text box used for entering of an ID. The validation specifications for the ID field are:

1. The user must enter some input (i.e., it is required), and

2. It must be a valid social security number.

These requirements are enforced via three validator controls: the **RequiredField-Validator, RegularExpressionValidator**, and the **ValidationSummary**. After placing a text box txtID and a Label "ID" next to the text box, we add a **RequiredFieldValidator** next to the txtID text box also. Refer to Figure 11–7. Now that the validator control is on the form, we need to change some of its properties. Table 11–3 shows these properties and their values.

Note that when the control is first added to the form, as shown in Figure 11–7, the string says "RequiredFieldValidator." However, after changing the properties to the values shown in Table 11–3, you'll see in Figure 11–8 that the Text property value of "x" appears

Table 11–2   Validator Controls

Control	Type of Validation	Description
RequiredFieldValidator	Required Entry	Requires that the user enters data in the field
CompareValidator	Compares values	Compares the value in the field to a constant value or the value in another control, using a comparison operator
RangeValidator	Range checking	Checks that the user's entry falls in the specified range
RegularExpressionValidator	Pattern matching	Checks that the user's entry matches a pattern defined by a regular expression, such as a required number of digits or a formatted value like a zip code, telephone number, or social security number
CustomValidator	User-defined	Checks the user's entry using validation logic that you write
Validation Summary	Gathers summary information	Displays a summary of all of the messages from the other validation controls

Table 11–3   Properties for the RequiredFieldValidator

Property	Value
Text	x
ControlToValidate	txtID (name of the text box to be validated)
ErrorMessage	ID is required
Font	
Bold	True
Name	Arial

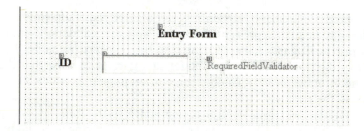

Figure 11–7   *A Web Form with a RequiredFieldValidator added*

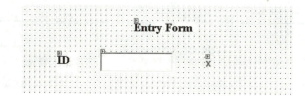

Figure 11–8   *The RequiredFieldValidator after Changing Some Property Values*

on the form where the string **RequiredFieldValidator** had been. This will be invisible on the form unless it is determined that the field is invalid (empty). If the field is empty, the "x" will appear. In addition, the value of the **ErrorMessage** property will be set to "ID is required" which will be displayed later with the **ValidationSummary** control.

Now we add a **RegularExpressionValidator** control to the form next to the **RequiredFieldValidator**. Figure 11–9 shows the form after the control has been first added. A regular expression is a special string that includes a number of characters that describe the valid syntax of another string. Visual Basic includes a number of predefined expressions that can be used for fields such as phone numbers, social security numbers, zip codes, and Internet email addresses. In our example, the ID must be a valid social security number. In the properties window for **RegularExpressionValidator1**, go to the **ValidationExpression** property and click on the ellipses, which brings up a regu-

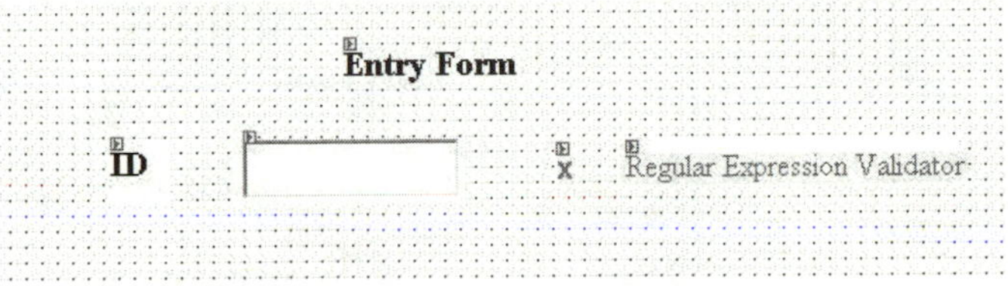

Entry Form

ID ☐ X Regular Expression Validator

Figure 11-9   *A Web Form with a RegularExpressionValidator added*

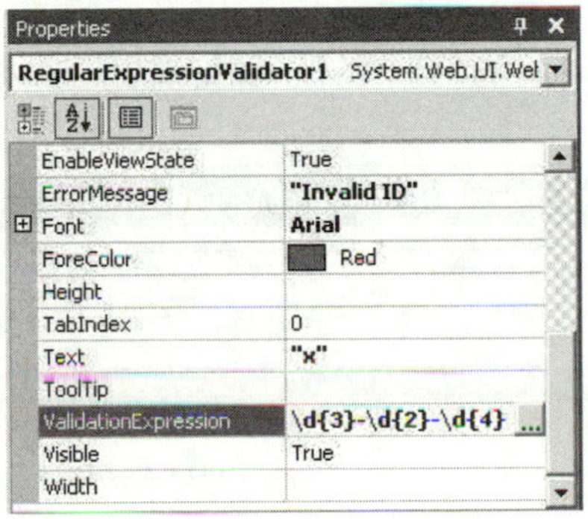

Properties ▯ ✕

RegularExpressionValidator1 System.Web.UI.Wet ▼

EnableViewState	True
ErrorMessage	"Invalid ID"
⊞ Font	Arial
ForeColor	■ Red
Height	
TabIndex	0
Text	"x"
ToolTip	
ValidationExpression	\d{3}-\d{2}-\d{4} ...
Visible	True
Width	

Figure 11-10   *Properties Window for RegularExpressionValidator1*

lar expression editor. Select the entry "U.S. Social Security Number." Figure 11–10 shows the properties window for **RegularExpressionValidator1** with the **Validation-Expression** property containing a regular expression for a social security number as \d{3}-\d{2}-\d{4}. Figure 11–11 shows the form after both validator controls have been added and their property values have been changed.

The final validator control to be added to this form is the **ValidationSummary** control. Figure 11–12 shows the form with this control added. This control displays the value of the **ErrorMessage** properties for all the errors that are detected on the Web Form. It is automatically invoked when any validator control detects an error. Note that there is no code we have to associate with any event in order to get the error message displayed. The default property values for this control can be used.

The next two figures show the running application after the user has incorrectly entered the data for the ID field. In Figure 11–13, the user did not enter any data, so the

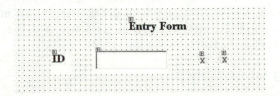

Entry Form

ID ☐ X X

Figure 11-11   *The RegularExpressionValidator after Changing Some Property Values*

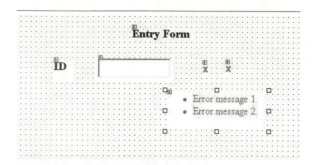

Figure 11–12   *ValidationSummary Control Added to Web Form*

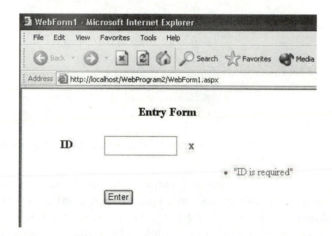

Figure 11–13   *ValidationSummary Control Displaying Error When No Data is Input*

error displayed is "ID is required." In Figure 11–14, the user typed in only three digits instead of a valid social security number, so the error "Invalid ID" is displayed. Note the "x" next to the text box displayed to indicate that that control contained errors.

Adding a Second Web Form

Now that the first form is complete we add a second form to the Project. The steps required are very similar to adding a second form for a Windows Application.

Select the Add Web Form item from the Project menu, as shown in Figure 11–15. This will bring up the Add New Item dialog box shown in Figure 11–16, from which you should select the Web Form icon. This will add the second form to the Project Explorer Window, as shown in Figure 11–17.

Completing the Application

The purpose of this application is to show how to pass information from the first form to the second form. After validating the input, the first form will cause the second form

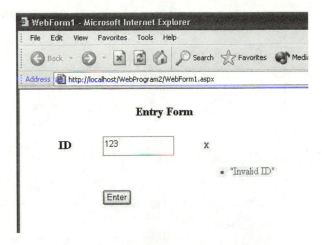

Figure 11–14 *ValidationSummary Control Displaying Error When Invalid Data is Input*

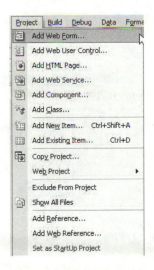

Figure 11–15 *Adding a Second Web Form Using the Project Menu*

to be displayed with the ID that was entered and a text box with the name "Gary Bronson." The interface for WebForm2 is shown in Figure 11-18.

After the ID has been entered and validated on WebForm1, we use the HyperLink control to display the second form (Web page). The HyperLink control is located in the Web Form Tool box. The HyperLink control allows us to associate a URL with a button. If the button is clicked, the control will request the page specified in the URL. The caption on the button is set via the **Text** property. For our applications it will display "Next Page." The **NavigateURL** property is set to refer to the URL we are requesting, in our case WebForm2. Figure 11–19 shows the Properties Window for HyperLink1 and shows the **NavigateURL** property after the value is chosen.

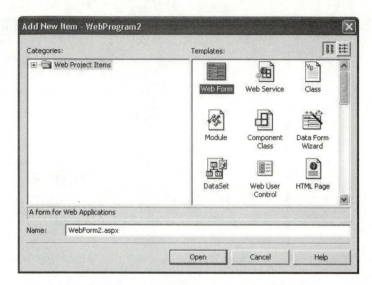

Figure 11–16   *The Add New Item Dialog Box*

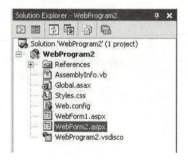

Figure 11–17   *The Solution Explorer Window Showing Two Web Forms*

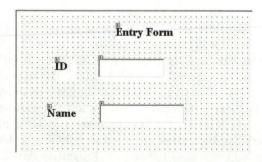

Figure 11–18   *Interface for WebForm2*

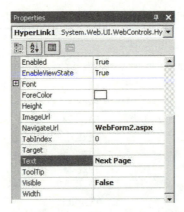

Figure 11–19 *Properties Window for NavigateURL Property*

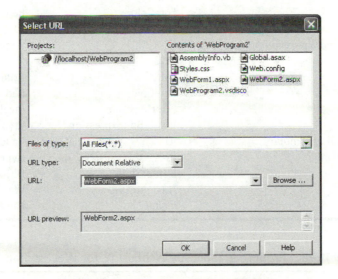

Figure 11–20 *Select URL Dialog Box*

To select a value, click on the ellipses. This brings up the "Select URL" dialog box shown in Figure 11–20.

WebForm2.aspx is chosen because it refers to the second Web form, WebForm2. The **Visible** property of the HyperLink is first set to **False**. After the user data is validated, the **Visible** property of the HyperLink is set to **True** and the **Visible** property of the Button btnEnter is set to **False**. Tables 11–4 and 11–5 are the Properties Tables for WebForm1 and WebForm2.

Let's examine the code used for WebProgram2. When the program starts, the browser will render WebForm1. The user types in a social security number into the ID

Table 11–4   Properties Table for WebForm1 for WebProgram2

Object	Property	Setting
Label	ID	lblEnter
	Text	Entry Form
Label	ID	lblID
	Text	ID
TextBox	ID	txtID
	Text	(blank)
Button	ID	btnEnter
	Visible	True
RequiredFieldValidator	ID	RequiredFieldValidator1
	Text	x
	Font	Arial
	ForeColor	Red
	ErrorMessage	ID is required
RequiredExpressionValidator	ID	RequiredExpressionValidator1
	Text	x
	Font	Arial
	ForeColor	Red
	ErrorMessage	Invalid ID
	ValidationExpression	\d{3}-\d{2}-\d{4}
ValidationSummary	ID	ValidationSummary1
HyperLink	ID	HyperLink1
	BorderStyle	Outset
	NavigateURL	WebForm2.aspx
	Visible	False

Table 11–5   Properties Table for WebForm2 for WebProgram2

Object	Property	Setting
Label	ID	lblEnter
	Text	Entry Form
Label	ID	lblID
	Text	ID
TextBox	ID	txtID
	Text	(blank)
Label	ID	lblName
	Text	Name
TextBox	ID	txtName
	Text	(blank)

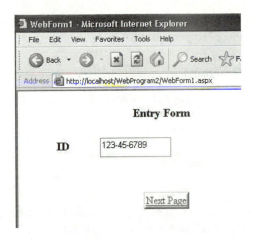

Figure 11–21   *WebForm1 after a Valid ID is Entered*

text box and then clicks on the Enter Button. If the ID is a valid social security number, the Enter Button becomes invisible and the "Next Page" HyperLink becomes visible. Figure 11–21 shows what the Web page looks like at this point.

The user then clicks on the "Next Page" HyperLink control, which brings up WebForm2 shown in Figure 11–22. This causes the server to access the page (WebForm2) defined by the **NavigateURL** property, to execute the code in that page on the server (as shown in Procedure Code for WebForm2), and then to send the completed page back to the client computer.

The btnEnter_Click event code of WebForm1 follows. After the ID has been entered and validated, the **Add** method of a Session object is used to save the ID that has been entered and associate it with the identifier "SocSecNum". This is needed in order to

Figure 11–22   *WebForm2, which has the ID entered on WebForm1*

retain the ID for the second form. In addition, the code makes the Enter Button invisible and the "Next Page" HyperLink visible.

Event Code 11–2 for WebForm1

```
Private Sub btnEnter_Click(ByVal sender As System.Object, ByVal e As _
    System.EventArgs) Handles btnEnter.Click
  Session.Add("SocSecNum", txtID.Text)
  btnEnter.Visible = False
  HyperLink1.Visible = True
End Sub
```

The code for WebForm2 simply accesses the Session object associated with the identifier "SocSecNum" and puts that value into the ID text box. The name "Gary Bronson" also is displayed in the txtName text box.

Procedure Code for WebForm2

```
Private Sub Page_Load(ByVal sender As System.Object, ByVal e As _
    System.EventArgs) Handles MyBase.Load

  txtName.Text = "Gary Bronson"
  txtID.Text = Session.Item("SocSecNum")

End Sub
```

Exercises 11.3

1. What is a session object used for?

2. What are validator controls used for? Give examples of three types of validator controls.

3. Add a text box named txtGender to WebForm1 and have the user enter either "M" or "F" after entering the social security number in the ID text box. If the string entered is not an "M" or "F," display an error message on the page. (*Hint:* Use a **CompareValidator** control.)

4. Enhance WebForm2 so that it also displays the gender that was entered on WebForm1. (*Hint:* Add another name-value pair to the Session Object.)

5. Modify Program 5–3 (on page 253), which you wrote as a Web-based application in Section 11.2, Exercise 3, to include a validator control that checks that the income entered is a positive number.

11.4 Using Databases with Web Applications

In order to build business type applications, a Web program needs to be able to access and update a database. Fortunately, database functions for Web applications are very similar to what was done for Windows applications in Chapter 9. Data adapters and datasets are used for making a connection and storing and manipulating the data. However, there are some programming differences that will be discussed in this section.

Displaying Data from a Database on a Web Form

The application we will build allows a user to retrieve and update data about their account profile. Specifically, the user will enter their ID (social security number), as in the previous exercise. The program will validate the ID, and if valid, will find the associated record in the customer database that contains that ID. The program will then display on the Web Form the name and full address of that customer (i.e., all the information that is found in the customer record for that ID). If the ID is not found in the database, a message will appear on the screen.

The initial design of the form is shown in Figure 11–23 and is similar to WebForm1 used in WebProgram2. It contains the same validator controls. However, this application will have only one form and therefore will not need the HyperLink control.

Because we will be accessing a database, we need to set up a database connection, configure a data adapter, and generate a dataset. The details of the setup can be found in Chapter 9. This application will use a database table called Customer which contains the fields ID, LastName, FirstName, Address, City, State and Zip. After the initial database setup is completed, the components are visible in the tray below the Web form as shown in Figure 11–24.

In order to display the customer information on the Web page, **Label** and **TextBox** controls are added to the Web form as shown in Figure 11–25.

Aside from the labels and text boxes for each field in the database record, there is also a Label lblMessage which is used to print out a message if the ID is not found in the database. It's important to note that the **Visible** property of all these fields is set to

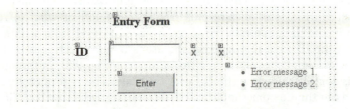

Figure 11–23 *Initial Web Form Interface for WebProgram3*

Figure 11–24 *Component Tray after Database Access is Set up*

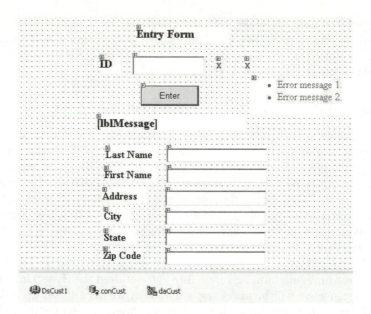

Figure 11–25   *Final Design Interface for Web Form*

False at design time so that they are not displayed when the user first enters an ID. If the ID is found in the database, the **Visible** property is set to **True** and the labels and text boxes are then displayed with the data for that customer. Refer to Table 11–6 for the Properties Table of the Web Form.

In WebProgram2, we described how the ID field is validated. After this validation is complete, the program needs to access the database and search for a record matching that ID field. Figure 11–26 shows the initial Web page that is displayed.

If the ID is found, the information is displayed as shown in Figure 11–27.

The code that is used for this application is shown in Event Code 11–3. The method to find the exact matching ID works as follows. The **Fill** method is used to fill the dataset with all customer records. The specification of what to retrieve is done in the setup of the data controls. However, we need to find from within all the records in the dataset the ID field that matches the user's input, which is stored in `txtID.Text`. This will be accomplished through a **Do While** loop that will go through all the records until one is found. Note that the **DsCust1.Customer.Count** property contains the number of records in the Customer table and that the first row is row 0. A Boolean variable `found`, initially set to **False**, is needed to indicate when a match has been found. When this occurs, `found` is set to **True** which will cause the loop to terminate. Otherwise, the loop terminates when all the rows have been searched (`rownum` is equal to `Count`).

When a match is found, the title on the page is changed to "Customer Data" and the **Visible** property of all the labels and text boxes is set to **True**. The **Text** property of each text box is set to the value of each of the remaining fields from the Customer table. If a match is not found and we have searched all the records, the found variable would still be **False**. We test it after the loop has terminated to see if the message "ID not found in Database" is displayed as shown in Figure 11–28.

Table 11–6 Properties Table for WebProgram3

Object	Property	Setting
Label	ID	lblEnter
	Text	Entry Form
Label	ID	lblID
	Text	ID
TextBox	ID	txtID
	Text	(blank)
RequiredFieldValidator	ID	RequiredFieldValidator1
	Text	x
	Font	Arial
	ForeColor	Red
	ErrorMessage	ID is required
RequiredExpressionValidator	ID	RequiredExpressionValidator1
	Text	x
	Font	Arial
	ForeColor	Red
	ErrorMessage	Invalid ID
	ValidationExpression	\d{3}-\d{2}-\d{4}
ValidationSummary	ID	ValidationSummary1
Button	ID	btnEnter
	Visible	True
Label	ID	lblMessage
	Text	(blank)
	Visible	False
Label	ID	lblLname
	Text	Last Name
	Visible	False
TextBox	ID	txtLname
	Text	(blank)
	Visible	False
Label	ID	lblFname
	Text	First Name
	Visible	False
TextBox	ID	txtfName
	Text	(blank)
	Visible	False
Label	ID	lblAddress
	Text	Address
	Visible	False

(continued)

Table 11–6 (continued)

Object	Property	Setting
TextBox	ID	txtAddress
	Text	(blank)
	Visible	False
Label	ID	lblCity
	Text	City
	Visible	False
TextBox	ID	txtCity
	Text	(blank)
	Visible	False
Label	ID	lblState
	Text	State
	Visible	False
TextBox	ID	txtState
	Text	(blank)
	Visible	False
Label	ID	lblZip
	Text	Zip
	Visible	False
TextBox	ID	txtZip
	Text	(blank)
	Visible	False

Figure 11–26 *Initial Web Form Where User Enters ID*

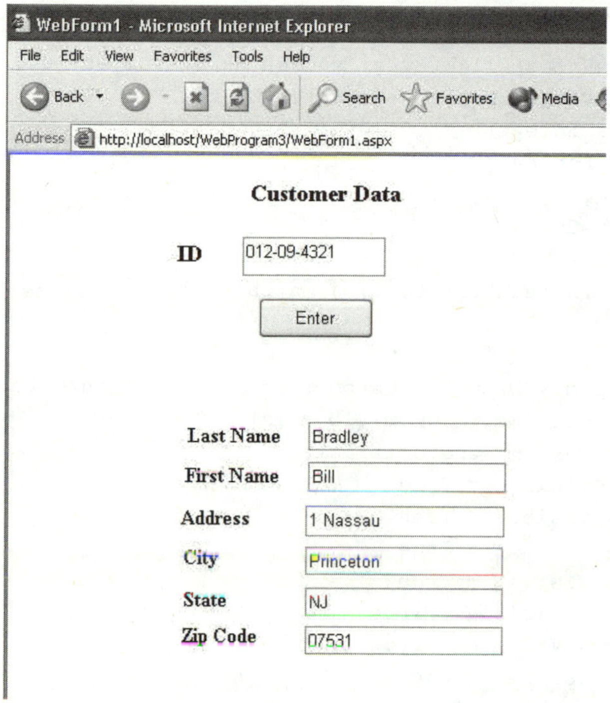

Figure 11–27 *Web Page with Data from Customer Database*

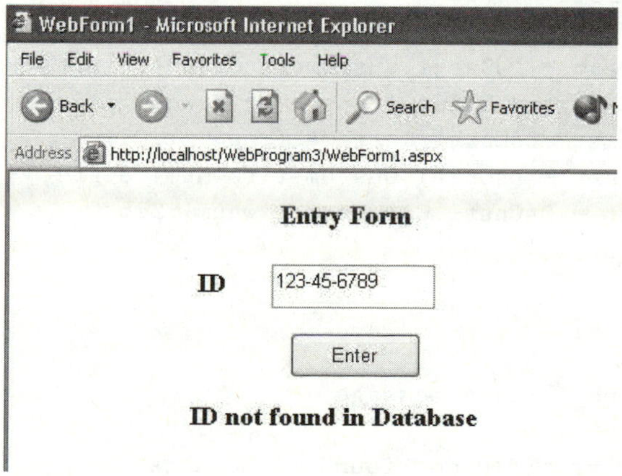

Figure 11–28 *Web Page with Message When ID Is Not Found in Database*

Event Code 11–3

```
Private Sub btnEnter_Click(ByVal sender As System.Object, ByVal e As _
    System.EventArgs) Handles btnEnter.Click
  Dim rownum As Integer
  Dim found As Boolean

  daCust.Fill(DsCust1)
  lblMessage.Text = ""
  'search through database to find matching ID
  rownum = 0
  found = False
  Do While rownum < DsCust1.Customer.Count And found = False
    If DsCust1.Customer(rownum).ID = txtID.Text Then
      lblTitle.Text = "Customer Data"
      txtLname.Visible = True
      lblLname.Visible = True
      txtFname.Visible = True
      lblFname.Visible = True
      txtAddress.Visible = True
      lblAddress.Visible = True
      txtCity.Visible = True
      lblCity.Visible = True
      txtState.Visible = True
      lblState.Visible = True
      txtZip.Visible = True
      lblZip.Visible = True
      txtLname.Text = DsCust1.Customer(rownum).LastName
      txtFname.Text = DsCust1.Customer(rownum).FirstName
      txtAddress.Text = DsCust1.Customer(rownum).Address
      txtCity.Text = DsCust1.Customer(rownum).City
      txtState.Text = DsCust1.Customer(rownum).State
      txtZip.Text = DsCust1.Customer(rownum).Zip
      found = True
    End If
    rownum = rownum + 1
  Loop
  'if ID not found - print message
  If found = False Then
    lblMessage.Text = "ID not found in Database"
  End If
End Sub
```

Updating Data on a Web Form

Now that we have a Web application that enables you to find a customer record in a database based on an ID number, we will modify the application so that you can edit

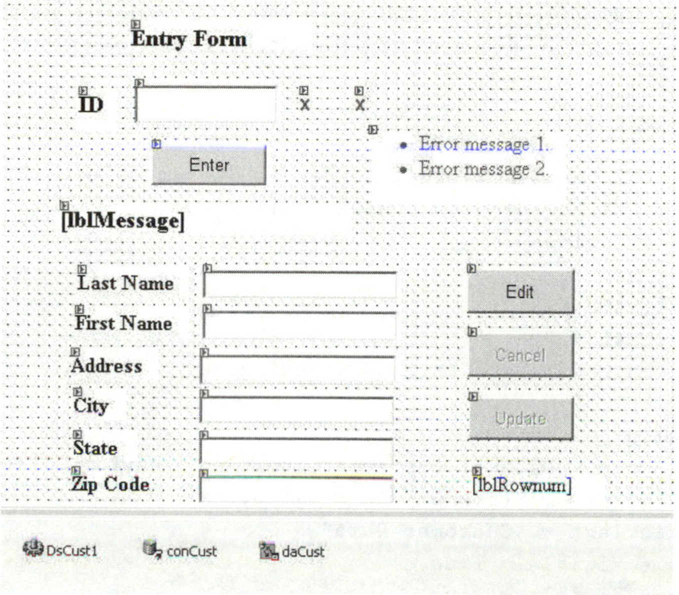

Figure 11–29   *Interface for WebProgram4 to Edit a Database Record*

the record and update the database. The new form, which is shown in Figure 11–29, is the same as the form that was used in WebProgram3 but with some additional buttons: Edit, Update, and Cancel.

If the user wants to edit any number of fields in a record, the Edit Button is clicked to initiate the editing process. After changing some of the fields, the user must either click on the Update Button to write these changes to the database, or the Cancel Button to stop the editing process and restore the values displayed on the screen to their original values.

At design time, the **Visible** property of these new buttons is set to **False** so they do not appear on the screen until the record is found. Only the Edit Button has its **Enabled** property set to **True** at design time. After the user clicks on the Edit Button, the Update and Cancel buttons become **Enabled** and Edit becomes disabled.

The code for the Enter Button's Click event is shown in Event Code 11–4. Note that the `While` loop is essentially the same as the code in the previous program. However, there is one important addition. The row number of the record that is being displayed needs to be saved in case an Edit occurs. Unfortunately, just saving this value in a variable is not adequate because the "state" information is not saved when the form moves from the client to the server and back again. Another technique that can be used to overcome this, besides storing this value in the Session object, is to create an invisible **Label** control (lblRownum) on the form and display the row number in it. In the program that follows it occurs at the end of the `While` loop. Also, you'll see that the `Fill` method of the data adapter is called in each event procedure to fill the dataset with the records from the database. After the `While` loop has either found the record or searched through the entire database table, if a matching record is found, the Edit, Cancel and Update Buttons are displayed by setting their **Visible** property to **True**.

Event Code 11-4

```
Private Sub btnEnter_Click(ByVal sender As System.Object, ByVal e As _
    System.EventArgs) Handles btnEnter.Click
  Dim found As Boolean

  daCust.Fill(DsCust1)
  lblMessage.Text = ""
  'search through database to find matching ID
  rownum = 0
  found = False
  Do While rownum < DsCust1.Customer.Count And found = False
    If DsCust1.Customer(rownum).ID = txtID.Text Then
      lblTitle.Text = "Customer Data"
      txtLname.Visible = True
      lblLname.Visible = True
      txtFname.Visible = True
      lblFname.Visible = True
      txtAddress.Visible = True
      lblAddress.Visible = True
      txtCity.Visible = True
      lblCity.Visible = True
      txtState.Visible = True
      lblState.Visible = True
      txtZip.Visible = True
      lblZip.Visible = True
      txtLname.Text = DsCust1.Customer(rownum).LastName
      txtFname.Text = DsCust1.Customer(rownum).FirstName
      txtAddress.Text = DsCust1.Customer(rownum).Address
      txtCity.Text = DsCust1.Customer(rownum).City
      txtState.Text = DsCust1.Customer(rownum).State
      txtZip.Text = DsCust1.Customer(rownum).Zip
      found = True
      ' Save the current rownum in an invisible Label
      lblRownum.Text = rownum
    End If
    rownum = rownum + 1
  Loop
  'if ID not found - print message
  If found = False Then
    lblMessage.Text = "ID not found in Database"
  Else
```

```
      btnEdit.Visible = True
      btnCancel.Visible = True
      btnUpdate.Visible = True
   End If
End Sub
```

Figure 11-30 shows the Web page after a match has been found.

Note that both the Enter and Edit Buttons are enabled while the Cancel and Update Buttons are disabled. Once the user clicks on the Edit Button, the Enter and Edit Buttons become disabled while the Cancel and Update Buttons are enabled. Refer to Event Code 11-5 for the btnEdit_Click procedure code.

Event Code 11-5

```
Private Sub btnEdit_Click(ByVal sender As System.Object, ByVal e As _
    System.EventArgs) Handles btnEdit.Click
  btnUpdate.Enabled = True
  btnCancel.Enabled = True
  btnEdit.Enabled = False
  btnEnter.Enabled = False
End Sub
```

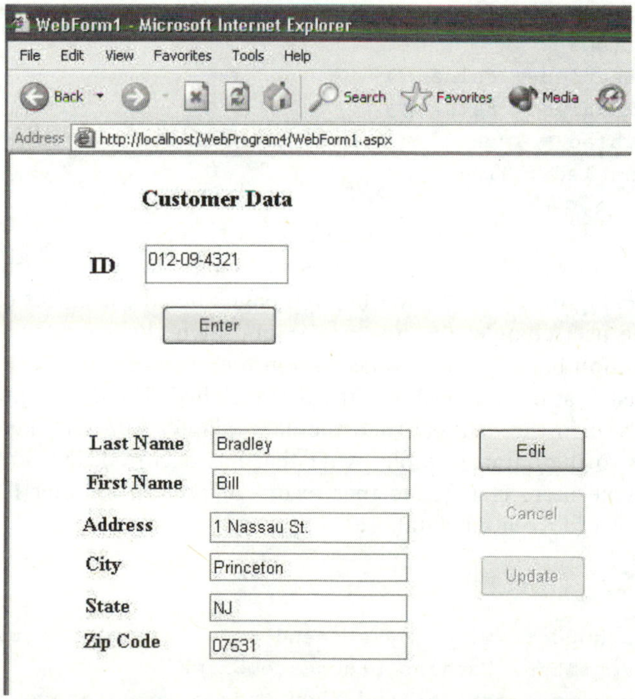

Figure 11-30   *New Web Page After Match Is Found in Database*

After the user clicks on the Edit Button, any changes that are made to any of the displayed fields can be saved to the database by clicking on the Update Button. If the user decides not to make these changes, a click on the Cancel Button will restore the displayed fields to their original value. Refer to Event Code 11–6 for the btnCancel_Click procedure. Note that the first statement executed is to retrieve the row number that was saved in the Label lblRownum. The Val function is used to convert the string to an integer. After that, the dataset is filled and the text boxes are restored to the values from the database. The Edit and Enter Buttons are enabled and the Update and Cancel Buttons are disabled.

Event Code 11–6

```
Private Sub btnCancel_Click(ByVal sender As System.Object, ByVal e As _
    System.EventArgs) Handles btnCancel.Click
  rownum = Val(lblRownum.Text)
  ' Restore original values from dataset
  daCust.Fill(DsCust1)
  txtLname.Text = DsCust1.Customer(rownum).LastName
  txtFname.Text = DsCust1.Customer(rownum).FirstName
  txtAddress.Text = DsCust1.Customer(rownum).Address
  txtCity.Text = DsCust1.Customer(rownum).City
  txtState.Text = DsCust1.Customer(rownum).State
  txtZip.Text = DsCust1.Customer(rownum).Zip
  ' Reset buttons
  btnUpdate.Enabled = False
  btnCancel.Enabled = False
  btnEdit.Enabled = True
  btnEnter.Enabled = True
End Sub
```

In our example, the user decides to change the Address from Nassau St. to Nassau Street. Figure 11–31 shows the Web page after the user has clicked on the Edit button.

The user changes St. to Street and then clicks on the Update button to save the information back to the database. As in the btnCancel_Click procedure, the row number must first be retrieved and the dataset filled. The data that is in all the text boxes is first saved to the dataset. Then the data adapter's Update method is called to save the dataset to the database table. After that has occurred, the buttons are reset so the user may make more changes to that record or type in another ID to retrieve another customer record from the database.

Event Code 11–7

```
Private Sub btnUpdate_Click(ByVal sender As System.Object, ByVal e As _
    System.EventArgs) Handles btnUpdate.Click
  ' Save values into dataset and then update to database
```

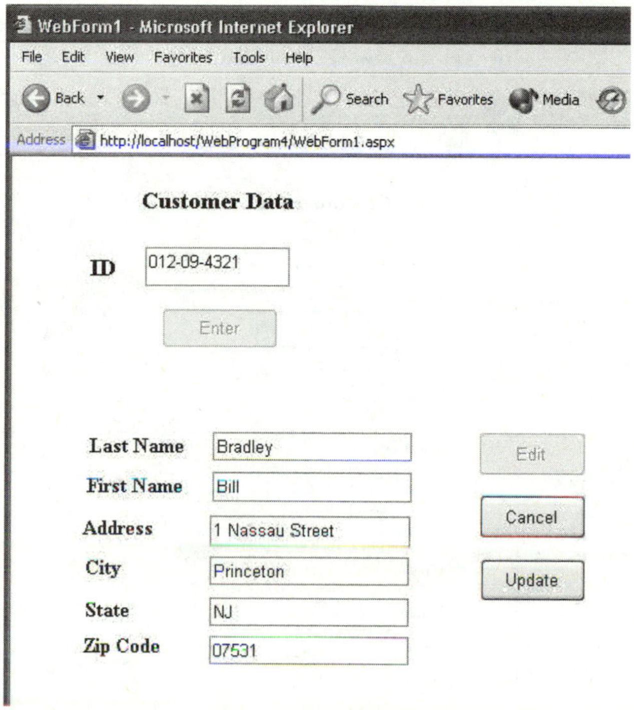

Figure 11–31 *Edit Button is Clicked*

```
    rownum = Val(lblRownum.Text)
    daCust.Fill(DsCust1)
    DsCust1.Customer(rownum).LastName = txtLname.Text
    DsCust1.Customer(rownum).FirstName = txtFname.Text
    DsCust1.Customer(rownum).Address = txtAddress.Text
    DsCust1.Customer(rownum).City = txtCity.Text
    DsCust1.Customer(rownum).State = txtState.Text
    DsCust1.Customer(rownum).Zip = txtZip.Text
    ' Save record to database
    daCust.Update(DsCust1)
    ' Reset buttons
    btnUpdate.Enabled = False
    btnCancel.Enabled = False
    btnEdit.Enabled = True
    btnEnter.Enabled = True
End Sub
```

Figure 11–32 shows the Web page after the user has made the change to the record and the new data has been written to the database.

Figure 11–32 *Database Has Been Updated*

Using a DataGrid on a Web Form

In Chapter 9 we used a DataGrid to display data from a database. A DataGrid also can be used with a Web application. However, there are some differences when working in a Web application. Both the data adapter and the dataset exist in the code running on the Web server, as opposed to the client. There are other programming differences, as this section will describe, between the Web DataGrid and the Windows versions.

The following program displays all the records from the Customer table into a Web DataGrid. Just as with Windows Forms, the **DataSource** property contains the name of the dataset to which the DataGrid will be bound. The **DataMember** property also is used to specify the table name when a dataset contains more than one table. An important property for DataGrids is the **EditItemIndex** property, which contains the index of the row that the user is editing when the user is editing a record. This property is zero-based, so the first record in a dataset has an EditItemIndex value of 0. If editing is not taking place, the value of this property is −1. The example below does not use this property, but it is important in applications that support editing the data in the DataGrid.

An important method of the DataGrid control is the **DataBind** method. This binds the DataGrid to the dataset at run-time, enabling the data from the dataset to be displayed in the DataGrid.

In this example, we will simply use a DataGrid to display the data from the Customer database. First we set up the data connection to the Customer database with the conCust connection, daCust data adapter, and DsCust1 dataset. Then we add a DataGrid dgCust to the Web Form as shown in Figure 11–33. After setting the **DataSource** property to DsCust1, the DataGrid on the Web Form displays the field names from the dataset.

To fill the DataGrid with data from the Customer database, the **Fill** method is called in the Web Form's Page_Load event procedure. The **DataBind** method is then called to bind the data from the dataset to the DataGrid. Event Code 11–8 shows the Page_Load procedure.

Event Code 11–8

```
Private Sub Page_Load(ByVal sender As System.Object, ByVal e As _
    System.EventArgs) Handles MyBase.Load
  'Put user code to initialize the page here
  daCust.Fill(DsCust1)
  If Not Page.IsPostBack Then
    dgCust.DataBind()
  End If
End Sub
```

It is important to note the **If** statement in this procedure. Every Web Form has a predefined object named Page which contains general information about the Web Form. The Page object supports a Boolean property named **IsPostBack**. If **IsPostBack** is equal to **False**, then this Web page is being loaded for the first time. If it is equal to **True**, then the Web page is being reloaded from the server. In the code above, the data binding only occurs if the page is being loaded for the first time. Figure 11–34 shows the Web page that is displayed when the application is run.

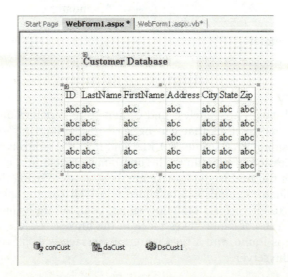

Figure 11–33   *DataGrid Control Interface on a Web Form*

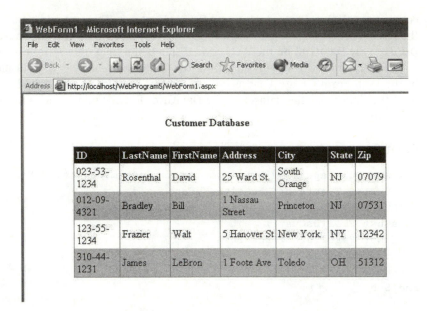

Figure 11–34 *Displayed Web Page When Application is Run*

11.5 Chapter Review

Key Terms

ASP.NET	server
browser	Session object
client	validator control
cookie	Web server
DataBind method	URL
PostBack	

Summary

1. Web pages are stateless and cannot store variables on their own. There are several mechanisms that can be used to maintain information such as cookies, a Session object, strings in URLs, and invisible controls on the Web pages.

2. A Session object allows the programmer to store a number of name-value pairs with the **Add** method; these are then retrieved using the **Item** method.

3. Validator controls can be added to a Web Form to ensure that a required field is set, to check for a range of values, compare the value to a set of values, and so on. The validation takes place in the browser on the client computer. If a problem is found with a field, an error message is displayed and the page is not sent to the server.

Test Yourself—Short Answer

1. The type of validator control that enables you to validate the format of a zip code or social security number is a _____ validator.
2. The method used to bind a DataGrid to a dataset is _____.
3. Web pages are _____, meaning they cannot store variables.
4. The small green arrow displayed on a Web Form in the upper-left corner of a control indicates that the control is a _____ control.

Programming Projects

1. Rewrite the calculator project, Programming Project 1 in Chapter 4, as a Web application.
2. Write a Web application (Price Calculator) where you input a price, a percent discount, and display the calculated sale price. Use a validator control to check that the value of the discount is between 1 and 99. Figure 11–35 shows the Web Form interface without the validator control.
3. Write a Web application (Service Signup) that requires the user to enter information in all the fields as shown in Figure 11–36. Use **RequiredFieldValidator** controls on all fields as well as other validation controls where necessary. Remember that there are some predefined ValidationExpressions available. The following are additional requirements on some of the fields:

   - The state must be entered as two capital letters (e.g., NJ). (*Hint:* Use a Regular-ExpressionValidator where the expression is set to [A-Z][A-Z].)
   - The zip code must be a valid format.
   - The email address must be a valid format.
   - The password must be at least 4 digits or letters and both passwords must match. (*Hint:* Use a RegularExpressionValidator where the expression is set to \w\w\w\w.*) For the two password text boxes, set the **TextMode** property to Password so that the passwords are not displayed.

   Figure 11–37 shows the run time version of the form.

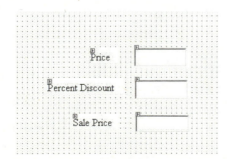

Figure 11–35   *Web Form Interface for Price Calculator*

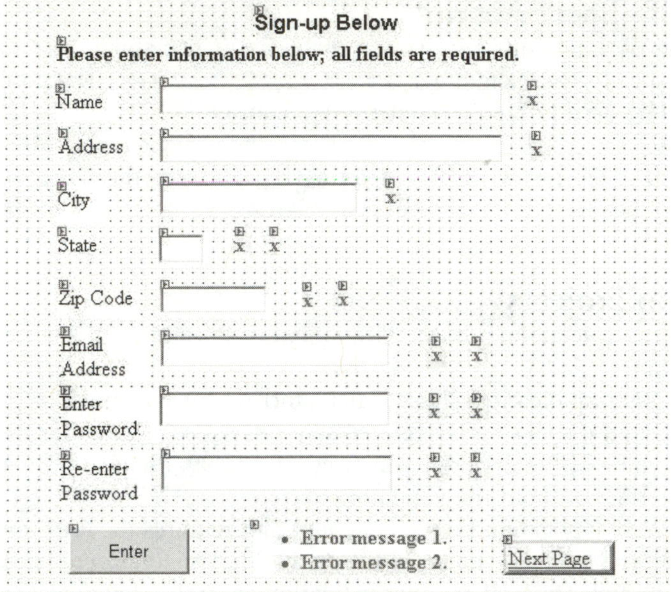

Figure 11–36 *Web Form1 Interface for Service Signup*

After completing the first Web Form, add a second Web Form as shown in Figure 11–38. Add a Hyperlink, that becomes visible after all the entered information is valid, to the first Web Form. Using session objects on the second Web Form, make the first text box contain the Name from the first form and make the second text box contain the E-mail Address from the first form.

4. Rewrite Program 9–1 from Chapter 9 as a Web application. This program accesses the Phonebook table from the Company database and allows the user to navigate through the dataset.

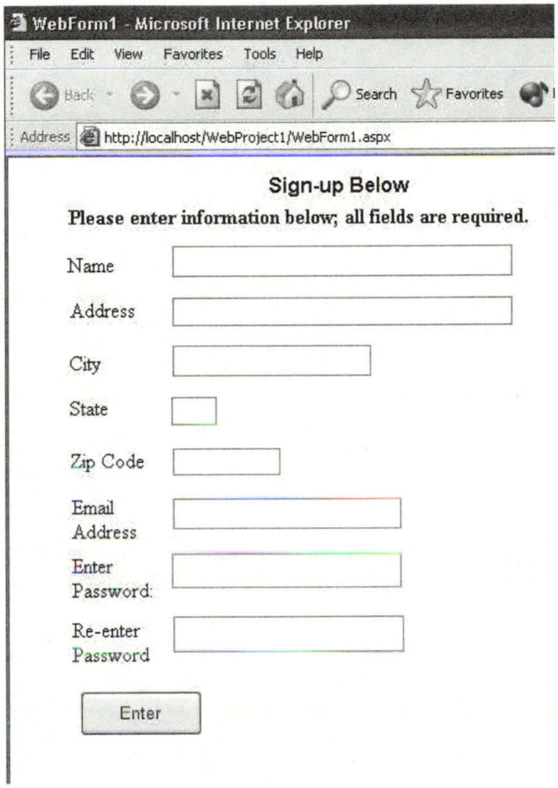

Figure 11–37   *Web Form1 at Run-time*

Figure 11–38   *Web Form2 Interface for Service Signup*

Introduction to Classes

Goals

In contrast to procedural programming, where software is organized by what it does to the data (its function), object-oriented programming organizes software as a collection of discrete objects that include both data and functional behavior.

As such, procedural programs are constructed as a sequence of transformations that convert input data into output data. In a well-constructed procedural program, each transformation is captured within an individual procedure, which in Visual Basic is coded as either a procedure or a function. The method for converting inputs to outputs is described by an algorithm. Thus, procedural code is frequently defined as an algorithm written in a programming language.

In object-oriented programming, the packaging and processing of data is handled in a much different manner. Both the data and the processing that can be applied to it are combined and packaged in a new unit called an object. Once suitable objects are defined, object-oriented programming is concerned with the interactions between objects. Note that this way of thinking about code does not remove the necessity of understanding data and their related operations and algorithms. It simply binds the data and procedures in a new package—an object—and then concerns itself with the interactions between objects. One advantage to this approach is that once objects are defined for one application they can be used, without reprogramming, in other applications.

Visual Basic provides the ability to create user-defined objects. Central to this ability is the concept of an abstract, or programmer–defined, data type. In this chapter we explore the implications of permitting programmers to define their own data types, and then present the Visual Basic mechanism for constructing abstract data types.

Programmer Notes

Program and Class Libraries

The concept of a program library began in 1954 with the introduction of FORTRAN, the first commercial high-level language. The FORTRAN library consisted of a group of completely tested and debugged mathematical routines that were provided with the compiler. Since that time, every programming language has provided its own library of functions. In Visual Basic, this library is referred to as the *intrinsic program library* and includes functions such as **Format**, **Str**, **Val**, **Asc**, and **Rnd**. The advantage of library functions and procedures is that they significantly enhance program development and design by providing code that is known to work correctly without the need for additional testing and debugging.

With the introduction of object-oriented languages, the concept of a program library has been extended to include class libraries. A *class library* is a library of tested and debugged classes. Generally, the class is provided in a form that cannot be changed by the user, but can be accessed and incorporated into a user's application.

One of the key practical features of class libraries is that they help realize the goal of code reuse in a significant way. By providing tested and debugged code consisting of both data and function members, class libraries furnish large sections of prewritten and reusable code ready for incorporation within new applications. This shifts the focus of writing application programs from the creation of new code to understanding how to use predefined objects and stitching them together in a cohesive way. A prime example of this are the visual object classes—consisting of Check boxes, List boxes, Dialogs, Buttons, and Group boxes provided in Visual Basic.

12.1 Classes and Class Modules

The programming environment changed dramatically in the 90s with the emergence of Windows applications. Providing a graphical user interface (GUI) where a user can easily move around in even a single window, however, is a challenge using procedural code. Programming multiple and possibly overlapping windows on the same graphical screen increases the complexity enormously.

Unlike a pure procedural approach, an object-oriented approach fits well in graphical windowed environments, where each window can be specified as a self-contained rectangular object that can be moved and resized in relation to other objects on the screen. Within each window other graphical objects (controls), such as CheckBoxes, GroupBoxes, Labels, and TextBoxes, can be placed and moved with ease.

Central to the creation of objects is the concept of abstraction and an abstract data type, which is simply a user-defined data type, as opposed to the built-in data types provided by all languages (such as integer and floating point types). Permitting a programmer to define new data types forms the basis of Visual Basic's object orientation.

Abstract Data Types

To gain a clear understanding of what an abstract data type is, consider the following three built-in data types supplied in Visual Basic: Integers, Singles, and Strings. When using these data types we typically declare one or more variables of the desired type, use them in their accepted ways, and avoid using them in ways that are not specified. For example, we would not use the subtraction operator on two strings. Because this operation makes no sense for strings, it is not defined for this data type. Although we typically don't consider it, each data type consists of *both* a type of data, such as integer or float, *and* specific operational capabilities provided for each type.

Programmer Notes

Procedural and Pure Object-Oriented Languages

Most high-level programming languages can be categorized into one of two main categories: *procedural* or *object-oriented.* FORTRAN—again, the first commercially available, high-level programming language—is procedural. This makes sense because FORTRAN was designed to perform mathematical calculations that used standard algebraic formulas. These formulas were described as algorithms, and then the algorithms were coded using function and subroutine procedures. Other procedural languages that followed FORTRAN include BASIC, COBOL, Pascal, and C.

Currently there are many object-oriented languages: Smalltalk, Eiffel, C++, Java, and Visual Basic.NET. The first requirement of a pure object-oriented language is that it contain three specific features: Classes, Inheritance, and Polymorphism. (Each of these features is described in this chapter.) In addition to providing these features, however, a "pure" object-oriented language must always, at a minimum, use classes. In a pure object-oriented language all data types are constructed as classes, all data values are objects, and every operation only can be executed using a class member procedure or function. *It is impossible in a pure language not to use object-oriented features throughout a program.* This is not the case in a hybrid language.

In computer terminology, the combination of data and its associated operations is defined as a *data type*. That is, a data type defines *both* the types of data and the types of operations that can be performed on the data. Seen in this light the Integer data type, the Single data type, and the String data type provided in Visual Basic all are examples of *built-in* data types that are defined by a type of data and specific operational capabilities provided for initializing and manipulating the type. In a simplified form this relationship can be described as

Data Type = Allowable Data + Operational Capabilities

Thus, the operations that we have been using in Visual Basic are an inherent part of each data type we have been using. For each of these data types the designers of Visual Basic had to carefully consider, and then implement, specific operations.

To understand the importance of the operational capabilities provided by a programming language, let's take a moment to list some of those supplied with Visual Basic's built-in data types. The minimum set of the capabilities provided by Visual Basic's built-in data types is listed in Table 12–1.

Table 12–1   Required Data Type Capabilities

Capability	Example
Define one or more variables of the data type	`Dim a As Integer`
Assign a value to a variable	`a = 10`
Assign one variable's value to another variable	`a = b`
Perform mathematical operations	`a + b`
Perform relational operations	`a > b`
Convert from one data type to another	`a = 7.2`

Now let's see how all of this relates to abstract data types (ADTs). By definition an *abstract data type* is a user-defined type that describes both a type of data and the operations that can be performed on it. Such data types are required when we wish to create objects that are more complex than simple integers and strings. When we create our own data types we must consider both the type of data we are creating and the capabilities we will provide to initialize and manipulate it.

Programmer Notes

Abstraction

Abstraction is a concept that is central to object-oriented programming. In its most general usage, an abstraction is an idea or term that identifies general qualities or characteristics of a group of objects, independent of any one specific object in the group. For example, consider the term "car." As a term this is an abstraction: it refers to a group of objects, each containing the characteristics associated with a car, such as a motor, passenger compartment, wheels, steering capabilities, brakes, and so forth. A particular car, such as "my car" or "your car," is not an abstraction. All are real objects that are classified as "type car" because they have the attributes associated with a car.

Although we use abstract concepts all the time, we tend not to think of them as such. For example, the words tree, dog, cat, table, and chair are all abstractions, just as car is. Each of these terms refers to a set of qualities possessed by a group of particular things. For each of these abstractions there are many individual trees, dogs, and cats, each of which conforms to the general characteristics associated with the abstract term. In programming we are much more careful to label appropriate terms as abstractions than we are in every day life. And you have already encountered a programming abstraction with data types.

Just as "my car" is a particular object of the more abstract "type car," a particular integer, "5" for example, is a specific object of the more abstract "type integer," where an integer is a signed or unsigned number having no decimal point. Thus, each type—integer, character, and floating point—is considered an abstraction that defines a general type of which specific examples can be observed. Such types, then, simply identify common qualities of each group and make it reasonable to speak of integer types, character types, and single types.

Having defined what we mean by a type, we can now create the definition of a data type. In programming terminology a *data type* consists of *both* an acceptable range of values of a particular type *and* a set of operations that can be applied to those values. Thus, the integer data type not only defines a range of acceptable integer values, but also defines what operations can be applied to those values.

Although users of programming languages such as Visual Basic ordinarily assume that mathematical operations such as addition, subtraction, multiplication, and division will be supplied for integers, the designers of Visual Basic had to carefully consider what operations would be provided as part of the integer data type. For example, the designers of Visual Basic included an exponentiation operator, though this operation is not included in either the C or C++ languages. (In these languages exponentiation is supplied as a library function.)

The set of allowed values is more formally referred to as a data type's *domain*, and the following table lists the domain for Visual Basic's numeric data types.

Visual Basic's Numeric Data Types

Data Type	Domain
Byte	0 to 255
Integer	−2,147,483,648 to 2,147,483,647
Long	−9,223,372,036,854,775,808 to 9,223,372,036,854,775,807
Single	−3.402823E38 to +3.402823E38
Double	−1.79769313486231E308 to +1.79769313486231E308

All of the data types listed in this table are provided as part of the Visual Basic language. As such, they are formally referred to as *built-in*, *intrinsic*, or *primitive* data types (the three terms are synonymous). In contrast to built-in data types, Visual Basic permits programmers to create their own data types; that is, to define a type of value with an associated domain and operations that can be performed on the acceptable values. Such user-defined data types are formally referred to as *abstract data types*. In Visual Basic abstract data types are called *classes*.

As a specific example, assume that we are programming an application that uses dates extensively and wish to create our own Date data type independent of Visual Basic's built-in type. Clearly, from a data standpoint, a date must be capable of accessing and storing a month, day, and year designation. Although from an implementation standpoint there are a number of means of storing a date, from a user viewpoint the actual implementation is not relevant. For example, a date can be stored as three integers—one each for the month, day, and year, respectively. Alternatively, a single long integer in the form *yyyymmdd* also can be used. Using the long integer implementation the date 5/16/98 would be stored as the integer 199805. For sorting dates, the long integer format is very attractive because the numerical sequence of the dates corresponds to their calendar sequence.

The method of internally structuring the date, unfortunately, supplies only a partial answer to our programming effort. We must still supply a set of operations that can be used with dates. Clearly, such operations could include assigning values to a date, subtracting two dates to determine the number of days between them, comparing two dates to determine which is earlier and which is later, and displaying a date in a form such as 6/3/96.

Note that the details of how each operation works is dependent on how we choose to store a date (formally referred to as its data structure), and only is of interest to us as we develop each operation. For example, the implementation of comparing two dates will differ if we store a date using a single long integer as opposed to using separate integers for the month, day, and year, respectively.

The combination of the storage structure used for dates with a set of available operations appropriate to dates would then define an abstract Date data type. Once our Date type is developed programmers that want to use it need never be concerned with *how*

```
' Data Declaration Section
'    Declaration of all variables
' Methods Implementation Section
'    Procedures and Functions that can
'    be used on the above declared variables
```

Figure 12–1   *Class Code Format*

dates are stored or *how* the operations are performed. All that they need to know is *what* each operation does and how to invoke it, which is as much as they know about Visual Basic's built-in operations. For example, we don't really care how the addition of two integers is performed, only that it is done correctly.

In Visual Basic an abstract data type is referred to as a *class*. Construction of a class is easy and we already have all the necessary tools in variables and general procedures. What Visual Basic provides is a mechanism for packaging these two items together in a self-contained unit that is referred to as a *class module*. Let's see how this is done.

Class Construction

A class defines both data and procedures. This is usually accomplished by constructing a class in two parts: a data declaration section and a methods implementation section. As illustrated in Figure 12–1, the declaration section declares the data types of the class. The implementation section is then used to define the procedures and functions that will operate on this data.

First, note that a class consists of code only. The variables, procedures, and functions provided in the declaration and implementation sections of the code are collectively referred to as *class members*. Individually, the variables are referred to as both *member variables* and as *instance variables* (the terms are synonymous), while the procedures and functions are referred to as *member methods*.

As a specific example of a class, consider the following definition of a class that we will construct and name CLDate.

The CLDate Class Code—Version 1

```
' Data Declaration Section
Private intMonth As Integer
Private intDay As Integer
Private intYear As Integer

' Methods Implementation Section
Public Sub setdate(ByVal mm As Integer, ByVal dd As Integer, ByVal yyyy As _
    Integer)
  intMonth = mm
  intDay = dd
  intYear = yyyy
End Sub
```

```
Public Function showdate() As String
   Return Format(intMonth, "00") + "/" + Format(intDay, "00") + "/" _
      + Format(intYear Mod 100,"00")
End Function
```

This class consists of both variable declarations and general procedure code. Note that we have separated the declarations and remaining code into two sections—a declaration section and an implementation section. Both of these sections contain code that you should be very familiar with.

The *declaration section* declares all variables that are to be members of the class. Although the initial capital letter is not required, it is conventionally used to designate a class data member. In this case the data members Month, Day, and Year are declared as integer variables. The keyword Private in each declaration defines the variable's access rights. The Private keyword specifies that the declared data member only can be accessed by using the procedures and functions defined in the *implementation section*. The purpose of the Private designation is specifically meant to enforce data security by requiring all access to private data to go through member methods. This type of access, which restricts a user from seeing how the data is actually stored, is referred to as *data hiding*. Although a variable can be declared as Public, doing so permits any procedure or code that is not a part of the class module to access the variable.

Specifically, we have chosen to store a date using three integers: one each for the month, day, and year, respectively. We also will always store the year as a four-digit number. Thus, for example, we store the year 1998 as 1998 and not as 98. Making sure to store all years with their correct century designation will eliminate a multitude of problems that can crop up if only the last two digits, such as 98, are stored. For example, the number of years between 2002 and 1999 can be quickly calculated as 2002 − 1999 = 3 years, whereas this same answer is not so easily obtained if only the year values 02 and 99 are used. Additionally, we are sure of what the year 2000 refers to, whereas a two-digit value such as 00 could refer to either 1900 or 2000.[1]

The general procedures in the class have been declared as Public. This means that these class methods *can* be called from any code not in the class. In general, all class methods should be Public; as such, they furnish capabilities to manipulate the class variables from any code or Form module outside of the class. For our class we have initially provided one procedure, named setdate, and one function, named showdate. These two methods have been written to permit assignment and display capabilities.

Specifically, the setdate procedure expects three integer parameters: mm, dd, and yyyy. The body of this procedure assigns the data members intMonth, intDay, and intYear with the values of its parameters. Finally, the last function declaration in the implementation section defines a function named showdate. This function has no parameters and returns the values stored in intMonth, intDay, and intYear as a formatted string having the form mm/dd/yy. The single statement in this function needs a little more explanation.

---

[1]These problems are all included under the designation "The year 2000 problem."

Although we have chosen to internally store all years as four-digit values that retain century information, users are accustomed to seeing dates where the year is represented as a two-digit value, such as 12/15/99. To display the last two digits of the year value, the expression `year Mod 100` can be used. For example, if the year is 1999, the expression `1999 Mod 100` yields the value 99, and if the year is 2001, the expression `2001 Mod 100` yields the value 1. Formatting this value using a **Format**[2] function (refer to Online Help for more information on the **Format** function) with the "00" format string ensures that this latter value is displayed with a leading 0, as the string 01. We will see shortly how our class can be used within the context of a complete program. But first we have to code this class using a class module.

Creating a Class Module

Creating a class requires inserting a class module into a project and then adding the class code to that module. The steps used to insert a class module are almost identical to those for inserting a code module. They are:

1. Open up either an existing or new project.
2. Choose the Add Class option from the Project menu (See Figure 12–2). Choosing this option brings up the Add New Item window shown in Figure 12–3. Note the Class template is highlighted.

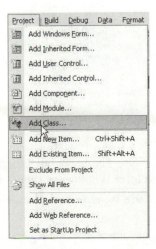

Figure 12–2   *The Add Class Module Option*

---

[2]Although there is a FormatDateTime method, the older Format function, which is very flexible, is used here to help illustrate the concept of classes.

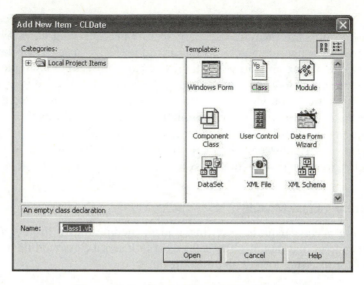

Figure 12–3 *The Add Class Module Window*

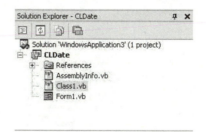

Figure 12–4 *The Project Window Containing a Class Module*

3. Select Open Button (see Figure 12–3). Doing this will add a class module to the Solution Project Explorer Window, as shown in Figure 12–4.

4. Click on the Class Code Window and change the name of the Class from the default name Class1.

5. After the Public Class name statement (first line), type the class member variables declarations.

6. After this, type the header and code for each class method.

Figure 12–5 shows the code window for a class that we named CLDate (Step 4). By convention the first letter of a class name is capitalized. In this case we have chosen to

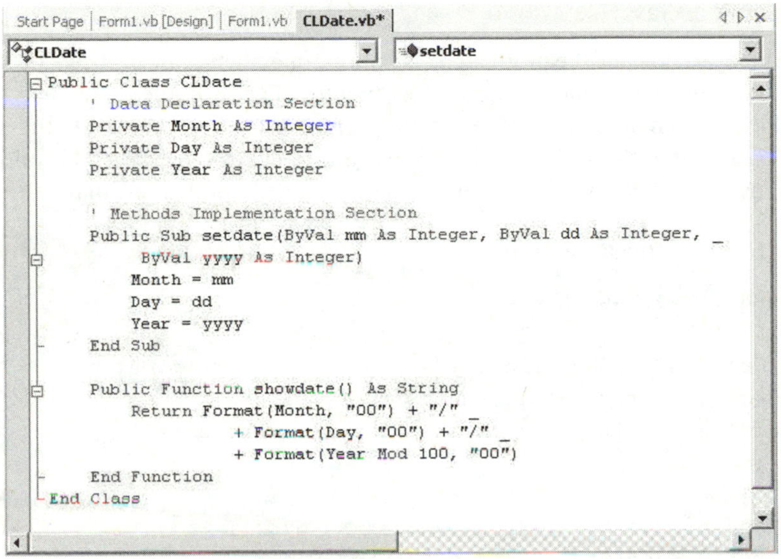

```
Start Page | Form1.vb [Design] | Form1.vb | CLDate.vb*                    ◁ ▷ ×

CLDate                               ▼    setdate                          ▼

⊟ Public Class CLDate
        ' Data Declaration Section
        Private Month As Integer
        Private Day As Integer
        Private Year As Integer

        ' Methods Implementation Section
        Public Sub setdate(ByVal mm As Integer, ByVal dd As Integer, _
            ByVal yyyy As Integer)
            Month = mm
            Day = dd
            Year = yyyy
        End Sub

        Public Function showdate() As String
            Return Format(Month, "00") + "/" _
                    + Format(Day, "00") + "/" _
                    + Format(Year Mod 100, "00")
        End Function
 └ End Class
```

Figure 12–5   *The Code Window for the CLDate Class*

capitalize the first three letters. Note that, unlike a form module, which contains both a form and a code window, a class module contains a code window only.

Saving a Class Module

To save the module:

- Select the <u>S</u>ave Option from the <u>F</u>ile's submenu, or
- Select the Save <u>A</u>s option from the <u>F</u>ile's submenu, or
- Press the file icon on the Toolbar when the Class Name combo box displays the Class you wish to save.

If you are using a class, your project will consist of at least two modules: a form module and a class module. Both modules should be saved. To switch between modules you can double-click on the desired module within either the Solution Project Explorer or Object Browser windows, save a form module, make sure it is active on the screen and repeat the steps you used to save the class module. The <u>O</u>bject Browser window is activated via the <u>V</u>iew menu or by pressing the F2 function key.

Note that this procedure saves only the class module—it does not save any other modules associated with a project. You will need to save the Form module(s) separately or invoke the Save A<u>l</u>l from the <u>F</u>ile menu or from the toolbar.

Using a Class

Once a class has been created, its public members can be used by any module within any project that includes the class module. For example, if we use the graphical interface shown in Figure 12-6 as Program 12-1's interface with the properties in Table 12-2, enter the code listed as Program 12-1's procedure code, and insert the CLDate class into the project, we will have a completed application that uses the CLDate class.

Program 12–1's Procedure Code

```
Dim firstdate As New CLDate()

Private Sub btnDisplay_Click(ByVal sender As System.Object, ByVal e As _
    System.EventArgs) Handles btnDisplay.Click
  txtShow.Text = "The date is " & firstdate.showdate()
End Sub

Private Sub btnSet_Click(ByVal sender As System.Object, ByVal e _
    As System.EventArgs) Handles btnSet.Click
  Dim mm, dd, yyyy As Integer

  txtShow.Clear()
  mm = Val(txtMonth.Text)
  dd = Val(txtDay.Text)
  yyyy = Val(txtYear.Text)
  firstdate.setdate(mm, dd, yyyy)
End Sub

Private Sub btnExit_Click(ByVal sender As System.Object, ByVal e As _
    System.EventArgs) Handles btnExit.Click
  Beep()
  End
End Sub
```

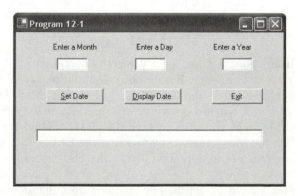

Figure 12–6   *Program 12–1's Graphical User Interface*

Table 12-2   Program 12-1's Properties Table

Object	Property	Setting
Form	Name	frmMain
	Text	Program 12-1
Label	Name	lblMonth
	Text	Enter a Month:
Label	Name	lblDay
	Text	Enter a Day:
Label	Name	lblRate
	Text	Enter a Year:
TextBox	Name	txtMonth
	Text	(blank)
TextBox	Name	txtDay
	Text	(blank)
TextBox	Name	txtYear
	Text	(blank)
Button	Name	btnSet
	Text	&Set
Button	Name	btnDisplay
	Text	&Display
Button	Name	btnExit
	Text	E&xit
TextBox	Name	txtShow
	Text	(blank)
	TabStop	False

In reviewing this code, realize that a class module only creates a data type. *It does not create any objects of this class type.* This is true of all Visual Basic types, including the built-in types such as integers and strings. Just as a variable of an integer type must be declared, variables of a user-declared class must also be declared. Variables defined to be of a user-declared class are referred to as objects, and objects are declared using the New keyword. Thus, the second statement in the **(Declarations)** section is a declaration statement that creates a new object of type CLDate class. Now note the syntax for referring to an object's method. This syntax is

object-name.method-name(arguments)

where *object-name* is the name of a specific object and *method-name* is the name of one of the methods defined for the object's class. Because we have defined all class methods as Public, a statement such as firstdate.setdate(mm,dd,yyyy) is valid inside an event procedure and is a call to the class' setdate procedure. This statement tells the setdate procedure to operate on the firstdate object with the arguments mm, dd, and yyyy. It is important to understand that, because all class data members were specified as **Private**, a statement such as firstdate.intMonth = mm is invalid from any procedure not in the class module. We are, therefore, forced to rely on member procedures to access data member values. For this same reason, a statement such as txtShow.AppendText(firstdate) is invalid within the btnDisplay_Click procedure, because the **AppendText** method does not know how to handle an object of class CLDate. Thus, we have supplied our class with a procedure that can be used to access and display an object's internal values. Figure 12–7 illustrates a sample output using Program 12–1.

Programmer Notes

Interfaces, Implementations, and Information Hiding

The terms interface, implementation, and information hiding are used extensively in object-oriented programming literature. Each of these terms can be equated to specific parts of a class' declaration and implementation sections. An *interface* consists of the methods that are available for a programmer to use a class. Thus, a programmer should be provided with documentation as to the names and purpose of each class method, and how to correctly call and use each method. As such, the interface should be all that is required to tell a programmer how to use the class.

The *implementation* consists of all the information contained in a class module. It is how the class is constructed. This information should not be needed by a user of the class.

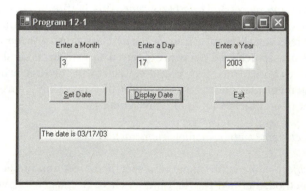

Figure 12–7 *A Sample Output Using Program 12–1*

The implementation or class module is the essential means of providing information hiding. In its most general context, *information hiding* refers to the principal that how a class is internally constructed is not relevant to any programmer who wishes to use the class. That is, the implementation can and should be hidden from all class users, precisely to ensure that the class is not altered or compromised in any way. All that a programmer need know to correctly use a class should be given in the interface information.

Terminology

There is at times confusion about the terms classes, objects, and other terminology associated with object-oriented programming. We will take a moment now to clarify and review the terminology.

A *class* is a programmer-defined data type out of which objects can be created. *Objects* are created from classes; they have the same relationship to classes as variables do to Visual Basic's built-in data types. For example, in the declaration

```
Dim firstdate As Integer
```

firstdate is said to be a variable, while in Program 12–1's declaration

```
Dim firstdate As New CLDate
```

firstdate is said to be an object. If it helps you to think of an object as a variable, do so.

Objects also are referred to as *instances* of a class, and the process of creating a new object is frequently referred to as an *instantiation* of the object. Each time a new object is instantiated (created), a new set of member variables belonging to the object are created. The particular values contained in these member variables determine the object's *state*.

Seen in this way, a class can be thought of as a blueprint out of which particular instances (objects) can be created. Each instance (object) of a class will have its own set of particular values for the set of member variables specified in the class (**Declaration**) section.

Note that a class also defines the operations that are permitted to be performed on an object's data members. Users of the object need to know *what* these operations can do and how to activate them through method calls, but unless run-time or space implications are relevant, they do not need to know *how* the operation is done. The actual implementation details of an object's operations are contained in the implementation section, which can be hidden from the user. Other names for the operations defined in a class implementation section are *procedures*, *functions*, *services*, *methods*, and *behavior*. We will use these terms interchangeably throughout the remainder of this chapter.

Programmer Notes

Values and Identities

Apart from any behavior that an object is supplied with, a characteristic feature that objects share with variables is that they always have a unique identity. It is an object's identity that permits distinguishing one object from another. This is not true of a value, such as the number 5, because all occurrences of 5 are indistinguishable from one another. As such, values are not considered as objects in object-oriented programming languages such as Visual Basic.

Another distinguishing feature of an object and a value is that a value can never be a container whose value can change, while an object clearly can. A value is simply an entity that stands for itself.

Now consider a string such as "Chicago." As a string, this is a value. However, because Chicago could also be a specific and identifiable object of type *City*, the context in which the name is used is important. Note that when the string "Chicago" is assigned to an object's Name attribute, it reverts to being a value.

Exercises 12.1

1. Define the following terms:

   a. class
   b. object
   c. declaration section
   d. implementation section
   e. instance variable
   f. member method
   g. data member
   h. information hiding

2. Enter and execute Program 12–1 on your computer.

3. a. Write a class definition for a class named `CLTime` that has integer data members named `Secs`, `Mins`, and `Hours`. The class should contain two methods named `settime` and `showtime` that can be used for setting and displaying a `CLTime` object.

   b. Include the class prepared for Exercise 3a in a complete working program.

4. a. Write a class definition for a class named `Complex` that has floating point members named `Real` and `Imaginary`. The class should contain two methods named `setcomplex` and `showcomplex` that can be used for setting and displaying a `Complex` object.

   b. Include the class prepared for Exercise 4a in a complete working program.

5. Determine the errors in the following class declaration section:

   ```
   Public Empnum As Integer

   Public Name As String
   ```

6. a. Provide data input validation for Program 12–1 to ensure that only months between 1 and 12 are accepted.

   b. Provide data input validation for Program 12–1 to ensure that only days between 1 and 31 are accepted for the months 1, 3, 5, 7, 8, 10, and 12; that only days between 1 and 30 are accepted for the months, 4, 6, 9, and 11; and that only days between 1 and 29 are accepted for month 2.

7. a. Add another member method named `convrt` to the `CLDate` class in Program 12-1 that accesses the month, year, and day member variables and display and then return a long integer that is calculated as *year * 10000 + month * 100 + day*. For example, if the `CLDate` is 4/1/96, the returned value is 19960401. (Dates in this form are useful when performing sorts, because placing the numbers in numerical order automatically places the corresponding CLDates in chronological order.)

   b. Include the modified `CLDate` class constructed for Exercise 7a in a complete Visual Basic program.

8. a. Add an additional member method to Program 12-1's class definition named `leapyr`, that returns a 1 when the year is a leap year and a 0 if it is not a leap year. A leap year is any year that is evenly divisible by 4 but not evenly divisible by 100, with the exception that all years evenly divisible by 400 are leap years. For example, the year 1996 is a leap year because it is evenly divisible by 4 and not evenly divisible by 100. The year 2000 was a leap year because it is evenly divisible by 400.

   b. Include the class definition constructed for Exercise 8a in a complete Visual Basic program. The program should display the message "The year is a leap year" or "The year is not a leap year" depending on the `CLDate` object's year value.

9. Modify the `CLDate` class in Program 12-1 to contain a method that compares two `CLDate` objects and returns the larger of the two. The method should be written according to the following algorithm:

Comparison method

  Accept two CLDate values as arguments.

  Determine the later CLDate using the following procedure:

   Convert each CLDate into an integer value having the form yymmdd.

     Which can be accomplished using the algorithm described in Exercise 7.

   Compare the corresponding integers for each CLDate.

     The larger integer corresponds to the later CLDate.

  Return the later CLDate.

10. a. Add a member method to Program 12-1's class definition named `DayofWeek` that determines the day of the week for any `CLDate` object. An algorithm for determining the day of the week, assuming a date of the form mm/dd/ccyy, known as Zeller's algorithm, is the following:

If mm < 2 Then

   mm = mm + 12

   ccyy = ccyy − 1

Endif

$$T = dd + Int(26*(mm + 1)/10) + yy + Int(yy/4) + Int(cc/4) - 2 * cc$$

$$DayofWeek = T \text{ Mod } 7$$

$$If\ DayofWeek < 0\ Then\ DayofWeek = DayofWeek + 1$$

Using this algorithm *Day-of-week* will have a value of 0 if the CLDate is a Saturday, 1 if a Sunday, and so on.

b. Include the class definition constructed for Exercise 10a in a complete Visual Basic program. The program should display the name of the day (e.g., Sun.) for the CLDate object being tested.

12.2 Constructors

When an object is instantiated via a declaration, Visual Basic also provides a means of initializing member variables. This is accomplished via a special method called a *constructor*.

In Section 12.1, we wrote the method setdate that sets the member variables of the CLDate class. This could have been accomplished via a constructor. A constructor is denoted by a method named New. The following is the constructor for the CLDate class:

```
Sub New(ByVal mm As Integer, ByVal dd As Integer, ByVal yy As Integer)
    intMonth = mm
    intDay = dd
    intYear = yy
End Sub
```

The method can be placed anywhere in the class code window. Typically it appears in the beginning, as it relates to the creation of the object. To invoke the constructor, the program that creates the object would have the declaration

```
Dim firstdate As New CLDate(2, 22, 52)
```

Now when declaration executes, not only is the object created, but the member variable Month is set to 2, Day is set to 22, and Year is set to 52.

Visual Basic[3] provides a feature with methods called *overloading*. Overloading means that you can define multiple methods with the same name but different argument lists. This ability is particularly useful with constructors where we might want to allow a user of a class the ability to create an object with member variables initialized, or just

---

[3]Constructors and overloading are standard object-oriented programming language concepts and not particular to Visual Basic.

create the object without any initialization. To overload the constructor for the CLDate class we can add the following:

```
Sub New()

End Sub
```

This creates a second version of a constructor for the CLDate. It performs no initialization of member variables. The declaration statement for using it would be

```
Dim firstdate As New CLDate()
```

How does Visual Basic decide which version of the two constructors to use when the object is instantiated? The decision is based on the number and type of the arguments in the declaration. In our case, if the declaration has three integer arguments, the first constructor is used; if there are no arguments, then the second constructor is used. Note that if the declaration had one argument, an error would occur because there would be no constructor that would match the number and type used in the declaration.

The use of a constructor with arguments provides a second way of initializing member variables, the other being coding a specific method such as setdate. Constructors are preferable to specific methods for one time initialization of member variables. Note that once an object is created, the constructor method cannot be invoked again for that object. If a program needs to reinitialize member variables after the object is created, the only way to do so would be to create another method.

Arrays of Objects

We saw in Chapter 8 how useful arrays are. As you might suspect, Visual Basic allows for the creation of arrays of objects. The usage of object arrays is the same as with any type. The program that follows will clearly demonstrate this. The only difference with arrays of objects is creating and initializing them.

The code to create an array of objects named adate is:

```
Dim i As Integer
Dim adate(5) As CLDate

For i = 0 To 4
   adate(i) = New CLDate(3, i, 2003)
Next
```

Look at the line where adate is declared. It differs in two ways from other object instantiations we have seen. First, after the object name (adate) is the specification of the number of array elements (five). This is in line with the way arrays of other types are specified. Second, the Class name, CLDate, is not preceded by New. That is because you cannot initialize all five array elements at one time. The initialization is done in the

Table 12–3   The Properties Table for Program 12–2

Object	Property	Setting
Form	Name	frmMain
	Text	Program 12–2
Button	Name	btnDisplay
	Text	&Display
Button	Name	btnExit
	Text	E&xit
ListBox	Name	lstBox1
	TabStop	False

Figure 12–8   *A Sample Output Using Program 12–2*

For loop with the statement adate(i) = New CLDate(3, i, 2003). This will initialize, via the constructor method, each of the five elements one at a time. The second argument is set to i to allow us to differentiate each array element.

Program 12–2 shows how arrays of objects can be used in an entire program. Note the way the method **showdate** is called when used with arrays. Table 12–3 lists the objects and properties for Program 12–2. Figure 12–8 shows the screen after the Display Button is clicked.

Program 12–2 Procedure Code

```
Private Sub btnDisplay_Click(ByVal sender As System.Object, ByVal e As _
    System.EventArgs) Handles btnDisplay.Click
  Dim i As Integer
  Dim adate(5) As CLDate
```

```
For i = 0 To 4
   adate(i) = New CLDate(3, i + 1, 2003)
Next

For i = 0 To 4
   lstBox1.Items.Add(adate(i).showdate)
Next
End Sub

Private Sub btnExit_Click(ByVal sender As System.Object, ByVal e As _
   System.EventArgs) Handles btnExit.Click
   Beep()
   End
End Sub
```

Exercises 12.2

1. Enter and execute Program 12-1 on your computer.

2. Enter and execute Program 12-2 on your computer.

3. a. Construct a class named CLTime that has integer data members named Secs, Mins, and Hours. The class should contain two methods named settime and showtime that can be used for setting and displaying a CLTime object and include a Constructor that initializes all member variables to 0.

   b. Include the class constructed in Exercise 3a in a complete working program.

4. a. Write a class named Complex that has floating point members named Real and Imaginary. The class should contain two methods named setcomplex and showcomplex that can be used for setting and displaying a Complex object and include a Constructor that initializes all member variables to 0.

   b. Include the class constructed in Exercise 4a in a complete working program.

5. Construct a class named CLCircle that has integer member variables named Xcenter and Ycenter and a floating point data member named Radius. The class should contain two methods named setradius and setcenter to set the radius and center values, respectively, and two methods named showradius and showcenter to display these values. Additionally, the class should include a Constructor that initializes all member variables to 1.

   b. Include the class constructed in Exercise 5a in a complete working program.

6. a. Construct a class named System that has character data members named Computer, Printer, and Screen, each capable of holding 30 characters, and floating point data members named Comp_price, Print_price, and Scrn_price. The class should include a Constructor that initializes all strings to the NULL value and all numeric values to 0. Additionally, include methods that permit a programmer to both set and display member values.

   b. Include the class constructed in Exercise 6a in a complete working program.

7. a. Construct a class named `Student` consisting of an integer student identification number, an array of five floating point grades, and an integer representing the total number of grades entered. The Constructor for this class should initialize all `Student` member variables to zero. Included in the class should be member procedures to (1) enter a student ID number, (2) enter a single test grade and update the total number of grades entered, and (3) compute an average grade and display the student ID followed by the average grade.

b. Include the class constructed in Exercise 7a within the context of a complete program. Your program should declare two objects of type `Student` and accept and display data for the two objects to verify operation of the member procedures.

12.3 Access Procedures Set and Get

An *access procedure*, which is frequently referred to simply as an *accessor*, is any member method that accesses a class's private data members. For example, the procedure `showdate` in the `CLDate` class is an access procedure. Such procedures are extremely important because they provide the only public means of access to these data members.

When constructing a class, it is important to provide a complete set of access procedures. Each access procedure does not have to return a data member's exact value, but it should return a useful representation of the value. For example, assume that a date such as 12/25/98 is stored as a long integer member variable in the form 982512. Although an accessor procedure could display this value, a more useful representation typically would be either 12/25/98 or December 25, 1998.

Besides being used for output, accessors also can provide a means of data input. For example, the `setdate` procedure in the `CLDate` class is an example of an input access procedure. Although the Constructor accesses a class' private member variables, as event procedures these two procedures are not formally classified as accessors.

Accessor procedures are considered so important that Visual Basic designates a specific procedure, named `Property`, explicitly for access purposes. The `Property` procedure is special in that it houses two methods used for inputting (`Set`) and accessing (`Get`) values of member variables. These two methods are further described in Table 12-4.

Table 12-4 Visual Basic's Property Procedures

Name	Description	Usage
Property Get	Read a data member's value	*variable* = *objectname.procedure()*
Property Set	Assign a data member's value	*objectname.procedure* = *expression*

As an example of constructing `Property Get` and `Set` methods, consider the `CLDate` class that we have used throughout this chapter. For convenience, this class' member variable declaration section is repeated below:

```
' The CLDate class data declaration section
Private intMonth As Integer
Private intDay As Integer
Private intYear As Integer
```

For this class we need to construct three `Property` procedures, each having a `Set` and `Get` method. Below is the procedure for the `Month` member variable.

```
Property Month() As Integer
  Get
    Month = intMonth
  End Get
  Set(ByVal Value As Integer)
    intMonth = Value
  End Set
End Property
```

The utility of the `Set` and `Get` methods occurs when the `Month` property is referenced in the code where the `CLDate` object is used. Assume the following is code in a Form module:

```
Dim firstdate As New CLDate()

firstdate.Month = 5
MessageBox.Show("Month = " & firstdate.Month)
```

The first executable statement, `firstdate.Month = 5`, assigns the `Month` property a value of 5. It does so by executing the `Set` code of the `Month` `Property` procedure. This code assigns `intMonth`, in the `CLDate` class module, the value of 5 (`intMonth = Value`). The second statement displays the value of the `Month` property. It does so by executing the `Get` method code, which returns the value stored in the member variable intMonth.

Our last version of the `CLDate` class is listed as Version 3 below:

The CLDate Class—Version 3

```
Public Class CLDate
  ' Data Declaration Section
  Private intMonth As Integer
  Private intDay As Integer
  Private intYear As Integer
```

```
'Constructor
Public Sub New()

End Sub

' Property methods
Property Month() As Integer
  Get
    Month = intMonth
  End Get
  Set(ByVal Value As Integer)
    intMonth = Value
  End Set
End Property

Property Day() As Integer
  Get
    Day = intDay
  End Get
  Set(ByVal Value As Integer)
    intDay = Value
  End Set
End Property

Property Year() As Integer
  Get
    Year = intYear
  End Get
  Set(ByVal Value As Integer)
    If Value < 1000 Then
      MessageBox.Show("Enter a 4-digit Year")
    Else
      intYear = Value
    End If
  End Set
End Property
End Class
```

Except for the Property Set procedure for the Year member variable, all of the Set and Get procedures are straightforward variations of the Month Property procedure. The Property Set procedure for the Year member variable includes additional processing to ensure that the final assigned value resides in the range 0 to 99.

Program 12–3 uses this version of the CLDate class within a complete application. The interface for this program is shown in Figure 12–9 and the objects and properties are shown in Table 12–5.

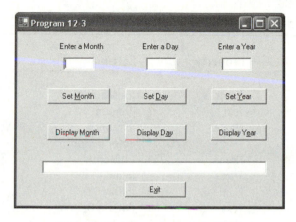

Figure 12–9   *Program 12–3's Interface*

Program 12–3's Procedure Code

```
Dim firstdate As New CLDate()

Private Sub btnExit_Click(ByVal sender As System.Object, ByVal e As _
    System.EventArgs) Handles btnExit.Click
 Beep()
 End
End Sub

Private Sub btnSMonth_Click(ByVal sender As System.Object, ByVal e As _
    System.EventArgs) Handles btnSMonth.Click
  firstdate.Month = Val(txtMonth.Text)
End Sub

Private Sub btnSDay_Click(ByVal sender As System.Object, ByVal e As _
    System.EventArgs) Handles btnSDay.Click
  firstdate.Day = Val(txtDay.Text)
End Sub

Private Sub btnSYear_Click(ByVal sender As System.Object, ByVal e As _
    System.EventArgs) Handles btnSYear.Click
  firstdate.Year = Val(txtYear.Text)
End Sub

Private Sub btnDMonth_Click(ByVal sender As System.Object, ByVal e As _
    System.EventArgs) Handles btnDMonth.Click
  txtShow.Text = "The Month has been set to " & firstdate.Month
End Sub
```

Table 12–5   Program 12–3's Properties Table

Object	Property	Setting
Form	Name	frmMain
	Text	Program 12–3
Label	Name	lblMonth
	Text	Enter a Month:
TextBox	Name	txtMonth
	Text	(blank)
Label	Name	lblDay
	Text	Enter a Day:
TextBox	Name	txtDay
	Text	(blank)
Label	Name	lblYear
	Text	Enter a Year:
TextBox	Name	txtYear
	Text	(blank)
Button	Name	btnSMonth
	Text	Set &Month
Button	Name	btnSDay
	Text	Set &Day
Button	Name	btnSYear
	Text	Set &Year
Button	Name	btnDMonth
	Text	Display M&onth
Button	Name	btnDDay
	Text	Display D&ay
Button	Name	btnDYear
	Text	Display Y&ear
Button	Name	btnExit
	Text	E&xit
TextBox	Name	txtShow
	Text	(blank)
	TabStop	False

```
Private Sub btnDDay_Click(ByVal sender As System.Object, ByVal e As _
    System.EventArgs) Handles btnDDay.Click
  txtShow.Text = "The Day has been set to " & firstdate.Day
End Sub
```

```
Private Sub btnDYear_Click(ByVal sender As System.Object, ByVal e As _
    System.EventArgs) Handles btnDYear.Click
  txtShow.Text = "The Year has been set to " & firstdate.Year
End Sub

Private Sub txtMonth_Enter(ByVal sender As Object, ByVal e As _
    System.EventArgs) Handles txtMonth.Enter
  txtShow.Clear()
End Sub

Private Sub txtDay_Enter(ByVal sender As Object, ByVal e As _
    System.EventArgs) Handles txtDay.Enter
  txtShow.Clear()
End Sub

Private Sub txtYear_Enter(ByVal sender As Object, ByVal e As _
    System.EventArgs) Handles txtYear.Enter
  txtShow.Clear()
End Sub
```

Exercises 12.3

1. Enter and run Program 12–3 on your computer.

2. a. Modify the Month Set Property method in Program 12–1 to ensure that only months between 1 and 12 are accepted. If an invalid month is entered, the modified procedure should display an error message using a MessageBox.Show method.

   b. Modify the Day Set Property method in Program 12–1 to ensure that only days between 1 and 31 are accepted for the months 1, 3, 5, 7, 8, 10, and 12; that only days between 1 and 30 are accepted for the months 4, 6, 9, and 11; and that only days between 1 and 29 are accepted for the second month. If an invalid day is entered, the modified procedure should display an error message using a MessageBox.Show method.

   c. Modify the Day Set Property procedure written for Exercise 2b to account for leap years. (*Hint:* See Exercise 8a in Section 12.1.)

3. a. Construct a class named CLTime that has integer data members named Secs, Mins, and Hours. The class should contain three Property procedures, one pair for each member variable. Additionally, include a Constructor that initializes all member variables to 0.

   b. Include the class written in Exercise 3a in a complete working program.

4. a. Write a class named Complex that has floating point member variables named Real and Imaginary. The class should contain Property procedures, one pair for

each member variable. Additionally, include a Constructor that initializes all member variables to 0.

    b. Include the class written in Exercise 4a in a complete working program.

5. a. Construct a class named `CLCircle` that has integer member variables named `Xcenter` and `Ycenter` and a floating point member variable named `Radius`. The class should contain three Property procedures, one pair for each member variable. Additionally, the class should include a Constructor that initializes all member variables to 1.

    b. Include the class written in Exercise 5a in a complete working program.

Programmer Notes

Encapsulation, Inheritance and Polymorphism

An *object-based language* is one in which data and operations can be incorporated together in such a way that data values can be isolated and accessed through the specified class functions. The ability to bind the member variables with operations in a single unit is referred to as *encapsulation*. In Visual Basic encapsulation is provided by its class capability.

For a language to be classified as object-oriented it must also provide inheritance and polymorphism. *Inheritance* is the capability to derive one class from another. A derived class is a completely new data type that incorporates all of the member variables and methods of the original class with any new member variables and methods unique to itself. The class used as the basis for the derived type is referred to as the *base* or *parent* class, and the derived data type is referred to as the *derived* or *child* class.

Polymorphism permits the same method name to invoke one operation in objects of a parent class and a different operation in objects of a derived class.

12.4 An Example: Constructing an Elevator Object

Now that you have an understanding of how classes are constructed and the terminology used in describing them, let us apply this knowledge to a particular application. In this application we simulate the operation of an elevator. We assume that the elevator can travel between the 1st and 15th floors of a building and that the location of the elevator must be known at all times.

For this application, the location of the elevator corresponds to its current floor position and is represented by an integer variable ranging between 1 and 15. The value of this variable, named `Curfloor` (for current floor), effectively represents the current state of the elevator. The services that we will provide for changing the state of the elevator will be a Constructor to set the initial floor position when a new elevator is put in service, and a request function to change the elevator's position (state) to a new floor.

Putting an elevator in service is accomplished by declaring a single class instance (declaring an object of type Elevator), and requesting a new floor position is equivalent to pushing an elevator button. To accomplish this, a suitable class definition is:

```
Public Class Elevator

  ' Data Declaration Section
  Const MAXFLOOR As Integer = 15
  Private Curfloor As Integer

  ' Constructor
  Public Sub New()
    Curfloor = 1
  End Sub

  ' Methods Implementation Section
  Public Sub request(ByVal newfloor As Integer, ByVal frmMainRef As frmMain)

    If newfloor < 1 Or newfloor > MAXFLOOR Then
      frmMainRef.txtError.Text = "An invalid floor has been selected"
    ElseIf newfloor > Curfloor Then
      frmMainRef.lstFloor.Items.Add("Starting at floor " & Curfloor)
      Do While newfloor > Curfloor
        Curfloor = Curfloor + 1
        frmMainRef.lstFloor.Items.Add("Going Down - now at floor " & Curfloor)
      Loop
      frmMainRef.lstFloor.Items.Add("Stopping at floor " & Curfloor)
    ElseIf newfloor < Curfloor Then
      frmMainRef.lstFloor.Items.Add("Starting at floor " & Curfloor)
      Do While newfloor < Curfloor
        Curfloor = Curfloor - 1
        frmMainRef.lstFloor.Items.Add("Going Up - now at floor " & Curfloor)
      Loop
      frmMainRef.lstFloor.Items.Add("Stopping at floor " & Curfloor)
    End If
  End Sub
End Class
```

Note that we have declared one member variable, Curfloor, and implemented one method and a Constructor. The member variable, Curfloor, is used to store the current floor position of the elevator. As a private member variable it can only be accessed through methods in the class. The method request defines the external services provided by each Elevator object and the Constructor is used to initialize the starting floor position of each Elevator type object. The Constructor is straightforward. Whenever an Elevator object is first accessed it is initialized to the first floor.

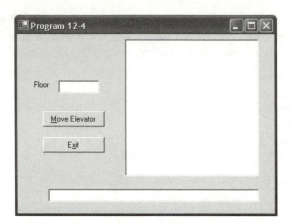

Figure 12–10 *Program 12–4's Interface*

The `request` procedure defined in the implementation section is more complicated and provides the class' primary service; it is used to alter the position of the elevator. Essentially this procedure consists of an `If-Else` statement having three parts: if an incorrect service is requested an error message is displayed, if a floor above the current position is selected the elevator is moved up, and if a floor below the current position is selected the elevator is moved down. For movement up or down, the procedure uses a **Do/While** loop to increment the position one floor at a time, and reports the elevator's movement to a lstFloor object located on `frmMain`.

It is worth noting two points with respect to the notation used here. First, because the **lstFloor** control is not on the current class module (class modules cannot contain visual objects), the complete designation for where the object resides must be given. This is done by passing, as an argument, the name of the form (`frmMain`). The parameter `frmMainRef` holds this reference. To refer to any object on the form, prefix the object name with the form reference. Hence the full name of the object, `frmMain.txtError`, must precede the Text method name. This is the standard way of having code on one module access objects and methods defined on a different module. Next, the request method is over ambitious precisely because it references an object not contained within the class. Theoretically, a class should be self-contained and not require any object outside of the class for it to be executed correctly. (In Exercise 4 we will explore how to reconstruct this class to adhere to this requirement.)

Program 12–4 includes this class in a working program. The interface for this program is shown in Figure 12–10 and the objects and properties are shown in Table 12–6.

Program 12–4's Procedure Code

```
Private a As New Elevator()

Private Sub txtFloor_Enter(ByVal sender As Object, ByVal e As _
    System.EventArgs) Handles txtFloor.Enter
```

Table 12-6   Program 12-4's Properties Table

Object	Property	Setting
Form	Name	frmMain
	Text	Program 12-4
Label	Name	lblFloor
	Text	Enter a floor:
TextBox	Name	txtFloor
	Text	(blank)
Button	Name	btnFloor
	Text	&Move Elevator
Button	Name	btnExit
	Text	E&xit
List box	Name	lstFloor
	TabStop	False
TextBox	Name	txtError
	TabStop	False

```
   txtError.Clear()
End Sub

Private Sub btnFloor_Click(ByVal sender As System.Object, ByVal e As _
    System.EventArgs) Handles btnFloor.Click
  lstFloor.Items.Clear()
  a.request(Val(txtFloor.Text), Me)
End Sub

Private Sub btnExit_Click(ByVal sender As System.Object, ByVal e As _
    System.EventArgs) Handles btnExit.Click
  Beep()
  End
End Sub
```

Program 12-4's procedure code is extremely simple, precisely because all of the work in moving the elevator is contained within the class' **request** method. Note that this method is called in the standard way by preceding the method's name with a period and an object's name. A sample run using Program 12-4 is illustrated in Figure 12-11.

The basic requirements of object-oriented programming are evident even in as simple a program as Program 12-4. Before a form module can be written, a useful class must be constructed. This is typical of programs that use objects. For such programs, the design process is front-loaded with the requirement that careful consideration of the

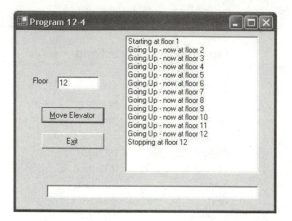

Figure 12–11   *A Sample Run Using Program 12–4*

class—its declaration and implementation—be given. Code contained in the implementation section effectively removes code that would otherwise be part of a form's responsibility. Thus, any program that uses the object does not have to repeat the implementation details within its form's procedures. Rather, the form's procedures are only concerned with sending arguments to its objects to activate them appropriately. The details of how the object responds to the arguments and how the state of the object is retained are hidden within the class construction.

Exercises 12.4

1. Enter Program 12–4 in your computer and execute it.

2. Modify Program 12–4 to put a second elevator in service. Have this second elevator move to the 12th floor and then move to the 5th floor.

3. Verify that the **Constructor** method in Program 12–4 is called by adding a message within it that is displayed each time a new object is created. Run your program to ensure its operation.

4. The `Elevator` class violates pure class construction rules because one of its methods accesses an object that is not in the class. Modify the `Elevator` class to remove this violation. To do so, provide the class with a procedure named `oneup` and `onedown`, which adds and subtracts 1, respectively, to and from the current value of `Curfloor`. Then modify the `btnMove_Click` procedure to incorporate an `If-Else` similar to the one used in `request`.

5. a. Modify the `CLDate` class that is used in Program 12–3 to include a **nextDay** method that increments a date by one day. Test your procedure to ensure that it correctly increments days into a new month and into a new year.

   b. Modify the `CLDate` class that is used in Program 12–3 to include a **priorDay** method that decrements a date by one day. Test your method to ensure that it correctly decrements days into a prior month and into a prior year.

6. a. In Exercise 3 in Section 12.3 you were asked to construct a `CLTime` class. For this class include a **tick** method that increments the time by one second. Test your method to ensure that it correctly increments into a new minute and into a new hour.

   b. Modify the **Time** class written for Exercise 6a to include a **detick** method that decrements the time by one second. Test your method to ensure that it correctly decrements time into a prior hour and into a prior minute.

7. a. Construct a class that can be used to represent an employee of a company. Each employee is defined by an integer ID number—a name consisting of no more than 30 characters, a floating point pay rate, and the maximum number of hours the employee should work each week. The services provided by the class should be the ability to enter data for a new employee, the ability to change data for a new employee, and the ability to display the existing data for a new employee.

   b. Include the class definition created for Exercise 7a in a working Visual Basic program that asks the user to enter data for three employees and displays the entered data.

   c. Modify the program written for Exercise 7b to include a menu that offers the following choices:

      i. Add an Employee

      ii. Modify Employee data

      iii. Delete an Employee

      iv. Exit this menu

      In response to a choice, the program should initiate appropriate action to implement the choice.

8. a. Construct a class that can be used to represent types of food. A type of food is classified as basic or prepared. Basic foods are further classified as either Dairy, Meat, Fruit, Vegetable, or Grain. The services provided by the class should be the ability to enter data for a new food, the ability to change data for a new food, and the ability to display the existing data for a new food.

   b. Include the class definition created for Exercise 8a in a working Visual Basic program that asks the user to enter data for four food items and displays the entered data.

   c. Modify the program written for Exercise 8b to include a menu that offers the following choices:

      i. Add a Food Item

      ii. Modify a Food Item

      iii. Delete a Food Item

      iv. Exit this menu

      In response to a choice, the program should initiate appropriate action to implement the choice.

12.5 Knowing About: Inside and Outside

Just as the concept of an algorithm is central to procedures, the concept of encapsulation is central to objects. In this section we present this encapsulation concept using an inside-outside analogy, which should help your understanding of what object-oriented programming is all about.

In programming terms, an object's attributes are described by data, such as the length and width of a rectangle, and the operations that can be applied to the attributes as described by procedures and functions.

As a practical example of this, assume that we will be writing a program that can deal a hand of cards. From an object-oriented approach, one of the objects that we must model is clearly a deck of cards. For our purposes, the attributes of interest for the card deck are that it contains 52 cards consisting of four suits (hearts, diamonds, spades, and clubs), with each suit consisting of thirteen values (Ace to Ten, Jack, Queen, and King).

Now consider the behavior of our deck of cards, which consists of the operations that can be applied to the deck. At a minimum we will want the ability to shuffle the deck and to deal single cards. Let's now see how this simple example relates to encapsulation using an inside-outside concept.

A useful visualization of the inside-outside concept is to consider an object as a boiled egg, such as shown in Figure 12–12. Note that the egg consists of three parts: a very inside yolk, a less inside white surrounding the yolk, and an outside shell, which is the only part of the egg visible to the outside world.

In terms of our boiled egg model, the attributes and behavior of an object correspond to the yolk and white, respectively, which are inside the egg. The innermost protected area of an object, its data attributes, can be compared to the egg yolk. Surrounding the data attributes, in a similar manner as an egg's white surrounds its yolk, are the operations that we choose to incorporate within an object. Finally, in this analogy, the interface to the outside world, which is represented by the shell, represents how a user gets to invoke the object's internal procedures.

The egg model, with its egg shell interface separating the inside of the egg from the outside, is useful precisely because it so clearly depicts the separation between what should be contained inside an object and what should be seen from the outside. This

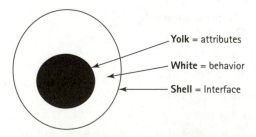

Figure 12–12 *The Boiled Egg Object Model*

separation forms an essential element in object-oriented programming. Let's see why this is so.

From an inside-outside perspective, an object's data attributes, the selected algorithms for the object's operations, and the ways these algorithms are actually implemented are always inside issues, hidden from the view of an object user. On the other hand, the way a user or another object can actually activate an inside procedure, is an outside issue.

Now let's apply this concept to our card deck example. First, consider how we might represent cards in the deck. Any of the following attributes (and there are others) could be used to represent a card:

1. Two integer variables, one representing a suit (a number from 1 to 4) and one representing a value (a number from 1 to 13).

2. One character value and one integer value: the character represents a card's suit, and the integer represents a card's value.

3. One integer variable having a value from 0 to 51: the expression **Int** (number / 13 + 1) provides a number from 1 to 4, which represents the suit, and the expression (number Mod 13 + 1) represents a card value from 1 to 13.

Whichever one we choose, however, is not relevant to the outside. The specific way we choose to represent a card is an inside issue to be decided on by the designer of the deck object. From the outside, all that is of concern is that we have access to a deck consisting of 52 cards having the necessary suits and numerical values.

The same is true for the operations we decide to provide as part of our card deck object. Consider just the shuffling for now.

There are a number of algorithms for producing a shuffled deck. For example, we could use the Visual Basic random number function, **Rnd,** or create our own random number generator. Again, the selected algorithm is an inside issue to be determined by the designer of the deck. The specifics of which algorithm is selected and how it is applied to the attributes we have chosen for each card in the deck are not relevant from the object's outside. For purposes of illustration, assume that we decide to use the Visual Basic **Rnd** function to produce a randomly shuffled deck.

If we use the first attribute set previously given, each card in a shuffled deck is produced using **Rnd** at least twice; once to create a random number from 1 to 4 for the suit, and then again to create a random number from 1 to 13 for the card's value. This sequence must be done to construct 52 different attribute sets, with no duplicates allowed.

If, on the other hand, we use the second attribute set previously given, a shuffled deck can be produced in exactly the same fashion as above, with one modification: the first random number (from 1 to 4) must be changed into a character to represent the suit.

Finally, if we use the third representation for a card, we need to use **Rnd** once for each card, to produce 52 random numbers from 0 to 51, with no duplicates allowed.

The important point here is that the selection of an algorithm and how it will be applied to an object's attributes are implementation issues *and implementation issues are always inside issues.* A user of the card deck, who is outside, does not need to know how the shuffling is done. All the user of the deck must know is how to produce a shuffled deck. In practice, this means that the user is supplied with sufficient information to correctly invoke the shuffle function. This corresponds to the interface, or outer shell of the egg.

Abstraction and Encapsulation

The distinction between inside and outside relates directly to the concepts of abstraction and encapsulation. *Abstraction* means concentrating on what an object is and does before making any decisions about how the object will be implemented. Thus, abstractly, we define a deck and the operations we want to provide. (Clearly, if our abstraction is to be useful, it needs to capture the attributes and operations of a real-world deck.) Once we have decided on the attributes and operations, we can actually implement them.

Encapsulation means separating and hiding the implementation details of the chosen abstract attributes and behavior from outside users of the object. The external side of an object should provide only the necessary interface to users of the object for activating internal procedures. Imposing a strict inside-outside discipline when creating objects is really another way of saying that the object successfully encapsulates all implementation details. In our deck-of-cards example, encapsulation means that users need never know how we have internally modeled the deck or how an operation, such as shuffling, is performed; they only need to know how to activate the given operations.

Code Reuse and Extensibility

A direct advantage of an inside-outside object approach is that it encourages both code reuse and extensibility. This is a result of having all interactions between objects centered on the outside interface and hiding all implementation details within the object's inside.

For example, consider the object shown in Figure 12–13. Here, any of the two object's operations can be activated by correctly stimulating either the circle or square on the outside. In practice the stimulation is simply a method call. We have used a circle and a square to emphasize that two different methods are provided for outside use. In our card-deck

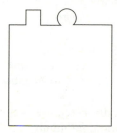

Figure 12–13   *Using an Object's Interface*

example, activation of one method might produce a shuffled deck, while activation of the other method might result in a card suit and value being returned from the object.

Now assume that we want to alter the implementation of an existing operation or add more functionality to our object. *As long as the existing outside interface is maintained, the internal implementation of any and all operations can be changed without the user ever being aware that a change took place.* This is a result of encapsulating the attribute data and operations within an object.

In addition, as long as the interface to existing operations is not changed, new operations can be added as they are needed. From the outside world, it looks as though all that is being added is another function call accessing the inside attributes and modifying them in a new way.

12.6 Common Programming Errors

The more common programming errors initially associated with the construction and use of classes are:

1. Failing to make data members **Private**.
2. Failing to make member methods **Public**.
3. Failing to include an appropriate **Constructor** method.

12.7 Chapter Review

Key Terms

abstract data type
class
class library
class members
constructor
data type
declaration section
implementation section

inheritance
instantiation
intrinsic program library
member methods
member variables
object
polymorphism

Summary

1. A *class* is a programmer-defined data type. *Objects* of a class may be defined and have the same relationship to their class as variables do to Visual Basic's built-in data types.
2. A class definition consists of a declaration and implementation section. The most common form of a class definition is:

```
' Data Declaration Section
'    Declaration of all variables
```

```
' Methods Implementation Section
'    Procedures and Functions that can
'    be used on the above declared variables
```

The variables, procedures, and functions declared in the class declaration section are collectively referred to as *class members*. The variables are individually referred to as *class member variables* and the procedures and functions as *class member methods*.

3. The keywords **Private** and **Public** are formally referred to as *access specifiers* because they specify the access permitted to the class' variables and procedures. Once an access specifier is listed, it remains in force until another access specifier is given. The **Private** keyword specifies that a class member is private to the class and can only be accessed by member methods. The **Public** keyword specifies that a class member may be accessed from outside the class. Generally, all data members should be specified as **Private** and all member methods as **Public**. This ensures that variables declared as **Private** within the Data Declaration section can only be accessed through member methods, and that the member methods are available and can be called from outside the class.

4. Objects are created using the **New** keyword. For example, if CLDate is the name of a class, the statement

```
Dim firstdate As New CLDate()
```

declares firstdate as an object of type CLDate.

5. Visual Basic provides a method, called a Constructor, that is automatically called when an object is first referenced. Its purpose is to initialize each created object.

6. An *access procedure* is any member method that accesses a class' private data members. Visual Basic provides for a Property procedure that contains two access methods: **Set** and **Get**. The purpose of the **Get** method is to read a data member's value, while the **Set** method is used to assign a value to a data member. **Set** and **Get** methods are used in pairs that share a common property name. The **Get** method is called using the syntax:

```
variable = objectname.method()
while the Set method procedure is called using the syntax:
objectname.method = expression
```

Test Yourself—Short Answer

1. In an object-oriented language, the data and the procedures are bound together in the _____.
2. A data type is defined as a combination of data and the _____.
3. An abstract data type is more frequently called a _____.
4. In what type of module would you find a class definition? _____.
5. A Class module consists only of code and is broken down into two sections, the _____ section and the _____ section.

6. The name of the method that creates an object is _____.

7. A class module creates a user-declared class, which is referred to as an _____.

8. The keyword that is used to declare an object is _____.

9. When an object is created from a class it is referred to as an _____, which gives the class instantiation.

10. Another word for instantiated is _____.

Programming Projects

1. Using Property Get and Set methods (see Program 12–3) create a class module (CLName) and the form shown in Figure 12–14 that permit the following operations:

   Assign a value to a CLName object's FirstName member (Property Set method)

   Assign a value to a CLName object's LastName member (Property Set method)

   Read a value from a CLName object's FirstName member (Property Get method)

   Read a value from a CLName object's LastName member (Property Get method)

   Read values from both FirstName and LastName members and concatenates the two together with a space embedded between the names (similar to showdate() method in Program 12–1 in the chapter)

   The First Name and Last Name should be stored in such a way that the first letter of each name is capitalized and the remaining letters of the name are stored in lowercase. The Property Set methods should handle this conversion. (*Hint:* Use the **ToUpper, ToLower,** and **Substring** methods to build the strings for first and last names in the Set methods.) You might create a function (Proper) to perform the conversion.

Figure 12–14   *Form for Exercise 1*

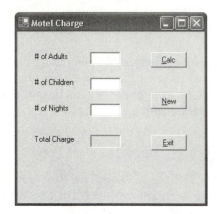

Figure 12–15 *Form for Programming Project 2*

Clicking the form's "Show Whole Name" Button should call (and display) a method in the class module that joins the first and last names together (e.g., Tommy Melbourne).

2. The following is the repeated description of the Motel 8 project initially described in Section 3.8, Exercise 8:

A night's stay at Motel 8 costs $30 per adult and $10 per child. There is no discount for a stay of multiple nights. Additionally, there is a 5% state and local tax that is computed on the sum of the nightly charges.

From this description, and using a Form like the one shown in Figure 12–15, create a class module CLMotel8 that permits the following operations:

a. Assign a value to a CNMotel8 object's Adults member (Property Set method).
b. Assign a value to a CNMotel8 object's Children member (Property Set method).
c. Assign a value to a CNMotel8 object's Nights member (Property Set method).
d. Read a value that returns the computed charge for a stay at the Motel 8 based upon the values in the Adults, Children, and Nights members (similar to showdate() method in Program 12–1).

Your code can execute the class module's Property Set method for number of adults, number of children, and number of nights and the class method (show-charge()) when the Calc Button is clicked. Pressing the New Button can call the Class **Constructor** method. You should set the Adults, Children, and Nights properties to 0 (in the class module). Additionally, clear all text boxes.

Figure 12–16 *Form for Programming Project 3*

3. All hourly employees at Acme Ltd. are paid time and a half for all hours worked over 40. Create an employee class (CLEmployee) that has the following properties:

FirstName
LastName
HoursWorked
HourlyRate
BasePay
OvertimePay
GrossTotalPay

Your project should use a form like the one shown in Figure 12–16. It should also create Property Set methods in the class module that permit direct assignment of object properties First Name through Hourly Rate, and assign to the remaining object properties values based upon the following rules:

    i. Base Pay is calculated by multiplying hours worked (up to a maximum of 40) times hourly rate.

    ii. Overtime Pay is calculated by multiplying hours worked in excess of 40 times hourly rate times 1.5.

    iii. Gross Total Pay is the sum of Base Pay and Overtime Pay.

The Set Properties Button should call the Property Set methods for the current instance (object) of class CLEmployee (and compute values for the Base Pay, Overtime Pay, and Gross Total Pay properties). Additionally, the Base Pay, Overtime Pay, and Gross Total Pay Buttons should display the appropriate values in the disabled text box control (by calling the class module's Property Get methods).

Supported ASCII Character Codes

(ASCII values from 32 to 127)

Value	Symbol	Value	Symbol	Value	Symbol
32	(space)	64	@	96	`
33	!	65	A	97	a
34	"	66	B	98	b
35	#	67	C	99	c
36	$	68	D	100	d
37	%	69	E	101	e
38	&	70	F	102	f
39	'	71	G	103	g
40	(	72	H	104	h
41	)	73	I	105	i
42	*	74	J	106	j
43	+	75	K	107	k
44	,	76	L	108	l
45	-	77	M	109	m
46	.	78	N	110	n
47	/	79	O	111	o
48	0	80	P	112	p
49	1	81	Q	113	q
50	2	82	R	114	r
51	3	83	S	115	s
52	4	84	T	116	t
53	5	85	U	117	u
54	6	86	V	118	v
55	7	87	W	119	w
56	8	88	X	120	x
57	9	89	Y	121	y
58	:	90	Z	122	z
59	;	91	[	123	{
60	<	92	\	124		
61	=	93	]	125	}
62	>	94	^	126	~
63	?	95	_	127	DEL

Additional Controls

In this appendix, we present additional information on the ListBox control that was described in Chapter 4. We also present two controls provided in the standard Toolbox that have not been previously described: the Scroll Bars and ComboBox.

The ListBox Control

The ListBox control is extremely useful for presenting a small list of items, such as might be obtained from a file, array, or user-input. Some of the more common properties of list boxes are shown in Table B–1.

Table B–1 Common ListBox Properties

Property Name	Description
Name	Gets or sets the name of the list box.
Items	Stores the items of the list box; this property is an object that has its own set of properties and methods.
Items.Count	Gets the number of items stored in the **Items** property.
SelectedIndex	Gets or sets the index of the currently selected list box item. This returns a value of −1 if no item is selected.
SelectedItem	Gets or sets the currently selected item when the **SelectedItem** property is not −1.
Sorted	Gets or sets a Boolean value where the value True indicates the items in the list box are sorted alphabetically.

Figure B–1   *The ListBox Control*

Figure B–1 shows the ListBox control. The items in a list box may be stored in the Items property at design time or run-time. To specify items at run-time, use the Items.Add property. To specify items at design time, create a list box on a form and select the list box. In the Properties window, select the **Items** property and click on the ellipses button as shown in Figure B–2.

Click on the ellipses button which opens the String Collection Editor dialog box as shown in Figure B–3. You may now type in each list item on a separate line. When finished, click the OK button.

Figure B–2   *List Box Items Property*

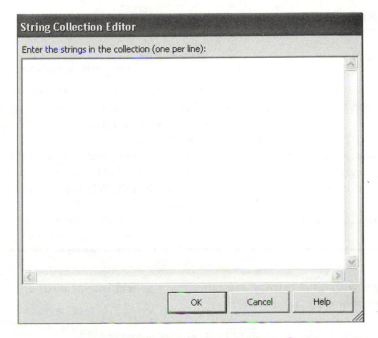

Figure B-3 *String Collection Editor Dialog Box*

For example, if we have a list box named lstItem, the value of the expression `lstItem.Items.Count` is the number of items in the current list. Within a list box, each item is uniquely identified by an integer index value ranging from 0, which corresponds to the first list item, to the value Count −1, which corresponds to the last list item. Thus, for a list box named lstItem, the value of the expression

```
lstItem.Items(lstItem.SelectedIndex)
```

is the string currently highlighted in the list box.

Finally, a list box provides a number of methods, the most commonly used of which are listed in Table B-2.

For example, if we have a list box named lstItem and a text box named txtItem, the statement:

```
lstItem.Items.Add(txtItem.Text)
```

causes the string contained in the text box to be added to the list displayed in the list box. If the list box's **Sorted** property is **True**, the added item is inserted in alphabetical

Table B–3   Commonly Used ListBox Methods

Method	Description
`Items.Add(Item)`	Add an `Item` to the list displayed in the list box.
`Items.Insert(Index, Item)`	Inserts item `Item` into the list box at index `Index`; this causes all subsequent items to move up a position in the list box.
`Items.Remove(Item)`	Remove the `Item` from the list displayed in the list box.
`Items.Removeat(Index)`	Removes the item at index location `Index`; this causes all subsequent items to move down a position in the list box.
`Items.Clear()`	Remove all items from the list displayed in the list box; the value of `Items.Count` becomes 0.

order within the existing list; otherwise, the item is appended to the end of the list. In a similar manner, the statement

```
lstItem.Items.Removeat(lstItem.SelectedIndex)
```

causes the currently selected item in the list to be removed.

Program B–1, whose design time interface is shown in Figure B–4, illustrates a typical list-handling application. Table B–3 lists the objects and properties for this program.

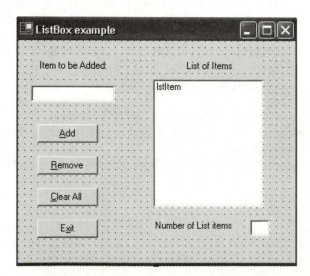

Figure B–4   *Program B–1's Design Time Interface*

Table B–3   Program B–1's Properties Table

Object	Property	Setting
Form	Name	frmMain
	Text	List Box Application
Label	Name	lblList
	Text	List of Items
ListBox	Name	lstItem
	Sorted	True
Label	Name	lblItem
	Text	Item to be Added:
TextBox	Name	txtItem
	Text	(Blank)
Label	Name	lblCount
	Text	Number of Items
TextBox	Name	txtCount
	TabStop	False
Button	Name	btnAdd
	Text	&Add
	TabStop	False
Button	Name	btnRemove
	Text	&Remove
	TabStop	False
Button	Name	btnlear
	Text	&Clear All
	TabStop	False
Button	Name	btnExit
	Text	E&xit
	TabStop	False

Program B–1's Event Code

```
Private Sub frmMain_Load(ByVal sender As System.Object, ByVal e As _
    System.EventArgs) Handles MyBase.Load
  lstItem.Items.Add("Zebra")
  lstItem.Items.Add("Lion")
  lstItem.Items.Add("Antelope")
  lstItem.Items.Add("Monkey")
  lstItem.Items.Add("Dog")
  lstItem.Items.Add("Cat")
  txtCount.Text = lstItem.Items.Count
End Sub
```

```
Private Sub btnAdd_Click(ByVal sender As System.Object, ByVal e As _
    System.EventArgs) Handles btnAdd.Click
  If Len(txtItem.Text) > 0 Then
    lstItem.Items.Add(txtItem.Text)
    txtItem.Text = ""    ' Clear Text box
    txtItem.Focus()
    txtCount.Text = lstItem.Items.Count
    txtItem.Refresh()
  Else
    Beep()
  End If
End Sub

Private Sub btnRemove_Click(ByVal sender As System.Object, ByVal e As _
    System.EventArgs) Handles btnRemove.Click
  Dim itemno As Integer

  itemno = lstItem.SelectedIndex
  If itemno >= 0 Then
    lstItem.Items.RemoveAt(itemno)
    txtCount.Text = lstItem.Items.Count
  Else
    Beep()
  End If
  txtItem.Focus()
End Sub

Private Sub btnClear_Click(ByVal sender As System.Object, ByVal e As _
    System.EventArgs) Handles btnClear.Click
  lstItem.Items.Clear()
  txtItem.Clear()
  txtCount.Text = 0
  txtItem.Focus()
End Sub

Private Sub btnExit_Click(ByVal sender As System.Object, ByVal e As _
    System.EventArgs) Handles btnExit.Click
  Beep()
  End
End Sub
```

Except for the btnExit_Click event, which we have used throughout the text, the remaining four event procedures use methods and properties specifically applicable to list boxes. The first event procedure, which is the Form load event code, uses the **Items.Add** method to initialize the list. Because a list box may also be set at design

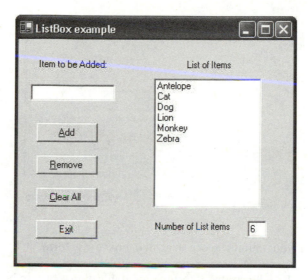

Figure B–5   *Program B–1's Initial Run-Time Interface*

time, this instead could have been done using the String Collection Editor dialog box. Because the list box's **Sorted** property was set to **True** at design time, the list will appear in the alphabetical order shown in Figure B–5. Note also that the count displayed in the picture box is obtained using the **Items.Count** property's value.

The `btnAdd_Click` event procedure first determines that the text box contains a string by checking for a string length greater than zero. If such a string is present in the text box it is added to the list, and the new **Items.Count** value is displayed. In a similar manner, the `btnRemove_Click` event procedure first determines that an item has actually been selected from the list before the **Items.Removeat** method is invoked. Finally, the `btnClear_Click` event procedure invokes the **Clear** method to clear all items from the list. In each of these event codes the focus is reset back to the text box in preparation for another item to be added to the list.

The ComboBox Control

A ComboBox control can be considered as a ListBox control that includes a text box. Therefore, you should be familiar with the ListBox control as a prerequisite to reading this section. The difference in usage between the list box and combo box is that a list box should be used when you want to limit the list of choices presented to a user, while a combo box, with one exception, should be used to provide a list of *suggested* choices, to which the user can enter an item that is not on the list.

Additionally, because the list of choices presented in a combo box is, with one exception, only displayed as a drop-down list when the user clicks on the box's down-facing arrowhead, a combo box can save a considerable amount of space on a form.

Figure B–6   *The ComboBox Control*

When you initially place a combo box on a form, it appears as shown in Figure B–6.

Figure B–7 illustrates the three available types of combo boxes, each of which is described in Table B–4.

Like a list box, all three combo box types have a **Sorted** property and the **Items.Add** and **Items.Remove** methods for adding and removing items from the list. Additionally, there is a **DropDownStyle** property for setting the combo box's type. For example, assuming the three combo boxes shown in Figure B–5 are named cbo0, cbo1, and cbo2, respectively, the following Form Load event code can be used to create the same list for each box.

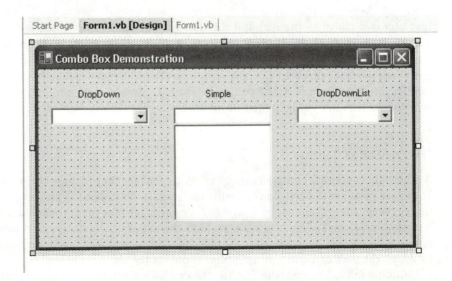

Figure B–7   *The Three Types of ComboBoxes As They Appear at Design Time*

Table B–4   Available ComboBox Types

DropDownStyle Value	Description
DropDown	By either clicking on the down-facing arrowhead of pressing the Alt + Down Arrow when the box has the focus, a text box and a drop-down list is presented. A user can enter an item in the text box either by selecting it from the list or by directly typing into the text box. The entered item does not have to be in the list.
Simple	The complete list is displayed at run-time only if the box has been made large enough at design-time; otherwise, a vertical scroll bar is automatically displayed. As with the DropDown box, an item can be entered in the text box by either selecting it from the list or by directly typing into the text box. The entered item does not have to be in the list.
DropDownList	This is essentially a list box, whose items are displayed only when the down-facing arrow is clicked. As such, a user cannot type into the text box, but can only select an item in the list.

```
Private Sub Form_Load(ByVal sender As System.Object, ByVal e As _
    System.EventArgs) Handles MyBase.Load

  cbo0.Text = ""
  cbo0.Items.Add("Zebra")
  cbo0.Items.Add("Lion")
  cbo0.Items.Add("Antelope")
  cbo1.Text = ""
  cbo1.Items.Add("Zebra")
  cbo1.Items.Add("Lion")
  cbo1.Items.Add("Antelope")
  cbo2.Items.Add("Zebra")
  cbo2.Items.Add("Lion")
  cbo2.Items.Add("Antelope")
End Sub
```

Assuming that the **Sorted** property for each box has been set to **True**, Figure B–8 shows how each combo box appears at run-time. As is seen in this figure, the lists *do not* initially appear in either the DropDown and DropDownlist boxes; the lists will appear in these boxes when the down-facing arrows are clicked. Note, however, that the Simple box is the exception to this drop-down format. The list appears in a Simple

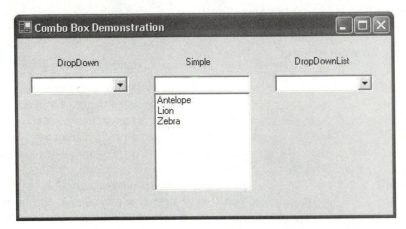

Figure B-8 *The Combo Boxes at Run-Time*

combo box as it would in a normal list box, and in this case is in alphabetical order because the **Sorted** property has been set to **True**.

Figure B-9 shows how the list appears when the down arrow is clicked on the DropDown combo box. If a user clicks on any item in the list, the selected item will automatically appear in the text box; alternatively, any item, whether it is in the list or not, can be directly typed into the text box.

Figure B-10 shows what happens when an item in the Simple combo box is selected. As shown, the selected item is automatically displayed in the text box. As with the DropDown box, a user also can enter any item directly into the text box, whether it is in the list or not.

Finally, Figure B-11 shows the selection of an item from an activated DropDown-List list. As with DropDown, this list is activated by clicking on the down-facing arrow-

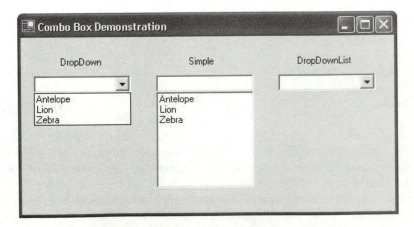

Figure B-9 *Activation of the DropDown Combo Box*

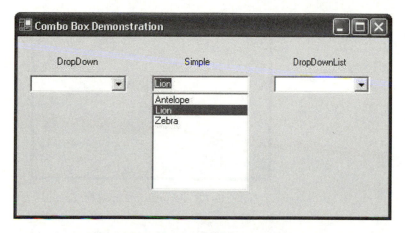

Figure B–10 *Selection of a Simple List Item*

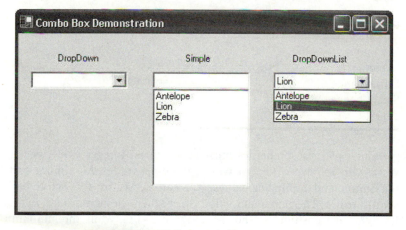

Figure B–11 *Selection of a DropDownList Item*

head. Unlike the DropDown list, however, a user may not type into the text box because only items in the list can be selected. Thus, a DropDownList combo box is effectively a list box presented as a drop-down list.

ScrollBar Controls

Two additional controls for entering input numbers are the Horizontal and Vertical Scroll Bar controls. Except for their visual orientation (horizontal or vertical), both controls work the same way. In this section we present the Horizontal Scroll bar as an example for using either type of Scroll bar.

Figure B–12 illustrates a form with a Horizontal Scroll Bar. The Scroll bar is placed on a form in the same manner as all other toolbox controls; either by double-clicking the control or clicking and dragging the control to the desired form location.

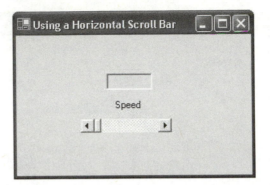

Figure B-12 *A Horizontal Scroll Bar Control*

In addition to a typical control's properties and events, Scroll bar controls have the following five unique properties that should be explicitly set at Design:

Property	Default Value
Maximum	100
Minimum	0
LargeChange	10
SmallChange	1
Value	0

Each of these properties must be set to an integer value, because Scroll bars only work with integers. The first two of these properties, **Maximum** and **Minimum**, set the maximum and minimum values that can be set by the Scroll bar's thumb slide and scroll arrows. The maximum value is set when the Scroll bar's thumb slide is moved to its rightmost position, as shown in Figure B-13a, while the minimum value is set when the thumb slide reaches its leftmost position, as shown in Figure B-13b. For the Scroll bar shown in these figures, the **Maximum** and **Minimum** values are set at 210 and 0, respectively.

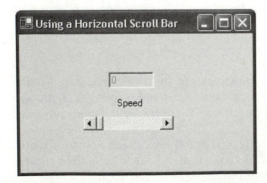

Figure B-13a *Thumb Slide at Maximum Value*

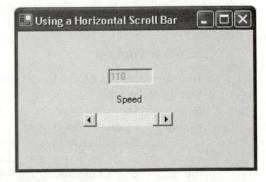

Figure B-13b *Thumb Slide at Minimum Value*

The Value property determines the thumb slide's initial position and can be set to any integer value between **Minimum** and **Maximum**. When the Value setting is the same as the **Minimum** setting, the thumb slide is initially located at its leftmost position. If the **Value** setting is the same as the **Maximum** setting, the thumb slide will initially be at its rightmost position.[1] For the Scroll bar previously shown in Figure B-12, the Value setting is 105; because this is halfway between the **Maximum** and **Minimum** values, the initial thumb slide position is in the middle of its scrollable area.

The **SmallChange** value determines the change in value whenever the Scroll bar's arrows are clicked or the thumb slide is moved. The **LargeChange** value determines how much the value is changed by clicking within the slide area on either side of the thumb slide.

For monitoring a Scroll bar's movement, either by clicking the arrows, moving the thumb slide, or clicking within the scroll area, the following two events are used:

Event	Description
ValueChanged	Occurs after the scroll arrows have been clicked and after the thumb slide has been moved to its final new position.
Scroll	Occurs while the thumb slide is being moved.

For the Scroll bar (hsbSpeed) shown in Figures B-13a and B-13b, Event Procedures B-1 and B-2 provide the code used to display the values shown in the associated text box (txtSpeed). The first event code causes the text box display to change as the thumb slide is being moved, and the second event code changes ensures the display also changes when the arrows are used.

Event Procedure B-1

```
Private Sub hsbSpeed_Scroll(ByVal sender As Object, ByVal e As _
    System.Windows.Forms.ScrollEventArgs) Handles hsbSpeed.Scroll
  txtSpeed.Text = hsbSpeed.Value
End Sub
```

Event Procedure B-2

```
Private Sub hsbSpeed_ValueChanged(ByVal sender As Object, _
    ByVal e As System.EventArgs) Handles hsbSpeed.ValueChanged
  txtSpeed.Text = hsbSpeed.Value
End Sub
```

---

[1]The value of Minimum can be larger than the value of Maximum. In this case the Scroll bar will cause values to change from larger to smaller.

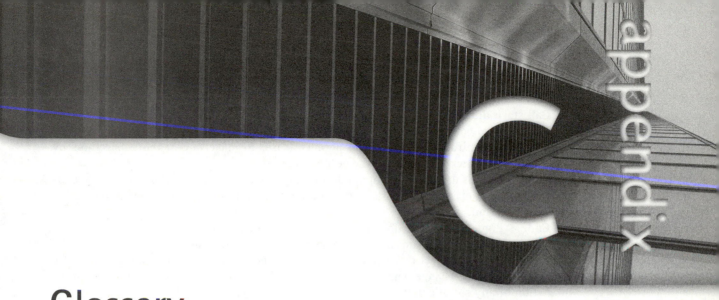

Glossary

Accelerator key: Any key sequence that initiates an action by pressing the Alt key and a designated letter. An accelerator key is created by preceding the designated letter with an ampersand, &, in an object's Text property. Also referred to as a hot-key sequence.

Access key: Any key sequence that permits a user to open a menu or shift focus to a control by pressing the Alt key and a designated letter. The access key is always underlined.

Application: A collection of visual objects and procedural code that constitutes a complete program. Synonymous with the terms program and project.

Argument: A value or expression that is passed into a subprogram (subroutine, procedure, or function).

Array: A group of variables, all of the same type, that share a common name. Individual variables that comprise the array are referred to as array elements. Each array element is distinguished from another by its position in the array, which is designated by an integer value known as an index number.

Bitmap: A rectangular arrangement of dots arranged to make a picture. Also referred to as a raster.

Boolean expression: An expression that evaluates to one of two values, **True** or **False**.

Bound Controls: Controls that can be linked to database fields and are used to display the values in the fields to which they are linked. Also referred to as data-aware controls, they include CheckBoxes, Label, TextBox, and PictureBox controls.

Break mode: Temporary suspension of program execution in the development environment. In break mode, you can examine, debug, reset, step through, or continue program execution.

Breakpoint: A selected program line at which execution automatically stops. Breakpoints are not saved with your code.

Built-in: A data type, object type, function, or subroutine that comes with the Visual Basic language. Built-in data types are also referred to as primitive types.

Button: A control that is used to initiate an event procedure when it is clicked.

Call stack dialog: Lists the procedure calls in an application that have been started but are not yet completed. Available only in break mode.

CheckBox control: A control that permits a user to make one or more selections by placing a check mark next to the desired item.

Class: A class defines both data and procedures that usually are accomplished by constructing a class in two parts: a data declaration section and a methods implementation section.

Code: Procedural instructions that are used to produce a result.

Code window: The window in which code is written and displayed.

Collection: An object that contains a set of related objects. An object's position in the collection can change whenever a change occurs in the collection; therefore, the position of any specific object in the collection may vary.

ComboBox control: A control that is a combination of a List box and Text box control.

Comment: A remark used to document code. A comment is designated by an apostrophe followed by text, or by the keyword **Rem** placed at the start of a line. Remarks are nonexecutable code.

Compile time: The period during which source code is translated to executable code.

Control: An object that can be placed on a form with its own set of recognized properties, methods, and events. Controls are used to receive user input, display output, and trigger event procedures. Most controls can be manipulated using methods. Additionally, some controls are interactive, which means that they are responsive to user actions, whereas other controls are static, which means that they are accessible only through code.

Constant: A value that cannot change during program execution. It can be either a string constant, a number, or a symbolic constant.

Constructor: A method that automatically initializes class member variables.

Current record: The record in a dataset that is available for modification or examination.

Data adapter: Handles the transfer of data to and from the data source and an application.

Dataset: The current set of records associated with a data control.

Data control: A control that incorporates the Microsoft Jet engine for accessing databases, and is used to view database records in connection with bound controls.

Data grid control: A control having rows and columns, that is used to display data in a similar manner to a spreadsheet.

Data source: A source of data such as a database.

Data type: The characteristic of a variable that determines what kind of data it can hold. Data types include Byte, Boolean, Integer, Long, Currency, Single, Double, Date, String, Object, and user-defined types, as well as specific types of objects.

Debug: To locate and eliminate errors in a program.

Declaration statement: A statement used to declare variables and constants.

Design time: The time during which an application is constructed within the development environment by adding controls, setting control or form properties, and so on.

Development environment: A set of software, presented as a unified environment, in which the software developer can efficiently work. Microsoft Visual Basic is an example of a development environment.

Dialog box: A box that requests user input. A modal dialog requires input before an application can continue, while a modeless box permits shifting the focus from the box and allows an application to continue without the box being closed.

Directory List box: A control that displays available directories on the current disk drive.

DLL: Dynamic Link Library; a file having the extension .DLL that is used to hold procedures that are dynamically linked to an application.

Drive List box: A control that displays available disk drives.

Drop-down: A list that is displayed in a drop-down fashion by either the clicking of a down-facing arrowhead or the action of an accelerator key.

Embedded object: An object that is created in one application and then embedded in a second application. All of the data associated with the embedded object is copied to and contained within the embedding application.

End-of-File (EOF): A condition that evaluates to True when the end of a sequential file or the end of a dataset object has been reached.

Error trapping: Detecting an error and invoking code when the designated error occurs.

Event: Any user or system action to which an object responds.

Event procedure: A Sub procedure that is attached to an object and initiated by an event.

Event-driven Program: A program that executes code based on user- and system-initiated events.

EXE: A standalone application that is executed as an individual process. Also refers to controls that are built in to Visual Basic and are displayed in the standard Toolbox.

Expression: A syntactically correct arrangement of constants, variables, operators, functions, and subroutines that evaluates to a single value.

Field: A single item that represents an attribute or entity of a database record.

File List box: A control that displays a list of file names that match the value set in the Pattern property.

Focus: The state that defines the currently active control. A control can receive focus by being tabbed to, clicked on, selected by access keys, or designated by program code.

Form: Forms are containers for controls. At run-time a form becomes either a window or a dialog box. Forms can be of two types, MDI or SDI.

Form-level: A variable, declared in the General Declaration section that is accessible by all procedures on the form.

Format: The specification for how data will be displayed.

Function: A general procedure that directly returns a single value.

(General) Declarations section: The section of a code module that is used to declare module-level variables and symbolic constants.

General procedure: A user-defined procedure that can be either a **Sub** or **Function** procedure.

Global variable: A variable that is available to all modules and can be accessed by any procedure in the project.

Graphical User Interface (GUI): The graphical portion of a program that is visually presented to a user for interaction with the procedural code.

GroupBox: A control used to contain other controls. Typically used to provide containers for Radio buttons in which each GroupBox provides a separate set of options.

Handle: A small square on a control that is visible at design-time and can be used to resize the control. Also referred to as a sizing handle.

Horizontal scroll bar: A control that uses a horizontal scroll bar to set a numerical value. One end of the control corresponds to a minimum value and the opposite end corresponds to a maximum value.

Hot key: *See* Accelerator key.

Immediate window: A debug window that is active during break mode, and can be used to immediately evaluate an expression or determine the value of a variable.

Index: A number that specifies an element's position in an array.

Key field: One or more combined fields on which records in a database are organized and searched.

Keyword: A word that has a special meaning in Visual Basic. Unrestricted keywords may be used as identifiers, but doing so precludes their use for the feature normally associated with the keyword. Restricted keywords can be used only for their intended purpose.

Label control: A control that is used to provide the user with information about a form and the controls on a form. For example, a TextBox typically has a Label control next to it to indicate the purpose of the TextBox.

Linked object: An object created in one application that is linked to a second application. When an object is linked, a reference to the object is inserted into the second application, rather than the actual object. Unlike an embedded object, a linked object's data is stored in and managed by the application that created it.

ListBox control: A control that displays a list of items from which one or more may be selected.

Local scope: The scope of a symbolic constant or variable in which visibility is limited to the declaring procedure.

Logic error: An error that causes an erroneous, unexpected, or unintentional result due to a flaw in the program's logic.

Logical operator: The **And, Or,** and Not operators used to construct compound relational expressions.

Message box: A dialog box that displays a message and one or more options that must be selected before an application can continue executing.

Method: A procedure that is connected to an object. The method is invoked by providing an object name, followed by a period, followed by the method's name.

Microsoft Jet database engine: A database management system that retrieves data from, and stores data into, user- and system-databases. The Jet engine can be thought of as a data manager component with which other data access systems, such as Visual Basic and Microsoft Access, are built.

Modal dialog box: A dialog box that requires input from a user and must be closed before an application can continue.

Modeless dialog box: A dialog box where focus can be shifted from the box, and one in which an application can continue without the box being closed.

Module: A set of declarations followed by procedures. Can be a form module, a code module, or a class module. Each module is stored as a separate file.

Module level: Code within the General Declaration section of a module that is available only to procedures within the module.

Multiple Document Interface (MDI): An application that can support multiple windows from one application instance. An MDI application consists of a main window that contains internal windows referred to as child windows. The main window and its child windows can all be visible at the same time.

Numeric expression: Any expression that evaluates to a number. Elements of the expression can include any keywords, variables, constants, operators, and subroutine calls.

Object: An instance or occurrence of a class.

OLE object: Object Linking and Embedding. An object that can be transferred and shared between applications, either by linking or embedding.

One-to-many relationship: An association between two tables in which the primary key value of each record in the primary table corresponds to the value in the matching field or fields of a number of records (or no record) in the related table.

Option button control: A control that permits selection of a single item from a group of items. If additional sets of options are required, a GroupBox control is used to contain the additional option controls.

Parameter: A variable used by a procedure whose value is initialized outside of the procedure and transferred to the procedure when the procedure is called.

Pass by Reference: A transfer of data to a procedure in which the procedure has access to the memory location of the argument being passed. This permits the procedure to alter the value of the argument.

Pass by Value: A transfer of data to a procedure in which a copy of an argument's value is passed to the procedure.

PictureBox control: A control used to display a graphic image.

Primary key: One or more fields whose value or values uniquely identify each record in a table. A table can have only one primary key.

Procedure: A named sequence of statements executed as a unit. **Function, Property,** and **Sub** are types of procedures. A procedure name is always defined at the module level. All executable code must be contained in a procedure. Procedures cannot be nested within other procedures.

Procedure template: An empty procedure that consists only of a header line and either an **End Sub** or **End Function** statement.

Project: The collection of elements that constitute an application.

Project window: A window that displays all of the forms, modules, and elements that comprise a project. Also referred to as the Project Resource window.

Property: A named attribute of an object. Properties define object characteristics, such as size, color, screen location, and the state of an object, such as **Enabled** or **Disabled**.

Public scope: The scope that permits a procedure or variable to be called from all project modules.

RadioButton control: The RadioButton control provides a user with a set of one or more choices, only one of which can be selected. Radio buttons always operate as a group, where selecting one radio button immediately deselects and clears all the other buttons in the group.

Random-access file: A file in which all records are fixed-length, and records may be read or written in any order.

Record: A group of related fields.

Run-time: The time during which a program is executing.

Scope: Defines the availability of a variable, procedure, or object, which is referred to as its visibility. For example, a variable declared as **Public** is available to all procedures in all modules in a project, unless the **Option Private** module is in effect. When **Option Private** module is in effect, the module itself is private and, therefore, not visible to other projects. Variables declared in a procedure are visible only within the procedure and lose their value between calls unless they are declared as **Static**.

Single Document Interface (SDI):   An application that supports a single, visible document at a time. An SDI application can contain multiple windows, but only one can be visible at a time.

Session ID: A unique identifier assigned to a Web connection to enable the Web server to differentiate between Web connections/sessions.

Session object: An object that stores a Session ID and name-value pairs containing data that enables a Web server to obtain state information about a Web connection.

Single Document Interface (SDI):   An application that supports a single visible document at a time. An SDI application can contain multiple windows, but only one can be visible at a time.

Sizing handle: A small square on a control that is visible at design-time and can be used to resize the control.

SQL statement: An expression that defines a Structured Query Language (SQL) command, such as SELECT, UPDATE, or DELETE, and includes clauses such as WHERE and ORDER BY. SQL statements typically are used in queries.

Static variable: A variable whose value is retained between procedure calls.

String expression: Any expression that evaluates to a sequence of contiguous characters. Elements of the expression can include a function that returns a string, a string literal, a string constant, a string variable, a string variant, or a function that returns a string variant.

Structure: A data type that stores different types of data, known as members, under a single variable name.

Subscript: See index.

Sub procedure: A procedure that only returns values through its parameter list.

Symbolic constant: A constant that has been named using the **Const** keyword.

Syntax: The set of rules for formulating grammatically correct language statements.

TextBox control: A control used for data entry and display.

Timer control: A control used to automatically execute an event at a specified interval of time.

Toolbar: A set of icons, referred to as buttons, which are used as shortcuts for menu options.

Toolbox: A window containing controls that can be placed on a form at design-time.

Transaction: A series of changes made to a database's data and structure. The beginning of a transaction starts with a **Begin Trans** statement, transactions are committed using a **Commit Trans** statement, and all changes made since the last **Begin Trans** statement can be undone using a **RollBack** statement.

Twip: A unit of measurement that is equivalent to 1/20 of a point and 1/1440 of an inch.

Validator control: A control on a Web form used to automatically validate input data.

Variable: A named location containing data that can be modified during program execution. Each variable has a name that uniquely identifies it within its scope. Variable names must begin with an alphabetic character, must be unique within the same scope, cannot be longer than 255 characters, and cannot contain an embedded period or type-declaration character. Variables declared in a procedure are visible only within the procedure and lose their value between calls unless they are declared as **Static**.

Vertical scroll bar: A control that uses a vertical scroll bar to set a numerical value. One end of the control corresponds to a minimum value and the opposite end corresponds to a maximum value.

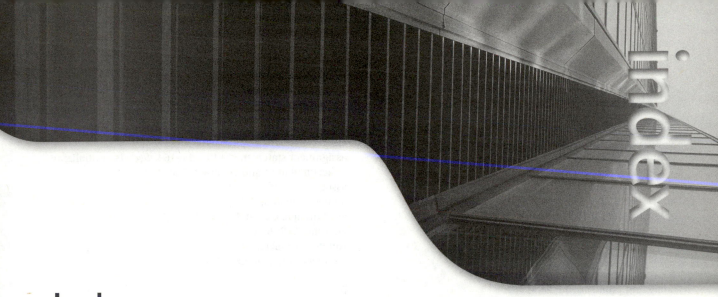

Index